GAMES

GAMES

BY JESSIE H. BANCROFT, M.P.E.

FELLOW, AMERICAN ASSOCIATION FOR THE ADVANCEMENT OF SCIENCE; FELLOW, AMERICAN ACADEMY OF PHYSICAL EDUCATION; FELLOW, AMERICAN PHYSICAL EDUCATION ASSOCIATION. FORMERLY DIRECTOR PHYSICAL TRAINING, BROOKLYN PUBLIC SCHOOLS; FORMERLY ASSISTANT DIRECTOR PHYSICAL TRAINING, PUBLIC SCHOOLS, NEW YORK CITY. AUTHOR OF *THE POSTURE OF SCHOOL CHILDREN*

Revised and Enlarged Edition of
Games for the Playground,
Home, School, and Gymnasium

THE MACMILLAN COMPANY

NEW YORK   MCMXLVIII

TABLE OF CONTENTS

v

FOREWORD

The changes in this book consist mainly of additions, required by the amazing spread of the play spirit and its practical applications in education and community life since the book was first issued in 1909. So thoroughly is the material in the original collection a part of game programs that but few items could be eliminated without lessening the usefulness of the volume; but the wider use now made of many games that were not in the original book, the invention by instructors of many other games whose popularity warrants their inclusion, together with many finds from new research in foreign countries, constitute the sources from which new material has been derived.

To each section of the book new games have been added. Most significant perhaps is the need for including the major ball games, such as regulation Football, Basketball, Hockey, and other highly organized athletic games. When this book was first published these advanced games were issued in a separate volume, as appealing to a distinct field, mainly of older players; but these games are no longer the exclusive quarry of the college, or the sporting club for adults. They have sifted down through the high school to the elementary school, the playground, and the camp, in a way that indicates great increase of skill among both players and instructors. Similarly, interest in simpler recreative games and sports has become so general among players of all ages that both types of games, the simple and advanced, are now needed within the same covers.

Major ball games have, in this period, undergone a marked evolution. There is scarcely one that has not had numerous changes either in rules of play, size of teams, the lay-out of court or field, specifications for equipment, or all of these details. In some instances the very vocabulary has changed. No simple transfer from the earlier volume was therefore possible, and the major games here presented have been newly written and brought up to date with official rules.

Other important educational trends have been given ample space in this revision. Conspicuous is the increased use of skill games and lead-up games. The former train fundamental skills in handling balls, clubs, bats, rackets, and other implements of play. A new chapter on *Balls and How to Play Them* explains the most important technique required in such skill. Lead-up games are also preparatory for the major games. They introduce players gradually to various features of any given advanced game, such as highly organized team work, more complicated rules, or more varied applications of skill. Another educational trend which is provided for in this volume is the earlier introduction into game programs of carry-over games, such as Tennis, Golf, and others popular with adults. Equipped in school or college with some facility in one or more of these games, a young person goes out into life with a lasting interest in some specific form of wholesome exercise and with a key to companionships that may mean much for his future. Another new section gives *Track and Field Events* — running, jumping, and weight-throwing contests — which are now a part of most educational and popular game programs.

For adults the last decade has shown a large increase in the use of games for social gatherings, so that in making a substantial enlargement of the section on *Social and Quiet Games* many have been added that have been highly successful with adults, as well as new ones for younger players. At the other extreme very little tots have been remembered in all sections. A chapter has been added on *Games for One or Two*, to reach the lonely child, the handicapped, the adult invalid or convalescent, or the isolated individual, all of whom need diversion and amusement more, perhaps, than those who play in groups. The author's recent research in foreign countries has resulted in some valuable new finds, with excellent playing values, from France, England,

Italy, Czechoslovakia, Russia, Holland, China, Monaco, and elsewhere, many of which, though traditional in their own countries, are quite different from any heretofore published or played in America.

Practical features of the original volume that have been especially serviceable have been continued. These include helps to teachers, and — one of the most useful devices — the arrangement of the games in each section alphabetically, by title, so that any game may be readily turned to without reference to the Index; but there is also an Index, with many cross references to facilitate finding games that may be known under different names.

Altogether the volume covers a much larger amount of material and a wider range of interest than in its original form, while continuing all that has been most useful. It has been brought abreast of the great development of the subject and aims to be equally helpful for both the trained and untrained player or teacher or leader, in the ever increasing field of sport and play. Those subjects have not only become indispensable in educational programs, but with shorter working hours and much idle time due to unemployment, there is a greater community demand for such activities. If one addresses a public more informed and skillful, one also addresses a need more urgent and universal.

JESSIE H. BANCROFT

MENTON, FRANCE
July, 1937

INTRODUCTION

INTRODUCTION

PURPOSE AND PLAN. — This book aims to be a practical guide for the player of games, whether child or adult, and for the teacher or leader of games. A wide variety of conditions has been considered, including schools, playgrounds, gymnasiums, athletic fields, summer camps, adult house parties and country clubs, settlement work, children's parties, and the environment of indoors or out-of-doors, city or country, summer or winter, the seashore, the woodland, or the snow. The games have been collected from many countries and sources, with a view to securing novel and interesting as well as thoroughly tried and popular material, ranging from traditional to modern gymnasium and athletic games. An especial effort has been made to secure games for particular conditions. Among these may be mentioned very strenuous games for older boys or men ; games for the school-room ; games for large numbers ; new gymnasium games and those which make use of natural material such as stones, pebbles, shells, trees, flowers, leaves, grasses, holes in the sand or earth, and diagrams drawn on the ground.

The description, classification, and arrangement of the games have been made with the steadfast purpose of putting them into the most workable form, easily understood, with suggestions for getting the most sport and playing value out of them. The grading of games is essentially a graded course for schools.

The ball games requiring team play have been described according to an analytic scheme which makes it possible to locate at a glance information about the laying out of the ground ; the number, assignment, and duties of players ; the object of the game ; and rules, fouls, and score. The various kinds of balls are described with methods of playing them. Diagrams for all kinds of games have been supplied unsparingly, wherever it seemed possible to make clearer the understanding of a game

3

by such means, and pictorial illustration has been used. The music for all singing games is given with full accompaniment. Suggestions for the teaching and conduct of games are given, with directions for floor formations. Means of counting out and choosing sides and players are described, and one section is devoted to forfeits, stunts, and contests. Athletic procedure is explained at length from the difference between amateur and professional standards, through the organization of different kinds of match games and tournaments, to handicaps, prizes, and officials.

Under each of the main divisions chosen — miscellaneous active games, social and quiet games, singing, beanbag, ball, and track and field games — the material is in alphabetic order to facilitate ready reference, although a general alphabetic Index is appended. In short, the book aims to bring together all related material and every available device for making it readily accessible and easily understood.

* * *

SOURCES AND NATURE OF MATERIAL. — The material in this volume, aside from that accumulated through a long experience in the teaching and supervision of games, has been collected through (1) special original research and (2) bibliographical research. Much original research has been made among the foreign population of New York City, where practically the entire world is accessible, but also in other sections of the United States.

Original research This has resulted in some entirely new games that the writer has not found elsewhere in print. Among these may be mentioned the Greek Pebble Chase, the Russian Hole Ball, the Scotch Keep Moving, the Danish Slipper Slap, and, from our own country, among others, Chickadee-dee from Long Island, and Hip from New Jersey. Entirely new ways of playing games previously recorded have been found, amounting not merely to a variation but to a wholly new form. Such is the method here given for playing Babylon, a form gathered from two different Scotch sources. Another example is the game of Wolf, for which additional features have been found that add greatly to its playing value, especially the rule whereby the wolf, when discovered by the sheep who are hunting for him, shall take a jump toward the sheep before his chase after them begins; or, should he discover them first, the requirement that they take three steps toward him before the chase begins. Such points add greatly to the sport of a game, and with the spoken formulas that accompany them form a rich find for both student and player.

One may not well refer to the original research without mention of the charm of the task itself. It has been one of the sunniest, happiest lines possible to follow, attended invariably with smiling faces and laughter on the part of old or young, native or foreign, the peasant people or those more sophisticated.

The bibliographical research has covered a wide field. Heretofore the principal sources in English for the collector of games have been the invaluable and scholarly folklore compilations of Mr. William Wells Newell (*Songs and Games of American Children*) and Mrs. Alice B. Gomme (*Traditional Games* in the *Dictionary of British Folk Lore*). The earlier British collection by Strutt (*Sports and Pastimes of the English People*) has also been a source of great value. In the United States considerable collecting and translating of games have from time to time been done by the physical training magazine, *Mind and Body*. For all modern athletic games an invaluable service has been rendered by Messrs. A. G. Spalding and Brothers in the publication, since 1892, of the *Spalding Athletic Library* originally directed by Mr. A. G. Spalding and Mr. James E. Sullivan. The author is greatly indebted to all of these sources. In addition, hundreds of volumes have been consulted in many fields including works of travel, reports of missionaries, etc. This has resulted in games from widely scattered sources, including European countries, the Orient, the Arctic regions, and the North American Indians. While in such a mass of material there are some games that are found in almost all countries, so that one is continually meeting old friends among them, a very considerable harvest of distinctive material has been gathered, eloquent of environment or of temperamental or racial traits. Such, among many others, are the Japanese Crab Race; the Chinese games of Forcing the City Gates and Letting Out the Doves; the Korean games with flowers and grasses; the North American Indian games of Snow Snake and Rolling Target; and the poetic game of the little Spanish children about the Moon and Stars, played in the boundaries marked by sunshine and shadow.

But the object of the book has been by no means to present only novel material. There is an aristocracy of games, classic

Standard material   by all the rights of tradition and popular approval, without which a collection would be as incomplete as would an anthology of English ballads without *Robin Hood*, *Sally in Our Alley*, or *Drink to Me Only with Thine Eyes*. These standard games are amply represented, mingled in the true spirit of American democracy with strangers from foreign lands and the new creations of modern athletic practice.

The games, old and new, are full of that intimation of environment which the novelist calls local color, often containing in the

Local color and humor in games   name alone a comprehensive suggestiveness as great as that of a Homeric epithet. Thus our familiar Cat and Mouse appears in modern Greece as Lamb and Wolf; and the French version of Spin the Platter is My Lady's Toilet, concerned with laces, jewels, and other ballroom accessories instead of our prosaic numbering of players. These changes that a game takes on in different environments are of the very essence of folklore, and some amusing examples are to be found in our own country. For instance, it is not altogether surprising to find a game that is known under another name in the North called, in Southern States, "Ham-Ham-Chicken-Ham-Bacon!" The author found a good example of folklore-in-the-making in the game usually known as "Run, Sheep, Run!" in which a band of hidden players seek their goal under the guidance of signals shouted by a leader. As gathered in a Minnesota town, these signals consisted of colors — red, blue, green, etc. This same game was found in the city environment of New York under the name of Oyster Sale, and the signals had become pickles, tomatoes, and other articles strongly suggestive of a delicatessen store. The butterfly verse for Jumping Rope is obviously another late production of the folklore spirit.

The lover of childish humor will find many delightful examples of it among the games, as where little Jacky Lingo feeds bread

and butter to the sheep (Who Goes Round My Stone Wall?);
or the Mother, trying the Old Witch's apple pie, discovers that
"It tastes exactly like my child Monday!" The tantalizing
"nominies" or "dares," as in Fox and Geese, and Wolf, and the
ways in which players are trapped into false starts, as in Black
Tom, are also highly amusing.

* * *

PRINCIPLES OF SELECTION. — In the selection of material for
this work, a marked distinction has been made between games,
on the one hand, and on the other, the unorganized play and
constructive activities included in many books of children's
games. While the term "play" includes games, so that we
"play games," it applies also to informal play activities, such
as a child's "playing horse," "playing house," or playing in the
sand. In such unorganized play there are no fixed rules, no
formal mode of procedure, and generally no climax to be achieved.
The various steps are usually spontaneous, not predetermined,
and are subject to individual caprice. In games, on the contrary, as in Blind Man's Buff, Prisoners' Base, or Football,
there are prescribed acts subject to rules, generally penalties for
defeat or the infringement of rules, and the action proceeds in a
regular evolution until it culminates in a given climax, which
usually consists in a victory of skill, speed, or strength. In a
strictly scientific sense, games do not always involve the element
of sport or play, being used in many forms among primitive
peoples for serious divinatory purposes. It is perhaps needless
to say that all of the games in the present collection are for the
purpose of sport and recreation.

The hundreds of games here published are selected from a
far larger number. No game has been included that has not been
considered to have strong playing values, by which **Playing**
term is meant, in addition to other qualities, and **values**
above all others, the amount of sport and interest attending it.
The points of play that contribute to the success of a game have
been secured from experience, and unfamiliar games have been
thoroughly tested and the points of play noted for older or

younger players, large or small numbers, or other circumstances.[1]

Games may be analyzed into certain elements susceptible of classification, such as the elements of formation, shown in the

Elements of games circle form, line form, or opposing groups; other elements are found in modes of contest, as between individuals or groups; tests of strength or skill; methods of capture, as with individual touching or wrestling, or with a missile, as in ball-tag games; or the elements of concealment, or chance, or guessing, or many others. These various elements are like the notes of the scale in music, susceptible of combinations that seem illimitable in variety. Thus in the Greek Pebble Chase, the two elements that enter into the game — that of (1) detecting or guessing who holds a concealed article, and (2) a chase — are neither of them uncommon elements, but in this combination make a game that differs in playing value from any familiar game, and one affording new and genuine interest, as evidenced by the pleasure of children in playing it. Indeed, the interest and sport were fully as great with a group of adult Greek men who first demonstrated this game for the author. This element of guessing which player holds a concealed article is found again in a different combination in the Scotch game of Smuggling the Geg, where it is used with opposing groups and followed by hiding and seeking. This combination makes a wholly different game of it, and one of equal or even superior playing value to the Pebble Chase, though suited to different conditions.

Because of this wonderful variety in combinations, leading to entirely different playing values, the author has found it impossible to agree with some other students of games, that it is practicable to select a few games that contain all of the typical elements of interest. Such limitation seems no more possible than in painting, poetry, music, or any other field of spontaneous imitative or creative expression. There will doubtless always be some games that will have large popular following, playing on the

[1] In the adaptation of games the author wishes to make most appreciative acknowledgment of the help of a staff of skilled assistants in the public schools including special concentration on the subject by Miss Lillian McConville. Also, in foreign bibliographical research, of the assistance of Mrs. Marie Talbot-Constant.

"psychology of the crowd" as well as on that of the players. Thus we have the spectacle of so-called national games, Baseball and Football in America, Handball in Ireland, Pelota in Spain, and so on; but natural expression through games has always been and probably always will be infinitely varied, and it should be if the psychology of the subject is to be taken as a guide.

In the arrangement of material there has many times been a strong temptation to classify the games by their historic, geographic, psychologic, or educational interests; by the playing elements contained in them; or by several other possible methods which are of interest chiefly to the academic student; but these have each in turn been discarded in favor of the original intention of making the book pre-eminently a useful working manual for the player or leader of games.

The same games are found not only in many different countries and localities, but under different names and with many variations in the form of playing them. This has necessitated **Varying** a method of analytical study which has been fol- **modes of play** lowed with all of the games. A card catalogue has been made of them, and in connection with each game notation has been made of the various names under which it has been found, and details of differences in rules. In unofficial games the choice of rules or directions has been determined chiefly by the playing values previously alluded to, those directions having been selected which experience has shown make the most interesting game. Sometimes these differences are so great as to amount to a different game, or one suited to different ages of players. In a few instances, as with Prisoners' Base, Captain Ball, Zigzag Ball, etc., it has seemed best to present several typical forms of the same game with an analytic statement of the differences, leaving the leader to select the form best adapted to his conditions. At no time, however, has there been any attempt to present all games or all forms of any one game. That would be merely to make a compendium of all possible material. A purposeful selection has been made throughout.

The choice of names could not well be made on any one principle. Wherever feasible, the name that has seemed to have the widest vogue has been adopted. In other instances it has ap-

peared best to make a different selection to avoid too great
similarity in names.   Some games, especially those from foreign
sources, came without names and have had to be christened.   In
the case of several modern adaptations of old games, a name
bestowed by some previous worker has been continued, if espe·
cially descriptive or appropriate.

Occasional distinction has been made between games for
masculine or feminine players; but the modern tendency of
Games for athletic practice is away from such distinctions.
boys and This is a question that varies so much with the
girls, men previous training and condition of players on the
and women one hand, and with personal opinion or prejudice
on the other, that it has been thought best to leave it for decision in each individual case.

* * *

THE USES OF GAMES. — The use of games for both children
and adults has a deep significance for the individual and the
community through the conservation of physical, mental, and
moral vitality.

Games have a positive educational influence that no one can
appreciate who has not observed their effects.   Children who are
slow, dull, and lethargic; who observe but little of what goes on
around them; who react slowly to external stimuli; who are, in
short, slow to see, to hear, to observe, to think, and to do, may be
completely transformed in these ways by the playing of games.
Sense The sense perceptions are quickened: A player
perceptions comes to see more quickly that the ball is coming
toward him, that he is in danger of being tagged, or that it is his
turn; he hears the footstep behind him, or his name or number
called; he feels the touch on the shoulder; or in innumerable
other ways he is aroused to quick and direct recognition of, and
response to, things that go on around him.   The clumsy, awk-
ward body becomes agile and expert; the child who tumbles
down today will not tumble down next week; he runs more
fleetly, dodges with more agility, plays more expertly in every
way, showing thereby a neuromuscular development.

The social development through games is fully as important and as pronounced. Many children, whether because of lonely conditions at home or through some personal pecu- **Social** liarity, do not possess the power readily and pleas- **development** antly to co-operate with others. Many of their elders lack this facility also, and there is scarcely anything that can place one at a greater disadvantage in business or society, or in any of the relations of life. The author has known case after case of peculiar, unsocial, even disliked children, who have come into a new power of co-operation and have become popular with their playmates through the influence of games. The timid, shrinking child learns to take his turn with others; the bold, selfish child learns that he may not monopolize opportunities; the unappreciated child gains self-respect and the respect of others through some particular skill that makes him a desired partner or a respected opponent. He learns to take defeat without discouragement and to win without undue elation. In these and in many other ways are the dormant powers for social co-operation developed, reaching the highest point at last in the team games where self is subordinated to the interests of the team, and co-operation is the very life of the game.

Most important of all, in the training that comes through games, however, is the development of will. The volitional aspect of the will and its power of endurance are plainly **Will training** seen to grow in power of initiative; in courage to give "dares" and to take risks; in determination to capture an opponent, to make a goal, or to win the game. But probably the most valuable training of all is that of inhibition — that power for restraint and self-control which is the highest aspect of the will and the latest to develop. The little child entering the primary school has very little of this power of inhibition. To see a thing he would like is to try to get it; to want to do a thing is to do it; he acts impulsively; he does not possess the power to restrain movement and to deliberate. A large part of the difficulty of the training of children at home and at school lies in the fact that this power of the will for restraint and self-control is undeveloped. So-called "willfulness" is a will in which the volitional power has not yet been balanced with this inhibitive power. One realizes in this way the force of Matthew Arnold's definition of character as "a completely fashioned will."

There is no agency that can so effectively and naturally develop power of inhibition as games. In those of very little children there are very few, if any, restrictions; but as players grow older, more and more rules and regulations appear, requiring greater and greater self-control — such as not playing out of one's turn; not starting over the line in a race until the proper signal; aiming deliberately with the ball instead of throwing wildly or at haphazard; until again, at the adolescent age, the highly organized team games and contests are reached, with their prescribed modes of play and elaborate restrictions and fouls. There could not be in the experience of either boy or girl a more live opportunity than in these advanced games for acquiring the power of inhibitory control, or a more real experience in which to exercise it. To be able, in the emotional excitement of an intense game or a close contest, to observe rules and regulations; to choose under such circumstances between fair or unfair means and to act on the choice is to have more than a mere knowledge of right and wrong. It is to have the trained power and habit of acting on such knowledge — a power and habit that mean something immeasurable for character. It is because of the lack of such balanced power that contests in the business world reach the point of winning at any cost, by fair means or foul. If the love of fair play, a sense of true moral values, and above all, the power and habit of will to act on these can be developed in our boys and girls, it will make immeasurably for the uplift of the community.

The natural interests of a normal child lead him to care for different types of games at different periods of his development. Evolution of In other words, his own powers, in their natural play interests evolution, seek instinctively the elements in play that will contribute to their own growth. When games are studied from this viewpoint of the child's interests, they are found to fall into groups having pronounced characteristics at different age periods.

Thus, the little child of six years enjoys particularly games in which there is much repetition, as in most of the singing games; games involving impersonation, appealing to his imagination and dramatic sense, as where he becomes a mouse, a fox, a sheepfold, a farmer, etc.; or games of simple chase (one chaser for one runner) as distinguished from the *Games for* group chasing of a few years later. His games *various ages* are of short duration, reaching their climax quickly and making but slight demand on powers of attention and physical endur- ance; they require but little skill and have very few, if any, rules, besides the mere question of "taking turns." In short, they are the games suited to undeveloped powers in almost every particular but that of imagination.

Two or three years later these games are apt to seem "babyish" to a child and to lose interest for him. His games then work through a longer evolution before reaching their climax, as where an entire group of players instead of one has to be caught before the game is won, as in Red Lion, Pom Pom Pullaway, etc. He can watch more points of interest at once than formerly, and choose between several different possible modes of play, as in Prisoners' Base. He gives "dares," runs risks of being caught, and exercises his courage in many ways. He uses individual ini- tiative instead of merely playing in his turn. This is the age of "nominies," in which the individual player hurls defiance at his opponents with set formulas, usually in rhyme. Players at this time band together in many of their games in opposing groups, "choosing sides" — the first simple beginning of team play. Neuromuscular skill increases, as shown in ball play and in agile dodging. Endurance for running is greater.

When a child is about eleven or twelve years of age, some of these characteristics decline and others equally pronounced take their place. "Nominies" disappear and games of simple chase (tag games) decline in interest. Races and other competitive forms of running become more strenuous, indicating a laudable instinct to increase thereby the muscular power of the heart at a time when its growth is much greater proportionately than that of the arteries, and the blood pressure is consequently *Team play* greater. A very marked feature from now on is the closer organization of groups into what is called team play. Team play bears to the simpler group play which precedes it an analogous relation in some respects to that between modern and primitive warfare. In primitive warfare the action of the participants was homogeneous: that is, each combatant performed the same kind of service as did every other combatant and largely on individual initiative. The "clash of battle and the clang of arms" meant an individual contest for every man engaged. In contrast to this there is, in modern warfare, a distribution of functions, some combatants performing one kind of duty and others another, all working together to the common end. In the higher team organizations of Basket Ball, Baseball, Football, there is such a distribution of functions, some players being forwards, some throwers, some guards, etc., though these parts are often taken in rotation by the different players. The strongest characteristic of team play is the co-operation whereby, for instance, a ball is passed to the best thrower, or the player having the most advantageous position for making a goal. A player who would gain glory for himself by making a sensational play at the risk of losing for his team does not possess the team spirit. The traits of character required and cultivated by good team work are invaluable in business and social life. They are among the best possible traits of character. This class of games makes maximal demands upon perceptive powers and ability to react quickly and accurately upon rapidly shifting conditions, requiring quick reasoning and judgment. Organization play of this sort begins to acquire a decided interest at about eleven or twelve years of age, reaches a strong development in the high schools, and continues through college and adult life.

Such are the main characteristics of the games which interest a child and aid his development at different periods. **Relation between development and play** They are all based upon a natural evolution of physical and psychological powers that can be only hinted at in so brief a sketch. Anyone charged with the education or training of a child should know the results of modern study in these particulars.

The studies in psychology of play by Karl Groos (*The Play of Animals* and *The Play of Man*), and the chapter by Professor William James on *Instinct* show how play activities are expressions of great basic instincts that are among the strongest threads in the warp and woof of character — instincts that should have opportunity to grow and strengthen by exercise, as in play and games. We have come to realize that play, in games and other forms, is nature's own way of developing and training power. As Groos impressively says, "We do not play because we are young; we have a period of youth so that we may play."

The entire psychology of play bears directly on the subject of games. Indeed, although the study of games in their various aspects is of comparatively recent date, the bibliography bearing on the subject, historic, scientific, psychologic, and educational, is enormous and demands a distinct scholarship of its own.

It is highly desirable that a teacher should know the significance of certain manifestations in a child's play interests. If they should not appear in due time, they should be en- **Age** couraged, just as attention is given to the hygiene of **classification** a child who is underweight for his age. But it should not be inferred that any hard and fast age limits may be set for the use of different plays and games. To assign such limits would be a wholly artificial procedure, yet one toward which there is some-times too strong a tendency. A certain game cannot be pre-scribed for a certain age, as one would diagnose and prescribe for a malady. Nothing in the life of either child or adult is more elastic than his play interests. Play would not be play were this otherwise. The caprice of mood and circumstance is of the very soul of play in any of its forms.

The experience of the writer has been chiefly away from dog-matic limitations in the use of games. Very young players and adults alike may find the greatest pleasure and interest in the same game. Previous training or experience, conditions of fatigue, the circumstances of the moment, and many other considerations determine the suitableness of games. To illustrate, the author has known the game of Three Deep, which is one of the best gym-nasium games for men, to be played with great interest and ability by a class of six-year-old boys; and the same game stupidly and uninterestedly bungled over by a class of much older boys who had not had previous training in games and were not alert and resourceful. Similarly, the comparatively simple game of Bombardment may be interesting and refreshing for a class of tired business men, while high-school pupils coming to care largely for team play may prefer Battle Ball, a more closely organized game of the same type. In general, boys and girls dislike the mode of play they have just outgrown, but the adult often comes again to find the greatest pleasure in the simpler forms, and this without reaching second childhood.

The grading of games, as for elementary or high school, constitutes a graded course based on experimental study of children's

Graded course of study on games

interests. This grading of the games for schools is made, not with the slightest belief or intention that the use of a game should be confined to any particular grade or age of pupils, but largely, among other considerations, because it has been found advantageous in a school course to have new material in reserve as pupils progress. The games have usually been noted for the earliest grade in which they have been found, on the average, of sufficient interest to be well played, with the intention that they be used thereafter in any grade where they prove interesting.

The relation of games to a school program is many-sided. To sit for a day in a class room observing indications of physical

Relation of games to school life

and mental strain and fatigue is to be convinced beyond question that the schoolroom work and conditions induce a tremendous nervous strain, not only through prolonged concentration on academic subjects, but through the abnormal repression of movement and social intercourse that becomes necessary for the maintenance of discipline and proper conditions of study. As a session advances, there is needed a steady increase in the admonitions that restrain neuromuscular activity as shown in the unnecessary handling of books and pencils and general restlessness; also restraint of a desire to use the voice and communicate in a natural outlet of the social instinct. One is equally impressed with the prolonged continuance of bad postures, in which the chest is narrowed and depressed, the back and shoulders rounded forward, and the lungs, heart, and digestive organs crowded upon one another in a way that impedes their proper functioning and induces passive congestion. In short, the nervous strain for both pupil and teacher and the need for vigorous stimulation of respiration and circulation, for an outlet for the repressed social and emotional nature, for the correction of posture, and for a change from abstract academic interests are all largely indicated. Nothing can correct the posture but formal gymnastic work selected and taught for that purpose; but the other conditions may be largely and quickly relieved through the use of games. Even five minutes in the class room will do this — five minutes of lively competition, of laughter, and of absorbing involuntary interest. The more physical activity there is in this the better, and fifteen minutes of even freer activity in the fresh air of the playground is more than fifteen times better.

The gameless school recess is a sad apology for such complete refreshment of body and mind. A few pupils take the center of the field of play, while the large majority, most of whom are in greater need of the exercise, stand or walk slowly around the edges, talking over the teacher and the lesson. An organized recess, by which is meant a program whereby only enough classes go to the playground at one time to give opportunity for all of the pupils to run and play at once, does away with these objections, if some little guidance or leadership be given the children for lively games. The best discipline the writer has ever seen, in either class room or playground, has been where games are used, the privilege of play being the strongest possible incentive to instant obedience before and after. Besides, with such a natural outlet for repressed instincts, their ebullition at the wrong time is not so apt to occur. Many principals object to recesses because of the moral contamination for which those periods are often responsible. The author has had repeated and convincing testimony of the efficacy of games to do away with this objection. The game becomes the one absorbing interest of recess, and everything else gives way before it.

The growth of large cities has been so comparatively recent that we are only beginning to realize the limita- **Sociological** tions they put upon normal life in many ways **and economic** and the need for special effort to counterbalance **significance** these limitations. The lack of opportunity for **of games** natural play for children and young people is one of the saddest and most harmful in its effects upon growth of body and character. The number of children who have only the crowded city streets to play in is enormous, and anyone visiting the public schools in the early fall days may readily detect by the white faces those who have had no other opportunity to benefit by the summer's fresh air and sunshine. The movement to provide public playgrounds for children and more park space for all classes in our cities is one connected vitally with the health, strength, and endurance of the population. The crusade against tuberculosis has no stronger ally. Indeed, vital resistance to disease in any form must be increased by such opportunities for fresh air, sunshine, and exercise. This whole question of the building up of a strong physique is an economic one, bearing directly on the industrial power of the individual, and upon community expenditures for hospitals and other institutions for the care of the dependent and disabled classes.

The crippling of moral power is found to be fully as much involved with these conditions as is the weakening of physical power. Police departments have repeatedly reported that the opening of playgrounds has resulted in decrease of the number of arrests and cases of juvenile crime in their vicinity; also in decrease of adult disturbances resulting from misdeeds of the children. They afford a natural and normal outlet for energies that otherwise go astray in destruction of property, altercations, and depredations of many sorts, so that the cost of a playground is largely offset by the decreased cost for detection and prosecution of crime, reformatories, and related agencies.

It would be a mistake to think that the children of the poor are the only ones who need the physical and moral benefit of normal childish play. One is forced to the conclusion that many children **Children of** of the rich are even more to be pitied, for the **the rich** shackles of conventionality enslave them from the outset. Many are *blasé* with opera and picture exhibits — typical forms of pleasure for the adult of advanced culture — without ever having had the free laughter and frolic of childhood. That part of the growing-up process most essential for character is literally expunged from life for them. One need spend but an hour in a city park to see that many children are restrained from the slightest running or frolic because it would soil their clothes or be otherwise "undesirable." The author recalls a private school for girls in which laughter was checked at recess because it was "unladylike."

In contrast to this barbarous repression are some delightful instances of provision for normal childish play and exercise for such children. In one of our large Eastern cities a **Teachers of** teacher was employed for several seasons to play **games** games with a group of children on a suburban lawn to which all repaired twice a week. This was genuine play, full of exercise and sport and laughter. In another Eastern city a teacher was similarly employed for many seasons to coach a Basket Ball team in the small rear area of the typical city residence. Teachers of physical training and others are doing much to organize this sort of exercise, including tramping clubs and teams for cross-country runs, and the encouragement of Tether Ball and other games suited to limited conditions.

As a nation we are slow to learn the value of recreation. We go to the extremes of using it either not at all or so excessively as to exhaust nervous energy to the point where "the day we most need a holiday is the day after a holiday." This may be different when we learn more fully that the recuperative power of short intervals of complete relaxation has a genuine investment value. The increased output of energy afterward, the **Investment-** happier spirits, prolonged endurance, clearer think- **value of** ing, and the greater ease and pleasure with which **recreation** work is done, more than compensate for the time required. Some large manufacturing concerns, stores, and offices have found it greatly to their advantage to give a daily recess period to employees at the firm's expense, the loss of working time being compensated in the quality of the output following, which shows, for instance, in the fewer mistakes that have to be rectified.

For the brain worker such benefit from periods of relaxation is even more apparent. Our strenuous and complicated civiliza- tion makes more and more necessary the fostering of **Brain** means for complete change of thought. When this **workers** can be coupled with invigorating physical exercise, as in active games, it is doubly beneficial; but whether games be active or quiet, the type of recreation found in them for both child and adult is of especial value. It affords an emotional stimulus and outlet, an opportunity for social co-operation, an involuntary absorption of attention, and generally an occasion for hearty laughter, that few other forms of recreation supply.

The games in this volume for house parties and country clubs are given with the hope of making games more available for adults, though with the knowledge that guests on such occasions take in a wide range of ages, and many games for young people are included. These are equally appropriate for the home circle. In addition, the so-called gymnasium games offer some of the finest recreative exercise.

The author would like to make a special plea for the playing together of adults and children. The pleasure to the child on **Play of** such occasions is small compared to the pleasure and **adults with** benefit that may be derived by the grown-up. To **children** hold, in this way, to that youth of spirit which appreciates and enters into the clear-eyed sport and frolic of the child is to have a means of renewal for the physical, mental, and moral nature. In a large city in the Middle West there is a club formed for the express purpose of giving the parents who are members an opportunity to enjoy their children in this way. The club meets one evening a week. It is composed of a few professional and business men and their wives and children. It meets at the various homes, the hostess being responsible for the program, which consists of musical or other numbers (rendered partly by the children and partly by the adults), of occasional dancing, and of games, some of which must always call for the mutual participation of the children and their elders. A more beautiful idea for a club could scarcely be devised. It is also a tragic fact that, lacking such an occasion, many parents have little opportunity to enjoy their children, or, alas! even to know them.

Another illustration may indicate even more strongly the benefits from such social gatherings of adults and children. In a **Games in** small town where the young boys and girls spent **country life** more evenings than seemed wise in places of public amusement, a teacher of physical training not long ago opened a class for them expressly to meet this situation. The program included games, dancing, and formal exercise, and a special effort was made to teach things of this sort that might be used for gatherings at home. The class fulfilled its object so well that the parents themselves became interested and began to attend the sessions and participate in the games until they were an integral part of all that went on — a wholesome and delightful association for all concerned, and one that practically ended the tendencies it was designed to overcome.

A very real factor in the failure of American country life to hold its young people is the lack of stimulation, and organization through trained guidance for the play activities of the young. It is a mistaken idea that country children and youths have through the spaciousness of environment alone all that they need of play. Organization and guidance are often needed more than for the city children whose instincts for social combination are more acute.

* * *

ORIGINS. — One may not close even a brief sketch of games and their uses without reference to the topic of origins. This has been studied chiefly from two different viewpoints, that of ethnology, in which the work of Mr. Stewart Culin is pre-eminent, and that of folklore, in which in English Mrs. Gomme and Mr. Newell have done the most extensive work. Both of these modes of study lead to the conclusion that the great mass of games originated in the childhood of the race as serious religious or divinitory rites. Indeed, many are so used among primitive peoples today. Very few games are of modern invention, though the development of many to the high point of organization and skill in which we know them is very recent. Basket Ball was a deliberate invention, by Dr. James Naismith, then of Springfield, Massachusetts, in 1892; Base Ball and Tennis, as we know them, were developed during the nineteenth century from earlier and simpler forms; Indoor Base Ball was devised by Mr. George W. Hancock, of Chicago, in 1887; Battle Ball and Curtain Ball, both popular gymnasium games, were devised by Dr. Dudley Allen Sargent, of Harvard University.

In ethnology the study of the origin and distribution of games "furnishes," says Mr. Culin, "the most perfect existing evidence of the underlying foundation of mythic concepts upon which so much of the fabric of our culture is built." The most scientific work on the entire subject of games lies in this direction. As revealed by board and other implement games the element of sport does not originally inhere in a game, the procedure being a rite of magic or religion, pursued mainly as a means of divination. In Mr. Culin's opinion, "the plays of children must be regarded apart from games, being dramatic and imitative, although copying games as they [the children] copy other affairs of life, and thus often preserving remains of ceremonials of remote antiquity."

From the folklore viewpoint Mrs. Gomme and Mr. Newell have brought to bear on games a wealth of knowledge of old customs and beliefs, discerning thereby a significance that might otherwise pass unnoticed and unappreciated. Thus we have the recognition of old well-worship rites in the little singing game "Draw a Bucket of Water"; of ancient house ritual in some of the dramatic games; in others the propitiation of deities that preside over the fertility of the fields; survivals of border warfare; old courtship and marriage observances; and many other rites and customs. Sometimes this recognition is merely one of analogy or association, leading to a surmise of the origin of a game; sometimes it is supported by old records and drawings, or references found in early literature. While often not so exact as the strictly scientific method, this folklore study throws a flood of light on the heritage of games that passes from child to child, giving to the subject added dignity and worth. One comes to appreciate that the childhood bereft of this heritage has lost a pleasure that is its natural right, just as it would lose if brought up in ignorance of Jack the Giant Killer, Beauty and the Beast, or Robinson Crusoe.

The class of games studied by the folklorists mentioned includes mainly those of active and dramatic character as distinguished from the board and implement games. Mrs. Gomme sees in their form, method of playing, the dialogue often included, and the fact of their continuance from generation to generation, an expression of the dramatic instinct, and considers them a valuable adjunct in the study of the beginnings of the drama. The student of games must find of great interest Mrs. Gomme's classification by formation, the line form being considered to represent, or to have grown out of, a contest between people from different countries or localities; the circle formation a representation of customs prevailing in one village, town, or tribe, and so on, with the arch form or tug of war, the winding-up games (as in Snail), etc.

Viewed in this light of their origin, games are especially fascinating. They take one back to the atmosphere that pervades romance: to quaint chronicles of kings and courtiers setting forth in brilliant train for some game that is the heritage of the child of today; to ladies in waiting on the Queen playing Babylon; to shepherds congregating on the moors, or early village communities dividing, over some forerunner of our college Football; to village lads and lasses dodging through the cornstalks with Barley Break, or milkmaids playing Stool Ball with their stools. For while it is rightly said that the serious occupations of adults at one period become the games of children at another, the statement omits an intermediate fact that strongly impresses the student of games: namely, that these activities, which at first were serious rites, have been used for sport by adults themselves before being handed down to children; as though the grown folk should masquerade for a time in their outworn garments before passing them on to following generations. Considering the varied interests that find expression in these games, one is further impressed by the fact that humanity passes thus in review its entire range of experience, transmuting into material for sport the circumstances of love and hatred, sorrow and rejoicing, fear and veneration. Nothing is too exalted or humble, too solemn or fearsome, to be the subject of these frolic events. Nature in all her panoply is here in dramatized form or reference — earth, stone, fire, and water; verdure and the kingdom of living things from beast to man; the seasons and the planets. Industry, love and war, fiends and deities, death itself and the hereafter, all pass in review, for one who sees the hidden significance, like a panorama of existence, as they passed, a plaything and a jest, before the gods of Olympus. It would seem as though humanity viewing in long perspective its own experiences, had found them all at last fit subjects to

"Beget the smiles that have no cruelty."

* * *

One dares to hope that this little craft, bearing as it does such a freight of gladness, may leave behind a wake of cheer, and laughter, and happiness.

JESSIE H. BANCROFT

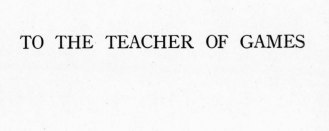

TO THE TEACHER OF GAMES

TO THE TEACHER OF GAMES

THE following suggestions are made with a view to the use of games under any circumstances, though many of them apply especially to large numbers of players under the guidance of a teacher or leader, as in playgrounds and schools.

The leader or teacher of a playground should approach his or her work largely in the spirit of the host or hostess whose duty it is to see that each individual guest is happy and has opportunity to share all of the pleasures of the occasion. But much more than this is involved in the relation of teacher and pupil. The teacher of games, or leader of children's play, needs, like all teachers, to have a sympathetic personal understanding of the players; a quick insight into character and motive; a knowledge of what to look for in the child's development at different periods, as indicated in the Introduction; and to be, in short, guide, philosopher, and friend.

The teacher should never hesitate, from questions of personal dignity, to participate in the play of children. Nothing can more quickly gain the respect and affection of a child than such participation. Every adult can doubtless recall the extreme pleasure experienced in childhood when some grown person entered into the childish play. In schools, where there is necessarily so much of formal discipline and dealing with large numbers *en masse*, one of the most valuable effects of games is to produce a more natural and sympathetic relationship between teacher and pupil, and a fuller appreciation on the part of the teacher of child nature. This effect from the use of games has been noted by scores of teachers, even those who were at first opposed to such use.

Every teacher will have his or her individual methods for teaching, discipline, and management of games. The following general suggestions, however, are the result of experience, and may be of assistance to the novice, at least.

The best method of teaching a game is to make a full explanation of it before the pupils take their places to play. If this be in **How to teach a game** a schoolroom, illustrative diagrams may often be drawn on the blackboard, and it is sometimes helpful, there or elsewhere, to have a few pupils go slowly (not running) through the general form of the game to illustrate it to the others. In a playground the same method may be used by having the players sit, if that be feasible, or by halting them in a march or after gymnastic exercises, to listen to the explanation. Never try to teach and play a game at the same time. The only exception to this rule should be where there is a large and disorderly crowd with which to deal. Then it may occasionally be best to start a game to gain interest and attention, and then halt for further explanation.

It often becomes necessary for the sake of discipline and unity to unite all of the players in a playground in one game. Com- **Class and group games** paratively few games, however, are successful when played by very large numbers. Classes may often be brought to order and attention in a playground by the simple device of marching, the march to end in one game for all of the players, or several games in groups.

An indication that too many players are taking part in a game is almost invariably to be found in a lack of interest on the part of the players, arising usually from the infrequency with which each player gets an opportunity to participate. The ultimate test of any game, however, from the recreative standpoint must be one of interest, and this is often found among players who are not participating in the action if competition be close. A teacher should watch closely for waning interest, and may often save the situation by dividing the players into two or more groups.

A resourceful teacher will find many ways of adapting games to large numbers. Among such devices may be mentioned (1) increasing the number of runners and chasers; for instance, in the game of Cat and Rat, there may be several cats and several rats; (2) in the circle games of simple character, especially the singing games, the circle may be duplicated, thus having two concentric circles, one within the other; (3) in many ball games it will be found possible to put more than one ball in play, as in Bombardment or Circle Club Bowls. Such suggestions as this are often made in the present volume in connection with the description of the games.

Group play, by which is meant the division of a large number of players into smaller squads or groups, is undoubtedly the best method for getting the best sport and the greatest playing values out of most games. Such a division of players is not always an easy matter to inaugurate, untrained players being inclined to follow the teacher from point to point in the playground. This may be obviated by appointing group leaders, each of whom should understand the game to be played and be appointed to take charge of it. Older children and almost invariably the children who are disorderly or inclined to disturb the general harmony and discipline of the playground are the best ones to charge with such responsibility. This method serves the double purpose of quelling their disorderly propensities by occupying them in a position of responsibility, and takes care of a group of players at the same time. When the group method is used in schools, it is advisable to appoint the leaders of the groups, or to allow the children to elect them, before leaving the class room for the playground.

The choice of games to be played should be left to a vote or to the suggestion of the players. The teacher's **Choice of** function in this regard is to suggest, not to dictate. **games** In schools this choice may generally best be made in the class room, before a class goes to the playground.

A teacher should be ready with suggestions for new games or occupation of some sort when interest wanes in a game that is being played; but a new game should not be suggested until there is evidence that players are tired of the old one. Do not make the mistake of thinking that children want to play games incessantly during a half-day session of a playground. Children like quiet pursuits occasionally as well as do adults, and it is well to alternate active games with such quiet periods and also with marching, gymnastics, folk dancing, or periods of free activity. So-called quiet games will be found useful under such circumstances.

Each playground leader or teacher should be provided with a whistle. This saves a great deal of strain on the voice, and should
Discipline be understood from the outset to command instant quiet, all play to be suspended when it is heard. The most joyous play goes always with the best discipline. Both children and adult players like strength and decision in a teacher or leader. Indeed, they instinctively place themselves under the leadership of the decided and dominant characters among themselves. It has been the experience of the author that discipline in schools is greatly helped by the playing of games, partly because the privilege of play or the fear of its loss is one of the strongest incentives to order at other times, but also because of the happy outlet afforded for normal tendencies and the disciplinary training of the games themselves.

Get the playing values out of games. By this is meant, see that every child gets as much opportunity as possible for participation
Playing values in the actual physical exercise of the game and in all the phases of play that make him a successful, alert, resourceful player. The result of this and the test of it will be the amount of interest and sport in the games. *Do not make the games too serious. In purely recreative games get laughter and frolic. The discipline of silence comes with advanced team games.*

Encourage timid pupils to give dares and to take risks. No class of players needs more sympathetic or tactful understanding and help from a teacher than the timid. Such children often suffer greatly through their shyness. They should first be brought into play in some form of game that does not make them conspicuous; one, for instance, in which they do what all the other players do, or merely take turns. Such children should be encouraged by praise of their successful efforts, and especial care should be taken not to call attention to their failures.

See that the selfish or the most capable children do not have the lion's share of the play; the opportunities should be equally distributed. It is often necessary for a teacher to distinguish between self-assertiveness, which is a natural phase of the development of the sense of individuality, or selfishness and "bullying," which are exaggerated forms of the same tendency. Both may need repression and guidance, but only the latter are reprehensible.

Encourage each pupil to be alert to see when it is his turn and to be quick in play. Every game should be a sense-training game, developing power for quick perception of external stimuli and quick and expert reaction to such stimuli.

In chasing games, encourage interesting chases, the runner to take unexpected turns and dodges, making capture difficult. The shortest distance between two points for a chase often makes a dull game, devoid of sport.

Young players will need to be helped to use reason and judgment in games, as to when to run risks of capture, how to attack the opponent's weakest point, etc.

Do not treat children as though they were made of glass and fear to see them tumble down. Every child, boy or girl, ought to be able to bear a few falls, knocks, and bruises. This is nature's way of training a child to be more observant or agile. Besides, physical hardihood is one of the best possible results from the playing of games. Do not coddle a child who has received an injury. Cultivate a stoic spirit. If it is a slight injury, have the child go on with his play and he will soon forget it. If it requires treatment of any sort, take the player at once away from the playground or vicinity of the other players and apply first-aid remedies until medical assistance can be obtained.

Team play is one of the highest forms of play. The teacher should look for the beginning of the tendency toward it as shown in a fondness for the play of opposing groups, **Team play** manifest from ten to twelve years of age. This tendency should be encouraged and developed into more closely organized types of team games. The greatest value of team play lies in the co-operation of the players, all working together for a common end, a player's thought and effort being to do what is best for his team rather than to use his skill for individual glory. (See paragraph on *Team Play*, page 50.)

The number and difficulty of rules and regulations governing a game go through a steady increase as children grow older. The games for very little children have practically no rules except the following of turns in rotation. Later come such games as those in which a player's turn comes only on a given signal, and it is a foul to start before this signal, as in relay races. Many other **Enforcement** types of rules appear as the games progress. These **of rules** reach their culmination in ball games where, amid the excitement of a game, a player must exercise heedfulness and restraint in the method of playing upon a ball, the range of movement allowed from a given base, and many other points.

A teacher should understand clearly that the inhibitive power of the will necessary for the observation of rules is a slow and late development, and that its training by means of rules is one of the most important educational features in the use of games. (See Introduction.) Players should therefore not be expected to take part in a game that is much beyond their power in this regard. A teacher should not announce a rule unless sure that it is reasonable to expect the players to observe it. Having announced a rule, however, enforce it to the full extent. To condone the infringement of a rule is equivalent to a lie in its injury to the moral nature of a player. It is a weak-willed teacher who does not enforce rules. Players will respect far more a strict disciplinarian than a weak one. Every player who infringes a rule should suffer the full penalty therefor. Only by such means can there be trained the strength of will to avoid such infringement in the future, for it should be repeated that such infringements are not always the result of intentional cheating. They indicate very often an undeveloped power of will, and the teacher should be able to discriminate between the sneaking cowardice that would win unfairly and mere lack of power. Both causes, however, should lead to the same result of suffering the full penalty for any infringement of rules.

Teach players to play to win — with all their might. But with this cultivate a sense of honor. Have them realize that any **Honor** victory not earned strictly by their own merits or those of their team is a disgrace rather than a cause for congratulation. No better opportunity can ever be found for inculcating the knowledge that to be trusted is far greater than to be praised. A player should scorn rewards not based on merit, and should be led to feel that a defeat resulting from an honest trial of strength is an honorable defeat; that the real issue is as much concerned with the amount of effort put forth as with the comparative results of it measured with some other player. A defeated player should be led to recognize and do honor to the prowess of his adversary, and so to congratulate him honestly. A sense of superior power should never degenerate into gloating over a defeated adversary or into contempt for his weaker ability. Many thrilling examples of honest mutual admiration between victor and vanquished may be gleaned from the history of warfare, as when Grant handed back the sword of surrender to Lee.

In athletic games players should learn that to question or dispute the decision of judges or other officials presiding over games is thoroughly unsportsmanlike and a species of dishonor. Having once placed themselves under officials, decisions must be accepted without cavil at the time. The natural desire to learn how a decision was reached in an athletic event must be held in check until the judges have opportunity to announce fouls or other features of scoring that determine the result. It should always be borne in mind, by both players and coaches, that the officials, each of whom is concentrating on some one feature of the play, know what happens far more accurately than the general observer. It is also thoroughly unsportsmanlike and counts as a foul, disqualifying a player, to receive directions or coaching of any sort from an instructor during a game.

FLOOR FORMATION. — The terms "formation" and "floor formation" are commonly used to designate the placing of players in the playground and gymnasium in the lines, circles, groups, or opposing sides, necessary for the starting of a game. Commonly used are the following formations, illustrated in the accompanying diagram :

File formation. — Players stand in a single file, one behind the other.

Rank formation. — Players stand in line side by side.

Relay formation — **single** (*for teams in sprints and relay races*). — Each team stands in single file with distinct space between files ; leaders toe a starting line and as they run the next players move up.

(*See other relay formations on page* 202.)

Single circle or ring formation. — Players stand in a circle one and one as in single file. They may all face inward toward the center of the circle, or outward with backs toward the center, or alternated, one facing inward

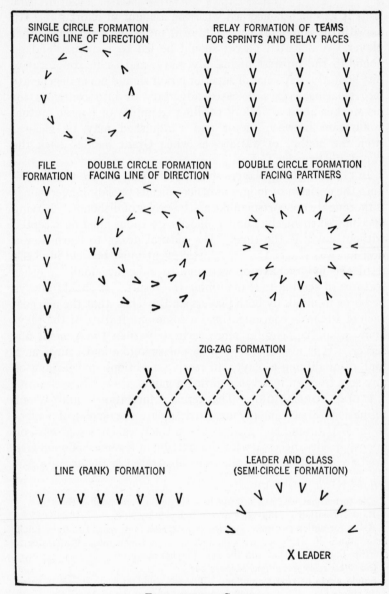

FORMATION FOR GAMES
(See also Relay Races, page 202.)

and one outward; or they may all face in the direction around the circle in which they are to run or play, called the line of direction. For the latter see on accompanying diagram "*Single circle formation facing line of direction.*"

Double circle formation. — Two circles are concentric, one inside the other. In some games the two circles face each other as partners; in others they all face in the same line of direction; or the two circles may move or play in opposite directions.

(*For Spoke, Star, or Circle relay, see page* 202.)

Zigzag formation. — Players stand in two ranks, usually full-arm distance apart, the two ranks facing each other with a considerable distance between ranks, varying in different games. Each player stands opposite an opening in the opposing rank. In some games each two ranks so facing represent a team; in other games the players of two different teams stand alternately side by side in each rank. There are also other variations. The play of the ball is zigzag from rank to rank as described in "Zigzag" games.

Leader and class. — This formation is used in a considerable number of games. A leader stands in front of a group of players, the play being from him to each one of them in turn. The group may stand in a straight rank in front of him or in a semicircle.

To direct players into a formation quickly and without confusion requires a clear knowledge of methods on the part of the teacher. Some methods are here offered.

For all formations pupils should be trained to move quickly. Formations made from marching order may often be done on the double-quick.

CIRCLE OR RING FORMATION. — For *small numbers* no formal procedure is needed to get the players into a ring formation. For very little children the teacher should simply stretch his or her own hands sideways, taking a child by each hand to show what is wanted, and telling the others to form a circle. All will naturally clasp hands in the same way. Children should be urged to move quickly for such formations. For some games the hands remain clasped. For others the hands are dropped (unclasped) after the ring is formed. The distance between players may be gauged by the stretch of the arms when the hands are clasped, making the ring larger or smaller. With older players the teacher's participation in the formation of the circle is not necessary, the mere command to "Form circle!" being adequate.

For *large numbers* the ring formation is best achieved from a line standing in single file. The players should march or run, the leader of the file describing a circle and joining hands with the rear player of the file, all of the others joining hands similarly with their neighbors.

DOUBLE OR CONCENTRIC CIRCLES. — Where there are to be two circles, one within the other, as in Three Deep, Zigzag Ball, or some of the singing games for large numbers, players should march in a column of twos (two by two), and the leaders should describe a circle until the ends meet. All then face inward.

Another method of forming concentric circles is to form a single circle, and have every alternate player step inwards. Or the players may number off by twos, and those bearing the odd (or even) numbers take one or two steps toward the center of the circle. All numbering-off methods, however, are comparatively slow.

OPPOSING TEAMS OR LINES. — For assigning large numbers of players quickly in opposing teams or lines, the order "Teams, line-up!" may be sufficient; otherwise the following methods are among the most orderly:

I. The players "fall in" for a march in single file. They march up the center of the room or ground; the first player turns to the right and the next to the left, and so on alternately, taking stations at the opposite sides of the room or ground; they are thus separated into two opposing groups, those which turn to the right forming one group or team, and those to the left another.

This method is even quicker if players march in columns of twos or fours, alternate ranks turning to alternate sides.

II. Players may be required to march in columns of twos (two abreast), halt, and those in one file of the column step to one side of the playground instead of marching to the front and separating, as in I, and those in the other file to the opposite side.

Where an even division of running ability or height for catching balls is necessary, players should be sized when lining up for either of the above methods.

III. When players in a gymnasium or playground have already been numbered for gymnastic purposes, the odd numbers may be directed to one end of the playground to form one team, and the even numbers to the opposite end for the other team.

GROUP FORMATIONS. — To get players into many small groups, a division may often best be made from the marching formations. Players may be brought for this purpose into columns of four (marching four abreast) or more, halted, and each file in turn directed to some particular location in the playground.

Where time is not a consideration, or the number of players is smaller, more deliberate methods of counting out, choosing sides, etc., may be used, described in the chapter on "Counting-out."

A word should be said of the differing psychological effects of the various formations.

The circle or ring formation has a pronounced tendency toward a spirit of unity among players. Each player may see and become somewhat acquainted with all other players in a group, in a way not practicable in any other formation. Anyone who has met strangers at a dinner party or a committee meeting gathered at a round table will comprehend the significance of this. In the kindergarten, this principle is used largely, each day's exercises opening with the pupils in a circle. A game in circle formation is therefore often one of the best means of making acquainted players who are strangers to each other, and of giving a sense of united interest to a heterogeneous group.

The sense of being united in a common interest, or *esprit de corps*, may be gained to some extent in some general forms of playground activities such as marching. As children grow into the tendency to enjoy group or team play, the competitive spirit becomes very strong, and games in which the players work in competitive teams, as in relay races, or in opposing sides, as in Bombardment, may serve the purpose of continuous mutual interest. As a rule the competitive spirit is strong in games in the line and group formations, and, indeed, is usually the basis of such formations.

COUNTING–OUT; CHOOSING SIDES

COUNTING–OUT; CHOOSING SIDES AND TURNS; "WHO'S IT?"

Counting-out rhymes and other methods of choosing players for games form one of the most interesting topics in the whole study of children's games. Such rhymes and methods are found in use all over the world and are prehistoric, having descended like the great mass of children's games from the serious practices of adults in the childhood of the race. Classic literature has innumerable references to such customs, as in the *Iliad*, where the heroes cast lots in the cap of Atrides Agamemnon to know who shall go forth to battle with Hector, or choose by similar means their places in the funeral games for Patroclus. Many instances of the use of these practices are recorded in Scripture, including the famous one of the casting of lots for the seamless garment. Much collecting and investigating have been done as to these methods, several collections of counting-out rhymes, covering hundreds of examples, having been made in the interests of folklore, the history of magic, etc. Such rhymes are found in Asia, Africa, Europe, and America, not to mention the Sandwich Islands and other places presenting primitive conditions. The largest collection and most thorough study published in America was that made by Mr. H. Carrington Bolton of the Smithsonian Institution. These rhymes unquestionably originated in old superstitions and rites, including incantations of the old magicians and practices of divination by lot. The doggerel of counting-out rhymes is often traceable to old Latin formulas used for these purposes, a fact that shows the absurdity and artificiality of purposely manufactured rhymes.

In the majority of games it is necessary to assign various players to their parts in some manner that shall be strictly impartial. Thus, one player may have to be chosen to be "It" — that is, to take the prominent, arduous, or often disadvantageous or disagreeable part; for example, the part of "Black Tom" in the game of that name, the "blind man" in blindfold games, etc. In many other games the players have to determine who shall have the first turn, or the order of rotation in which all shall play, as who shall be the first back in leapfrog, etc. In still other games, such as Prisoners' Base, Black and White, and many ball games, opposing sides or teams have to be chosen.

Some games have their own distinctive methods of assigning parts, but in most cases any method may be used. A few of the most popular, practical, and useful methods are given here. (See also *Floor Formations* in previous chapter.)

For very little children, the teacher or leader should choose or assign the players for the different parts, such as who shall be the first cat or mouse in the game of "Kitty White," or who shall go into the center in many of the singing games. This method is often used by the hostess for parlor games in children's parties, though many other methods may be used. For older players, the following methods will be found helpful.

COUNTING-OUT. — This is a very popular method among children. One player in the group, generally self-appointed, but sometimes chosen by popular consent, does the "counting out." He repeats a rhyme or jingle, touching one player on the chest for each accent of the verses. He always begins with himself and then touches the first one on his left, and so on around the circle or group in regular order. Any player to whom falls the last word is "out"; that is, he is eliminated from the succeeding counting and is not to be "It," generally a matter for rejoicing. Such a player steps out of the group at once. This counting is continued, the verses being repeated over and over, until only two players are left, when the formula is again gone over, the one to whom the last word falls being free, and the remaining player "It." When a verse is not long enough to go around the entire group, the player at his discretion may lengthen it by adding "One, two, three, — out goes he!" (or she); or "O–U–T spells out!"

From many verses the following, without which no collection could well make its appearance, are chosen as typical for the purpose:

> "Onery, twoery, tickery tee,
> Hanibal, Crackible, turnablee.
> Whing, whang, muskadan,
> Striddledum, straddledum, twenty-one!"

The following counting-out rhyme is famous in literary annals as having been taught to Sir Walter Scott before his open fire by that dainty little maiden, Marjorie Fleming:

> "Wonery, twoery, tickery seven;
> Alibi, crackaby, ten and eleven;
> Pin, pan, muskydan;
> Tweedle-um, twoddle-um,
> Twenty-wan; eeerie, ourie, owrie,
> You, are, out!"

The following are old and popular forms:

"Enna, mena, mina, mo,
Catch a nigger by the toe;
If he hollers, let him go,
Enna, mena, mina, mo!"

"Aina, maina, mona, mike;
Bassalona, bona, strike;
Hare, ware, frown, hack;
Halico, balico, wee, wo, wy, whack!"

"Monkey, monkey, bottle of beer;
How many monkeys are there here?
One, two, three, out goes he (or she)!"

"Little fishes in a brook,
Father caught them with his hook,
Mother fried them in a pan,
Father ate them like a man."

> "One and two and three, four, five,
> Hopping Rabbit much alive;
> Hunter sees him, Piff! Puff! Pooh!
> Rabbit finished, that is you!"
> (*Last verse from the Russian*)

HOLDERS. — A favorite method of choosing players, especially with boys, is that called "holders" or "hand holders." When a group of boys decides to play a game, one suddenly shouts, "Picker-up!" picks up a pebble and hands it to another boy. The one who picks it up is called the stone picker, and is "out" to start with; that is, he does not have to take part in the guessing of hands which follows.

Mr. Beard, who has recorded from observation this method of choosing players, gives an additional point which the writer has not happened upon. He says: "The first player has scarcely shouted 'Picker-up!' before another cries 'Wipe-'er-off!' and a third, 'Stone-holder!' 'Picker-up hands the stone to Wipe-'er-off. Picker-up is then free. Wipe-'er-off makes a great show of wiping the stone off on his trouser leg, and hands it to Stone-holder. Wipe-'er-off is then free, and Stone-holder puts his hands behind him,' etc. This preliminary of handing the stone is often omitted, especially where a large group is to play, as the first holder of the stone has in a large group a good chance to go 'out' as the guessing proceeds."

The person who holds the stone (a coin, button, or any small object may be used) places his hands behind his back so that the other players may not know in which hand he disposes the stone, and then holds his closed fists out in front of him, with the backs of the hands (knuckles) upward. The first player on his left steps forward and touches the hand in which he thinks there is no stone. The holder opens that hand; if the guess has been correct, the guesser is "out" and the holder must go through the same performance with the next guesser. Should the one who guesses touch the hand which holds the stone instead of the empty hand, then he must become holder, taking the stone and going through the same play with it, the holder from whom he took it being "out." In other words, the object of the guessing is to choose the hand which is empty, a successful guess putting the guesser out, a wrong guess making him the next holder and putting the preceding holder out.

DRAWING CUTS. — In this method of choosing players, a blade of grass or hay or a slip of paper is provided for each player in the group. These should all be cut of approximately the same length, with the exception of one which should be quite short. One player, the holder, holds these in a bunch in one hand, first getting even all of the ends that are to show. The other ends are concealed in the hand, so that it is impossible, by looking at the extended ends, to tell which is the short piece. Each player in the group then draws one of the slips or pieces, the one who gets the short piece being "It."

If desired, the slips may be put in a hat or box, the players drawing without looking in. This method is quite suitable for parlor games, where it is much used.

TOSS-UP. — The toss-up is a very simple and popular method of choosing players. It consists in tossing a coin in the air and allowing it to land on the ground, to see which side will fall uppermost, each player having previously chosen a side, or, in other words, taken his chance on that side landing upward. Generally a coin is used, but a stone will do as a substitute, one side being marked. Shells may also be used, the throw to be determined by the light or dark side or the convex or concave side falling upward. The method of tossing is the same for any of these articles. One player tosses the coin in the air, the players having chosen "heads" or "tails"; the side of the coin having the date on it is called "heads," the other side "tails." The side wins which falls uppermost. If a coin or shell does not lie flat on the ground, but rests edgewise, the toss does not count. When this method is used by a group of players, each player is considered out who makes a lucky guess. Any player who guesses the wrong side takes the next turn for tossing the coin. Sometimes it is required that the choice (of heads or tails) shall be made while the coin is in the air, probably to avoid any juggling on the part of the tosser.

RACING; LAST OVER; ETC. — A popular method of determining who shall be "It" for a game is for the players to race to a certain point, the last one to reach it being "It." Or one of a group of players deciding on a game may say "Last over the fence!" when all climb or vault over a fence, the last one over being "It." In the gymnasium this method is sometimes used when the players are grouped in the center of the floor. Upon hearing the shout "Last over!" they all scatter and jump over any available piece of apparatus, bars, horse, etc., the last one to vault being "It."

The Wabanaki Indians use an interesting method, combining counting-out and racing. The players being gathered in a group, each player puts out two fingers, resting them on the ground, a stone, or any convenient place. A counting-out rhyme is then used, one finger being touched for each accent. A finger is doubled under whenever a verse ends on it, until only three fingers are left. The owners, whether they be two or three players, immediately start on a run, the counter chasing them. The one caught is "It."

Some games have each their own distinctive method of choosing players, as in Duck on a Rock. These methods are described with the games wherever they have been obtainable.

CHOOSING SIDES. — For many games the players are divided into two opposing groups or teams. When there is no special leader or captain for each group, some of the above methods of counting-out or choosing are used for assigning players to one side or the other. In most games, however, where there are opposing groups, a captain or leader is first selected. This part sometimes goes to the person who first shouts for it, but it is more usual for the players to choose captains, as special qualities are generally needed in persons in that position, and even young children are glad to place themselves under strong leadership. Captains or leaders, however, may be chosen by any of the previously mentioned methods, or they may be selected by a teacher or leader.

Two captains or leaders having been chosen, each chooses his own players, the choice being made alternately one at a time, the first captain selected generally having first choice. A good captain will select his players for the playing qualities needed in the particular game to be played. These qualities will vary in different games, and different players may be chosen for excellence in one particular direction, such as swift running, agile dodging, boldness in giving dares and taking risks; in ball games, skill in catching or throwing, or other forms of play; and in all games, the ability to "play fair," and to co-operate generously and with good temper. A player may be unskillful, and yet very valuable as a general helper if he possesses the qualities for co-operation. The unpopular player is nearly always a selfish person, one who disregards rules or tries to win unfairly. Aside from the general contempt engendered by such qualities, a player having them is undesirable because he gets his side into disputes or runs a greater risk of increasing the opponent's score with fouls.

ORGANIZED ATHLETICS

ORGANIZED ATHLETICS

AMATEUR AND PROFESSIONAL STANDARDS. — One of the most important questions in athletics is the distinction between amateur and professional standards, as only on a basis of clear distinction between these two classes of players can competition be kept equal and a true spirit of sport maintained.

The amateur plays for the pleasure of the game and for its physical, mental, moral, and social benefits. Amateur skill is that which may be cultivated in the leisure time available from the serious business and affairs of life. As soon as a player exceeds this amount of attention to a game, he gains an unfair advantage and thus places himself in another class.

A professional player in any game or sport is one who plays, not alone for the pleasure and benefit of the game itself, but as a business, devoting to it an amount of time that develops skill beyond the average attainable by one who takes it up as a recreation. Professional players usually follow a game partly or wholly as a means of income. Thus the entire status of the professional in sport, including his interest, motive, and skill, is on a different plane from that of the amateur.

From the classic days of Greece to the present time, playing for money, or for prizes of monetary value, has been considered the main distinction between the amateur and the professional in sport. This includes compensation as an instructor or coach as well as for playing the game. To play with or against a professional has also been held to disqualify an amateur as such and rank him as a professional. The money reward, however, is merely a symbol of a fundamental difference in spirit, motive, and attainment. There is no stigma in being a professional athlete; there is a stigma in competing with amateurs when one's interest and motives in, and advantages for, a game make competition unequal.

ATHLETIC ORGANIZATION. — There are athletic organizations, national in scope, that prescribe uniform rules for games, establish amateur standards, and conduct championship competitions. Competition may be in the form of an individual contest, a group contest, or the more highly developed and complicated form of contest called team play.

INDIVIDUAL COMPETITION is characteristic of track and field athletics and of some ball games. In track and field games, the competition is essentially individual, even when a group, competing for the honor of their college or organization, is called a team. In such cases the combined score of the different contestants — whether all enter each event, as in the pentathlon, or each appears in only his specialized events — determines the winning team; but there is none of the more complicated interplay between different players that distinguishes the term "team play."

Some of the most popular ball games are essentially individual competition. This is true of golf, tennis, handball, and squash.

CLASS ATHLETICS offer a form of competition in which all of the members of a class, or a given percentage of them, try their skill in systematic succession in an event, the combined score making a class record.

INTRAMURAL GAMES are those played within one institution, as distinguished from games involving outside competition, *intramural* meaning "within the walls."

TEAM PLAY.[1] — The term "team," as applied to games, means a group of players combining efforts for a common end. The highest form of team organization is that in which the individuals support and aid each other, each taking an understood part, to a common end. To comprehend a complicated situation, to adjust one's self instantly to it, to play any part that helps, however inconspicuous, to unite with others for a common result make for good team work. Well-trained teams act as a unit, and the game is as much one of wits as of muscle. It has been stated that real team play is peculiar to the Anglo-Saxon race.

MATCH GAMES. — A match game, or championship game, is one played to determine which of two or more contestants is the

[1] See also paragraph on *Team Play*, page 31.

superior player, the championship being awarded to the player or team that wins. Such match games take various forms, according to the number of contestants. The simplest form of challenge is that in which one player, team, or organization challenges another, there being only the two concerned. Football is a game played in this way; a given team challenges individually only a few organizations in a season, as it is too hard a game for tournaments. Three or four hard games are the most that should be expected of a football team in a season. A club or organization may conduct open championship games for a given class of institutions, as colleges; or for a certain geographical territory, as a city, or state, or district; or such competition may be national or international in scope. For many of the more popular games, such as tennis, golf, polo, rowing races, etc., the official national or international organization for that particular game conducts championship games annually, or at longer intervals, while the modern Olympic Games throw open worldwide competition.

TOURNAMENTS. — Baseball, basketball, hockey, and other games which make lighter demands on the players than football, and which may therefore be played against a considerable number of competing teams, are played in tournaments. A tournament may take the form of a round-robin series or an elimination series.

ROUND-ROBIN SERIES. — In this plan of competition, each team plays every other team. It is therefore used when not too many organizations are competing — usually from three to five. In such a series, team A plays B, C, D, and E; team B plays A, C, D, and E; and so on, until each team has played every other team.

The winning team is that one which wins the greatest number of games, or the largest percentage of the total number of games played, in the series.

ELIMINATION SERIES. — This plan is used where so many teams are to compete that it would be impracticable for each team to play every other. Then it is decided by lot, or by assignment by the officials in charge, which two teams shall play against each other in the first and succeeding trials. For example, it may be decided that in the first trials A and B shall play against each other, C and D against each other, etc. The winning team in each of these pairs is then paired by the same method with one other winning team ; the winners from the second series of games are paired off, and so on, until, finally, all are eliminated except the final winning team, which is the champion of the series.

In one or more of this series of trials there may be an odd team without a competitor. This is called a "bye," and that team is assigned to play with a team in the following series; in other words, it is not compelled to compete in its particular series in order to have the right to compete in the following series.

CHAMPIONSHIPS. — The winner in a championship contest is said to hold the championship title, and this is held until some other player or team wins in subsequent games. Sometimes the winning contestant must be met and defeated in order that the title may pass to another; this is the case in some games of individual competition, such as the national and international championships in golf and tennis. Sometimes the championship is annual, the 1937 champion, for example, holding the championship only for that year, and not necessarily entering the 1938 games of the same class, so that the 1938 champion may, or may not, have to defeat the previous year's champion in order to win. Sometimes, especially in track and field events, it is a record, as well as an individual, that is competed against. Thus, the intercollegiate record in the running high jump for a given year may be unbroken (unsurpassed) for many subsequent years, and yet each year's games will have its champion, who makes the highest record for that particular year, though it may be less than the highest intercollegiate record.

In any games the same champion may hold the title indefinitely by winning in successive years.

HANDICAPS. — When a very wide margin of difference exists between the ability of two players, competition between them would obviously be impracticable were one not handicapped. A handicap is an extra burden placed on the more proficient player whereby he allows to the less proficient a certain number of points on his score, or an equivalent, before a comparison in the two scores begins. Just what form the handicap will take varies for different games. For example, in golf a certain number of strokes are allowed the less proficient player by the one who is handicapped; in a contest in high jumping a certain height is expected of the more proficient contestant in addition to the height cleared by his competitor; in a race, the handicapped player must cover a greater distance.

The official organization for each game that is susceptible of handicap regulations has established a systematic method and scale for handicaps.

A scratch player is one who starts or plays at par. That is, he starts from the regular starting line. In a handicap race the runner who is handicapped is a "scratch man," and those to whom he gives an allowance start in front of him. The term is derived from the scratch, or starting line in a race, though applied to other events.

PRIZES AND TROPHIES. — These are usually limited in form or value in all amateur sports; that is, an amateur may not compete for a money prize, or for trophies of great intrinsic value, nor may he sell his trophies.

A championship or title is essentially an honor, and there may or may not be tangible evidence of it in the form cf a prize or trophy. Sometimes each contestant in match games is given a permanent souvenir in the form of a pin or medal, while the champion receives in addition a loving cup or other prize or trophy to hold until won at subsequent games by some other contestant.

NONCOMPETITIVE AWARDS. — Believing that the true spirit of amateur sport is often defeated through overemphasis on competition, a plan for noncompetitive awards has arisen that has been highly successful in some schools. The awards are for participating in a minimum amount and variety of exercise, irrespective of beating someone else in each particular kind.

OFFICIALS. — For informal games it is not usual to have officials; for all challenge or match games, they are essential.

The head official of a game is usually either an Umpire or Referee, the particular title being specified in the official rules for each game. The duties pertaining to these two titles are sometimes identical, though in games where both officials are engaged, the duties are different. Other officials customary for ball games are Linesmen, who judge of certain phases of a game in relation to boundary lines; Scorer; Timekeeper; and in track and field games, Judges for the various events; Inspectors; Clerk of the Course; and Marshal.

The method of selecting officials is prescribed by the official rules of all games. The head official, at least, must be approved by both parties to a contest.

The success of a match game depends immeasurably on the officials and too much care cannot be taken in their selection. While every official of a game should preferably be experienced as a player of the game over which he officiates, it does not follow that every player, however expert, would make a good official. Keen, quick perception, an immediate working knowledge of rules, power of accurate judgment and quick decision, absolute impartiality, superiority to any personal considerations, and a strong unflinching will to enforce rules and decisions — these are some of the qualities needed for a successful official.

For some games, there are, in some localities, central committees that form lists of authorized officials; and the custom is spreading of training officials.

MISCELLANEOUS ACTIVE GAMES

MISCELLANEOUS ACTIVE GAMES

✓ ALL UP RELAY

10 to 60 or more players
Playground; gymnasium; schoolroom

Intermediate
to senior high school

The players line up in single relay formation behind a starting line. Directly in front of each team, at the opposite end of the running space (which should be from twenty to fifty feet long), are drawn two circles, each three feet in diameter, and placed side by side, with rims touching. In one of the circles of each pair place three Indian clubs.

On a signal, number one of each file runs forward and, with one hand only, changes the clubs from one circle to the other. Each club must be made to stand, and none must touch the outline of the circle. As soon as each player finishes this, he touches off the next player and passes off, back of the line.

This second player, on receiving the touch-off, runs forward to the circles and changes the clubs from the second ring back to the first, observing the same rules of procedure. Each player in turn does this, the file winning whose last player is first to dash over the starting line on his return.

This is a very popular game for athletic contests, especially for younger girls. When used in this way, an especially careful observation should be kept for fouls by official judges. One foul is scored against a team for (a) each time a runner starts over the line without the "touch-off"; (b) each time both hands are in play at once in changing the clubs; (c) each club that is not replaced after falling; (d) each club that is left standing anywhere but within the circle for which it was intended. When played thus, according to strict athletic rules, the teams win in the order of finishing plus the smallest score on fouls. Thus, if team A finishes first with six fouls, team B finishes second with four fouls, and team C finishes third with no fouls, team C wins, being given first place, team B second place, and team A third place. The score would be written as follows:

Teams	Order of Finishing	Number of Fouls	Order of Winning
A	1	6	3
B	2	4	2
C	3	0	1

✓ ANIMAL BLIND MAN'S BUFF

10 to 30 or more players   *Elementary grades*
Parlor; gymnasium; playground

One player is blindfolded and stands in the center of a circle with a wand, stick, or cane in his hand. The other players dance around him in circle until he taps three times on the floor with his cane, when they must stand still. The blind man thereupon points his cane at some player, who must take the opposite end of the cane in his hand. The blind man then commands him to make a noise like some animal, such as a cat, dog, cow, sheep, lion, donkey, duck, parrot. From this the blind man tries to guess the name of the player. If the guess is correct, they change places. If wrong, the game is repeated with the same blind man.

The players should disguise their natural tones and height, to deceive the blind man.

Where there are thirty or more players, two blind men should be placed in the center.

There is much sport in this game for either children or adults or both together. The author has known it to be the occasion for great merriment under all three circumstances.

ANIMAL CHASE

10 to 30 or more players   *Intermediate grades*
Playground; gymnasium

Two pens are marked off in distant corners of the playground. One player, called the chaser, stands at one side of one of these pens. The other players stand within the pen that is nearest the chaser. All of the players in the pen are named for different animals, there being several players of each kind. Thus there may be a considerable number each of bears, deer, foxes, etc. The chaser calls the name of any animal he chooses as a signal for the players to run. For instance, he may call "Bears!" whereupon all of the players who represent bears must run across to the other pen, the chaser trying to catch them.

Any player caught before reaching the opposite pen changes places with the chaser.

The particular point of difference between this and some other similar chasing games is that the chaser may not know just which of the players in the pen will start out in response to the name of the animal that he calls.

ARROW CHASE

8 to 16 players   *Children or adults*
                          Out of doors

This game is especially adapted to surroundings where a very devious chase may be given, with many opportunities for the runners to go out of sight, double back on their course, etc., as in a village or the country.

The players are divided into two teams. One of these teams, each member having a piece of chalk, starts out on a run over any route chosen by their leader. Every ten feet the runners must chalk a small arrow somewhere along their path, the object of the hunting party being to overtake these runners, discovering their course by the arrows. No attempt is made to get back to a goal, as in many other games of chase.

The hunting team at the starting place counts two thousand to give the runners a full start, and then pursues them. The runners will use all possible finesse in making it difficult to find their arrows, although it is a rule of the game that the arrow must be in plain sight, though not necessarily from the point of view of the course taken. It may be marked on the farther side of a post, stone, etc., or at a considerable height, or near the ground, but never under a ledge or where it might not be seen plainly by any one standing in front of it.

The runners will naturally take a course that will eventually bring them back to the starting point, the chasers, however, trying to overtake them before they can accomplish this.

BADMINTON
(See *Ball Games*.)

BAND OBSTACLE RACE

10 to 60 players　　　　　　　　　*Junior high school*
Gymnasium　　　　　　　　　　　　　*to adults*

This is a relay race. In front of each team is laid a flexible band three and one-half feet long and about three inches wide, made of webbing or other pliable material. Different-colored bands are effective.

At the signal to start, Number One picks up the band, holds it taut overhead, pulls it down behind his back (still holding it with both hands) and steps back over it. He then passes the band to Number Two and sits down on the floor. Number Two steps over the band in the same way, passing it to Number Three, and so on down the line. When the last player has done this, he sits down crosslegged, holds the band taut overhead between both hands, pulls it behind his back and under him to the front and hands it to the next player. Each one thus passes the band under himself in a sitting position. When it gets to the end of the line, the last player, after going through this same performance, stretches out his legs straight in front of him, holds the band taut and pulls it up under his legs and body, beginning at the foot, and so on up the back until it is stretched overhead. From this position the next player takes it and goes through the same process. The last player to receive the band lies flat on his back, passes the band under himself from head downward, and returns to the sitting position to hand the band to the next player. The team first to get the band back to its last player with the lying-down stunt wins.

This is here given by courtesy of the National Council of Girls' Clubs, of England.

BARLEY BREAK

6 to 18 players　　　　　　　　　*Intermediate grades*
Playground; gymnasium　　　　　　*to junior high school*

A long, narrow strip of ground is needed for this game, divided into three spaces measuring from ten to fifty feet square. The central one of these three spaces is called the barley field. In each of the three stand a couple of players (or more, as hereinafter described). The couple in the center are obliged to link arms; therefore the center place is the most difficult and is considered disadvantageous. The couples in the other spaces advance, singly or together, into the barley field, trampling the barley by dancing around the field as much as they can without being caught. These couples need not link arms. When one of these is caught, he must remain inactive in the barley field until his partner is also caught. The couple owning the barley field may not step beyond its limits, nor may the couple being sought take refuge in the field opposite to their own. When the two are caught, they become warders of the barley field, changing places with the previous couple, and any others who have been caught return to their own fields. The game is made interesting by not confining the effort to catching two members of the same couple in succession. Both couples in the adjoining fields should venture far into the barley, taunting the couple who have linked arms by calling "Barley break!" These, in turn, will assist their object by making feints at catching one player and turning suddenly in the opposite direction for another.

The number of players may be increased by putting three couples in the center (barley field) and two or three couples at each end.

This game is centuries old and used to be played at harvest time around the stacks in the cornfields.

BASTE THE BEAR

10 to 30 or more players   *Elementary grades*
Playground; gymnasium; parlor   *to junior high school*

One player is chosen to be bear, and sits in the center on a stool. The bear chooses a second player to be his keeper. The keeper stands by the bear, each of them holding an end of a short rope about two feet in length and knotted at either end to give a firm hold. The rest of the players stand around in a circle enclosing these two. The object of the players is to tag (baste or buffet) the bear, without themselves being tagged by the bear or his keeper. The players may only attack the bear when the keeper calls, "My bear is free!" Should a player strike at the bear before the keeper says this, they change places, the striker becomes bear, the former bear becomes the keeper, and the keeper returns to the ring. The keeper does his best to protect his bear by dodging around him on all sides to prevent the attacks of the players who dodge in from the circle to hit him. Should the keeper or bear tag any player, the same exchange is made; that is, the player tagged becomes bear, the former bear the keeper, and the keeper returns to the ring.

Should a rope not be conveniently at hand, the game may be played in any of the three following ways: (1) The bear and his keeper may clasp hands; (2) a circle may be drawn around the bear beyond which the keeper may not go; or (3) the keeper may be subjected to the general rule of not going more than two steps away from the bear in any direction.

Where there are more than thirty players, two or more rings should be formed, each having its own bear and keeper.

This is an old game, popular in many countries. It contains excellent sport, with opportunity for daring, narrow escapes, and much laughter.

BEAR IN THE PIT

10 to 30 players   *Intermediate grades*
           Playground; gymnasium

A bear pit is formed by the players joining hands in a circle with one in the center as a bear. The bear tries to get out by breaking apart the bars (clasped hands), or by going over or under these barriers. Should he escape, all of the other players give chase, the one catching him becoming bear.

This is a favorite game with boys, and is not so rough a game as Bull in the Ring, the means of escape for the bear being more varied. He can exercise stratagem by appearing to break through the bars in one place, and suddenly turning and crawling under another, etc.

BEND AND STRETCH RELAY

10 to 60 players   *Primary grades*

Schoolroom

This game consists in a sideways passing of two beanbags and two dumbbells alternately. This amount of apparatus should be placed on the floor in the outer aisle beside each player in one of the outside rows, say, that to the left of the pupils.

On the command "Go!" each player in this first row picks up a dumbbell, raises it overhead, and there passes it to his own right hand, which is then extended sideways at shoulder level, where the next player takes it. The dumbbells are passed across the room in this manner, each player stretching his arms high overhead when he passes a bell from his left to his right hand. The last player who receives a bell places it on the floor beside him in the outer aisle.

As soon as the first player has passed the first dumbbell, he picks up a beanbag by bending down to the left, then straightens upward, passes the bag over his head to his own right hand, and then bends deeply to the right and places the beanbag on the floor at his right side. He immediately straightens to an erect position, when the next player bends, takes up the bag, passes it over his head, and bends to place it on the floor at his right side.

As soon as he has disposed of the first beanbag, the leader of each line reaches for the second dumbbell. This time the bell is passed simply from hand to hand in front of the body instead of overhead.

As soon as the second bell has left his hand, the leader of each line picks up the second beanbag, which is the last piece of apparatus to be passed. The passing of the second beanbag is different from that of the first. The pupils face sideways to the left, their feet resting in the aisle, and drop the bag behind them to the floor with both hands, at the same time bending slightly backward. The next player bends forward, picks up the bag with both hands, and then leans backward, with his hands stretched high overhead, and drops the bag in his turn in the aisle behind him. The line wins whose last player first receives the second beanbag. The player in the last line receiving this beanbag should stand instantly and hold the bag overhead, the winning line being selected by this signal.

This game was originated by Mr. Joseph Cermak.

BIRD CATCHER

10 to 60 players   *Primary grades*
Schoolroom; playground

Two opposite corners are marked off at one end of the ground or room, the one to serve as a nest for the birds and the other as a cage. A mother bird is chosen and takes her place in the nest. Two other players take the part of bird catchers and stand midway between nest and cage. If played in the schoolroom, the remaining players sit in their seats; if on a playground, they stand beyond a line at the farther end of the ground which is called the forest. All of these players should be named for birds, several players taking the name of each bird. The naming of the players will be facilitated by doing it in groups. If in the class room, each row may choose its name, after which the players should all change places, so that all of the robins or orioles will not fly from the same locality.

The teacher calls the name of a bird, whereupon all of the players who bear that name run from the forest to the nest, but the bird catchers try to intercept them. Should a bird be caught by the bird catcher, it is put in the cage, but a bird is safe from the bird catchers if it once reaches the nest and the mother bird. The players should be taught to make the chase interesting by dodging in various directions, instead of running in a simple, straight line for the nest.

The distance of the bird catchers from the nest may be determined with a little experience, it being necessary to place a handicap upon them to avoid the too easy capture of the birds.

BIRD'S NEST

2 to 10 players   *Elementary*
Country; out-of-doors

Two or more players are vultures and the rest are song birds. Each bird makes a nest about the size of a bird's nest, weaving it of grasses and twigs or making it of burrs. In each nest is placed a stone. When ready, the vultures blind their eyes while the birds scatter and hide their nests in bushes, trees, or on the ground. They are given five minutes in which to do this and then the vultures go out to find the nests. Each bird must stay within ten steps of his nest and call to the vulture, or make other efforts to attract his attention away from the nest.

The vultures have ten minutes in which to find the nests, which they gather in; the one who has the most nests is the winner.

For the next game the vultures change places with some of the birds.

This game is from Russia.

✓ BLACK AND WHITE

10 to 100 players ·   *Intermediate grades*
Gymnasium; playground; schoolroom   *to junior high school*

One player is chosen as leader, the rest being divided into two equal groups. Each player in one group should tie a handkerchief on the left arm to indicate that he belongs to the Whites; those in the other division are called the Blacks. The players stand around the ground promiscuously, the Whites and Blacks being mingled indiscriminately.

The leader is provided with a flat disk which is white on one side and black on the other, and preferably hung on a short string to facilitate twirling the disk. He stands on a stool at one side or end and twirls this disk, stopping it with one side only visible to the players. If the white side should be visible, the party known as the Whites may tag any of their opponents who are standing upright. The Blacks should therefore drop instantly to the floor, as in Stoop Tag. Should the black side of the disk be shown, the party of Blacks may tag the Whites. Any player tagged drops out of the game. The party wins which puts out in this way all of its opponents. The leader should keep the action of the game rapid by twirling the disk very frequently.

This is an excellent game for keeping players alert, and may be the source of much merriment.

BLACKBOARD RELAY

10 to 60 players   *Intermediate grades*
Schoolroom   *to junior high school*

As here explained, this game is adapted to grammar (sentence construction and punctuation). It may be made to correlate with almost any school subject, as explained.

The class is seated with an equal number of pupils in each row. A piece of crayon is given to the last players in each row, all of whom at a given signal run forward and write on the blackboard at the front of the room a word suitable to begin a sentence. Upon finishing the word, each player returns at once to his seat, handing the crayon as he does so to the player next in front of him. This second player at once runs forward and writes one word after the first one, to which it must bear a suitable relation. In this way each player in the row adds to the sentence being written by his own row, the last player being required to write a word that shall complete the sentence, and to add punctuation marks.

The points scored are 25 for speed (the first row to finish scoring the maximum, and the others proportionately in the order of finishing), 25 for spelling, 25 for writing, and 25 for grammatical construction, capitals, and punctuation. The row wins which scores the highest number of points.

The following modes of correlation are suggested for this game:

Arithmetic. — Each relay of pupils writes and solves on the blackboard a problem dictated by the teacher just before the signal to leave their seats. The line wins which has the largest number of problems correct. Multiplication tables may also be written, one step for each pupil.

English. — Grammar or punctuation, as explained previously; spelling, the teacher announcing the word for each relay as they leave their seats; authors, each pupil to write the name of an author belonging to a certain period or country; each pupil to write the name of some poem, play, story, essay, or book by an author whose name is given at the outset of the game; or the names of characters from a given literary work or author; or the next line or passage from a memorized selection.

Geography. — The names of mountain ranges, rivers, capital cities, boundaries, products.

History. — The names (related to a given period if desired) of famous men — statesmen, military men, writers, artists, musicians; of battles, discoveries, etc.

BLACK TOM

10 to 30 or more players　　　　　　　　*Primary grades*
Playground; gymnasium　　　　　　　　*to junior high school*

Two parallel lines are drawn on the ground with a space of from thirty to fifty feet between them. All of the players except one stand beyond one of these lines. In the middle territory between the lines the one player who is chosen to be It takes his place, and cries, "Black Tom! Black Tom! Black Tom!" repeating the words three times as here given; whereupon the other players must all rush across to the opposite line, being chased by the center player, who catches any that he may. Anyone so caught joins him thereafter in chasing the others.

The particular characteristic of this game lies in the fact that the center player, instead of saying "Black Tom," may trick or tantalize the runners by crying out "Yellow Tom," or "Blue Tom," or "Red Tom," or anything else that he chooses. Any player who starts to run upon such a false alarm is considered captive and must join the players in the center. This is also true for any player who starts before the third repetition of "Black Tom."

Another way of giving a false alarm is for any one of the center players except the original It to give the signal for running. Any runner starting in response to such a signal from any of the chasers, except the original It, thereby becomes captive and must join the players in the center.

The first one to be caught is center player, or It, for the next game.

The game as here given is played in Brooklyn, N. Y. The same game is played in the South under the title of "Ham-ham-chicken-ham-bacon!" the word "bacon" being the signal for the run, any player starting without hearing it having to join the center players.

BLIND BELL

5 to 100 players　　　　　　　　　　*Elementary grades*
Parlor; gymnasium; playground

All the players but one are blindfolded and scatter promiscuously. The one who is not blindfolded carries a bell loosely in one hand, so that it will ring with every step. If desired, this bell may be hung around the neck on a string or ribbon. The blindfolded players try to catch the one with the bell, who will have to use considerable alertness to keep out of the way. Whoever catches the bellman changes places with him.

Where there are over twenty players, there should be two or more bellmen. This is a capital game for an indoor party.

BLIND MAN'S BUFF

10 to 30 or more players   *Elementary grades*
Parlor; gymnasium; playground

One player is chosen to be blindfolded and stands in the center. The other players join hands and circle around him until the blind man claps his hands three times, whereupon the circle stops moving and the blind man points toward the circle. The player at whom he points must at once step into the circle; the blind man tries to catch him and when he is caught must guess who the player is. If the guess is correct, they change places. If not correct, or if the blind man has pointed at an empty space instead of at a player, the circle continues and the game is repeated. The player who is called into the circle will naturally try, by noiseless stepping, dodging, etc., to give the blind man some difficulty in catching him, but when once caught must submit without struggle to examination for identification.

This is one of the oldest recorded games and is found in practically all countries. The ancient Greeks called it "Brazen Fly."

BODY GUARD

10 to 30 or more players   *Intermediate grades*
Playground; gymnasium

A small space is marked off at one end of the ground as a "home" or goal. One player is chosen to be the Panjandrum, an important personage requiring a body guard. Two other players are chosen to be the guard. The game starts with these three players in the home ground and the balance of the players at large. The three issue forth, with the two players who act as body guard clasping each other by the hand and preceding the Panjandrum as a shield. The object of the game is for the players at large to touch or tantalize the Panjandrum without being tagged by his guard

The guard will dodge around their charge to avoid these attacks, and the Panjandrum himself may evade them by moving around his guard. Whenever a guard succeeds in tagging a player, the Panjandrum and his guards return at once to the home; whereupon the player tagged changes places with the Panjandrum, and the game goes on as before.

BRONCHO TAG

(Hook-on Tag)

One player is chosen as chaser; the other players form groups of three, each of which stands in a file three deep, numbers two and three each with an arm around the waist of the player in front, thus forming a "broncho." The chaser tries to attach himself similarly to the rear player of any group — that is, to become the tail of the broncho. If he succeeds, the head of the broncho must become chaser. The chief sport of the game is in the efforts of the broncho to avoid having a new tail. He does this by switching and dodging to keep his head always toward the chaser.

BULL IN THE RING

10 to 30 or more players   *Junior high school*
Playground; gymnasium

All but one of the players stand in a circle with hands firmly clasped. The odd player stands in the center and is the bull. The bull tries to break through the ring by parting the hands of any of the players. If he breaks through, the two players whose hands he parted immediately give chase to him, and the one catching him becomes the bull.

This is a very rough game.

BUNCH OF IVY

20 to 60 or more players   *Intermediate grades*
Parlor; gymnasium; playground

The players in pairs form a ring. The inner player of each
couple kneels. The outer player of each couple holds the upraised hand of the kneeling partner and circles around her, asking
the following questions. The partners reply as indicated, men-
tioning each time one hour later by the clock, until six o'clock has
been reached.

"What time does the king come home?"
"One o'clock in the afternoon."
"What has he in his hand?"
"A bunch of ivy."

This dialogue and the accompanying movement of the players
should be rhythmic and spirited in time. As the kneeling players
say "A bunch of ivy," they begin clapping their hands in the
same rapid time; whereupon the outer players run around the
entire ring to the right until each player has returned to her
partner, once for one o'clock, twice for two o'clock, etc., until
six o'clock has been reached. The players change places each
time after this series of circling, the outer players kneeling, and
those who formerly knelt, standing. The time of both the
dialogue and the running should be rapid to keep the game
spirited. The larger the circle that may be described around
each kneeling player by the partner the better.

BUYING A LOCK

5 to 30 or more players   *Elementary grades*
Playground; schoolroom

> Oh, here we all go to buy us a lock;
>   What kind of a lock shall it be?
> We'll buy a broom handle; if that will not do,
>   With a poker we'll try it alone.
> But if neither the broom nor the poker will do,
>   We'll open it then with a stone.

This game is suitable for very little children. They stand in a
long line or rank side by side, holding hands. While repeating the

verse, one end of the line winds in under the raised arms of the last two players at the opposite end, but instead of passing entirely through, as in many other winding games, the player next to the last only turns far enough to face in three quarters of a circle, or so that the players will eventually, when all have so turned, be brought into single file, one standing behind the other. In this position the arms are dropped over the shoulder, so that the player's own left arm crosses his chest with the clasped hands (his own left and his neighbor's right) resting on his right shoulder. Each player should clasp his neighbor's hands at the start, so that the palm of his own left hand faces forward and the palm of his own right hand faces backward.

When the whole line has been "locked" in this way, the players unwind in reverse order, still repeating the verse.

When players are familiar with the winding and unwinding process, the game may be played in circle formation instead of line formation; that is, it will start with all of the players facing inward as they clasp hands to form a circle, and the locking or winding will bring them facing in single file around the circle.

This is a favorite game with little girls in China, and is here given with the kind permission of Dr. Isaac T. Headland and Messrs. Fleming H. Revell & Co., from the book entitled *The Chinese Boy and Girl*.

CAT AND MICE

5 to 60 players   *Primary grades*
                         Schoolroom

One player is chosen to be cat, and hides behind or under the teacher's desk. After the cat is hidden, the teacher beckons to five or six other players, who creep softly up to the desk, and when all are assembled, scratch on it with their fingers, to represent the nibbling of mice. As soon as the cat hears this, she scrambles out from under the desk and gives chase to the mice, who may save themselves only by getting back to their holes (seats). If a mouse be caught, the cat changes places with him for the next round of the game. If no mouse be caught, the same cat may continue, or the teacher may choose another at her discretion.

A different set of mice should be chosen each time, so as to give all of the players an opportunity to join in the game.

This is a favorite schoolroom game for little children. They should be taught to add sport to the play by giving the cat quite a chase before returning to their seats, instead of seeking safety in the shortest and most direct way.

CAT AND RAT

10 to 30 or more players   *Primary grades*
Playground; gymnasium; parlor

One player is chosen for cat and one for rat. The others all form a circle with clasped hands. The cat stands outside of the circle and the rat inside. The game opens with a conversation between the cat and rat.

The cat says:
"I am the cat."
The rat says:
"I am the rat."
"I will catch you!"
"You can't!"

This last defiance is a signal for a chase. The cat tries to get into the circle, and the rat tries to evade him. Both may run in and out of the circle, but the players will assist the rat by raising their hands to let him run under, and they will try to foil the efforts of the cat by preventing his breaking through the circle, either inward or outward.

When the rat is caught, he joins the circle and the cat becomes rat, a new cat being chosen from the circle players.

This game is a great favorite with young children, and though very similar in its general form to Bull in the Ring, the slight difference of the circle assisting the rat and hindering the cat makes a great difference in the playing qualities of the game, rendering it much less rough than Bull in the Ring.

CATCH AND PULL TUG OF WAR

10 to 100 players   *Junior to*
Gymnasium; playground   *senior high school*

Any number of players may engage in this contest, which is one of the best for a large number, containing as it does both excellent sport and vigorous exercise.

A line is drawn down the middle of the playing space. The players are divided into two teams and stand one team on either side of the line. The game starts on a signal and consists in catching hold of an opponent by any part of his body, as hand, arm, or foot, reaching over the line, and so pulling him across the boundary. Any number of players may try to secure a hold on an opponent and any number may come to his rescue and try to resist his being pulled over the line, either by pulling him in the opposite direction or by trying to secure a hold on one of the opponents. A player does not belong to the enemy until his entire body has been pulled over the line. He must then join his captors in trying to secure players from across the line. The team wins which has the largest number of players at the end of time limits.

CATCH OF FISH

10 to 30 or more players   *Intermediate grades*
Playground; gymnasium

This is one of the very strenuous games, and affords opportunity for some very good exercise and sport.

A line is drawn across each end of the playground, beyond which the players stand in two equal teams, one at one end and one at the other. The players of one team clasp hands to form a fish net. The players in the other team are fish. At a given signal both advance toward the center of the playground, which represents a stream, the object of the fish being to swim across to the opposite shore without being caught in the net. To do this they will naturally dodge around the ends of the net.

The net should enclose or encircle any fish that it catches. The fish so caught may not try to break apart the clasped hands forming the net, but may escape only through the opening where the two ends come together. Should the net break at any point by an unclasping of hands, the fish are all allowed to escape, and the players go back to their respective goals and begin over again. Any fishes caught in the net are thereafter out of the game until all are caught. After the net has made one catch, the sides exchange parts, those of the fish that are left forming the new net, and the first net crossing to the other side and becoming fish. The two sides thus exchange places and parts, until all on one side are caught.

For a large number of players it is better to have two small nets instead of one large one, the dodging being livelier and the progress of the game more rapid in every way.

CATCH THE CANE

10 to 30 or more players　　　　　　　　　　*Intermediate*
Playground; gymnasium; schoolroom;　　　　*grades to adult*
　　parlor

The players, who should be numbered consecutively, stand in a circle or semicircle. One player stands in the center of the circle or in front of the semicircle, with his index finger on the top of a cane, wand, or closed umbrella, which stands perpendicularly to the floor. Suddenly he lifts his finger from the cane, at the same time calling the number assigned to one of the players in the circle. The person whose number is called must run forward and catch the cane before it lies on the floor. If he fails, he must return to his place in the circle; if successful, he changes places with the center player.

This game may have a great deal of sport in it if the action be kept lively and the one who is calling the numbers gives them in unexpected order, sometimes repeating a number that has recently been given, then giving a few in consecutive order, and then skipping over a long series, etc.

FOR THE SCHOOLROOM. — When played in the schoolroom, the player with the cane should stand in the center of the front of the room. The other players — part of the class at a time — may be lined up in front of the first row of desks, or only the players seated in the first row of seats may be called, according to the number of their row. At the discretion of the teacher this row may change to the rear row of seats, each line moving up one seat to make room for them.

This is an admirable game for making alert and active, children who are slow or dull.

CENTIPEDE

9 to 12 players   *Intermediate grades*
Gymnasium; seashore   *to senior high school*

The players sit in a circle on the floor, with their feet stretched out and mingled in a promiscuous pile. One player, who is leader and stands outside the circle, touches one of the feet (he may mark it slightly with a piece of chalk if desired), and calling on some player by name, commands him to tell to whom the foot belongs. When this player has named someone, the leader commands the owner of the foot to stand up. If the guess be wrong, the leader chases the mistaken player and whips him with a knotted hand-kerchief. If the guess be right, the guesser is released from the game, sits down at one side, and chooses the next one to be It, while the one who was It takes a place in the circle.

This game lends itself especially to the gymnasium or seashore, where the dressing of the feet is inclined to be uniform.

The game is played by the modern Greeks.

CHANGING SEATS

20 to 60 players   *Primary and*
Schoolroom   *intermediate grades*

This game is played in several different forms. The following are very popular:

CHANGING SEATS — I

The teacher gives the command, "Change right!" Thereupon each pupil slips from his own seat to the one across the aisle to the right, the pupils in the farthest right-hand row standing in the outside aisle. The next order may be, "Change left!" Then all of the pupils slip back to their own seats, and the row that stood resumes its own.

In the same way the orders, "Change forward!" and "Change backward!" may be given, the row of pupils left out each time merely standing in the aisles.

CHANGING SEATS — II

In this form of the game the players in the displaced row run around the room and take the vacant row of seats on the opposite side.

CHARLEY OVER THE WATER

10 to 30 or more players   *Primary grades*
Parlor; gymnasium; playground

One player is chosen to be Charley; if there be more than twenty players, there should be two or more Charleys, to make the action more rapid. Charley stands in the center; the other players join hands in a circle around him and dance around, repeating the rhyme:

> "Charley over the water,
>   Charley over the sea.
> Charley catch a blackbird,
>   Can't catch me!"

As the last word is said, the players stoop, and Charley tries to tag them before they can get into that position. Should he succeed, the player tagged changes places with him.

CHICKADEE–DEE

5 to 10 players   *Intermediate grades*
Dark room

This game is a good one for the loft of an old barn on a rainy day. The writer obtained the game from a group of boys, who found it one of their chief sports used in this way.

It is necessary to prepare in advance a rather large, soft bag; an oat sack or potato bag may be used. This should be nearly filled with dry leaves or some substitute, and the end gathered up and tied with a string, so as to leave quite a hilt or handle for a firm grasp. All light is shut out of the place, so that the sense of hearing will be the only guide in the game.

One player, who is It, is seated on the floor in the center of the loft or room, and holds the sack. The object of the game for this player is to tag or touch any of the other players with the sack without leaving his sitting position on the floor. The object of the other players, who are scattered promiscuously, is to approach as near as possible to the center player, taking him unaware with a taunting cry of "Chickadee-dee!" close to his ear.

The game starts in perfect silence and darkness. A player steals up to the center man, calls "Chickadee-dee!" and darts back again as quickly as possible, the center man whirling his bag around in a circle and hitting out with it in the direction of the voice, trying to hit this player. While he is doing this, another player from some other direction repeats the call of "Chickadee-dee!" close to his ear, and darts back or dodges. Any tactics may be used for dodging, such as dropping to the floor, jumping, or the more usual modes of dodging.

Any player hit with the bag exchanges places with the one in the center.

CHICKEN MARKET

5 to 20 or more players *Elementary grades*
Indoors; out of doors

This is one of the traditional dramatic games.

One player is chosen to be market man and another buyer; the rest of the players are chickens; they stoop down in a row and clasp their hands under their knees. The buyer approaches the market man and asks, "Have you any chickens for sale?" The market man answers, "Yes, plenty; will you walk around and try them?" Whereupon the buyer goes up to different chickens and tests them by laying over the head his clasped hands, palms downward and pressing inward. The buyer pretends to be dissatisfied with some of the chickens, saying, "This one is too tough," "This one is too old," "This one is too fat," etc., until at last he finds one that suits him, the chickens being supposed to go through this ordeal without smiling.

When a chicken is found that appears to be satisfactory, the buyer and the market man take him by the arms, one on either side, he still remaining in his first position with hands clasped under the knees, and swing him forward and backward three times. Should he stand this test without loosening his own grasp, he is supposed to be all right, and the buyer leads him off to the opposite side of the playground, or home. The game continues until all of the chickens are sold. Any chicken that smiles or whose arms give way in the swinging test must pay a forfeit, all of the forfeits being redeemed at the close of the game. Where there are more than ten players, there should be two or more buyers and sellers.

This game is played in various countries: in England as a "Sale of Honey Pots," in China as a "Fruit Sale," etc. The version here given is from Italy.

CHICKIDY HAND

5 to 30 or more players   *Primary grades*
Playground; gymnasium

One player is chosen to be It, and stands near a post with the fingers of his hands interlocked. The other players, each clasping his own hands in the same way, crowd around the post and touch it with the clasped hands. The one who is It counts ten, whereupon the players all run, the one who is It trying to tag any of them. None of the players may unclasp their hands until they are tagged, whereupon they are prisoners and clasp hands with It, forming a line which thereafter is the tagging line, though only the original It may tag the other players. The game is a contest between the tagging line, which tries to recruit and retain its numbers, and the free players, who try (1) to avoid being captured for the tagging line, and (2) to reduce the tagging line by breaking through it; but the players in the line must resist this. Each time that the line is broken, the one of the two players (whose hands were parted) who stands toward the head of the line is dropped out of the game. A free player may not be tagged after he has thrown himself upon (touched) a pair of hands that he is trying to part. The last player caught by the tagging line is the winner and becomes It for the next game.

CHINESE CHICKEN

5 to 30 or more players   *Primary grades*
Playground; gymnasium; schoolroom; seashore

This game is played with small blocks of wood or bean bags. Stones, or, at the seashore, bathing slippers, may be used instead. These are placed in straight rows of five to fifteen each, with intervals of about ten inches between them. The players are divided into groups numbering from five to ten each, and line up as for a relay race, each before one row of blocks or bags.

The game is played in the same way by each row of players; and while the game may be competitive between the different groups, in its original form it is for one group only. The first player in a group represents a "lame chicken," and hops on one foot over each bag until the end of the line of bags has been reached. The last bag is then kicked away by the "lame" (lifted) foot, after which it must be picked up and carried back over the same route to the first end of the line, when the same player hops back on the opposite foot, kicks away a second bag, picks it up and returns, and so on until he fails. Only one foot may touch the ground at a time, and may touch it but once in each space between the bags. No bag may be touched except the one at the end of the line, which is afterward picked up, and this must be secured without putting the lame foot upon the ground.

When the "chicken" infringes any of these rules, he must at once give place to another. The winner is the player who has at the end of the game the greatest number of bags.

This is a Chinese game, taken by kind permission of the author from Miss Adèle Fielde's *A Corner of Cathay*. The Chinese children play it with their shoes in place of the bean bag or block of wood.

CHINESE WALL

10 to 60 or more players   *Junior to*
Playground; gymnasium   *senior high school*

The Chinese wall is marked off by two parallel lines straight across the center of the playground, leaving a space between them of about ten feet in width, which represents the wall. On each

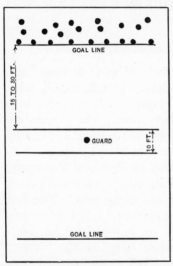

side of the wall, at a distance of from fifteen to thirty feet, a parallel line is drawn across the ground. This marks the safety point or home goal for the besiegers.

One player is chosen to defend the wall, and takes his place upon it. All of the other players stand in one of the home goals. The defender calls "Start!" when all of the players must cross the wall to the goal beyond, the defender trying to tag as many as he can as they cross; but he may not overstep the boundaries of the wall himself. All so tagged join the defender in trying to secure the rest of the players during future sorties. The game ends when all have been caught, the last player taken being defender for the next game.

CHINESE WALL

This is a capital game for both children and older players, as it affords opportunity for some very brisk running and dodging, especially if the playground be wide. It differs from Hill Dill and several other games of the sort in that there is a more limited space in which the center catcher and his allies are confined.

CIRCLE RACE

10 to 30 or more players   *Intermediate grades*
Playground; gymnasium   *to senior high school*

The players stand in a circle a considerable distance apart and face around in single file in the same direction. At a signal all start to run, following the general outline of the circle, but each trying to pass on the outside the runner next in front of him, tagging as he passes. Any player passed in this way drops out of the race. The last player in the circle wins. On signal from a leader, the circle faces about and runs in the opposite direction. As this reverses the relative position of runners who are gaining or losing ground, it is a feature that may be used by a judicious leader to add much merriment and zest to the game.

CIRCLE SEAT RELAY

10 to 60 players   *Primary to*
Schoolroom   *Intermediate grades*

This game starts with the players all seated, and with an even number in each row. At a signal, the last player in each row runs forward on the right-hand side of his seat, runs around the front desk, and returns on the left-hand side of his own row. As soon as he is seated, he touches the player next in front on the shoulder, which is a signal for this one to start. He runs in the same way. This is continued until the last player, which in this case is the one sitting in the front seat, has circled his desk and seated himself with hand upraised. The line wins whose front player first does this.

This is one of the best running games for the schoolroom. As in all such games, seated pupils should strictly observe the rule of keeping their feet out of the aisles and under the desks.

Players must observe strictly the rule of running forward on the right-hand side and backward in the next aisle, else there will be collisions.

CLAM SHELL COMBAT

2 to 30 players   *Children or adults*
                      Out of doors; seashore

Each of the players is provided with an equal number of clam shells; the players then pair off in twos for the combat. Which of the two shall have the first play is decided by the players each dropping a clam shell from a height of three feet. The one whose shell falls with the hollow or concave side down has the first play. Should it be a tie, the trials are repeated until one player is chosen in this way. The play then opens with the unsuccessful player putting a clam shell on the ground, when the opponent throws another shell at it, trying to break it. If he succeeds, the opponent must put down another shell. This is kept up indefinitely, until a player's shells have all been won by the opposing thrower, or until the thrower fails to hit a shell or his own breaks in doing so. Whenever one of these things occurs, he loses his turn, and must put down a shell for the opponent to throw at. The player wins who retains an unbroken shell the longest.

Where there is a considerable number of players, they may be divided into opposing parties, the players stepping forward in turn at the call of their respective captains.

This is a Korean game, reported by Mr. Culin.

CLUB SNATCH

10 to 60 players.   *Intermediate grades*
Playground; gymnasium   *to junior high school*

This is one of the best competitive chasing games.

A goal is marked off across each end of the playground. Midway between the goals, an Indian club is placed; a handkerchief or other similar object may be used, placed on some support — on a stake driven into the ground, laid over a rock or stool, or hung on the end of a branch. A stone or dumb-bell laid on the ground may be substituted. In line with the club a starting base is marked on each goal line.

The players are divided into two equal teams, each having a captain. Each team takes its place in one of the goals. The object of the game is for one of the runners to snatch the club and return to his goal before a runner from the opposite goal tags him, both leaving their starting bases at the same time on a signal. The players on each team run in turn, the captains naming who shall run each time.

The captains toss for first choice of runners; the one who wins names his first runner, who steps to the running base, whereupon the competing captain names a runner to go out against him, trying to select one of equal or superior ability. Thereafter the captains take turns as to who shall first designate a runner.

When there is a large number of players, or very limited time, a different method may be used for selecting the runners. All of the players should then line up according to size, and number consecutively by couples. That is, the first couple would be number one, the second, number two, the third, number three, etc. The couples then divide, one file going to one team and the other to the opposite team. The players run thereafter according to number, the numbers *one* competing, and so on. Each player may run but once until all on the team have run, when each may be called a second time, etc. To avoid confusion, the players who have run should stand to one side of the starting base, say the right, and those who have not run, to the left.

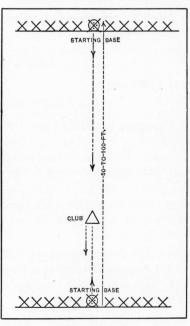

CLUB SNATCH

The first runners, having been called by their respective captains to the starting bases, run on a signal; the players may reach the club together and go through many false moves and dodges before one snatches the club and turns back to his goal. Should he succeed in reaching the goal before the other player can tag him, his team scores one point. Should he be tagged before he can return with his trophy, the opponent scores one point. The club is replaced after each run. In either case both players return to their original teams.

When each runner has run once, the teams exchange goals and run a second time. The team wins which has the highest score at the end of the second round.

For large numbers of players there may be several clubs, each having corresponding starting bases on the goals, so that several pairs of runners may compete at once. One club for twenty players, ten on each side, is a good proportion. For young players the club may be placed nearer one goal than the other at first, as shown in the diagram.

This is a capital game as here developed with the feature of scoring, and may be made very popular.

COCK STRIDE

3 to 15 players   *Intermediate grades*
Playground; gymnasium

This game is usually played with boys' caps, but knotted handkerchiefs or balls of crumpled paper may be used. One player is the cock; he is blindfolded and stands in a stride position with his feet wide apart sideways. The other players stand in turn at a point five to ten feet behind him, and throw their caps forward as far as possible between his legs. After the caps are all thrown, each player moves forward and stands beside his own cap. The cock then crawls on all fours, still blindfolded, until he reaches a cap. The player whose cap is first touched at once becomes an object of chase by the other players, who are at liberty to "pommel" him when he is captured. He then becomes cock for the next round of the game.

CONKERS

Indefinite number   *Intermediate grades*
Out of doors

This is an outdoor game usually played by boys. Each boy carries a store of empty horse-chestnut shells threaded on a string, as a source of supply. Each boy has also one shell on the end of a string held in place by a knot. Two boys, as opponents, try each to break the shell of the other by banging his single shell against the opponent's. According to the number of shells he has broken, a player is called a "Oner," or "Twoer," or "Threer," and so on. If a boy succeeds in breaking the shell of a player who has gained two victories (that is, has already broken two opponent's shells), he gains two points for this victory; if he breaks the shell of a boy who has already broken five shells, he gains five points. This is kept up until the supply of empty shells is exhausted, the boy having the largest score being the winner.

This is an English game, as indicated by the term "conkers," for chestnuts.

CORKSCREW

8 to 60 players　　　　　　　　　　　*Intermediate grades*
Gymnasium　　　　　　　　　　　　*to junior high school*

CORKSCREW

This is a relay game with from four to twenty players in each file. A jump standard or other obstacle is placed at the far end of the room. Each team stands with back toward this obstacle, and with a space of four feet between players. The player at the rear of the team is Number One. On signal, the Numbers One start forward on the left and run completely round Number Two, *clockwise*, keep right on down past the left hand of Number Three, and circle that player in the same way, and so on down the line. When the last player has been circled, the runner returns on the opposite side of the file, keeping on to the far end of the room, there goes around the obstacle and back to his original place. As soon as Number One has circled Number Three, Number Two starts after him, circling each player down the line, and follows around the obstacle.

When Number One gets back to his own place he stands there and Number Two, returning, circles him, *counterclockwise*, and stands on his place, etc., until each member of the team has returned to his original place. The team whose last player is first to get back wins.

This is one of the games which make a very

humorous effect if done rapidly.   No player may touch another
with his hands in circling.

By courtesy of the National Council of Girls' Clubs, England.

COUPLE RACE

8 to 40 players   *Intermediate grades*
Parlor; gymnasium   *to junior high school*

The players are in relay teams of from four to twenty players.
Each team is divided into equal halves which stand in files facing each other from opposite ends of the room, as in a shuttle
relay.   On a signal, the Number One players of the two teams
run toward each other, clasp both hands when they meet, turn
completely under their arms toward an understood side of the
room, still holding hands; they then return to their own starting lines, touch this with the foot, and return to the center,
where they once more clasp hands and turn under arms in the
opposite direction; they then return each to his starting line
and sit crosslegged on the floor.   The next couple may not start
until the first players are thus seated, but they then go through
the same play.   The team whose last couple is first to be seated
wins the game.

CROSSING THE BROOK

5 to 60 or more players   *Primary grades*
Playground; gymnasium; schoolroom

This game is a great favorite with little children.   A place representing a brook is marked off by two lines on the ground.   For
little children in the first year of school (about six years old) this
may start with a width of two feet.   The players run in groups
and try to jump across the brook.   Those who succeed turn
around and jump back with a standing jump instead of a running
jump.   On either of these jumps the player who does not jump
across the line representing the bank gets into the water and
must run home for dry stockings, being thereafter out of the

game. The successful jumpers are led to wider and wider places in the brook to jump (a new line being drawn to increase the distance), until the widest point is reached at which any player can jump successfully. This player is considered the winner.

CROSS TAG

5 to 30 or more players   *Intermediate grades*
Playground; gymnasium

One player is chosen to be It. He calls out the name of another player, to whom he at once gives chase. A third player at any point in the chase may run between the one who is It and the one whom he is chasing, whereupon this third player becomes the object of the chase instead of the second. At any time a fourth player may run between this player and the chaser, diverting the chase to himself, and so on indefinitely. In other words, whenever a player crosses between the one who is It and the one being chased, the latter is at once relieved of the chase and ceases to be a fugitive. Whenever the chaser tags a player, that player becomes It. Considerable sport may be added to the game by the free players trying to impede the chaser and so help the runner — getting in the way of the former without crossing between the two, or any other hindering tactics.

DO THIS, DO THAT

10 to 60 or more players   *Primary grades*
Playground; gymnasium; schoolroom; parlor

All the players stand facing one of their number who is the leader. The one who is leader assumes any gymnastic position or imitates any action, at the same time saying "Do this!" and the others immediately imitate. Should the leader at any time say "Do that!" instead of "Do this!" any player who imitates the action performed must be seated, or pay a forfeit, whichever form of penalty has been decided on at the beginning of the game. Three mistakes of this kind put a player out of the game, even when forfeits are the penalty.

The leader may choose any gymnastic positions that are familiar, such as chargings, head bendings, trunk bendings, arm movements, knee bendings, hopping, jumping, dancing steps, etc.; or imitate familiar actions such as hammering, sawing, washing, ironing, sewing, stone cutting, shoveling, riding horseback, etc.

DROP THE HANDKERCHIEF

10 to 30 or more players   *Primary grades*
Indoors; out of doors

All of the players but one stand in a circle. The odd player runs around on the outside of the circle, carrying a handkerchief, which he drops behind one of the circle players. The main idea of the game is to take the circle players unaware with this. Those who form the ring must look toward the center, and are not allowed to turn their heads as the runner passes them. The one who runs around with the handkerchief will resort to various devices for misleading the others as to where he drops it. For instance, he may sometimes quicken his pace suddenly after dropping the handkerchief, or at other times maintain a steady pace which gives no clew.

As soon as a player in the circle discovers that the handkerchief has been dropped behind him, he must pick it up and as rapidly as possible chase the one who dropped it, who may run around the outside of the circle or at any point through or across the circle, his object being to reach the vacant place left by the one who is chasing him. The circle players should lift their hands to allow both runners to pass freely through the circle. Whichever player reaches the vacant place first stands there, the one left out taking the handkerchief for the next game.

This is one of the oldest known games and is found throughout the world. The writer has heard it described by Cossacks, Japanese, Italians, and people of many other nationalities.

DUCK ON A ROCK

5 to 30 or more players   *Intermediate grades*
Playground; gymnasium

Each player is provided with a stone, called a "duck," about the size of a baseball. A large rock or post is chosen as the duck rock, and twenty-five feet from it a throwing line is drawn. On this duck rock one player places his duck and stands by it as guard. This guard is selected at the outset by all of the players throwing their ducks at the duck rock from the throwing line. The one whose duck falls nearest to the rock becomes the first guard. The other players stand behind the throwing line and take turns in throwing at the guard's duck on the rock with their stones, trying to knock it from the rock. After each throw a player must recover his own duck and run back home beyond the throwing line. Should he be tagged by the guard while

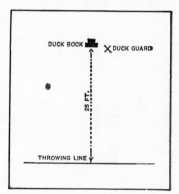

DUCK ON A ROCK

trying to do this, he must change places with the guard. The guard may tag him at any time when he is within the throwing line, unless he stands with his foot on his own duck where it first fell. He may stand in this way as long as necessary, awaiting an opportunity to run home; but the moment he lifts his duck from the ground, or takes his foot from it, he may be tagged by the guard. Having once lifted his duck to run home with it, a player may not again place it on the ground.

The guard may not tag any player unless his own duck is on the rock. Before he may chase the thrower, he must therefore pick up his own duck and replace it should it have been knocked off. This replacing gives the thrower an opportunity to recover his own duck and run home; but should the duck not have been displaced from the duck rock, the thrower may have to wait either at a safe distance or with his foot on his own duck if he can get to it, until some other thrower has displaced the duck on the rock, and so engaged the time and attention of the guard. Several players may thus be waiting at once to recover their ducks, some of them near the duck rock with a foot on their ducks, others at a distance. Any player tagged by the guard must change places with him, placing his own duck on the rock. The guard must quickly recover his duck and run for the throwing line after tagging a player, as he in turn may be tagged as soon as the new guard has placed his duck on the rock.

A stone that falls very near the duck rock without displacing the duck may also prove disastrous to the thrower. Should a stone fall within a hand span (stretching from finger tip to thumb) of the duck rock without knocking off the duck, the guard challenges the thrower by shouting "Span!" whereupon he proceeds to measure with his hand the distance between the duck rock and the stone. Should the distance be as he surmises, the thrower of the stone has to change places with him, put his own duck on the rock, and become the guard. This rule cultivates expert throwers.

When used in a gymnasium, this game may best be played with bean bags, in which case one bag may be balanced on top of an Indian club for the duck on the rock.

The modern Greeks play this game with a pile of stones instead of the one rock or stake with the duck on top. The entire pile is then knocked over, and the guard must rebuild the whole before he may tag the other players. These variations make the game possible under varied circumstances, as on a flat beach or playground where no larger duck rock is available, and add considerably to the sport.

DUMBBELL TAG

5 to 30 or more players   *Intermediate grades*
Gymnasium; playground; schoolroom   *to senior high school*

The players stand, scattered promiscuously, one of their number, who is It, being placed in the center at the opening of the game. A dumbbell is passed from one player to another, the one who is It trying to tag the person who has the dumbbell. If he succeeds, the one tagged becomes It.

A great deal of finesse may be used in this game : in appearing to hand the dumbbell in one direction, turning suddenly and handing it in another, etc. Players may move around freely, and the action is frequently diversified with considerable running and chasing.

In the schoolroom this may be played with the players either seated or standing.

EVERY MAN IN HIS OWN DEN

5 to 30 or more players   *Junior high school*
          Playground; gymnasium

Each player selects for himself a den ; a post, tree, or other objective point may serve for this, or the corner of a building, or if in a gymnasium, a piece of apparatus.

One player opens the game by running out from his den. The second player tries to catch (tag) him. The third player may try to catch either of these two, and so on. The object of the different players is to make captives of the others, as any player caught must thereafter join his captor in trying to catch others, thus eventually aggregating the different players into parties, although each starts separately, and anyone may be the nucleus of a group should he be successful in catching another player. The players may only be caught by those who issue from a den after they themselves have ventured forth. For instance, Number Two goes out to catch Number One. Number Three may catch either Two or One, but neither of them may catch him. The last player out may catch any of the other players. At any time a player may run back to his den, after which his again issuing forth gives him the advantage over all others who may then be out, as he may catch them. As the players are gradually gathered into different parties, the game becomes more concentrated, and the side wins that captures all of the players.

One player may catch only one opponent at a time.

EXCHANGE

(Numbers Change; French Blind Man's Buff)

10 to 30 or more players   *Children or adults*
Parlor; gymnasium; playground

One player is blindfolded and stands in the center. The other players sit in chairs in a circle around him. It is advisable to have the circle rather large. The players are numbered consecutively from one to the highest number playing.

The game may start with the players sitting in consecutive order, or they may change places at the outset to confuse the blindfold player, although the changing of places takes place very rapidly in the course of the game. The blindfold player calls out two numbers, whereupon the players bearing those numbers must exchange places, the blindfold player trying meanwhile either to catch one of the players or to secure one of the chairs. Any player so caught must yield his chair to the catcher. No player may go outside of the circle of chairs, but any other tactics may be resorted to for evading capture, such as stooping, creeping, dashing suddenly, etc.

This game may be one of the merriest possible games for an informal house party. The writer recalls one such occasion when a prominent manufacturer was blindfolded and had located two players whose numbers he called for exchange, one of them a newly graduated West Point lieutenant, the other a college senior. The business man stood in front of the chair occupied by the lieutenant and close to it, taking a crouching attitude, with his feet wide apart and arms outspread ready to grasp the victim when he should emerge from his chair. Noiselessly the lieutenant raised himself to a standing position in his chair, and then suddenly, to shouts of laughter from the company, vaulted over the head of his would-be captor, while at the same moment the collegian crawled between his feet and took possession of the chair.

FACE–THE–CORNER RELAY

12 to 30 players   *Intermediate grades*
Playground; gymnasium

This is a relay game in unusual formation. A line is drawn around a room or gymnasium, three feet from the wall, to form a "running lane." The players are divided into four equal teams, which line up, each facing a corner behind a diagonal starting line drawn four feet inward from the corner. The leader of each team has a flag or kerchief to hand to the next player. As in all such games, this should not be on a stick that may be poked into the eyes or lead to other accidents.

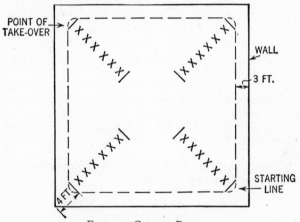

FACE-THE-CORNER RELAY

On signal, the first player in each team starts running to the right around the edge of the room, keeping within the running lane. When a player gets back to his team, he hands the flag to the next player, who has moved up to the starting line, and then takes his place behind a line at the rear of his team. When the last player of a team returns to the starting line, he holds the flag above his head and cries: "Home!" The first to get home of course wins the game.

In overtaking a runner, a player may run outside the lane, but he must immediately return to it.

FARMER IS COMING (THE)

10 to 30 or more players   *Intermediate grades*
Playground; gymnasium

One player, chosen to be the farmer, is seated. The remaining players, standing at a distance, select a leader who taps some of them on the shoulder as an invitation to go with him to the farmer's orchard for apples. Thereupon they leave their home ground, which has a determined boundary, and approach as near to the farmer as they dare. The game is more interesting if they can do this from various sides, practically surrounding him. Suddenly the farmer claps his hands and all players must stand still, while the leader calls out, "The farmer is coming!" The players try to get safely back to their home ground, the farmer chasing them. He may not start, however, until the leader has given his warning. Any player caught by the farmer changes places with him.

For the parlor or class room. — This game adapts itself well to indoor use, the farmer sitting on a chair in the middle of the room if in a parlor, or at the teacher's desk if in a schoolroom. The players are home when in their seats, and the farmer, to catch them, must tag them before they are seated.

This is a particularly enjoyable game for an older person to play with children, the former enacting the farmer.

FENCE TAG

4 to 30 or more players   *Primary and*
Indoors; out of doors; schoolroom   *intermediate grades*

This game is a great favorite with boys for outdoor play, but may also be used in the gymnasium, various pieces of apparatus being used in lieu of a fence.

A certain length of fence is chosen for the game. The one who is It gives the other players a slight start in which to vault over the fence, when he immediately vaults over and tries to tag them. This tagging may be done only when both players are on the same side of the fence.

The dodging is made almost or quite entirely by vaulting or dodging back and forth across the fence within the length or boundaries previously determined. Any player tagged must change places with the one who is It.

FOR THE SCHOOLROOM. — This game may be used in the schoolroom by vaulting over the seats. When played in this way, it is not allowable to reach across seats or desks to tag a player.

The tagging must be done in the same aisle in which the tagger stands.

FIRE ON THE MOUNTAINS

10 to 30 or more players   *Intermediate grades*
Playground; gymnasium

A number of stools are placed in a circle with considerable space between them, there being two stools less than the number of players. If played out of doors, a stone may be used to sit on in place of a stool, or the players may stand, each on a spot or base marked on the ground. One of the odd players is a leader, and sits or stands in the center; the remainder are circle men and each takes his place on a stool or base, the other odd man standing anywhere in the circle between the bases. The object of the game is

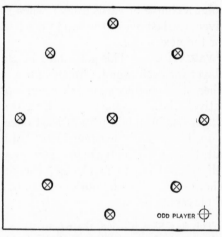

FIRE ON THE MOUNTAINS

for the circle men to change places on a signal given by the leader, each player trying to secure a stool and avoid being the odd man. The longer the distance between stools or bases the greater the sport. The running must be done in a circle outside of the bases, and no crosscuts through the circle are allowed. The player in the center repeats in rapid time the following lines:

> "Fire on the mountains, run, boys, run!
> You with the red coat, you with the gun,
> Fire on the mountains, run, boys, run!"

At any time, at the close of the verse, or unexpectedly, by way of interruption to it, the center player will call "Stool!" or "Base!" when all of the players must change bases. There will thus be one odd player left out.   This player then steps one side and is out of the game, taking with him a stool belonging to one of the players, so that the number of stools is reduced by one ; if bases are used, one is crossed out to show it is out of the game.   The center player, who remains caller throughout, then repeats the verse and the signal for changing.

For each round of the game one player and one stool are taken out of the circle, until but two players and one stool are left. These two finish the game by circling the stool and some objective point a couple of yards away ; when the signal to change is then given, the last one of the two to reach the stool becomes the leader for the next game.

VARIATION. — This game may be played without eliminating a player for each round.   In this form, each player who is left out when stools or bases are taken must pay a forfeit, but continues actively in the game.   The forfeits are redeemed when each player has been odd man at least once.

In this form of the game, instead of having one leader throughout, the leader (center man) should try to secure a stool for himself when the others change, the odd man becoming leader. There should then be but one stool or base less than the number of players.

This is a Scotch game, the references to signal fires on the mountains, red coats, and guns having an obviously historic origin.   For parlor use, see the similar game, " Going to Jerusalem."

FLOWERS AND THE WIND

4 to 30 or more players   *Primary grades*
                Indoors; out of doors

This game is suitable for little children.   The players are divided into two equal parties, each party having a home marked off at opposite ends of the playground, with a long neutral space between.   One party represents a flower, deciding among themselves which flower they shall represent, as daisies, lilies, lilacs, etc.   They then walk over near the home line of the opposite party.   The opposite players (who represent the wind) stand in a row on their line, ready to run, and guess what the flower chosen by their opponents may be. As soon as the right flower is named, the entire party owning it must turn and run home, the wind chasing them. Any players caught by the wind before reaching home become his prisoners and join him. The remaining flowers repeat their play, taking a different name each time. This continues until all of the flowers have been caught.

FOLLOW THE LEADER

5 to 60 or more players　　　　　　　　　　*Primary grades*
Playground; gymnasium; parlor; schoolroom

One player, who is especially resourceful or skillful, is chosen as a leader. The others all form in single file behind him, and imitate anything that he does. The leader aims to keep the line moving, and should set particularly hard tasks for them, such as climbing or vaulting over obstacles, under others, jumping to touch high points or objects, going through difficult feats, jumping certain distances, taking a hop, skip, and jump, walking backward, turning around while walking, walking or running with a book on the head, etc. Anyone failing to perform the required feat drops out of the game or goes to the foot of the line; or at the pleasure of the players may pay a forfeit for the failure and continue playing, all forfeits to be redeemed at the close of the game.

FORCING THE CITY GATES

10 to 30 or more players　　　　　　　　*Junior high school*
Playground; gymnasium

Two captains are selected, who alternately choose players until all are in two groups. The two sides then line up in two straight lines, facing each other about ten feet apart, and holding hands, each line representing the gates of a city. The captains dispose their men in line as they see fit, but it is advisable to alternate the larger or stronger players with the smaller or weaker ones, to equalize the strength at the points of attack. The captain of one side then names one of his players, who steps forward and tries to break through the hands of the opposing side, or he may dodge under them. If he does not succeed in one place, he may try in another, but may not have more than three trials. Should he succeed in breaking the opposing line or dodging under, he returns to his side, taking the two whose hands had been parted or evaded, as prisoners to re-enforce his side. Should he fail in the third attempt, he is to remain on the side of his opponents. The captains alternate turns in sending forth a man to "force the city gates." The players taken from the opposing side must thereafter work for the side to which they are taken captive, each prisoner being placed in the line between two of the original team. The side wins which eventually secures all of the opposing players. The action may be made more rapid where a large number are playing by sending out two or more players at once.

This is a Chinese game, recorded by Dr. Headland, who has kindly supplied additional points to the author. Some modifications for large numbers have been found advisable under American school conditions.

FORTRESS

10 to 100 players   *Children or adults*
               Out of doors; gymnasium

This is one of the very strenuous games based on the idea of warfare. The underlying idea is exactly opposite to that of Robbers and Soldiers, being a game of attack and defense rather than of chase and capture.

A fortress is marked on the ground, in the shape of a large square or oblong, the size differing with the area at disposal and the number of players. It should be not less than twenty-five by forty feet in dimensions. One or more sides of this may be situated so as to be enclosed by a wall or fence. A line should be drawn five feet inside of the fortress boundaries and another five feet outside of it; these mark the guard lines or limits for making prisoners. Each party should also have its prison — a small square marked in the center of the fortress for the defenders, and another at some distant point for the besiegers.

The players are divided into two equal teams, each under the command of a general, who may order his men at any time to any part of the battle. One team of players are defenders of the

fortress, and should scatter over it at the beginning of the attack
and keep a sharp lookout on unguarded parts at any time. The
other players, forming the attacking party, scatter under the
direction of their general to approach the fortress from different
directions. This may be done in a sudden rush, or deliberately
before attacking. At a signal from their general, the besiegers
attack the fortress.

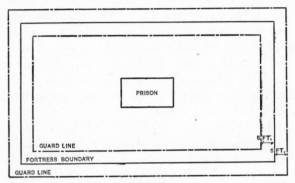

FORTRESS

The method of combat is entirely confined to engagements
between any two of the opposing players, and is in general of the
nature of a "tug of war." They may push, pull, or carry each
other so long as they remain upright; but wrestling or dragging
on the ground are not allowed. Any player so forced over the
guard line becomes a prisoner to his opponent and is thereafter
out of the game. If he be a besieger, captured by a defender,
he is placed within the prison in the center of the fortress, and may
not thereafter escape or be freed unless the generals should make
an exchange of prisoners. Should he be a defender, pulled over
the outer guard line by a besieger, he is taken to the prison of the
attacking party, subject to the same rules of escape. In the
general engagement, players of equal strength should compete,
the strong players with strong ones, and *vice versa*. The com-
manders should each give general directions for this to their men
before the engagement opens.

The battle is won by either team making prisoners of all of the opponents. Or it may be won by the besiegers if one of their men enters within the guard line inside the fortress without being touched by a defender. Should a player accomplish this, he shouts "Hole's won!" Whereupon the defenders must yield the fortress, and the two parties change places, defenders becoming besiegers, and *vice versa*. The possibility of taking the fortress in this way should lead to great alertness on the part of the defenders, as they should leave no point unguarded, especially a fence which the enemy might scale. The guard line should be drawn inside any such boundaries, and a player entering in this way must of course get inside the guard line as well as over the fence. The attacking team on its part will use all possible devices for dashing into the fortress unexpectedly, such as engaging the players on one side of the fort to leave an unguarded loophole for entering at another.

The attacking general may withdraw his forces at any time for a rest or for conference; either general may run up a flag of truce at any time for similar purposes. Under such conditions the generals may arrange for an exchange of prisoners; otherwise there is no means of freeing prisoners.

FOX AND FARMER

(Follow Chase)

10 to 30 or more players   *Primary grades*
Gymnasium; playground

The players stand in a circle with arms stretched sideways, resting on each other's shoulders, thus making a wide distance between. One player is chosen for runner and one for chaser. The game starts with the runner in one of the spaces under the outstretched arms of the players, and the chaser in a similar position on the opposite side of the circle. At a signal from a leader both start, the runner weaving in and out between the players or dashing across the circle in any way that he sees fit; but the chaser must always follow by the same route. If the runner be caught, he joins the circle; the chaser then takes his place as runner and chooses another player to be chaser.

The leader (who may be one of the players) may close the chase if it becomes too long by calling "Time!" when both runners must return to their places in the circle, new ones taking their places.

For large numbers there may be two or more runners and an equal number of chasers, or the players may be divided into smaller groups.

With various modifications, this game is found in many countries. As given here, it is of Italian origin.

FOX AND GEESE

(Fox's Tail)

(For other games sometimes known by this title, see *Broncho Tag*, *Fox Trail*, and *Naughts and Crosses*.)

10 to 30 or more players   *Junior and*
Playground; gymnasium   *senior high school*

One player is chosen to be fox and another to be gander. The remaining players all stand in single file behind the gander, each with his hands on the shoulders of the one next in front. The gander tries to protect his flock of geese from being caught by the fox, and to do this spreads out his arms and dodges around in any way he sees fit to circumvent the efforts of the fox. Only the last goose in the line may be tagged by the fox, or should the line be very long, the last five or ten players may be tagged as decided beforehand. It will be seen that the geese may all co-operate with the gander by doubling and redoubling their line to prevent the fox from tagging the last goose. Should the fox tag the last goose (or one of the last five or ten, if that be permissible), that goose becomes fox and the fox becomes gander.

A good deal of spirit may be added to the game by the following dialogue, which is sometimes used to open it:

The fox shouts tantalizingly, "Geese, geese, gannio!"
The geese reply scornfully, "Fox, fox, fannio!"
Fox: "How many geese have you today?"
Gander: "More than you can catch and carry away."

On this challenge the fox begins his chase for the end goose.

This game is found in almost all countries, under various names and representing different animals.

FOX AND SQUIRREL

20 to 60 players   *Primary grades*

Schoolroom

The players sit in their seats facing toward the aisles, so that each two adjacent lines have their feet in the same aisle and face each other. The game consists in passing or tossing some object (the squirrel), such as a beanbag, basket ball, or hand ball, from one player across the aisle to another and back again, zigzagging down each aisle, to be followed at once by a second object (the fox); the effort being to have the fox overtake the squirrel before the end of the line is reached.

With very little children, passing is better than tossing; but with older children, or even with little ones when more experienced, it is well to use the game as a practice for tossing and catching. The action should be very rapid. The game makes much sport for young children, and they are very fond of it.

FOX TRAIL (DOUBLE RIM)

(Fox and Geese; Half Bushel)

(See also *Fox Trail, Single Rim.*)

3 to 30 or more players   *Intermediate grades*

Out of doors; indoors; snow

This form of Fox Trail, like the Single Rim game, is distinctively a snow game, but may be used anywhere if a large diagram may be marked on the ground or floor. This game differs from the Single Rim in the size and complexity of the diagram, there being two rims to the wheel instead of one. It also differs in the fact that there is one more player than the number of dens for the foxes, and in the methods by which the foxes may run or be chased.

I. A large diagram is drawn on the ground, resembling a wheel with two rims. In the snow this is trampled with the feet like a path; on bare ground or damp sand it may be drawn with the foot or a stick ; in the gymnasium or on a pavement it may be drawn with chalk.   The outer rim should measure from thirty to forty feet in radius ; the inner rim should be ten feet from this. Across the circles are drawn straight lines resembling the spokes of a wheel, the number being governed by the number of players. Where these spokes touch the outer rim, a den or goal is marked for the foxes, there being one goal less than the number of foxes.

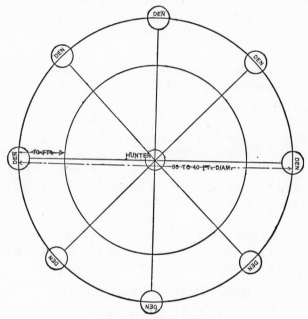

Fox Trail (Double Rim)

One player, who is chosen as hunter, stands at his goal in the center or hub of the wheel.   The balance of the players, who are foxes, take each a place in a den on the outer rim, with the exception of the odd fox, who stands elsewhere on the rim, trying to get a den whenever he can.   The object of the game is for the foxes to run from den to den without being caught by the hunter. The method of running, however, is restricted.   Both foxes and hunter are obliged to keep to the trails, running only on the lines of the diagram.

It is considered poor play to run from den to den around the outer rim, as there is practically no risk in this. The foxes may run in any direction on any trail, on the spokes of the wheel, or on either of the rims. They may turn off on the intersecting trail at any point, not being obliged to run entirely across to the opposite side of the rim, as in the simpler diagram given for the other game of this name. No fox, however, may turn back on a trail; having once started, he must keep on to the next intersecting point. Whenever the hunter succeeds in tagging a fox, the two players change places, the fox becoming hunter and the hunter fox.

This game is excellent sport, and is one of the most interesting and popular of the chasing games. It is one of the very few distinctive snow games.

II. As **Fox and Geese** this game is played by having only one fox instead of a hunter, the rest of the players being geese who start the game standing on the outer, or goose, rim. The hub of the wheel is called the goose shed, and the inner ring the fox ring. The object of the geese is to get from their ring to the goose shed without being caught by the fox. He may tag them only when they are on the spokes of the wheel, but not on the outer rim or when they are in contact with the goose shed. If a goose is tagged it at once becomes the fox and the former fox a goose. The old fox (now a goose) must run quickly, as the new fox may tag him immediately.

FOX TRAIL (SINGLE RIM)

(Fox and Geese; Half Bushel)

(See also *Fox Trail, Double Rim*)

3 to 20 players   *Primary grades*

Out of doors; snow; seashore; gymnasium

This is one of the few distinctive snow games, but may be played anywhere if a large diagram may be outlined on the ground. It is very popular with children, and makes an admirable game for older players as well. See the more complicated form, with double-rim diagram, preceding this.

A large circle from fifteen to thirty feet in diameter should be marked on the ground and crossed with intersecting lines like the spokes of a wheel, there being about five such lines (ten spokes).

The more players there are, the larger should be the circle and the greater the number of spokes; but there is no fixed relation between the number of spokes and players. If played in the

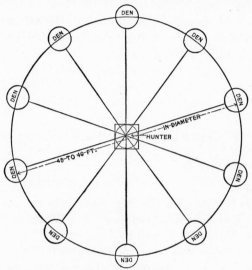

Fox Trail (Single Rim)

snow, this diagram may be trampled down with the feet; if on the fresh earth or sand, it may be drawn with the heel or a stick; or if in a gymnasium or on a pavement, marked with chalk.

One player is chosen to be It, or hunter. He stands in the center, that is, on the hub of the wheel. The other players scatter around the rim and are foxes. They are not stationed at any one point as in the Double Rim game, but run or stand anywhere around the rim when not dashing across the spokes. The object of the game is for the foxes to cross the wheel to some opposite point without being tagged by the hunter. They may only run, however, on the prescribed trails, — that is, on the lines of the diagram. In this form of the game (the Single Rim diagram) they may run only straight across, and are not at liberty to turn an angle at the hub and seek refuge over any other trail than the direct continuation of the one on which they started. The hunter changes places with anyone whom he tags.

FRENCH TAG

4 to 60 or more players   *Intermediate grades*
Indoors; out of doors

In this form of tag certain boundaries are agreed upon beyond which players may not run, though they may climb or jump over any obstacles within the boundaries.

Any player who goes outside of the bounds is at once declared to be It by the pursuer. Otherwise the game is like ordinary tag, any player who is tagged by the chaser becoming It. (See *Tag.*)

FROG IN THE MIDDLE

10 to 30 or more players   *Primary grades*
Parlor; gymnasium; playground

One player is chosen for the frog, and sits in the center on the floor with his feet crossed in tailor fashion. Where there are more than twenty players, it is well to have at least two such frogs. The other players stand in a circle around the frog, repeating, "Frog in the sea, can't catch me!" They dance forward toward the frog and back, tantalizing him and taking risks in going near him, the object of the game being for the frog to tag any one of them, whereupon he changes places with such player. The frog may not at any time leave his sitting position until released by tagging another player.

GARDEN SCAMP

10 to 30 or more players   *Primary grades*
Playground; gymnasium; schoolroom; parlor.

This game is a great favorite with children, and may be made an opportunity for much sport with youths and older players.

All but two of the players form a ring by clasping hands, the enclosure serving as the garden. Within this, one of the odd players who is assigned to be the scamp takes his place. The other odd player, the gardener, moves around on the outside of the circle.

The gardener calls to the scamp inside, "Who let you in my garden?" and the scamp answers, "No one!" whereupon he starts to run away, the gardener chasing him. The gardener must take the same path followed by the scamp in and out under the arms of the players, who must lift their hands to let them pass. The gardener must also go through all of the movements performed by the scamp, who may jump "leapfrog" over any player in the circle, turn somersaults, crawl between the legs of a circle player, double unexpectedly on his path, circle around one of the players, or resort to any other device for making the chase difficult. If the scamp be caught, he becomes gardener, and the gardener joins the circle. The former scamp, now gardener, chooses a new scamp to go into the circle.

Should the gardener fail to follow in the exact path of the scamp, or to perform any of the feats or antics of the scamp, the gardener must at once join the ring, and the scamp then has the privilege of choosing a new gardener.

FOR THE SCHOOLROOM. — This game may be played by the entire class forming a circle around the room as close to the seats as possible to leave room for the chase outside the circle. Where seats can be turned up, this should be done, to give the runners opportunity to cross and recross the center space easily. The scamp, however, may vault over seats in his efforts to escape or delay the gardener.

GOING TO JERUSALEM

10 to 60 or more players   *Intermediate grades*
Parlor; gymnasium; schoolroom   *to junior high school*

A row of chairs is placed in the center of the room, so that they face alternately in opposite directions, one chair to one side, the next to the opposite side, etc. There should be one chair less than the number of players. The game is most interesting when played with musical accompaniment.

The game starts with all the players seated in the row of chairs except one. This odd one is the leader, and his first object is to recruit the players for his trip to "Jerusalem." He carries a cane and walks around the row repeating, "I'm going to Jerusalem! I'm going to Jerusalem!" in singsong. Every few moments he stops at his discretion and knocks with his cane on the floor behind the chair of some player. Immediately the player thus summoned rises from his chair and follows the leader, sometimes having a lively scramble to encircle the row of chairs and catch up with him. The next player knocked for follows this one, and so on, until all are moving around in single file. The leader may reverse his direction at pleasure. This general hurry and confusion for the start may, with a resourceful leader, add much to the sport of the game.

When the players are all recruited, they continue to march around the row of chairs, the main object of the game being the scramble for seats when the music stops, or upon some other signal to sit if there be no music.

The musician will add to the interest of the game by varying the time of the march from slow and stately time to "double quick." At any moment, after all the players are marching, the music may stop suddenly. Whenever this happens, the players all scramble for seats. There will be one odd player left without a seat. This player is thenceforth out of the game and retires to one end of the room, taking with him one of the chairs. This continues until there are only two players encircling one chair, and the one who secures it wins.

Where two players reach a chair at nearly the same time, the chair belongs to the one who first reached it, or who is sitting more fully on it. Sitting on the arm of a chair does not count, nor touching it with the hands or knees.

FOR THE GYMNASIUM. — When played in a gymnasium, a row of gymnasium stools may be used instead of chairs, and the gathering up of the players omitted, the game starting with the stools empty.

FOR THE SCHOOLROOM. — When played in the schoolroom, the game starts with all of the players ready to march, the first part of the game, in which they are recruited, being omitted. The class should march in serpentine form up one aisle and down the next, etc., instead of encircling a row of seats. There should be for a large class from one to six less seats than the number of players. For instance, one seat should be counted out in each row or each alternate row. The seat that is not in play may be designated by turning it up, if of that variety, and by placing a book on the desk belonging to it.

Wherever played, the game may be carried on without music, simply by the leader's, or teacher's, beating time and stopping when players are to sit; or he may give a signal or a command to "Sit!"

GOOD MORNING

10 to 60 or more players   *Primary grades*
Schoolroom; parlor

This is a very pretty sense-training game — cultivating discrimination through the sense of hearing. Little children are very fond of it, and it is most interesting and surprising to note the development of perceptive power through the playing of the game.

One player blinds his eyes. He may do this by going to a corner of the room and facing the wall, with his hand over his eyes; or a very pretty method is to have him go to the teacher, with his face hidden in her lap, and her hands on either side of his head, like the blinders of a horse.

The teacher then silently points to some other player in the class, who rises at once and says, "Good morning, David!" (or whatever the child's name may be). The little guesser, if he has recognized the voice, responds with, "Good morning, Arthur!" (or other name). If he does not guess the voice after the first greeting, the child may be required to repeat it, until the guesser has had three trials. Should he fail on the third trial, he turns around to see who the player was, and changes places with him. If he names the right player, the guesser retains his position until he fails to guess the voice of the one greeting him, one player after another being required to stand and give the greeting "Good morning!"

When pupils have become somewhat proficient in the guesser's place, the others should be required to change their seats after the guesser has blinded his eyes, so that he will not be assisted in his judgment by the direction from which the voice

comes, which is very easily the case where the other players are
in their accustomed seats.

Of course the greeting will be varied according to the time of
day, being "Good afternoon!" or "Good evening!" as may be
appropriate. Occasionally, in a school game, a pupil from another room may be called in. Should a strange voice be heard
in this way, the little guesser is considered correct if he answer,
"Good morning, stranger!"

GUESS WHO

10 to 30 or more players   *Primary grades*
              Playground; gymnasium; parlor; schoolroom

Where there are more than ten players, it is desirable to have
them separated into several groups. Each group has a leader,
and lines up in rank (side by side), with the leader in the middle.
One odd player stands in front of the line, facing it.

The odd player asks:

"Have you seen my friend?"

The line answers,

"No."

First player:

"Will you go and find him?"

"Yes."

"Put your finger on your lips and follow me!"

The player in front then turns around and, with finger to his
lips, runs to another part of the ground, all of the row falling in
behind and following him, each player with finger on lips. When
they have reached a new position, the first player stops with his
back to the line, which re-forms in a new order under the direction
of its leader, so that the players do not stand in the same relative
positions as when the odd player faced the line. One player from
the row selected by the leader now steps forward behind the odd
player and says, trying to disguise his voice, "Guess who stands
behind you!"

If the odd player guesses correctly, he retains his position,
turns around, and the dialogue begins over again. If the guess

be wrong, the one who is It changes places with the one whose name he failed to guess.

GYPSY

5 to 10 players   *Primary grades*
Indoors; out of doors

This is one of the traditional dramatic games, obviously an abbreviated form of *Mother, Mother, the Pot Boils Over!*

One player is selected for gypsy, and one for the mother. The others are children. The gypsy remains in hiding while the mother says to her children, pointing to the different ones in turn:

> "I charge my children every one
> To keep good house while I am gone;
> You and you, but specially you,
> Or else I'll beat you black and blue."

The mother then goes away and blinds her eyes. During her absence the gypsy comes in, takes away a child, and hides her. The gypsy repeats this until all of the children are hidden. The mother returns and finds her children gone, whereupon she has to find them. When all have been found and brought back home, all chase the gypsy.

HANG TAG

10 to 100 players   *Primary grades*
Playground; gymnasium

One player is It, or chaser, and changes places with any other player whom he can touch (tag). In this form of the game, however, any player may escape being tagged by hanging from anything overhead which will enable him to lift his feet from the floor. When played out of doors, where there are trees, players will naturally jump to catch hold of the branches of the trees. On a playground or in a gymnasium pieces of apparatus may be used for the same purpose. A player is considered immune if, instead of hanging by his hands, he throws himself across some obstacle, such as a fence, which enables him to lift his feet from the ground. The game is very uninteresting if players each choose a place and remain close to it in the intervals of the game; but it may be made full of sport if each will take risks and run from point to point, taunting the one who is It by going as near him as possible, or allowing him to approach closely before springing for the overhead support. The one who is It may not linger near any player to the extent of trying to tire him out in the hanging position, but must move rapidly from one to another.

A very interesting form of this game for the gymnasium allows no two players to hang from the same piece of apparatus; the last one taking possession has the right to remain hanging on the apparatus, the one before him being obliged to run at once for another place. This keeps the players moving and makes the game very lively.

TREE TOAD. — This is a form of Hang Tag played by the modern Greeks. It is played where there are trees, the players jumping to clasp the trunk of the tree as a means of lifting their feet from the ground when the branches are too high to reach. This makes a very funny, vigorous, and interesting form of the game, to be played in a grove or shaded lawn.

HAVE YOU SEEN MY SHEEP?

10 to 30 or more players   *Primary grades*
Playground; parlor; gymnasium; schoolroom

The players stand in a circle. One walks around on the outside, and touching one of the circle players on the back, asks, "Have you seen my sheep?" The one questioned answers, "How was he dressed?" The outside player then describes the dress of someone in the circle, saying, for instance, "He wears a red necktie; he is dressed in gray and has low shoes." The one questioned then names the player whom he thinks this describes, and if right, at once begins to chase him around the outside of the circle. Each of the circle players must be very alert to recognize himself in the description given by the outside player, for immediately that he is named he must run around the outside of the circle, chased by the player who guessed, and try to reach his own place before being tagged. The one who gives the description does not take part in the chase. Should the runner be tagged before returning to his place, he must take the place of the questioner, running in his turn around the outside of the circle and asking of some player, "Have you seen my sheep?"

IN THE SCHOOLROOM. — The players remain seated, with the exception of the one who asks the first question of any player he chooses. This player at once stands, guesses the player described, and chases him around the room, the one chased trying to gain his seat before being caught. If caught, he becomes questioner; if not caught, the same questioner and guesser play as before.

HIDE AND SEEK

The following games of hiding and seeking will be found in alphabetical order:

Gypsy Hide and Seek	Sardines
I Spy!	Smuggling the Geg
Ring-a-lie-vio	Ten Steps
Run, Sheep, Run!	Wolf
Yards Off	

HIDE AND SEEK

2 to 20 or more players   *Primary grades*
Indoors; out of doors

This is a simple form of "I Spy," played by very little children. One covers his eyes or *blinds* and the others hide. When securely hidden, they call "Coop!" and the one who is It goes in search of them. The call of "Coop!" may be repeated at the discretion of the hider. In this game the object is won when the searcher discovers the hidden players. There is no race for a goal as in "I Spy."

HIGH WINDOWS

10 to 30 or more players   *Intermediate grades*
Playground; gymnasium

All of the players but one join hands in a circle. The odd player in the center runs around on the inside of the circle and hits one of the players with a wisp of grass, if the game be played out of doors, or tags him if played indoors. Both players then run out of the circle, it being the object of the player who was tagged to catch the odd player before he can run three times around the outside of the ring. As the runner completes his third time around, the players in the circle cry "High Windows!" and raise their clasped hands to let both of the players inside. Should the one who is being chased succeed in entering the circle without being tagged, he joins the circle and the chaser takes his place in the center. Should the chaser tag the pursued before he can circle the ring three times and dodge inside at the close, the chaser returns to the circle and the one caught goes again into the center.

It is permissible to vary the chase by running away from the immediate vicinity of the circle. Should the chase then become too long, the circle players may call "High Windows!" as a signal for the runners to come in. This call is made at the discretion of a leader, whether he be one of the circle players appointed for that purpose, or a teacher

HILL DILL

10 to 30 or more players   *Intermediate grades*
Playground; gymnasium

Two parallel boundary lines are drawn from thirty to fifty feet apart; or the game is often played between the curbings of a street, which serve as boundaries. One player is chosen to be It, and stands in the center. The other players stand in two equal parties beyond the boundary lines, one party on each side. The center player calls out, "Hill, dill! come over the hill!" The other players then exchange goals, and as they run across the open space the one in the center tries to tag them. Any who are tagged assist him thereafter in tagging the others.

This game is not well adapted to very large numbers of players, as it brings two opposing parties running toward each other in the exchange of goals. It is especially suited to conditions where a very wide central field lies between the goals, thus giving opportunity for the players to scatter.

HIP

5 to 30 or more players   *Intermediate*
Playground   *to junior high*

All of the players stand in an informal group. One of them is provided with a stick about the size of a broomstick and about two feet long. He throws this as far as he can, at the same time calling the name of one of the other players. The one who threw the stick and all the others, except the one whose name is called, then scatter in a run. The one who is called must pick up the stick, whereupon he becomes "Hip" and must chase the other players. Any player whom he catches he touches with the stick (pounding not allowed), and that player at once joins him in trying to catch the others. Anyone caught by the second player, however, must be held by him until Hip can come and touch the prisoner with the stick, whereupon he also joins Hip's party. As the number of players with Hip increases, there may be some pretty lively "tussling" on the part of players who are caught, pending the arrival of Hip to touch them with the stick, as he may have several to reach in this way, and the interval may be considerable in which the captor must hold his victim. The game ends when all of the players have been touched by Hip.

HOME TAG

4 to 60 or more players   *Intermediate grades*
Indoors; out of doors   *to senior high school*

One player is It, or chaser, and changes places with anyone whom he can touch (tag) outside of the safety places called homes. One or more such places are chosen to which the players may run at any time for safety. It is advisable to have these homes widely separated, as at opposite ends of the playground. If the players resort to these homes too frequently to make a good game, the chaser may call

> "Three times three are nine;
> Who does not run is mine."

Whereupon every player must run out from his home or goal, or change places with the tagger.

HOPPING RELAY RACE

10 to 100 players   *Intermediate grades*
Playground; gymnasium; schoolroom   *to adult*

A starting line is drawn on the ground, behind which the players stand in two or more single files, facing a goal. The goal should be ten or more feet from the starting line, and may consist of a wall, or a line drawn on the ground. At a signal the first player in each line hops on one foot to the goal, touches it with his hands (stooping for this if it be a line on the ground), and hops back to the end of his line, which should have moved forward to fill his place as he started. He takes his place at the rear end of the line. He tags the first player in the line as he passes him, and this player at once hops forward to the goal. Each player thus takes his turn, the line winning whose last player first reaches the rear of his line and there raises his hand as a signal.

If the game be repeated, the hopping in the second round should be on the opposite foot.

FOR THE SCHOOLROOM. — This may be played in the classroom by having an equal number of pupils in each row of seats. The players remain seated until it is their turn to hop, each hopping from his own seat to the forward blackboard and back to his seat again; or the distance may be made greater by continuing past his seat to the rear wall and then back to his seat again. The game starts with those in the rear seats. Each pupil as he takes his seat tags the pupil seated next in front of him, who takes this as a signal to start. The line wins whose player in the front seat first returns and raises a hand to show he is seated.

HOP SCOTCH

1 to 10 players   *Primary and*
Playground; street   *intermediate grades*

Games of hopping and jumping through a diagram, and playing a stone or puck through it, are probably seen in more countries and more frequently than any other kind of game. One can easily imagine these to be the forerunners of sword dances.

Several forms of Hop Scotch are here given. These include the form played in America for generations — followed by Italian, French, Monagasque, and English forms, selected because of their distinctive features of play as well as for their different diagrams. Certain procedures and rules apply to all games and may be stated as follows:

General Rules

DIAGRAM OR COURT. — This is outlined with chalk on a pavement, or with a stick on the ground.

STONE OR PUCK. — The traditional game is played with a flat stone, such as that used for "skipping" over water; but in cities where stones are not easily found, a rubber heel makes an admirable substitute.

THE PLAY consists in hopping or jumping into the different sections of the diagram and out again in a prescribed manner and order, with or without playing a stone (puck). In all hopping games it is a miss to change the hopping foot during any given play, or to touch the other foot or any part of the person to the ground, except where the game calls for that, as sometimes in straddling. It is also a miss to touch a line with the hopping foot.

Straddling consists in jumping to a stride position in two spaces, one foot on each side of the line. Straddling is usually in the nature of a rest from hopping, as the weight may not only be on both feet, but the feet in some games are allowed to rest wholly on the ground unless "toes only" are specified.

Jumping (both feet together) is subject to the same rules about not touching lines or ground as hopping.

THROWING AND KICKING STONE (PUCK). — When the stone is thrown it must land wholly within the space intended; for it to touch or cross a line is a miss. When it is kicked out it must always go out over the base or end lines and not over the side lines.

The stone may be shoved by the hopping foot to a more advantageous position within its square or space before being kicked out. The player may hop around in this space as much as he pleases before, during, or after touching the stone, so long as he observes all rules about not touching lines or ground.

For throwing the stone or puck the player must stand outside the baseline and in most games must be in a hopping position when making the throw. He may bend forward, but must not touch the lines or ground within them with his foot or any part of his person.

PLAYERS are not limited as to number. They take turns in regular order. Any player missing gives way at once to the next player; when his turn comes around again he begins by playing over the particular play on which he missed, unless otherwise specified, as in part of the Italian game. All players begin with the first play, or stunt, unless otherwise directed, as in the English game (Hop Scotch V) in which a player begins with the play on which the previous player failed.

It is a miss also to (*a*) play out of turn, and (*b*) to make the wrong play.

WINNING. — The player wins who has gone through the entire game with the fewest number of turns (misses), everyone else having played. That is, if he should be fortunate enough to play the entire series without a miss, he has not won until every other player has had his turn and missed.

I. American Hop Scotch

I. HOP SCOTCH

This is the form best known in America, where it has been played for generations. It is also found in most other countries.[1]

OBJECT. — The first person completing the stunts described after all players have had an equal number of turns, wins.

PUCK. — Players may provide their own pucks, which may be of any material but not exceed 3½ inches in length, width, or other dimension.

COURT. — The court shall be outlined according to the accompanying diagram, lines being of uniform width approximating five eighths of an inch, chalked, or painted, upon a smooth and level cement surface.

STARTING POSITION. — Contestants shall stand in hopping pose on one foot beyond the base line of court with puck in one hand.

Stunt No. 1

a. Toss or drop puck into square 1.

b. Hop into square 1.

c. Kick puck out of square over baseline.

d. Hop out of square over base line. Do not step out.

e. If no error has been made, proceed to stunt No. 2.

[1] The rules here given are those adopted by the National Rules Committee on Athletics and Games of the National Recreation Association, for use in tournaments, and are reproduced by their courtesy.

STUNT No. 2

a. Toss puck into square 2.

b. Hop into square 1, then into square 2.

c. Kick puck directly out over baseline.

d. Retrace course by hopping to square 1, then out over baseline. If no error has been made, proceed to Stunt No. 3.

STUNT No. 3

a. Toss puck into triangle marked 3.

b. From starting position straddle first two squares; that is, leap in, landing with right foot in 1, left foot at the same instant in 2.

c. Jump from both feet and land on one (either) in triangle.

d. Kick puck toward or beyond baseline. If it stops in a square of smaller number without resting on a line, it must be retrieved as follows:

e. Return with straddle into 1 and 2, right foot in 2. Raise either foot and while hopping kick puck out beyond baseline.

f. Hop out over baseline.

If puck went entirely out from the kick in 3, straddle in 1 and 2, and leap out beyond baseline, landing on one foot.

STUNT No. 4

a. From starting position, toss puck into triangle No. 4.

b. Advance as in Stunt 3 to triangle 3 and hop into triangle No. 4.

c. Retrieve puck as in Stunt 3.

d. Hop into 3 and return as in Stunt 3. If no error has been made, proceed to

STUNT No. 5

a. From starting position toss puck into triangle No. 5.

b. Advance as in Stunt 4 and hop into triangle No. 5.

c. Retrieve puck and return as before. If no error has been made, proceed to

STUNT No. 6

a. From starting position, toss puck into triangle No. 6.

b. Advance as in Stunt 3 to No. 3.

c. Leap to alight with right foot in triangle 4 and left foot in 5, at the same time, and jump from both feet to land on one foot in triangle 6.

d. Retrieve puck as before.

e. Return by leaping to alight with right foot in 5 and left foot in 4 at the same time, jump into 3 with one foot only, leap into 2 and 1 with right in 2 and left foot in 1 at the same time, and jump out beyond baseline to land on one foot. If no error has been made, proceed to

STUNT No. 7

a. From starting position, toss puck into rectangle No. 7.

b. Advance as in Stunt No. 6 and leap to land on both feet at same time in rectangle 7.

c. Walk about in 7, moving puck with foot or feet alone until in position to retrieve it by kicking it out over baseline or into a space of smaller number.

d. Return by raising one foot and hopping into triangle 6, and continue out as before. If no error has been made, proceed to

STUNT No. 8

a. From starting position, toss puck into semicircle No. 8.

b. Advance as before to 7 and when ready to progress to space 8, raise either foot and hop out of rectangle into semicircle, landing on one foot.

c. Retrieve puck as before.

d. Return by leaping to land both feet at the same time in rectangle 7 and when ready continue as in Stunt 7. If no error has been made, proceed to

STUNT No. 9

a. From starting position toss puck into arc No. 9.

b. Advance as in Stunt No. 8.

c. Retrieve while in hopping position in semicircle by picking up the puck by hand from arc No. 9.

d. Return as in Stunt No. 8, carrying puck in hand.

STUNT No. 10

a. From starting position, toss puck into arc No. 10.

b. Advance as in Stunt No. 9 and hop into arc No. 10.

c. Retrieve as in Stunt No. 9.

d. Hop into semicircle 8 and return as before, stopping for a few seconds' rest in No. 7 if desired.

STUNT No. 11

a. From starting position, without tossing or carrying puck, advance as in Stunt 8 to semicircle.

b. Leap to land on both feet at the same time with right in arc 9 and left in arc 10.

c. About face and reverse position of feet by a leaping half turn.

d. Return by jumping to land on one foot in semicircle and continue out according to Stunt No. 8.

FOULS, ERRORS, OR MISSES

The following are penalized by loss of turns:

1. Tossing puck while not in proper hopping position back of baseline. Leaning over is allowable.

2. Puck, on throw, does not come to rest entirely within designated space so that a vertical line dropped from any edge of puck intersects one of the court lines.

3. Puck, on kick, comes to rest so that a vertical line dropped through any part of it touches a court line.

4. Puck, on kick, passes out of court over a side line, not the baseline.

5. Touching any court line with footwear or coming to rest on a foot so that a vertical line dropped through the footwear would touch a line.

6. Any irregularity in progression as judged by the umpire.

II. HOP SCOTCH

(Italian)

The player throws the stone into a square, hops and straddles through the entire diagram, omitting the square containing the stone by hopping over it; he also hops over the blank spaces, of which there are two, one in the middle of the diagram and a second one near the far end. He then returns in the same way except to stop in the square preceding the one where the stone is; while standing there he bends over, picks up the stone and hops out with it. Any puck may be used instead of a stone. See *General Rules*.

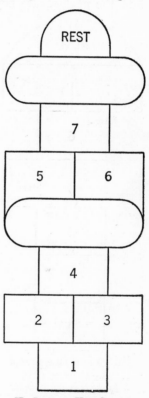

II. ITALIAN HOP SCOTCH
(*Spaces are twelve to twenty inches deep.*)

The stone is thrown successively into 1, 2, 3, 4, 5, 6, 7, and "Rest," but not into the two blank spaces. If the stone lands accidentally, either on a throw or a bound, in the middle blank space, the player loses his turn and the next time that he plays must begin by doing over the last number that he did right. If the stone lands accidentally in the second blank space, the player loses his turn and has a harder penalty, for the next time he must begin the game all over again, throwing into square 1.

Hopping is done on one foot in single spaces (1, 4, 7,) and by straddling (on the toes) the double spaces (2–3, 5–6). The two blank spaces and the square containing the stone are omitted, the player hopping over them; he lands in "Rest" on both feet, heels down, jumps to a reverse position and retraces his course in the same way, except for stopping to pick up the stone, as explained in first paragraph

Having finished the game in this way, expert players top off by hopping and straddling through the diagram with eyes shut, but without playing the stone.

III. HOP SCOTCH

(French)

1. — Standing outside the baseline, the player throws the stone into each square in succession, as numbered, each time hopping into the next square beyond by hopping over the square containing the stone; there he reverses his position, hops into the square with the stone, and kicks the stone out over the baseline with his free foot; he then hops out and throws for the next higher square.

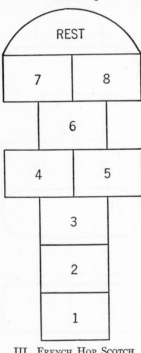

III. FRENCH HOP SCOTCH
("MARRAINE")

(Spaces are twelve to twenty inches deep.)

It is a miss if the stone is not kicked out over the baseline but stops short of it in the diagram. The double squares are straddled, the single ones made with a single hop going through; that is, the foot may touch the ground in those squares but once.

2. — After throwing from the baseline to all squares including 8, and successfully kicking the stone out, the player stands beyond the semi-circle at the head of the diagram and reverses the play (8, 7, 6, 5, 4, 3, 2, 1), throwing in from there and kicking out over the circle. In hopping in for each of these plays he must hop over the space marked "Rest," landing astride in 7–8. If the stone is in one of these squares, he lifts the opposite foot, which leaves him on one foot in the square with the stone, and kicks the latter out. This is the method in all the double squares.

3. — **HOUSES.** — Having completed plays 1 and 2, the player may stand outside the baseline and throw the stone into any square he selects, or let it land where it may; that square then becomes his "house," and in it he writes his initials. Thereafter, in whatever play being made, he may come to rest in his house whenever he reaches it, by standing there on both feet; but no other player may set foot in his house, having to hop over it in the play. As each player has the privilege of taking a house after completing the series, the game becomes very difficult when there are several houses.

4. — Throw the stone into square 1, hop into that square, and by little shoves of the hopping foot send the stone into square 2; hop into 2 and send it in the same way into 3, and so on through the diagram and back again, hopping always on the same foot. The stone must not stop on a line or it is a miss. There are no "houses" in this play, and the double squares are hopped in their order as numbered, not straddled.

5. — Instead of throwing the stone, the player places it on the back of his outstretched hand and hops and straddles through the entire diagram and back again without the stone falling off.

6. — This is done with the stone on the head.

7. — Same, with the stone held on the toe of the hopping foot.

8. — Hop through and back without the stone, but with the eyes shut.

The French game is called "Marraine" (Godmother). It is here included by courtesy of St. Hubert's, The Riviera School, at Cannes, France.

IV. HOP SCOTCH

(English)

The player jumps through the squares as numbered, holding the stone between his feet. Of course he must jump on both feet at once, and in the game's most difficult form he is allowed only

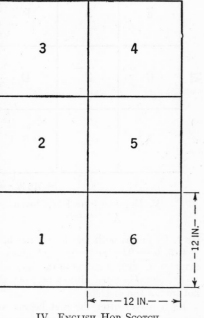

IV. English Hop Scotch

one jump for each square, a jump within the square being a miss. To drop the stone is also a miss.

This is also played with two partners to a team; at a miss the second partner begins at the square where his partner missed.

V. HOP SCOTCH
(Hop-and-Jump)

This is one of the English Hop Scotch games that is played without a stone or puck, but only by jumping and straddling through the diagram, always on both feet.

1. — The player stands outside of the square marked 1 on the first side of the diagram, jumps into 1 with both feet, then jumps to a straddle position

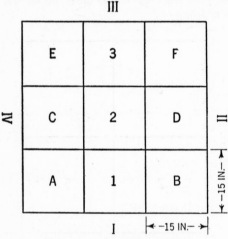

V. Hop-and-Jump Hop Scotch
(English)

with feet in the squares on his right and left (marked *a, b*), jumps again to 1 with both feet, and then jumps out of the diagram backward, beyond the baseline from which he started.

2. — From the same starting position the player jumps over square 1 into square 2; from there he jumps to a straddle in the squares to right and left (marked *c, d*); jumps both feet again into 2, then jumps backward to 1, and backward out.

3. — From the same starting position the player jumps over 1 and 2 to 3; from there he straddles (to *e, f*), jumps both feet into 3 again, then backward to 2, to 1, and out.

4, 5, 6. — The same series of plays is repeated from each side of the diagram in turn, standing in the places marked II, III, IV.

The jump-in must always be from a standing jump, both feet at once, not from a run or step.

Each player after the first begins where his predecessor missed. The game may consist of one round, or a series of rounds, the one first through being the winner in either case; or the play may be continued until one player wins by going through the entire series without missing.

VI. HOP SCOTCH
(Snail Hop Scotch)

This takes its name from the resemblance of the diagram to a snail. In French it is called "Escargot" (snail). It is found in many countries.

The game is entirely one of hopping and uses no stone or puck. The player hops on one foot through the diagram (one hop only to each "square" or space), until he reaches the center space marked "Rest." There he may stand on both feet. When rested he hops out again over the same course. He may stand as long as he wishes in any other space to get his balance or rest, but only on the hopping foot, and may not take any extra hops there.

When a player has successfully hopped to "Rest" and out again, he writes his initials on any space in the diagram that he may choose (except "Rest"), thus making that his "house."

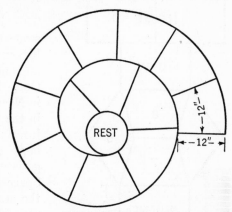

VI. Snail Hop Scotch

Thereafter in hopping through he may rest in his house on both feet, but no other player may step into it. Instead, when other players come to his house, they must hop over it, still on one foot.

VII. HOP SCOTCH

(Monte Carlo Hop Scotch)

This game of Hop Scotch, from Monte Carlo, in the Principality of Monaco, presents some difficulties in the points of play different from any previously described, and has an entirely different diagram.

FIRST SERIES. — The player stands at the base of the diagram, outside of Space Three, and throws the stone in by hand to Space One, by sliding it over the ground. He has then to hop through the spaces on one foot in consecutive order, avoiding the space containing the stone and those marked Neutral. To do this he has to hop over Space Three into Space Two, then to Three and then to Four; then to Space Five, a difficult hop; across to Six, then to Seven and Eight, then over the second Neutral space, landing on both feet in the territory marked " Home," one foot on each side of the center line. For the return he jumps to an about-face in Home, straddling the center line, hops over Neutral to Eight, then to Seven, Six, Five, Four, Three, and Two, reaches over into One while standing on one foot, picks up the stone and hops out over Space Three. This is repeated, sliding the stone each time into the next higher space than it was before, and hopping first into Space One. The stone is never placed in Neutral or Home, and always in the hopping the space where it rests is omitted. Some of the hops are very difficult to negotiate, as for instance from Space Four to Space Six, when the stone is in Five, but good players do it.

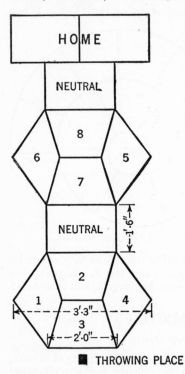

VII. Monte Carlo Hop Scotch

SECOND SERIES. — Standing in front of Space Three, the stone is kicked into the first Neutral space; the player is then to hop into One, Two, Three, Four (omit Neutral), Five, Six, Seven (omit Neutral), straddle and turn in Home as before; hop over upper Neutral to Eight, Seven, Six, Five, then into the first Neutral and shove the stone by foot with a hop into Space Four, then shove it to Three, Two, One, and out.

On the second play of this series the stone is thrown from the same place outside of Space Three into the second (upper) Neutral space, and the player hops through in consecutive order, omitting both Neutrals and straddling in Home. He returns by hopping into the upper Neutral and hops out (shoves) the stone from there through the entire series, not omitting the lower Neutral.

THIRD SERIES. — This is played the same as the First Series except that the player stands with his back to the diagram and throws the stone backward over his head into each space in consecutive order. If the stone does not land in the space intended, the player loses his turn. Having thrown into a space, the player then faces the diagram and hops and picks up the stone as in the First Series, and repeats this for each space.

FOURTH SERIES. — This is played the same as First and Third Series except that the stone is balanced on the back of the hand and thrown from that position, the thrower facing the diagram. The hopping and recovery are the same as in the First Series.

HORSESHOE PITCHING

(See also Quoits and Ring-Toss.)

2 or 4 players   *Juniors; adults*
Pitcher's box   *Stakes; horseshoes*

Horseshoe Pitching is probably the ancient form of Quoits and other ring-toss games, but requires a peculiar skill of its own that has held the interest of adults for generations.

The game consists of tossing horseshoes toward, or over, a stake driven in the ground. The highest score is for a shoe encircling the stake, called a "ringer."; otherwise the shoe landing nearest to the stake scores.

STAKES. — PITCHER'S BOX. — In official games two stakes are used, a round being pitched from one stake and then from the other alternately. In informal games one stake only may be used. Each stake is in the center of a pitcher's box. The box is six feet square, made by sinking in the ground wooden strips two by four inches (or two by six), the two-inch edge showing, but not more than one inch above ground level. The two stakes should be forty feet apart for men and thirty feet for women and juniors. The entire box should be filled with clay to a depth of six inches, or at least a three-foot center area so filled, so that the clay extends eighteen inches on all sides of the stake; the clay must be moist. A stake of iron, three feet long and one inch in diameter, is driven in the center of each pitcher's box so that it is eight inches above ground and inclined one inch toward the opposite stake.

HORSESHOES. — Two pairs of horseshoes are needed, each pair marked for identification. The shoes are specified to weigh two and a half pounds, to measure seven and a half inches in length and seven inches in width. Toe and heel calks must not extend more than three quarters of an inch, and the opening between heel calks must be not more than three and one-half inches inside clearance. Juniors play with smaller and lighter shoes.

PLAY. — The first player is chosen by toss of a coin; thereafter the first pitch in a new game goes to the loser in the preceding game. Each player pitches his two shoes in succession, one after the other, both players pitching for the same stake. On the next turn both pitch from the opposite box, and so on alternately throughout the game.

PITCHING. — For this the player stands anywhere he chooses within the pitcher's box; beside the stake is the usual place; the pitch is made with a step forward, but this must not take him over the front line of the pitcher's box. That is called the foul line, and any shoe delivered with the foot on or over this line does not score.

The shoe is held between the fingers of the right hand, swinging downward, and gets an impetus from a rhythmic swing forward and back from the right shoulder before being released on a forward step. It is slightly lofted as thrown, falling in an arch. In skillful play the shoe falls with the calks toward the ground, or, in the case of a ringer, the calks on the farther side of the stake, though the latter is not essential. It is permissible to wear a glove or wrap the fingers with tape. Immediately that a first player has pitched his second shoe, he must step out of the pitcher's box and stand back of an imaginary line that is even with the stake, while the second player is pitching. Failing to take such a position, he is not allowed to score on the shoes just pitched. The second player is not allowed before pitching to walk over to the opposite stake and examine the lie of the opponent's horseshoes.

The shoes must fall within the opposite pitcher's box, otherwise they do not score. If a shoe is broken, as by hitting the stake, another shoe, the frame of the pitcher's box, or any other object, it is removed and the player allowed another pitch.

MEASUREMENTS. — After all shoes are pitched, the closest shoe to the stake scores, and also any shoe which encircles the stake, called a "ringer." Measurements for both of these are made with calipers and a straight-edge. To be a ringer a shoe must encircle the stake far enough for a straight-edge to touch both heel calks without touching the stake.

GAME. — Fifty points constitute a game. The player wins who first makes this score. Three such games are a usual match between two players. Women and juniors often play a game of twenty-one points.

SCORE. — A shoe closest to the stake scores *one* point. Both shoes closer to stake than opponent's score *two* points.

A ringer scores *three* points.

A double ringer scores *six* points, the highest score a contestant can make.

Ties. — All equals count as ties and no points are scored.

If each contestant has one ringer on the stake at the same time, they cancel each other (*i.e.* no score), but each player is credited with having pitched a ringer. In such a case the next closest shoe scores.

If each player has a double ringer no points are scored.

If one player has two ringers and the opponent one, the two-ringer player scores *three* points.

If all four shoes are equal distance from the stake, no score is made. The last player has the next pitch.

Touching Stake. A shoe touching the stake or leaning against it is a closest shoe.

A shoe leaning against the stake and an opponent's shoe lying on the ground and touching the stake are considered a tie and do not score.

Shoes Moved. A shoe moved by an opponent's shoe is counted in its new position.

A shoe which becomes a ringer by being moved by another shoe scores as a ringer for its owner.

A ringer knocked off the stake by another shoe loses its ringer score for the one who originally pitched it.

HOUND AND RABBIT

10 to 60 or more players   *Primary grades*
Playground; gymnasium; schoolroom   *to junior high school*

A considerable number of the players stand in groups of three, with their hands on each other's shoulders, each group making a small circle which represents a hollow tree. In each tree is stationed a player who takes the part of rabbit. There should be one more rabbit than the number of trees. One player is also chosen for hound.

The hound chases the odd rabbit, who may take refuge in any tree, always running in and out under the arms of the players forming the tree. But no two rabbits may lodge in the same tree; so as soon as a hunted rabbit enters a tree, the rabbit already there must run for another shelter. Whenever the hound catches a rabbit, they change places, the hound becoming rabbit and the rabbit hound. Or the hound may at any time become a rabbit by finding shelter in an empty tree, whereupon the odd rabbit who is left without shelter must take the part of the hound.

This game may be made very lively, and has much sport in it even for adults. The trees should be scattered promiscuously, so that both rabbits and hound may have many opportunities to dodge and run in various directions, with false starts and feints that add zest and interest to such a game.

For large numbers of players it is advisable to give each a better chance to participate actively in the game by having the rabbits and trees change parts whenever a rabbit is caught. The hound and the rabbit who was caught then choose their successors.

HOW MANY MILES TO BABYLON?

10 to 100 players   *Intermediate grades*
                Indoors; out of doors

The players are divided into two lines and stand facing each other, with a distance of about ten feet between. Each line numbers off in twos, and the players in each line take hold of hands. The following dialogue takes place between the two lines, all of the players in a line asking or answering the questions in unison.

The lines rock forward and backward during the dialogue from one foot to another, also swinging the clasped hands forward and backward in time to the rhythm of the movement and the words. The time should be rapid.

The first line asks:
"How many miles to Babylon?"

Second line:
"Threescore and ten."
"Will we be there by candle light?"
"Yes, and back again."
"Open your gates and let us through."
"Not without a beck [curtsy] and a boo [bow]."
"Here's a beck and here's a boo,
Here's a side and here's a sou;
Open your gates and let us through."

As the players in the first line say, "Here's a beck and here's a boo," they suit the action to the words, drop hands, and make each a curtsy, with wrists at hips for the "beck," and straighten up and make a deep bow forward for the "boo"; assume an erect position and bend the head sideways to the right for "Here's a side," and to the left for "Here's a sou." Then the partners clasp hands and all run forward in eight quick steps in the same rhythm as the dialogue that has been repeated, each couple passing under the upraised hands of the opposite couple, which represent the city gates. Having taken the eight steps, the running couple turns around, facing the other line from the opposite side. This is done in four running steps, making twelve steps in all. The couples that made the gates then turn around in four running steps (a total of sixteen steps or beats) until they face the first line, when they in turn begin the rocking motion and the dialogue, "How many miles to Babylon?" This is repeated indefinitely, each line being alternately the questioners and the gates.

The time in which the lines are repeated and the accompanying movements should be very brisk and rapid, so as to give life and action to it. The start forward in the run when the couples pass through the gates should be made with a decided stamp or accent on the first step; and the last step with which they turn in place, facing the line after they have passed through the gates, should have a similar accent. The questions and answers should be given with varied intonation to avoid monotonous singsong.

Mrs. Gomme ascribes the origin of this game to a time when toll was required for entrance into a city, or for the carrying of merchandise into a walled town. The form here given is of Scottish origin, gathered by the writer, and is different from any published versions that have been consulted.

HUCKLE, BUCKLE, BEANSTALK

5 to 60 players   *Children*
Schoolroom; parlor   *to adults*

This game is a form of Hide the Thimble.

A thimble, cork, ring, or other small object may be used for hiding. All of the players leave the room save one, who places the object in plain sight but where it would not be likely to be seen, as on the top of a picture frame, in a corner on the floor, etc. It may be placed behind any other object, so long as it may be seen there without moving any object. This hiding will be especially successful if some hiding place can be found near the color of the object; for instance, if the object be of metal, to hang it from the key of a door, put it in the filigree of a vase, etc. When the object has been placed, the players are called into the room, and all begin to look for it. When one spies it, he does not at once disclose this fact to the others, but quietly takes his seat, and when seated, says, "Huckle, buckle, beanstalk!" which indicates that he knows where the object is. The game keeps on until all of the players have located the object, or until the teacher or leader calls the hunt closed. The first one to find the object hides it for the next game.

HUNT (THE)

10 to 30 or more players   *Intermediate grades*
Playground; gymnasium

The ground is marked off with two goals at opposite ends by parallel lines drawn entirely across it. The space between the lines should measure from thirty to fifty or more feet. One player is chosen for hunter, who stands in the center. The other players are named in groups from various animals; thus there will be several lions, several tigers, etc. These groups are divided so that part stand in one goal and part in the other, the number of players being equal in each goal when the game opens.

The hunter, standing in the center, calls the name of any animal he chooses, whereupon all of the players bearing that name must change goals. The hunter tries to catch them while they are in his territory. The first player caught must thereafter help the hunter in catching the others. The second player caught changes places with the first, the first one then being placed in a "cage" at one side of the playground and is out of the game. The game ends when the hunter has caught all of the animals.

There are several games very similar to this, but all of them have distinctive points that make them quite different in playing. In the present game the hunter has the advantage of chasing players running from both directions, but there is a comparatively small number of these, and he is placed at the disadvantage of not usually knowing just which players bear the names of certain animals.

HUNT THE FOX

20 to 60 or more players *Intermediate grades*
Playground; gymnasium

The players stand in two parallel lines or files facing to the front, with about five feet distance between the files, and considerable distance between each two players in a file, so that the runners may have space to run between them. The head player of one file is a fox and the head player of the opposite file the hunter.

At a signal the fox starts to run, winding in and out from one side to the other of his file until he reaches the bottom, when he turns and comes up the opposite file. The fox is not obliged to run between each two players, but may skip any number that he wishes, and choose his own track. The hunter must follow in exactly the same trail, being obliged, should he make a mistake, to go back to the point at which he diverged from the path of the fox. If the fox succeeds in getting back to the head of the second file without being caught, he is considered to have escaped, and

takes his place at the foot of his own file.   Should he be caught
by the hunter, he changes places with the latter, the hunter going
to the foot of the fox's file, and the fox taking the hunter's original
place at the head of his file.   The second player in the fox's file,
who should have moved up to the front to keep the lines even,
is then fox for the next chase.

HUNT THE SLIPPER

10 to 30 or more players   *Children to adults*
Parlor; seashore; gymnasium

All of the players but one sit in a circle, with the feet drawn up
and knees raised so that a slipper may be passed from hand to
hand of each player under his knees.   Where both boys and girls
are playing, it is desirable to have the girls alternate as much as
possible with the boys, as the slipper is more readily hidden under
their skirts.   The players pass the slipper or bean bag around the
circle under the knees, the object being on their part to evade the
vigilance of the odd player, who runs around on the outside of
the circle trying to touch the person who holds the slipper.   Many
devices may be resorted to for deceiving the hunter, such as appearing to pass the slipper when it is not in one's hands, or holding
it for quite a while as though the hands are idle, although it is not
considered good sport to do this for very long or often.   The
players will use every means of tantalizing the hunter; for instance, when he is at a safe distance, they will hold the slipper up
with a shout, or even throw it to some other person in the circle,
or tap the floor with it.   When the hunter succeeds in catching
the player with the slipper, he changes places with that player.

When the circle of players is very large, the odd player may
take his place in the center instead of outside the circle.

INDIAN CLUB RACE

10 to 100 players   *Intermediate grades*
Gymnasium; playground   *to adults*

This game is an adaptation of the Potato Race.   See also the related
game *All Up Relay*.

Teams stand in single relay formation. A small circle is marked on the ground to the right of the first player in each file, and just within the starting line. A series of six small crosses is also marked on the ground in front of each line, at intervals of six feet apart, continuing in the same direction as the file, the first one being ten or fifteen feet from the starting line. An Indian club is placed on each cross. At a signal, the first runners rush forward, each picks up a club, returns, and places it (standing upright) within the small circle, beside his starting place, returns for another, and so on until all six clubs are within the circle. The first players, having finished, pass to the rear of their respective lines, which move up to the starting line.

At a signal each in the next row of players takes a club and returns it to one of the crosses, returning for another, etc., until all are placed. The next runners return the clubs to the circle, and so on until each player in the files has taken part. The file wins whose last player is first to get back to the starting line after placing the last club. In case of a tie, the last three players from the tied files may be required to repeat the play.

INDIAN CLUB RACE

This is one of the best games for training in self-control, and a teacher should strictly enforce the rules. Any player starting over the line before the signal, or standing with the foot beyond it before starting, should go back and start over again. Whenever a club falls down, or is not placed on the cross or in the circle, the player who placed it must go back and stand it upright or in the right place or it counts as a foul.

IRON TAG

(See *Wood Tag*)

I SAY, " STOOP! "

5 to 60 or more players   *Primary grades*
Playground; gymnasium; schoolroom

This game is a variation of the old familiar game "Simon Says," but calls for much more activity than the latter game.

The players stand in a circle, and in front of them the leader or teacher. The teacher says quickly, "I say, stoop!" and immediately stoops himself and rises again, somewhat as in curtsy. The players all imitate the action; but when the leader says, "I say, stand!" at the same time stooping himself, the players should remain standing. Any who make a mistake and stoop when the leader says, "I say, stand!" are out of the game.

This may be made a very amusing little game to fill in a few dull moments, and when used in the schoolroom, it serves to refresh tired minds very quickly. The leader should speak and move very rapidly and make unexpected variations in the order in which the two commands are given.

I SPY

(See *Hide and Seek* for list of other games of this type.)

3 to 30 or more players   *Children to adults*
Out of doors; indoors

One player is chosen to be the spy, who blinds his eyes at a central goal while the other players scatter and hide. The spy counts one hundred, upon the completion of which he announces his readiness to take up the hunt by shouting aloud:

> "One, two, three!
> Look out for me,
> For I am coming and I can see!"

Or he may shout only the word "Coming!" as he leaves the goal, or merely the last count, "One hundred!" The spy endeavors to detect as many hidden players as possible, and for each player must dash back to the goal, hit it three times, and call out, "One, two, three for ——," naming the player. Should he make a mistake in identity, the player really seen and the one named by mistake are both free and may return to the goal without further danger. As soon, however, as a player knows he has been detected by the spy, he should race with the latter for the goal, and should he reach it first, should hit it three times and call out, "One, two, three for me!" Any player who can thus make the goal after the spy has started on his hunt may save himself in this way, whether he has been detected or not. Should all of the players save themselves in this way, the same spy must blind for the next game. This, however, seldom happens. The first one caught by the spy, that is, the first one for whom he touches the goal, becomes spy for the next game.

JACK BE NIMBLE

10 to 60 players   *Primary grades*
     Indoors; out of doors; schoolroom

This game is suitable for very little children. Some small object about six or eight inches high is placed upright on the floor to represent a candlestick. This may be a small box, a book, bottle, or anything that will stand upright; or a cornucopia of paper may be made to answer the purpose. The players run in single file and jump with both feet at once over the candlestick, while all repeat the old rhyme:

> "Jack be nimble,
> Jack be quick,
> And Jack jump over the candlestick."

When there are more than ten players, it is advisable to have several candlesticks and several files running at once. In the schoolroom there should be a candlestick for each two rows of players, and these should encircle one row of seats as they run.

I. JACKSTONES, WITH BALL

Played by one player alone   *Intermediate grades*
    or by two or a group   *to adult*

Jackstones are small, pronged, metal objects which come in various sizes; but for the games here given those measuring $\frac{3}{4}$ inch in diameter are recommended. Six of these are used for children, but adults sometimes use as many as twelve. A small semihard rubber ball is used in the first series, being about the size of a golf ball. Any smooth, level surface may be used to play on.

BABY GAME — ONES. — Scatter all jacks upon the playing surface by a single movement of the right hand. Toss the ball, pick up one jack, and after ball has bounced once, catch the ball in the same (right) hand. Transfer the jack to the left hand and proceed as before until all six jacks are in the left hand.

TWOS. — Jacks are picked up by twos; otherwise proceed as in Ones. Same for *Threes*, *Fours* (four and then two, or two then four), *Fives* (one and then five, or five then one), and *Sixes* (all at once).

DOWNS AND UPS. — All jacks and ball in right hand. Toss ball upward, lay down all jacks and catch ball in right hand. Throw ball up again, pick up all jacks, and catch ball in right hand.

EGGS IN BASKET. — Scatter jacks, toss ball, pick up one jack, right hand only used, and *while ball bounces once*, transfer jack to the left hand. then catch ball with the right hand. When all jacks have been picked up and transferred to the left hand, the jacks are all put in the right hand and scattered again. Proceed through twos, threes, fours, fives, and sixes.

CRACK THE EGGS. — Scatter jacks with right hand. Toss ball with right hand and while ball bounces once, pick up one jack with right hand, "crack" (tap) it on the playing surface, and catch ball in right hand which is still holding the jack. Transfer the jack to the left hand and proceed as before until all jacks are picked up. Scatter again and proceed by twos, threes, etc., through sixes.

DOWNCAST. — Scatter jacks with right hand. Toss ball with right hand, pick up one jack with right hand, and catch the ball in the right hand after it has bounced once, same as in Baby Game. Bounce the ball downward and transfer the jack to the left hand, then catch the ball with the right hand. (This differs from Upcast in that the ball is bounced by turning the palm of the hand toward the ground and then letting go of the ball.) Proceed through sixes.

PIGS IN THE PEN. — Place left hand on the playing surface, finger tips and wrist touching the surface and forming the pen. Toss the ball upward and while it bounces once, pick up one jack with right hand and push it into the pen, then catch the ball in the right hand. Thumb and forefinger are lifted from the playing surface when jack is pushed in, but any jack or jacks left outside the thumb constitute a "miss." Scatter again with the right hand and proceed as before, putting jacks into the pen by twos, then by threes, etc., through sixes.

PIGS OVER THE FENCE. — Place left hand at right angles to the playing area, little finger resting on the playing surface. This forms the wall or fence. Scatter the jacks, toss the ball upward with the right hand,

and pick up one jack with the right hand. While ball bounces once, place the jack on the far side of the left hand (over the fence). When all six jacks are picked up, rescatter with the right hand and proceed by twos, threes, etc., through sixes.

SWEEPS. — Scatter jacks, toss ball, and while ball bounces once, place fingers on one jack and without lifting it from the playing surface, sweep it across the surface with the right hand until it is close to the body. Then pick it up and catch the ball with the same hand. Sweep all jacks singly; then rescatter and proceed sweeping by twos, then by threes, etc., through sixes.

SCRUBS. — Scatter jacks, toss ball, pick up one jack and scrub it across the playing surface with a backward and forward movement. Keep jack in right hand and after ball has bounced once, catch the ball in the same hand. Transfer jack to the left hand and proceed until all six jacks have been "scrubbed." Rescatter and scrub by twos, then threes, etc., through sixes.

DOUBLE BOUNCE. — This is played the same as the Baby Game, but ball must bounce *twice* before it is caught. Play through sixes.

BOUNCE, NO BOUNCE. — Scatter jacks with right hand. Toss ball upward, pick up one jack while ball bounces once and catch the ball in the right hand. With jack still in right hand, toss the ball upward with the right hand, transfer the jack to the left hand, and catch the ball in the right hand *without allowing it to bounce*. Continue until all jacks have been transferred to the left hand; then rescatter and proceed by twos, threes, etc.

FOULS OR MISSES. —

1. Using wrong hand to catch the ball.
2. Failure to pick up the proper number of jacks required by ones, twos, etc., that is, picking up three jacks while playing twos, or four jacks while playing fives, etc.
3. Clothesburn. Allowing the ball or jacks to touch the body or clothing while catching the ball, except the hand used to catch the ball.
4. Two hands. Catching the ball with both hands.
5. Drop jack and drop ball. Failure to hold the ball or jacks until movement is completed.
6. Touching any other jack while attempting to pick up a jack or group of jacks.
7. Double grab. Trying twice for the same jack or group of jacks.
8. Double bounce in any game, except Double Bounce.
9. Changing sitting or standing position after jacks have been scattered. Plays must be made from original position.
10. Failure to begin a turn with the proper stunt. (This should always be the one on which the player missed on his last turn.)

The rules given above are those adopted by the National Rules Committee on Athletic Games of the National Recreation Association, and are here reproduced, by kind permission of the Association, from *88 Successful Play Activities*, published by the National Recreation Association, New York City.

II. JACKSTONES, WITHOUT A BALL

In the following games Jackstones probably bear a closer resemblance to traditional Knucklebone than those previously described. Like Jackstones I, this is a traditional American form.

ONES. — Scatter the jacks, select one for tossing, choosing one that is interlocked, or so near to others that it could not easily be removed in the afterplay without stirring them; or else one that has rolled so far away that it would be hard to play.

Toss the jackstone and while it is in the air pick up one of the others and, holding it in the palm of the hand, catch the tossed one in the same hand. Place to one side the jack picked up, toss, pick up another, and so on until all five have been picked up and set aside.

TWOS. — Same as Ones, but two are picked up at once and the catch made with both in the hand; set the two aside, toss and pick up two more, and at last the one odd one.

Same for Threes (three and two), Fours (four and two).

OVER AND BACK. — Scatter and select one for tossing. Toss the jackstone, pick up one, catch, toss the two and catch them on the back of the hand; toss them both from the back of the hand and catch in the palm of the hand. Set one aside and proceed in the same way until all have been picked up.

SCATTERS. — (*A*) Select and toss one jackstone and while it is in the air pick up one and catch; toss both and catch both on the back of the hand; toss both from the back of the hand and catch in the palm. So far this is the same as Over and Back.

(*B*) Toss both and pick up a third, hold it and catch the other two; toss the three, catch them on the back of the hand, toss, catch them in the palm; continue until all are picked up, each time tossing all that are in the palm and catching them on the back of the hand as in *A*. In the final play all six will be tossed from the palm, caught on the back of the hand, tossed from there, and caught in the palm.

PIGS IN PENS. — Scatters. Spread the left hand, palm downward, and touch the fingertips to the floor as for a chord on the piano. Select a jackstone and toss it with the right hand. While it is in the air move one of the other jacks so that it rests between the thumb and first finger of the left hand and could easily be grasped by them; catch the tossed jack with the right hand; toss again and place another jack between the left forefinger and second finger, and so on until four jacks are placed in the four openings between fingers. Without any assistance from the right hand, lower the palm of the left hand and close the fingers so that the jackstones are held firmly. Toss the jackstone with the right hand and catch it in the palm of the left hand, still holding the jacks between the fingers. Toss the sixth jack with the right and catch it in the same way in the left palm, making two in the left palm and four between the fingers.

SWEEPS. — Scatters. Place the left hand as for Pigs in Pens, toss a jackstone with the right hand, and while it is in the air put one jackstone in front of the tip of the left thumb. Catch the tossed stone in the right hand. In similar manner the other four jacks are placed at the tips of the fingers. Lift the left hand, toss the jack, and while it is in the air gather all five of the jacks that have been placed, with one sweep into the right hand and catch the tossed one. Finish by tossing all six and catching on the back of the right hand; toss again from the back of the right hand and catch in the palm.

As in all previous games, no jackstone must be moved except those that are being played. The whole play is much quicker and more difficult than with the ball.

III. JACKSTONES PLAYED WITH PEBBLES

(" SCRATCHES ")

This selected series of plays is from Czechoslovakia, and is doubtless one of the original forms from which modern Jackstones are descended. The game is traditional and popular in all parts of the country.

Five small, smooth stones, or pebbles, are used for this game. They should be as nearly round as possible and about one-half inch in diameter, though smaller stones are preferred by very skillful players. Modern jackstones, made of pronged iron, may be used instead, but require less skill.

SLUGSNAIL. — The player places four stones at the corners of a square and a fifth stone on the back of his hand. Without displacing the latter he gathers up, one after the other, the four on the ground, holding them against the palm until all four are in his hand and the fifth still on top. Not one of the gathered stones must fall out or it is a miss and the play must be done over, or, if competitive, the player loses his turn.

ONES. — The player scatters all five stones, then picks up one, tosses it in the air, picks up another stone and catches the tossed one, all with the same hand. He then throws one of the two in his hand into the opposite hand and repeats until all stones are in the second hand. If there is more than one player.

the winner is the one who goes through the entire play without a fault or miss, or else the one who finishes first.

With more skillful players the picked stones remain in the playing hand until at the end five stones are in this hand. To drop a stone is a miss.

TWOS. — Same as Ones but with two stones tossed in the air and caught after two are gathered up; transfer two and repeat.

THREES; FOURS. — Same as above, but toss, gather, and catch three at a time, then four at a time.

HORSIE. — The player throws all five stones in the air and tries to catch them on the back of the same hand. Those which remain on the hand he again throws and catches in the palm. In competition play the one wins who ends with the largest number of stones in hand.

THUMBER. — An additional stone is used called a "thumber." This is placed between the thumb and first finger (crotch of thumb) and is held there while the previously described plays are gone through. It must not fall out or be thrown or put aside with the other stones during the play.

IV. JACKSTONES, WITH PEBBLES

(" KNUCKLEBONES ")

From the island of Mauritius, Indian Ocean, comes a game called Knucklebones, but played with pebbles. The game has winning and losing features not encountered elsewhere by the author.

(1) Each player has ten stones plus a master stone; the ten are about thumb-end size, of a height to be readily picked up yet not rounded enough to roll easily off the back of the hand. These ten are held in the hand, tossed, and as many as possible caught on the back of the hand. Those not caught are left on the ground where they fall and the next play is made with the remainder.

(2) Toss stones from back of hand and catch all in the palm. If any are dropped it is a miss and the turn is lost. If caught, all these stones are laid aside as winnings. Those that fell in the first toss are now played, as many as possible being picked up each time the master stone is tossed.

(3) Toss master stone, pick up as many as possible and hold them while catching the toss. In picking up the stones the player must avoid three; that is, he must not pick up three, or leave three on the ground, or hold three in his hand. For example, if there are six on the ground he must pick up one, two, four, or five, but not three and leave three. He must not touch any but those picked up. Those picked up are not tossed for catching on the back of the hand, but laid aside as winnings.

(4) The same player continues picking up stones and laying them aside until he misses or has all of his own stones in his winning pile. In the latter case the next player has a turn.

A player missing leaves the balance of his unplayed stones where they have fallen on the ground so that an opponent may have his chance to play them.

(5) When a player follows one who has missed, he first plays his own stones until all are won, and then plays those of his opponent's stones which were left on the ground after a miss, adding them to his own pile of winnings. The object of the game is for any one player to get all of the stones into his possession or to have the largest number at the end of the playing period.

History. — The modern game of Jackstones is undoubtedly a direct descendant of the ancient game of Knucklebone shown in the accompanying reproduction of a Pompeiian fresco. Both games may have originated in pebble jackstones. In Europe, on the Riviera, where Roman tradition is still influential, butchers today cut and cure knucklebones for tne game. Lamb knee bones are used for children and women and sheep bones for men, the top of the fibula being cut, bleached, and sometimes colored. These are for sale in toy stores in sets of five in a box, called *osselets*.

As descended through many generations in a French family, the simple form of the game is played with five bones, one to be tossed, the others placed at the corners of an imaginary six-inch square. One is picked up for each toss and held while the toss is caught until at last all five are in the hand. This series of plays is made four times, first with the bones placed convex side upward, then in turn the opposite side, the "S" side, and the cut side. The game is won when all four series are played continuously without a miss. Two or more players take turns. (Included by courtesy of Mme. Juliette Duringer.)

JACOB AND RACHEL

10 to 30 or more players   *Primary grades*
Playground; gymnasium; parlor

All of the players but two form a circle with clasped hands. The two odd players are placed in the center, one of them, "Jacob," being blindfolded. The object of the game is for Jacob to catch the other player, "Rachel," by the sound of her voice; but Rachel is supposed to be rather coy, and to do all in her power to avoid being caught by Jacob, even though she answer his questions.

Jacob begins the game by asking, "Rachel, where art thou?" Rachel replies, "Here am I, Jacob," and immediately tiptoes to some other point in the ring, trying to evade Jacob's outstretched hands as he gropes for her. Rachel may stoop to evade being caught, or may dash from one side of the ring to the other, or resort to any tactics except leaving the ring. Jacob may repeat his question whenever he wishes, and Rachel must answer each time.

When Rachel is caught, Jacob returns to the ring, Rachel is blindfolded and chooses a new Jacob, this time taking the aggressive part and seeking him with the question, "Jacob, where art thou?" etc.

When the game is played by both boys and girls, the names are used properly, but where all boys or all girls are playing, the same names are used, but one of the party is personated by a player of the opposite sex.

JAPANESE CRAB RACE

2 to 60 or more players   *Junior high school*
Gymnasium; playground   *to adults*

If there be but few players for this game, it may be played as a simple race, without the relay feature, as here described. For large numbers the relay idea will be advisable.

The players are lined up behind a starting line, in from two to five single files, each containing the same number. Opposite each file, at a distance of from twenty-five to forty feet, there should be drawn a circle about three feet in diameter. The game consists in a race run backward on feet and hands (or "all fours") to the circles. To start, the first player in each file gets in position, with his heels on the starting line and his back to the circle for which he is to run; and all start together at a signal, the player who first reaches his circle scoring one point for his team. Others follow in turn.

Until one has tried this, it would be difficult to realize how thoroughly the sense of direction and the power to guide one's movements are lost while running in such a position. It is one of the jolliest possible games for the gymnasium, camp, or picnic.

JAPANESE TAG

4 to 60 or more players   *Intermediate grades*
Indoors; out of doors

One player is chaser, or It, and tries to touch or tag some one of the other players, the one tagged then becoming chaser. In this form of the game, however, whenever a player is touched or tagged, he must place his left hand on the spot touched, whether it be his back, knee, elbow, ankle, or any other part of the body, and in that position must chase the other players. He is relieved of this position only when he succeeds in tagging someone else.

As in other tag games where there are large numbers of players, several players may take the part of the tagger, or It, at the same time.

JUMPING RELAY RACE

10 to 60 or more players
Playground; gymnasium; schoolroom

The players are lined up in relay formation from ten to fifty feet from a finish line which should be parallel to it. At a signal the first players in each file jump forward with both feet at once and continue the jumping to the finish line, when they turn and *run* back to the starting line, and touch off the next players who jump and run in turn. The file wins whose last player first gets back to the starting line.

JUMP THE SHOT

(Sling Shot)

10 to 60 or more players   *Junior to*
Playground; gymnasium   *senior high school*

For this game a shot bag, such as is used to weight the ends of the rope that is drawn over jump standards, may be used, and the game takes its name from this. This bag, however, being heavy and hard, may lead to accidents by hitting the ankles of players, and other things are more desirable unless the players be expert. A bean bag, sand, or oat bag will do just as well, tied to the end of a rope.

The players stand in a circle, with one in the center holding a rope with a weight on the end. The center player swings the rope around to describe a large circle on the floor, with a sufficient length of rope to place the bag in line with the feet of those in the circle. The circle players jump to avoid being caught around the ankles by the rope. Anyone caught in this way must retire from the circle, the player winning who longest retains his place.

KEYS

6 to 20 players   *Elementary*
Playground

This is a Russian game which makes possible on an open playground a play similar to Puss in the Corner.

The players scatter over the playground and each player draws around himself a circle from two to three feet in diameter. One player who is "Key-man" goes to one of the circle players and says: "Where are the keys?" This player points to some other circle-man and says: "Go and knock there." The Key-man then goes to the one designated; but as soon as he turns his back, the first player and others in his vicinity try to exchange places. Whenever such an exchange takes place, the Key-man tries to secure one of the circles by reaching it when no other player is on it, and the one left out then becomes Key-man.

If the play goes on too long without the Key-man's getting a place, he may say: "The keys are found!" when all must change places and give him a better chance to seize one.

LADY OF THE LAND

4 to 10 players   *Children*
Indoors; out of doors

This is one of the old dramatic games in which various parts are enacted by the different players.

One player takes the part of a lady and stands alone on one side. Another represents a mother, and the balance are children, from two to eight in number, whom the mother takes by the hand on either side of her, and approaches the lady, repeating the following verse; the children may join with her in this if desired:

> "Here comes a widow from Sandalam,
> With all her children at her hand;
> The one can bake, the other can brew,
> The other can make a lily-white shoe;
> Another can sit by the fire and spin;
> So pray take one of my daughters in."

The lady then chooses one of the children, saying:

> "The fairest one that I can see
> Is pretty [Mary]; come to me."

Mother:

> "I leave my daughter safe and sound,
> And in her pocket a thousand pound.
> Don't let her ramble; don't let her trot;
> Don't let her carry the mustard pot."

The mother then retires with the other children, leaving the daughter chosen with the lady. This daughter sits down behind or beside the lady. As the mother retires, the lady says, under her breath, so that the mother may not hear:

> "She shall ramble, she shall trot;
> She shall carry the mustard pot."

This entire play is repeated until all of the children have been chosen and left with the lady. The mother then retires alone, and after an interval in which several days are supposed to have elapsed, calls to see her children. The lady tells her she cannot see them. The mother insists, and the lady finally takes her to where they are sitting.

The mother goes to one child and asks how the lady has treated her. The child answers, "She cut off my curls and made a curl pie and never gave me a bit of it!" The mother asks the next child, who says she cut off her ear or fingers, etc., and made a pie, not giving her a bit of it. When all have told the mother what the lady has done to them, they all rise up and chase the lady; when captured, she is led off to prison.

This is one of the oldest traditional dramatic games, and is found in some form in almost all countries. Sometimes the mother is supposed to be poor, and bestows her children upon the wealthy lady of the land for adoption. It is thought possibly to have come from the country practice in European countries of hiring servants at fairs.

LAME FOX AND CHICKENS

10 to 30 or more players   *Primary grades*
Playground; gymnasium

One player is chosen for the fox, and stands in a den marked off at one end of the playground. The rest are chickens, and have a chicken yard at the opposite end of the ground. The chickens advance as near as they dare to the den of the fox and tease him by calling out: "Lame fox! Lame fox! Can't catch anybody!" The lame fox may take only three steps beyond his den, after which he must hop on one foot, trying to tag the chickens while hopping. All tagged become foxes and go home with him, thereafter sallying forth with him to catch the chickens. They must all then observe the same rule of taking but three steps beyond the den, after which they must hop. Should any fox put both feet down at once after his three steps while outside the den, the chickens may drive him back. Care should be taken that the hopping be not always done on the same foot, though a fox may change his hopping from one foot to the other. The chicken last caught wins the game and becomes the first lame fox in the new game.

Where more than thirty players are engaged, the game should start with two or more foxes.

This game of "Lame Fox and Chickens" has sometimes been called "Lame Goose."

It is admirable for players of all ages, but, like all "dare" games, is especially good to overcome timidity. Timid children should be encouraged to venture near the fox and to take risks in giving their challenge.

LAST COUPLE OUT

(Widower; Last Pair Pass)

11 to 31 or more players
Playground; gymnasium

Junior high school
to adults

An odd number of players is required for this game. One is chosen for catcher, who stands at one end of the playground with his back to the other players. The other players stand in couples in a long line behind him, facing in the same direction that he faces. The catcher should be not less than ten feet in front of the first couple.

When the catcher calls, "Last couple out!" the last pair in the line runs toward the front, the right-hand one on the right side of the double line, and the left-hand one on the left side, and try to join hands in front of the catcher. The catcher may not chase them before they are even with him, and may not turn his head to see when or from where the runners are coming. They should try to gain their end by varying the method of approach, sometimes both circling far out beyond him on either side, or one of them doing this and the other running in close toward the lines.

If the catcher succeeds in catching one of the players before that player can clasp hands with his partner, these two, catcher and caught, form a couple and take their places at the head of the line, which should move backward one place to make room for them, and the other player of the running couple becomes catcher. If neither is caught, they are free; *i.e.* out of the game.

In the Scotch and Swedish forms of this game, the title is "Widow" or "Widower," the catcher supposedly taking the part of the bereaved one and trying to get a mate. It has been suggested that the game has descended from old methods of marriage by capture.

LAST MAN

10 to 60 players   *Intermediate grades*
Schoolroom   *to adults*

This is a schoolroom adaptation of the game usually known as "Three Deep," or "Third Man." It is one of the most interesting and popular schoolroom games.

One player is chosen to be runner and another chaser. The remaining players are seated. The game starts with quite a distance between runner and chaser. The first object of the game is for the chaser to tag (touch) the runner. Should he do this, they immediately change parts, the previous chaser having to flee instantly for safety with the previous runner, now chaser, after him. The greatest sport of the game comes in, however, in the way the runner may save himself at any time from being tagged by the chaser by standing at the rear of any row of seats and calling "Last man!" As soon as he does this, the one sitting in the front row of that line of seats becomes liable to tagging by the chaser, and must instantly get up and run. As soon as he has left his seat, the entire line moves forward one seat, leaving a seat at the rear for the "last man." There may be no moving of this kind, however, until the runners are out of the aisle.

As in all running games in the class room, the seated players must keep their feet under the desks and out of the aisles.

It will be seen that all of the players must be very alert to watch the actions of the runner, but especially those sitting in the front seats, as at any moment one of them may have to become runner. The last man must never fail to call out the words "Last man!" when he takes his stand at the rear of a row of seats. He is not considered to have taken refuge until he does this.

LEAPFROG

2 to 100 players   *Intermediate grades*
Playground; gymnasium   *to adults*

The Back. — Any player who bends over to make a back for others to leap over is called the "back." He must rest his hands on his knees or near them to make a firm back. It is against the rules for any player making a back to throw up his back or bend it lower while a player is leaping over it; but each player, before jumping, may say "High back!" or "Low back!" which the one who is down must adjust before the jumper starts. He then must do his best to keep the back perfectly level and still, unless the game calls for a different kind of play. In some games the back stands with his back toward the jumpers, and in others with his side toward them. If he is to stand on a certain line, he must "heel it" if with his back toward them, or, if his side be toward them, stand with one foot on either side of the line.

The Jumper. — The player who leaps must lay his hands flat on the back at the shoulders and not "knuckle," *i.e.* double under his fingers. Any player transgressing this rule must change places with the back. The back must be cleared without touching him with the foot or any part of the body except the hands. Such a touch is called "spurring," and the transgressor must change places with the back if the latter stands upright before the next player can jump over him. If he does not stand upright in time, he remains back. When a leap is made from a starting line or taw, the jumper may not put his foot more than half over the line. Good jumpers will land on the toes with knees bent and backs upright, not losing the balance.

I. LEAPFROG WITH ONE BACK

1. OVER AND DOWN. The first player makes a back, standing either with his back or his side toward the one who is to leap over. The next player runs, leaps over the back, runs a few steps forward so as to allow space for a run between himself and the first player, and in his turn stoops over and makes a back. This makes two backs. The third player leaps over the first back, runs and leaps over the second, runs a short distance and makes a third back, etc., until all the players are making backs, when the first one down takes his turn at leaping, and so on indefinitely.

VARIATION. — This may be made much more difficult by each player moving only a few feet in advance of the back over which he has leaped; this will then leave no room for a run between the backs, but means a continuous succession of leaps by the succeeding players.

2. LEADER AND FOOTER. One player is chosen to be "back," and he chooses a leader, generally the poorest jumper, and a "footer" — the best jumper. A starting or "taw" line is drawn on the ground and the back stands with his side parallel to it. The other players line up in single file at some distance, with the leader at the head and the footer at the rear of the line. The footer dictates the way in which the back is to be cleared and his distance from taw. For instance, he may, having put a long distance between the back and the line, require a run of a limited number of steps, or a hop and skip (specifying the number), before the jump. The leader makes the first jump as prescribed by footer, and the others, in turn, including the footer. Any player failing in the feat becomes back. Any player who is doubtful of success may call upon the footer to perform the feat. If the footer fails, he becomes the back. If the challenge be successfully met, the one making the challenge becomes back.

3. LEAPFROG RACE. The players are lined up in two or more single files, as for the simplest form of leapfrog, but the game is a race between the different files.

The first player takes his place on the starting or taw line and makes a "back," with his head away from the file. The next player immediately jumps over and makes a back one pace forward of the first player. The third jumps over the backs of the two and makes a third back, and so on until all are down, when the first player jumps over all in succession, but steps one side when he has vaulted over the last back. The others all follow.

The line wins which is first reduced to one player in the position of "back." In other words, when every player in the line has jumped over the back of every other player.

A BURLESQUE on this game, which has in it some good sport and exercise, consists in crawling between the feet of the players instead of jumping over their backs. This may be done for every player in the line, or the two methods alternated, leaping over the back of one, crawling between the feet of the next, etc.

4. PAR. — The distance of the back from the jumping line is advanced after each round a "foot and a half," measured in a certain way called a "par." The game starts with the back at a given distance from the line. After each player has "overed," the back places one foot with the outer edge on the line on which he has been standing, puts the heel of the other foot against the instep so that the second foot will be at right angles to the first, and marks a new line at the point where the toes come. The new line is thus the length of one foot in advance of the first line, plus the width of the other foot at the instep. The players then leap again from the starting line, and as the back moves farther away, they add to their leaps each time, as becomes necessary for the greater distance, as follows: (1) leap; (2) hop and leap; (3) hop twice and leap; (4) hop three times and leap; (5) hop, skip, jump, and leap.

Any player failing to "over" changes places with the back.

5. SPANISH FLY. — The leader (first over) sets feats for the others to perform, as in Follow the Leader, any player who fails taking the place of the back. The following feats are popular:

The jumper leaps over, touching the back with one hand only and waving his cap with the other.

The jumper leaps over without touching the back.

The jumper makes a quarter turn while going over.

6. HATS ON DECK. — The leader, as he vaults, places his cap on the back, and must clear without touching it. Each player, in turn, adds his hat to the pile, the last player having to jump over all. If anyone knocks over the pile, he must become back, and the game begins over again. If all jump successfully, the last one over then jumps again, removing his hat as he goes over without disturbing the others, and so on until all have been removed.

7. HATS FULL OF WATER. — The jumper places his own hat on his head upside down and balances it there while leaping over the back.

II. LEAPFROG WITH TWO OR MORE BACKS

1. BUNG THE BUCKET. The players are divided into two teams. Half of them form one continuous "back," on which the other half jump, one at a time, until all are seated. The players who form the "back" stand one behind another, the first player resting his head against the stomach of one who stands upright, backed by a wall or fence. Each player in turn grasps the coat-tail or waist of, and rests his head or shoulder against, the player next in front. They should thus make one long, even, and solid "back" or row of backs. These are called the buckets. The other players are called the bungs, and stand at some little distance to get a run for the leap. They will naturally select their best leaper as the first of their line, as he may not move forward after he has once landed on the backs, and it is desirable that he should leave as much space behind him as possible for the others to sit on.   None of the players may move forward after once landing on the backs.   If all of the bungs succeed in seating themselves without any break occurring among the buckets, it counts one in favor of the buckets.   When such a breakdown occurs, the two teams change places, the bungs taking the place of the buckets; otherwise the game is repeated with the same bungs and buckets.   The team wins which has the highest score to its credit at the end.

2. JOHNNY RIDE A PONY. — The players are divided into two even teams, except for one leader, one team being the ponies and the other the riders, or Johnnies.   The ponies form one long back as follows: one player stands upright against a wall or fence; the first one back of him stoops in front of this leader, bracing his head against him; the other players grasp each the waist of the player in front, and stoop with the heads against him or turned to one side (away from the jumper).   When the backs (ponies) are ready, the riders all run toward them from the side, each rider vaulting from the side on to the back of one pony. The ponies try in every way, except by straightening up, to throw their riders while the leader counts fifty.   If a rider be made to touch even one foot to the ground, the ponies have won and score a point, the riders exchanging places with them.   If the ponies fail in this attempt, they must be ponies again.   The side wins which has the higher score at the end.

3. CAVALRY DRILL. — **A.** Two players make a back.   They stand with backs to the jumpers and place their inside hands on each other's shoulders with arms extended at full length to leave a space between.   The jumper places a hand on each of the inside shoulders.   The push will be away from the center and the backs will need to brace themselves for this.

B. A back is made by two or more players standing close together with sides toward the jumpers, thus making a back several widths deep to jump over.

For whichever form of back is used, any player failing to clear the back without touching it is out of the game, the first two failing becoming backs for the next round when all have jumped. For large numbers of players this may be played as a competition between different groups.

4. SADDLE THE NAG. The players are divided into equal teams, with a chief for each. One of the chiefs stands with his back to a wall or fence, and all of his team bend their backs as for leapfrog, the first with his head against the chief, and the rest, one behind the other, in a line stretching out in front of him. Each player in the line braces his shoulder against the stooping player next in front, or each may grasp the forward player around the waist. The heads should all be turned to the same side. One of the opposite team then leaps on the back of the player farthest from the wall, and tries to make his way over the backs of the entire line to the chief to "crown" him; that is, to place his hand on his head. The players who are making "backs" try in every way, without rising to a standing position, to throw this player off and so prevent his crowning their chief. Each player of the "out" team tries in turn to crown the chief. Should they be unsuccessful the sides change. If one or more players succeed in crowning the chief, each successful player has a second chance before the teams change. The team that succeeds in oftenest crowning its opponent's chief wins the game. The limit of the game is usually placed at six trials for each side.

5. SKIN THE GOAT. — This differs from Saddle the Nag in the gradual lengthening of the line of backs, though there are similar features in the two games. The players in this game are not divided into opposing teams.

One player stands with his back against a wall or fence. Another player stoops, with his head against the breast or stomach of this first player. A third player jumps upon the back thus made and tries to "crown" the player standing against the wall, that is, to place his hand on his head. The player who is making the "back" tries in every way (except by straightening up) to throw the player off his back and so prevent his crowning of the standing player. If the "back" succeeds in doing this, the one whom he throws off takes his place behind this stooping player in the same general position, grasping him around the waist and bending his head to one side or against the forward player, thus lengthening the line of backs. Another player then jumps on the backs, tries to make his way to the one who is upright and crown him. Any player who succeeds in crowning the upright player changes places with him, the one winning who has done this the most times when the play ends.

6. **TWO–DEEP LEAPFROG.** — All players but two (runner and chaser) stand in a circle facing inward, each making a low "back" by grasping his ankles. The game starts with the runner outside of the circle on one side and the chaser on the opposite side. The runner may save himself by leaping over any back, at once stooping to make a back himself. The player over whom he jumped becomes vulnerable at once and must run to save himself. Before the game begins players must decide whether or not runners may go through the circle.

LETTING OUT THE DOVES

3 to 30 players   *Primary grades*
Indoors or out of doors

This game is particularly suitable for young children. The players stand in groups of three. One in each group, usually the smallest, represents a dove; one a hawk, larger than the dove or a swifter runner; and the third the owner of the birds. The dove stands in front of the owner, holding her by the hand. The hawk stands behind, also held by the hand. The owner throws the dove from her with a gesture of the hand, first toward herself and then away, as a dove might be tossed for flight in the air, and the little dove sails away, with arms floating like wings. When the dove has a sufficient start, so that the larger and swifter hawk may not get her too easily, the owner throws the hawk in the same way. The hawk runs with outstretched arms also as though flying, and tries to catch the dove, but is obliged to run over exactly the same route as the dove. At her discretion the owner claps her hands as a signal for the two pet birds to return to her, the dove trying to get back without being caught by the hawk. The clapping for the return of the birds is always done with hollowed palms to make a deep sound. The owner gives this when the dove has reached the farthest point to which she thinks it best for her to go, the judgment for this being determined sometimes by the gaining of the hawk on his prey. The dove may not turn to come home until the signal be heard.

It is well to make an imaginative atmosphere for little children for this game by telling them of the way doves and hawks are trained as pets.

This game is played by little girls in China, and is one reported by Dr. Headland in his charming book, *The Chinese Boy and Girl*. Some additional points are given here, kindly supplied by Dr. Headland to the author.

LOST CHILD (THE)

10 to 30 or more players   *Primary grades*
Schoolroom; parlor; playground; gymnasium

This is a quiet game designed to test the memory, and makes an interesting variation when players are tired of active games. The players are all seated, with the exception of one, who is sent from the room. Or if the game be played in an open playground, this one player may blind his eyes in a corner of a wall or fence or behind a bush. When this player is well out of sight and hearing, the leader or teacher beckons one of the players, who leaves the group and hides. If in the schoolroom, this may be done under the teacher's desk or in a wardrobe. The rest of the players then change their seats, and the one who is blinding is called back and tries to tell which player is hidden. When successful, this first guesser may be seated and another chosen to blind. Otherwise the first guesser blinds again.

MARBLES

(Ringer)

Playground   *Intermediates to adults*

Play with marbles is one of the most skillful of traditional games and its appearance is usually considered a sure sign of the return of spring. It is one of the very interesting and perennially popular playground activities, played by both boys and girls, and not unknown in colleges. Some city playgrounds have organized marble tournaments on a district, neighborhood, and city-wide basis. The rules adopted by recreation executives, under the auspices of the National Recreation Association, are as follows:

RINGER is played in a ring ten (10) feet in diameter, with thirteen (13) marbles arranged in the center on a cross. The object is to shoot these marbles out of the ring, the player shooting the largest number of marbles out of the ring in any one game being the winner of that game. From two to six may play in one game in Ringer, except that in championship matches only two play. In preliminary eliminations as many as six play in one game. All tournament play is for fair, and marbles must be returned to owners after each game.

Rule 1 — Equipment

1. — The playing surface shall be a smooth level area of ground, hard clay, or other suitable substance. The ring is inscribed upon this area, 10 feet in diameter (inside measurement), and all play is within this ring. The outline of the ring shall be approximately one-half inch wide and one-half inch deep to aid the judge in determining whether marble or shooter is out. (A local committee may use another method.)

2. — With the center of the ring as a point of intersection, mark or paint two lines at right angles to each other to form a cross, which shall be a guide for placing the playing marbles. It is recommended that markings be omitted when a cardboard or metal spacing gauge is used. Place one marble at the center and three each on the four branches of the cross, each marble three inches away from the next one.

3. — The lag line is a straight line drawn tangent to the ring and touching it at one point. The pitch line is a straight line drawn tangent to the ring, directly opposite and parallel to the lag line.

4. — Playing marbles shall be round and made of glass, and shall be not more than five eighths of an inch in diameter. All marbles in any one playing ring must be of uniform size. (A local tournament committee may use agate or glass marbles.)

5. — Shooters shall be round and made of any substance except steel or any other metal, and shall be not less than one-half inch nor more than six eighths of an inch in diameter, by exact measurement.

Rule 2 — Plan of Game

1. — The lag is the first operation in Ringer. To lag, the players stand toeing the pitch line or knuckling down upon it, and toss or shoot their shooters to the lag line across the ring. The player whose shooter comes nearest the lag line, on either side, wins the lag.

2. — Players must lag before first game. The player who wins the lag shoots first, and the others follow in order as their shooters were next nearest the lag line. The same shooter that is used in the lag must be used in the game following the lag. Starting succeeding games, the winner of previous game shall shoot first, but the other plays shall lag for order.

3. — On all shots, except the lag, a player shall knuckle down so that at least one knuckle is in contact with the ground, and he shall maintain this position until the shooter has left his hand. Knuckling down is permitted, but not required, in lagging.

4. — Starting the game, each player in turn shall knuckle down just outside the ring line, at any point he chooses, and shoot into the ring to knock one or more marbles out of the ring.

5. — One or more marbles knocked out of the ring are credited to the player knocking them out, and the player continues to shoot from the spot where shooter comes to rest. Marbles knocked only part way out of the ring are left where they come to rest and the next player is permitted to shoot at them. A player whose shooter goes outside of the ring, after success in shooting a marble out, continues shooting from the ring line, taking roundsters if desired.

6. — After a miss, a player picks up his shooter wherever it lies until his next turn and then is permitted to take roundsters and shoot from any point of the ring line.

Rule 3 — Playing Regulations

1. — Marbles knocked out of the ring shall be picked up by the player who knocks them out.

2. — Whenever a marble or shooter comes to rest in the ring groove, it shall be considered out of the ring because the inner edge of the depression is the outer edge of the ring. If its center is inside the ring, it shall be considered inside the ring.

3. — When a shooter slips from a player's hand, if the player calls "slips" and the referee is convinced it is a slip and if the shooter does not travel more than 10 inches, the referee may order "no play" and permit the player to shoot again. The referee's decision is final.

Rule 4 — Scoring

1. — The scorer counts all marbles each player scores, the player first obtaining seven (7) marbles being declared the winner of that game, providing that on obtaining the seventh marble the shooter also goes out of the ring. If shooter remains in the ring on this shot, the marble or marbles knocked out on this shot are respotted on cross line, the shooter being picked up, the shot counting as a miss.

2. — In games where more than two players are engaged, if two or more players lead with the same score, those in the tie shall play a new game to break the tie.

3. — A player refusing to continue a game once it is started shall be disqualified, and if only two players are engaged, the game shall be forfeited to the offended player.

4. — The score of a forfeited game shall be 13–0.

Rule 5 — Officials

1. — The officials shall be a Referee and a Scorer; if a Scorer is not available, the Referee shall keep score.

2. — The Referee shall have complete charge of the play. He shall interpret these rules and have power to make decisions on any points not specifically covered by these rules. He shall have authority to disqualify players for unsportsmanlike conduct. He shall have authority to order from the playing field, or its vicinity, the coach or other representative of any player who conducts himself improperly.

3. — The Scorer shall keep a record of the game, marking score of each player, shot by shot, and at the termination of each game, shall notify the Referee of the score, and the Referee shall announce the winner. The Scorer may assist the Referee in enforcing the rule against coaching, and may call to the attention of the Referee any infraction of the rules.

Rule 6 — Penalties

A player shall not —

1. — Raise his hand until the shooter has left his hand. This violation is known as "histing."

2. — Move his hand forward until the shooter has left his hand. This violation is known as "hunching."

3. — Smooth or otherwise rearrange the ground, or remove any obstacles. He may request the Referee to clear obstructions.

Penalty. — If any marbles were knocked out or dislocated on the shot, they shall be restored to their place and the player shall lose his shot.

4. — Change shooters during the course of any game, except that he may choose a new shooter on each lag, provided he uses that shooter in the subsequent game.

Penalty. — The player shall be disqualified from the game.

5. — Communicate in any way with his coach during the course of the game.

Penalty. — Forfeiture of all marbles he has knocked out of the ring, said marbles to be returned to the game and placed on the cross.

6. — A coach shall not give instructions to either his own or any other player engaged in the game.

Penalty. — Coach shall be ordered from the playing field if, after being warned once, he continues his violation.

7. — Players must not walk through the marble ring.

Penalty. — Referee may require the forfeiture of one marble, said marble to be returned to the ring and placed on the cross.

Rule 7 — Age of Players

1. — The tournament is open to boys or girls of fourteen years or under.

2. — A boy or girl who becomes fifteen on or after July 1 of the current year is eligible to play, and one who becomes fifteen any time before July 1 is not eligible to play.

3. — Each municipal unit (borough, town, city, or county recreation system) shall have but one entry in the state or interstate tournaments.

Rule 8 — Definitions

The term **marbles** in these rules is used to denote the object marbles only, variously known as **mibs, miggs, commies, hoodles, ducks,** etc.

The term **shooter** is used to denote the offensive marble, variously known as the **taw, moonie, glassie,** etc.

Knuckling down is the act of resting a knuckle or knuckles on the ground when shooting.

Shooting is the act of holding a shooter between the thumb and first finger and releasing it by force of the thumb.

Hunching is the act of moving the hand forward across the ring line when shooting from the ring line, or forward from the point at which the shooter came to rest when shooting inside the ring. (Forbidden.)

Histing is the act of raising the hand from the ground in shooting. (Forbidden.)

Roundsters is the privilege of taking a different position on the ring line for shooting and is permitted only at the start of the game or on a turn after a shooter has passed out of the ring.

For fair is playing for sportsmanship only, when marbles are returned at the end of each game to their owners. All marble tournament games are "for fair."

Lofting is the act of shooting in an arch through the air to hit a marble.

Spinning is the act of causing the shooter to strike a marble, making it travel, while the spin causes the shooter to lose momentum. This is perhaps the most difficult shot in the game.

Bowling is the act of rolling a shot on the ground to hit a marble.

A **match** may be decided in one, three, or five games. It is not the total high score, but the games won that determine the winner of each match.

These rules are here given by courtesy of the National Recreation Association from their book, *88 Successful Play Activities.*

MASTER OF THE RING

2 to 30 or more players   *Junior to senior*
Playground; gymnasium   *high school*

A circle is drawn on the ground. The players stand shoulder to shoulder inside the circle, with arms folded either on the chest or behind the back. The play starts on a signal, and consists in trying to push one's neighbor with the shoulders out of the circle. Any player overstepping the line drawn on the ground drops out of the game. Any player who unfolds his arms or falls down is also out of the game.

The Master of the Ring is he who in the end vanquishes all of the others.

MAZE TAG
(Line Tag; Right Face)

15 to 100 players   *Intermediate grades*
Playground; gymnasium; house party   *to senior high school*

All but two of the players stand in parallel lines or ranks, one behind the other, with ample space between each two players and each two ranks; all the players in each rank clasp hands in a long line. This will leave aisles between the ranks, and through these a runner and chaser make their way.

The sport of the game consists in sudden changes in the direction of the aisles, brought about by one player who is chosen as leader and stands aside, giving the commands, "Right face!" or "Left face!" at his discretion. When one of these commands is heard, all of the players standing in the ranks drop hands, face in the direction indicated, and quickly clasp hands with the players who are then their neighbors on the right and left. This brings about a change of direction in the aisles, and therefore necessitates a change of direction in the course of the two who are running.

The success of the game depends largely upon the judgment of the leader in giving the commands, "Right (or left) face!" They should be given quickly and repeatedly, the leader often choosing a moment when the pursuer seems just about to touch his victim, when the sudden obstruction put in his way by the change in the position of the ranks makes necessary a sudden change of direction on his part. The play continues until the chaser catches his victim, or until a time limit has expired. In either case two new players are then chosen from the ranks to take the places of the first runners.

It is a foul to break through the ranks or to tag across the clasped hands.

MENAGERIE

10 to 60 or more players   *Children*
Indoors.   *to adults*

This game may be one of the funniest possible for a house party. The players sit around the room or in a circle. One player who has ready wit is chosen to be ringmaster, or there may be different showmen or ringmasters for each group of animals. The ringmaster takes his place in the center, and will be more effective if furnished with a whip. He shows off in turn different troops of animals, pointing out from two to eight players for each troop, according to the number who are taking part. These must come forth into the center of the ring and go through their paces as indicated by the showman. He may thus display the growling and clawing bear, the hopping and croaking frog, the leaping kangaroo, the roaring and ramping lion, the humped and swaying camel, the stubborn, balking, and braying donkey, the screaming and wing-flapping eagle, the hooking and mooing cow, the neighing and galloping horse, the snarling and springing tiger, the flopping and barking seal, the scratching and cackling hen, etc.

For instance, the ringmaster may say : "Ladies and gentlemen : I will now exhibit to you a marvelous troupe of snorting hippopotami. Such graceful carriage has never before been seen in these ponderous animals. They have learned to gambol in our Northern clime with even greater grace than they showed in their native jungles. They show almost human intelligence. Sit up there !" (cracking his whip) "Snort to the right ! Snort to the left !" etc.

When all of the animals in the menagerie have been displayed, they may all join in a circus parade, each retaining his distinctive character.

MIDNIGHT

(Twelve O'clock at Night)

10 to 30 or more players   *Primary grades*
Playground; gymnasium; schoolroom

One player is the fox and the others sheep. The fox may catch the sheep only at midnight. The game starts with the fox standing in a den marked in one corner of the playground, and the sheep in a sheepfold marked in the diagonally opposite corner. The fox leaves his den and wanders about the meadow (playground), whereupon the sheep also come forth and scatter around, approaching as close to the fox as they dare. They keep asking him, "What time is it?" and he answers with any hour he chooses. Should he say "Three o'clock," or "Eleven o'clock," etc., they are safe; but when he says "Midnight!" they must run for the sheepfold as fast as possible, the fox chasing them. Any sheep caught changes places with the fox, and the game is repeated. When played in a class room, only a few children should be selected for sheep.

This game is enjoyed by children of almost any age.

It affords an excellent opportunity for daring and for finesse. Timid children should be encouraged to take risks, approaching near the fox, and surrounding him on all sides. All should be taught to make the chase varied and difficult for the fox, instead of running in a straight line for the goal. The fox has opportunity for much stratagem in choosing for the moment when he says "Midnight!" one in which the players are standing where he could easily catch or corner them. He may also gain advantage by appearing to start in one direction and suddenly changing to another. These elements add zest to the game, cultivate prowess, and make the children brighter and more alert.

MOON AND MORNING STARS

5 to 20 players   *Primary grades*
Out of doors

This game is played when the sun is shining. One of the players is the moon, and takes her place in a large area of shadow, such as would be cast by a large tree or a house. As the moon belongs to the night, she may not go out into the sunshine.

The other players are morning stars, and as they belong to the daylight, their place is in the sun. The morning stars dance around in the sunlight, venturing occasionally into the shadow where the moon is, saying:

> "O the Moon and the Morning Stars,
> O the Moon and the Morning Stars!
> Who dares to tread — Oh,
> Within the shadow?"

The moon tries to catch or tag them while they are in the shadow. Any star so caught changes places with the moon.

This game is played by Spanish children.

MOTHER, MAY I GO OUT TO PLAY?

5 to 10 players
Indoors or out

Primary to
intermediate grades

This is one of the old traditional dramatic games and is found in many countries.

One player represents a mother, and the rest are her children, and stand in front of her in a line. One or all of them ask the mother the following question, the mother answering as indicated:

"Mother, may I go out to play?"

"No, my child; it is such a wet day."

"Look how the sun shines, mother."

"Well, make three round curtsies and be off away."

The children thereupon make three "round curtsies" by whirling around and dipping down suddenly to spread the skirts out. They then run away and pretend to play. Soon they return and knock at the door. The mother asks:

"What have you been doing all this time?"

"Brushing Jennie's hair and combing Jennie's hair."

"What did you get for it?"

"A silver penny."

"Where's my share of it?"

"The cat ran away with it."

"Where's the cat?"

"In the wood."

"Where's the wood?"
"Fire burnt it."
"Where's the fire?"
"Moo cow drank it."
"Where's the moo cow?"
"Sold it for a silver penny."
"What did you do with the money?"
"Bought nuts with it."
"What did you do with them?"
"You can have the nutshells, if you like."

The last words being rather disrespectful, the mother at once chases the children, calling, "Where's my share of the silver penny?" The players being chased, reply, "You may have the nutshells!" The mother thus catches the children, one after another, and pretends to punish them.

MOTHER, MOTHER, THE POT BOILS OVER!

5 to 11 players
Indoors; out of doors

Primary to
intermediate grades

This is a traditional dramatic game.

One player represents an old witch, another a mother, another the eldest daughter, another a pot boiling on the hearth, and the balance are children, named for the days of the week, Monday, Tuesday, etc.

The old witch hides around the corner of a house or other convenient place, and peeps out, while the mother says to her eldest daughter, "I am going away, and I want you to let nothing happen to your sisters." To the others she says, "Monday, you take care of Tuesday, and Tuesday, you take care of Wednesday," etc., until she comes to the last child, when she says, "And Saturday, take care of yourself." Then to the eldest, "Be sure and not let the old witch take any of your sisters. You can also get the dinner, and be sure not to let the pot boil over."

The mother then goes away and stays at a distance out of sight. As soon as the mother has gone, the old witch, stooping, lame, and walking with a stick, comes and raps with her knuckles on the supposed door.   The eldest daughter says : "Come in !   What do you want?"

Old Witch.   Let me light my pipe at your fire ; my fire is out.

Eldest Daughter.   Yes, if you will not dirty the hearth.

Old Witch.   No, certainly ; I will be careful.

The eldest daughter lets her in and goes about her work, setting the table or looking on the shelf, when the old witch suddenly stoops down and blows the ashes on the hearth ; whereupon the pot makes a hissing sound as though boiling over, and the old witch catches hold of Monday and runs away with her.

The eldest daughter cries out, "Mother, mother, the pot boils over !"

The mother calls back, "Take the spoon and skim it."

"Can't find it."

"Look on the shelf."

"Can't reach it."

"Take the stool."

"Leg's broken."

"Take the chair."

"Chair's gone to be mended."

Mother, "I suppose I must come myself !"

The mother then returns, looks about, and misses Monday. "Where is my Monday?" she demands of the eldest daughter. The daughter says, "Under the table."   The mother pretends to look under the table, and calls "Monday !" then says, "She isn't there."   The daughter suggests various places, up on the shelf, down in the cellar, etc., with the same result.   Finally, the eldest daughter cries and says : "Oh, please, mother, please ! I couldn't help it, but someone came to beg a light for her pipe, and when I looked for her again she had gone and taken Monday with her."

The mother says, "Why, that was the old witch !"   She pretends to beat the eldest daughter, and tells her to be more careful in the future, and on no account to let the pot boil over.   The eldest daughter weeps, promises to be better, and the mother again goes away.   The old witch comes again, and the same thing is repeated until each child in turn has been taken away, the old witch pretending each time to borrow a different article that is used around the fire, as the poker, the kettle, etc. Finally, the eldest daughter is carried off too.

The pot, which has boiled over with a hissing sound each time the old witch has come to the hearth, now boils over so long and so loudly that the mother hears it and comes back to see what is the matter. Finding the eldest daughter gone too, the mother goes in search of them to the witch's house. On the way she meets the old witch, who tries to turn her from her path by speaking of various dangers.

The mother asks of her, "Is this the way to the witch's house?" and the witch replies, "There is a red bull that way."

"I will go this way."

"There is a mad cow that way."

"I will go this way."

"There is a mad dog that way."

Finally, the mother insists on entering the witch's house. The witch refuses to let her in, saying:

"Your shoes are too dirty."

"I will take them off."

"Your stockings are too dirty."

"I will take them off."

"Your feet are too dirty."

The mother grows angry at this, pushes her way into the house, and calls her children. The witch is supposed, prior to this, to have cooked the children, made them into pies, and put them in a row, naming them apple pie, peach pie, etc. They stand or sit with their faces or heads covered.

The mother approaches them and says, "You have some pies?"

The old witch says, "Yes, some very nice apple pie." The mother proceeds to taste the apple pie and says, "This needs more sugar." The witch pretends to stir in more sugar, whereupon the mother tastes again and says, "Why, this tastes exactly like my child Monday!" Monday thereupon uncovers her face and says, "It is Monday!" The mother shakes her and says, "Run away home!" which she does.

This is gone through with each pie in turn, the mother finding them in need of more salt or longer cooking or some other improvement before she discovers in each case one of her children. When all have been sent home, the mother, joined by the children, chases and catches the witch.

This is one of the oldest traditional games, of which many versions are given by Mrs. Gomme and Mr. Newell, both from Great Britain and America. Several incidents here given the present writer has gathered directly from players of the game. According to Mrs. Gomme, the game probably illustrates some of the practices and customs associated with fire worship, worship of the hearth, and ancient house ritual. The magic pot boils over when anything is wrong and as a warning to the mother that she is needed. The incident of the witch taking a light from the hearth is very significant, as, according to an old superstition, the giving of a brand from a hearth gave the possessor power over the inmates of the house. The sullying of the hearth by the old witch in blowing the ashes has also an ancient significance, as fairies were said to have power over inmates of a house where the hearth or threshold had been sullied.

MOUSETRAP

10 or more players   *Elementary*
Playground; parlor

The players stand in two concentric circles, the very small circle in the center being made by from three to six players who take hold of hands; this is the mousetrap. The other players stand at some distance outside of the trap in another circle and do not hold hands.

On a signal from the leader, the two circles start moving in opposite directions until the leader says "Stop!" At this the trap players lift their hands and the mice march in, around, and out of the trap. Suddenly the leader says "Snap!" when the trap is shut quickly by dropping the hands and some of the mice will be caught. These mice then join the trap, making it larger. The play is repeated until the mice are all caught.

This game is from Russia.

MUMBLETY–PEG

Playground   *Juniors; adults*

Games of tossing an open knife so that the blade will stick in the ground are almost universal. The following rules, used in American playgrounds and camps, are here given by kind permission of the National Recreation Association from their *88 Successful Play Activities*.

GENERAL RULES

Players must either sit or kneel on the ground.

Best out of three long games or seven short games determines winner.

Knife must stick into ground so that judge can get the thickness of at least two fingers between the ground and knife handle.

Boy Scout knife will be considered as official.

Belt punch will be considered as the "blade."

Long games shall be for boys.

Short games shall be for girls.

To be done with right hand only except where indicated.

PENKNIFE RULES (LONG GAME)

FRONT. — Knife on palm of right hand with blade toward finger tips; toss knife upward and inward, causing blade to stick in ground.

BACK. — Place knife on back of right hand and toss as for front.

PUNCH. — Make a fist with right hand. Place knife handle across the fingernails with blade toward thumb; twist hand quickly toward the left, sticking blade into the ground.

SNAPS. — Hold blade between thumb and forefinger of left hand with handle pointing toward the right. Strike the handle downward sharply with right hand, causing blade to stick into the ground.

SEVEN PENNIES. — Hold blade between thumb and first finger of right hand with handle away from contestant and snap knife away from tosser, sticking it into the ground. This must be done seven times in succession.

AROUND THE HORN. — Hold blade of knife between the index finger and thumb of right hand, as for **Pennies,** and swing the knife, with handle toward the ground, around the head from left to right; then snap away from tosser as in **Seven Pennies.**

SHAVE THE PEG. — Place blade between the first and second fingers and hold with thumb, have handle pointing away from body and point of blade toward person tossing; snap knife away from tosser.

CUT LEFT. — Hold knife as for **Pennies** and snap downward across left arm, striking left wrist with the right.

CUT RIGHT. — Opposite to **Cut Left.**

HEADINGS. — Same as for **Seven Pennies** except that the handle of knife is touched against the forehead before snapping.

CHINNINGS. — Same as **Headings** except that chin is touched with handle.

SNAPS. — See above; must be done three times in succession.

DROP IN AND PULL OUT. — Hold knife handle between thumb and forefinger of right hand and drop the knife through a hole made by touching the tips of the forefinger and thumb of the left hand. After blade sticks in ground, pull knife back through the hole by the blade, with the handle touching ground and the index finger and thumb holding blade; snap as in **Seven Pennies.**

SHAVE THE BARBER. — Hold left hand with palm in and little finger toward the ground. Place knife flat against the palm of left hand with cutting edge toward tosser and handle toward the ground. With the fingers of the right hand pull blade of knife toward the contestant, giving a downward snap.

LADY DIVES. — Hold right hand vertical, with back of it toward the players; place point of knife against the heel of the hand and the handle against the finger-tips; push upward and forward, giving a loop effect to the knife.

PINWHEEL. — With the handle at right angles to the right hand and the arm at right angles to the body, hold the point of the blade loosely between thumb and first finger; flip the knife toward the left with a downward push of the thumb.

KICK 'EM OUT. — Place handle of knife flat on palm of left hand with the blade protruding over the little finger side; strike blade downward with right hand.

COPS' CLUB. — Hold knife as for **Seven Pennies,** but flip toward tosser. Immediately strike upward with same hand, causing knife to spin in opposite direction.

TONY CHESTNUT. — Starting at toe, place point of blade on end of shoe and snap away from player. Repeat same at knee, again at the chest, and then from front part of the head. The toe may be elevated and the point of the knife may be placed against thumb when snapping from chest.

FINGERS. — Same as **Pennies** except that the blade is held between the thumb and each finger consecutively and two snaps are made with the first finger and thumb and one with the second, third, and little fingers.

JOHNNY JUMP THE FENCE. — Stick knife into ground at an angle and about one foot away place left hand with palm toward the knife and little finger touching the ground; with the right hand strike the knife up and forward, causing it to go over the left hand or fence and stick into the ground.

O–U–T PERIOD. — Place point of knife on left wrist and with right thumb and forefinger on top of knife snap to ground; at the same time say "O," repeat at elbow and say "U," repeat at shoulder and say "T." Make a fist as in **Punch** and place knife along fingernails with blade toward little finger side; twist wrist inward quickly and say "period." These last four stunts must be performed consecutively in order to complete the game.

PENKNIFE RULES (SHORT GAME)

FRONT. — Same as **Long Game**.
BACK. — Same as **Long Game**.
PUNCH. — Same as **Long Game**.
RABBIT'S EARS. — Extend index and little fingers; hold the second and third fingers closed with thumb; rest knife on extended fingers with blade toward thumb side; stick knife into ground with inward twist of wrist.

SNAPS. — Same as **Long Game.**

FIVE PENNIES. — Same as **Long Game** except that five flips are made in succession instead of seven.

SLICE THE HAM. — With left palm toward the player place point of knife against the thick of the hand near the little finger side, handle of knife toward the thumb side of hand. With right forefinger and thumb on end of the handle, pull the knife toward the contestant.

LADY DIVES. — Same as **Long Game.**

SHAVE THE PEG. — Same as **Long Game.**

CUT RIGHT. — Same as **Long Game.**

CUT LEFT. — Same as **Long Game.**

O–U–T PERIOD. — Same as **Long Game.**

MUMBLETY–PEG BASEBALL

SURFACE. — The game is best played on a board of soft wood, such as pine or cypress. It can be played, however, on any smooth surface where the ground is soft enough to allow the knife to stick.

THE KNIFE. — A regulation Scout knife is the official knife. The small blade shall be open to its full extent; the large blade shall be open only half way.

PLAYERS. — Two or more players shall play as individuals, taking their turn and keeping their own score.

THE GAME. — The game may be played by innings as in baseball. In this case, each player shall have three outs before the knife is passed on to the next player. Or it may be played until one of the players has twenty-one runs; in this case the knife is passed on each time an out is made.

PLAY. — The knife shall be placed so that the large blade is sticking into the surface with the end of the knife resting on the surface. The index finger shall be placed near the end of the knife and lifted so as to flip the knife end over end. The position in which it comes to rest determines the move or score the player makes. If the knife comes to rest with the small blade sticking in the surface, a "home-run" is scored. If only the large blade is sticking in the surface, a "three-base hit" is scored. If both the large and small blade are sticking in or touching the surface, a "two-base hit" is scored. If the large blade is sticking in with the end of the knife resting on the surface, a "single" is scored. If the knife rests on its back, one strike is recorded. Three strikes constitute one out. If the knife rests on its side, an out is scored. Men on bases are advanced only the number of bases scored; *i.e.* if a man is on first and a "two-base hit" is scored, the man on first is advanced only to third base.

MY LADY'S TOILET

10 to 30 or more players   *Primary and*
Parlor; schoolroom   *intermediate grades*

This is a French form of a game known in America as Spin the Platter. Each of the players is named for some article of My Lady's toilet, such as her gown, necklace, evening coat, slippers, bracelet, etc. All sit in a circle except one, who stands or crouches in the center and spins a plate or tray, at the same time saying, "My Lady wants her necklace"; or names some other article of the toilet. The player representing the article thus named must rush to the center and catch the plate before it stops spinning and falls to the ground. If successful, the player takes the place of the spinner. If unsuccessful, she returns to her place and pays a forfeit, which is redeemed at the end of the game. The speaker should name the different articles while carrying on a flow of narrative, as, for instance: "My Lady, being invited to a ball at the king's palace, decided to wear her *blue gown*. With this she called for her *silver slippers*, her *white gloves*, her *pearl necklace*, and a *bouquet* of roses. As the evening was quite cool, she decided to wear her *white opera coat*," etc. The speaker will make several opportunities for introducing mention of the ball, and whenever she says anything about the ball, all the players must jump up and change places, the spinner trying to secure one for herself in the general confusion. One odd player will be left without a place, and she becomes spinner. When boys are playing, they may appropriately take the parts of carriage, horses, footmen, the escort, etc.

NUMBERS CHANGE

(See also *Exchange.*)

10 to 30 or more players   *Intermediate*
Parlor; playground; gymnasium; schoolroom   *grades*

The players stand in a large circle and are numbered consecutively. One player takes his place in the center. He calls two numbers, and the players whose numbers are called must change places while the center player tries to secure one of their places.

The one who is left without a place changes places with the center player.

FOR THE SCHOOLROOM. — This game may be adapted by selecting two players as chasers, who take their places in the front of the room. These players are not blindfolded, as in the parlor form of the game. All of the other players are seated, having been numbered. The teacher calls two numbers, when the players bearing those numbers must rise at once and exchange seats, the two chasers trying to catch them before they can get to their seats.

When a game is played under these circumstances, it is not permissible for the chaser to take a vacant seat; he must catch the player who is running for it. No player, having once left his own seat, may return to it, but must keep up the chase until he is caught or reaches the seat for which he is running.

This game gives opportunity for some very lively chasing, with good running and dodging up and down the aisles. As in all running games in the class room, the seated players should keep their feet out of the aisles.

For young children it may be found desirable to have only one chaser. It generally adds to the interest of the game to have a general exchange of seats at the opening of the game, immediately after the numbers have been assigned, and before the chasing is commenced, as then the person who calls the numbers is at a loss to know how near or distant those called may be in relation to each other, and this element adds much to the sport of the game.

ODD MAN'S CAP

10 to 30 or more players   *Junior high school*
Playground; gymnasium

Twelve players make the best-sized group for this game; where there are more players, they should be divided into small groups. All but one of the players stand in a circle with considerable space between each two. The odd man stands in the center. Each player is provided with a stick about two feet in length; canes or wands may be used as substitutes, but the shorter sticks are better; they may be whittled from branches or bits of wood, and should not be pointed at the ends. The odd man tosses his cap or a cloth bag toward the circle. The players endeavor to catch it on their sticks, and keep it moving from one to another, so as to evade the odd man, who tries to recover his property. Should he succeed, he changes places with the one from whom he recovered it. The sticks must be kept upright in the air. A dropped cap may be picked up only by hand, not on a stick. The sticks must always be held upright. An old stiff hat, or a cap or bag wired around the edge to keep it spread open, makes the best game.

This game holds the interest of the players intently and is full of sport.

OLD BUZZARD

5 to 30 or more players *Elementary*
Playground

This is one of the old dramatic games, probably better known in America than any other of this type.

One player is chosen to represent the "Old Buzzard"; another player represents a hen, and the remainder are chickens. All the players circle around the buzzard, saying in chorus:

> "Chickany, chickany, crany crow;
> I went to the well to wash my toe;
> And when I came back a chicken was gone."

The hen finishes by asking alone, "What o'clock is it, old buzzard?" The buzzard crouches on the ground during the repetition of the verse, going through the pantomime of building a fire with sticks, and in answer to the question may name any hour, as eight o'clock, nine o'clock, ten o'clock. So long as the buzzard does not say twelve o'clock, the players continue to circle around, repeating the verse, the final question being asked each time by a different player, until the buzzard finally says, "Twelve o'clock!" When this occurs, the ring stands still, and the following dialogue takes place between the buzzard and the hen:

Hen. Old buzzard, old buzzard, what are you doing?
Buz. Picking up sticks.
Hen. What do you want the sticks for?
Buz. To build a fire.
Hen. What are you building a fire for?
Buz. To broil a chicken.

Hen.   Where are you going to get the chicken?

Buz.   Out of your flock!

The buzzard, who keeps a crouching attitude with face downcast during this dialogue, suddenly rises on the last words and chases the players, who scatter precipitately.   When a player is captured, the buzzard brings him back, lays him down, and dresses him for dinner, while the rest of the players group around.   The buzzard asks of the captured chicken, "Will you be picked or scraped?" and goes through the motions of picking feathers or scaling fish, as the chicken decides.   The buzzard then asks, "Will you be pickled or salted?"   "Will you be roasted or stewed?" each time administering to the recumbent chicken the appropriate manipulations.   At the end he drags the victim to a corner, and the game goes on with the remainder of the players.

OLD MAN TAG

10 to 60 players   *Primary grades*

Schoolroom

The players are in groups of two rows each, which play together. These two rows face away from each other.   Thus the first and

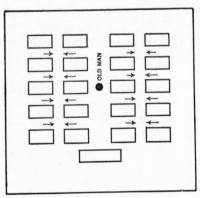

OLD MAN TAG

second row will turn respectively to the right and left, with their feet in the aisles, toward which they then face. This will leave a free aisle between them, in which the "old man" may run about. The third and fourth rows play together, facing away from each other, and leaving a free aisle for their old man or tagger. This will bring the second and third rows with their feet in the same aisle.

For each group one player is selected to be old man or tagger. The teacher gives a signal, whereupon all of the players stand. The object of the game is for the old man to tag any player who is standing. The players may avoid this by sitting whenever the old man approaches them. Should he succeed in tagging any player, that player must remain seated until the end of the game, but any player who sits to escape tagging must rise again as soon as the old man has moved away from his vicinity. The player is considered to have won who longest avoids the old man.

Children are very fond of this game in many grades, and it may be made very lively, the old man dodging rapidly up and down his aisle, and the other players bobbing quickly up and down from their seats.

OLD WOMAN FROM THE WOOD

(For boys, see *Trades*.)

10 to 60 or more players   *Intermediate grades*
Parlor; playground; schoolroom

The players are divided into two even parties, which face each other from a short distance. One party advances toward the other, remarking, "Here comes an old woman from the wood." The second party answers, "What canst thee do?" whereupon the old woman replies, "Do anything!" The second party then says, "Work away!" whereupon all the players in the first party proceed to imitate some occupation in which an old woman might engage, and which they have previously agreed on among themselves, such as sewing, sweeping, knitting, digging a garden, chopping wood, kneading bread, stirring cake, washing, ironing, etc. The opposite party tries to guess from this pantomime the occupation indicated. Should they guess correctly, they have a turn to perform in the same way. Should they be unable to guess correctly, the first party retires, decides on another action, and returns. This form of the game is generally played by girls. Boys play the same game with different dialogue under the name of "Trades."

When played in a playground or gymnasium, where there is free space for running, a successful guess should be followed by a chase of the actors by the guessing party, any players caught before a designated goal line is reached having to join the party of their captors. The party wins which secures all of the players.

OVER–THE–LEGS RELAY

12 to 80 players
Gymnasium

Intermediate grades
to adults

Players are divided into two or more teams. Each team forms in a rank, with its players facing alternately right and left; they take hold of hands, stretch arms to full length, and sit on the floor with legs stretched straight in front of them — "long sitting position." Heads should be in a straight line.

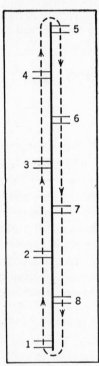

On signal, Number One of each team rises, jumps over the legs of each player down his side of the line, and similarly up the opposite side of his line, and immediately sits in his original place. When seated, he touches off the next runner, who is the neighbor on his right facing in the same direction. Number Two hurdles through a similar tour, jumping last over the legs of Number One, before sitting and touching off his right-hand neighbor, Number Three. The players all run thus in consecutive order from one side and then the other, as indicated in the diagram. The team wins whose last player is first to sit and raise his arm.

This makes a humorous number if run through quickly between more serious items in an exhibition.

OVER-THE-LEGS
RELAY

By courtesy of Miss Dorothy C. Clark of the Polytechnic, London.

OYSTER SHELL

10 to 100 players
Playground; gymnasium

Intermediate
grades

Two parallel lines are drawn across the center of the playground, with a space of ten feet between them, which is neutral territory. At a considerable distance beyond each line, and parallel to it, a second line is drawn, the space beyond being a refuge for any players of the party belonging to that side. This second line should preferably be at a considerable distance from the starting line, so as to give plenty of opportunity for a good chase during the game.

The players are divided into two equal teams which take place one on either side of the neutral territory. Each team chooses a color, light or dark, corresponding to the light or dark side of an oyster shell or some other small object which is used in the game.

A neutral odd player who acts as leader takes his place in the center of the neutral territory and tosses the oyster shell into the air. If there is no such leader available, the parties may choose captains to toss the shell alternately. The shell is allowed to fall on the ground. If the light side falls upward, the light team must turn and run for the goal at the opposite end of the ground, the other team chasing them. Anyone captured (tagged) must carry his captor back to his home goal on his back. A team scores one point for each prisoner caught. These may be easily counted, as the prisoners carry their victors home pick-a-back. The team first scoring fifty or one hundred points (according to the number of players) wins the game; or the winners may be determined by the largest score when the game ends.

Because of the carrying home of the victors by the players who are caught, it is advisable that some means be adopted to have opponents of nearly equal size. This is easily done by having the players line up according to size at the opening of the game and assigned alternately to the different sides. In any event, the tall players should be placed opposite each other, and the smaller players *vis-à-vis*.

This game is from the ancient Greeks, and is said to have arisen from a custom of exiling wrangling political opponents by writing their names on an oyster shell and sending from the city the one whose name fell uppermost when the shell was tossed. Some modern adaptations are here given.

PARTNER TAG

4 to 100 players   *Intermediate grades*
Indoors; out of doors; schoolroom   *to senior high school*

All of the players but two hook arms in couples. Of the two who are free, one is It or chaser, and the other the runner. The runner may save himself by locking arms with either member of any couple he chooses. Whenever he does so, the third party of that group becomes runner and must save himself in like manner. If the runner be tagged at any time, he becomes It or chaser, and the chaser becomes runner.

To get the proper sport into this game, the couples should run and twist and resort to any reasonable maneuver to elude the runner, who is liable at any time to lock arms with one of them and so make the other a runner.

For large numbers there should be more than one runner and chaser.

PEBBLE CHASE

5 to 30 or more players   *Junior high school*
Gymnasium; playground   *to adults*

One player, who is the leader, holds a small pebble between the palms of his hands, while the others stand grouped around him, each with his hands extended, palm to palm. The leader puts his hands between the palms of each player, ostensibly to drop therein the pebble which he holds, as in the game called "Button, button." The player who receives the pebble is chased by the others, and may only be saved by returning to the leader and giving the pebble to him. This chase may begin as soon as the players suspect who has the pebble. Each player should therefore watch intently the hands and faces of the others to detect who gets it, and immediately when he suspects one, start to chase him. It is therefore to the interest of the player who gets the pebble to conceal that fact until the attention of the group is distracted from him, when he may slip away and get a good start before he is detected. He may do this whenever he sees fit, but may not delay after the leader has passed the last pair of hands. The leader will help to conceal the fact of who has the pebble by passing his hands between those of the entire group, even though he should have dropped the pebble into the hands of one of the first players.

If the pebble holder gets back to the leader and gives him the pebble before being tagged, he continues with the group. If the pebble holder is caught before he can get back to the leader, he must pay a forfeit or change places with the leader, whichever method is decided on before the game opens.

In a crowded playground it is well to require that the chasers follow over exactly the same route as the pebble man. Under such conditions, the game is more successful if limited to ten players to a group.

This game is from the modern Greeks. It is found to bear transplanting excellently, being full of interest and sport.

PINCH–O

5 to 30 or more players   *Intermediate*
Gymnasium; playground   *grades*

This is a game of chase, an advancing line (rank) of players turning and fleeing from an odd player in front of them when a signal is given.

The player who is It walks backward, being about ten feet in front of the others, who advance slowly forward in a line, holding hands. The player on one end of the line calls "Pinch!" and at once squeezes or pinches the hand of the player standing next. This player slightly presses the hand of the one on his other side, and so on across the line until the pressure is felt by the last player on the opposite end, who at once calls out "O!" Immediately that the "O" is heard, the entire line is liable to be tagged by the one who is walking backward in front of them, and they therefore instantly turn and run for "home," a place determined beyond certain boundaries at one end of the ground. The one who is It gives chase, and anyone tagged by him must join him in tagging the players when the game is repeated. The game ends when all are caught, the last player to be caught being the winner, and taking the part of the odd player for the next round.

PITCH PEBBLE

4 to 10 players   *Children*
Out of doors; seashore   *to adults*

This game may be played with pebbles, shells, or nuts, each player having two or four of such articles. The object of the game is to throw these pebbles into a hole about four inches in diameter, which should be made in the ground. The first part of the game is concerned with determining the order in which the players shall take turns. Ten feet from the hole a place is marked, from which the players throw in turn until each has had enough turns to have thrown all of his pebbles. The one who has succeeded in landing a pebble nearest the hole becomes the first player, and takes his stand on a second mark drawn one fourth nearer the hole, all the players meanwhile having gathered up their pebbles again. These are all given to the successful player, and he pitches them in a mass toward the hole, becoming the owner of as many as fall into the hole. Any pebbles that do not go in the hole are gathered up by the player who in the original throwing came out second in trying to get near the hole, and he, in turn, throws these in mass, standing also at the nearer throwing point from which his predecessor threw. All of the players take turns in this way until all of the pebbles have been appropriated. The player wins who gets the most pebbles. Pebbles won are not thrown again, but kept for score.

For good players the distances from the hole may be increased.

POISON

10 to 30 or more players   *Intermediate grades*
Gymnasium; playground; seashore   *to senior high school*

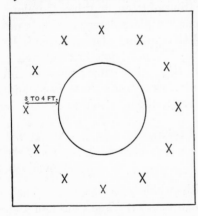

3 TO 4 FT.

POISON

A circle is marked on the floor or ground considerably smaller than an outer circle formed by the players, clasping hands. Each player tries, by pulling or pushing, to induce the others to step within the smaller circle, but endeavors to keep out of it himself. Anyone who touches the ground within the inner circle, if only with one foot, is said to be poisoned. As soon as this happens, the player or players so poisoned become catchers; the other players shout "Poisoned!" and at once break the circle and run for safety, which consists in standing on wood. The merest chip will answer, but growing things are not counted wood. If played in a gymnasium, iron may give immunity instead of wood. Anyone caught before reaching safety, or in changing places afterward, joins the catchers, and when all have been caught, the ring is once more surrounded.

POISON SNAKE

10 to 30 or more players　　　　　　　　　*Junior high school*
Gymnasium; playground　　　　　　　　　　　*to adults*

The players join hands to form a circle. About fifteen Indian clubs or tenpins are placed in the center of the circle, with spaces between them in which a player might step. The players then try, by pushing or pulling their comrades by means of the clasped hands, to make them knock over the clubs. Any player who overturns a club or who unclasps hands must at once leave the circle, the club being replaced. The first players so leaving start a "scrub" circle; players disqualified in the scrub

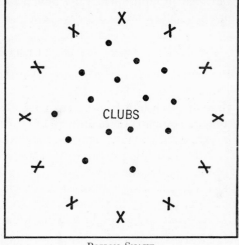

POISON SNAKE

circle start another in their turn, etc. The player wins who is left in the original circle. Where several circles have been formed, the several winners may form a circle at the close and play to determine the final winner.

This game has possibilities for much sport and skill. The agility with which players leap over or pass between the clubs is as important a part of

the game as the pulling and pushing. The clubs should be sufficiently
scattered to make it possible for a player to save himself in this way. Children may need to have this feature of the game pointed out to them. The
game is equally interesting to children or adults, but obviously requires
athletic suits for girls or women.

POM POM PULLAWAY

5 to 30 or more players   *Intermediate grades*
Out of doors   *to junior high school*

This game is often played between the curbings of a city street,
but is suitable for any open play space which admits of two lines
drawn across it with a space of from thirty to fifty feet between
them. All players stand on one side behind one of the dividing
lines, except one player who is It and who stands in the center of
the open ground. He calls any player by name and adds a
formula, as below:

> "John Smith, Pom Pom Pullaway!
> Come away, or I'll fetch you away!"

Whereupon the player named must run across the open space to
the safety line on the opposite side, the one who is It trying meanwhile to catch him before he reaches that line. If he gets over
safely, he remains there until all of his comrades have joined him
or have been caught. Anyone caught by the one who is It joins
the latter in helping to catch other players as they dash across the
open space, but the one originally It remains the caller throughout the game. After all of the uncaught players have crossed to
one side, they try in the same way to return to their first goal.
The first one to be caught is It for the next game.

Players should give the chaser as much difficulty as possible in catching
them by making feints in one direction and suddenly running in another, or
by running diagonally instead of straight across, etc.

POTATO RACES

Four forms of Potato Race are here given as follows:
Potato Race I. Individual competition. Placing potatoes on marked
spots; gathering them up not a part of the game.

POTATO RACE II. Team competition. One player places the potatoes on spots; the next gathers them up, etc.

POTATO SHUTTLE RELAY. Alternate placing and gathering up.

POTATO SPOON RACE. Only gathering up of potatoes.

POTATO RACE — I

(For individual competitors)

2 to 60 or more players   *Intermediate grades*
Playground; gymnasium   *to adults*

The simpler and usual Potato Race is played in two forms: (I) the players competing as individuals; and (II) competing as teams. The following description is for individual competition; the team game is described as Potato Race II. There are other forms of playing the individual game, the one given here being for an athletic competition.

The competitors should each wear a large number pinned across the shoulders on the back, where it may be read plainly by the judges. The competition is carried on in heats, as many players as the playing space will allow playing in each heat. Potatoes should be used, or blocks of wood are officially permissible. These wooden blocks may be procured of potato shape, and are better than those of cubical form, as the latter are apt to land on the corners and bound.

A starting line is drawn across the ground. At right angles to it a row of potatoes is placed for each player in the heat. The potatoes should be on spots marked two yards apart and eight in number. The first potato should be two yards from the receptacle, which is usually placed on the starting line, one beside each competitor. This receptacle should be a pail, basket, box, or can, not over two feet in height, with an opening not over thirty-six inches in circumference, or a circle one foot in diameter may be drawn on the ground. The potatoes are replaced on the marks before the beginning of each heat, the game in this form consisting solely of gathering them up, not in placing them. There is no rule against tossing a potato into the receptacle, but it is poor policy to do so, as it increases the risks of failure.

The contestants start, as for a race, in response to the starter's signals, "On your marks!" "Get set!" "Go!" The game consists in picking up the potatoes one at a time and placing them in the receptacle. The potatoes may be picked up in any order desired. A potato dropped, however, must be picked up before another potato be touched, or the player is disqualified. Similarly, a potato missing the receptacle or bounding out of it must be placed in it before the next potato be touched, or the player is disqualified. When all the potatoes have been placed in the receptacle, the player finishes by dashing across a finish line (a tape, or strand of worsted, stretched five feet back of the receptacle). As in all races in athletic form, a player is disqualified for interfering with any other competitor, or for touching the finish tape with the hands or arms; the tape should be breasted. The winners in each heat play a final race; or, with large numbers competing, semi-finals before the finals. Where small numbers are competing, those finishing first, second, and even third, may be entered for the final trials. In case of a tie, both competitors are entered for the next (final, or semi-final) heat, or, if tied in the final heat, the tied competitors play again.

POTATO RACE — II

(Team competition)

10 to 100 players *Intermediate grades*
Playground; gymnasium; seashore *to adults*

The first description given below is for an informal game. This is followed by the rules for strict athletic procedure.

The ground is marked off with a starting line. At right angles to it are marked two or more rows of spots according to the number of teams competing, the spots being from three to six feet apart, each row containing from six to ten. On each spot is placed a potato; or a stone, block of wood, or any other object may be substituted; on the seashore bathing slippers may be used. Potato-shaped blocks of wood may be had as substitutes for potatoes, and are better than cubical blocks, which are apt to land on the corners and bound.

The players are divided evenly into competing teams which line up in single file behind the starting line, each file being in line

with one of the rows of potatoes. Beside the leader of each file
is a box or basket; or a circle may be drawn on the ground instead.
At a signal each leader runs forward, picks up a potato, brings it
back and puts it in the box, goes for another, etc., until all the
potatoes in his row have been gathered in. He may pick them up
in any order that he chooses. Immediately when the last potato
is placed, this player touches the outstretched hand of the next
player in his file, and at once leaves the playing space; he should
not line up again with his team. The next player in the file
starts out immediately on receiving the "touch off," replaces
the potatoes one at a time, and touches off the next player, who
gathers them in, and so on, alternately, until each player has
had his turn. The team wins whose last player is the first to
dash back over the starting line.

For an athletic contest for adults, the following rules are typical: There
should be eight potatoes for each team, placed two yards apart, the first
potato two yards from the receptacle. The receptacle should be either a
pail, basket, box, or can, not over two feet in height, having an opening
not over thirty-six inches in circumference. The finish line is a "tape"
(strand of worsted) stretched parallel with the starting line and five yards
back of the receptacle. There should be a judge of fouls for each team
and two judges at finish. Fouls are:

    1. Not placing a potato accurately on the spot.

    2. Leaving a potato outside the receptacle instead of in it, whether it
be dropped there or bound out.

    3. Starting over the line without or before the "touch off."

A foul corrected before the next step in the game is taken does not score
as a foul. The teams win first, second, third, and fourth places in the order
of finishing, if there are no fouls. Where fouls have been scored, the team
finishing first, with the fewest number of fouls, has first place, etc. In case
of a tie, the tied teams must play again to determine the winner.

Teams	Order of Finishing	Fouls	Order of Winning
A	2	0	First place
B	1	4	Third place
C	4	6	Fourth place
D	3	2	Second place

III. POTATO SHUTTLE RELAY

20 to 100 players   *Intermediate grades*
Playground; gymnasium; seashore   *to adults*

This first description is for an informal game. This is followed by rules for an athletic contest.

This is a form of potato race suitable for large numbers. The ground is marked off with two starting lines, one at either end of the ground. At even intervals between these two lines a row of from four to ten spots should be clearly marked on the ground, each row forming a line at right angles to the starting lines. There should be as many rows of this kind as there are teams.

On the first spot of each row should be placed a box, basket, or pail, and in it three or more potatoes, according to the number of spots. Stones, blocks of wood, or any other uniform objects may be used, as a substitute for potatoes, but the latter are best.

The players are in teams, each standing in two divisions in shuttle relay formation. Between the two divisions should stretch the row of spots. The receptacle should be on the spot near the first runner.

At a signal, the first runner of each team starts over the line, takes a potato from the box, places it on the first spot, returns, gets another potato, places it on another spot, and so on until all are placed; he need not observe strictly the consecutive order of the spots. He then runs forward and touches the outstretched hand of the first runner in the opposite file of his team. This runner must pick up the potatoes and replace them in the box one at a time, and then "touch off" the player facing him in the opposite file. Each player, as he finishes his part ("touches off" the next runner), should leave the running space entirely and not line up with his team. The line nearest the box serves as a finish line, and the team wins whose last runner, having replaced the last potato, is first to get over this line.

If a potato be dropped, the runner must pick it up and replace it in the box or on the spot, then make his play over again.

The above description is for a comparatively informal game. For a strict athletic contest for junior players the layout of the grounds should

be for four spots in each row, two yards between each, with the starting
lines two yards back of the first and fourth spots. The receptacle is placed
on the spot nearest the first runners, and should be a pail, basket, box, or
can, not over twenty-four inches in circumference at the opening. Three
potatoes are used.

The first runners start on signals, "On your marks!" "Get set!" (or
"Get ready!") "Go!" There should be a judge to score fouls for each
division of each team, and two judges at the finish.

In case of a tie, the tied teams play again.

Fouls consist in: 1. Placing a potato otherwise than on the mark.
2. Leaving a potato outside the receptacle instead of in it, whether it be
dropped outside or bound out. 3. Starting over the line without the
"touch off." Any foul corrected before going on with the next step in the
game does not score as a foul. Teams win in the order of finishing, plus
consideration of the record on fouls, as in Race II.

IV. POTATO SPOON RACE

6 to 60 players   *Intermediate grades*
Parlor; playground; gymnasium   *to adults*

This is a form of potato race that may afford much amusement,
especially for indoor companies. The players are divided into
two or more teams which compete against each other. Each
team lines up in single file, so that the leaders all toe a starting
line. Placed on the floor in front of each group, and stretching
ahead in the same direction, should be a row of potatoes at
intervals of two or three feet apart, one for each player in the
file. The larger and the more irregular in shape the potatoes
the better. There should be from six to ten potatoes for each
row. Each leader should be furnished with a teaspoon, and
beside the leader of each file should be a pan, box, or basket,
in which the potatoes are to be placed. At a signal each leader
starts forward, takes up a potato on the spoon, carries it to the
box or basket beside his first standing position, and places the
potato in it; he then hands the spoon to the next player and
passes off the playing field, not lining up again with his team.
The second player picks up the next potato, puts it in the box,
and so on, until all have played, the last one standing beside
the box with the spoon held aloft as a signal that he has finished.

It is not allowable to touch the potato with anything but the spoon.   Should a potato be touched otherwise, the player must replace it and pick it up again on the spoon.   Should a potato drop from the spoon, it must be picked up on the spoon where it dropped, and the play continued from that point.

PRISONER'S BASE

Prisoner's Base is one of the most popular games for both boys and girls who are beginning to care for team organization, and is capital for adults. It gives opportunity for vigorous exercise for all of the players, for the use of much judgment, prowess, and daring, and for simple team or co-operative work.

The game is found under many different forms.   Several, which offer marked or typical differences, each possessing distinct playing values, are given here.   These differences are in (1) the arrangement of the ground, and (2) the rules governing the players and game.

The differences in the grounds may be classed as follows:

I. The entire playground divided in two divisions, one belonging to each team, each division having a small pen for prisoners at the rear. (Diagram I.)

II. The main part of playground neutral territory, with home goals for the opposing teams at opposite ends, with prisons in, near, or attached to them.   (Diagrams II, V.)

III. The main part of playground neutral territory, with home goals for both teams at the same end, attached or separate, and prisons at the opposite end, either (1) on the same side of the ground as the home goal, or (2) on the enemy's side of the ground.   (Diagrams III–IV.)

The rules for play for the second and third types of ground are fundamentally the same, though differing in details, and they differ from those for Diagram I.   The playing qualities of the games for the last three diagrams, however, are very distinct because of the different methods of the enemies' approach to each other (which make differences in the risk of "dares"), and because of the differing risks in rescuing prisoners and taking the enemy's goal by entry.

It has seemed best to make a selection of the typical forms, and leave the leader of games free to choose his own.   The first form is the simplest for beginners and younger players, and makes a good introduction to the game for such players.

Stealing Sticks is still another form of Prisoner's Base.   The main difference lies in the carrying away of the enemy's property.

Prisoner's Base and related games are supposed to have descended from the days of border warfare.   They are very old, and Strutt mentions a "Proclamation at the head of the Parliamentary proceedings early in the reign of Edward the Third, . . . where it [Prisoner's Base] is prohibited

in the avenues of the palace at Westminster during the sessions of Parlia·
ment, because of the interruption it occasioned to the members and other
in passing to and fro." The game at that time was played by adults.

PRISONER'S BASE — I

10 to 30 or more players   *Intermediate grades*
                    Playground; gymnasium

The ground is divided into two equal parts, with a small base
or prison marked off at the farther corner of each division.   From
five to fifteen players guard each side.   They venture into the

enemy's ground, and, if caught, are
put into the prison, where they must
remain until tagged by one of their
own side who is free.   Both prisoner
and rescuer may be tagged and
brought back to prison before reaching their own ground.   The game is
won when one side makes prisoners
of all of its opponents, or when a free
man enters the opponents' prison, but
this last may be done only when there
are no prisoners there.

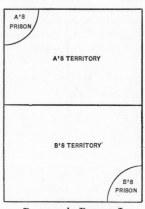

PRISONER'S BASE — I

This form of Prisoner's Base differs from
others in greater simplicity, both as to the
arrangement of the ground and the rules of play.   It is therefore better for
younger players or beginners in the game.

The differences in detail consist in:

1. The ground being divided by a line through the center into two opposing territories.   In other forms, the main playground is neutral territory,
each party having a small home goal marked within it.

2. In this game (No. I) a player cannot "give a dare" without venturing
into the opponents' territory, and any opponent may tag him.   In other
forms, the tagging, being on neutral territory, is controlled by limitations
as to which player was last to leave his home goal, and makes a more com-
plex game.

The rules about (1) a prisoner and his rescuer both being liable to cap·
ture on the way home, and (2) to winning by entering the enemy's prison,
with the restriction that no prisoners must be there, are also distinctive
features.

PRISONER'S BASE — II

10 to 30 or more players　　　　　　*Intermediate grades to*
Playground; gymnasium　　　　　　*junior high school*

Two captains are chosen who select players alternately until all are disposed in two teams of equal numbers. A large goal is marked off at each end of the ground, with a small base or prison in one rear corner of it. The wide, open space between the goals is neutral territory. The objects of the game are to enter the opponent's goal or to make prisoners of all of his men.

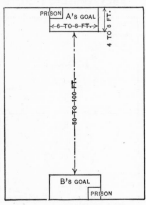

PRISONER'S BASE — II

The entrance of one player within the enemy's home goal means victory for his side. As one player advances for this purpose, or "gives a dare," the opponents send out a player to tag him, when the first side immediately sends out a second player to "cover" or protect the darer by trying to tag his opponent. The second side then sends out a second player to "cover" their first man. He is at liberty to tag either of the other two players. In this way any or all of the players may be out at one time, though it is unwise to leave the goal unguarded. Any player may tag any man from the opposite side who left his goal before he did, but none who came out after he did. Whenever a player returns to his home goal, which he may do at any time, the man who went out to cover him must return also, and of course the man who went out to cover this second one, etc. The issuing forth of players, or their return to the home goal, is subject at all times to the direction of the captain, though not dependent on it, and much independence of judgment should be exercised by the various players. The captain may also designate one player to guard the home goal and one to guard the prisoners whenever he chooses.

Any player caught (tagged) is placed in the opponents' prison ("prisoner's base"), where he must remain until rescued by one

of his own side.   The prisoner may reach as far out of the prison
as possible, so long as one foot is within it.   When there are several
prisoners, they may take hold of hands or otherwise touch each
other, as by the feet (this is optional with the prisoners), and
reach forward as far as possible, to be tagged by a rescuer, so
long as one of them (the last caught) keeps one foot within the
prison goal.   In such a line the first one caught should be farthest
from the prison, the next one caught holding his hand, and so on
in the order of capture.   A guard should always be at hand to
intercept any attempts at rescue.   A prisoner and his rescuer
may not be tagged while returning home, but the rescuer may be
tagged before he touches the prisoner.   One rescuer may free
only one prisoner at a time.   Whenever a player is caught, all of
the others return to their home goals (except prisoners), and a
fresh start is made in the game.

Much finessing is possible by engaging the enemy on one side
of the ground, while a good runner is held in reserve to dash into
the enemy's goal on the other side.   Or one player may, by a wide
detour, creep around unnoticed to the rear of the enemy's goal and
enter it from that side.

Each side should have a captain to maintain discipline, to take
general direction of the game, and to decide with the opposing
captain any disputed points.

This game is more complicated than the one of the same name previously described.   It is well for beginners to start with the first game.   The
author can testify from vivid recollections the hold which this form of the
game may have for successive seasons on its devotees.   Sometimes a "dare
line" is drawn a few feet in front of each home goal, which challenges the
opponents to a special thrill of venturesomeness.   The game in this form,
as a small boy said to the author, is "the national game of Minneapolis."

PRISONER'S BASE — III

6 to 30 or more players   *Intermediate grades*
Playground; gymnasium   *to senior high school*

The ground is divided according to the accompanying diagram ;
the players, who are divided into two equal teams, with a captain
for each team, being stationed respectively in the goals marked

A and *B*, which are at the same end of the ground instead of at opposite ends, as in Prisoner's Base II. In the present form of the game, the prison belonging to each side is located directly opposite its own home goal at the farther end of the ground, instead of near its own goal, as in II. Rescue of a prisoner is by entry of the opponent's prison, not by tagging the prisoners; so there is no object in the prisoner's reaching out of the prison, as in the previous forms of the game.

The two teams decide which shall commence by counting out, holders, drawing lots, or some other form of choice. One member of this side then runs out to the middle of the ground and gives a "nominy," or "dare," calling, "Chevy, chevy, chase! One, two, three!" As soon as he has called this (but not before), he is liable to be tagged by the opponents, who try to catch him before he can run home again. Should he reach home in safety, the opponents take their turn in sending a man to the middle to give a "dare" in the same way. A player need not run home, however, but may remain at large, another player from his side running out to cover or protect him by trying to tag the opponent. Several players from each team may be out in this way at one time. A player may be caught by any man who left his home goal after he did, but by none who left before him. Each player must therefore keep a sharp watch on his opponents to know which of them may tag him and which he may tag. This is continued until a prisoner is caught, when he is taken by his captor to the prison belonging to the side capturing him. A captor may not be tagged while taking a prisoner to prison, and is allowed to go back to his goal afterward without tagging. If a player can reach the opponent's prison without being tagged by an opponent, he releases the first prisoner taken there. Both may return home without being tagged. The object of the game

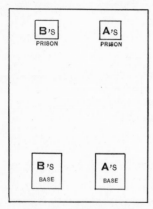

PRISONER'S BASE — III

is to place all of the players of the opponent's side in prison, and when that is accomplished, to take possession of the opponent's home goal. When this is done, the two teams change sides and begin again, the losing side being first to send a man into the field.

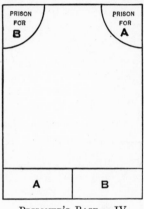

PRISONER'S BASE — IV

This differs from the preceding game only in the laying out of the ground, the prison for each party being on the opponent's side of the ground instead of on the side of the home goal. This arrangement decreases the risk in rescuing prisoners. All of the rules for the game are the same as in III.

PRISONER'S BASE — IV

PRISONER'S BASE — V

10 to 30 or more players　　　　　*Intermediate grades*
Playground; gymnasium　　　　　*to senior high school*

In this form of prisoner's base the ground is marked out in a square or oblong, the dimensions varying with the number of

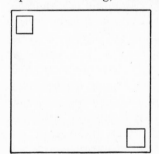

players and their age or ability as runners. For average players a ground measuring sixty by sixty feet is recommended. The two end boundaries serve as base lines, the territory beyond each belonging to the team on that side. In this respect the game differs from those previously described, in which a limited home goal is marked for each team. About ten feet from the base line, near the

PRISONER'S BASE — V

left-hand corner of the square or oblong, a small prison is marked for each team.

The first object of the game is to make prisoners of all the opponents. The second object of the game is to make runs into

the enemy's territory and back again without being caught
(tagged). Three such runs entitle the player making them to
select a player from the opposing team as a prisoner, or to free
one prisoner from his own team. Should a player be made a
prisoner, any runs he may have made into the enemy's territory
up to that time are lost in his account, and when freed, he must
begin his score of runs over again to count three. A player
returning home after a run into the enemy's territory may not
capture a prisoner or free one of his own men from prison on the
way. A player may not be tagged after crossing the opponents'
baseline until he starts back. In returning home after such a
run, a player may be tagged by any opponent who left his own
goal after the runner left his own goal (not the enemy's goal),
but not by any who started out before the runner started. This
rule applies to the capture of opponents at any time, any player,
for instance, on team A, being liable to capture by any opponent
on team B who left his baseline *after* the A man, but not any
who left it *before* he left his own. Similarly, he may capture
any player on team B who ventured forth before he did, but
must be on his guard against any who came out after he did.
Stepping over the side lines while being chased is equivalent
to being caught; but this does not apply when escorting a
prisoner or at any other time.

Prisoners may stretch out of the prison as far as possible so long
as one foot is within it. As the number of prisoners increases,
they may stretch out in one long file from the prison, provided
each touches a hand or foot, or some other part of the next player.
In such a file, the first prisoner captured should be the farthest
away from the prison, the last one captured with at least one
foot in the goal, and the others in relative order. After the first
prisoner is caught, the game centers more on freeing or preventing
the freeing of prisoners than on runs into the enemy's goal.

This is the form of Prisoner's Base preferred by Mr. Joseph Lee of Boston,
and described by him in *Playground* (No. 8). Mr. Lee says:

"The interest of the game depends very much on locating the prison in
such a way as to give the right balance between the forces of offense and
defense. If it is placed close to the baseline of the side by which the capture has been made, it is almost impossible to free the prisoner if there is

any defense at all. The game is often spoiled by this mistake. On the other hand, it must not be placed too far out, for if it is, it becomes impossible to win the game, because the line of prisoners, when the side is nearly all caught, then extends to a point so much nearer their own baseline than to that of their opponents that even the slowest runner on the losing side can get down and free a prisoner before the fastest runner on the opposite side can get out to stop him. The art of laying out the ground is to have the prison placed far enough out to make the freeing of the first prisoner reasonably easy, without being so far out as to make the catching of the last one impossible. In general, the game can be made lively and comparatively unscientific by making the distance between the baselines (the lines on which the two sides are lined up) short, the field wide, and the prisons far out; and can be made more difficult and less eventful by making it long and narrow, with the prisons close in. If this latter tendency is carried too far, however, freeing prisoners and making runs become at last impossible, and the game is entirely stopped. . . . The game, of course, is at its best when there is most going on and of the most thrilling sort — a lot of players making runs and freeing and defending prisoners — with flight and rally, charge and rout, and triumph and despair."

PUSS IN A CORNER

5 to 30 or more players   *Primary grades*
Schoolroom; playground; gymnasium; parlor

All of the players but one are disposed in the corners or at con-venient goals that will answer the same purpose. The odd player goes from one to another, saying, "Pussy wants a corner!" The player to whom this is addressed replies, "Go to my next-door neighbor." Any two of the other players meanwhile watch their opportunity to beckon to one another for exchanging places. They try to make this exchange of signals and to dash across from place to place when the attention of Puss is attracted in some other direction, as Pussy must try to secure a corner by rushing to any place that is vacant when the players thus exchange.

The sport of the game consists very largely in tantalizing Puss by making many exchanges, or, on the other hand, in Puss's suddenly dashing for some vacant place without giving previous evidence of knowing of it. Whenever Puss secures a corner, the odd player left out becomes Puss.

Puss, when not succeeding in getting a corner as soon as desirable, may call "All change!" when all of the players must exchange places, and in the general flurry Puss should secure a place.

Out of doors. — This game may be very delightfully adapted to outdoor play by each player taking a tree as a "corner," when the dodging and running may be much more varied and interesting than in the usual space of a parlor or gymnasium.

PUSS IN THE CIRCLE

10 to 30 or more players　　　　　　　　　　　*Primary grades*
Playground; gymnasium

A large circle is marked on the ground or floor. One player, who is Puss, stands in the center of this circle; the other players stand outside of the circle surrounding it. These players may be tagged by Puss whenever they have a foot inside of the circle. They will make opportunity for this by stepping in and out of the circle, teasing Puss in every possible way to tag them. Anyone whom Puss touches becomes a prisoner and is another Puss, joining the first Puss in the circle to help tag the others. The last one tagged is the winner of the game.

This is one of the games particularly suited to make a timid child courageous, and a teacher or leader using the game with little children should urge such timid children to take an active part in the game.

QUOITS

(See also *Ring-Toss* and *Horseshoe Pitching*.)

2 or 4 players　　　　　　　　　　　　　*Juniors; adults*
1 or 2 pins in pitcher's box; 4 to 8 quoits

I. THE FORMAL OR OFFICIAL GAME of Quoits requires two pins sunk each in a bed of clay in a pitcher's box, the latter made as for Horseshoe Pitching. The pin (spike) is driven into the ground until the head is level with the surface. It is of iron, the head being about three quarters of an inch in diameter, with a point sunk in the exact center for measuring. The distance between pins is fifty-four feet (eighteen yards) and both players pitch from the same box, first from one and then the other, alternately. A pitcher may never stand in advance of the pin, though he may stride it if not toeing beyond its center.

The official quoit is of metal, ring-shaped, with a four-inch opening, a rim two and a half inches wide, and one side convex. This side must always be uppermost in throwing.

SCORE. — A quoit encircling the pin is called a "ringer"; one touching the pin but not encircling it a "hobber." The score is made on ringers, hobbers, and nearest quoits. The latter are measured with calipers from the center of the pin to the nearest point of the quoit.

A game is twenty-one points whether scored by one of two players or four players in partners.

Ringer, three points.

Double ringer, six points.

Ringer topped by opponent, six points for pitcher of last ringer.

Triple ringer, nine points for pitcher of last ringer.

Hobber, two points.

Two hobbers, four points.

Hobber topped by another, two points for one nearest pin or resting on it.

Two opposing hobbers on pin do not score; next nearest quoit scores.

Three hobbers, two are a tie and do not score; third one scores one point.

Ringer and hobber, five.

Ringer topped by opponent's hobber, three for ringer.

Ringer topped by two opposing hobbers, seven for pitcher of hobbers.

Ringer and hobber (same pitcher) topped by opponent's hobber, three for ringer.

Double ringer topped by hobber, six for pitcher of second ringer.

Ringer topped by opponent's ringer and hobber, eight points for pitcher of last two.

Nearest quoit to pin scores one point if neither a ringer nor a hobber has been pitched.

Two nearest quoits by same pitcher, one point for each.

Two nearest quoits at same distance from pin, if opponents, are a tie and do not score; the nearest of the other two scores one point.

II. INFORMAL GAME. — Quoits are often played on one stake in an informal game. The scoring is the same as for the formal game, the player standing behind a throwing line drawn at a distance of from twenty to thirty feet from the pin.

RAILROAD TRAIN

10 to 100 players   *Primary grades*
Parlor; schoolroom; out of doors

Each player is named for some object on a train, such as engine, baggage car, dining car, smokestack, boiler, cylinders, wheels, oil, coal, engineer, porter, conductor, etc. One person is chosen to be the train master. He says in narrative form: "We must hurry and make up a train to go to Boston. I will take Number One *engine* and some *coal;* have the *bell rope* in order; be sure that the *cushions* are brushed in the *sleeping car*," etc. As he names these objects, the player bearing each name runs to the starter and lines up behind him, each putting his hands on the shoulders of the one in front, the first one placing his on the shoulders of the starter. When all are on the train, the starter gives the signal for going, and the whole train moves out on its journey, which at the discretion of the starter will be up hill over obstacles, down hill from others, around loops and curves, etc.; and he may, under suitable circumstances, find a convenient place for a grand "smash-up" at the end.

For large numbers there should be several starters, starting several trains at once, and these may race for a given point at the end.

RED LION

5 to 30 or more players   *Intermediate grades*
Playground; gymnasium   *to junior high school*

A place is marked out at one side or end of the ground called the den. In this stands one player who is called Red Lion. The other players choose one of their number as a chief, who does not run, but stands at one side and directs the movements of the others. The chief calls "Loose!" to the Red Lion. After hearing this signal, the lion is free to run out whenever he chooses. The players venture near to the den, taunting the lion with the lines:

"Red Lion, Red Lion, come out of your den!
Whoever you catch will be one of your men."

When the Red Lion thinks the players are sufficiently near to give him a good opportunity to catch one, he makes a sudden sortie and catches any player that he can. The player is not his prisoner until the Lion has held him and repeated three times "Red Lion!" Both the Lion and his prisoner must hurry back to the den, as all of the other players may turn upon them at once to drive them back with blows. This is generally restricted to hitting with caps. Thereafter, when the Red Lion issues forth, he must take the prisoner with him, hand in hand, both of them endeavoring together to catch one of the other players by putting their arms over his head.

The Red Lion and his man may not issue, however, from their den until the chief calls "Cow catcher!" or some other signal, as explained below. As in the previous case, when a prisoner is caught, he and his captors hurry to the den to avoid the buffeting of the other players. Each time that the Red Lion goes forth, all of his prisoners must go with him. The method in which they go, however, and in which they capture their prey, will be determined by the signals of the chief. When he calls "Cow catcher!" they must all run out in a long string, hand in hand, and capture their prisoner by any two in the line slipping their clasped hands over his head. If the chief calls "Tight!" the Red Lion and his men go forth in the same way, holding hands, and try to capture a player by surrounding him and so take him to the den. Should the chief call "Doubles!" then the Red Lion and his men come forth two by two, and try to capture their prisoners. The order in which these varied commands are given is entirely at the discretion of the chief.

At any time when the Red Lion and his men are out on the hunt, any of the other players may try to break apart the clasped hands of the hunters. Whenever this is done, the lions must rush back to their den, being driven back and buffeted by the outside players. The game ends when all of the men have been captured by the Red Lion's party. The last man to be caught is the winner, and becomes Red Lion for the next game.

RELAY RACES

Relay races are those in which teams, instead of individuals, compete against each other, so that the winning team cannot be determined until all players have run or played. The succession of players in a team occurs in regular order, determined by their line-up at starting. Each player after the first may start only after he has received a "touch-off" (touch of the hand) or some object handed him, or had some other play or interchange with the preceding runner, this varying in different games. There are many forms of relays. The main forms for all but Track Relays are:

(1) **SINGLE RELAYS,** in which all teams are lined up in single file behind the same starting line, thus facing in the same direction. (*Diagram A*)

(A) Single Relay Formation

(B) Shuttle or Double Relay
(*Three teams of ten players each.*)

(2) **SHUTTLE OR DOUBLE RELAYS,** in which each team is divided in halves which face each other from behind two starting

lines that are some distance apart. See game, **Shuttle Relay.**
(*Diagram B*)

(3) **SPOKE OR STAR RELAY** (sometimes called **Circle Relay**), in which the files ray out from a central point. (See game, *Spoke Relay,* page 230.)

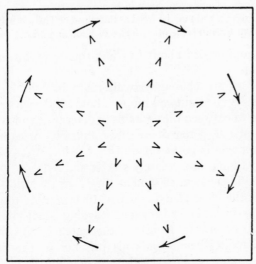

(C) SPOKE OR STAR RELAY

The relay races in the following list appear in alphabetical order in this section on Miscellaneous Active Games. Relay races for balls, beanbags, and track events appear in their respective sections.

All-up Relay
Band Obstacle Race
Bend and Stretch Relay
Blackboard Relay
Circle Seat Relay
Couple Race
Face the Corner Relay
Hopping Relay Race
Indian Club Race
Japanese Crab Race

Jumping Relay Race
Over the Legs Relay
Potato Races
Shuttle Relay
Single Relay
Spoke Relay (Circle Relay)
Stunt Races
Tag the Wall Relay
Wand Race

RING–A–LIEVIO

(Ring′a-lee′ve-o)

10 to 30 or more players   *Junior high school*

Out of doors

This is a form of Hide and Seek in opposing parties. Players who are caught are prisoners and may be freed as described. The method of capture also differs from that in some other forms of Hide and Seek.

A small goal or den about five feet square is drawn at some central point.

Two leaders are chosen who alternate in choosing players, until all are disposed in two groups. Lots are drawn or counting out resorted to between the captains to determine which side shall start out first. The remaining group takes its place in the den while the opponents go to some distant point, from which they call "Ready!" and immediately scatter and hide.

The group in the den, as soon as they hear the call "Ready!" start out for the chase, leaving one of their number to guard the den. Whenever a player is caught (tagging is not enough; the player must be firmly secured), the catcher calls "Caught! Caught! Caught!" and leads his prisoner to the den. The object of the game is to make prisoners of all of the hiding team. A prisoner may be freed from the den by one of the players from his group running out from his hiding place and tagging him. This may only be done, however, by the rescuer's getting both feet in the den. Should this be accomplished, the rescuer calls "Ring-a-lievio!" as he dashes through the den, and both run for safety. The den keeper tries to catch them as they run away, but may not chase them beyond certain boundaries, which must be determined beforehand. Only one prisoner may be freed at a time. Prisoners are most easily freed when there are several in the den at once and the den keeper's attention is distracted to one side of the den while the prisoners are freed from the other.

This game, like all hiding games, is especially adapted to open spaces, offering many hiding places, such as the edge of a wood, a garden, park, or playground having considerable shrubbery, or to a village street.

RING-TOSS

(See also *Quoits* and *Horseshoe Pitching*.)

2 or 4 players
Indoors; out of doors

Juniors; adults
5 stakes; 4 or 8 rings

Five stakes are driven in the ground in formation as shown in the diagram; or, for indoor use, they may be fastened in a board. The center stake should be eighteen inches above the surface and each of the four shorter ones eight inches above it. The short stakes are ten inches outward from the center. A tossing point, to be toed by each player when throwing, is marked ten or fifteen feet directly in front of one of the shorter stakes. Each player has two rings of wood or rope, not more than one-half inch thick and six inches in diameter, inside measurement. Each pair of rings is colored alike for identification. Players take turns in tossing and at each turn toss both rings. The best

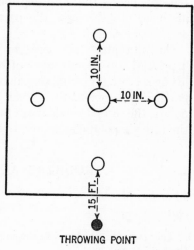

THROWING POINT

RING-TOSS

technique is to hold the ring between the fingers, and with a loose wrist motion toss it edgewise. The object is to land the ring on one of the stakes, this being the only play that scores. The rings are left on the stakes, or wherever they fall, until each player has had his turn, as some rings affect the score of others, which cannot be completed until all are played.

GAME. — Fifty points constitute a game. The first player (or partners) to score this number wins the game.

SCORE. — The center stake scores two points; farther stake five points; right, left, and near stakes one point each.

Topping rings on right, left, and near stakes have no effect on the score of previous players; each ring there scores one point for its thrower whether or not other rings are there before or after it.

On the farthest stake, topping an opponent's ring cancels his score for that ring and adds it to the topper's score. Thus, the first player, having a score of five for one ring, loses this, and the opponent scores ten, — five for his topper plus the five scored by his predecessor. In partnership play, a partner of the first player in the case just mentioned might in turn top the opponent's ring and deprive him of his score, adding it to his own. In this case the partner would make fifteen points on this one ring.

On the center stake a player topping another's ring does not deprive the previous player of his score, but adds one point to his own score for every ring that was there before him, whether partner's or opponent's. Thus the first ring having scored two points, the second would score three points, the third four points, the fifth six points, etc.

ROBBERS AND SOLDIERS

10 to 100 players　　　　　　　　　　*Intermediate*
Out of doors　　　　　　　　　　　*grades to adults*

This game is best played in the country, where there are woods in which the robbers may hide.

The players are divided between robbers and soldiers, there being about ten robbers to fifty soldiers (the proportion of one to five). The larger and stronger players are usually selected for the robbers. The soldiers have one General who directs their movements, and the robbers a Captain. The robbers are given five or ten minutes' start from the prison. The soldiers stand at this place, marked as their fort or prison, until the General gives the command for the search to begin. The object of the robbers is to hide so that the soldiers may not find them, and when found, to resist capture if possible. They may hide by climbing trees or dodging behind them, conceal themselves in underbrush, under dead leaves, etc. If played aright, the game should be a very strenuous one, the resistance offered by the robbers requiring several soldiers to overcome. A robber may resist all of the way to prison. A guard is appointed by the General for the prison, and prisoners may run away at any time if not prevented by the guard.

The soldiers, in attempting to locate the robbers, will use many devices besides a simple hunt. For instance, they will form a large circle and gradually work in toward the center, thus surrounding any robbers who may be hidden within the territory so covered. The game is won when all of the robbers have been made prisoners. Old clothes are quite in order for this game.

The soldiers will find whistles of advantage for signaling each other for help.

This game has been a favorite one for many generations with the boys at a large school near Copenhagen.

ROLLING TARGET

2 to 30 players   *Junior high school*
Gymnasium; playground

This game consists in shooting or hurling a stick or gymnasium wand through a rolling hoop. The hoop may be from six inches to two feet in diameter. The smaller hoop is adapted only to expert players; it is well to begin with a hoop the size of a barrel hoop. Old automobile tires serve well as hoops, and another modern adaptation is to throw beanbags or potatoes instead of sticks.

Where there are numerous players, they are divided into opposing teams, which alternate in throwing at the target (hoop). These players take places at intervals of about five feet along one side of the playground, each holding a spear (stick) to hurl at the hoop as it passes him. Another player stands at one end of the ground and sends the hoop rolling the full length of the space covered by the playing team; its course should be from ten to twenty feet distant from the line-up of the team and parallel to the latter.

As the hoop passes him, each player in turn hurls his spear at it. This is best done with the spear held horizontally at a height of about the middle of the hoop. Each spear that successfully goes through the hoop scores one point for its team. Each team has three rounds, and then gives place to the opponents. The team first scoring one hundred points wins the game.

When there are not enough players to put into teams, each player scores independently, the first to make twenty points winning.

For obvious reasons of safety, no player should be allowed on the side toward which the spears are hurled.

This is an adaptation of one of the hoop and pole games played by the North American Indians, and is almost the only game of theirs that has not been previously adopted by the whites. The instant success of the game with boys, who ask to stay after school to play it, would indicate a valuable acquisition. Different tribes of Indians play with different sized hoops, the illustration showing a very small one. The author is indebted for this to the remarkable collection, *Games of the North American Indians*, by Mr. Stewart Culin.

ROPE JUMPING
(Skipping)

3 to 100 players   *Primary to*
Playground; gymnasium   *intermediate grades*

Jumping a rope is admirable for both boys and girls, combining much skill with invigorating exercise. It should always be done on the toes, with a "spring" in the ankles and knees to break the jar.

There are numerous kinds of jumps or steps.

SINGLE JUMP is a jump from both feet at once, the rope passing under them each time they leave the ground. It is a "choppy" jump, usually employed only when the rope is turned very rapidly.

DOUBLE JUMP consists of a fairly high jump and then a little spring or low jump, both being made with both feet at once unless a hop on one foot is specified. The rope passes under the feet during the higher jump, the little spring being a preparation. This has more rhythm and ease than the single jump.

SKIPPING is a run combined with a low, quick hop made by each foot immediately after its forward step. The rhythm is step-*hop*, step-*hop*, step-*hop*. Ground is gained by the hop (skip) as much as by the step, and it is during this skip that the rope usually passes under the foot.

ROCKING is done without gaining ground. One foot is kept a step forward of the other, the weight shifting or rocking from one to the other to let the rope pass under each in turn.

STUNT STEPS are readily adapted from dance steps or gymnastic movements.

COUNTING. — Jumping for endurance, to see how long one can keep it up, is strongly to be deprecated. All of the rope jumping here described is chosen for skill, agility, interest, and sport. Where repetition of a jump is called for, twenty-five jumps are enough for primary grades and fifty for older players. Rope jumping is used by many adult athletes and ball players as a conditioning exercise, the counts being extended to one hundred. No player with a weak heart should do rope jumping. For others it is excellent exercise.

The different series following are for:
I.   Small single rope.
II. One large rope.
III. Two large ropes.
IV. Large single rope and small individual rope.
V.   Rope jumping for large numbers.

The small single rope or individual rope should be about six feet long for the average player. A good general rule is to have it just long enough to reach to the shoulders on each side while the player is standing on it.

A rope not made with handles at the ends should have a knot tied at either end, to prevent untwisting and to give a firm hold. Every jumper knows how to twist the ends around the hands to shorten too long a rope.

A long rope should be heavy and from ten to twenty feet in length. It should be turned by two players while one or more jump, as indicated. When not needed in athletic competition, any player failing in the jumping should change places with one of the turners; that is, should "take an end."

I. SMALL SINGLE ROPE

1. Standing in one place, the jumper turns the rope forward and jumps on the toes of both feet for from ten to fifty counts. Prolonged jumping to the point of exhaustion should not be done. See note on *Counting* in general directions.

2. Standing in one place, jump five counts on one foot and then five on the other.

3. Jump as in 1 and 2, but turn the rope backward instead of forward.

4. Running and skipping, the rope turned forward.

5. Running and skipping, the rope turned backward.

6. Running and skipping, one player in the rope and two others running and turning the rope. The one who is skipping repeats the verse:

> "Butterfly, butterfly, turn around;
> Butterfly, butterfly, touch the ground;
> Butterfly, butterfly, show your shoe;
> Butterfly, butterfly, twenty-three to do."

7. All of the above with two jumpers, each turning one end of the rope, the inner hands resting on each other's shoulders.

8. As in 7, but with two jumpers, one standing behind the other instead of side by side, a hand of the rear jumper being placed on a hip of the one in front. Each turns one end of the rope.

II. One Large Rope

1. The rope should be turned toward the jumper, who should run under.

2. Rope turned away from the jumper, who runs under.

3. Run in; jump once and run out on the opposite side; the rope turned toward jumper.

4. Run in, jump once, run out on the opposite side; rope turned away from jumper.

5. Repeat 3 and 4, jumping five or more times before running out.

6. Run in, jump once, and run out backward.

7. The player runs in and jumps while the turners say, "Salt, pepper, mustard, cider, vinegar," increasing the speed with which the rope is turned as the word *vinegar* is said.

8. **ROCK THE CRADLE.** — The turners of the rope do not make a complete circle with it, but swing it from side to side in a pendulum motion. In this position the player runs in and jumps from one to five times and runs out on the other side.

9. Run in (*a*) with the rope turned toward the jumper, and then (*b*) away from the jumper, and jump five times and run out,

the hands meanwhile being placed in some particular position, such as held out sideways at shoulder level, clasped behind, placed on the shoulders, or head, or hips, etc.

10. Run in, first with the rope turned toward the jumper and then away from the jumper, and jump in various ways — as on both feet at once; on one foot; on the other foot; on alternate feet with a rocking step, changing from one foot to the other.

11. **CHASE THE FOX.** — The jumpers, instead of taking single turns until each has missed, choose a leader or fox who goes through the various jumps as described, all of the others following in single file. For instance, the fox runs under the rope without skipping; the others all follow. The fox then turns and runs back; the others follow. The fox runs in and takes any of the jumps described above and runs out, the others in turn following.

12. Repeat all of the above jumps, running in in pairs, threes, etc.

13. **CALLING IN.** — A player runs in and jumps three times, calling someone in by name on the second jump. They jump once together, and the first player runs out on the opposite side. The second player, in turn, calls someone in on his second jump, etc.

14. A player runs in, calls someone in on the first jump, and continues jumping to five and then runs out. The player called in calls another on his first jump, etc., until there are five jumping at one time. It will probably be necessary for players to run out on opposite sides.

15. **BEGGING.** — Two players run into the rope and jump together side by side. While jumping, they change places. One player starts this by saying, "Give me some bread and butter"; and the other, while changing, answers, "Try my next-door neighbor." This is continued until one trips.

16. A player runs in, turns halfway around in two jumps, and runs out on the same side.

17. A player runs in, turns all the way around in two jumps, and runs out on the opposite side.

18. **WINDING THE CLOCK.** — A player runs in, counts consecutively from one to twelve, turning halfway around each time, and then runs out.

19. **DROP THE HANDKERCHIEF.** — A player runs in, and while skipping, drops his handkerchief, and on the next jump picks it up again, reciting the lines:

> "Lady, lady, drop your handkerchief;
> Lady, lady, pick it up."

20. **BAKING BREAD.** — A player runs in with a stone in his hand, and while jumping places it on the ground, straightens up, picks up the stone again, and runs out.

21. A player runs in and works his way while skipping toward one end of the rope. He says to the turner at that end, "Father, give me the key." The turner says, "Go to your mother." The player then jumps to the opposite end of the rope and says, "Mother, give me the key"; and the turner at that end answers, "Go to your father." This is continued a certain number of times, or until the player trips.

22. **ROCKING,** as described with the steps, the rope turned as for Rock the Cradle.

III. Two Large Ropes

In this series two ropes are turned at one time, and this requires considerable skill on the part of the turners and a great deal on the part of the jumpers. When two ropes are turned inward toward each other, the turn is called "Double Dodge," or "Double Dutch." When the two ropes are turned outward, away from each other, the turn is called "French Rope."

1. While the two ropes are turned inward, the players run in, jump, or skip over each rope in turn as it comes, and run out on the opposite side.

2. Number one is repeated, taking the fancy jumps described under I for the single rope.

3. The two ropes are turned outward, and the players run in, jump, and run out, as described above.

4. **CHASE THE FOX.** — This is played with the ropes turning either Double Dodge, or French Rope, and any of the fancy jumps mentioned previously are taken, the players going through in single file, following a leader, the fox, who chooses the feat which all are to perform.

IV. Large Single Rope and Small Individual Rope

While two turners keep the large rope turning, a player turning and skipping his own small rope goes through the following feats:

1. The player stands in and jumps five times, both the large and small ropes starting together. He then runs out forward.

2. While turning and skipping his own individual rope, the player runs under the large rope.

3. The player runs in while his own rope is turning, jumps five times, and runs out on the opposite side.

4. The player stands in, jumps five times, and runs out backward.

5. The player runs in while turning his individual rope backward, jumps three times, and runs out.

6. A player jumps in the large rope, at the same time turning and jumping in his own individual rope. Another player runs in, facing him, in the small rope, jumps with him, and then runs out again without stopping either rope.

V. Rope Jumping for Large Numbers

RELAY ROPE JUMPING. — Rope jumping may be made one of the most interesting competitive games for large numbers, lined up in relay formation and jumping in turn over a long rope. There should then be one rope for each line. A score should be kept for each team, each feat successfully performed by a player scoring one point for his or her team. For each round, each player in all teams should perform the same feat.

KEEP THE KETTLE BOILING. — Another excellent use of rope jumping for large numbers is described by the National Recreation Association in its collection of *88 Successful Play Activities*, under the title of "Keep the Kettle Boiling." "Ropes are placed at suitable intervals around the playground or radiating from the center. The players form in twos, threes, or fours, and at a signal all run round the course, jumping each rope in turn. The object of the game is to keep the jumping continuous; the ropes should therefore be quite low at first. Later they may be raised slightly, but they should be adjusted to the capacity of the weakest jumper."

ROUND AND ROUND WENT THE GALLANT SHIP

4 to 30 or more players   *Primary grades*
Indoors; out of doors

This is a simple little game for very little children, consisting merely in dancing around in a circle with clasped hands as the following verse is recited, and "bobbing" down quickly as the ship goes to the bottom of the sea:

> "Three times round went our gallant ship,
> And three times round went she;
> Three times round went our gallant ship,
> Then she sank to the bottom of the sea."

A tumble as the ship goes down adds much to the spirit of the play.

RUN, SHEEP, RUN!

10 to 30 or more players   *Intermediate grades*
Out of doors

This is a form of Hide and Seek, but the hiding and the seeking are done by teams instead of individually, each team acting under the direction of a captain. Any number of players may take part, but from four to six on a side are perhaps best.

Two captains are chosen, who in turn alternately choose players until all the players are divided into two teams. One team becomes a searching party (chosen by lot, "holders," or counting out between the captains) and remains at the goal, while the other team goes out with its captain, who directs the various individuals where to hide, after agreeing with his team on a series of signals to be used, as described below. When all are hidden, this captain goes back to the searchers, who at once start out on the hunt under the direction of their captain, who may divide or dispose of his team as he sees fit. The captain of the hiding team remains with the searchers, calling out signals to his hidden men which will enable them to approach nearer to the goal by dodging from one hiding place to another, always trying to keep out of sight of the searchers. Neither team, however, may run for the goal until its own captain shouts "Run, sheep, run!" The captain of the hiding party is generally the first one to give this signal, and he does so whenever he thinks his men are well placed to make the goal. The captain of the searchers naturally gives the signal to his players as soon as he hears his competitor calling it, as the game is won by the team of which one player first reaches the goal.

Should any member of the searching party catch sight of an opposing player before all run for the goal, he tells his captain, who at once shouts, "Run, sheep, run!"

Any signals may be agreed on between the captain of the hiding party and his men; the following are examples:

"Red!"   meaning "Danger."

"Green!"   meaning "Go around the house to the left."

"Blue!"   meaning "Go around the house to the right."

"Purple!" meaning "Stand still."

"Yellow!" meaning "Keep on going in the same direction and get nearer to the goal."

SARDINES

10 to 30 or more players   *Juniors; adults*
Playground; house party

This is a game of hide and seek that reverses some of the usual methods of playing the game. The player chosen to be It, instead of blinding goes out himself to hide, while all of the other players stay at the goal. While one of their number counts one hundred, they must all either blind their eyes or be shut in one room to give the hider a fair chance. After counting, they shout "One hundred!" and all start out to hunt for the hider. Any player discovering him must, after making sure that none of the others observe him, hide in the same place with the hider. If necessary, he must linger near until there is opportunity to do this without being discovered. If there should not be room to hide in the same place, the finder must take a seat in plain sight near the hiding place. Sometimes a large number of players will be seated in a room or in a group out of doors, while the last unfortunate hunters try to locate some clever hiding place which is obviously near but hard to detect. Of course, it is better for the players actually to hide with the first hider, if practicable, which probably suggested, on occasion, being "packed in like sardines."

This is one of the most interesting house party games for young people for either out of doors or within.

SCHOOLROOM AUTOMOBILE RACE

20 to 30 players at once   *Elementary grades*
Schoolroom

This schoolroom game is played with most of the class sitting, being a relay race between alternate rows. The first child in each alternate row, at a signal from the teacher, leaves his seat on the right side, runs forward around his seat and then to the rear, completely encircling his row of seats, until his own is again reached. As soon as he is seated, the child next behind him encircles the row of seats, starting to the front on the right side and running to the rear on the left side. This continues until the last child has encircled the row and regained his seat. The row wins whose last player is first seated. The remaining alternate rows then play, and lastly the two winning rows may compete for the championship.

The interest may be increased by calling the race an international one, the teacher providing small flags of different nations, or the children may cut and paint these of paper. The first child in each row chooses the country he will represent by the selection of a flag at the beginning of the game. This he places on the rear desk, and it is held aloft by the last player when he regains his seat, indicating that his country has come in first, second, etc., in the automobile race.

SCHOOLROOM TAG

10 to 60 players   *Primary to*
Schoolroom   *intermediate grades*

A circle about three feet in diameter is drawn on the floor in the front of the room and serves as a goal. One player is chosen to be It, and stands ten feet from the goal. The other players sit at their desks. The one who is It calls the name of some player, who must at once rise and try to run through the goal and return to his seat without being tagged. In order to do this, he may have to make quite a detour before passing through the goal, or he may be able to run through it at the opening of the chase. The chaser must also run through the goal before he may tag the runner. If the chaser succeeds in tagging the runner, he continues to be chaser, and calls the name of another player to run. If the runner gets to his seat without being tagged, he changes places with the other and becomes It.

SHADOW TAG

4 to 60 players   *Primary grades*
Out of doors

This is a very pretty form of tag, suitable for little children, and they delight in playing it. It hardly need be said that it requires a sunny day.

The player who is It tries to step or jump on to the shadow of some other player, and if successful, announces the fact by calling the name of the player. That player then becomes It.

The teacher or leader will need to encourage the children to venture boldly into the open spaces, where the shadows become apparent, rather than to huddle on one side of the ground, where the chaser cannot reach the shadows.

SHUFFLEBOARD

2 or 4 players   *Junior high school to adults*
Floor; pavement; ship deck   *8 wooden disks; cues*

The game consists in "shooting" (shoving) flat wooden disks over a diagramed surface to score according to where they finally rest. A player may displace his opponent's disks as well as land his own.

EQUIPMENT. — Disks are of wood one inch in thickness and six inches in diameter. Eight of these are needed for a game and are painted for opposing teams, four being blue and four red.

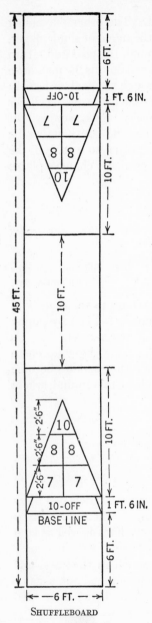

SHUFFLEBOARD

Special cues about five feet long (six feet three inches maximum) are used for playing the disks. Cues are round to within a few inches of the lower end, where they broaden into a blade three inches wide which is curved to fit the disks.

This equipment may be had ready made, or it is easily constructed, especially with a turning lathe.

COURT. — The court is a narrow lane six feet wide and forty-four feet eight inches in length. Six feet from each end is drawn a baseline, and one foot four inches inward from this another line, the two enclosing a space called a "10-off" area. It is from here that disks are shot. Still farther in towards the center is a triangle seven and one-half feet from the 10-off area to its apex. This triangle is divided into five spaces, each two and one-half feet in height, with scoring values marked in each, as in the illustration. The points of the two triangles are fifteen feet distant from each other; two and one-half feet inward from each point or apex is drawn a dead line across the court. The two dead lines are ten feet apart.

THE GAME may be played as singles (*i.e.* by two opposing players) or as doubles (*i.e.* by four players in opposing teams of two each).

In either singles or doubles a player places his disks in his half of the 10-off area and shoots them from there towards the scoring area at the opposite end of the court. He may not himself step on or over the base line. For violation of either of these rules he loses five points from his score.

In singles the two players stand side by side at the same end, one playing from the right half of the 10-off area, and the other from the left. Right plays first, then left, and so on alternately until all the disks are shot. The players then exchange places for the next round and so on until a game score is reached. The winner of the game is first to play in the next game.

In doubles two opponents play side by side from one end of the court and the other two from the opposite end. Partners are thus at opposite ends from each other. All eight disks are played from one end and then from the other. Each team plays only its own colored disks and the two opponents at a given end alternate in play: thus, of the two opponents at one end, red plays a disk, then blue a disk, then red, etc., until all eight are played. The disks then go to the other end.

SCORE. — Fifty points constitute a game.

A disk scores the value of the area in which it is finally at rest after all eight disks have been shot, so the score cannot be determined until the eight plays have been made. Thus a disk may be shot to space eight, but, if a later disk sends it to ten or seven, and it remains there at the close of the play, its score is ten or seven; or should it rest in the 10-off area, that number of points is taken from the player's score. If a disk is hit out of the scoring area or so that it rests on a line, it scores nothing, whether sent to this position by the original player or his opponent.

Disks that do not pass the farther dead line are out of play ("dead") and must be at once removed from the court.

If each side makes more than fifty points the higher score wins.

A tie is settled by shooting the eighth disk twice from each end, the side thus achieving the higher score being the winner.

SHUTTLE RELAY

(Double Relay)

20 to 100 players
Playground; gymnasium

Intermediate grades
to senior high school

This form of relay race is especially adapted to large numbers in limited space. The action is more rapid than in the single relay, although each runner runs only half as far.

TEAM 1	TEAM 2	TEAM 3
10, V	X	✶
8, V	X	✶
6, V	X	✶
4, V	X	✶
2, V	X	✶

50' TO 100'

TEAM 1	TEAM 2	TEAM 3
1, Λ	X	★
3, Λ	X	★
5, Λ	X	★
7, Λ	X	★
9, Λ	X	★

SINGLE RELAY

The players are divided into two or more teams of equal size, and each team, in turn, arranged in two divisions which stand facing each other in single file, with the leader of each division toeing a starting line. The starting lines should be from fifty to one hundred and fifty feet apart. On signal, the leaders on one side of the ground (Numbers One) run forward and "touch off" (touch the outstretched hand of) the leaders of the file facing them (Numbers Two). On receiving the touch-off Numbers Two run to touch Numbers Three, who have moved up to the starting line, Threes give the touch-off to Fours, Fours to Fives, and so on until both divisions of the team have run. Each player thus runs only in one direction instead of two, as in the single relay, unless it is understood that the play is to keep on for another round.

Each player, as he gives the touch-off passes off the field past the rear of the file he has reached, if the game is being run as an athletic event. In most other races, each runner lines up with the file he has reached, standing at its rear, and moving forward with the file one place each time a runner leaves the mark, so that at the end each file stands lined up on the opposite side of the field from which it started.

The team wins whose last player is first to dash across the starting line opposite him, if it is an athletic event. In less formal races, in which the runners line up at the rear of the file, the team wins whose last runner is first to reach this position and raise his arm as a finish signal.

If the game is played with strict observance of athletic rules, the first runners should be started with the signals, "On your mark!" "Get set!" (or "Get ready!") and "Go!" There should be a judge to watch fouls for each division of each team, and two judges at the finish. Fouls consist in starting over the line, even with part of the foot, before being touched off, or in a failure to actually touch. The teams win in the order of finishing, plus consideration of the number of fouls, as described for the Potato Shuttle Relay.

SIEGE

10 to 30 players   *Intermediate grades*
Out of doors; barn

This game is suitable for a barn; the greater the number of open doors and windows available in the barn the better.

The players are divided into two equal parties, one of which personates defenders, and takes their places in the barn, with the doors and windows open. The other party is the besiegers, and is stationed outside the barn. The fighting is done by means of weeds specially prepared for the purpose. The weeds commonly called redroot or iron-weed are very good for this. The stems, measuring about a foot and a half in length, are stripped except for a small leaf or tuft of leaves at one end. On the opposite end the root is cut away so as to leave only a small knob which will serve to weight the missile.

The game opens with each party provided with a pile of this ammunition, which is thrown at the opponents through the doors and windows of the barn. A player hit once with a dart is considered "wounded," but may keep on playing. A player hit twice is "killed," and is out of the game. Each party must keep within its own bounds.

The party wins which has the fewest killed at the end of the game.

This was a favorite game with a group of Long Island boys, from one of whom the author obtained it.

SINGLE RELAY RACE

10 to 100 players   *Primary grades*

Playground; gymnasium

This game differs from the track event known as a Relay Race. The form here given is one of the best for engaging in strenuous exercise all of a large number of players in a limited playing space.

A wall or fence is chosen for a goal, or a line may be drawn across the ground for this purpose, or a goal object may be placed for each team, around which each player on the team must run. From fifty to a hundred feet back of this goal, or objective point, and parallel to it, a line is drawn to serve as a starting line.

The players are divided into two or more groups of equal numbers. Each group lines up in single file behind the starting line. If possible, there should be at least five feet distance sideways between the files. The first player of each file stands toeing the starting line, and at a signal runs forward to the goal,

SINGLE RELAY FORMATION

touches it with his hand if it is a wall or fence, or with his foot if it is a line on the ground, or runs around it if it is an object. He then runs back to his line and touches the outstretched hand of the next player (called the "touch-off"), who should have moved forward to toe the starting line. As soon as this touch is received, this player in turn runs forward, touches the goal, and returns in the same way. Each player as he returns leaves the playing space by the rear for a strictly athletic game, or, in other games, lines up with his file at the rear. In the latter case, the last runner on each team lifts his arm as a finish-signal when he joins the file. The file moves up one place each time that a runner starts, so that the next player will toe the starting line.

In an athletic race the file wins whose last runner is first to dash across the starting line on his return run. If desired, each runner may hold a flag in his hand and pass it to the next player, instead of merely touching the hand. This flag should not be on a stick, which is dangerous for the eyes of the runner receiving it.

Starting over the line before being touched by a returning runner is a foul. Where athletic procedure is not observed, this starting over the line may be penalized by having the transgressor go back and start over again. In an athletic event it disqualifies the team, unless the competing teams have made an equal or greater number of fouls.

Where this game is played in strict athletic form, the first start is made in response to the usual signals: (1) "On your mark!" (2) "Get set!" (or "Get ready!") (3) "Go!" In competitive events of this sort, crossing the starting line before being touched off is a foul; also touching a goal object around which the players may have to run. There should be a judge of fouls for each team and two judges at the finish. The team wins which finishes first with the fewest number of fouls, as explained for the Potato Race. The simple "touch-off," and not the handing of flags, is customary in athletic procedure.

SKIP–AWAY

(See *Slap Jack*)

SKYTE THE BOB

NOTE. — The word "skyte" means a sharp, glancing blow, and as here used indicates the way in which the stones are thrown at the "bob."

This game is played with buttons and stones. Each player is provided with one or more buttons called "men." A small, flat stone about the size of a quarter may be used as a man in place of a button. In addition, each player is provided with a flat stone called a "pitcher." A flat stone, small, but somewhat larger than the pitchers, is placed on the ground as a base on which the men are piled, and is called the "bob." The game consists in hitting the bob with a pitcher so as to knock over the pile of men, the men becoming the property of the thrower or not, according to their position as they fall.

From fifteen to twenty-five feet from the pile of men a line is drawn from which the players throw. Each player in turn toes the line and throws his pitcher so as to strike the bob or base under the pile of men, his object being to make these men fall off. Any men that are knocked off, and lie nearer to the pitcher where it fell than to the bob, become the property of the player who threw the pitcher. The second player then takes his turn, but his play is more difficult than that of the first player, as any men that he drives nearer to the first player's pitcher belong to the latter. Any man which lies nearer to the second player's pitcher, however, than to the bob or to the first player's pitcher, belongs to this second player. This is continued by the different players in succession, the player winning who has the largest number when all of the men are disposed of, or when all have thrown.

SLAP CATCH

(Hands Up)

The players stand in a circle, with one in the center. Those in the circle bend their elbows, which should touch the sides, and extend their hands in front, with palms downward. The object of the one in the center is to slap the hands of any player in the circle while thus extended. The circle players may bend the hands downward or sideways at the wrist, but may not withdraw the arms, or change the position of the elbow. Anyone slapped in this way changes places with the one in the center.

The success of this game will depend upon the alertness of the one who is in the center, who should dodge quickly and unexpectedly from one part of the circle to another, with many feints and false moves that will keep the circle players uncertain where he is going to slap next. Played in this way, the game calls for much alertness on the part of all concerned. The circle should not be too large, or the action will be too slow to be interesting.

SCHOOLROOM.—In the schoolroom this is played in groups with the players seated instead of in a circle. Two rows face each other to form a group, with feet drawn well under the seats. The one who is It walks up and down the aisle.

SLAP JACK

(Herr Slap Jack; Skip-Away)

10 to 30 or more players   *Primary grades*
Playground; gymnasium; parlor

The players stand in a circle, clasping hands. One player runs around the outside of the circle and tags another as he runs. The player tagged immediately leaves his place and runs in the opposite direction. The object of both runners is to get back first to the vacant place. Whoever succeeds wins, and remains in that place, the one left out becoming runner the next time.

This is sometimes varied by having the players bow and shake hands as they meet, lock arms and swing once around, or go through some other performance to avoid a collision. This adds an element of self-control, but detracts from the vigor and sport of the game. This game is one of the standard favorites for little children.

SCHOOLROOM.—In the schoolroom this game is played with all of the pupils seated except one. The odd player walks or runs through the aisles, touches some player, and runs on around the room in the direction he is going. The one touched at once leaves his seat and runs around the room in the opposite direction. The one wins who first gets back to the vacant seat. Dodging through aisles to shorten distance is not allowed; the run must be around the outer aisles of the room.

SLIPPER SLAP

10 to 30 or more players   *Primary grades*
Indoors; out of doors

This game is played with a slipper, or a piece of paper folded in several thicknesses to present a surface of about three by eight inches, firm but flexible. This may be crumpled at one end to form a sort of handle, if desired.

One player is chosen to stand in the center. The others stand in a circle, shoulder to shoulder, so that the center player cannot see what goes on behind their backs. The players then pass the slipper from hand to hand behind their backs, taking every favorable opportunity to slap the one in the center with it; but instantly that this is done the player holding the slipper must put it again behind his back and pass it to the next player, to avoid being caught with the slipper in his hand. The one in the center should try to catch any player who thus slaps him before the slipper is passed to another player.

Very rapid action and much sport may be had from this game. It is rulable to hit the center player with nothing but the slipper, but the players will use any other feints they choose to mislead him as to who holds the slipper, pretending to pass it, or making a false move as though to hit him, etc. The center player must catch one of the circlemen with the slipper actually in his hands to have it count. Should this be done, he changes places with that player.

This game may be played in the schoolroom, the class being divided into groups of ten or twelve players each. It is also an excellent parlor game, and is full of sport if played by quick, alert players.

This game is from Denmark.

SMUGGLING THE GEG

10 to 30 or more players   *Children to adults*
Out of doors; camp

This is an old Scotch game, evidently an outgrowth of smuggling. The "geg" is a small treasure or object easily handled, such as a pocket knife, key, marble, etc.

The players are divided into two even teams, one called the "Outs" and the other the "Ins." A den about four feet by six in size is marked on the ground in some central place. Both teams agree on boundaries beyond which it is unfair to go, though the space available for play should be very considerable. It is determined by lot or by counting out which of the teams shall be the first Outs, or smugglers, this being the more desirable position. The Outs have the geg, or treasure, which they give to one of their number in a manner that leaves his identity unknown to the Ins. They may do this by going out of sight around a corner of a building and choosing one of their number to take the geg, or by standing in a row within sight of the Ins, with their backs to a wall or fence, and pass the geg from hand to hand behind their backs, making many feints and passes intended to deceive the onlookers.

When the geg has been deposited with one of their number, the Outs run and hide, but before reaching their final hiding place, must give a call of "Smugglers!" This is the signal for the Ins to start on the chase. The object of the Ins is to catch the one player among the Outs who is custodian of the geg. The identity of this player may be a sheer matter of surmise on their part, when they will have to challenge any player whom they may catch. If the player holding the geg can return to the den without being caught, his team wins, and again goes out for the next game. But if the holder of the geg be caught before he gets to the den, the Ins win the game, and become the Outs for the next round.

Whenever one of the Ins catches one of the Outs, the latter is not a prisoner until he is "crowned"; that is, the pursuer must hold him, take off his cap, and place the palm of his hand on the prisoner's head, when he must cease to struggle. The pursuer then demands, "Deliver up the geg!" which must be done at once should this particular smuggler be the one who holds it. This fact is then shouted aloud, and all of the players return to the den.   If the player caught should not have the geg, he is allowed to go free.

Of course it is to the interest of the Outs to engage the attention of the Ins as much as possible upon players who do not hold the geg, thus to give the holder of it a chance to make the den and so win for his party.

SNOW DART

2 to 10 players
For the snow

Children
to adults

This game is played with a wooden dart about eight inches long, whittled out of wood about the size of a broomstick, pointed

SNOW DART

abruptly at one end, and sloping gradually to the other.   A narrow track or slide is made down the side of a hill or inclined place, about sixty feet in length.   At four different points in this track snow barriers or bumpers are made.   The track is iced by throwing water over it and letting it freeze.

The dart is started at a point at the top of the track.   It is not rulable to shove it; it must simply be placed on the track and move of its own weight.   The object of the game is to pass the dart in this way over as many of the barriers as possible without its leaving the track.   Each player scores one point for each barrier over which the dart passes without leaving the track, the one having the highest score at the end of the playing time winning. The players take turns in sliding the dart.   Any player who can successfully pass his dart over all four barriers four times in succession wins, irrespective of other scores.   If desired, the players may play in partners.

This game is an adaptation from one played by the Cree Indians.   For it the author is indebted to Mr. Stewart Culin's *Games of the North American Indians.*

SNOW SNAKE

2 to 10 or more players   *Children*
For the snow   *to adults*

This game is played by skimming or skipping sticks over the hard surface of the snow, as stones are skipped over the water. Each player is provided with from three to five small sticks. These may be especially whittled, or they may be pieces of branches. A perfectly smooth stick is best, and one that has some weight to it. Each stick is notched, one notch on the first, two on the second, three on the third, etc.

The players stand at a given line and take turns in skimming their sticks over the surface of the snow, each player throwing but one stick at a time. When each player has thrown, the stick that has gone the farthest scores for the thrower according to the number of notches on it. For instance, if the stick had but one notch, it scores one point for the player; a three-notched stick scores three points, etc. The sticks are then gathered up and put to one side, and each player in turn throws the next stick in his bunch, the successful player of the first round having the first throw in the second round, and scoring in similar manner. This is continued until all of the sticks have been thrown. This may close the game, which is won by the highest scorer, or it may be repeated indefinitely, either with a time limit or until a certain score is reached.

This game is an adaptation of one played by the Wabanaki Indians. The Northern Indians have many games belonging to the Snow Snake class.

SPANS

2 to 10 players   *Intermediate grades*
Out of doors; indoors

This is a game played by snapping buttons against a wall, their landing point determining a score. Each player has a button. One of the players lays his button on the ground near a wall or fence. The others, in turn, snap their buttons against the wall so as to rebound near to that of the first player. Should the button snapped drop within one hand reach or span (*i.e.* the distance between stretched thumb and fingers) of the button first laid down, it scores two points for the player throwing it. If it comes within two such spans of the first button, it scores one point. Should it hit this button and bounce away within but one span, it counts four points. Should it so bounce within two spans, it scores three points; and should it go farther than this, it scores but one point. The number of points in the game, twenty-five or fifty, is agreed on at the outset. The players take regular turns, and the first to score the required number wins the game.

SPIN THE PLATTER
(See also *My Lady's Toilet*.)

10 to 30 or more players　　　　　　　　　　　*Children*
Parlor; schoolroom

All the players are numbered and seated in a circle, except one, who stands in the center and twirls a platter, tray, or some other round object. As he starts it spinning, he calls any number that he chooses, and the player bearing that number must at once spring forward and try to catch the platter before it ceases to spin and falls to the floor. If successful, he returns to his place in the circle. If not successful, he takes the place of the spinner and pays a forfeit. The forfeits are all redeemed at the end of the game.

This game may also be played by calling the players by name instead of numbering them.

SPOKE RELAY
(Circle or Star Relay)

9 to 60 or more players　　　　　　　　　*Junior high school*
Playground; gymnasium

The players stand in three or more divisions in single file, facing to a common center. In this formation they radiate like the spokes of a wheel. On a signal from a leader, the outer player of each file faces to the right. On a second signal, these outer players all run in a circle in the direction in which they are facing. The object of the game is to see which runner will first get back to his place. The one winning scores one point for his line. Immediately upon the announcement of the score, these runners all step to the inner end of their respective files, facing to the center, the files moving backward to make room for them.

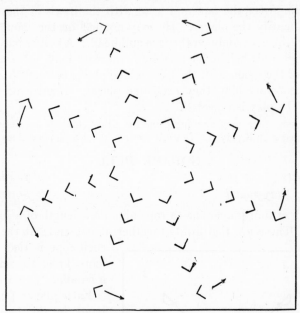

SPOKE RELAY

The signals are repeated, and those who are now at the outer end of each file face and then run, as did their predecessors. The line scoring the highest when all have run wins the game.

This game may be varied by having the players start facing either outward or in the direction of the run; and they may go through the game without any commands except for the start of the first runners.

SPOONING

10 to 30 players   *Children*
Children's party; adult house party   *adults*

All but one of the players stand in a circle. The odd player is blindfolded and placed in the center. He is given two silver tablespoons. The players in the circle clasp hands and move around until the blindfolded player clicks the spoons together, at which signal the circle must stand still.

The blindfolded player then goes up to anyone in the circle, and by feeling over the face and head with the bowls of the spoons must identify the player. He may not feel on the shoulders or around the neck, only on the face and head. A player may stoop to disguise his height for this, but otherwise may not evade the touch of the spoons. If the blindfolded player correctly identifies the one before him, they exchange places. If incorrect in his guess, the play is repeated.

This may be a very amusing game for either children or adults. The author has seen it played with great success under both conditions.

SQUARE PULL

4 Players   *Intermediate —*
Camp; playground   *to junior high*

Each of four players has a rope about the length of a jumping rope. These are tied firmly together at one end; at the other,

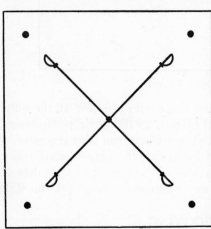

SQUARE PULL

each rope is tied into a loop knot to serve as a handle.

Each player puts one hand in the handle of his rope, and the four stride out in four opposite directions as far as the ropes will stretch. Two yards farther out from each player is set up an Indian club or other object which he is to try to pick up. The game consists of a tug-of-war, each player trying to pull the others far enough in his direction to enable him to pick up his club. The one who first does this wins.

This is a Russian game.

SQUIRREL AND NUT

10 to 60 players   *Primary grades*

Schoolroom

All of the pupils but one sit at their desks with heads bowed on the arms as though sleeping, but each with a hand outstretched. The odd player, who is the squirrel, and carries a nut, runs on tiptoe up and down through the aisles, and at his or her discretion drops the nut into one of the waiting hands. The player who gets the nut at once jumps up from his seat and chases the squirrel, who is safe only when he reaches his nest (seat). Should the squirrel be caught before he reaches his nest, he must be squirrel the second time. Otherwise the player who received the nut becomes the next squirrel.

It is scarcely necessary to say that the other players wake up to watch the chase.

SQUIRREL IN TREES

10 to 100 players   *Primary grades*

Schoolroom; playground; gymnasium

This game is very like Hound and Rabbit, but is a little less exciting, and under some circumstances better adapted to very young children.

Most of the players stand in groups of three, with hands on each other's shoulders, forming hollow trees. In each tree is a player representing a squirrel, and there is also one odd squirrel without a tree. The teacher or leader claps her hands, when all of the players must run for other trees, and the odd squirrel tries to secure a tree, the one who is left out being the odd squirrel next time.

STAGE COACH

10 to 60 or more players   *Intermediate*

Parlor; schoolroom; gymnasium

A leader is chosen who has a faculty for telling a story. This leader gives to each of the players the name of some part of a stage coach or of its contents. Thus, one may be the whip, one the wheels, one the cushions, one the windows, others the brake, driver, harness, horses, passengers, including specifically the fat old gentleman, the woman with the bandbox, etc.

Where there are many players, several may be given the same name, though it is desirable that these should not all be seated near together. The leader then tells a story in which the various parts of a stage coach are mentioned, and whenever he names one of these parts or articles, the player or players bearing that name must get up instantly, whirl around once, and sit down again. Any player failing to do this must pay a forfeit. Whenever the story teller says "Stage Coach!" all of the players must get up and turn around. At the end of this story he will manage to have the stage coach meet with a catastrophe, and as soon as he says "The stage coach upset!" all of the players must change seats. The leader takes this opportunity to secure one for himself, and the player who is left without a seat becomes leader for the next game, or must distribute the forfeits. For large numbers there should be several more players than chairs.

The leader may say, for example: "It being a beautiful spring day, the *old lady with the bandbox* [here the old lady must get up and turn around] decided to visit her daughter, and so took a *seat* in the *stage coach* [everybody turns around]; she found the *cushions* [cushions turn around] very comfortable until the *fat old gentleman* [fat old gentleman turns around] got in, when the place seemed to her very crowded, and she was glad to open the *windows;* the *driver* cracked his *whip,* the *wheels* creaked, the *horses* strained at the *harness,* and away they started on their journey," etc.

The interest of the game may be enhanced by connecting the stage coach, its passengers, and the journey with some well-known story, as of Mr. Pickwick and Sam Weller, or Rebecca of Sunnybrook Farm.

STAKE GUARD

(See also *Duck on a Rock*.)

10 to 30 players   *Intermediate grades*
Playground; gymnasium   *to junior high school*

This game is one of the forms of Duck on a Rock, and in this form is well adapted to use indoors as well as out of doors. The game differs from the ordinary games of Duck on a Rock chiefly in the limited territory to which the guard is confined.

A stake is driven in the ground (or if in a gymnasium, an Indian club is placed) in the center of a square plainly marked, and measuring from eight to twelve feet. A throwing line is drawn twenty or more feet from the stake. The game is played with beanbags, and begins with the choice of a guard. This choice is made by all of the players standing on the throwing line and throwing their bags at the stake. The player whose bag falls farthest away from the stake becomes the first guard.

The stake guard places his bag on top of the stake (or club). The other players line up on the throwing line. Upon a given signal from a leader or captain, all of the players throw their bags simultaneously at the stake, trying to displace the bag on top of it. Knocking over the club accomplishes the same purpose. Each player must then try to regain his bag, but in doing this he may be tagged by the guard. If this be done, he changes places with the guard. The guard may only tag a player, however, within the limits of the square surrounding the stake, beyond which he may not go; and he may do this only after he has replaced his own bag on top of the stake.

Any player failing to recover his bag at once will watch for an opportunity to do so when the guard is next occupied in replacing his own bag. Any player thus waiting for his bag may linger near the boundaries of the center square.

Should the guard succeed in tagging a player within the square, that player must at once place his own bag on the stake; and the guard must try to get his bag and escape from the square before this new guard can place his bag and tag him. As soon as a player recovers his bag and escapes from the center square, he should go at once to the starting line, and may throw again immediately for the center bag. The game progresses better, however, if all of the throwing be done simultaneously, the returning players waiting for a signal from the leader before throwing.

As players become proficient, the game may be made more skillful and interesting by increasing the distance between the throwing line and the stake, and also by lessening the size of the square drawn around the stake, in which the guard is confined.

STATUES

(See *Step*)

STEALING STICKS

(See also *Prisoner's Base.*)

10 to 30 or more players   *Intermediate grades*
Playground; gymnasium   *to junior high school*

STEALING STICKS

The ground is divided into two equal parts, with a small goal marked off at the rear of each part, in which six sticks are placed. Each player who reaches the enemy's goal safely may carry one stick back to his own goal, and may not be caught while carrying it back. If caught in the enemy's territory before reaching the goal, a player must remain a prisoner in the goal until touched by one of his own side; neither may be caught while returning. Any player may catch any opponent, except under the rules just stated. No stick may be taken by a side while any of its men are prisoners. The game is won by the side gaining all of the sticks.

This game is known also by the name of Scots and English and probably originated in border warfare. The players sometimes contribute some article of wearing apparel to the pile of property that is to be stolen instead of using sticks for the purpose. Caps and coats are the usual donations.

STEP

(*Statues*)

5 to 30 or more players   *Children*
Playground; gymnasium   *to adults*

The ground is marked off by two parallel lines from fifty to two hundred feet apart. One player, who is chosen to be counter, stands on one of these lines with his back to the other players, who line up on the opposite line.

The object of the game is for the players who are lined up in the rear to advance forward until they cross the line where the counter is stationed. They may only advance, however, by short stages, during which the player in front counts ten.

The game starts by this forward player's counting ten loudly and rapidly, the other players moving forward while he does this; but immediately when he says "Ten!" they must stand still, and he at once turns to look at them. He will call the name of any player or players whom he sees moving, and any so called must go back to the starting line and begin over again. This counting of ten by the one player and moving forward of the others continues until all have crossed the line where the counter stands. The last one over changes places with him for the next game.

This game is a great favorite, especially with girls, though the writer has known many boys to play it persistently. The players will learn to use much caution in moving forward, often stopping before the count of ten, to be sure that they shall not be caught in motion. The progress thus made may seem slower than that of those who dash forward to the last moment, but as with the famous hare and tortoise, this slower but continuous method often wins.

STATUES. — This form of the game is adapted to a small room or limited space. Instead of running forward, each player then merely changes his pose, the one who is It calling (after his count of ten) the name of anyone whom he sees in motion.

STILL POND; NO MORE MOVING!

(Still water, still water, stop!)

5 to 30 or more players   *Primary to*
Parlor; gymnasium; playground   *intermediate grades*

One player is blindfolded; the others scatter promiscuously. The blindfolded player is led to the center of the playground, and asked:

"How many horses has your father in his stable?"

He replies, "Three."

"What color are they?"

"Black, white, and gray."

"Turn around three times and catch whom you may."

The blindfolded player is then spun around so as to confuse his sense of direction. He then says, "Still pond; no more moving!" whereupon the other players must stand still, being allowed only three steps thereafter. The blindfolded player begins to grope for the others. When he catches one, he must guess by touching the hair, dress, etc., whom he has caught. If he guesses correctly, the player changes places with him. If incorrectly, he must go on with his search. The players may resort to any reasonable devices for escaping the hands of the groping blind man, such as stooping or dodging, so long as they do not take more than three steps. When caught, a player may try to disguise his identity by making himself shorter, etc.

STONE

10 to 30 or more players   *Intermediate grades*
Playground; gymnasium

A large circle is drawn on the ground or floor in the center of the play space. At either end of the ground a goal is marked off. One player, chosen to be stone, sits on the floor in the circle. The other players stand around outside the circle, taunting the stone by stepping over into his territory. Suddenly, and the more unexpectedly the better, the stone rises and runs for the other players, who are only safe from tagging when behind one of the goals. Anyone so tagged becomes a stone and joins the first

stone in sitting near the center of the circle.   They also join him
in chasing the other players whenever he gives the signal.   This
continues until all the players have been tagged.

STOOP TAG

("Squat" Tag)

4 to 60 or more players   *Primary grades*
Indoors; out of doors   *to senior high school*

One player is It and chases the others, trying to tag one of them.
A player may escape being tagged by suddenly stooping or
"squatting"; but each player may stoop but three times.   After
the third time of stooping, the player may resort only to running
to escape being tagged.   Any player tagged becomes It.

For large numbers of players there should be several taggers.

STUNT RACES

10 to 100 players   *Children to*
Indoors; out of doors   *adults*

An almost endless variety of stunts, feats, obstacles, and
handicaps may be required of runners in either single or shuttle-
relay races.   The chapter on *Stunts and Contests; Feats and Forfeits* contains many of the most interesting of these, and others
are described in relay games.   Typical examples of positions of
the body that may be required throughout a race are to be found
in the Hopping Race, Jumping Race, and Japanese Crab Race;
the use of obstacles to be negotiated during the run are illustrated
in the Potato Race and Leapfrog; feats to be performed at the
end of the run are shown in the All-Up Relay, while Couple Race
illustrates what may be done when the two runners meet in shuttle
relays.

In selecting feats or stunts to be used in these ways, the conditions under which a game is to be used will largely determine
the choice: that is, whether the game is to cultivate skill or
agility, or whether it is for sheer fun as on social occasions.

SUN DIAL

2 to 10 players   *Primary to*
Gymnasium; playground; seashore   *intermediate grades*

A circle from twelve to twenty feet in diameter is drawn on the ground. This is intersected with straight lines, like the spokes of a wheel, which divide it into twelve sections, numbered consecutively and clockwise from one to twelve.

One player is blindfolded, placed in the center (on the hub of the wheel), and turned around several times to confuse his sense

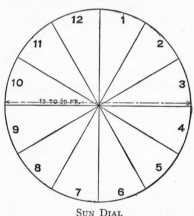

SUN DIAL

of direction. He then walks around inside the rim while counting twelve, or repeating the verse:

>"Dickery, dickery, dock;
> The mouse ran up the clock;
> The clock struck ten,
> He ran down again,
> Dickery, dickery, dock."

He stops on the last word, and the number of the space in which he stands is scored to his credit; for instance, if he stops in section eight, it scores eight points for him; if in section three, it scores three points, etc. Should he stop with one foot on a line or outside the circle, he scores nothing. The players take turns, each having but one trial at a turn. The game is won by the player first scoring twenty-five or fifty points, as may be decided.

SWIM TAG

3 to 10 players   *Children;*
Water   *adults*

This is the game of Tag played while swimming, one player being It and trying to tag the others. In its simplest form he may tag any part of the person, but the game may be made more difficult by requiring that he touch the arm, shoulder, head, foot, etc. The one in danger of being tagged may save himself by being in touch with some specified object, such as a raft, canoe, buoy, or rock; or some stipulated position may give him immunity, such as floating or ducking.

TAG

The game of plain, old-fashioned Tag may be made great sport, especially if suddenly and unexpectedly commenced in a group of players when other interests seem to lag.

The game has many variations, a considerable number of which are here given, each variation making practically a different game.

This game is found in all countries and is prehistoric. It is supposed to have arisen from the idea of fleeing from an evil spirit, and in those forms from which immunity is found by touching wood or iron or taking some particular position, that especial feature is supposed to have originated in the idea of breaking the spell of the pursuing evil.

The following tag games will be found in their alphabetical order:

Broncho Tag	Hang Tag
Cross Tag	Home Tag
Fence Tag	Japanese Tag
French Tag	Shadow Tag
Iron Tag	Stoop Tag (Squat Tag)
Maze Tag (Line Tag; Right Face)	Swim Tag
Old Man Tag	Tag
Partner Tag	Whip Tag
Schoolroom Tag	Wood Tag

TAG

4 to 60 players   *Primary grades*
Indoors; out of doors

Tag in its simplest form may be started by any one of a group of players suddenly turning to another, touching (tagging) him and saying "You're It!" when all must flee from the one who is It.

The player who is It may chase and tag any other player whom he chooses, but will aid his own ends by suddenly turning his attention from one player to another, or by doubling back on his course, or by resorting to any of the other feints that give an unexpected turn to a game of chase.

The players who are being chased will add to the zest of the game by venturing as close as possible to the one who is It, calling to him and taunting him with their proximity and suddenly dodging away. When a player is hard pressed or breathless, or does not wish to play, he may become immune from tagging by crossing any one finger over its neighbor on either hand, as the forefinger over the middle finger. It is considered "babyish," however, to resort to this unless there is some very good reason. A player who has had a good fair chase ought to be willing to be It if caught.

Any player whom the chaser tags immediately becomes It, but the chaser, in touching him, must say "You're It!" At his own discretion he may add "No fair," which means that the one who has just become It may not turn at once and tag him. A venturesome player, however, will omit this, especially if he should tag another player from behind, and trust to his own powers of dodging for getting safely away. Where there is a large number of players, two or more may be chosen to be It.

See also Swim Tag for water sport.

TAG THE WALL RELAY

10 to 60 players *Primary grades*
Schoolroom

The players should all be seated, an even number in each row of seats. At a signal, the last player in each line runs forward and tags the front wall. As soon as this player is out of the aisle, the others all move backward one seat. This leaves the front seat vacant, and the runner having touched the wall returns immediately and takes this vacant front seat. As the player sits he raises his hand, which is a signal for the player who is now the last one in the line to run forward, the line moving backward one place as soon as he is out of the aisle. He, in turn, having touched the wall, takes the vacant front seat. The play is continued in this way until everyone in the row has run.

The line wins whose player, sitting at the start in the front seat, first returns to his seat.

As in all schoolroom games where there is running, the seated players should be very careful to keep their feet under the desks, so there will be nothing in the aisles over which the runners may trip.

This is one of the best classroom games and is very popular.

TEN STEPS

10 to 30 or more players   *Intermediate grades*
Playground; indoors

This is a game of Hide and Seek and like all such games is best played where there is plenty of space and many hiding places. The distinctive feature of this game is the peculiar limitation put on the opportunity to hide, which may even free the blinder from his task. The one who is It, or hunter, blinds his eyes and counts ten while the other players run for hiding places. As soon as the one who is blinding says "Ten!" the players must all stand motionless wherever they happen to be, while he turns at once to look for them. Any player whom he sees moving must come back to the goal and start over again. The hunter repeats this five times, and any player not entirely out of sight the fifth time the hunter turns must change places with him, the original hunter becoming a spectator of the game. Having called "Ten!" and turned to look for moving players five times, the hunter (or the one taking his place, as explained above) counts one hundred, to give the players time to reach final hiding places, and the game proceeds as in regular I Spy.

THIMBLE RING

10 to 30 or more players   *Primary to*
Indoors; out of doors   *intermediate grades*

All of the players but one stand in a circle, each one clasping with his left hand the right wrist of his left-hand neighbor. This leaves all of the right hands free and all of the left hands occupied. The odd player stands in the center of the circle, and tries to detect who holds the thimble that is passed from hand to hand. Each player in the circle places his right hand first in the hand of his neighbor on the right and then in the hand of the neighbor on the left, keeping this movement going rhythmically, while the entire circle repeats the lines:

> "The thimble is going, I don't know where;
> It is first over here and then over there."

When the player in the center thinks he knows who has the thimble, he goes up to him and says: "My lady's lost her thimble. Have you it?" If correct, these two players change places. If incorrect, the one who is It demands of the player addressed to find it. This player, in turn, has one guess. If correct, he takes the place of the one who has the thimble, the one who was It taking the vacant place in the circle, and the one who held the thimble going to the center. Should the player be incorrect in his guess, he changes places with the one in the center.

VARIATION. — The same game is played by stringing a ring on a piece of twine which is long enough to go around the circle, the ends being tied together to make a circle of the twine. The players, facing inward, all take hold of the twine with both hands, palms downward, and slide the ring over it from one to the other. They keep up a constant movement of the hands to mislead the center player as to the situation of the ring.

THIRD MAN

(See also *Three Deep* and *Last Man*.)

15 to 100 players   *Primary grades*
Playground; gymnasium   *to adult*

This game is another form of the game commonly known as Three Deep, but instead of being played in the circular formation, the players are scattered irregularly over the playground.

I. All of the players but two take partners and scatter in any irregular way. The players forming each couple stand facing each other, with the distance of a long step between them. To make a success of the game, the distance should be considerable between the various couples.

Of the two odd players, one is runner and the other chaser, the object of the latter being to tag the runner. The runner may take refuge between any two players who are standing as a couple.

The moment that he does so, the one toward whom his back is turned becomes third man, and must in his turn try to escape being tagged by the chaser. Should the chaser tag the runner, they exchange places, the runner immediately becoming chaser and the chaser being liable instantly to tagging.

II. Instead of facing each other, the partners may stand side by side and hook the near arms. The runner then saves himself by hooking the outer arm of any player, when the original partner, having been made a third man, becomes It and immediately runs for a similar play.

THIRD SLAP

5 to 30 or more players   *Intermediate grades*
Playground; gymnasium; schoolroom

The players should be divided into groups of from five to ten each. One in each group is chosen to be It; the others line up in front of him, all standing at a distance of from thirty to fifty feet from a goal previously decided on. The players in the line hold their hands extended forward the length of the forearm, the elbows being bent and touching the sides; the palms should be turned downward.

The one who is It tries to slap the hands of any of the players, who may evade him by bending the hands downward, upward, or sideways, at the wrist, but may not withdraw the arm or change the position of the elbow. Any player who receives three slaps, whether on one or both hands, immediately upon receiving the third slap, chases the one who is It toward the goal. Should the slapper be caught before he reaches the goal, he must continue as before, but if he succeeds in reaching the goal in safety, he changes places with his pursuer, who becomes It, or slapper, for the next round.

This game may have much sport in it if the one who is taking the part of slapper be very alert and agile in his movements, dodging quickly from one player to another, and making many false moves to throw the players off their guard as to where he is going to strike next. This game is very popular with children, and is an amusing diversion for young people for house parties.

THREE DEEP

(See also *Third Man, Last Man,* and *Broncho Tag.*)

15 to 60 players   *Intermediate grades*
Playground; gymnasium   *to adult*

This game is one of the standard favorites for both children and adults.
In any of its forms it may be made one of the jolliest possible, and also one
of the best for making slow and dull players alert and active.   The author
has seen many a class of slow-minded children waken to much quicker
mental action as well as greater physical agility by this game.   For adult
players it may be thoroughly delightful.   The writer recalls a class of
adult business men in a Y.M.C.A. gymnasium who resorted even to leapfrog tactics in the strenuous sport they put into the form first described.

I. — All of the players but two form in a double ring, facing inward ; that is, in two concentric circles, with one player directly
behind another.

There are several methods of getting players into this formation.   One
method is to have the players march in column two abreast, form in a circle,
and all face inward.   Another method is to have the players form in a
circle in single file; one player steps in front of his neighbor on the right,
and each alternate player in quick succession around the circle does the
same, thus accomplishing the end of bringing all of the players in couples
one behind another.

The two odd players, one of whom is runner and the other
chaser, start outside of the circle, generally one of them being on
one side of the circle and the other opposite.   The object of the
game is for the chaser to tag the runner.   The runner may save
himself by stopping in front of any couple standing in the circle,
whereupon, that file having been made "three deep," the outer
player or third man becomes at once liable to tagging, and in his
turn becomes runner and tries to evade the chaser.   He may seek
refuge in the same way in front of a couple.

Should the chaser tag the runner, they exchange places, the
runner immediately becoming chaser, and the chaser being liable
instantly to tagging.

It will thus be seen that great alertness is necessary on the part
of anyone standing on the outside of the circle, as at any moment
the runner may take refuge in front of his file or couple, making

him the third man and liable to be tagged. It is not permissible for any third man to take refuge in front of the couple standing immediately on his right or left when he becomes third man.

Both runner and chaser may dash through the circle, but may not pause for a moment within the circle, except when the runner claims refuge in front of some couple. When players are inclined to confuse the play by hesitating while running through the circle, this privilege of running through is sometimes forbidden, all the chasing being confined to the outside of the circle.

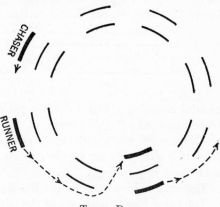

THREE DEEP

II. — VARIATION. — This game may be varied by having the players who form the circle stand face to face, with a distance of one long step between each two, instead of all facing toward the center of the circle. In this form of the game the runner takes refuge between the two forming the couple, the one toward whom his back is turned being the third man. Both runner and chaser may run between the two circles of players.

III. TWO DEEP. — In this form the players stand in a single circle instead of in twos. Otherwise the game is the same as Three Deep, the runner saving himself by stepping in front of any player. The latter thereby becomes vulnerable for tagging and must run immediately. The action is more rapid than in Three Deep.

TIP–CAT

4 to 20 players   *Intermediate grades*
Playground   *to junior high school*

This game is played with a "cat" and bat usually of home construction. The "cat" is a stick from four to six inches long and one or two inches thick, whittled to a point at each end. The bat is a stick of from one to four feet long and about two inches thick, either flat or rounded. Broomsticks are often used from which to make the cat and bat.

The "cat" is batted by hitting it a sharp blow with the bat on one end as it lies on the ground (left end is better); as it jumps into the air, the Batter strikes at it again, trying to send

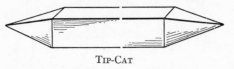

it as far as possible. Two forms of the game are here given.

TIP-CAT

I. — A three-foot circle is drawn on the ground and thirty feet from it a pitcher's line. Players are in two teams which take turns at bat. The opposing team is scattered as fielders with one member acting as pitcher. The pitcher is either chosen by the captain of his team or the players take turns in pitching.

The play is in several stages like baseball.

The game begins with one of the batting team beside the circle as batter, the opponents in the field and their pitcher on his line holding the cat. The pitcher tries to throw the cat into the ring. If it lands inside the ring, the batter is out and the next batter of his team takes his place; if the cat lands on the ring, the batter is entitled to one turn at batting it from where it lies; if it lands outside the ring, he has three turns at batting from that point. The batter tries to send the cat as far as possible. If it does not go more than five feet, he is out, the next batter of his team takes his place, and the cat is pitched again. If, however, it goes a greater distance than five feet, the batter estimates the fewest number of steps (usually leaps) in which an opponent could cover the distance from the point where the cat fell to the ring, and he names this requirement; for instance: "I give you six steps (or fifteen or any number of steps). The captain of the opposing team then selects his best jumper, who has three chances to cover the distance in the required number of steps. He may start with a run, but the first step is counted from the point where the cat landed. If he fails to cover the distance, the batting team scores the number of steps designated, and its next batter moves up to bat. If the jumper is successful, the teams change places, the jumper's team coming to bat to have its inning.

This is one of the oldest and most popular boys' games. Like many traditional games, it is played with different details in different localities, such as measuring the distance with the bat instead of requiring opponents to step it off. The form here given is that used in England, from whence the game probably came to America.

II. STARLING TIP-CAT. — This form of Tip-Cat, played in Czechoslovakia, has some distinctive details of play and scoring. Like the American and English games, it is played by two teams of from two to ten members each, uses the same kind of whittled "cat" and bat, but has a batting circle three yards in diameter. The batting team plays in order, each member having three tries in succession at playing the cat (called the "starling"). The batter stands in the circle and tosses the cat, hitting it with the bat to any point outside. When successful, it is picked up and thrown from where it fell toward the circle, by anyone on the opposite team, whose members are scattered over the field. If the cat falls in and stays in the circle, or on the line, the batter is retired and the next one of his team goes to bat; but if it falls or bounds outside the circle, the batter has three tries at "horsing," which consists in getting the cat into the air by hitting one end with the bat and then batting it back into the field. Should the horsed starling fall in the circle, the player's next try must be from where it lies; should it fall outside the circle but near it, he must play it next from the center of the circle.

The horsing player may not prepare or alter the ground by digging under the starling, or building it up with stones or earth. On a grassy field he may pull the grass from around the points, but may not touch or move the starling. It is permissible to turn a point of it for better direction, but this may be done only with the bat.

After his third try at horsing, the batter estimates the distance of the last lie to which he has batted the starling in terms of bat-lengths and calls this number. If one of the opponents agrees with him, the distance is not measured but is scored for the batting team; if his estimate is challenged, measured, and found to be too great (too many bat-lengths), nothing is scored; if too low, that figure is scored for the batting team.

That team wins which has the highest score after each team has had three times at bat. Teams change places after each member of the batting team has had his turn.

TOMMY TIDDLER'S GROUND

5 to 30 or more players   *Primary grades*
Playground; gymnasium

The ground is divided by a line into two equal parts. One of these belongs to Tommy Tiddler, who stands on his side of the line and may not cross it. All of the other players are on the other side of the line, and venture across the line into Tommy Tiddler's ground, taunting him with the remark,

> "I'm on Tommy Tiddler's ground,
> Picking up gold and silver!"

Tommy may tag anyone on his ground, and anyone so tagged changes places with him. The players will learn to add to the interest of the game by venturing as near Tommy Tiddler as possible and being very tantalizing in inducing him to run after them. Tommy Tiddler, on his part, will find opportunity for considerable finesse, such as in appearing to give his attention entirely to one player, then suddenly turning and dashing for another.

TOSSING WANDS

10 to 60 or more players   *Junior high school*
Gymnasium; playground; schoolroom

This game is played in two forms, line form and circle form.
LINE FORM. — The players stand in two lines or ranks facing each other, all those in one line being provided with gymnasium wands about three feet in length. A leader is appointed who either counts or commands as a signal for tossing the wands back and forth from one line to the other: as, "One, two, three —

toss!" This is even more effective if gymnastic movements be taken on the three counts, as bending the trunk forward with the wand downward, stretching the arms upward with the wand overhead, extending it forward at shoulder height, and then tossing to the opposite player. The signals for this would be "Bend! Stretch! Out! Toss!" Or the lines may stand facing in the same direction, when the toss will be backward over the head.

The wands should first be held in the hand with the palms upward, and caught with the hands in the same position. Later, the hand position should be reversed, the wand being grasped with the downward-turned palms.

CIRCLE FORM. — When players are proficient in catching in opposite lines or ranks, they should form a circle, facing around in single file, each player being provided with a wand which is tossed backward over the head and caught by the player behind. This may be done best rhythmically with the exercises and commands mentioned above, "Bend! Stretch! Out! Toss!" The wand should be caught with the palms outward.

Any player failing to catch a wand drops out of the game. With a little practice, however, this usually resolves itself into a quick drill rather than a game; but it is a most interesting, skillful, and diverting play.

TRADES

10 to 60 or more players   *Junior high school*
                        Indoors; out of doors

This game is the boys' form of the game played by girls as Old Woman from the Woods. The players divide into two equal parties. One party retires and decides on some trade or occupation, whereupon they advance toward the second party, saying:

> "Here are some men from Botany Bay.
> Got any work to give us today?"

The second party asks, "What can you do?" The first party answers, "Anything." The second party says, "Set to work, then!" whereupon they go through pantomimic motions descriptive of the occupation chosen, such as planing, sawing, or hammering, for the carpenter; the motions of the bricklayer, tailor, cobbler, motorman, etc. The second party guesses what this pantomime indicates. Should they guess correctly, they have a turn at representing a trade. Should they fail, the first party has another trial.

When played in a playground or gymnasium, where there is a good running space, a successful guess should be followed by a chase of the actors by the guessing party, any players caught before a designated goal line is reached having to join the party of their captors. The party wins which secures all of the players.

The following activities and occupations were shown by one class of city boys: milking cows, grinding coffee, hanging wall paper, traveling salesmen (displaying and measuring goods), rooting a baseball team, Marathon race, picking cherries, basketball game, oiling sewing machine, blowing up bicycle tires, running a lawn mower, bricklaying.

TREE PARTY

5 to 60 players   *Children;*
Out of doors   *to adults*

In days of nature study this game is especially appropriate. It may be used on any ground or strip of woodland where there is a variety of trees, the game consisting in identifying the trees.

A tag or card is fastened on one or more trees of each variety within certain prescribed limits. These cards may be made as fanciful or as rustic as desired. Birch bark is very appropriate for them, and for either birch bark or a conventional card a pretty element may be added by writing some appropriate quotation or verse, after the Japanese custom. The main object of each card, however, is to bear a number. Each player is provided with a card or slip of paper containing a list of numbers corresponding to those on the trees. Thus, if fifteen trees are numbered, there should be fifteen numbers on each player's card.

The players, having been provided each with a card and pencil, wander at will over the designated territory. Whenever a number is discovered on a tree, the player, if he knows the name of the tree, writes it on his own card opposite the corresponding number. For most companies, popular rather than botanical names of the trees are permissible. At a signal — a bell, whistle, horn, or call — the players all assemble. The host or hostess then reads a correct list, each player checking the card that he holds. The player wins who has the largest number of names correct.

The writer has known this game to be a most beautiful diversion for a lawn party on a large estate, and has a feeling appreciation of how many trees most people will find it hard to name in even a familiar strip of woodland.

TRIPLE CHANGE

10 to 60 or more players *Intermediate grades*
Playground; gymnasium; parlor *to senior high school*

The players form a circle, with the exception of three who stand in the center. Those forming the circle and those in the center number off in threes. The players in the center take turns in calling each his number, as "One!" "Two!" or "Three!" whereupon all of the players in the circle who hold that number quickly change places with each other, the one who called the number trying to catch one as he runs to a new place. Any player so caught changes places with the caller. For instance, the center player may call "Three!" whereupon all of the Numbers Three in the circle must change places. They may do this by changing with a near neighbor, or tantalize the one who called by running across the circle.

The center players take turns in calling numbers. For instance, if the first one fails to secure a place, then the second of the center group calls. Should the first succeed in catching one of the other players, the player so caught will await his turn in the center until Numbers Two and Three have each had a turn at calling before he calls a number.

TUG OF WAR

(See *Catch and Pull Tug of War* and *Wand Tug of War;* also *Contests for Two,* under " Stunts and Contests; Feats and Forfeits.")

TWO DEEP

(See *Variation* under *Three Deep*)

UNDER THE CUCKOO'S NEST

5 to 30 players   *Primary grades*
House party; out of doors

One player is chosen as leader, and stands up, generally with his back against a wall or post, while a second player, who is the cuckoo, bends down, as for leapfrog, with his head against the leader. The other players stand around in a circle, each placing a finger on the back of the cuckoo. The leader then "counts off" the fingers of the players with the following rhyme, indicating a finger for each accent of the rhyme:

> "The wind blows east, the wind blows west,
> The wind blows under the cuckoo's nest.
> Where shall this or that one go?
> Shall he go east or shall he go west?
> Or shall he go under the cuckoo's nest?"

The player whose finger is indicated by the last word of the rhyme must then go to any place directed by the cuckoo, who, if he has any intimation of the identity of the player, may use considerable tact in choosing a difficult or interesting place; as on some high point to which it is difficult to climb, or under some low object under which it is hard to crawl, some distant place, etc. One player, however, must be directed to hide under the cuckoo's nest, and this player takes a position at the feet of the cuckoo. This is a favored position. When all of the players have been thus disposed, the leader calls, "Pom, pom, cooketty coo!" As soon as this call is heard, the players run back and touch the cuckoo on the back until the last one is in. This last one becomes the cuckoo for the next repetition of the game.

VAULTING SEATS

10 to 60 players   *Intermediate grades*
Schoolroom

This game is played the same as Changing Seats, except that the pupils vault over the seats instead of sitting in them. The game may be played anywhere above the third year.

The teacher gives the order "Right, jump!" whereupon all of the pupils jump over their seats toward the right-hand side of the room. The row that is displaced, now standing in the right-hand aisle, runs at once around the room to the left-hand aisle. The teacher then repeats her command. The directions for the vaulting should be varied and unexpected, several being given to the right, then several to the left, etc.

The method of vaulting is to place one hand on the edge of the desk at the back of the seat to be vaulted over, and one hand on the desk that goes with the seat to be vaulted over. The hand should preferably be placed halfway between the two aisles, to assist both the jump and the landing. While placing the hands, pupils should crouch in a position ready to spring, with the heels raised, knees spread outward, and back straight and erect. They should land in the same position, as the bend of the ankle, knee, and hip joints breaks the jar of landing.

WAND RACE

10 to 30 or more players   *Intermediate grades*
Parlor; gymnasium; schoolroom   *to adults*

An objective line, fence, or wall is chosen, and from ten to twenty feet from it and parallel with it a starting line is drawn. The players stand behind this line and toe it. If there is a large number, they form in competitive files as for a relay race, the leaders of each division toeing the line. Each leader balances on the forefinger a gymnasium wand, the other hand being placed on the hip, and walks forward to the objective line, all starting at a given signal. Should the wand be dropped, it must be picked up and the effort resumed from the place where this happened.

The first one to reach the objective line wins; or, if a relay, scores for his division. The division wins that gets the largest score. If desired, the winners, *i.e.* those scoring for the different lines, may "play off" against each other, after all of the other players have had their turn. For a parlor game a cane or umbrella may be used.

WAND TUG OF WAR

10 to 100 players   *Junior high school*
Playground; gymnasium

This game is played with wooden gymnastic wands, from three to five feet in length, and not less then one inch in diameter.

There should be half as many wands as there are players. A line is drawn across the center of the floor or playground. The players are divided into two divisions, one standing on each side of the dividing line, so that each player faces an opponent. These grasp each the end of a wand, held horizontally between them. At a signal a tug of war begins, each player trying to pull his opponent across the line. Anyone who puts a foot on the ground of the opponent's territory ceases the struggle and must come across the line. The division wins which has the greatest number of players on its side of the line at the end.

The game is best played in two or three five-minute intervals, with rests between.

WATCHDOG

10 to 20 players   *Very young children*
Kindergarten or party

This is a game for very little children. They are all seated on the floor in a ring. One child is chosen to be Watchdog and sits on a chair in the center of the ring, eyes shut or blindfolded. Under the chair is placed a "bone," which is a spool or a small block. The leader points to one of the children in the circle, who tries to get the bone and back to his place without waking the Watchdog. If he makes a noise in the circle, the Dog growls; if near the chair, the Dog wakens, barks, jumps from his chair, and the child who was trying to get the bone changes places with him.

If the child from the circle succeeds in getting the bone without disturbing (being heard by) the Watchdog, he hides it behind him or under him and tries not to show by his expression that he has it. All of the children in the circle call: "Watchdog! Watchdog! Wake up!" The Dog gets down from his chair and walks around the circle trying to tell which child has the bone. He has three guesses. If correct, he is the Watchdog again. If he fails to guess right, he loses his turn and the one who has the bone becomes Watchdog.

WATER SPRITE

10 to 30 or more players   *Primary grades*
                 Playground; gymnasium

The players stand in two lines facing each other, with a large open space representing a river between. One player, representing the water sprite, stands in the middle of the river and beckons to one on the bank to cross. This one signals to a third player on the opposite bank or side of the river. The two from the banks then run across to exchange places, the water sprite trying to tag one of them. If the water sprite is successful, he changes places with the one tagged.

This is a Chinese game, reported by Miss Adèle M. Fielde, and is based upon the superstition that a water sprite waits in the middle of a stream to entice people into it, probably an outgrowth of spring freshets.

WEATHERCOCK

10 to 60 players   *Primary grades*
                      Schoolroom

This game, besides offering much sport, may be made to serve a useful purpose in familiarizing children with the points of the compass.

The class having learned which directions are north, east, south, and west, one player, who represents the weather bureau, stands in front of the others (or the teacher may take this part), and calls out which way the wind blows. For instance, when he says, "The wind blows north," the players turn quickly toward the north; if he says "west," the players turn to the west; whenever he says "whirlwind," the players all spin around quickly three times on the right heel.

The interest will depend very largely on the rapidity and variety with which the leader calls the various points of the compass. For older children, halfway points may be named, as northwest, southeast, etc.

WEE BOLOGNA MAN

2 to 60 or more players   *Primary grades*
Parlor; playground; schoolroom

> "I'm the wee Bologna Man.
> Always do the best you can,
> To follow the wee Bologna Man."

A leader who can be very brisk in movement and resourceful in ideas stands in front of the other players and repeats this verse rapidly, imitating each time he repeats the verse some one action characteristic of the members of a band. For instance, the first time he may go through the pantomime of playing a fife; the next time, without any pause between, he may imitate the beating of a drum; the next, playing a fiddle, trombone, flute, cymbals, triangle, or imitating the drum major, etc. All of the other players follow his movements.

The sport will depend largely upon the rapidity of the time and the vivacity that is put into the movements.

FOR THE SCHOOLROOM. — The head players in the different lines of seats should take turns in being the Bologna Man, and the movements should be such as will afford effective exercise. For instance, the first player will stand and repeat the verse while hopping on one foot, the entire class joining in the hopping. The moment he is through, the leader of the next row should jump up, face the class, and repeat the verse, going through some other motion, such as hopping on the other foot; he, in turn, to be succeeded by the next leader, etc. Many gymnastic movements will suggest themselves, such as jumping on both feet, jumping forward down the aisle frog fashion, jumping high in place, running in place, stretching the arms out sideways and bending sideways like a walking beam, whirling both arms around like a windmill, taking a dance step, etc.

This is one of the Scotch plays, and like most Scottish things of the sort, should be done in brisk time.

WHIP TAG

(Light the Candle; Beetle-Goes-Round)

10 to 30 or more players   *Junior high school*
Playground; gymnasium

This game may be played with a knotted towel, though it is perhaps more skillful and interesting when played with a "beetle," a small cylindrical sack about twenty inches long, stuffed with cotton, and resembling in general proportions a policeman's club.

All but one of the players stand in a circle with hands behind their backs. The odd player runs around the outside carrying the beetle, which he drops in the hands of any player in the circle. That player immediately turns to chase his right-hand neighbor, beating him as much as he can find opportunity for while he chases him around the circle and back to his place. It is obviously to the interest of this neighbor to outrun the beetle and escape a buffeting.

The one holding the beetle then takes the place of the first outside player, that one joining the ring. The new beetle man, in turn, runs around on the outside and drops the beetle in any hands which he chooses.

The sport of this game depends on the alertness of the players, as not only the one who receives the beetle but his right-hand neighbor must know when and where the beetle lands, and turn quickly for the chase. The player running around the outside will add to the zest of the game by trying to deceive the ring players as to where he is going to place the beetle, quickening or slowing his pace, or resorting to other devices to keep them on the alert.

WHITE BEAR

10 or more players   *Elementary*
Out-of-doors

This is a game from Russia, as the white bear might suggest. The Bear lives on a field of ice which, for the game, may be a stump, or rock, or hillock; a clear space is outlined around it for a distance of from thirty to fifty feet, which is the White Sea, and in that the fishes are scattered irregularly.

The Bear says growlingly: "White Bear is hungry today; he goes fishing," whereupon he jumps into the sea, chases the fish until he catches one, and takes it home with him to his icy rock. He repeats this once; then, having two helpers, and being quite lazy himself, he orders the helpers to go hunting and bring him a fish. The two helpers jump into the sea, face each other, and clasp hands. They then try to catch a fish by putting their arms over his head; such a catch they take back to the rock. This they repeat when White Bear again tells them he is hungry, and as soon as there are two couples the Bear sends both out for a catch. This is kept up, each additional couple joining the fishers, until all the fish are caught, the last one becoming the next Bear.

The fish may never swim outside the boundary marked for the Sea.

WHO GOES ROUND MY STONE WALL?

10 to 30 or more players   *Primary grades*
              Indoors; out of doors

There are two ways of playing this game. The one first described is better suited to schools and general playground conditions; the second is quite distinct, and may have better sport for parlor use.

The players stand in a circle, numbering preferably twenty or less, with a little space between each two players, and not holding hands. They represent a sheepfold, but later, as each is chosen from the circle, he takes the part of a sheep. One player is chosen to be Jacky Lingo, who walks around outside of the circle. Another, who is the shepherd or owner of the sheep, stands in the center of the circle.

The owner says, "Who goes round my stone wall?" The outside player answers, "Nobody; only little Jacky Lingo."

"Pray don't steal any of my fat sheep."

Jacky Lingo answers: "Unless I take one-by-one, two-by-two, three-by-three! Follow me!"

As Jacky Lingo says his last line, he taps three different players on the back, one for "one-by-one," another for "two-by-two," and a third for "three-by-three." If a large number be playing, he may tap two for each count instead of one, making six in all.

As the players are tapped, they step out from the sheepfold and line up back of Jacky Lingo, each one in the line placing his hands on the shoulders of the one next in front. This is continued until all the players are taken by Jacky Lingo, who then runs off around the ground with them. The owner goes after them, faces Jacky Lingo, and says, "Have you seen anything of my black sheep?"

"Yes; I gave them a lot of bread and butter and sent them up there" (pointing to left or right).

"Then what have you got behind you?"

"Only a few poor black sheep."

"Well, let me see! Here are my black sheep!"

The owner then tries to catch the sheep, and this Jacky Lingo tries to prevent. Any sheep in the line may be touched by the owner, and when so touched he steps out of the line and stands aside until all are caught.

VARIATION. — When played indoors or on the turf, the game may be played by the owner's being blindfolded and taking a position on hands and knees — "all fours." The dialogue is the same as given above, and the gathering in of the sheep by Jacky Lingo the same, except that the players do not line up behind him. They simply stray over the ground when he takes them from the fold. When all are scattered in this way, they begin to cry, "Baa-a! baa-a!" and the owner, still on all fours and blinded, tries to catch them. The first one caught becomes shepherd the next time.

WINK

9 to 25 players
House party

Children
to adults

An uneven number of players are required for this game. Enough chairs are placed in a circle to allow one chair to each two players and one for the odd player, that is, half as many chairs as there are players, with one player over. A player sits in each chair, all facing inward. Behind each chair stands a second player, who acts as guard. There should be one empty chair with a guard behind it. This odd player winks at someone sitting in the circle, who at once tries to slip out of his chair without being tagged by his guard and take his place in the empty chair. He may not go if he is tagged by his guard. The object of the guards should be to avoid being the keeper of an empty chair, and therefore the one who has to wink. The players try to evade the vigilance of the guards by the quickness and unexpectedness of their movements. The guards may not keep their hands on their prisoners, but must have them hanging at their sides until they see their players winked at. They may not dash around the sides of the chairs which they guard, but must stay behind them all the time.

Nodding the head may be used instead of winking, but is more apparent to the guards.

WOLF

5 to 30 or more players   *Junior high school*
Out of doors

This is an admirable hide-and-seek game where there are many hiding places, as in a village or the country.

One player is chosen for the wolf, who goes off and hides. The rest of the players are sheep, with one of their number as leader. A place is chosen for a pen where the sheep must stay and blind their eyes while the wolf is hiding. This pen may be a tree or rock or a square or circle drawn on the ground. The leader counts one hundred, to give the wolf time to hide. The sheep then start out, but must all follow their leader "like sheep," looking for the wolf in each place where the leader may search for him. This game differs from most other hiding games in that the searchers are the ones who have to flee for safety when the hider is discovered. As soon as the wolf is spied, the leader cries:

> "All my sheep
> Gather in a heap;
> For I spy the woolly, woolly wolf!"

The sheep at once stand still until the wolf has taken a jump toward them, which he must do before he may chase them; but immediately that the wolf has made his leap, the sheep all turn and run for the sheep pen, the wolf following. As the wolf may not run until he hears the word "wolf" at the end of the leader's lines, the latter often tantalizes the wolf by saying, "I spy the woolly, woolly — lamb!" or "the woolly, woolly — cat!" or names any other animal he chooses, with a pause before the name, to prolong the suspense of the impatient wolf, finally ending with "the woolly, woolly — wolf!"

Any sheep tagged by the wolf becomes a wolf and joins the wolf the next time, hiding either in the same den with him or in a separate den. When there is more than one wolf, the leader halts his sheep whenever he spies a wolf, whether it be the original wolf or not, and all of the wolves join in the chase when the sheep run back to the pen. The game ends when all of the sheep have been caught.

The wolf has several resources at his command for catching sheep in addition to a simple chase. If at any time while in hiding he spies the sheep before they spy him, and considers their position in relation to the goal advantageous to himself, he may call, "Stand your ground, three feet!" whereupon the sheep must instantly stand still and then take three steps toward the wolf and stand again until he jumps toward them, when the chase for the sheep pen begins. The wolf may also exercise considerable finesse by running directly for the pen if he be in a position to reach it quicker or more directly than by chasing the sheep. Should he reach the pen first, he may then tag the sheep as they run in. One sheep may act as a decoy to engage the attention of the wolf while the others run into the pen.

WOOD TAG

3 to 30 or more players   *Intermediate grades*
Out of doors; gymnasium

This is a game of tag. When there are more than thirty players, it is desirable to have two or more who are It, or taggers. The players venture as near as possible to the one who is It, taunting him by crying, "Ticky, ticky, touch wood!" Any player may seek immunity from being tagged by touching a piece of wood. No growing thing, however, such as a tree or shrub, is to be considered as wood. No player may stay very long in any place of safety, and the moment his hand or foot be taken from the wood he is liable to be tagged. A player who is not near wood may gain a few minutes' respite by calling out "Parley!" but he must stand perfectly still in the place where he then is, the tagger being able to tag him if he makes the slightest move of any part of his body. When such a player decides to run again, he calls out, "Parley out!"

This game affords opportunity for a great deal of sport through the making of false starts and the daring approach to the one who is It, who, in turn, may make sudden and unexpected sorties in different directions.

VARIATION. — This game is also played as Iron Tag by touching iron to give immunity instead of wood. Either game is good for water sport as well as on land.

This game is very ancient, and has evidently come from an old superstition that to touch iron or some other particular substance gave immunity from the spell of evil spirits.

WRESTLING

(See *Contests for Two* under "Stunts and Contests; Feats and Forfeits.")

YARDS OFF

3 to 30 or more players　　　　　　*Intermediate grades;*
Out of doors　　　　　　　　　　　　　*adults*

This is a form of I Spy or Hide and Seek, and seems indigenous to New York. All players properly caught by the spy become prisoners, but may be freed in a prescribed way. The procedure which gives time for hiding is also distinctive.

Two players are chosen, one to be It and one for stick thrower. All the players stand grouped around a goal, and the stick thrower throws a stick as far away from the goal as he can. As soon as the stick touches the ground, all of the players, including the thrower, but not the one who is It, scatter and hide. The one who is It must walk to the stick (never run), take it up, bring it back, and stand it up, resting against the goal. He then starts to hunt for the hidden players. He must run back and touch the goal for any player whom he discovers, saying, "One, two, three,

for — !" naming the player. Anyone caught in this way becomes a prisoner at the goal. Any player who has not been detected by the spy may run in to the goal at any time and throw
the stick away, whereby all of the prisoners, *i.e.* those who have
been spied and previously caught, become free and hide again.
Whenever this freeing of prisoners happens, the spy must return
to the goal, walk to the stick, pick it up, walk back with it to the
goal again, and go on with the play as before. This continues
until the spy has touched the goal for all of the players, though
they need not all be prisoners at once. Any player spied who
reaches the goal before the spy, is thereafter free; *i.e.* out of the
game. The last one caught becomes spy for the next game.

SOCIAL AND QUIET GAMES

SOCIAL AND QUIET GAMES

AUTHOR'S INITIALS

2 to 60 players
Parlor; schoolroom

Each player is given a piece of paper on which are written various series or groups of words, each group descriptive of some author, and each word beginning with one of his initials in regular order. The player wins who guesses the largest number of authors. The following are suggested; others may be devised:

1. Juveniles firmly conquered (James Fenimore Cooper).
2. Name honored (Nathaniel Hawthorne).
3. Bright humor (Bret Harte).
4. One wholesome humorist (Oliver Wendell Holmes).
5. Really lasting stories (Robert Louis Stevenson).
6. Cheerful laborer (Charles Lamb).
7. Tender, brilliant author (Thomas Bailey Aldrich).
8. Heroism wisely lauded (Henry Wadsworth Longfellow).
9. Just, gentle writer (John Greenleaf Whittier).
10. Poetry bridged skyward (Percy Bysshe Shelley).
11. Clever delineator (Charles Dickens).
12. Rare brain (Robert Browning).
13. Weird imagination (Washington Irving).

AUTOMOBILE TREASURE HUNT

Out of doors   *Adults*

This is a popular game for adults and is suited to the environment of a small town or city or of a country home or camp.

A "treasure" or prize is hidden somewhere within easy automobile distance, say a half-hour's ride; the guests go out in automobiles to find it and are told to be back in an hour. Clues are written on inconspicuous slips of paper numbered consecutively, and each is fastened, as with a thumb tack, to some spot indicated by the previous clue. The couple or car party first to find the treasure wins it, drawing lots as to which individual shall have it.

The placing of clues should be done a half day in advance of the hunt; it is advisable that someone go over the trail to check their accuracy. The clues should be posted so that they do not require handling by the treasure seekers. Much ingenuity and sport are possible in their preparation. The following examples in prose and verse are from highly successful treasure hunts:

The hostess announced, "Clue Number One is posted on the side of the house." (This required considerable hunting, as which side was not specified, and the clue might be under a vine, on a veranda post, in a cellar window, or otherwise hidden.) When found it read: "Clue Number Two is on the second railing under a bridge." (Bridge not specified.) When found, this read: "For Clue Number Three go down the Ridge Road to second turning and find clue on a large maple tree in front of a white house with green blinds," etc. — Here are some clues in verse.

1. First you must find a tall brick structure,
     An engineering feat of old;
   'Twas used for many and many a year
     And still stands firm and bold.
                    (Old water tower)

2. On a lonely dirt road near a beacon light,
     Just over the railroad track,
   You'll find the clue at the foot of a pole
     That is painted shiny and black.

3. Next seek a wired enclosure
     Where a game is played with a ball;
   But if you win, have naught of love,
     For love is nothing at all.
                    (Tennis courts)

4. The man who owns the nursery
     Won't let you pick a bouquet
   So look in the northwest corner
     Of the lawn where he plays croquet.

5. East on highway Number Three
     A house is ready for a spree;
   At this number, one-twenty-nine,
     The treasure you will surely find.
       (*And supper was ready, also.*)

"B" GAME

House party   *Juniors; adults*

Each player is given a sheet of paper with numbered questions prepared like the following list. The answer to each question is to be written opposite it, and must consist of the letter B as an initial and added to it the number of letters designated, the whole conforming to the definition given. The following examples will illustrate:

1. B and one letter, meaning to exist. — Be.
2. B and two letters, forming a sack. — Bag.
3. B and three letters, forming a storehouse. — Barn.
4. B and three letters, side of a stream. — Bank.
5. B and three letters, a young creature. — Baby.
6. B and three letters, a bag of goods. — Bale.
7. B and three letters, without hair. — Bald.
8. B and three letters, a surety. — Bond.
9. B and three letters, timber. — Beam.
10. B and three letters, a vegetable. — Beet. — **Bean.**
11. B and three letters, a poet. — Bard.
12. B and three letters, a drink. — Beer.
13. B and three letters, a globule. — Bead.
14. B and three letters, part of a bird. — Beak.
15. B and three letters, a vessel. — Boat.
16. B and four letters, an appendage. — Beard.
17. B and four letters, a tree. — Beech.
18. B and four letters, to commence. — Begin.
19. B and four letters, a strand. — Beach.
20. B and four letters, a receptacle. — Basin.
21. B and four letters, a kind of meat. — Bacon.
22. B and five letters, a combat. — Battle.
23. B and five letters, a hound. — Beagle.
24. B and five letters, a signal. — Beacon.
25. B and five letters, a cup. — Beaker.
26. B and eight letters, a demon. — Beelzebub.

The player wins who answers correctly the largest number. This game may be devised for any initial letter.

BARGAIN COUNTER

House party   *Juniors; adults*

Each player is provided with a paper and pencil. The following is either written on the papers in advance, or by the players from dictation, minus the underscoring. Each player is then required to find in the text the names of twenty-five textiles that may be purchased in a dry goods store, none to be mentioned twice, indicating each by underscoring. The player wins who has the largest number correct.

Dolly Varden, immaculately dressed, sat in the window ledge and heard from the church near by the mellow chords of the organ dying slowly away. Her silken hair was well drawn back from her forehead low and broad. Clothed as she was in pink and green, she made one think of the spring. She was considered musical; I considered her brilliant in every way. I was before the dresser, getting ready to go out, and taking a forkful of cold slaw now and then, or some mock duck. "I want to send a line north, Henrietta," said Dolly, bringing ham sandwiches; for she saw I felt hungry. She then wrote this letter: "I marvel, veterans, if you pause in your good work for lack of cash, merely as is represented. You should canvass for a book or paper, Caleb, some handy volume, possibly a duodecimo. Hairsplitting terms like this I do not often employ, but, blessings on the head of Cadmus! linguists must sometimes use their hands as well as their wit, weed gardens, if need be, but spare the mullein, for it seems to me like a flower. Always remember that, though the light burns dim, it yet will burn."

BARNYARD BEDLAM

(Peanut Hunt)

House party   *Children; adults*

From one to five pounds of peanuts are hidden around the house before the guests arrive. The number of peanuts depends on the size of the company. The players are divided into teams say of five or six players each, each team with a Captain who is provided with a paper bag. Each team is named for some animal whose cry they are to imitate, such as *cat, cow, dog, turkey, hen, donkey,* etc.

The object of the game for each team is to gather as many peanuts as possible in the time allotted, say twenty minutes. Only the Captain may touch the nuts and put them in the bag; but whenever a team-member finds a peanut he stands by it and gives the call of his team — that is, the cry of the donkey, horse, or what not — to attract his Captain. The Captain is supposed to come quickly and gather the nuts pointed out to him by this player; but, as many animals call at once, the resulting chorus is very funny. There should be a prize for the team gathering the greatest number of nuts.

BEAN PORRIDGE HOT

Two players   *Children; adults*

This traditional hand-slapping game for two players has much sport in it if done rapidly, though at first it may have to be played slowly. Two players sit facing each other, near together, and while repeating in unison the verses given below, slap each his own knees or palms, or his partner's palms, in the rhythm of the lines and in the order indicated.

Bean . . . . . . porridge . . . . hot,
(*Knees*)   (*own palms*)   (*both hands of opponent*)
Bean . . . . . . porridge . . . . cold,
(*Knees*)   (*own palms*)   (*both hands of opponent*)
Bean . . . . . . porridge . . . . in the . . . . pot
(*Knees*)   (*own palms*)   (*right to opponent's right*)   (*own palms*)
Nine . . . . . . days . . . . . old.
(*Left to oppo-*   (*own palms*)   (*both hands of opponent.*)
nent's left*)

The same play is repeated with the second stanza. The two complete stanzas are:

> Bean porridge hot,
>   Bean porridge cold,
> Bean porridge in the pot
>   Nine days old.

> Some like it hot,
>   Some like it cold,
> Some like it in the pot
>   Nine days old.

BEAST, BIRD, OR FISH

Parlor; schoolroom   *Intermediate grades*

The players stand or are seated, preferably in a circle. One player stands or sits in the center with a soft ball, made by crushing paper or knotting up a handkerchief. This is thrown at one of the players by the one in the center, who says quickly, "Beast, bird, or fish!" then repeats one of these classes and immediately counts ten, whereupon the player who has been hit by the ball must name some beast or bird or fish, according to the class last named by the thrower. This must be done before the latter has finished counting ten. For instance, the thrower will say as he throws, "Beast, bird, or fish! — Bird!" whereupon the player hit by the handkerchief must name a bird while the thrower counts ten. This must not be a repetition of any bird previously named in the game. Should the player who is hit by the ball fail to meet the requirements, he changes places with the thrower. Should he succeed, the thrower repeats the game by hitting some other player.

IN THE SCHOOLROOM this game may be played with all the players but one in their accustomed seats.

An old English form of this game substitutes the words "Fire, air, or water" for "Beast, bird, or fish," the players being required to name some animal that lives in the air or water when those elements are named, but to keep silence when fire is named. In this form the game is supposed to be a survival of fire worship.

BLACK MAGIC

Party   *Juniors; adults*

This is a guessing game for social parties. Two players who are confederates are necessary. One, who says he can guess any object chosen by the group, leaves the room. The remaining players decide on any object in the room, and the guesser is recalled. The host, or whoever is the other confederate, points to one object after another, saying: "Is it this?" or "Is it that?" The guesser says "No," until directed by his confederate's clue. The correct object is the third pointed at after one that is black·

BROWN FAMILY (THE)

Party   *Children; juniors*

Several players, representing the Brown Family, go out of the room. They include Mr. and Mrs. Brown, their children, Ebenezer and Sallie (or any names selected), Mr. Brown's brother, sister, uncle, aunt, cousins, mother-in-law, and as many more as there are persons in the group. One by one these are brought in by the host or leader and introduced to the company, their embarrassment or bravado under such circumstances being displayed in various mannerisms, attitudes, gestures, or remarks, which are to be imitated by everyone present. Thus the host may say, "I will introduce to you Mr. Brown"; or "Allow me to make you acquainted with Mrs. Brown"; "It is my pleasure and privilege to present to you Mr. Brown's father-in-law." Whereupon the person mentioned acts shy, or nods pompously, or bows deeply, saying: "I am greatly honored"; or hobbles hurriedly, remarking "Queer looking people you have here, aren't they?" or struts brusquely, nodding over his shoulder; or squints near-sightedly trying to make out the company; or hides his face; or tries to run away; or simpers and titters; etc.; etc. At the end the seated company votes on which of the Brown Family was most polite, and which the most entertaining. Anyone not imitating the Browns' actions or remarks must pay a forfeit.

BUZZ

Parlor; schoolroom   *Juniors; adults*

This is a quiet game, as distinguished from those requiring much muscular activity. One of the players starts the game by saying "One"; the next says "Two," the next "Three," etc., until the number "Seven" is reached, when the word "Buzz" is substituted for it. The next player says "Eight," and so on up to a multiple of seven, such as fourteen, twenty-one, twenty-eight, etc., on each of which the word "Buzz" should be used instead of the right number. The word "Buzz" is also substituted for any number in which the word seven occurs, even though it should not be a multiple of seven, such as seventeen, twenty-seven, thirty-seven, etc. When seventy is reached, the counting proceeds as "Buzz-one," "Buzz-two," etc., and seventy-seven is "Buzz-buzz."

Whenever a player says a number instead of "Buzz," or says "Buzz" in the wrong place, or calls out a wrong number, he must pay a forfeit and start the game over again by saying "One."

The game may also be played by having each player who misses drop from the game. Where this is done, and the player retains his seat but is silent, the game becomes even more confusing for the players who remain.

CAKE SALE

Party   *Juniors; adults*

Each player is given a card or sheet of paper prepared with the following questions, or they may be dictated at the time. The one wins who has the largest number of answers correct.

What kind of cake would you buy for—

1. Sculptors? (Marble cake.)
2. Politicians? (Plum cake.)
3. Geologists? (Layer cake.)
4. Advertisers? (Cream puffs.)
5. Dairymen? (Cream cake.)
6. Milliners? (Ribbon cake.)
7. His Satanic Majesty? (Angel's food.)
8. Babies? (Patty cakes.)
9. Lovers? (Kisses.)
10. The betrothed? (Bride's cake.)
11. Gossips? (Spice cake.)
12. Carpenters? (Plain [plane] cake.)
13. Idlers? (Loaf cake.)
14. Pugilists? (Pound cake.)
15. One who lives on his friends? (Sponge cake.)
16. Dynamiters? (Raisin cake.)
17. Invalids? (Delicate cake.)
18. Convalescents? (Sunshine cake.)
19. "Boodlers"? (Doughnuts.)
20. Those who sample all these too much? (Stomach ache.)

CAT PARTY

5 to 30 or more players
House party

Each player is provided with a sheet of paper on which are written the following questions. Each question is to be answered with a word, of which the first syllable is cat. The player wins who writes the largest number of correct answers, the list of answers being read by the host or hostess at the close of the time allowed for the game.

Examples of questions are given below:

1. What sort of cat is allowed in a library? (Catalogue.)
2. What sort of cat makes you think of reflected sounds? (Catacoustics.)
3. What sort of cat unites well with a toilet article? (Catacomb.)
4. What sort of cat requires a physician's attention? (Catalepsy.)
5. What sort of cat is feared by soldiers? (Catapult.)
6. What sort of cat is bad for the eyes? (Cataract.)
7. What sort of cat is to be dreaded? (Catastrophe.)
8. What sort of cat is allowed on the table? (Catsup.)
9. What sort of cat goes to Sunday school? (Catechism.)
10. What sort of cat do girls most detest? (Caterpillar.)
11. What sort of cat makes small boys weep? (Cat-o'-nine-tails.)

CHAIN OF EVIDENCE

House party   *Adults*

This game is probably an outgrowth of the one called "Murder," but it has more sheer nonsense and fun in it.

One person, chosen as the District Attorney, calls the company to order and announces that a serious crime has been committed on the premises, such as a theft of jewels, and it becomes his duty to question all present. Each person questioned must tell a possible (though it is seldom plausible) story of how he happened to be connected with the suspicious circumstances in which he finds himself placed by the previous speaker; for in answering questions, each one must mention the name of one of the other guests in a way that involves the latter in a manner difficult to explain. The sport of the game lies in these explanations and in the implication of other persons, and usually becomes so hilarious that the crime is entirely forgotten. The person mentioned be-comes the next one to be questioned. For example:

Attorney. Mr. Morer, you have heard your hostess say that she heard a strange noise in the hall just before discovering the loss of her jewels at two o'clock in the morning, and on opening her door to investigate, saw you going down the stairs. Will you please explain to us, Mr. Morer, how you happened to be going down stairs at that remarkable hour?"

Mr. M. There was a mouse nibbling in my room and I went down to find a mouse trap. As I passed the front door I saw the handle turn, slipped behind a portiere and saw Miss Ivory come in with a flash light.

Atty. Miss Ivory, you were with the company all the evening; you retired to your room at half past eleven, when the others retired?

Miss I. I did.

Atty. How did you come to be entering the house at two o'clock?

Miss I. I had left my bridge score in the car and could not sleep until I had it; so I went out to the garage to get it. As I started back to the house I saw Prof. Goggles climbing out of the dining room window.

Atty. Prof. Goggles! What explanation have you to offer, sir, of such remarkable conduct?

Prof. G. I had accidentally dropped my necktie out of my window, which is directly above the dining room, and I thought I could locate it most accurately by going out that way. I went down the back stairs so as not to waken the household; as I started down, a figure in a dark cloak came up noiselessly and brushed past me. I turned to look at it, and in the moonlight from the window — hem! — I am very sorry to tell you, sir, that I recognized the coiffure of Mrs. Peroxide. etc., etc.

CHARADES

House party   *Children; adults*

This is one of the oldest and most popular of the acting-guessing games, having a more elaborate procedure than Dumb Crambo, which it somewhat resembles.

The company is divided into two groups, one of which goes out of the room and decides on a word to be acted, which the other group, as audience, is to guess. Words of two or more syllables are selected, and the acting group is divided into as many sub-groups as there are syllables, each acting one of the syllables; then at the end the entire acting group joins in presenting the whole word at once. Impromptu spoken dialogue is used, and, in its traditional form in European countries and in early American usage, some costuming is quite a feature. Many households have a "dress-up" chest of garments, lengths of material, and accessories for such occasions, but improvisations are often more interesting and humorous, as a shawl or rug wrapped around one for a cloak or pinned on for a train, an umbrella fastened on for a sword, a towel pinned to the head by one corner to simulate a veil, etc.

Actable words are numerous. A few suggestions are:

Artificial (*art-i-fish-all*)
Persuaded (*purse-wade-Ed*)
Understandable (*under-stand-able*)
Perspicacity (*purse-pick-a-city*)

Television (*tell-a (I or eye) vision*)
Seasonable (*sea-son-able*)
Culmination (*cull-my-nation*)
Intrusive (*in-true-sieve*)

CODE TELEGRAM

House party; camp   *Juniors; adults*

Arrange in advance a paper for each player about the size of a telegraph blank and divided in five large columns for words, with one small column at the left for letters of the alphabet. In this left-hand column write five letters that spell a one-syllable word, such as C, H, E, S, T. At the top of each column write the generic name of some class of things with which all are familiar, such as *Tree, Automobile, Magazine, Flower, City*. The number of columns may vary, and also the words at the top.

	Tree	Automobile	Magazine	Flower	City
C	Catalpa	Cadillac	Century	Carnation	Chicago
H	Hemlock	Haynes	Harper's	Hibiscus	Hoboken
E	Elm	Elgar	Élite	Edelweiss	Erie
S					
T					

The game consists in filling in the columns with words beginning with the letters listed in the left-hand column. The diagram will show how this is done. When a time limit has expired, say of ten minutes, one person reads the names he has written. When anyone else has one of the same words, the count is nought. For each word that appears on only one paper, that player receives a score of one. The player wins who has the largest score, and may receive a prize or favor.

VARIATION. — This game is also played without the column headings, but instead a requirement that a sentence be written in which each word begins with one of the letters of the given word arranged in the same order — in this case, C–H–E–S–T. The results are often very laughable.

COSTUME RACE

House party   *Adults*

This game has so much sport for adults that it is well worth the trouble of gathering together the material needed for it. The game is best played by the men of the party as here described. They stand in relay teams of from three to five each. These teams are lined up at one end of the room. A couple of yards in front of each team is a basket containing articles of clothing, mostly women's dress. The more old-fashioned and ridiculous these garments, the greater the fun. In each basket should be a dress skirt, either long, short, or trained; then a man's vest, which is to be put on in lieu of a waist or blouse (it must be large, as it is to go over a man's coat); then a hat, a bandana handkerchief for the neck, a pair of gloves of man's size, and a ridiculous parasol, either child's size or for women. At a signal the first man from each team goes forward to the basket, puts on these garments over his own street or evening suit in any order that he chooses, runs in them to the far end of the room, touches the wall, returns to the basket, removes the garments and puts them into the basket, and then goes on to his team and touches off the next player. He, in turn, goes through the same performance. The team whose last player gets back first wins the race.

A large part of the fun of this game consists in the appearance and acting of men in women's clothing, as well as in the out-of-style and incongruous garments that may be collected for it.

CRAMBO

Each player is provided with two slips of paper, and also with another full sheet of paper and a pencil. On one of the slips he writes a question. This may be as serious or absurd as fancy dictates. On the other slip of paper he writes a word, either a common or proper noun. The slips containing the questions are then collected in a box or hat, and those containing the nouns in another receptacle. The questions are thoroughly mixed and passed around, each player drawing one. The same is done with the nouns.

Each player must then write a verse which shall answer the question and contain the word that he has drawn, no matter how irrelevant it may be. A time limit is generally given for this performance, varying with the facility of the players.

The following may serve as examples. The author recalls a very grave banker, not suspected of humor, who drew the question, "How long should you roast a leg of mutton?" The word drawn was "Finger." He wrote:

> "To roast the mutton, let it linger
> Longer than to roast your finger."

Another business man drew the question, "What is the difference between doughnuts and sponge cake?" The word was "Youth." He wrote:

> "Sponge cake is delicate and sweet to the taste,
> While doughnuts are tough as thunder;
> And the youth who partakes of the first in haste
> Will tackle the latter with wonder."

The game may be made more difficult by each player writing on a third slip of paper a verb or an adjective, these to be collected and redistributed with the nouns and questions.

CROSS QUESTIONS

All but one of the players sit in two rows facing each other, those directly opposite each other being partners. The odd player walks around the rows behind the others, asking questions of any player facing him from the farther row. The question must be answered, not by the player addressed, but by his partner or *vis-a-vis*, who sits with his back to the questioner.

Any player answering a question addressed directly to him, or failing to answer one addressed to his partner, or giving an incorrect answer to a question, changes places with the questioner, or pays a forfeit, as may have been decided on beforehand.

FOR THE SCHOOLROOM. — When played in the schoolroom, the adjacent rows should form a group and face each other so as to leave free aisles between the groups in which the questioners may walk, as shown in the diagram of Old Man Tag (page 176).

The game may be made to correlate with almost any subject in the school curriculum, the questioner asking, for instance, for capital cities, boundaries, mountains, etc., for geography; for dates or the names of heroes in great events, for history; or even for brief problems in mental arithmetic.

DONKEY'S TAIL

Party   *Children; adults*

An outline drawing is made of a donkey minus his tail. The figure should be about three feet long and on a cotton sheet or large piece of paper. This is fastened against the wall at about shoulder height. Each guest is provided with a paper tail and a pin with which to pin it on the donkey; but he is to place it while blindfolded and start from at least ten feet away from the donkey. The anatomy of the creature becomes more and more astounding as the game goes on. The person who puts the tail nearest to where it belongs is given a prize.

DUMB CRAMBO

Parlor   *Juniors; adults*

The players are divided into two groups. One group goes outside of the room, and those remaining choose some verb, which is to be guessed and acted by the other party. The outside group is then told some word which rhymes with the chosen verb. They consult among themselves, decide on a verb which they think may be the right one, enter the room, and without speaking act out the word they have guessed. The inside group must decide from this pantomime if the correct verb has been guessed. If not, they shake their heads. If right, they clap their hands. No speaking is allowed on either side. If the outside group is wrong in their guess, they retire and try another word, repeating this play until they hit upon the right word, when the two sides change places.

EGGSHELL RACE

Parlor; camp   *Children; adults*

Prepare eggshells by making a small hole in either end and blowing out the yolks and whites, one shell for each player. The players stand back of the starting line at one end of the room and, at a signal, start to propel the empty eggshells over the floor by fanning them — preferably with a palm leaf fan — to the goal line at the opposite end of the room. The player whose eggshell crosses the goal line first wins.

No eggshell may be touched or blown with the breath, but only propelled by the fan. The movements of the empty eggshell are quite erratic, and there is as much fun for those who look on as for those who play.

FAMOUS PEOPLE

Party   *Juniors; adults*

Each player is given a paper and pencil. The leader of the group names some letter of the alphabet, and each one writes the names of as many famous people, dead or living, as he can think of whose surnames begin with this letter. A signal to stop is given in two or three minutes. The player wins who has the largest number of names at the end.

FIND THE RING

Parlor; schoolroom   *Children*

The players sit in a circle, holding in their hands a long piece of string tied at the ends so as to form a circle large enough to go around, a small ring having been put upon this string. One player is chosen to stand in the center. The players who are seated then pass the ring from one to another, the object being for the player in the center to detect who has the ring. The other players will try to deceive him by making passes to indicate the passage of the ring when it really is not in their vicinity. When the player in the center thinks he knows who has the ring, he calls out the name of that player. If right, he sits down, and that player must take his place in the center. This game may be played by the players repeating the following lines as the ring is passed around the circle:

"Oh, the grand old Duke of York,
    He had ten thousand men;
    He marched them up the hillago,
    And marched them down again.

"And when they were up they were up,
    And when they were down they were down;
    And when they were halfway up the hill,
    They were neither up nor down."

FISHERMEN

4 to 15 players   *Elementary*

Each child fastens to his belt a heavy thread or lightweight cord which will snap easily if stepped on. It should be just long enough to trail slightly on the ground; on the loose end he ties some small object to serve as a fish. This may be a lead sinker, an empty spool, a bunch of twigs, or anything heavy enough to trail.

On signal, each player tries to step on the fish of some other player so as to snap the thread and allow him to gather in the fish. At the same time he tries to save his own fish from a similar fate, but may not touch any fish line with his hands. Any player who loses his fish is out of the play. The winner is the one who at the end has the most fishes.

This and several other games from the Russian are included by courtesy of Mademoiselle Marie Barsky.

FLOWER MATCH

Out of doors   *Children*

This is one of the pretty Oriental games recorded from Korea by Mr. Culin, and is played by the children of that country, Japan, and China.

The players each gather a handful of meadow bloom — blossoms and grass indiscriminately, not selecting the contents of the bunch. All sit down in a group. The first player lays out one from his pile, say a buttercup. All of the players around the circle try to match this, that is, each one who has buttercups lays all of them in a pile with that of the first player, who appropriates the entire pile when this has gone around the circle. Then the next player lays out something which all must try to match. The one wins who has the largest number of grasses or blossoms all counted together at the end. Different sorts of grasses and leaves count in this game as well as different kinds or colors of blossoms.

GRASS BLADE

Out of doors   *Children*

This is a pretty game for little children, recorded by Mr. Culin, as played by the children of Japan, China, and Korea.

Each child gathers a handful of grass, soft, flexible grass blades being best for the purpose. The players are all seated in a group. One child makes a loop of a blade of grass by holding the two ends in his hand. Another child loops a blade of grass through this and the two pull; the one whose grass blade breaks loses, and the two pieces as trophies are given to the successful player, who then matches his grass blade with the next, and so on around the circle until his grass blade breaks, when he loses his turn and the next player has a similar turn. The one wins who has the greatest pile of trophies at the end.

HAND–SLAPPING GAMES

(See *Scat* and *Bean Porridge Hot*)

HANDS UP — HANDS DOWN

Schoolroom   *Intermediates to seniors*

This is a schoolroom adaptation of Up Jenkins, and is designed especially for use as children assemble in a class room before the opening of the school session. The only material required is a

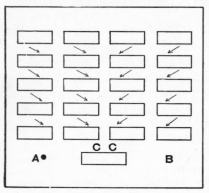

HANDS UP, HANDS DOWN

small paper or worsted ball of a size that may be hidden in the clenched hand.

The players are divided into two groups, each group seated, partly facing the other (indicated by arrows in the diagram) with a captain standing before each side at C.

The side starting the game is given a small ball of paper or worsted, and at the command of the captain

of the *opposing* side the players pass the ball rapidly from one to another. Each player makes the motion of passing, so as to deceive the opposing group as to the whereabouts of the ball.

The captain and players of the opposing group meanwhile keep a sharp lookout for the ball without leaving their seats.

After a short time of passing, the captain who started the passing (Group B, diagram) calls suddenly, "Hands up!" and immediately all passing in Group A must cease, and all hands must be raised high overhead and tightly clenched, so the player having the ball when the passing ceased may not disclose the fact.

The B captain again gives a sudden command of "Hands down!" Immediately all hands are brought down softly on the desk in front of each player of Group A, hands wide open, palms downward, and again the player with the ball tries to hide it under his hand.

The players of Group B who think they know who has the ball raise their hands. No player may speak unless called by his captain. When called, he may say, "Under J.'s right hand" (or left hand, as the case may be). J. raises the right hand, and if the guesser be mistaken, places that hand in his lap, it being thereafter out of commission, so to speak. No other player of Group A moves a hand. Should the ball be found under the hand raised, the opposing group, *i.e.* Group B, receives as many points as there are hands left upon the desks. Otherwise, the search continues, the captain of Group B asking players of his group to order a hand raised, or orders it himself, until the ball is discovered. Group B now takes the ball and passes it from one to another, and Group A gives commands through its captain. The side making a score of three hundred points wins. A side loses ten points when a player talks or calls for a hand to be raised without the permission or call of the captain.

HEN ROOST

Party; schoolroom   *Junior high school*

Each of the players except one chooses a word, which should be the name of some object, and in answering any questions put to him in the game he must introduce this word which he has chosen into each answer. The odd player takes the place of questioner. He may ask one or more questions of each player, as he sees fit, the dialogue taking any turn he chooses, the following being suggestive of the general tone of it:

The questioner says: "I heard that you got into the hen roost yesterday. How did you get in?"

Answer: "With the dictionary."

To the next player: "What did you find there?"

Answer: "A horse."

To the next player: "What did you give him to eat?"

Answer: "A sofa pillow," etc.

Any player who laughs, or who fails to answer promptly or correctly to the question, must change places with the questioner. Forfeits may also be required if desired.

HIDE THE THIMBLE

(Magic Music)

5 to 60 players   *Children*
Schoolroom; parlor   *to adults*

One player is sent from the room; while absent, one of those remaining hides a thimble, a cork, or some small object which has been previously shown to the absent one. When the object is hidden, the absent player is recalled, and proceeds to hunt for the hidden object. While he is doing this, the others sing or clap their hands, the sound being very soft and low when the hunter is far away from the object, and growing louder as he approaches it. The piano music is desirable, but for schoolroom use singing is found to be more interesting for all, as well as often more practicable. For very little children hand clapping is pleasing and sometimes more easily used than singing. Instead of music or clapping, the watching players often call out, "Warm!" "Very Warm!" "Hot!" to indicate the hunter's nearness to the object, or "Cold!" "Very Cold!" "Freezing!" as he goes away from it.

HORNS

Indoors; schoolroom   *Children to seniors*

This game is played very much like "Simon says." It is a quiet game that may be played with all of the players seated, their forefingers placed on their knees or on a table or desk in front of them. One who is leader says:

"All horns up!"

"Cat's horns up!" or

"Cow's horns up!"

whereupon he lifts his own forefingers, pointing upward. Should he name an animal that has horns, all of the players lift their fingers in similar manner, but should he name an animal such as a cat, that has no horns, any player that lifts his fingers in imitation of the leader is out of the game.

INDOOR TREASURE HUNT

House party   *Juniors to adults*

There are several ways of conducting this:

I. A number of "treasures" (sometimes peanuts!) may be hidden so that a small part is visible — as, back of a picture, in a vase or jar, in a book, under a pillow or rug, etc. The person collecting the largest number is winner and, if peanuts have been used, receives a prize in addition to a store of nuts.

II. **CRYPTIC CLUES.** — One prize or "treasure" may be hidden and a series of cryptic clues lead to it. As in the outdoor Treasure Hunt, these are written on slips of paper and hidden. The final clue leads to the "treasure." Successful clues have been as follows:

"Find Clue Number One in this room, decapitate the last word of the first line, go into the hall. and follow its instruction."

When found, Clue Number One reads:
> "Tiger, tiger, burning bright
> In the forests of the night."

The word when decapitated is "right" and leads to the next clue.

When found, Clue Number Two may be the first of a series of arithmetic problems, such as: "Multiply 97608 by 53; find a volume on a bookshelf, in a position corresponding with the last figure of your answer, counting volumes from the left. This is Clue Three. Clue Number Four is shut in this book."

Clue Number Four: "Subtract 5269 from the answer to Clue Two and the answer will be the page in the biggest work in the library, where you will find Clue Five."

Clue Five may be a conundrum of which the answer is to be guessed and will lead to Clue Six.

Clue Six may be a series of words made from a reversed alphabet:

```
        a  b  c  d  e  f  g  h  i  j  k  l  m
Key: — |  |  |  |  |  |  |  |  |  |  |  |  |
        z  y  x  w  v  u  t  s  r  q  p  o  n
```

> Pvvk irtag lm urlfirmt, blf'iv wlrmt urmv.
> Tl fk gl gsv mligs dvhg illn;
> Gsviv urmw blfi mvcg xofv zg gsv hrtm
> Lu z orggov yildm dsrhp yilln.

Decoded this means:
> "Keep right on figuring, you're doing fine.
> Go up to the northwest room;
> There find your next clue at the sign
> Of a little brown whisk broom."

INITIALS

House party   *Juniors to adults*

For this game it will be necessary to prepare slips of paper, one for each player. At the head of the paper are written the initials of some person who will be present; under this a series of questions which the player drawing the paper is to answer. The papers are put in a box or hat and drawn by the players, or held in the hand with the initials concealed and drawn in that way. A certain time may be allowed, if desired, for the answering of the questions.

The answers must be written in each case immediately below the question, must consist of only as many words as there are initials at the top of the sheet, and the words of the answer must begin with the initials in their proper order. For example:

H. B. B.

1. To whom does this paper belong? (Henry B. Brown.)
2. What is his character? (Horrid, but bearable.)
3. What kind of hair has he? (Heavy, burnished brown.)
4. What kind of eyes has he? (Heavenly, bright blue.)
5. What books does he prefer? (Handsomely bound biographies.)
6. What animals does he prefer? (Howling big bears.)
7. What is his chief occupation? (Hammering bulky boxes.)
8. What do you surmise regarding his future? (He'd better beware.)
9. What does he think of the opposite sex? (Hebes! Bright beauties!)
10. What does he think of the world in general? (He's becoming bewildered.)

KALEIDOSCOPE

(Flower Garden)

5 to 30 or more players   *Primary grades*
Schoolroom; parlor; playground

This is a quiet game, and makes a pleasant and restful change from more active games. It may be correlated with geography, history, literature, and many other subjects.

The players are all seated, with the exception of from four to six, who stand in a line in front of their fellows, each being given, or choosing, the name of a color — red, violet, green, etc. The players who are seated then close their eyes, and those who represent colors change places in the line. When they are rearranged, those who are seated open their eyes, and being called upon individually, try to name the colors in their new arrangement, the game being a test of memory.

IN THE SCHOOLROOM, and for little children, to give more activity the colors should scatter and run around the room after being named, halting on a signal. The player who is to name them then runs around the room to the different ones as they stand scattered in this way, naming each as he reaches him.

CORRELATION. — This game may be correlated with any academic subject in which familiarity with proper names is desired; as in

History. — By using the names of generals or statesmen from a given period instead of the colors.

Geography. — The names of capital cities, states, rivers, etc.

Literature. — The names of the works of a given author; of the authors of a period; or of the characters in a book or play.

Nature study. — The names of birds, trees, flowers; or any other branch of nature study may be used.

LEAF BY LEAF

Out of doors   *Children; adults*

A basket of leaves is provided, no two of the leaves being alike. These may be leaves from trees, shrubs, or plants, or flowers may be used in the same way.

The players are each provided with a card or slip of paper and a pencil, and are seated. One leaf is handed to the first player, who passes it on to the next, and so on until it has made the round of the group. Each player, in turn, if he can identify the leaf, writes the name of it on a card. Each leaf is thus passed.

The host or hostess then reads a correct list, naming the leaves in the order in which they were passed. The player wins who has the largest number correct.

This is an especially pleasing game for nature students.

LITERARY LORE

House party; schoolroom   *Seniors to adults*

Each player is given a sheet of paper on which the following questions are written. The player wins who writes correct answers to the largest number of questions. This game may be worked up from the writings of any poet or author. Examples are given from Tennyson and Longfellow. The answers are appended here, but in playing the game they should be read by the host or hostess at the end.

TENNYSON

1. What poem is it that sings down the vale? — The Brook.
2. What is the poem whose father is king? — The Princess.
3. The poem that honors a friend who is gone? — In Memoriam.
4. The poem that rules in the spring? — The May Queen.
5. The poem that lives in the depths of the sea? — The Mermaid.
6. The poem once baked in a pie? — The Blackbird.
7. The poem from which all its dwellers have gone? — The Deserted House.
8. The poem that is a good-by? — The Farewell.
9. The poem whose dress was tatters and rags? — The Beggar Maid.
10. The poem that lets in light? — The Window.
11. The poem in which we see castles in Spain? — The Day Dream.
12. The poem that sees in the night? — The Owl.

LONGFELLOW

1. What poem is it that helps to shoe your horse? — The Village Blacksmith.
2. The poem that needs an umbrella? — The Rainy Day.   An April Day.
3. The poem that carries you across? — The Bridge.
4. The poem that finds you weary? — The Day Is Done.
5. The poem that keeps the time? — The Old Clock on the Stairs.
6. The poem that belongs to little people? — The Children's Hour.

LIVING WORDS

House party   *Juniors to adults*

In advance prepare placards enough, about 8 by 10 inches, so that each player may have one. On each is drawn in large size a letter of the alphabet, one half in red and the other half, a duplicate set, in black. A string should be attached to the two upper corners, long enough to go over the head and leave the placard hanging on the chest. If there are not enough players for two full alphabets, use selected letters, making a combination of the most-used vowels and consonants, such as *A E H M N O R S T.*

The player in charge of the game calls a word which may be made from these letters, having prepared a list in advance. The players wearing the red letters immediately rush to one side of the room and arrange themselves in the order that spells the word, while the black-letter team does the same on the other side. The team getting its word in order first scores one point. When the judge has recorded and announced the winner, the players go back to their team and another word is called. At the end of the list the team is pronounced winner which has the larger score.

From the letters mentioned, the following list of words are given as an example:

rest, man, those, more, hasten, north, roam, heart, shone, east, ham, roast, home, storm, moan, steam, shot, thorn, share, morn, near, sermon.

Longer words for older players make more fun.

LONDON

Indoors; schoolroom; seashore　　　　　　　*Juniors; seniors*

This is a quiet game in which the players are all seated. A diagram is drawn on a slate or a piece of paper of oblong shape, about six by ten inches in outside dimensions, if the surface admits of one so large. This is divided by a horizontal line every two inches. It is an advantage if the players have different colored pencils, but this is not necessary. A piece of paper is placed at the bottom of the diagram and blown over the diagram toward the top; or a small piece of glass or china called a "chipper" is used, the latter being nicked or snapped with the fingers. The first player snaps his chipper, and in whichever place it stops marks with a pencil a small round "*o*" to represent a man's head. The chipper is then returned to its starting place and the play is repeated. This is continued until the player has marked a head in each of the horizontal spaces; or should his chipper land a second time in a space in which he has already marked such a head, he makes a larger round under the head to represent the body of a man. The third time it lands in this place he makes a downward stroke for a leg, and the fourth time one for a second leg, which completes the man. Should three complete men be so drawn in one space, the player, without shooting again, draws what are called "arms," that is, a horizontal line from the figures across the space to the outside limits. This occupies the space

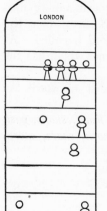

LONDON

completely and keeps the other player out of that space; that is, the other cannot put any men in it or add to any which he may already have started there.

The first player continues to play until the chipper lands on a line; a player whose chipper lands on a line or outside of the diagram loses his turn. The other player then takes his turn, and may start, continue, or complete men in any spaces which the first player has not occupied with three armed men, even though the latter may have started men in the space or have completed two of them. Each player may build only on his own men.

The player wins who succeeds in occupying the largest number of spaces with three armed men of his own drawing.

The space at the top of the diagram, called "London," is especially advantageous. No men are marked in it, but should the chipper land there at any time, the player may draw a head in every other space on the diagram, or add one mark to any one drawing he may have already in each space.

This game may be played on the **seashore** or playground or wherever the diagram may be drawn in hard earth.

For the **schoolroom** it is an interesting diversion for pupils who assemble early before the opening of the school session.

MINISTER'S CAT (THE)

Party; schoolroom　　　　　　　　　　　　　*Children; adults*

The first player says, "The minister's cat is an avaricious cat," using an adjective which begins with "*a*" to describe the cat.

The next player makes a remark about the cat, using the same initial letter for the adjective; for instance, that it is an "aggressive" cat.   This is continued, each player using a different adjective beginning with the letter "a," until the game has gone entirely around the circle.   The first player then makes a similar remark about the cat, using an adjective beginning with "b."   This goes around, and so on through the alphabet.   Any player who is slow to respond, or who fails, must either drop out of the game or pay a forfeit, as may be decided at the start.

MURDER

House party   *Adults*

This is a very popular game with house parties for adults. The host, or a chosen leader, should take as many playing cards from a deck as there are guests, making sure that the ace of spades is included.   Each guest draws one card, concealing it from the other players.   The one who draws the ace of spades is to be the murderer, and the leader explains to the company that when the lights are turned out someone will be murdered, that is, taken by the throat or stabbed in the back.   Anyone so assassinated is immediately to scream and fall to the ground.   After an interval of ten seconds, the lights will be turned up, and the district attorney will try to identify the murderer through questioning. The latter is supposed to make a getaway (without leaving the house) in the ten seconds before the lights are turned on.

The host takes his position by the light switch, turns off the lights, and the entire group scatters through the rooms.   When a scream is heard, the host counts the ten seconds, turns up the lights, and everyone must stand still.   The district attorney then proceeds to question each person in the group.

The district attorney should be carefully chosen by the host. It is better not to choose a lawyer, as the legal mind strays from facts that are interesting to the general player.   After taking a general survey of the position of players in relation to the one assassinated, the attorney asks the others to be seated, and each one in turn is called forward to be questioned.   Everyone but the murderer must tell the absolute truth.   He alone may fabricate.   Only three times may the attorney ask the direct question: "Are you the murderer?" and this only when he thinks he has found the culprit; this is the only question which the murderer must answer truthfully.

The district attorney's questions will probably be mostly in the line of discovering circumstantial evidence, such as: "Was the scream near you?" "Which room were you in?" "How did you come to be on the stairs?" "Did you hear anyone moving?" "Was it the sound of skirts or only of footsteps?" "Was it on your right or your left side?"

"Close your eyes and re-live the moment immediately after the outcry, being careful to recall such things as height of person passing you, texture of garment that touched you, scent, etc.

"Now open your eyes and tell us all you have remembered.

"Close your eyes again while we have those on trial pass by you one at a time. Indicate by raising your hand if you detect the scent, or hear the same sound, or have any other similar indication."

(See also *Trial by Jury* and *Chain of Evidence*.)

MUSIC BOX

House party; schoolroom   *Children; adults*

Each player is given a slip of paper and pencil. Someone who has a good repertoire of popular airs sits at the piano — or lacking a piano, may sing without words — and goes briefly through snatches of one air after another, each of the players writing on his slip of paper the name of the air, or leaving a blank if he be unable to name it. The one wins who names the largest number of airs correctly.

This is an admirable game to use for old ballads, such as "Annie Laurie," "Suwanee River," "My Old Kentucky Home," "Blue Bells of Scotland," etc., or for national airs, or for both together. In a company that is well up on current music, airs from current songs and popular operas may be used successfully.

MY LADY'S LAPDOG

Party   *Juniors; adults*

My lady's lapdog.
Two plump partridges and my lady's lapdog.
Three great elephants, two plump partridges, and my lady's lapdog.
Four Persian cherry trees, three great elephants, etc.

Five Limerick oysters, four Persian cherry trees, etc.

Six bottles of Frontignac, five Limerick oysters, etc.

Seven swans a swimming, six bottles of Frontignac, etc.

Eight flip flap floating fly boats, seven swans, etc.

Nine merchants going to Bagdad, eight flip flap, etc.

Ten Italian dancing masters going to teach ten Arabian magpies how to dance, nine merchants going to Bagdad, etc.

Eleven guests going to celebrate the marriage of the Princess Baldroubadour with the Prince of Tierra del Fuego, ten Italian dancing masters going to teach ten Arabian magpies, etc.

Twelve triumphant trumpeters triumphantly trumpeting the tragical tradition of Telemachus, eleven guests going to celebrate the marriage, etc.

The players sit in a circle; the one who is leader turns to the next player and says, "My lady's lapdog." This player turns to the one next him and repeats the phrase, which is thus handed around the circle. When it gets back to the leader, the leader turns to his neighbor and adds an item to that previously mentioned, saying, "Two plump partridges and my lady's lapdog." This goes around the circle, when the leader says, "Three great elephants, two plump partridges, and my lady's lapdog," and so on, adding each time different items according to the formula given above. Any player failing to repeat the list correctly pays a forfeit.

VARIATION. — For younger players, the following list may be found better:

A big fat hen.

Two ducks and a big fat hen.

Three wild geese, two ducks, and a big fat hen.

Four plump partridges, three wild geese, two ducks, etc.

Five pouting pigeons, four plump partridges, three, etc.

Six long-legged cranes, five pouting pigeons, etc.

Seven green parrots, six long-legged cranes, etc.

Eight screeching owls, seven green parrots, six long-legged, etc.

Nine ugly black turkey buzzards, eight screeching owls, etc.

Ten thousand domesticated chimney swallows, nine ugly black turkey buzzards, eight screeching owls, etc.

NAUGHTS AND CROSSES

(Tit-Tat-Toe)

Indoors; out of doors   *Intermediates*

A diagram is drawn on a slate, paper, or the ground, and consists of two vertical lines, crossed by two horizontal lines. One player chooses to write "naughts" (o) and the other "crosses"

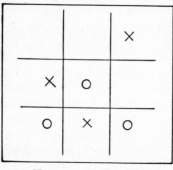

NAUGHTS AND CROSSES

(×). The players take turns in marking a naught or a cross in one of the nine places provided by the diagram, the object being to get three naughts or three crosses in a row. This row may be either vertical, horizontal, or diagonal.

A score is kept of the games won by each player, and a third score is kept of the games played in which neither player wins.

This game may be played at the **seashore,** on the **playground,** or wherever the diagram may be traced on the earth.

For **school** use it is an interesting diversion for pupils who assemble early before a session opens, or who remain in over a rainy noontime.

NIMBLE SQUIRREL

Schoolroom; parlor   *Intermediate to junior high school*

This is a device for mental arithmetic. It is one of which children are very fond. As the play element may enter very largely into the fanciful suggestions used by the teacher, it seems in place in a book of games.

The teacher states her problem in a manner similar to the following:

"There was a tree with fifty branches. A squirrel started on the first branch, jumped up three branches [to the fourth], came halfway down [to the second], went three times as high [sixth branch], fell halfway down [third branch], saw a dog, and ran to the top of the tree; fell to the ground and started over again;

went up eight branches, jumped past three branches," etc., finishing up with, "How many branches from the top was he?"

This game has been found intensely interesting for children through the upper grades of the elementary schools.

NUT RACE

House party; camp   *Children; adults*

Players are divided into teams of from three to five each, who stand in relay formation at one end of the room. Two players act as judges at the goal line — a straight line or string drawn across the opposite end of the room. Two bowls are provided for each team; one, containing peanuts in the shells, is placed at the starting line in front of the team, and the other, being empty, is placed on the goal line at the far end of the room.

The game consists in scooping up as many peanuts as possible on the back of one hand, like jackstones, carrying them to the bowl at the goal line, dumping them into this, and returning to the starting line to touch off the next player in the team. This next player then scoops up as many as he can hold in the same way, and repeats the performance, and so on until each player in each team has had his turn.

The game is won by the team which deposits the greatest number of peanuts in the bowl at the goal line. Any nuts falling off the hand in transit, or landing outside of the bowl at the end, may not be recovered and are not counted. Any nuts may be used, such as hazel nuts, walnuts, or chestnuts, and may be more difficult to play than peanuts.

OBSERVATION

5 to 60 players   *Children*
Parlor; schoolroom   *to adults*

This game is a test of visual memory. When played in a parlor, all the players are seated except one, who passes around a tray or a plate, on which are from six to twenty objects, all different. These may include such things as a key, spool of thread, pencil, cracker, piece of cake, ink bottle, napkin ring, small vase, etc. The more uniform the size and color of the objects, the more difficult will be the test. The player who carries the tray will pass at the pace of an ordinary walk around the circle, giving each player an opportunity to look at the objects only so long as they are passing before him. It is not allowable to look longer than this. The observer must then at once write down on a slip of paper the names of as many of the objects as he can remember. The player wins who writes correctly the longest list.

It is sometimes more convenient to have the articles on a table and the players all pass in a line before them.

IN THE SCHOOLROOM. — The objects should be placed on the teacher's desk, so shielded that pupils cannot see them except as they march past the desk. This they should do, returning at once to their seats and writing the list. Used in this way, the game may be made to correlate with nature study, the objects to be observed being grasses, shells, leaves, stones, woods, etc.

OUTDOOR TREASURE HUNT

(On foot)

Camp; party   *Children; adults*

This is similar to the Automobile Treasure Hunt, but it covers a smaller territory. Suggestive clues are:

"Look under the roof of the empty dog-house for Clue Number Three." This says:

"Clue Number Four is on the ninety-fourth post of a black-and-white fence." This in turn says that Clue Number Five is in an empty flower-pot back of Mr. James' house; etc.

PENNY WISE

House party   *Children; adults*

Each player is provided with a bright new penny, a piece of paper, and a pencil. On the paper are written beforehand, or to dictation, the following requirements, of course without the answers. The player wins who has the largest number of correct answers.

Find on the Lincoln penny the following:

The name of a song. — America.
A privilege. — Liberty.
A part of Indian corn. — Ear.
A part of a hill. — Brow.
Something denoting self. — Eye (I).
Part of a door. — Lock (of hair).
A gallant. — Beau (bow).
A piece of jewelry. — Ring.
A foreign fruit. — Date.
Trimming for a hat. — Feather.
What ships sail on. — Sea (C).
A perfume. — Scent (cent).
A religious edifice. — Temple.
A messenger. — One sent (cent).
A method of voting. — Ayes and Noes (eyes and nose).
A Chinese beverage. — Tea (T).
A gaudy flower. — Tulips (two lips).
Comfort. — Ease (E. E.).
A small animal. — Hare (hair).
A term of marriage. — United state.
An ancient honor. — Wreath.

PHOTOGRAPHER

House party   *Children; adults*

This is a game for a social party. Any number may participate, but two players are chosen as photographer and guesser.

The guesser leaves the room, and the photographer proceeds to take a photograph of one of the remaining players, using a large spoon instead of a camera. This gives opportunity for some ridiculous stage business in picture taking and a bit of fun. The guesser is then recalled and tries to guess whose picture was taken. He gets his cue from the photographer, who assumes the same posture as the person whose photograph he took, changing when the latter changes. It is well for the photographer to choose a restless person for his subject.

Or the entire company may assume the same position, so as to mislead the guesser.

After a successful guess, a new photographer and guesser are chosen.

PICTURE SHOW

Party   *Juniors; adults*

Each player is given a pencil and a strip of paper about three inches wide and ten or more inches long. He is told to draw a picture at the top of the slip — of an object, animal, person, landscape, or whatever he pleases — and that he will have three minutes in which to do this. When time is called, he is told to write at the bottom of the slip the name of what he has drawn and then to fold over the edge of the paper so that this writing cannot be seen. He then passes the slip to his neighbor on the right who in turn writes at the bottom a title for the picture, expressing what he thinks the drawing represents. He then folds the paper to hide his title and passes it on. This is repeated until each person in the group has written a title for each picture, when each is displayed to the company and the titles read aloud. They usually make much sport and may be pinned up as an art gallery for further examination. The company votes on the best artist, who then receives a decoration — another opportunity for sport.

PING-PONG DRIBBLE RACE

PING–PONG DRIBBLE RACE

10 to 30 players   *Children*
Parlor; gymnasium   *to adults*
Ping-pong ball, hoop, and ruler for each team.

The players are divided into relay teams which sit in line formation behind a starting line at one end of the room. The first player of each team is provided with a ping-pong ball and a ruler. Opposite this player, two thirds of the distance down the room, sits a player facing the team and holding a hoop through which the ball is to be dribbled. On a signal each leader bounces his ball and hits it with the ruler in a series of bounces along the floor and through the hoop, and then rolls it over a finish line drawn at the far end of the room. As soon as the ball is over the line, the player picks it up, runs back to his team, places the ball and the ruler on the starting line, and goes to the rear of the file. Number Two immediately picks up the ball and the ruler and goes through the same performance. The team whose last player returns first is the winner.

The ball must go through the hoop toward the finish line and the player may not touch the ball with his hand until it is over this line. The game may be prolonged by requiring a return dribble through the hoop to starting line.

By courtesy of Miss Dorothy C. Clark, London.

PLANTING A GARDEN

House party; camp *Children; adults*

Each player is provided with a sheet of paper and a pencil. The game consists in one player's writing down something that he has planted and the next player's stating what came up. Anything may be planted, though the questioner must have in mind something that could come up from what he writes. He must sign his initials. The names of the plants that come up must bear some direct relation, punning or otherwise, to the things planted.

For example, a player writes, "I planted a kitten; what came up?" The paper is handed to the next player, who writes, "Pussy willows."

After the questions are written, the papers are collected and redistributed, and each writes an answer to the question he has drawn. They are then collected again, and the hostess reads the questions and answers. Any question not answered must be replied to by the player who wrote it. Examples follow:

1. Plant an angry wise man; what will come up? — Scarlet sage.
2. Plant a box of candy; what will come up? — Candytuft.
3. Cupid's arrow; what will come up? — Bleeding heart.
4. Some steps. — Hops.
5. Days, months, and years. — Thyme.
6. Christmas Eve. — Star of Bethlehem.
7. Orange blossoms. — Bridal wreath.

8. A sermon. — Jack in the pulpit.
9. Cuff on the ear. — Box.
10. Grief. — Weeping willow.
11. Cinderella at midnight. — Lady's slipper.
12. A ship that has nowhere to go. — Portulaca (port you lack, ah!).
13. Star Spangled Banner and Union Jack. — Flags.
14. Claws and a roar. — Tiger lilies.
15. A Richmond caterpillar. — Virginia creeper.
16. Contentment. — Heart's-ease.
17. What a married man never has. — Bachelor's buttons.
18. Sad beauties. — Bluebells.
19. Labyrinth. — Maize.

POOR PUSSY

5 to 20 players   *Children*
Parlor   *to adults*

The players sit in a circle, except one who is chosen for Poor Pussy. Pussy kneels in front of any player and miaous. This person must stroke or pat Pussy's head and say, "Poor Pussy! Poor Pussy! Poor Pussy!" repeating the words three times, all without smiling. If the player who is petting Puss smiles, he must change places with Puss. The Puss may resort to any variations in the music of the miaou, or in attitude or expression, to induce the one who is petting to smile.

This may be made one of the most amusing games for adults at a house party. The writer has seen some of the most dignified professional people laughing until the tears came while playing this simple little game.

PRINCE OF PARIS

Party; schoolroom   *Children; adults*

A player is chosen as leader; the others are numbered consecutively from one up, and are all seated.

The leader, standing in front, says, "The Prince of Paris has lost his hat. Did you find it, Number Four, sir?" whereupon Number Four jumps to his feet and says:

"What, sir! I, sir?"

Leader. "Yes, sir! You, sir!"

No. Four. "Not I, sir!"

Leader. "Who, then, sir?"
No. Four. "Number Seven, sir."
Number Seven, as soon as his number is called, must jump at once to his feet and say:
"What, sir! I, sir?"
Leader. "Yes, sir! You, sir."
No. Seven. "Not I, sir!"
Leader. "Who, then, sir?"
No. Seven. "Number Three, sir!"
Number Three immediately jumps to his feet, and the same dialogue is repeated. The object of the game is for the leader to try to repeat the statement, "The Prince of Paris has lost his hat," before the last player named can jump to his feet and say, "What, sir! I, sir?" If he succeeds in doing this, he changes places with the player who failed in promptness, that player becoming leader.

Should any player fail to say "Sir" in the proper place, this also is a mistake, and the leader may change places with such player.

This game has much sport in it for house parties or other uses.

RECOGNITION

Party; schoolroom   *Children; adults*

Each player is given a card or slip prepared with the following questions, or the list may be dictated at the time.

What famous persons, historical or mythical, do these objects suggest?

1. Hatchet? (George Washington.)
2. A rail fence? (Abraham Lincoln.)
3. A kite? (Benjamin Franklin.)
4. A muddy cloak? (Sir Walter Raleigh.)
5. A lonely island? (Robinson Crusoe.)
6. A burning bush? (Moses.)
7. A ruff? (Queen Elizabeth.)
8. A glass slipper? (Cinderella.)
9. An apple? (William Tell.)
10. A silver lamp? (Aladdin.)
11. A smooth, round stone? (David.)
12. Long hair? (Samson.)

13. A dove? (Noah.)
14. A pomegranate seed? (Persephone.)
15. A spider web? (Robert Bruce.)
16. A key? (Bluebeard.)
17. A wolf? (Red Riding Hood.)
18. A steamboat? (Robert Fulton.)

SCAT

(Hand Slapping)

Anywhere *Intermediates*

One player holds on his upturned palm a ruler, a paper knife, or a small thin strip of wood. The other player takes this quickly and tries to "scat" or hit the opponent's palm with the ruler before he can withdraw his hand. The game will be made more interesting by feints on the part of the player who has to take the ruler, he giving several appearances of taking it before really doing so. When a player succeeds in hitting his opponent's hand with the ruler, they change parts in the game. Count is kept of the unsuccessful hits, the player winning who has the smallest score when the play ends.

This is one of the diversions useful for rainy-day recesses in school, or for pupils who congregate before a session opens.

SEEKING FOR GOLD

Out of doors; seashore *Children*

A handful of small pebbles is collected, and the players sit on the ground in a circle. One of the players scatters the pebbles on the ground in the center of the circle, as jackstones are scattered. This player then draws a line with his finger between any two of the pebbles, and tries to snap one of these two so that it will hit the other, as marbles are snapped at one another. If successful in hitting the pebble, the same player has a second turn, keeping each time the two pebbles hit. Should this player miss, another gathers up the pebbles, scatters them, draws a line between any two of them, snaps them, etc.

The one wins who at the close of the game has the largest number of pebbles. It will be seen that a small number of players is better for this game than a large group.   Nuts may be used instead of pebbles.

This game is played by children in China.

SHAKESPEAREAN ROMANCE (A)

House party; schoolroom   *Seniors; adults*

Each player is provided with a sheet of paper prepared with the following questions, or the questions may be dictated at the time.   Each question is to be answered with the title of one of Shakespeare's plays.   The player wins who has the largest number correct at the end of the time allotted for the game.

Other questions may be devised.

1. Who were the lovers?   (Romeo and Juliet.)
2. What was their courtship like?   (Midsummer Night's Dream.)
3. What was her answer to his proposal?   (As You Like It.)
4. About what time of the month were they married?   (Twelfth Night.)
5. Of whom did he buy the ring?   (Merchant of Venice.)
6. Who were the best man and maid of honor?   (Antony and Cleopatra.)
7. Who were the ushers?   (The Two Gentlemen of Verona.)
8. Who gave the reception?   (Merry Wives of Windsor.)
9. In what kind of place did they live?   (Hamlet.)
10. What was her disposition like?   (The Tempest.)
11. What was his chief occupation after marriage?   (Taming of the Shrew.)
12. What caused their first quarrel?   (Much Ado about Nothing.)
13. What did their courtship prove to be?   (Love's Labour's Lost.)
14. What did their married life resemble?   (A Comedy of Errors.)
15. What did they give each other?   (Measure for Measure.)
16. What Roman ruler brought about reconciliation?   (Julius Caesar.)
17. What did their friends say?   (All's Well that Ends Well.)

SIMON SAYS

Party; schoolroom   *Children to seniors*

The players sit around a table, or if played in the schoolroom, sit at their respective desks.   Each player makes a fist of each hand with the thumb extended.   One is chosen for leader, whom the others follow.

The leader says, "Simon says, 'Thumbs up!'" whereupon he places his own fists on the table before him with the thumbs upward. The players must all do likewise. The leader then says, "Simon says, 'Thumbs down!'" whereupon he turns his own hands over so that the tips of the thumbs touch the table, the others imitating him. He may then say, "Simon says, 'Thumbs wiggle waggle!'" whereupon he places his fist on the table with the thumbs upward and moves the thumbs sideways, the players imitating him.

If at any time the leader omits the words "Simon says," and goes through the movements simply with the words, "Thumbs up!" "Thumbs down!" or "Wiggle waggle!" the players must keep their hands still and not imitate his movements. Any player imitating him under these circumstances must either pay a forfeit or become leader, or both, as may be decided on beforehand.

SKETCHES

Schoolroom; party   *Intermediates to adults*

The game here described for use with history may be used simply as a diversion in describing animals or any inanimate objects; or it may be used to correlate with English (authors), picture study, etc.

Each player is provided with a sheet of paper and pencil and writes a description of some historical character; the object being to give a description that shall be perfectly truthful and yet puzzling or misleading for the other players who are to guess the identity of the character in the writer's mind.

One player is called on to read his description. The other players may have the privilege of asking questions that may be answered by "Yes" or "No" only; but it is considered much more of an honor to guess correctly without this assistance. The one guessing the character correctly reads his description next. A description for instance might read:

"The person whom I would describe was a very tall man; very vigorous; used an ax on occasion; had much to do with legislators; was widely known outside of his native country; and has been the subject of many biographies."

As this description would apply equally to Washington, Lincoln, Gladstone, and several others who might be mentioned, there is opportunity for considerable guessing before the right character is found.

TAXI DRIVER

One or two players   *Pencil and paper*

On a sheet of paper are written the figures 1 to 21, in three parallel lines across the page, each line of figures representing a street. The numbers represent houses, but they should not

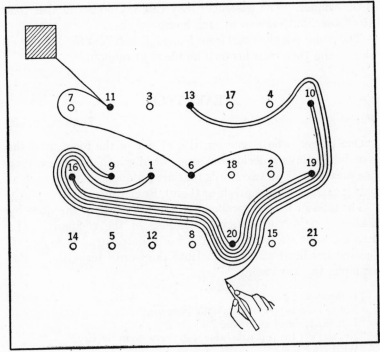

be in consecutive order. In the upper left-hand corner is drawn a little square for the garage of the taxi driver.

One player is the taxi driver and the other is a passenger. The passenger directs the driver to take him to a house, say, Number 11 on First Street, whereupon the driver must draw a line from the garage to house Eleven. The passenger may then say, "Drive me to Number 6 Grand Boulevard," and the driver draws a line from Number 11 to 6, but must not cross the previous line. This goes on until the driver cannot go to the address asked for without crossing one of his previous lines; that ends his turn. He then counts the number of houses that he has been able to visit; that is his record for that game. The players then change parts for a new diagram, the one who was driver becoming passenger and *vice versa*. The one who calls at the largest number of houses is the winner. The passenger may call any house number that he chooses, but may go to each house only once.

The game, which comes from Russia, is excellent for one player alone, who then calls his own numbers at random.

TEAKETTLE

Party   *Juniors; adults*

One player, who is guesser, is sent out of the room until the remaining players decide on some word which has more than one meaning, or on two words that are pronounced alike, such as pair (pear), weight (wait), hear (here), Rome (roam), prey (pray).

The guesser is then recalled and tries to discover the word by asking questions of different members of the company. The answers must always contain the word, but instead of saying it, the speaker must always substitute the word "teakettle." For example, the word being "Park."

"Is the word a long one?"
"Not as long as you may teakettle your car."
"Is it the name of an article?"
"No, and yet the teakettle belongs to everyone in the city."
"What color is it?"
"At times the teakettle is all imaginable colors — red, blue, green, pink, yellow."
"Does it make a noise?"
"No, the teakettle is absolutely silent."
It will be seen that some of the answers refer to an enclosure called a park, and some to parking a car, the double meaning of the word making confusion for the guesser.

The game is sometimes played by the players making remarks to the guesser without his asking questions, each remark to contain the word's substitute, "teakettle."

THIS IS MY ELBOW!

Party   *Children to seniors*

Players sit in a circle, one person in the center being It. The latter goes up to some player in the circle, takes hold of his own nose, and says: "This is my elbow!" The person thus addressed must immediately take hold of his own elbow and say: "This is my nose!" before It can count ten. If he does not do so before ten, or if he takes hold of the wrong part of the body, or if he says the wrong part, he changes place with It. The object is to confuse the players between the part that is touched and that which is named. For instance, touching the toe and saying: "This is my ear!" — hair, shoulder, knee, eye, forehead, or throat, etc.

TIDBITS FARMER (THE)

Party; schoolroom   *Intermediates; adults*

Each player should be given a card or slip of paper on which the following verses are written, the last of each line being left blank. The game consists in filling in the blank spaces each with a double letter of the alphabet, as indicated in parentheses. The player wins who has the largest number correct.

There is a farmer who is	(YY)
Enough to take his	(EE)
And study nature with his	(II)
And think on what he	(CC)
He hears the chatter of the	(JJ)
As they each other	(TT)
And sees that when a tree de	(KK)
It makes a home for	(BB)
A yoke of oxen will he	(UU)
With many haws and	(GG)
And their mistakes he will ex	(QQ)
When plowing for his	(PP)
He little buys but much he se	(LL)
And therefore little	(OO)
And when he hoes his soil by spe	(LL)
He also soils his h	(OO)

TIE–UP PRIZE HUNT

House party   *Juniors; adults*

There is a prize or favor for each player and each favor is tied to the end of a very long string, sometimes a whole ball of twine being used for one favor. Each player is given a free end of twine and must follow and disentangle it wherever it may lead him, winding it up into a ball until he finds his prize.

The placing of these strings should be done a day or two ahead of the party. A string may be carried from one room to another, upstairs or down, around the legs of furniture, behind pictures, into drawers and cupboards, and through any other maze which ingenuity suggests. Several strings may be wound around the same chair-leg so that players cross each other's path again and again. A time limit may be set on the hunt.

TIP, TAP, TOE

Indoors; out of doors   *Children; adults*

INDOORS. — A circle is drawn on a slate or paper, the size of it varying with the number of players, a larger circle being desirable for a large number of players. This circle is intersected with straight lines, so that it is divided into a series of wedge-shaped spaces, the number of lines and spaces being also at the discretion of the players, the larger the number of players the larger the number of spaces desirable and the greater the variation in scoring. In each of these spaces numbers are written in consecutive order, one for each space, 1, 2, 3, 4, etc., or the numbers may be done in multiples of five, — 5, 10, 15, 20, etc. The players take turns in rotation. The one whose turn it is shuts his eyes, takes a pencil, circles it around over the diagram while he says the following verse:

> "Tip, tap, toe, here we go,
> Three jolly sailor boys all in a row."

At the close of the verse the player places the point of the pencil on the diagram, still with his eyes closed. He then opens his eyes, and should the pencil have touched one of the numbered spaces, he marks down to his score the number written in that space, and crosses out that figure on the diagram. Thereafter that space does not count in playing. Should the pencil touch a dividing line or the line forming the circumference of the circle, or fall outside of the circle, or fall in a space in which the number has been crossed out, the player scores nothing, and loses his turn, the next one taking up the play.

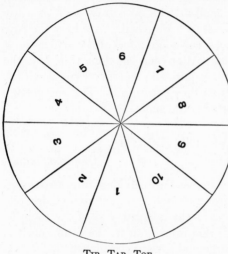

TIP, TAP, TOE

When all of the spaces have been crossed out, the player wins who has the largest score, but should any player at any time touch his pencil to the center of the circle, he wins the game.

OUT OF DOORS. — This game may be played out of doors by drawing the diagram on the earth with a sharpened stick, which is used afterwards as a pointer as a pencil is used on the paper diagram. If on hard earth the figures may be marked in the spaces as on a paper diagram, but the diagram should be drawn considerably larger than when on paper.

This is an admirable game for playing on the hard sand of the **seashore.** In that case little pebbles or shells are placed in the different spaces instead of numerals; one in the first space, two in the second, three in the third, etc. When a player places his stick or pointer in a space, he removes the pebbles from that place to a little pile, and the score is counted at the end by counting this pile of pebbles. Any space from which the pebbles have been removed is thereafter out of the game, as when the figures are crossed out on the paper diagram.

This game is supposed to have originated in early methods of allotting land.

TOUCH MEMORY

House party; camp   *Children; adults*

Players should be seated in a circle and the room darkened. Have from six to twelve small articles on a tray, such as a toy dog, a bottle, a spectacle case, a lead pencil, etc. Pass the tray around from player to player, each one to feel of the articles on it though he cannot see them. After each has done this, hide the tray, turn on the lights, and require all players to write down the names of as many articles as they can recall. The one getting the largest number correct wins the game.

TRAVELING CONES

Party   *Children; adults*

This is a relay game. Players are divided into two even-numbered teams, and in front of each team are two chairs, one at the starting line and one at the opposite end of the room at the finish line. A string is tied from chair to chair, and on it is laced an ice cream cone, large end toward the player.

The game consists in blowing the ice cream cone from the starting line to the finish and back again. The first team to get its cone back to the home line wins the game.

TRIAL BY JURY

House party   *Juniors; adults*

This is an excellent game for house parties for young people or adults. In advance two letters must be prepared and sealed in envelopes: One is merely a blank sheet or a bit of writing that has no relation to the game; the other contains a brief but graphic account of a murder or of a murderer's escape.

A resourceful member of the party is chosen as district attorney, and takes charge of the proceedings. He chooses two players from the group, to each of whom he gives a letter. They leave the room to read the letters and must not give any hint of the contents to each other or to other guests. They are then called in, one at a time, by the district attorney for questioning. He attempts to find out which one knows most about the murder, victim, locality, etc., and is therefore presumably the murderer.

The others of the group act as jury, discuss the evidence, and decide which of the two is guilty.

Each of the prisoners must answer truthfully and at once the first thing that occurs to him when a question is put or a subject mentioned. For example: The murderer escapes at dawn in a Ford car across a red bridge over a river, etc. The district attorney asks: "What occurs to you if I say river?" The accused must answer instantly without time for reflection. After a period of questioning, he is sent out, and the second prisoner called.

TWENTY QUESTIONS

House party; camp   *Juniors; adults*

This is a standard social game which usually makes good entertainment.

One person, who is It, decides on some famous person or thing anywhere in the world. When he says "Ready!" the other players try to guess what this is by his answers to their questions, which are limited to twenty in number. Any player may ask more than one question, unless the game requires regulation, when players may ask in turn. Each question must be of a kind that can be answered by "Yes," or "No," or "I do not know," as it is not allowable to say anything else until the object is correctly named.

It is well for the questions to begin with territory, element, or class of subjects, and narrow down to final details. For example: "Is it a person?" "Does it fly?" "Does it live in this country?" "Is it expensive? Large? Red? Blue? Hard? Soft?" etc.

Any person who first names the object correctly becomes It for the next round. If the object is named before the group has asked twenty questions, the same person must think of another object and be questioned again. The one who is It keeps tally of the number of questions asked.

VARIATION — Twenty Questions Race — " Third Degree." The game Twenty Questions may be made competitive by dividing the company into two or more groups or teams, each with a captain. The captains retire and decide on an object. Each then returns to his group and is questioned, the group or team winning which is first to guess right. The general procedure is the same as in the one-group game. If the teams overhear each other disturbingly, it is well to be in separate rooms.

UP, JENKINS!

Party; schoolroom   *Children to seniors*

This is one of the most popular current games among young people, being usually played to the accompaniment of much laughter and intense interest. It consists in the guessing by opposing parties of the hand under which a coin is hidden.

The players are divided into two parties. Each party has a captain, each player being captain in turn during successive rounds of the game. The players gather around a table, one party on one side and the others opposite. A coin, usually a quarter, is passed from hand to hand under the table by one of the parties in an endeavor to conceal from the opponents which individual holds it. The leader of the opposite party then calls, "Up, Jenkins!" when all of the hands of his opponents are brought from under the table and held up with palms outward toward the guessing party, fingers closed down tightly over the palms, the coin being hidden in one of the hands. The opponents may look at the hands from their side of the table in this way as long as they choose. The leader then commands "Down, Jenkins!" when the hands are slammed down simultaneously flat on the table, palms downward. This is done with enough noise to disguise the clink of the coin striking the table. The object of the game is for the opponents (those not having the coin) to guess under which hand the coin is laid, each hand supposed not to have it being ordered off the table. The captain of the guessing party, who alone may give these orders (though his players may assist him with suggestions), calls for the lifting of one specified hand at a time. The player named must lift the hand indicated, and that hand is thereafter to be taken from the table. If the guessing party can be successful in thus eliminating all of the empty hands so that the coin is left under the last hand, they are considered to have won, and the coin passes to them for the next round. If the coin be disclosed before the last hand be reached, the side holding it adds to its score the hands remaining on the table that were not ordered off. The side wins which has the highest score when the play stops, the time limits being indefinite.

For the **schoolroom** see also an adaptation called *Hands up — Hands down.*

WHAT IS MY THOUGHT LIKE?

Children's party; house party   *Juniors*

The players are seated in a circle or any convenient group. One of the number decides upon a "thought"; that is, he thinks of some person, object, or abstraction, without telling the others what it is. He then asks of each in turn, "What is my thought like?" Each answers anything he chooses. The first player then declares what his thought was, and asks of each, "Why is — (naming the object he thought of) like — (whatever such player answered)?" Each must find some likeness, however absurd, or pay a forfeit. For instance, the answers around the circle might be, "Your thought is like an umbrella," "like Napoleon," "Pinafore," "sadness," "my necktie," "a rose," etc. The questioner then says, "I thought of a lead pencil. Why is a pencil like an umbrella?" "Because it is oftenest black." The pencil may be like Napoleon because it can make a mark; like a rose because it is sometimes cut, etc.   If anyone happens to answer to the first question, "a pencil" (or whatever was thought of), he also must pay a forfeit.

WHO AM I?

Party   *Juniors; adults*

Each player has a placard hung on, or pinned to, his back, on which is written the name of some prominent person. Each other player who sees this makes some remark to him, or asks a question, appropriate to the name, and the game consists in each player's guessing his own name. He may ask two questions (only) of each of the other players. The one who first knows his own identity is the winner, and the others in order.

Examples:

Remarks: Good evening! We should have a dull time tonight without you.

I am much indebted to you for a great improvement in my business.

Yours was the only stock on which I had dividends last year.

Questions from the placard-wearer:

Am I an American? Yes. Living? No.

Was I a statesman? No. Captain of industry? No.

Was I a writer? No. Inventor? Yes.

Did I invent one thing or many? Many. Are they in general use? International, etc., until the player finds himself to be Mr. Thomas A. Edison.

WHOSE EYES?

Party   *Children; adults*

The company is divided into two groups. One of these goes out of the room and one member at a time returns, entering behind a curtain so hung that it hides the entire figure and the remaining group cannot see who enters. This player then sits with eyes close to two little holes in the curtain, just big enough for his eyes, and looks through at the company. The latter pass before these eyes slowly, in single file, and write down the name of the person whose eyes they think are looking out. This is repeated for each member of the absent group, when the guesser writes his name on his paper, exchanges this with his neighbor, and then checks the correct names on the paper he holds, as the host or leader tells who looked through first, second, third, etc. The number of correct guesses is scored for each individual and for the group as a whole. The groups then change places, the first "eyes" becoming guessers. The winning individual and group are those having the largest number correct.

WHOSE PORTRAIT?

House party   *Juniors; adults*

The hostess secures a photograph of each of her guests taken in infancy. If this can be done unbeknown to the originals, so much the better. For the game these portraits are displayed, each with a number, but with no other identifying marks visible, such as the name of the photographer or his city. The guests are then provided with pencil and paper and asked to write down the name of the person present whom he or she considers the original of each photograph. The one having the largest number of correct names is given a prize. There is great sport in the game and each guest must be careful not to express his feelings at seeing his own infantile portrait.

WOODLAND LOVERS (THE)

House party   *Seniors; adults*

Each player is given a paper on which the following is written or dictated, the words in parentheses being omitted and a blank space left. The game consists in each player's filling in these blank spaces with the name of some tree. The host or hostess at the end reads this list of words in order, the player winning who has the largest number correct. The same tree may be mentioned more than once.

He took her little hand in his own big (palm). "I love (yew), dear," he said simply. She did not (sago) away, for it had been a case of love at first sight. She murmured something in (aloe) voice. They had met one day upon a sandy (beech), and from that (date) onward, they cared not a (fig) for the outside world. Her name was (May Ple). She was a charming girl. Rosy as a (peach); (chestnut) colored hair; (tulips) like a (cherry); skin a pale (olive). In fact, she was as beautiful (as pen) or brush ever portrayed. The day he met her she wore a jacket of handsome (fir). He was of Irish descent, his name being (Willow) 'Flaherty. He was a (spruce) looking young fellow. Together they made a congenial (pear). But when did the course of true love ever run smooth? There was a third person to be considered. This was (paw paw). Both felt that, counting (paw paw) in, they might not be able to (orange) it. What if he should refuse to (cedar)! Suppose he should (sago) to her lover? And if he should be angry, to what point won't a (mango)? Well, in that case she must submit, with a (cypress) her lover in her arms for the last time, and (pine) away. But happily her parent did not constitute (ebony) skeleton at their feast. He was guilty of no tyranny to reduce their hopes to (ashes). They found him in his garden busily (plantain). He was chewing (gum). "Well," he said thoughtfully, in answer to the question: "Since (yew) love her I must (cedar) to (yew). You make a fine young (pear). Don't cut

any (capers) after you're married, young man! Don't (pine) and com-
plain if he is sometimes cross, young woman! I hope to see (upas) many
happy days together!"

YES AND NO

Supper party   *Children; adults*

This is a good game to use at a supper party to stimulate
conversation and create a bit of laughter.

Each guest should be provided with a little bundle of tokens
to be used as forfeits. These may be suited to the decorations
or suggest some holiday that is being celebrated, such as a little
bunch of green shamrocks, or flags, or tiny lead pencils. If these
are tied together in a bunch with a ribbon matching the table
decorations, they make a pretty item in the table coloring.

The object of the game is to give to your partner at table a
token whenever he or she says "Yes" or "No"; therefore the
conversation will be such as to trap your partner into the use of
these words.

Whenever "Yes" or "No" is used, the person using it is
given one of the tokens. The person who first gets rid of his
entire bunch of tokens is considered as winning the game and
awarded a prize or favor, and the partner who is given these
tokens is to receive a consolation prize.

ZOO

Party; schoolroom   *Intermediates*

Each player is provided with ten slips of paper, numbered con-
spicuously from one to ten, but arranged irregularly in a pile.
The players gather around a table or sit in a circle, each one
being given the name of an animal; the sport of the game will
consist largely in choosing unusual or difficult names, such as
yak, gnu, camelopard, hippopotamus, rhinoceros, Brazilian ant-
eater, kangaroo, etc.

Each player holds his slips with the numbers turned downward.
The first player turns up his upper slip so that the number is visible and lays it down in front of him. In doing this he must
turn it away from himself, so that the other players see it first;

the next player then does the same. Should the two slips happen to coincide in number — for instance, should the first player have turned up number three and the second player turn up number three, they must each at once call each other's names, as "Yak!" "Hippopotamus!" or whatever name was assigned to them. The one who first calls the other's name gives away his slip to that other, the object being to get rid of one's slips as fast as possible.

Should the slip turned up by the second player not correspond in number to that turned by the first, he also lays it down in front of him; the third player then turns up his, and this is continued around the circle until a slip is turned that corresponds in number with any that has already been turned up, when those two players must immediately call each other's names, as before explained. The player wins who first gets rid of all of his slips.

For **schools,** a class should divide into small groups, which may be made to correlate with geography or history, by using proper names from those subjects instead of names of animals.

For **older players** the game may be made very funny also by assigning to each player the name of a patent medicine instead of the name of an animal, and playing cards may be used instead of the numbered slips.

BOOKS ON SOCIAL GAMES

Social Games for Recreation, by B. S. Mason and E. D. Mitchell, A. S. Barnes and Company, Publishers, New York. A very large and valuable collection of games, active and quiet, for all kinds of social and recreative uses. Bibliography.

Partners in Play, Recreation for Young Men and Women Together, Prepared for the National Recreation Association and National Board, Y. W. C. A., by Mary J. Breen; A. S. Barnes and Company, Publishers, New York. Contains much direct help for young people themselves ("ages 12 to 30 and over"), though addressed especially to leaders and organizers. Packed with suggestions and some detailed directions. Bibliography for each field covered, including games, summer and winter sports, dancing and dancing games, cards, music, drama, arts and crafts, study, etc. For other special social uses, see publications of the National Recreation Association, New York.

Hoyle's Games, by Edmond Hoyle, A. L. Burt Co., Publishers, New York. For all kinds of card games.

STUNTS AND CONTESTS; FEATS AND FORFEITS

STUNTS AND CONTESTS; FEATS AND FORFEITS

Athletic stunts requiring skill, strength, or agility are a very interesting and amusing feature for gymnasiums and many other conditions, and contain possibilities for some excellent and vigorous physical development. As some of these may be used for forfeits (although some kinds of forfeits cannot take the place of athletic stunts), these two classes of amusements are included here in one chapter. The searcher for forfeits will do well, however, to look through the stunts and contests.

Further stunts for one and contests for two will be found in a *Handbook of Stunts*, by Martin Rodgers, published by The Macmillan Company.

I. Contests for Two : Wrestling Matches and Tugs of War

The following wrestling matches and races make very interesting and vigorous games. The wrestling matches are generally determined by the winning of the best two out of three trials.

These wrestling matches and races may of course be used also for forfeits.

BALANCE WRESTLE. — Two contestants stand each in a forward stride position, the right foot being lengthwise on a line (the same line for both contestants) and the left foot back of it, turned at right angles to the right foot with the heel touching the same line. The toes of the right feet should touch. In this position players grasp right hands. The objects of the game are to make the opponent (1) move one or both feet, or (2) touch the floor with any part of the body. A point is scored for the opponent whenever a player fails in one of these ways. After a trial has been made with the right hand and foot, the wrestle should be repeated with the left hand and foot extended, and so on alternately.

BOUNDARY TUG. — Two lines are drawn on the floor, five feet apart. Within this space two contestants face each other, the right toes touching and each stepping backward in a strong stride position with the left foot. Both players grasp a cane or wand, and each tries to pull the other across one of the boundary lines.

HARLEQUIN WRESTLE. — This is a one-sided wrestle between two persons. Each stands on one leg; they then grasp right hands and each tries to make the other lower his upraised foot to the ground, or touch the floor with his free hand. The opponent may not be touched with the free hand.

INDIAN WRESTLE. — Two players lie on their backs side by side, with adjacent arms locked. The feet should be in opposite directions. At a signal the adjacent legs are brought to an upright position and interlocked at the knees. The wrestle consists in trying to force the opponent to roll over from his position.

INTERFERING. — This is one of the hopping relays, but the shoulders may not be used in it. Two contestants fold arms, and each, while hopping on one foot, tries to make his opponent put the other foot to the floor. As neither arms nor shoulders may be used, this is done entirely by a side movement of the free leg.

KNEE AND TOE WRESTLE. — Two players sit on a mat, facing each other. The knees should be drawn up closely and the players should be near enough together to have the toes of each touch those of the opponent. Each player passes a stick under his knees, and then passes his arms under it and clasps his hands in front of his own knees. The wrestling begins at a signal and consists in each player trying to get his toes under those of his opponent and throw him backward.

LUNGE AND HOP FIGHT. — A circle six feet in diameter is drawn on the ground. One player takes a lunge position forward, so that his forward foot rests two feet within the circle. The second player stands in the circle on one foot with arms folded across the chest. The hopper tries to make the lunger move one of his feet. The lunger in turn tries to make the hopper put down his second foot or unfold arms. Either player is defeated also if he moves out of the circle. The lunger may use his hands and arms.

PUSH AND PULL. — Two lines are drawn on the floor at an interval of five feet. Within these lines two players take their places with two stout sticks, canes, or wands between them, each player grasping one end of each cane. The object of the feat is to push the opponent across the boundary line behind him, or to pull him over the nearer boundary line.

The relative positions of the opponents may be reversed and the same struggle gone through back to back, still holding the canes.

This differs from Boundary Tug in the way the wands are held and the fact of there being two wands.

ROOSTER FIGHT. — This is an old Greek amusement. A ring six feet in diameter is drawn on the ground. Two players are placed in this, who stoop and grasp each his own ankles. In this position they try to displace each other by shouldering. The player loses who is overthrown or who loosens his grasp on his ankles.

SHOULDER SHOVE. — For this, the players are divided into groups of five; each group marks on the ground a circle about eight feet in diameter. All five players stand within the circle. Four of them must fold their arms across the chest and hop on one foot. The object of the game is for these four players to push the fifth one, who is It, out of the circle with their shoulders. They may not use their hands. The fifth one may stand on both feet and use his arms. Should one of the hoppers place both feet on the ground or unfold his arms, he must leave the circle. The player who is It may avoid the hoppers by running and dodging. Should he be pushed out of the circle, the four hoppers are considered to have won the game.

WAND AND TOE WRESTLE. — Two players sit on the floor with knees bent and toes touching those of the opponent. One wand is held between them, which both grasp so that the hands are placed alternately; there should be a short space in the center between the hands. The object of the tug is to pull the opponent up and over the dividing line. This is an excellent form of wand wrestle and will hold the interest of a class for months, especially if a continuous score be kept for the same contestants.

WAND TWIST. — Two players stand and grasp at or near shoulder height a wand or cane held in a horizontal position. The object of one player is to raise or twist the wand out of the horizontal position, and of the other player to prevent this. The one who is trying to hold the wand in the horizontal position should have his hands next to each other in the center of the wand. The one who tries to twist the wand should place his hands outside of and touching those of the player who is resisting.

WAND WRESTLE. — One player holds a wand or cane at full arm's length above his head, the hands being at about shoulder width distant on the wand, which should be held horizontally. The other player tries to pull the wand down to shoulder height. He may pull it forward at the same time, as it may be almost impossible in some cases to lower it without this forward movement.

II. Stunt Races

ESKIMO JUMPING RACE. — Fold the arms across the breast with the knees rigid and the feet close together. Jump forward in short jumps of an inch or two.

This is the regular form of one of the games of the Eskimos, reported by Lieutenant Schwatka.

ESKIMO RACE ON ALL FOURS. — The performers stand with hands and feet on the floor, the knees stiff, the hands clenched and resting on the knuckles. The elbows should be stiff. In this position a race is run, or rather "hitched," over a course that will not easily be too short for the performers.

This is a game of the Eskimos, reported by Lieutenant Schwatka.

PAIL RACE. — The racers stand with each foot in a big bucket or pail, throughout the race, holding the handles in the hands.

PAPER RACE. — The racing players are each given two pieces of paper about ten by fifteen inches in size; folded newspapers will do. They are then required to go to the end of the room and return, placing one of the papers for each step, as it is a miss for the foot to rest on anything but paper. There is great sport in the race.

STUNT RACES.

The races given above, and most other races, can be used in relay form for large companies.

Many of the feats in this chapter may be used in races, to be performed at the end of, or during, the race.

III. Miscellaneous Stunts and Feats

ANKLE THROW. — This feat consists in tossing some object over the head from behind with the feet. A bean bag, book, or basket ball is held firmly between the ankles. With a sudden jump, the feet are kicked backward so as to jerk the object into an upward throw, which should end in its curving forward over the head. It should be caught as it comes down.

ARM'S LENGTH TAG. — Two players stand each with an arm extended at full length at shoulder level, and try to touch each other without being touched in return. This will require some rapid twisting, dodging, and bending. A touch on the extended hand does not count.

BACKSLIDING. — The hands are placed palm to palm behind the back with the fingers pointing downward and thumbs next to the back. Keeping the tips of the fingers close to the back and the palms still together, the hands are turned inward and upward until the tips of the fingers are between the shoulders, pointing upward toward the head, and the thumbs outside.

CATCH PENNY. — One elbow is raised level with the shoulder, the arm being bent to bring the hand toward the chest. Three or four pennies are placed in a pile on the bent elbow. Suddenly the elbow is dropped and the same hand moved downward quickly in an effort to catch the pennies before they fall to the ground.

CHINESE GET-UP. — Two persons sit on the floor back to back with arms locked, and retaining such relative positions they try to stand upright.

COIN AND CARD SNAP. — Balance a visiting card on the tip of the middle or forefinger. On top of the card place a dime or nickel; this should be exactly over the tip of the finger and in the middle of the card. Snap the edge of the card with a finger of the other hand, so that the card will be shot from under the coin and leave the coin balanced on the finger.

DOG COLLAR. — Two players on hands and knees on a mat, rug, or cushion face each other with about three feet distance between them. A knotted towel or a strap, or anything that will not chafe or cut the flesh, is thrown over both heads like a collar, being long enough to encircle the two. The head should be held well upward to prevent this from slipping off. At a signal, the players pull against each other, each trying to pull the opponent from the mat or to pull the collar from around his neck.

DOG JUMP. — The performer holds a stick horizontally between the forefingers of his hands, pressing with the fingers to keep it from falling. Keeping the stick in this position, he should jump over it forward and then backward. The same feat may be performed by pressing together the middle fingers of the two hands without a stick and jumping over them forward and backward, as a dog jumps through curved arms.

DOT AND CARRY TWO. — This is a spectacular feat of strength for three performers, A, B, and C. They stand in line, side by side, A standing in the center with B on his right and C on his left. He stoops down and passes his right hand behind the left thigh of B, and clasps B's right hand. He then passes his left hand behind C's right thigh, and takes hold of C's left hand. B and C pass each one arm around A's neck, and A, by raising himself gradually to a standing position, will find that he is able to lift the other two from the ground.

HAND STAND SALUTE. — A player is required to stand on his hands with legs stretched at full length in the air, and then wriggle the feet at the ankles.

HEEL AND TOE SPRING. — A line is drawn on the floor. The performer places his heels against this line, bends down, grasps the toes with the fingers underneath the feet and pointing backward toward the heels. He then leans forward slightly to get an impetus, and jumps backward over the line.

This same feat may be reversed. Standing in the same position, the performer toes a line and jumps over it forward.

JUG HANDLE. — The performer places his hands across the chest, with the tips of the middle fingers touching and the elbows extending on each side like a jug handle. Another player tries to pull the arms apart, either by working at them separately or together. Jerking is not permissible; the pull must be steady.

Until one has tried this, it is surprising to find that even a strong person cannot overcome a weaker one in this position.

LAST AND FIRST. — Place one foot immediately behind the other. On the rear foot place a small object, such as a light book, a slipper, or a small stick. With a sudden movement lift the forward foot, at the same instant hopping on the rear foot with a kicking movement forward, so as to throw the object forward beyond a given mark.

LATH AND PLASTER. — Rub the top of the head with one hand, and simultaneously pat the chest with the other hand. Reverse the movement, patting the head and rubbing the chest. Do each of these things with the hands changed, the hand that was on the chest being placed on the head, and *vice versa*.

PICK ME UP. — The performer is required to stand against the wall, drop a handkerchief at his feet, and without bending the knees stoop and pick up the handkerchief.

PICK UP AND PUSH UP. — A line is drawn about two feet from a wall, which is toed by the performer, facing the wall. Between the line and the wall is placed a stool directly in front of the performer. The player leans forward, puts the top of his head against the wall, picks up the stool with his hands, and pushes himself backward to an upright position, getting an impetus from the head only, and lifting the stool as he does so.

PINCUSHION. — On a chair having a cane or rush or wooden bottom a pin is stuck on the edge of the seat, or just under the edge, well around on one side toward the back. The performer starts sitting in the chair, and without leaving it, or touching his hands or feet to the floor, must reach around so as to remove the pin with his teeth.

PRAY DO. — A line is marked on the floor. The performer stands with his toes on the line, and without using his hands or moving his feet, kneels down and gets up again.

RABBIT HOP. — This should be done on a soft mat or cushion. The performer kneels; then sits back on the heels and grasps the insteps with his hands. From this position he leans suddenly forward, and while doing so pulls the feet up from the floor. In the instant that his weight is released, he hitches forward on the knees, the two knees moving forward alternately.

ROTARY. — Raise both arms above the head. Move both with a rotary motion in opposite directions, describing a circle in the air, with the right hand moving forward and with the left moving backward simultaneously.

Extend both arms in slanting position downward from the shoulders, elbows straight. Describe circles in the air with both arms, the hands at about the level of the hips, the right turning forward and the left backward.

"RUBBER NECK." — In this feat a kneeling performer is required to pick a card up from the floor with his teeth, both hands being behind his back. The card is placed in front of him at the length of his forearm and hand from one knee. This distance is measured by placing the elbow against the knee and stretching the forearm and the hand at full length on the floor; the point which the middle finger reaches is the point at which the card must be placed. The card has the ends folded down so as to rest like a small table on the floor. The nearer edge of it must rest on the line determined as above specified.

SCALES. — Hold a weight out at arm's length for a given time.

SIAMESE TWINS. — Two players (two boys or two girls), of about the same height and weight, stand back to back and lock arms. The object is to walk in one direction, using first the legs of one player and then those of the other. This may be done by one player moving his feet forward slightly. This is accomplished by both bending the knees, and the player on the side toward which progress is to be made sliding his feet forward. Bracing his feet in the new position, he straightens his entire body upright, drawing the rear player after him until both are in the same relative position as at the start. This constitutes one step, and is repeated over as long a distance as may be specified or desired.

SKIN THE SNAKE. — This is a feat for several performers — from five to fifty or more, and is suitable for the gymnasium. The players stand in a line, one behind another, with a short distance between. Each player bends forward and stretches one hand backward between his legs, while with the other hand he grasps that of the player in front, who has assumed the same position. When all are in position, the line begins backing, the player at the rear end of the line lying down on his back, and the next player walking backward astride over him until he can go no farther, when he also lies down with the first player's head between his legs. This backing and lying-down movement continues until all the players are lying in a straight line on the floor. Then the last one to lie down gets up and walks astride the line toward the front, raising the man next behind him to his feet, and so on until all again are standing in the original position. The grasp of hands is retained throughout.

It hardly need be said that this game is of Chinese origin. It makes a very funny spectacle, especially if done rapidly.

STOOPING PUSH. — Draw a line on the floor. Toe it with the feet spread wide apart. Reach around outside of the legs and grasp a light dumb-bell or other object of similar weight with both hands; throw or slide it forward on the floor from between the feet, the hands being kept together throughout. The object is to see how far the dumb-bell may be thrown without the player losing his balance.

TANTALUS. — The left foot and leg and left cheek are placed close against the wall. The right foot is then slightly lifted in an effort to touch the left knee. Having reached it, the position should be steadily maintained for a few moments.

THUMB SPRING. — This is similar to the Wall Spring, but differs both in method of execution and in general difficulty. The performer places the inner side of the thumbs against a wall, or the edge of a table or window sill may be used. No other part of the hands should touch this surface. The feet should then be moved as far backward as possible. The body will then be leaning forward; and from this position, without any movement of the feet, a sudden push should be made from the thumbs, the object being to recover the upright position. It is well to begin with a slight distance and work up to a greater one.

WALL PIVOT. — One foot is placed against a wall at about the height of the knee. The other foot is thrown over it, the body making a complete turn in the air, so that the free foot may touch the ground in time to sustain the weight before a tumble. Thus, if the right foot be placed against the wall, the left leg will be thrown over it and the body turned over toward the right, the left foot being replaced on the floor to receive the weight. This is usually easier if done with a short run, and is best practiced on a thick gymnasium mattress.

WALL SPRING. — The performer should stand facing a wall and a short distance from it. Keeping his feet in one spot, he should lean forward and place the palms of his hands flat against the wall; from this position he should then make a sudden push and spring backward to an upright position. With some practice, this may be done with a very considerable distance between the feet and the wall.

WOODEN SOLDIER. — The arms are folded across the chest. In this position the performer is required to lie down on the back and rise again to an upright standing position, without assistance from either hands or elbows.

WRIGGLE WALK. — The performer stands with heels together and toes pointed outward. Simultaneously he raises the right toes and the left heel, and turns them toward the same direction, the right toes inward and the left heel outward, pivoting on the opposite toe and heel. This is then reversed, so as to continue progress in the same direction. Resting on the toes and heel just moved, he lifts the opposite ones; that is, the left toes moving outward, the right heel moving inward, and so progresses for a specified distance.

IV. FORFEITS

Many of the things described in the previous sections of this chapter may be used as forfeits.

Forfeits are used in many games as a penalty for failure, and may be an occasion for much merriment. The usual method of collecting and disposing of the forfeits is for each player, when he fails, to deposit with some one person designated for the purpose some article which shall serve to identify him when the penalties are assigned. This may be a ring, some small article from the pocket, a bonbon, a pebble, or flower, a bit of ribbon, or other ornament of dress.

When the game is over, the forfeits are redeemed. For this purpose one player is chosen as the judge, who is seated. Behind him stands a player who takes one article at a time from the pile of collected forfeits, holds it over the head of the judge so that he may not see it, and says, "Heavy, heavy hangs over thy head."

The judge then asks, "Fine or superfine?" (meaning, boy or girl?)

The holder answers, "Fine," if a boy, and "Superfine," if a girl, and adds, "What must the owner do to redeem it?"

The judge then pronounces sentence. Part of the sport of this imposing of penalties for forfeits is the ignorance of the judge as to who is the owner of the forfeit.

The following penalties are appropriate for the paying of forfeits, and many of the feats previously described are also suitable.

The practice of forfeits is prehistoric, and is thought to have originated in the custom of paying ransom for immunity from punishment for crimes. As used in games of later years, the main object has been to make the offender ridiculous.

AFFIRMATIVE, THE. — A player is required to ask a question that cannot be answered in the negative. The question is, "What does y-e-s spell?"

BLARNEY STONE. — The player is required to pay a compliment to each person in the room in turn.

BLIND WALTZ. — Two players are blindfolded and told to waltz together.

CHEW THE STRING. — Two bonbons are wrapped in paper and tied each to a piece of string six yards in length. These are placed on the floor at a distance from each other, the free end of each string being given to one of the two players who are assigned to this penalty. At a signal, each player puts his piece of string in his mouth, and with hands behind back chews rapidly at the string, trying to get it all into the mouth. The one who first gets to his piece of candy is rewarded by having both pieces.

CONSTANTINOPLE. — The player is required to "Spell Constantinople, one syllable at a time." As soon as he gets to the letter "i," all of the other players shout the following syllable, "No!" The speller naturally thinks that he has made a mistake, and commences again. Each time that he gets to the letter "i," the same cry of "No" is made, and the poor victim may become very much confused, and doubt his own memory as to spelling before he discovers the trick.

CORDIAL GREETING, A. — This penalty is imposed upon two players at once. They are blindfolded and led to opposite corners of the room. They are then told to go toward each other and shake hands.

CRAWL, THE. — The player is required to leave the room with two legs and come back with six. He does this by bringing a chair with him when he returns.

DANGEROUS POSITION, A. — The player is required to sit upon the fire. This is done by writing the words "the fire" on a slip of paper, and then sitting on it.

ENNUI. — The player is required to yawn until he makes some-one else yawn.

FOOTBALL. — A ball the size of an orange is made of crumpled paper. It is placed on the floor, and the player is required to stand at a point three times the length of his foot from the ball. From this point he is required without bending the knees to kick the ball out of the way.

FORUM, THE. — The player is required to make a speech on any subject assigned by the judge.

FOUR FEET. — The player is required to put four feet against the wall. He does this by placing the feet of a chair against the wall.

GRASSHOPPER. — The player is required to hold one foot in his hand and hop on the other around the room.

HAND–TO–HAND. — A player is given some small article to hold in each hand, such as a flower or lead pencil, and required to stretch both arms at full length sideways, the right arm to the right and the left arm to the left. He is then required to bring both articles into one hand without bending shoulders or elbows; or, to state it differently, without bringing the hands any nearer together. This may be done by placing one of the objects on a table with one hand, turning around, and picking it up with the other hand.

HAYSTACK. — A player is required to make a pile of chairs as high as his head, and then take off his shoes and jump over them. (Jump over the shoes.)

HOTTENTOT TACKLE. — The player is required to cross the arms and grasp the left ear with the right hand and the nose with the left hand. He is then suddenly to release the grasp and reverse the position of the hands, grasping the right ear with the left hand and the nose with the right hand. This should be repeated several times in quick succession.

INSIDE AND OUT. — The player is required to kiss a book inside and outside without opening it. He accomplishes this seemingly impossible task by taking the book *out* of the room, kissing it there, coming back, and kissing it again *in* the room.

JINGLES. — The player is given two pairs of rhymes and required to write a verse of four lines ending with the prescribed rhymes. This same forfeit may be imposed on several different players at once, an added interest arising from comparison of the finished verses.

KNIGHT OF THE RUEFUL COUNTENANCE. — This requires two players, one who is assigned to be the knight and the other to be the squire.

The squire takes the knight by the arm and leads him before each lady present. The squire kisses the hand of each lady in turn, and after each kiss carefully wipes the knight's mouth with a handkerchief. The knight must display his grief at the loss of so many opportunities by preserving throughout an unsmiling countenance.

LITTLE DOG TRAY. — The player is required to crawl under the table on all fours and bark like a dog.

LITTLE GERMAN BAND, THE. — Three or four players are told to imitate a little German band, each being required to represent a certain instrument, and all to join in rendering some popular air, which should be assigned.

LITTLE SUNSHINE. — The player is required to walk around the room and bestow a smile on each person in turn.

LUNCH COUNTER. — An apple is suspended at head height on the end of a string from a chandelier or portière pole. The delinquent player is required to walk up to the apple and take a bite from it without help from the hands. For obvious reasons, only one person should be allowed to bite at an apple.

MOODS. — The player is required to laugh in one corner of the room, to sing in the second corner, to cry in the third, and to whistle or dance in the fourth.

NEGATIVE SIDE, THE. — The player is required to answer "No" to a question put to him by each member of the company in turn. This may be made very funny if he be required, for instance, thereby to express dislike for his favorite occupations or friends.

PILGRIMAGE TO ROME, A. — The judge announces that the player who is to redeem this forfeit is about to make a pilgrimage to Rome, and requests that each member of the company give him something to take on his journey. The pilgrim is then required to pass around the room while each person, in turn, presents him with some article, the more inappropriate or difficult or cumbersome to carry the better. These may consist, for instance, of a small chair, a sofa pillow, a house plant, a big basket, a lunch consisting of a nut, etc. These must all be carried at once, and when all have been collected, the pilgrim must make one entire round of the room before laying any of them down.

SAFETY POINT. — The player is required to put one hand where the other cannot touch it. He does this by placing the right hand on the left elbow, or *vice versa*.

SO NEAR AND YET SO FAR. — Two players are required to stand upon an open newspaper in such a manner that they cannot possibly touch one another. They will find the solution of the problem in placing the newspaper over the sill of a door, and then closing the door between them.

SPOON FOOD. — Two players are blindfolded and seated on the floor, each with a large towel or napkin pinned around the neck like a bib. Each is then given a bowl filled with corn meal or flour, and a spoon. When all is ready, the two players are told to feed each other. This forfeit makes as much sport for the rest of the company as for those engaged in its performance.

THREE QUESTIONS. — The delinquent player is sent out of the room. While he is gone, the remaining players decide on three questions, to which he must reply "Yes" or "No" before he knows what the questions are. When he returns, he is asked if he will answer the first question with "Yes" or "No." Having made his choice, the question is then repeated to him, often resulting in much laughter from the incongruity of the answer. The other questions are answered in the same way.

TIDBIT. — The player is required to bite an inch off the poker. He does this by holding the poker about an inch from his face and making a bite at it.

TOAST OF THE EVENING, THE. — The player is required to propose his or her own health in a complimentary speech about himself or herself.

UMBRELLA STAND. — A closed umbrella or a cane is held upright on the floor by pressing on the top of it with the forefinger. The player is then required to release his hold, to pirouette rapidly, and snatch the umbrella before it falls to the ground.

VERSE LENGTHS. — The player is required to repeat a verse or jingle, stating the number of the word after each word. For example :

"Yankee, *one*, Doodle, *two*, went, *three*, to, *four*, town, *five*," etc.

WALKING SPANISH. — The player is given a cane or closed umbrella. He rests this on the floor, places both hands on top of it, and then rests his forehead on the hands. While in this position, he is required to turn around three times, then suddenly stand with head erect, and walk straight ahead.

ZOO, THE. — The player is required to imitate a donkey or any other animal.

SINGING GAMES

SINGING GAMES

Singing games are suitable for primary grades. They are played in almost any environment, from a children's party indoors to any outdoor conditions, including the school yard or the public playground. Where there are too many children in a game to hold interest, double circles may be formed for the circle games, or the class may be divided into two or three groups, all singing the same game in unison.

DID YOU EVER SEE A LASSIE?

This is a game for very little children, and with a little suggestion as to the exercises or movements to be illustrated by the "lassie," may be the source of some very good exercise as well as a pleasing game.

All of the players but one form a circle, clasping hands. They circle around, singing the first two lines of the verse. While they are doing this, the odd player stands in the center and illustrates some movement which he chooses for the others to imitate. During the last two lines of the verse the players stand in place, drop hands, and imitate the movements of the center player, which he continues in unison with them.

Did you ever see a lassie, a lassie, a lassie,
Did you ever see a lassie do *this* way and *that?*
Do *this* way and *that* way, and *this* way and *that* way;
Did you ever see a lassie do *this* way and *that?*

When a boy is in the center, the word "lassie" should be changed to "laddie."

The player may imitate any activity, such as mowing grass, raking hay, prancing like a horse, or turning a hand organ; may use dancing steps or movements such as bowing, curtsying, skipping, whirling in dance steps with the hands over the head, etc.; or may take any gymnastic movements, such as hopping, jumping, and arm, head, trunk, or leg exercises, etc.

Did You Ever See a Lassie?

(*Directions on previous page*)

Did you ev - er see a las - sie, a

las - sie, a las - sie, Did you ev - er see a

las - sie do *this* way and *that?* Do *this* way and

that way, and *this* way and *that* way; Did you

ev - er see a las - sie do *this* way and *that?*

DRAW A BUCKET OF WATER

This game is played in groups of four, generally by girls. Two players face each other, clasping hands at full arm's length. The other two face each other from the other directions, with their arms crossing those of the first couple at right angles. Bracing the feet, the couples sway backward and forward, singing the following rhyme:

Draw a bucket of water, For my la - dy's daugh-ter,

One in a rush, Two in a rush,

Please, lit - tle girl, bob un - der the bush.

Draw a bucket of water,
For my lady's daughter.
One in a rush,
Two in a rush,
Please, little girl, bob under the bush.

As the last line is said, the players all raise their arms without unclasping the hands and place them around their companions, who stoop to step inside. They will then be standing in a circle

with arms around each other's waists. The game finishes by
dancing in this position around in a ring, repeating the verse
once more.

DUCK DANCE (THE)

1. I saw a ship a-sail-ing, A-sail-ing on the sea; And
2. There were com-fits in the cab-in, And ap-ples in the hold; The
3. Four and twen-ty sail-ors That sat up-on the decks Were
4. The cap-tain was a duck With a pack-et on his back, And

1st, 2d and 3d verses   D.C.

oh, it was la-den With pret-ty things for me.
sails were made of silk, And the masts were made of gold.
four and twen-ty white mice With chains a-bout their necks.
(Omit. . . . .

Last verse only   FINE

when the ship be-gan to move The cap-tain cried "Quack! quack!"

I saw a ship a-sailing, a-sailing on the sea;
And oh, it was laden with pretty things for me.
There were comfits in the cabin, and apples in the hold;
The sails were made of silk, and the masts were made of gold.

Four and twenty sailors that sat upon the decks
Were four and twenty white mice with chains about their necks.
The captain was a duck with a packet on his back,
And when the ship began to move the captain cried, "Quack!
     quack!"

The players hold hands and circle rapidly while singing.
After the last verse one of the players breaks the circle and with
his next neighbor raises his hand high to form an arch, calling
"Bid, bid, bid!" which is the call for ducks. The player on the
opposite side of the break in the circle proceeds to pass under
this arch, the entire circle following, all holding hands and
answering "Quack! quack! quack!"

When all have passed through, the two players at the opposite
end of the line raise their hands and cry, "Bid, bid, bid!" while
the two who first made the arch pass through, drawing the line
after them, and calling "Quack! quack! quack!" This passing
of the ducks under the gateway is continued during one or two
repetitions of the music. The players should repeat "Bid,
bid, bid!" and "Quack, quack, quack!" in rhythm during all
of this latter part of the play.

FARMER IN THE DELL

The farmer in the dell,
The farmer in the dell,
     Heigh-o! the cherry-oh!
The farmer in the dell.

The farmer takes a wife,
The farmer takes a wife,
     Heigh-o! the cherry-oh!
The farmer takes a wife.

The wife takes a child,
The wife takes a child,
    Heigh-o! the cherry-oh!
The wife takes a child.

The succeeding verses vary only in the choice in each, and follow in this order:

The child takes a nurse, etc.
The nurse takes a cat, etc.
The cat takes a rat, etc.,
The rat takes the cheese, etc.

The players stand in a circle with one of their number in the center, who represents the farmer in the dell. At the singing of the second verse, where the farmer takes a wife, the center player beckons to another, who goes in and stands by her. The circle keeps moving while each verse is sung, and each time the player last called in beckons to another; that is, the wife beckons one into the circle as the child, the child beckons one for the nurse, etc., until six are standing in the circle. But when the lines, "The rat takes the cheese," are sung, the players inside the circle and those forming it jump up and down and clap their hands in a grand confusion, and the game breaks up.

HUNTING

This game is especially enjoyed by little boys, for whom there is a comparatively small number of appropriate singing games.

The players all stand in two lines facing each other. They clap their hands in time with the song, and sing the first verse:

Oh, have you seen the Shah?
Oh, have you seen the Shah?
He lights his pipe on a starlight night.
Oh, have you seen the Shah?

> For a-hunting we will go,
> A-hunting we will go.
> We'll catch a fox and put him in a box.
> A-hunting we will go.

While the last verse is being sung, the two players at the top of the lines run forward, join hands, and run down between the lines to the foot, turn around, join the other hands, and return between the lines. When they have reached the head again, they unclasp hands and run down the outside of the lines, each on his own side, and take their places at the foot of the lines. By this time the verse should be finished, and it is then sung again, the two players who are now standing at the head running down through the middle, etc. This is repeated until all the players have run, when the two lines join hands in a ring and all dance around, repeating the verse for the last time.

For a large number of players several may run instead of two. The first two then represent foxes, the next four, prancing or galloping horses (all in time to the music), and four others for riders or hunters.

ITISKIT, ITASKET

This is a form of Drop the Handkerchief, differing somewhat in play, and also in that a verse is sung with the game.

All of the players but one stand in a circle with clasped hands; the odd player, carrying a handkerchief, runs around on the outside of the circle, singing the following verse:

> Itiskit, Itasket,
> A green and yellow basket;
> I wrote a letter to my love
> And on the way I dropped it.
> Some one of you has picked it up
> And put it in your pocket;
> It isn't you — it isn't you —

This last phrase is repeated until the player reaches one behind whom he wishes to drop the handkerchief, when he says, "It is you!" and immediately starts on a quick run around the circle.

Itiskit, Itasket

I - tis - kit, I - tas - ket, A green and yel - low bas - ket; I

wrote a let - ter to my love And on the way I dropped it. I
Some one of you has picked it up And put it in your pock - et; It

dropped it, I dropped it, And on the way I dropped it.
isn't you, it isn't you, It isn't you, it isn't you.

The one behind whom the handkerchief was dropped picks it up and at once starts around the circle in the opposite direction, the object being to see which of the two shall first reach the vacant place. The one who is left out takes the handkerchief for the next round.

Should a circle player fail to discover that the handkerchief has been dropped behind him until the one who has dropped it has walked or run entirely around the circle, he must yield his place in the circle to the handkerchief man, changing places with him.

KEEP MOVING

One player is chosen as leader. He repeats or sings the following formula, at the same time going through the motions indicated. The other players must repeat the formula and the motions with him. They may be either seated or standing. The rhythm should be very rapid:

One finger one thumb keep moving,
One finger one thumb keep moving,
One finger one thumb keep moving.
Tra-la! la-la! la-la!

(The thumb and index finger of one hand are separated and brought together, as when a bird's beak is being imitated with the fingers.)

Two fingers two thumbs keep moving,
Two fingers two thumbs keep moving,
Two fingers two thumbs keep moving.
Tra-la! la-la! la-la!

(The thumb and index finger of both hands are moved in similar manner.)

Four fingers two thumbs keep moving,
Four ——
Four ——
Tra-la! ——

(The thumb, index, and middle fingers on each hand.)

Six fingers two thumbs keep moving,
Six ——
Six ——
Tra-la! ——

(Add the ring finger.)

Eight fingers two thumbs keep moving,
Eight ——, etc.

(All the fingers.)

Eight fingers two thumbs one hand keep moving,
Eight fingers two thumbs one hand keep moving,
Eight fingers two thumbs one hand keep moving.
Tra-la! la-la! la-la!

(The finger motion is continued, and to it is added an up-and-down shaking of one hand.)

Eight fingers two thumbs two hands keep moving,
Eight ——
Eight ——
Tra-la! ——

(A similar movement of the other hand is added.)

Eight fingers two thumbs two hands one arm keep moving, etc.

(One arm is moved up and down with the shoulder, elbow, and wrist all active, while the movement of the fingers and of the opposite hand continues.)

Eight fingers two thumbs two hands two arms keep moving, etc.

(Add similar movement of the other arm.)

Eight fingers two thumbs two hands two arms one foot keep moving, etc.

(The toes of one foot are lifted (bending the ankle) and tapped on the floor as in beating time.)

Eight fingers two thumbs two hands two arms two feet keep moving, etc.

(Add similar movement of other foot.)

Eight fingers two thumbs two hands two arms two feet one leg keep moving, etc.

(Lift one leg with bent knee and replace the foot on the floor in rhythmic time, while all of the other parts mentioned are kept in motion as previously.)

Eight fingers two thumbs two hands two arms two feet two legs keep moving, etc.

(Add similar movement of the other leg.)

Eight fingers two thumbs two hands two arms two feet two legs one head keep moving, etc.

(Add a nodding movement of the head, forward and backward.)

This is a Scotch game and is full of sport, but will depend largely for its success upon the familiarity of the leader with the order of the movements, and, like most Scotch games, upon the rapid and sustained time in which it is kept going. It is especially good for the schoolroom, as it affords some excellent exercise without the players leaving their seats.

KING OF FRANCE (THE)

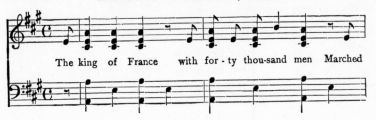

The king of France with for - ty thou-sand men Marched

up the hill and then marched down a - gain.

The King of France with forty thousand men
Marched up the hill and then marched down again.

The players stand in two rows or groups facing each other. Each group has a leader who stands in the center and represents a king leading his army.

The game or play is a simple one of imitation, in which the players perform in unison some action first indicated by one of the leaders.

The leaders of the two groups take turns in singing the verse, at the same time marching forward during the first line of the verse, and back again to their places during the second line, illustrating the action that is then to be taken by all. The verse is then sung by both groups while advancing toward each other and retreating, performing the movements indicated by the leaders. The movements illustrated by the leaders may be anything suitable to an army of men, the words describing the movement being substituted for the line, "Marched up the hill." Thus:

The King of France with forty thousand men
Waved his flag and then marched down again.

The following variations are suggested, each of which indicates the movements to go with it.

> Gave a salute, etc.
> Beat his drum.
> Blew his horn.
> Drew his sword.
> Aimed his gun.
> Fired his gun.
> Shouldered arms.
> Pranced on his horse.

It is scarcely necessary to say that a real flag and drum add much to the martial spirit of the game, and if each soldier can have a stick or wand over his shoulder for a gun, the *esprit de corps* will be proportionately enhanced.

KITTY WHITE

This is an admirable game for very little children. Their dramatic tendency should be given full rein in impersonating the soft movements of the kitty and mousie before the chase begins.

> Kitty White so slyly comes,
>   To catch the Mousie Gray;
> But mousie hears her softly creep,
>   And quickly runs away.
>
> Run, run, run, little mouse,
> Run all around the house;
> For Kitty White is coming near,
> And she will catch the mouse, I fear.

Kitty White

Kit-ty White so sly-ly comes To catch the Mous-ie Gray; But
mous-ie hears her soft-ly creep And quick-ly runs a-way. Run,
run, run, lit-tle mouse, Run all a-round the house; For
Kit-ty White is com-ing near, And she will catch the mouse, I fear.

One player is chosen for the mouse and stands in the center, and another for Kitty White, who stands outside of the circle. The other players join hands in a ring and move around, while singing the first four lines. Meanwhile Kitty White is creeping around outside of the circle, peeping in at little Mousie Gray. When the fourth line is reached, "And quickly runs away," the circle stops moving and drops hands while the mouse runs out and in through the circle, chased by Kitty White. For the last four lines, while the chase is going on, the players in the circle stand in place and clap their hands while singing "Run, run," etc.

When the mousie is caught, both return to the circle, and another mouse and kitty are chosen.

LEAVES ARE GREEN

This is a game for small children. The players join hands and form a ring. They dance around in a circle in time to the music, singing to the air of "Mulberry bush":

> The leaves are green, the nuts are brown;
> They hang so high they will not come down;
> Leave them alone till frosty weather;
> Then they will all come down together.

As the last words are sung, the children all stoop suddenly to the ground, to represent the falling nuts. This is more interesting if the time be rapid and if the players jump before stooping, which may lead to their tumbling over as the nuts do when they fall from the trees.

LET THE FEET GO TRAMP

> Let the feet go tramp! tramp! tramp!
> Let the hands go clap! clap! clap!
> Let the finger beckon thee.
> Come, dear friend, and skip with me.
> La, la la la, la la la, etc.

The players form a circle with from one to five in the center, according to the number of players. All of the players, both circle and center, sing the verse, suiting the action to the words with stamping of the feet for "Tramp, tramp, tramp!" and clapping of the hands for "Clap, clap, clap!" As the last line, "Come, dear friend, and skip with me," is sung, each child in the center beckons to one in the circle, who steps in and joins hands with the little partner as they stand facing each other. These partners in the center then dance around in time to the chorus "La, la," and the circle players may also join hands and dance in a circle.

Let the Feet Go Tramp

Let the feet go tramp, tramp, tramp, Let the hands go clap, clap, clap,

Let the fin-ger beck-on thee, Come, dear play-mate, skip with me.

Tra la la la la la la, La la la la la la la,

La la la la la la la, La la la la la.

LONDON BRIDGE

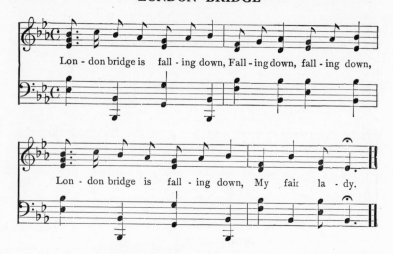

Lon - don bridge is fall - ing down, Fall - ing down, fall - ing down,

Lon - don bridge is fall - ing down, My fair la - dy.

London Bridge is falling down,
   Falling down, falling down.
London Bridge is falling down,
   My fair lady!

Build it up with iron bars,
   Iron bars, iron bars.
Build it up with iron bars,
   My fair lady!

Iron bars will bend and break,
   Bend and break, bend and break,
Iron bars will bend and break,
   My fair lady!

Build it up with gold and silver, etc.	Gold and silver will be stolen away, etc.
Get a man to watch all night, etc.	Suppose the man should fall asleep? etc.

Put a pipe into his mouth, etc.	Suppose the pipe should fall and break? etc.
Get a dog to bark all night, etc.	Suppose the dog should meet a bone? etc.
Get a cock to crow all night, etc.	Here's a prisoner I have got, etc.
What's the prisoner done to you? etc.	Stole my hat and lost my keys, etc.
A hundred pounds will set him free, etc.	A hundred pounds he has not got, etc.

Off to prison he must go, etc.

Two of the tallest players represent a bridge by facing each other, clasping hands, and holding them high for the others to pass under. The other players, in a long line, holding each other by the hand or dress, pass under the arch while the verses are sung alternately by the players representing the bridge and those passing under, those forming the arch singing the first and alternate verses and the last "Off to prison." As the words —

"Here's a prisoner I have got"

are sung, the players representing the bridge drop their arms around the one who happens to be passing under at the time. The succeeding verses are then sung to "Off to prison he must go." During this last one the prisoner is led off to one side to a place supposed to be a prison, and is there asked in a whisper or low voice to choose between two valuable objects, represented by the two bridge players who have previously agreed which each shall represent, such as a "diamond necklace" or a "gold piano." The prisoner belongs to the side which he thus chooses. When all have been caught, the prisoners line up behind their respective leaders (who have up to this time been the holders of the bridge), clasp each other around the waist, and a tug of war takes place, the side winning which succeeds in pulling its opponent across a given line.

Where a large number of players are taking part, say over ten, the action may be made much more rapid and interesting by forming several spans or arches to the bridge instead of only one, and by having the players run instead of walk under. There is thus much more activity for each player, and the prisoners are all caught much sooner.

This is a very ancient game, supposed to have originated in the custom of making a foundation sacrifice at the building of a bridge. The tug of war is thought by Mr. Newell possibly to signify a contest between powers of good and evil for the soul of the victim sacrificed.

LOOBY LOO

Here we dance, looby, looby, looby.
　Here we dance, looby, looby, light.
Here we dance, looby, looby, looby, loo,
　Every Saturday night.

Put your right hand in.
　Put your right hand out.
Give your right hand a shake, shake, shake,
　Hinkumbooby round-about.

Here we dance, looby, looby, looby, etc.

Put your left hand in, etc.

Here we dance, looby, looby, looby, etc.

Put your two hands in, etc.
Put your right foot in, etc.
Put your left foot in, etc.
Put your two feet in, etc.
Put your right elbow in, etc.
Put your left elbow in, etc.
Put your two elbows in, etc.
Put your right ear in, etc.
Put your left ear in, etc.
Put your head way in (bend deeply from the waist).

Looby Loo

Here we dance looby, loo - by, loo - by, Here we dance looby, loo - by, light;

Here we dance loo - by, loo - by, loo - by, loo,

Ev - 'ry Sat - ur - day night. Put your right hand in,

Put your right hand out, Give your right hand a

shake, shake, shake, Hin - kum - boo - by round a - bout.

The players stand in a ring, clasping hands. For the first two lines of the chorus —

> Here we dance, looby, looby, looby,
> Here we dance, looby, looby, light,

the players sway from one foot to the other, throwing the free foot across the other in sort of a balance movement in rhythm to the music. On the last two lines of this verse —

> Here we dance, looby, looby, looby, loo,
> Every Saturday night,

the circle gallops halfway around to the left for the first line, and reverses the action, returning to place on the last line.

For the alternate verses which describe action the movements are suited to the words; for instance, when the left hand is called for, the players lean far forward and stretch the left hand into the ring while singing the first line, turn around, and stretch the left hand outward for the second line, shake the hand hard on the third line, and on the last line jump or spin completely around.

This is a very ancient game, supposed to have originated in a choral dance, probably in celebration of the rites of some deity, in which animal postures were assumed or animal rites were an object. Later, it was an old court dance, stately and decorous as the minuet.

MUFFIN MAN

The players stand in a circle, with one or more in the center. The circle dances around and sings the first two lines of the following verse. They then stand still while the player or players in the center choose each a partner who enters the circle with him; they clasp hands and dance around, singing the last two lines:

Oh, have you seen the muffin man, the muffin man, the muffin man?
Oh, have you seen the muffin man that lives in Drury Lane, O!
Oh, yes, I've seen the muffin man, the muffin man, the muffin man,
Oh, yes, I've seen the muffin man that lives in Drury Lane, O!

(The) Muffin Man

Oh, have you seen the muf - fin man, the
Oh, yes, I've seen the muf - fin man, the

muf - fin man, the muf - fin man? Oh, have you seen the
muf - fin man, the muf - fin man, Oh, yes, I've seen the

muf - fin man that lives in Dru - ry Lane, O!
muf - fin man that lives in Dru - ry Lane, O!

Miss Newton has a very good adaptation of this game for the schoolroom or parlor, in which four or five players stand in corners. Each of
these chooses a partner at the end of the second line, and these groups of
two dance in a circle.

MULBERRY BUSH

Here we go round the mulberry bush,
The mulberry bush, the mulberry bush,
Here we go round the mulberry bush,
So early in the morning!

This is the way we wash our clothes,
We wash our clothes, we wash our clothes,
This is the way we wash our clothes,
So early Monday morning.

(Continued on next page.)

Mulberry Bush

Here we go round the mul - ber - ry bush, The
mul - ber - ry bush, the mul - ber - ry bush, Here we go round the
mul - ber - ry bush, So ear - ly in the morn - ing.

(See previous page.)

This is the way we iron our clothes,
   We iron our clothes, we iron our clothes,
This is the way we iron our clothes,
   So early Tuesday morning.

This is the way we scrub the floor,
   We scrub the floor, we scrub the floor,
This is the way we scrub the floor,
   So early Wednesday morning.

This is the way we mend our clothes,
   We mend our clothes, we mend our clothes,
This is the way we mend our clothes,
   So early Thursday morning.

This is the way we sweep the house,
  We sweep the house, we sweep the house,
This is the way we sweep the house,
  So early Friday morning.

Thus we play when our work is done,
  Our work is done, our work is done,
Thus we play when our work is done,
  So early Saturday morning.

The players stand in a circle clasping hands, and circle around, singing the first verse. In the second and alternate verses the action indicated by the lines is given in pantomime. In all verses the players spin around rapidly, each in her own place, on the repetition of the refrain, "So early in the morning."

This is one of the oldest traditional games, and probably one of the most widely known. It is considered to have originated as a marriage dance around a sacred tree or bush, our mistletoe custom having come from the same source.

NUTS IN MAY

(Sung to the air of "Mulberry Bush")

Here we come gathering nuts in May,
  Nuts in May, nuts in May.
Here we come gathering nuts in May,
  On a cold and frosty morning.

Whom will you have for nuts in May,
  Nuts in May, nuts in May?
Whom will you have for nuts in May,
  On a cold and frosty morning?

We'll have (Mary) for nuts in May,
  Nuts in May, nuts in May,
We'll have (Mary) for nuts in May,
  On a cold and frosty morning.

> Whom will you send to fetch her away,
> To fetch her away, to fetch her away?
> Whom will you send to fetch her away,
> On a cold and frosty morning?

> We'll send (Alice) to fetch her away,
> To fetch her away, to fetch her away.
> We'll send (Alice) to fetch her away,
> On a cold and frosty morning.

The players stand in two lines facing each other and holding hands, with a wide space between which will admit of advancing toward each other and retreating. The first line sings the first verse, advancing toward its opponents and retreating. The second line then advances and retreats and sings the second verse. The first line again advances and retreats, singing the third verse, naming some player who stands in the opposing line. The second line, unwilling to yield a player so easily, then advances and retires, singing the fourth verse, in which it suggests that someone be sent to take the one who has been selected for "nuts," and the first line then advances and retires, singing the last verse, in which it names some player from its own side whom it considers a good match for the player whom it has called from the opposite side.

The lines then stand still while these two players advance to the center, draw a mark on the ground, or throw a handkerchief down to serve the purpose, take hold of right hands across the line, and have a tug of war. The player who is pulled across the line becomes the captured "nut" and joins the side of her captors. The game is then repeated, with the change that the lines of players sing the verses that were sung by their opponents the previous time, the second line of players starting with the first verse. This should be continued until all of the players have taken part in the tug of war. The line wins which gets the most "nuts."

For large numbers of players, instead of a tug of war between two players only, the two lines may advance, each player joining hands with the one opposite, and all taking part in the tug of war. Still another method is to have the two players who are named join hands, with the players of their respective sides all lined up behind them for a tug of war, as in London Bridge.

OATS, PEAS, BEANS

Oats, peas, beans and bar - ley grows, Oats, peas, beans and

bar - ley grows. Nor you nor I nor no - bod - y knows How

oats, peas, beans and bar - ley grows. Thus the far - mer

sows his seed, Thus he stands and takes his ease,

Stamps his foot and claps his hands, And turns a - round to

view his lands. A - waiting for a part - ner,

A - waiting for a part - ner, So open the ring and

choose one in, Make haste and choose your part - ner.

Oats, peas, beans, and barley grows,
Oats, peas, beans, and barley grows.
Nor you nor I nor nobody knows
How oats, peas, beans, and barley grows.

Thus the farmer sows his seed,
Thus he stands and takes his ease,
Stamps his foot and claps his hands,
And turns around to view his lands.

A-waiting for a partner,
A-waiting for a partner,
So open the ring and choose one in,
Make haste and choose your partner.

Now you're married, you must obey.
You must be true to all you say.
You must be kind, you must be good,
And keep your wife in kindling wood.

The players form a ring, clasping hands, and circle about one of their number who has been chosen to stand in the center. They all sing the first four lines, when they drop hands, and each player goes through the motions indicated by the words: sowing the seed with a broad sweep of the arm as though scattering seed from the hand; standing erect and folding the arms; stamping the foot; clapping the hands; and at the end of the verse turning entirely around. They then clasp hands again and circle entirely around, singing:

Waiting for a partner,
Waiting for a partner,

standing still for the two lines above:

So open the ring and choose one in.

On these words the one in the center chooses one from the circle as a partner. The player who was first in the center then returns to the circle, and the one chosen as partner remains in the center while the game is repeated.

If large numbers are playing, four players may stand in the center instead of one, and in that case, of course, four partners will be chosen. This form of playing the game has traditional sanction, and at the same time adapts itself well to the large numbers that often have to be provided for under modern conditions of playing.

This is one of the games that Mr. Newell calls "world-old and world-wide." It is found in France, Italy, Spain, Germany, etc., was played by Froissart in the fourteenth century, and by Rabelais in the fifteenth. The game is supposed to have had its source in a formula sung at the sowing of grain to propitiate the earth gods and to promote and quicken the growth of crops. Mrs. Gomme notes that the turning around and bowing to the fields and lands, coupled with pantomimic actions of harvest activities, are very general in the history of sympathetic magic among primitive peoples, from which doubtless came the custom of spring and harvest festivals.

Mrs. Gomme also points out that the choosing of the partner indicates the custom of courtship and marriage at these sowing and harvest gatherings.

ON THE BRIDGE OF AVIGNON *

On the Bridge of Avignon
  Everybody walks and passes;
On the Bridge of Avignon
  Everybody passes by.
The ladies nid-nod this way,
  And the gentlemen bow this way,
On the Bridge of Avignon
  As they go walking by.

On the Bridge of Avignon
  Everybody walks and passes,
On the Bridge of Avignon
  Everybody passes by.
The ladies curtsy this way,
  And the gentlemen bow that way,
On the Bridge of Avignon
  As they go walking by.

On the Bridge of Avignon
  Everybody starts a-dancing.
On the Bridge of Avignon,
  Instead of walking by.
The trumpeters come this way
  And blow their trumpets that way,
To stop the dancing on the Bridge
  As they go marching by.

On the Bridge of Avignon
  Everybody stops a-dancing.
On the Bridge of Avignon
  Everybody walking by.
The ladies go home skipping,
  The ladies go home skipping,
They may not dance, they will not walk,
  So they go skipping by.

* (ă-vee-nyong)

On the Bridge of Avignon

On the Bridge of A-vi-gnon, Ev-'ry-bod-y walks and

pass-es. On the Bridge of A-vi-gnon, Ev-'ry-bod-y pass-es by.

The la-dies nid-nod this way, the gen-tle-men bow this

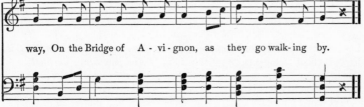

way, On the Bridge of A-vi-gnon, as they go walk-ing by.

In the beautiful city of Avignon, "a rose-red city, half as old as Time," situated in Provence in the South of France, is a famous old bridge on which, in the time of the troubadours, the ladies and gentlemen of the town use to promenade every evening. They were forbidden to dance round dances there; but it is said that where the Provençals walk there will they dance, and before the evening was over everyone would be dancing round dances. A very famous old song in France is about this bridge, and in adapting it for American children this story has been woven in.

The players are in two circles, one within the other. The little girls are inside, walking in one direction, and the boys in another circle outside walking in the opposite direction.

In the first stanza the ladies suit the action to the words by bowing with the head only, while the gentlemen gesture as lifting their hats. This is repeated several times.

In the second stanza the ladies stop, spread their skirts and curtsy, and the gentlemen bow with heels together, the left hand on the heart and the right hand making a large sweeping motion as though holding a plumed hat. This is repeated.

In the third stanza boys and girls pair off and begin dancing; then the boys become trumpeters and march around in their circle with hands held upward in front of the face as though blowing trumpets.

In the fourth stanza the trumpeters keep on marching while the girls stand still for a moment and then break the circle by skipping around the room with the boys skipping after them.

As the French version of this famous old song has been considerably altered in adapting it as an American action game, the original and translation are here given:

Sur le pont d'Avignon,	*On the bridge of Avignon,*
Tout le monde y passe et danse;	*Everybody passes and dances;*
Sur le pont d'Avignon,	*On the bridge of Avignon,*
Tout le monde y passera	*Everybody passes*
et danse en ronde.	*and dances in rounds.*
Les beaux Messieurs font comme ci,	*The fine gentlemen do like this,*
Et puis encor' comme ça;	*And then again like that;*
Sur le pont d'Avignon,	*On the bridge of Avignon,*
Tout le monde y passera	*Everybody passes*
et danse en ronde.	*and dances in rounds.*

This is repeated for the fine ladies, abbots, drinkers, soldiers, urchins.

ROUND AND ROUND THE VILLAGE

Go round and round the vil - lage, Go round and round the vil - lage, Go round and round the vil - lage, As we have done be - fore.

Go round and round the village,
Go round and round the village,
Go round and round the village,
As we have done before.

Go in and out the windows,
Go in and out the windows,
Go in and out the windows,
As we have done before.

Now stand and face your partner,
Now stand and face your partner,
Now stand and face your partner,
And bow before you go.

Now follow me to London,
Now follow me to London,
Now follow me to London,
As we have done before.

The players form a circle, clasping hands, with one player outside. In this game the circle stands still and represents the
houses of a village. The player outside sings the first verse dancing around the circle. On the second verse, "In and out the
windows," etc., the players forming the ring raise their clasped
hands to represent windows, and the outside player passes in
under one arch, out under the next, and so on, winding in and out
until the circle has been completed. She tries to get around by
the time the verse is finished, and then goes on singing the third
verse while she pauses in the circle and chooses a partner. These
two then run around the outside of the circle while singing the
last verse, "Follow me to London," etc., returning at the close to
the center of the circle, where they bow and part, the first player
taking her place in the ring. The game is then repeated, with the
second player running around the outside of the village.

Where large numbers are playing, several players may be chosen
instead of one, to run around the village and in and out of the
windows. In that case several partners will be chosen, and at
the close the first players will return to the circle, and the partners
whom they have chosen will go on with the game by running
around the village and singing the first verse again.

FOR THE SCHOOLROOM. — In the schoolroom two players
may be chosen to run "Round and round the village," starting
from different parts of the room. The remainder of the class
sits and sings while these players run up and down through the
aisles, each touching two or three pupils, who rise and run after
them. When the windows are mentioned, the seated players who
still have neighbors sitting across the aisles, stand, and clasp hands
with the neighbors to form an arch under which the runners make
their way.

VARIATIONS. — A good variation in this game, adapting it to
the modern city environment, with which many city children are
more familiar than they are with village life, is to substitute for

the words "Round and round the village" and "In and out the windows" the words, "Round and round the city" (presumably on elevated or subway trains) and "In and out the stations" or "In and out the subway." While this tampering with a traditional form of the game is questionable, there is no doubt that children much enjoy playing about things related to their own experiences. A gradual and probably unconscious adaptation to environment is one of the manifestations of the folklore spirit.

This is one of the very old traditional games, based on village customs. Mrs. Gomme traces it to the periodical village festivals at which marriages took place. In some of these it was customary for the young people to go through the houses in procession, a custom still observed in some parts of Europe.

SNAIL

This is a favorite game with very little children. For large numbers each verse may be repeated as needed to complete the winding or unwinding of the line.

> Hand in hand you see us well
> Creep like a snail into his shell,
>   Ever nearer, ever nearer,
>   Ever closer, ever closer,
> Very snug indeed you dwell,
> Snail, within your tiny shell.

> Hand in hand you see us well
> Creep like a snail out of his shell.
>   Ever farther, ever farther,
>   Ever wider, ever wider.
> Who'd have thought this tiny shell
> Could have held us all so well.

The players all stand in line holding hands; while singing the first verse they wind up in a spiral, following the leader, who walks in a circle growing ever smaller until all are wound up, still hold-

Snail

Hand in hand you see us well Creep like a
snail in-to his shell; Ev-er near-er, ev-er
near-er, Ev-er clos-er, ev-er clos-er, Ve-ry
snug in-deed you dwell, Snail,with-in your ti-ny shell.

ing hands.   The leader then turns and unwinds, until all are again
in one long line.

This " winding up " is a very old traditional feature in games, and is
supposed to have originated in tree worship.

GAMES FOR ONE OR TWO

GAMES FOR ONE OR TWO

Games are enjoyed by the solitary player perhaps even more than by those who play in groups. The lonely child, the convalescent of any age, the shut-in, the handicapped, the person who lives alone — for whom could such diversion and pleasure mean more?

Fortunately there are many games, quiet or active, which are not dependent on competition or other social aspects of play, but which, used by one alone, fascinate through skill, agility, knowledge, ingenuity, or other features. Each section of this volume contains such games; they are listed in the present chapter. Though often described for larger numbers, suggestions are given here for adapting the essential activity to one player. A second player will often add to the pleasure of such games, but they can be played without a partner. A separate list is given of additional games for which two players are necessary.

In these lists are games that call for muscular activity and others that may be played sitting still or lying down and that are suitable for the bedside or the convalescent's chair. Many of these require no implements of play; others use balls, pebbles, leaves and flowers, jackstones, marbles, beanbags, paper and pencil, or other easily acquired equipment. The most active games call for running, skipping, hopping, jumping, and many other athletic activities and skills which a child alone, or an older convalescent, might need or take pleasure in, but otherwise have no means of enjoying. Some games appeal to the sense of rhythm and dramatic instinct, while the paper and pencil games employ memory and mental agility or ingenuity.

In adapting these games to one player, one has only to overlook the directions for choosing sides or taking turns and go directly to the play itself, which is, after all, the real core and interest of the game. Similarly, references to competition, or to which player wins, have no significance, for the solitary player is playing for the fun of the game and not to beat someone else.

Among the best games for one alone are those which consist of a progressive series of skillful plays, such as Jackstones, Mumblety-Peg, the Ball Drills, or Rope Jumping. These work through to a climax of difficulty in true game evolution; whenever a miss is made, the player should do that feat over before going on, or, if very expert, go back to the beginning and repeat the entire series. To go through to the end without a mistake is to win triumphantly. This is just what one does in card games of Solitaire or Patience, which have fascinated mankind for centuries.

In many other games the skill, agility, or endurance called for provides a similar interest, though in these, instead of a series of plays of increasing difficulty, the same play is repeated over and over, but through a prescribed course which the player tries to cover without mistake, such as hopping over a row of obstacles. Of this kind are the Potato Races, Indian Club Race, Ball Jump Race, and Chinese Chicken. In these, one " races," as it were, with himself, tries to beat his own possibility of missing. He may even keep a record of mistakes and try each time to play through with a better score, or he may also race against time and endeavor with each repetition to play the game more quickly.

Games in which scoring is a main feature hold a keen interest. Among these are Pitch Pebble, Span, Sundial, Tip Tap Toe, Basketball and Baseball Distance-Throws, and surely the game of Golf played by the solitary golfer trying to achieve the ideal score of "par."

Among the quieter games, to match or name the leaves of flowers from a basket or bouquet, as in Flower Match or Leaf by Leaf, may be a delightful diversion for one alone; while in pencil and paper games the ingenious player will work out new series for Initials, Authors' Initials, or the "B" game, find new attributes for the Minister's Cat, write new Code Telegrams, or open new trails of Literary Lore. Possibly some paper or magazine would be glad to publish this new material. Those whose play must be from bed or chair will find many special games and occupations described in:

Hospital and Bedside Games, by NEVA L. BOYD, H. T. Fitzsimmons, Publisher, Chicago.

Amusements for Invalids, by MARY WOODMAN, Frederick A. Stokes and Co., Publishers, New York. Some card and board games; many diversions other than games.

See also titles after section on Social and Quiet Games, which include card games.

The lists which follow are given separately for the different sections of this book. In each section the games are arranged alphabetically by their titles so that one may turn readily to a game without consulting the final index. Ingenious players will find many other games to adapt in addition to those listed. Finally, no classification by age needs to be considered, for in playing by oneself, or with one person, the player enters a realm where such limitations do not exist and nothing but interest and fun have to be considered.

IN THE SECTION ON MISCELLANEOUS AND ACTIVE GAMES

For One (or Two)

All-Up (Relay)
Band Obstacle Race
Chinese Chicken
Crossing the Brook
Indian Club Race
Jack Be Nimble
Jackstones
Japanese Crab Race
Marbles
Mumblety-Peg

Rope Jumping
Pitch Pebble
Potato Races
Round and Round Went
    the Gallant Ship
Snow Dart
Snow Snake
Spans
Sundial
Tree Party

For Two

Arrow Chase
Blind Bell
Cat and Mice
Conkers
Do This, Do That
Follow the Leader
Fox Trail
Hide and Seek
Hide the Thimble

Hopping Race
I Say Stoop
I Spy
Jumping Race
Leap Frog
Moon and Morning Stars
Old Woman from the Wood
Poison
Poison Snake

Rolling Target
Shuffle Board
Slap Catch
Step

Tag Games
Ten Steps
Trades
Wee Bologna Man

IN THE SECTION ON SOCIAL AND QUIET GAMES

For One (or Two)

Pencil and Paper Games
Authors' Initials

Bean Porridge Hot
Buzz
Flower Match
Leaf by Leaf
Tip Tap Toe

"B" Game
Cat Party
Code Telegram
Initials
Literary Lore
Minister's Cat
Picture Show

For Two

Crambo
Dumb Crambo
Egg Shell Race
Famous People
Grass Blade
Horns
London

Naughts and Crosses
Scat
Simon Says
Sketches
Statues
Teakettle
Twenty Questions

IN THE SECTION ON FEATS AND FORFEITS

Almost the entire list of items will be found playable by one or two players.

IN THE SECTION ON SINGING GAMES

For One (or Two)

Did You Ever See a Lassie?   Looby Loo
King of France   Mulberry Bush
On the Bridge of Avignon

IN THE SECTION ON BEANBAG GAMES

For One (or Two)

Bag Pile   Beanbag Box
Beanbag Board   Beanbag Circle Toss
Beanbag Ring Throw

IN THE SECTION ON BALLS AND HOW TO PLAY THEM

Most of the types of technique described in this section are suitable for practice by one player or for competition between two players. In addition to the technique, the skill games listed for each of the major ball games (Basketball, Volleyball, Soccer Football, etc.) will be found to contain many that are very interesting for one or two persons.

IN THE SECTION ON BALL GAMES

For One (or Two)

Handball Drills I and II
Ball Jump Race
Baseball Distance Throw
Basketball Distance Throw
Clock Golf
Golf

Rosemary
Line Club-Bowls
   (Single and Double)
Russian Hole Ball
Three Holes
Wall-Ball Drill

For Two

Badminton
Ball Tag
Balloon Ball
Balloon Volleyball
Bounceball
Box Ball
Curtain Ball
Deck Hockey
Deck Tennis
Football Tag

Hand Tennis
Ice Hockey
Lawn Tennis
Paddle Tennis
Roley Poley
Soccer Pin Ball
Spongeball
Stool Ball
Table Tennis (Ping-Pong)
Tetherball

IN THE SECTION ON TRACK AND FIELD EVENTS

Numerous items of running, jumping, and weight throwing afford practice for one or competition between two.

BEANBAG GAMES

BEANBAG GAMES

BAG–PILE

10 to 100 players   *Intermediate*
Beanbags   *Gymnasium; playground; schoolroom*   *grades*

The players are divided into two or more equal teams which line up in ranks. At one end of each rank is a pile of from ten to fifteen beanbags. At a signal the first player in each rank takes a bag and passes it down the line, sending the others in succession as rapidly as possible. The last player in the line when he receives the beanbag lays it on the floor in front of him; and as each beanbag reaches him, he piles it on the first one, making a stack. Only the first bag must touch the floor. The stack must be able to stand without assistance, and the player who stacks the bags must have no help in his task. Should the bags fall over at any time, the player who stacked them must pick them up and pile them over again. The line which first succeeds in getting all of its bags stacked scores one. The last player, the one who stacked the bags, then carries them up to the front of the line and becomes the first passer for the next round of the game.

The line wins which first scores five or ten, as may be decided beforehand. The play should be very rapid.

BEANBAG AND BASKET RELAY

10 to 60 players   *Primary grades*
Schoolroom

Each player is provided with a beanbag. A waste-paper basket or a box is placed on the floor near the blackboard in front of each aisle. In line horizontally with the forward edge of each front desk, a chalk line is drawn on the floor at the end of

389

each aisle, which serves as a throwing line, from which players throw their beanbags into the baskets.

The game is a competition of skill rather than of speed. At a signal from the teacher, the first pupil in each row stands, places his toe even with the throwing line, and tosses his beanbag toward the basket. If the bag goes into the basket, it scores five. Should it lodge on the edge of the basket, it scores three. Should it fall outside, there is no score.

As soon as these first players have thrown, they return to their seats and the second row across the room steps forward and throws. This is continued until each player has thrown, and the line wins which has the highest score. There should be one scorekeeper for the entire game, who should draw a diagram on the board in which to write the score.

BEANBAG BOARD

(Faba Gaba)

2 to 30 or more players   *Primary grades*
Playground; gymnasium; schoolroom

This game consists in throwing beanbags through holes in an inclined board. The board should be preferably eighteen inches wide by three feet long. Near the lower end of it should be cut a square hole about the size of the beanbags. Higher up in the board a second hole about three inches larger should be cut. The board should be slanted by resting it against a wall or fence, or bracing one end of it in some other way, so that it is at an angle of about forty-five degrees.

The players stand at a throwing line from ten to fifteen feet from the board. Each player has five bags — or five may be used for the entire group of players, the bags being recovered for each thrower in turn. A bag thrown into the larger hole counts five; into the smaller hole ten. The player wins who first scores one hundred.

Where there are a large number of players, it is desirable to have more than one board, so that the players may be divided into several groups and make the game more rapid.

BEANBAG BOX

2 to 20 or more players   *Primary grades*
Playground; gymnasium; schoolroom

A small box measuring not less than six inches square should be fastened inside of one of eighteen inches and that in a third, leaving at least six inches margin between the boxes. This is set up on a slight incline with a stone or other object under its further end, or tipped up against the wall. From ten to twenty feet away from this a throwing line is drawn. Each player is provided with five beanbags and takes his place in turn on the throwing line, throwing all five bags at each turn. A bag thrown into the smallest box scores five points, one into the middle box ten points, and into the outside box fifteen points. The player who first scores one hundred wins.

This is a very popular game, and the paraphernalia for it may be easily improvised.

BEANBAG CIRCLE–TOSS

10 to 30 or more players   *Primary grades*
Gymnasium; playground; schoolroom   *Beanbags; balls*

There should be a beanbag for each of the players except one. All of the players form a circle, separated from each other by a small space. At a signal from a leader, each player turns toward his right-hand neighbor and tosses his beanbag to him, turning at once to receive the bag which is coming to him from the left. The game should move rapidly, but of course this is a matter of skill and may have to be acquired. With very little children it may be advisable first to play the game with a fewer number of beanbags, till they grow accustomed to tossing and turning quickly to catch. Balls may be used instead of beanbags if desired.

When the tossing has gone once or twice around the circle to the right, the direction should be changed to the left. It is well to have one of the beanbags of a different color from the others, so as to know when the circle has been completed. Any player failing to catch a bag must pick it up and toss it regularly to his neighbor.

BEANBAG RING–THROW

10 to 60 or more players   *Primary*
Playground; seashore; gymnasium   *grades*
     Beanbags; blocks of wood; stones; shells

I. This game may be played with beanbags, or when out of doors, especially at the seashore, with small blocks of wood, stones, or shells. The players should line up in relay formation. A small ring should be drawn on the ground measuring from twelve to eighteen inches in diameter, one opposite each file. The leaders toe a starting line drawn from ten to fifteen feet from the row of circles. Each file should be provided with six beanbags or other objects for throwing.

At a signal, the leader of each file throws each of his bags in succession toward the circle, and scores one point for each bag that lands within the circle. Any bag that touches the line does not count. The player then takes up his bags and runs back to the rear of the line, giving the bags as he passes to the front player of his row, who should have moved up to the starting line. These second players, in turn, all begin throwing on a signal. The line wins which has the highest score when all have thrown.

It is advisable to have someone to act as scorer for all of the lines; though it is practicable for the first player in each line to act as scorer for his line.

II. IN THE SCHOOLROOM. — When this game is played in the schoolroom, a circle should be drawn on the floor near the front blackboard opposite each aisle; across the end of each aisle, and even with the front row of desks, should be drawn a throwing line. The game should start with the six beanbags on each front desk. At a signal the front pupil in each row steps forward to the throwing line and throws the six bags in succession for his circle. Each bag that lands fully within the circle scores one point for him. No score is made for a bag that touches a line. He then steps to the blackboard in front of his aisle, and writes down his score; then gathers up the bags, places them on the front desk, and takes his seat. When he is seated the player next behind him steps forward to the throwing line and repeats the play; or if desired, the next row of players across the room may wait for the teacher's signal for doing this, as the game is played for a score and not on time limits.

The row wins which has the highest score when each of its players has thrown.

CATCH BASKET

10 to 60 players   *Primary;*
Schoolroom; gymnasium   *intermediate*
Beanbags; gas ball

The class stands in a circle around the room, each half constituting a team with a leader at one end. On a desk in the center of the room is placed a waste-paper basket. The game consists in throwing a beanbag or a ball (large, light gas ball preferable) into the basket, the teams alternating their turns. There is no interference, but an umpire stands in the center who returns the ball to the next player after each throw. The leaders throw first and each player in turn thereafter. Each time the ball lodges in the basket it scores one for the team throwing. A beanbag lodged on the edge of the basket scores as a goal. A player may throw but once at each turn. The game may be limited by time, the team winning which has the highest score at the end of ten or fifteen minutes; or it may end when each player has had a turn. The former method leads to quicker and more expert play, which should be encouraged.

CORNER SPRY

10 to 60 players   *Primary grades*
Playground; party; schoolroom   *to junior high school*
Beanbags; balls

The players are divided into four teams, one team stationed in each of the corners, called North, South, East, and West.

Four captains stand in the center, each with a beanbag, facing his corner of players, who stand in a row. The captain throws the beanbag to each player in turn in his group, who throws it back at once to the captain, and so on until the last player is reached. As the captain throws to his last player he calls "Corner

Spry!" and runs to the head of the row, the last player becoming captain. The team that first succeeds in having all of its players in the captain's place wins the game.

This game was originated by Miss Amy A. Young of Cleveland, Ohio.

CRISS–CROSS GOAL

10 to 60 players *Intermediate grades*
Schoolroom; gymnasium; playground

The class is divided into two teams. Each team is divided into two lines, which stand facing each other, as shown in the diagram.

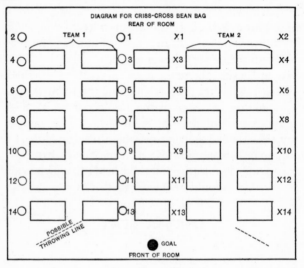

CRISS-CROSS GOAL

A waste basket is placed on the teacher's desk or hung higher if possible in the front of the room. Each team has one beanbag.

Player No. 1 holds the beanbag in each team.

At a signal each No. 1 tosses his bag to No. 2, No. 2 to No. 3, and so it continues to pass in a zigzag line till it reaches No. 14. No. 14, on receiving the bag, tries to throw it into the basket. If he misses, he runs forward, picks up the bag, runs back to his place and tries again; he continues trying until he or his opponent gets a bag in, which event finishes the inning.

The team in which No. 14 first receives the bag scores three points; and the team making the goal first scores one; so one team may score four points, or one three and the other one. The team wins which has the highest score at the end of the playing time.

If the distance from the basket seems too long, No. 14 may come forward a given distance to a chalk line and throw from that.

In order to pass around the privilege of throwing goal, the goal thrower in one game passes down to the other end of the line, the line moves up one place, and the next player in order throws for the goal in the next game. When everyone in one line has thrown for goal, the privilege passes to the other line.

Sometimes it is necessary to have umpires to watch for fouls, such as skipping a player in passing the bag.

DESK RELAY

20 to 60 players
Schoolroom

Intermediate
grades

The pupils sit on their desks facing the rear of the room and with the toes caught under the seats. The rear player on each line holds a beanbag. At a signal, the bag is passed over the head backward to the next player, who in turn passes it, and so on until it reaches the player at the front, who jumps down from the desk and hops on one foot to the rear of the room. As soon as this player has reached the rear seat, all the players in the line stand and move forward one desk. The rear player takes the desk thus vacated and starts the beanbag again.

The line wins whose beanbag first reaches the front of the room after the pupils have all changed seats until original places are resumed.

The teacher should indicate which foot is to be used in hopping, so that in successive playing of the game, each pupil will hop alternately on the right and left foot.

FETCH AND CARRY

10 to 60 players　　　　　　　　　　　　　*Primary grades*
　　　　　　　Schoolroom; playground

Each pupil is provided with a beanbag. A circle about fifteen inches in diameter is drawn with chalk on the floor directly in front of each aisle and close up to the front blackboard. At a

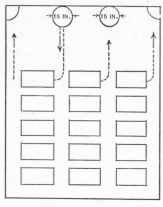

signal from the teacher the first pupil in each row of seats runs forward, places his beanbag in the circle in front of his aisle, and runs back to his seat. As soon as he is in his seat, the pupil back of him runs forward, places his beanbag in the circle, and returns to his seat. This is continued until every pupil in the row has deposited his beanbag, the signal for each player to start being the seating of the player in front. The row which gets all of its bags first into the circle wins, and scores one.

FETCH AND CARRY

The play is then reversed. The last player in each row runs forward, picks up a beanbag, and returns to his seat. As he sits, he touches the player in front on the shoulder, who then starts forward, but must wait for this signal. The row which first gets back to its seats, each player with a beanbag, wins and scores one.

As in all schoolroom games in which the players run through the aisles, those who are seated must be very careful to keep their feet under their desks, and never to start before the proper signal is given for their turn.

HAND–OVER–HEAD BEANBAG

10 to 60 players　　　　　　　　　　　　　*Primary grades*
　　　　　　　Schoolroom

This is a relay passing race, the different rows of pupils competing with each other in passing beanbags backward over the head.

The players should all be seated, there being the same number in each row of seats. On each front desk a beanbag should be laid. At a signal the first player in each row lifts the beanbag over his head and drops it (it should not be thrown) toward the desk behind him, immediately clasping his hands on his own desk. The next player catches or picks up the beanbag from his desk and passes it backward in the same manner. It is thus passed quickly to the rear of the line. When the last pupil receives it, he runs forward at once to the front of the line. As soon as he reaches the front desk, the entire row of players move backward one seat, and the player who ran forward takes the front seat, immediately passing the bag backward to the player next behind him.

The play thus continues until the original occupant of the front seat has again returned to it. Immediately, when he is seated, he should hold the beanbag up with outstretched arm, as a signal that his row has finished. The row wins whose leader first does this.

JUMP THE BEANBAG

10 to 60 players   *Intermediate grades*
                        Schoolroom

The class is divided into two equal divisions or teams. The teams stand in opposite outside aisles and face the center of the room. The game consists in a contest between the two divisions as to which shall finish first in the following relay, here described for one team.

The leader at the head or front of the line, having the beanbag in his hand, runs down the first aisle toward the rear, places the beanbag on the center seat of the row to his left (second row from standing line), vaults over the seat, and runs up the next aisle to the front of the room and so to the head of his division. He tags the player standing at the head of the line and passes behind the line to the rear, taking his place at the foot.

The player who has been tagged at the head of the line immediately runs down the first aisle, takes the beanbag from the seat, vaults over the seat, and passes down the next aisle to the rear of the room, and so to the foot of his line. He hands the beanbag to the player next to him, who passes it to his neighbor, and so it is passed up to the head of the line.

The player at the head of the line, immediately upon receiving the beanbag, runs down the first aisle, places it on the seat, vaults over the seat to the next aisle, and so to the head of his line, where he tags the player who has moved up to his place.

The game thus consists in an alternate placing and taking of the bag from the seat. The player who places the bag returns to the head of the line to tag the player standing there, and then passes behind the line to the foot; the player taking the beanbag returns to the rear of his line and passes the beanbag up the line.

The division whose original leader first gets back to his starting place wins the game.

PASSING RELAYS

There are several forms of this game, some of which are suited only to young children; others may be full of sport and interest for adults. The games may be adapted to comparatively small numbers or very large numbers. Several passing races will be found among the ball games. For beanbags, see:

> Bag Pile.
> Passing Race.
> Pass and Toss Relay (single line).
> Pass and Toss Relay (double line).

PASSING RACE

10 to 100 players   *Intermediate*
Playground; gymnasium; schoolroom   *to college*
Beanbags; dumbbells

The players stand in ranks, and bags are passed from one to another player down each line, starting on a signal for the first bag. Each rank should have about ten bags. The line wins which finishes first; that is, passes all of its bags to the end of the line.

The game may be varied by having each player pass the bags from one hand to the other before handing them to his neighbor, or by raising the bags overhead, or touching them to the floor, first with one hand, then with the other, before passing.

This makes an especially interesting game when dumbbells are used instead of beanbags, as they are harder to pass.

PASS–AND–TOSS RELAY (SINGLE LINE)

16 to 60 players   *Junior high school*
Gymnasium; playground; schoolroom

The players stand in two or more even ranks, facing sideways. The players at either end step one long pace forward of the ranks, to the points marked 1 and 10 respectively, as they are to catch the bag tossed from some other player.   Player Number One has

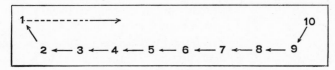

PASS-AND-TOSS RELAY (SINGLE LINE)

a bag and at the signal for starting runs toward the rear, and as he runs tosses the bag to Number Ten.   The line immediately moves forward one place, Number Two stepping into the place vacated by Number One.   As soon as Number Ten has caught the bag, he takes his place in line with the rank and passes the bag to his next neighbor, Number Nine.   The bag is then passed rapidly up the line until it is received by Number Three, who tosses it to Number Two.   Number Two, in his turn, as soon as he receives the bag, dashes for the rear, tossing the bag as he goes to the player standing at 10, who in this instance will be Number One.   The line again moves up, Number Three now stepping out to the place marked 1.

This play is continued until Number One is back in his original position.   The rank which first gets the bag around to Number One after he returns to his original position wins the game. Number One should hold the bag up at arm's length as soon as he gets it as a signal that his rank has completed its play.   As this feature adds much to the facility with which an umpire may judge of the winning rank, it may well be a required part of the play, the rank winning whose Number One is first to raise aloft his bag.

It adds much to the interest of the game to have a general umpire and scorekeeper who shall decide which is the winning line, and post the score where the players may see it.

PASS–AND–TOSS RELAY (DOUBLE LINE)

16 to 60 players　　　　　　　　　*Junior and senior high school*
Playground; gymnasium; schoolroom

The players are divided into two equal groups which compete against each other.　Each group is divided into two lines or ranks

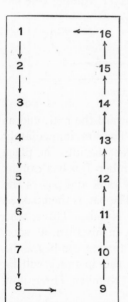

PASS-AND-TOSS RELAY
(DOUBLE LINE)

which stand facing each other.　There should be from ten to twenty feet of space between the two ranks.

The game consists of passing a beanbag up one of these lines to the end, when the last player runs across to the opposite line, tossing the bag as he goes to the end man in that line, who catches it and passes it down the line.　The same play is performed at the other end, the last player running across to the opposite line, tossing the bag as he goes to the last player there.　The lines move up or down one place each time a player runs across to the opposite rank.

This play is repeated until Number One reaches his original position again, and the bag is passed to him there.　Immediately on receiving it, he should lift it high, as a signal that the play is completed in his group.　The group wins whose first player is first to do this.

The game may be made a little more definite by Number One having some distinguishing mark, as a handkerchief tied on his arm.

When players have some proficiency in the game, as described, they may play with two bags instead of one, keeping both in play at once. In this form of the game the diagonal opposites start each a bag at the same time, that is, Number One and Number Nine. The game becomes thus just twice as rapid. The team wins whose Numbers One and Nine first succeed in both returning to their original positions, where they should hold the bags aloft.

A score should be kept, each team scoring two points for winning a game and one point for every time that its opponents' bags touch the floor, either through poor throwing or bad catching.

TARGET TOSS

10 to 60 players   *Intermediate*
Playground; seashore; gymnasium   *grades*
Beanbags; stones; shells

Three concentric circles should be drawn on the ground or floor, after the idea of a target. Their size will depend somewhat on the skill of the players, but for the youngest players the inner circle should be not more than two feet in diameter and the outer circle six feet in diameter. For those more skilled, smaller circles may be used. From ten to thirty feet from the outer rim of the largest circle a straight line is drawn on the ground, to serve as a throwing line. Each player throws three bags or other objects at each turn. If the bag stops within the center circle, it scores fifteen points; if between the center circle and the next larger one, it scores ten points; and if between the middle circle and the largest or outer one, it scores five points. For very little children a bag that lands on a line may score for the larger circle which it touches. For more expert players, a bag landing on a line does not score at all. The player wins who has the highest score in five rounds of the game.

TEACHER AND CLASS

5 to 60 players   *Primary grades*
Playground; gymnasium; class room

This game may be played with either beanbags or balls, and is one of the simplest and earliest tossing games, being generally used when pupils are first acquiring skill in handling a ball. With very rapid play and greater distance between the "teacher" and the "class," it may become very interesting, however, for older players.

One player is "teacher" or leader. The others stand in a line or semi-circle side by side, facing her, at a distance of from five to twenty feet. It is desirable to have from six to ten players for each "teacher" or leader.

The leader starts the game by tossing the bag or ball to each pupil in turn, who at once tosses it back to her. Each pupil missing goes to the foot of the line. If the leader misses, the player at the head of the line takes her place, the leader going to the foot. The action should be as rapid as possible.

VAULTING RELAY

10 to 60 players   *Schoolroom*   *Primary*

The players stand in line in the aisles between the desks, all facing to the right or left (facing open windows preferred). The first player at the front of each line will hold a beanbag in his right hand, if facing left, or in his left hand, if facing right. At the command "Start!" the beanbag must be passed toward the rear to each player, in turn, until the player at the end of the line receives it. Each player, after passing the beanbag, must place one hand on his desk and the other on the back of his chair, jump over his chair, turn, jump back again, and take his position in the aisle by the next seat, moving back one seat toward the rear of the line each time the beanbag has been passed, and so on until he returns to his place in line. The player receiving the beanbag at the end of the line must run to the head of the line and pass the bag to the next player. This continues until each player returns to his place in line.   The line wins whose original leader first gets back to his own place.

BALL GAMES SUITABLE FOR BEANBAGS

All Run
Arch Ball
Ball Chase
Ball Puss
Ball Tag
Call-Ball
Center Catch Ball
Circle-Ball
Club-Bowls
    Center Club-Bowls
    Circle Club-Bowls
    Line Club-Bowls (Single)
    Line Club-Bowls (Double)
Corner Spry
Dead-Ball
Dodgeball
Home Run

Line-Ball
Over-and-Under Relay
Overtake
Pig in a Hole
Ring Call-Ball
Roley Poley
Round Ball
Russian Hole Ball
Schoolroom Dodge Ball
Spud
Stride-Ball
Toss-Ball
Tree Ball
Zigzag Games
    Circle Zigzag
    Zigzag Ball I, II, III
    Zigzag Overhead Toss

BALLS AND HOW TO PLAY THEM

A SECTION ON TECHNIQUE, WITH LISTS OF LEAD-UP GAMES AND GAMES FOR TRAINING FUNDAMENTAL SKILLS

BALLS AND HOW TO PLAY THEM

A SECTION ON TECHNIQUE, WITH LISTS OF LEAD-UP GAMES AND GAMES FOR TRAINING FUNDAMENTAL SKILLS

BALLS

The simple, solid ball of a century ago is almost forgotten in the assortment of balls required for modern sport. The construction of balls has become both an art and a science. An outside of wood, leather, or rubber may give no inkling of what is within, for the core may be of sponge rubber, of cork wound with twine, rubber wound with yarn, packed leather strips encased in horsehair, or many other combinations of material according to whether a "lively," resilient ball is wanted or one more stolid in behavior. The technique of play in Baseball, Playground Baseball, Hockey, Golf, and many other games is largely influenced by the construction of the ball used.

LACED BALLS. — One of the greatest boons to modern sport has been the so-called "laced" ball, in which a rubber bladder is inflated and inserted in a leather case, which then is laced to close the opening. Such games as Basketball and Volleyball might never have really lived without these large, light-weight balls.

Official rules for major games always give specifications as to weight and size of ball, providing a margin for variation. Sometimes their construction is also specified.

HANDSIZEBALL. — This term is used to designate any ball that may be caught easily in one hand, as distinguished from larger balls or from the smaller official handball, used in the game of that name. A good handsizeball measures from two and one quarter to three inches in diameter. It may be of any material; but for children it is best if made of rubber, to weigh nearly or quite three ounces, and to have enough resiliency to rebound to a height of three feet when dropped from a height of six feet.

BALLOONS. — These are the toy balloons used by children, and are preferably ten or twelve inches in diameter when inflated, though smaller ones may be used. When the gas in a balloon is exhausted, if not convenient to refill it with gas, it may be blown up with the breath and will be found to float sufficiently in the air for purposes of the game, though the gas-filled balloons, with their tendency to rise, are better.

BEANBAGS. — These should be made of heavy, close-woven material, such as ticking, awning canvas, duck, or denim, and are from six to ten inches square when finished. They are stitched, turned, and stitched a second time, except for a small opening through which the beans are inserted. Hand sewing withstands the strain of play better than machine stitching. Dry beans or peas are used for filling, a half pound in weight being good for a bag of any size. For very little children the six- or eight-inch bag is best. An equipment should be half of one color and half of another as, for example, some red bags and some blue; or one set should be striped and the other plain. This aids in telling which bags belong to the opposing groups or players.

BALL TECHNIQUE

The play of each kind of ball requires a special technique. A large basketball, for instance, cannot be thrown and caught in the same manner as a comparatively small and solid base ball; a lightweight ball to be kept in the air, like a tennis or volleyball, cannot be played exactly as one that is to drop through a goal or roll on the ground.

In this section is a brief description of the most important modes of playing the various balls used in major games, such as Baseball, Basketball, Volleyball, Hockey, etc. It is now generally recognized that these fundamental skills, as they have been aptly called, are acquired with much more interest and zest in the form of simple competitive games, each requiring but one or two forms of play, than through individual practice. A list of such skill games is here given for each ball as used in the major game itself. This list is followed by another of lead-up games. These, though having a more advanced organization than the skill games, are yet much simpler than the major games and excellent to prepare players for the latter. A true lead-up game uses some of the technique of the major game; or its value may consist in accustoming players to certain forms of court or field, or to features of team play.

GENERAL TECHNIQUE

THROWING. — Handsizeballs of various kinds, from a tennis ball to a playground ball, are thrown either with a mere toss, or with the more skillful overhand or underhand throws here described.

OVERHAND THROW is from shoulder height. In the preparatory movement the ball is held in front of the chest in the right hand, the fingers of the left hand closed lightly over it. For the throw the arm is drawn backward, the elbow bent and the ball delivered with a forward thrust and snappy movement of the arm and hand. How much of the force of the rest of the body is put into the throw varies with the distance and speed desired. For a "long" ball, or a "hard" one, the body is turned, in the preparatory movements, with the left shoulder in the direction of the throw, weight on rear (right) foot, and, if needed, a bend of the rear knee. In delivering the ball, knees are straightened and the weight transferred forward so that the spring and force of the whole body reinforce the thrust of the arm.

UNDERHAND THROW. — The ball is held down at the side in the upturned palm, fingers spread. The throw is made with a full-arm swing at the side of the body. In most games the hand must be below the hip and six inches away from the body as it moves forward. The ball is released at, or below, waist or shoulder height, with a wrist motion to add impetus. In some plays a step forward is taken on the right foot as the arm swings forward and the ball is released.

CATCHING is almost always with both hands, which are cupped and ready for the ball. If above waistline the thumbs touch; if below waistline little fingers touch. With the impact of the ball the hands "give" — that is, are drawn in toward the body. The eye should be kept on the ball; the catcher should get in line with the ball and run in to meet it.

BOWLING is done with a straight-arm swing similar to that of the underhand throw, and the ball is held in the same way, but the body is bent to hold the ball near the ground. There is usually a preparatory run or change-step, ending, as the ball is delivered, with the weight on the opposite foot.

SERVING. — This is done by releasing the ball with one hand and hitting it with the other. The ball is held in the left hand, tossed (or the hand withdrawn), and while in the air is batted with the right hand or with any implement held in it for the game, such as a tennis racket. Detailed rules for serving vary with different balls and games. For some it is bounced and then batted.

VOLLEYING. — This consists in returning a ball "on the fly," that is, while it is in the air, before it touches the ground, and without catching it. It is hit or batted with the hand, open or closed, as the game requires, or with a racket or equivalent.

PIVOTING: QUICK TURN. — In many games a quick turn of direction must be made either from a stand or while running. This should be done with a pivot practiced until it is automatic. The turn is made on the heel or toe of one foot as the other foot is advanced ready for a step in the new direction — forward, backward, or sideways.

LIST OF SKILL GAMES FOR GENERAL BALL TECHNIQUE

Ball Puss
Ball Tag
Basketball Pivot-Race
Center Base
Center Club-Bowls
Circle Ball
Circle Dodgeball
Circle Zigzag
Cornerball
Corner Spry
Handball Drills

Line Club-Bowls
  (Single and Double)
Overtake
Pass-Ball Relay
Ring Call-Ball
Rosemary
Round Ball
Square Ball
Stride-Ball
Two-Team Circle Passing
Wall-Ball Drill

Zigzag Ball

BASEBALL TECHNIQUE

(See also *Playground Baseball Technique.*)

BALL. — The official baseball for adults approximates nine inches in circumference and five ounces in weight. For junior players a ball slightly smaller and lighter is used.

PITCHING. — The ball is pitched with an overhand throw as described on page 409. Rules require that the pitcher must face the batter, or anyone to whom he intends throwing the ball, that he may take but one step (in the direction of the throw), and must have at least one foot on the pitcher's plate. He may not make a feint at throwing. Infringement of any of these rules is called a "balk."

CATCHING. — As described on page 409.

BATTING. — A right-handed batter stands on the left-hand side of the plate and facing it, but with his head turned toward the pitcher so as to keep his eyes on the ball; his feet should be slightly apart and a few inches from the plate. He holds the bat in both hands, close together, with the left near the end. In the act of batting he steps forward and swings the bat forward in a horizontal plane parallel to the ground. A left-handed batter reverses the directions. After batting the ball, the bat should be dropped as the batter becomes a runner.

BUNTING consists in stopping the ball with the bat so that it drops and rolls only a short distance instead of hitting it for a long drive. The batter stands as for regular batting, but faces the pitcher, and holds the bat loosely, the left hand near the end but the right hand, palm upward, near the middle. The bat is held out in front, horizontally, and meets the ball without any swing.

LIST OF BASEBALL SKILL GAMES

Baseball Distance Throw	Baseball Target-Pitch
Baseball Grounders	Baseball Throw and Catch
Baseball Quick-Fielding	Bunt-Ball

LEAD-UP GAMES FOR BASEBALL

Baseball Hit-Pin	Bat and Tag
Baseball Overtake	Hand Batball

Long-Ball	Ten-Trips
Pass the Bat	Tip Cat
Skylark	Zigzag Passing Relays

BASKETBALL TECHNIQUE

BALL. — The basketball is a laced ball; that is, a rubber bladder inflated and inserted in a leather case, the opening of which is then laced together. Completed, the ball measures approximately thirty inches in circumference and is twenty ounces in weight.

UNDERHAND THROW WITH ONE HAND. — The ball is held in the right hand with fingers spread and wrist bent so that the ball is pressed against it. The arm is then swung at full length downward and backward. The right foot should ·be a step backward with the weight on it. As the ball is thrown, with a forward swing of the arm, the weight should be transferred to the forward foot so that the movement of the whole body is in the throw.

OVERHEAD THROW WITH ONE HAND. — The right arm is bent so as to hold the ball back of the right shoulder on the upturned hand, the right foot being back with the weight upon it. In the act of throwing, the knees are bent to give spring, and the weight is quickly transferred forward as the ball is delivered with a full stretch of the arm.

CHEST THROW OR PASS WITH BOTH HANDS. — The ball is held in front of the chest, fingers widely spread and elbows close at the sides. It is delivered with a quick throw or snap forward, and released just before the elbows are straight. A run may be used to add to the momentum of the throw.

UNDERHAND THROW OR TOSS WITH BOTH HANDS. — The ball is held in both hands between the knees, the feet apart, body and elbows slightly bent. The throw is a forward and upward toss, with the eyes looking at the basket, or point aimed for.

OVERHEAD SIDE THROW OR PASS WITH BOTH HANDS. — Standing with the side in the direction of the throw, the ball is held above the head with both hands, and thrown with a special push from the rear arm. At the same time the weight of the body is swung in the direction of the throw.

UNDERHAND SIDE THROW OR PASS WITH BOTH HANDS. — The ball is held in both hands extended downwards at arm's length and swung to one side with the weight on that foot. To deliver the ball, the arms are swung with a pendulum motion across the body and released on the opposite side. The weight should shift with the motion of the arms.

FORWARD OVERHEAD THROW WITH BOTH HANDS. — The ball is held in both hands above the head and thrown directly forward.

DRIBBLING. — This consists in one player advancing the ball by a series of quick bounces from the floor while he walks or runs forward. The ball is hit downward with the open palm of one hand, or both alternately, but never with both together, and should bounce not higher than the waist.

JUGGLING (UPWARD DRIBBLE). — The ball is bounced from the hand or lightly tossed upward above the head as the player advances.

Dribbling and juggling are means of circumventing the rule that there shall be no running with (carrying of) the ball. In some games (see *Basketball for Women*), not more than one bounce or step is allowed in either a dribble or a juggle.

BOUNCE-PASS WITH BOTH HANDS. — The ball is held at waist height and bounced on a slant by a sudden extension of both arms.

GOAL SHOOTING. — The player stands a short distance from the goal, as on the fifteen-foot free-throw line, and holds the ball at the chest with both hands as in the chest pass, but with fingers and forearms aiming upward at the basket; the elbows are held in toward the sides. With a slight spring from the knees and a forward thrust of the body, the arms are extended and the ball released. The eyes should be kept on the basket. It is a goal if the ball drops into the basket, touches or rolls on the rim and then goes through, or hits the backstop and then bounds through. Expert players throw long goals, that is, from a distance of thirty feet.

CATCHING. — The basketball is caught with both hands; if above the waist, fingers are spread with thumbs nearest each other; if below the waist, with little fingers nearest.

PIVOTING. — Described under *General Technique*, page 410.

LIST OF BASKETBALL SKILL GAMES

Basketball Distance Throw
Basketball Dribble Race
Basketball Dribble Relay
Basketball Goal Throw
Basket-Goal Clock-Throw
Basketball Follow-up Goal
Basketball Juggle Race
Basketball Ladder Run
Basketball Pass, Catch, and Goal
Basketball Pivot Race
Basketball Run-Throw-and-Catch Race
Basketball Side-Pass Race
Basketball Twenty-One

(See also *Over-the-Cord Catch*)

LEAD-UP GAMES FOR BASKETBALL

Battle-Ball
Bombardment
Boundary Ball
Captainball
Captain Basketball
Center Catch Ball II
Circle-Ball
Circle Pillar Ball

Cornerball
Couple Hit-Pin
Double Cornerball
Drive-Ball
Endball
Hand Bat-Ball
Keep-Ball
Nine-Court Basketball

Zigzag Relays

FIELD HOCKEY TECHNIQUE

BALL. — An official Field Hockey ball is covered with white leather, weighs slightly more than five ounces, and measures about nine inches in circumference.

DRIVE. — For the drive the hockey stick is gripped firmly by both hands close together at top of the handle, the left above. The feet are in a wide stance with left shoulder and foot in the direction of the drive, and as the stick is swung backward, the weight is on the right (rear) foot; as the stick swings forward for the drive, the weight sways to the left foot and the arms follow through until straight, but *at no time may the stick be lifted above* *shoulder height.* No undercutting or purposeful lofting of the ball is allowed (scoop stroke an exception).

SCOOP. — The scoop stroke consists in slightly lofting the ball to negotiate an obstacle. The blade is laid back with the tip under the ball, the right hand slipping down the handle for a quick forearm and wrist stroke.

DRIBBLE. — In dribbling, a player runs with the ball, carrying it along with him by a series of light strokes that do not send it out of reach. The left hand is at the top of the stick and the right about six inches below it. The ball is tapped by quick movements of the wrist, the arms being well away from the body and moving freely.

PUSH-PASS AND FLICK. — The stick is held at right angles to the ground and well away from the body, with the right hand a few inches down the handle. The ball is pushed along the ground as the player extends a forearm, ending with a flick of the wrist.

LEFT-HAND LUNGE. — A quick lunge is made to the left with the stick, held only in the left hand, swung downward and forward towards the ball. The opposite arm is flung backward as a balance.

STOPPING THE BALL. — To stop the ball a player gets in direct line with it and goes forward to meet it. The top of the stick is held forward so that the stick slants. This keeps the ball from bounding forward. As the stick contacts the ball, the arms should give. Some other play should immediately be made after stopping the ball, such as a dribble or pass.

STRAIGHT TACKLE. — This is used to stop an opponent who is dribbling straight toward one. The oncoming player should be faced squarely, and the position and grip of the stick the same as in stopping the ball.

HOLDING THE STICK WHEN NOT PLAYING THE BALL. — The stick is held horizontally across the body, the left hand at top with fingers around one side, the thumb around the other, the back of the wrist and hand facing forward. The weight of the stick rests in the right hand held where the stick begins to curve. This hand is cupped with the fingers on the outside of the stick. The grip is very loose so that the stick may be brought into play immediately by slipping the right hand into the desired position.

"STICKS!" — At no time may the stick be raised above shoulder level. This is a foul.

LIST OF FIELD HOCKEY SKILL GAMES

Field-Hockey Dribble Race
Field-Hockey Dribble and Drive
Field-Hockey Dribble and Turn
Field-Hockey Drive Relay I, II
Field-Hockey Goal Drive
Field-Hockey Scoop-Over Race

(See also *Keep-Ball*.)

FOOTBALL TECHNIQUE

(See *Rugby Football Technique* and *Soccer Football Technique*, given in their alphabetic order in this section.)

HANDBALL TECHNIQUE

BALL. — The official or regulation handball for men is very small, almost the size of a golf ball, made of rather hard rubber. In the women's game, and in junior and informal play, a larger ball is used, either a tennis ball or other handsizeball.

SERVING. — The server stands behind the short line, sixteen feet inward from the wall, and bounces the ball on the floor, then hits it against the wall with the open hand and a swinging stroke of the arm. It should strike the wall within sixteen feet of the ground and so hard as to rebound into the court beyond the short line.

RETURNING. — A served ball is returned to the wall, after it has bounced once in the court, by a stroke of the open hand hard enough to make it rebound again from the wall and into the court beyond the short line.

VOLLEYING consists in returning the ball on the fly before it has bounced from the floor. The stroke is the same as for serving and the ball must rebound into the court.

SKILL AND LEAD-UP GAMES FOR HANDBALL

Bounceball   Hand Tennis
Box Ball   Wall-Ball Drill

HOCKEY TECHNIQUE

(See *Field Hockey Technique* under "F" in this section.)

LAWN TENNIS TECHNIQUE

BALL. — A tennis ball is made of rubber filled with air under pressure. It is about two and one-half inches in diameter, and weighs about two ounces. The official ball is covered with white cloth.

FOREHAND DRIVE. — The racket should be gripped firmly in the right hand very near the end. The player stands on the right foot, left foot advanced, and with the left side of the body towards the net or the direction of the drive. He hits the ball with a full-arm swing, following through the stroke. At the same time the weight is transferred from the rear (right) foot to the left, turning the body so that the player faces in the general direction of the drive.

BACKHAND DRIVE. — The player stands with the right side of the body toward the net and swings the racket to his left side with a twist of the body, weight on the left foot, and then makes a swinging stroke to the right across the front of the body. The racket is tipped slightly toward the body with the thumb extended along its broad side, but the grip is otherwise the same as in the forehand drive. The same side of the racket is used to hit the ball as in the forehand, and the weight changes from the rear (left) foot to the right as the stroke is delivered.

SERVICE. — The ball is tossed in the air by the left hand and hit with a full-arm circular swing of the racket in the right hand, up, back, down, and forward, hitting the ball on the latter part of the swing. The left side of the body should be toward the net, with the left foot forward, but the weight on the right foot at starting. The weight is transferred to the left foot as the ball is struck. In tennis the ball is always put in play with such a serve.

There are many other tennis strokes.

Badminton	Hand Tennis
Bounceball	Paddle Tennis
Box Ball	Sponge Ball
Deck Tennis	Table Tennis (Ping-Pong)
Tennis Wall-Ball	Tetherball

PLAYGROUND BASEBALL TECHNIQUE

(Indoor Baseball)

BALL. — The ball used for Playground Baseball or Indoor Baseball is softer in construction than a regulation baseball, and slightly larger, measuring from twelve to fourteen inches in circumference.

PITCHING. — The pitcher must come to a stand with both feet on the plate and facing the batter before he makes any movement for pitching. He may then take one step forward in the act of throwing but must always have one foot on the plate when the ball leaves his hand. A right-handed pitcher stands with the right foot on or behind the pitching line and the left foot in advance. The ball is held in the right hand at the chest, lightly covered by the left hand. *In some games the pitching must be done entirely with the underhand throw,* but according to the size of the field and the section of the country the overhand throw is at times permissible. Just which is to be used should be distinctly understood.

BATTING and **BUNTING** are described under Baseball Technique.

Skill and Lead-up Games for Playground Baseball

(See the lists of games for Baseball.)

RUGBY FOOTBALL TECHNIQUE

BALL. — Rugby football is the so-called "oval" ball — a prolate spheroid about six by nine inches in the diameters. The official ball is of the laced-ball type — a rubber bladder inflated and inserted in a leather casing.

RUGBY PUNT. — The player holds the ball in his hands, drops it, and kicks it before it touches the ground.

RUGBY DROP KICK. — The player holds the ball, drops it, and kicks it after it has bounced.

RUGBY PLACE KICK. — The ball is set on end and kicked on the run. It is sometimes permissible for a team-mate to hold the ball in position by one finger placed against the upper end.

PASSING. — A pass is a throw or quick exchange of the ball between players, usually near together. The Rugby ball is thrown endwise, being firmly gripped in the fingers at the opposite end. Passes are forward and lateral, made from a stand or running.

LIST OF RUGBY SKILL GAMES

Rugby Distance Throw	Rugby Kicks for Distance
Rugby Kicks for Accuracy	Rugby Passes

Any of the ball-passing games played with the Rugby ball are excellent for skill in handling this ball of unusual shape.

SOCCER FOOTBALL TECHNIQUE

12 to 24 players   *Senior high to adult*

BALL. — The Soccer ball is a round, laced, leather-covered ball, somewhat smaller than a basketball. Practice games are often played with an inexpensive inflated rubber ball.

KICKING. — For kicking the ball the leg is raised backward with bent knee, the foot stiff with the toes pointed. The kick is made with a quick straightening of the leg forward, the ball being propelled either by the inside or outside of the instep, the foot being turned accordingly.

SOCCER PUNT. — The player drops the ball and kicks it before it touches the ground.

PASSING. — This is a short kick to send the ball between players who are near together, the ball being rolled along the ground. The passer uses either the inside of his left instep or the outside of his right when passing the ball toward the right. In passing it toward the left he kicks it either with the inside of the right instep or the outside of the left.

DRIBBLING. — This consists of a series of light taps with either foot, advancing the ball without sending it beyond easy reach, the player taking short running steps. The ball should be kicked underneath near the bottom, which gives it a backward spin and keeps it from going far.

FOOT TRAPPING. — To stop a rolling ball with the foot is called "trapping" it. The player gets in front of the ball, and, with the knee turned outward, contacts the ball with the arch of the foot, drawing the foot slightly backward at the moment to prevent the ball bounding off. Stepping or jumping on the ball should be avoided.

BODY TRAPPING. — A ball moving too high above the ground to be trapped by the foot may be stopped by the front of the thighs or abdomen. If the body gives with the impact of the ball the latter is less likely to bound out of reach. While it is a foul to stop the ball with any part of the arm, it is permissible in trapping a ball which is above the waist to spread the arms so that the ball is trapped between shoulder and chest.

HEADING. — A ball too high for foot or body trapping is often played by "heading," which consists in striking it with the front or side of the head so that it is sent in a new direction, as to a team mate, being equivalent to a pass. There should be no butting with the top of the head.

List of Soccer Skill Games

Soccer Dribble Relay   Soccer Foot-Trap and Pass
Soccer Dribble and Kick   Soccer Kick for Accuracy
Soccer Kick for Distance

Lead-up Games for Soccer Football

Baseball Hit-Pin   Soccer Line-Ball
Circle Stride-Ball   Soccer Line-Ball II
Football Tag   (Square Soccer)
Kick Long Ball   Soccer Pin-Ball
Socco-Smash Ball

TENNIS TECHNIQUE

(See *Lawn Tennis Technique*, under (L) in this section.)

VOLLEYBALL TECHNIQUE

BALL. — The volleyball is a laced ball, that is, it consists of a rubber bladder inflated and inserted in a leather case, the opening of which is then closed by lacing. A volleyball measures twenty-six to twenty-seven inches in circumference and weighs from seven to ten ounces, and has an air pressure of seven to eight pounds, being smaller in size and about half the weight of a basketball. Out of doors a twelve-ounce ball may be used. Balls for men and women are practically the same.

SERVING UNDERHAND. — The left side is turned in the direction the ball is to take, left foot forward, right foot back with the weight on it, knee bent. The ball is held in the left hand, palm upward, the left arm diagonally across the front of the body so that the ball is at, or below, waist height. The serve is made with a large circular swing of the right arm, starting backward at shoulder height and moving downward and forward in a circular motion. The heel of the right hand contacts the ball, still held on the hand, sending it upward and forward to go over the net. The weight shifts to the left foot with the swing of the arm, and the right foot follows in a further step so that the impetus of the whole body assists in the follow-through.

SERVING OVERHAND. — Standing as for the underhand serve, the ball is tossed from the left hand as the right arm swings backward, upward, and forward to contact the ball at a high point with the heel of the hand.

OVER THE NET. — The play of a volleyball is mostly upward and forward, the game being one that keeps the ball in the air. The spring of knees and thrust of arms and body are needed as much as with heavier balls.

RECEIVING differs as to whether the ball is high or low or is falling in front of the player or behind. To receive *a high ball* the player gets under it in crouching position, with feet apart, hands cupped, and thumbs together, so that the ball bounds from the palms. For a *low ball* the player crouches and the arms are extended downward and forward, hands cupped, little fingers touching; the ball then bounds from the heels of the hands or from the forearms. In either case the ball is directed toward a team mate who may volley it over the net. A *ball falling behind* a player is received with a quick about-face pivot and usually on outstretched arms on which the ball lands, to be sent upward and backward over the player's head to a team mate.

Catching or holding the ball is illegal.

RETURNING or **VOLLEYING** is done with one or both hands, either open or closed. If returned over the net with one hand, a swinging stroke is usual; a two-handed return is made with a pushing movement of the cupped hands. In either case, a step forward and the straightening of bent elbows and knees help to put the force of the whole body into the follow-through.

A "**SET–UP**" is a play to a team mate which will give the latter a good ball to volley over the net. It often consists of a high arc over the heads of intervening players.

"**KILLING THE BALL**," or "spiking" it, is usually done with a sudden "smash" downward with one or both hands to send the ball to the floor in opponent's court at short range.

PASSES. — A ball volleyed or deflected to a team mate as described above is called a pass.

List of Volleyball Skill Games

Volleyball Clock-Serve	Volleyball-Serve Relay
Volleyball Passing Race	Volleyball Serve-and-Return Relay

(See also *Basketball Distance Throw* adaptable for Volleyball Serve.)

Lead-up Games for Volleyball

Captainball	Drive-Ball
Cornerball	Hand Bat-Ball
Crossball	Keep-Ball II
Curtain Ball	Newcomb

Volleyball Keep-Over

BALL GAMES

BALL GAMES

All the ball games in this volume are grouped in this section in alphabetic order according to titles. They range from the simplest elementary plays through games suitable for all ages and degrees of skill, culminating in the major team or athletic games, such as Baseball, Basketball, Football, and Hockey, and such highly skillful carry-over games as Lawn Tennis and Golf.

Each major team game is accompanied by a special series of skill games which afford concentration and practice on one of the fundamental skills required for the game in question, examples of which are Baseball Quick Fielding, Basketball Passes or Goal Throws, Field Hockey Dribble and Drive, Rugby Kicks, etc. There are also for each major game a number of lead-up games which employ similar technique but are less highly organized or complicated than the major game; these are excellent for younger or less experienced players and prepare them to take part in the latter.

The fundamental technique required for the different balls, clubs, bats, rackets, etc., is described in the preceding section, *Balls and How to Play Them*, under the name of the major game in which it is used. Thus, under *Volleyball Technique* are described the most important methods of serving, receiving, returning, and passing a volleyball. Immediately following this technique is a list of the *Skill Games for Volleyball* and a second list of *Lead-up Games for Volleyball*.

Methods of organizing match games and tournaments are described in the introductory chapter on *Organized Athletics*.

Disputed points in any game or sport should be settled according to the rules of the National Committee in charge of that activity. Official rules are issued (annually in most cases) in *Spalding's Athletic Library*, published by the American Sports Publishing Company, New York. These inexpensive little volumes contain much valuable material in addition to Rules, such as suggestions for coaching and lists of books on the game in question.

ALL RUN

10 to 30 or more players   *Elementary and*
Playground; gymnasium   *intermediate*
Handsizeball; beanbag

This game is a gymnasium adaptation of the game known as Ball Stand.

A square is drawn on the ground or floor. All of the players gather within this, including one who holds the ball. The ball man throws the ball into the air, whereupon all of the other players run in any direction as far as they can. The thrower remains on his place, catches the ball, and as he does so cries "Hold!" Upon hearing this, all of the others must instantly stop running. The thrower then aims his ball at one of these other players, and if he succeeds in hitting him, the player hit must change places with the thrower. Should he miss, all of the players return to the square and the same thrower takes another trial.

ARCH BALL

10 to 100 players   *Intermediate*
Playground; gymnasium; schoolroom   *to senior high*
Basketball; beanbag; any substitute

This game is very similar to Pass Ball, but is here described under another name, as it differs from Pass Ball in (1) not having the run to a goal line; (2) admitting of variations, as in the passing of several articles; (3) being comparatively informal without the scoring of fouls and other strict observance of rules that class Pass Ball with athletic events.

I. The players line up in two or more single relay files; the leader of each file toes a line and holds a basketball or other object; at a signal he passes the ball backward over his head to the player next behind, who in turn passes it backward as rapidly as possible, and so on until it reaches the last player in the line. He at once runs forward, carrying the ball to the front of the line, which moves backward one place to make room for him. He toes the line and passes the ball backward over his head. The play continues until the captain reaches the end of the line, and runs forward with the ball to his original place at the head of the file. As he takes his place there, he holds the ball aloft as a signal that he has finished. The file wins whose captain is the first to do this.

II. The game may be made very enlivening by passing several articles in rapid succession, each of a different and contrasting character, such as a basketball, tennis ball, Indian club, heavy medicine ball, beanbag, light dumbbell, three- or five-pound iron dumbbell, etc. In this form of the game the last player must accumulate all of the articles before running forward with them, or the score may be made on the arrival of the last article at the rear of the line.

III. **FOR THE SCHOOLROOM.** — The players raise their seats where this is possible, and stand between the desk and the seat. Where the seats cannot be raised, the players may sit in the seats or on the desks. An even number of players should be in each line, and only alternate lines play simultaneously, so as to leave clear the necessary aisle space for running. Those at the front of the lines should hold a ball or any substitute for passing backward over the head, such as a beanbag, eraser, foot rule, or book. At a given signal the object is passed backward over the head to the next player in the rear, who in turn passes it backward, and so on down the line until the last player receives it. He runs forward on the *right*-hand side of his desk to the first seat. At the same time the other players in his row step into the aisle at the *left* of the desks and move backward one place. The line wins whose original leader first gets back to the front.

As in all games in the schoolroom in which part of the players are seated while others run, care should be taken that there are no feet in the aisle over which the runners might trip.

See also *Hand-over-Head Beanbag*, in which the entire class plays at once.

ARCH GOAL BALL

10 to 60 players   *Intermediate*
Playground; gymnasium   *to junior high*
Basketball

I. Relay formation, facing a basketball goal or any substitute. Each file has a basketball. At a signal each leader passes the ball backward overhead, the next player catches it and passes it in the same way, and so on to the end of the line. When the last player receives the ball, he runs forward and tries to throw it into the basket, standing on a line marked from five to ten feet from the goal. He is allowed but one throw, when he quickly takes his place at the front of his file (which moves backward one place to make room for him), and at once passes the ball backward overhead. The last player, in turn, runs forward, throws for goal, etc. This is repeated until each player in a file has thrown for the goal. Each goal made scores two points for the team. The team wins which has the highest score when all of the players have thrown.

II. This may also be played on time. Then each player throws until he succeeds in getting the ball into the basket. The team wins whose last man finishes first.

BADMINTON

(Battledore and Shuttlecock)

2 or 4 players   *Junior high*
Playground; gymnasium; ship deck   *to adult*
Shuttlecock (sponge ball); racket (or paddle)

Badminton is a game much resembling tennis, in which an object is batted over a net; but as this object is not a regular ball, the play, while very interesting and skillful, is slower and less highly specialized than tennis. These points make for popularity; and the smaller court, with any kind of surface feasible, renders the game adaptable to a wide range of conditions. Long played by the English, it is now in the recreational repertoire of American high schools, colleges, and playgrounds.

EQUIPMENT. — Badminton is played with a shuttlecock which is batted across the net instead of a ball. The shuttlecock consists of from fourteen to sixteen quills each about two and a half inches long, fastened in a cork which is about one inch in diameter. This is, however, very fragile, and a successful substitute, similarly light and erratic in play, has been found in a sponge ball (see the game of that name), scissored from an ordinary vegetable sponge to the size of a tennis ball. Badminton rackets are similar to tennis rackets, but smaller and lighter. Light weight wooden paddles make a substitute that is more durable.

COURT. — The court is slightly over half the size of a tennis court and its layout is similar to tennis with slight differences. A turf surface is best and usual, but any surface may be used.

The outside measurements of the court are twenty by forty-four feet. Across the center it is divided by a net, the upper edge of which is five feet above the ground. An alley line is drawn parallel to the side lines one foot six inches

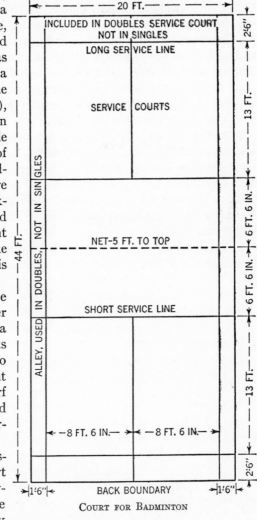

COURT FOR BADMINTON

inside them. A short service line is drawn six feet six inches on either side of the net and parallel to it. A long service line is thirteen feet back of this, leaving a back court of two feet six inches to the back boundary line. Parallel to the side lines is a center line drawn from the short service line to the boundary line, dividing the space into two courts. As in tennis, the use of the alley and back court varies with whether the game is singles or doubles (two or four players). For singles (two players) the side alley is not used, but the back court is then part of the receiving court; for doubles this is reversed, the side alley being then part of the service court, but not the rear court.

THE PLAY consists in batting and returning the shuttle over the net, not allowing it to touch the ground.

SERVING. — Each play starts with a service made by an underhand swing with the racket; that is, the shuttle, when hit, must be at or below waist height. If hit above that height the serve is considered an overhand stroke, counts as a fault, and puts the server out.

The server must be standing with both feet within his service court and the shuttle must go over the short service line into the diagonally opposite court without touching net or boundary lines.

In singles the first serve is from the server's right-hand court, and if good, his next serve is from his left-hand court, and so on alternately until he makes a fault.

In doubles the server stands in the right-hand court to serve while his partner stands in the left-hand court, the latter serving from the left-hand court when his turn comes. After the first hand, if the first serve is at fault and the server out, the serve goes to the opponents; but thereafter, both partners have a serve before the play goes to the opponents; that is, when the first server is out, his partner serves.

FAULTS. — In both singles and doubles the serving side is the only one to score, making its points on the opponent's faults; but if the serving side makes a fault, the player is out and the serve passes to the next player. Faults are:

Serving with an overhand stroke.
Serving when either server or receiver stands without both feet in the proper court.

Serving from the wrong court.

Serving into the wrong court, or short of the short service line, or outside of the opponents' court or boundary lines.

Serving short of the net or through it.

When the server makes feints before actually serving.

The receiver makes a fault :

If not standing with both feet in his proper court when the serve is made.

If he allows the shuttle to touch the ground before sending it back.

If his return sends the shuttle into or through the net or beyond the boundary lines.

Either player is at fault :

If he touches the net himself or with his racket.

If he reaches over the net to hit the shuttle. (Following through a stroke is not included in this.)

If the hit is not definitely a stroke on the shuttle.

If the shuttle is hit twice in succession by any player or players on the same side.

LET. — Some defects in play are not serious enough to count against the player and in certain circumstances he is allowed to take the play over. Such a play is called a "let."

A shuttle touching the top of the net in a service but going over, and otherwise a good play, is a let.

If a server making an ace, or a receiver making an otherwise legal and successful play has stood for that play in the wrong side of the court, or played out of turn, the player at fault may at once make a claim to have the mistake considered a let, on the supposition that it was an inadvertence. If the claim is made and the opponents allow it before another serve is made, it is a let.

SCORE. — Badminton is a defensive game, the score being made only by the serving side, on the opponents' faults. The penalty for a fault on the serving side is to put the server out.

A point scored is called an ace. A game is won by men on fifteen or twenty-one aces, as may be previously agreed; by women, on eleven aces.

In a game of fifteen aces, when each side has made thirteen points (called *thirteen all*), the side first scoring thirteen may lengthen the game by "setting" it at five, which means that the

side wins which then first makes five points.   Also, in a game of
fifteen aces, if the score reaches *fourteen all*, the side first scoring
fourteen may set the game at three; then the side which first
makes three points wins the game.

In the game of twenty-one aces, the score of *nineteen all*, or
twenty all, may be set respectively at five points or at three.

In the game of eleven aces, at a score of *nine all*, the game may
be set at five; or at a score of *ten all* it may be set at three.

Badminton originated in the Orient, whence it was brought by the English,
who are to be credited with its Western development.   It was originally
named, from the implements used, "Battledore and Shuttlecock."

BALL CHASE

4 to 20 players   *Primary;*
Playground; gymnasium   *intermediate*
Handsizeball or substitute

A row of caps is set against a wall or fence, or a series of holes
dug in the ground.   At a point ten or twenty feet from these all of
the players stand, and one selected as thrower throws a ball into
one of the caps or holes.   Any substitute may be used for a ball,
such as a small block of wood or a stone.   Should he miss, he
repeats the throw until he succeeds.   As soon as a ball lands in
a cap, the owner of the cap runs away, and all of the others chase
him until caught.

It will be seen that this game may best be played where there
is opportunity for considerable dodging around and behind obstacles.   The player being chased is exempt if he can get back to
his own cap before being caught by the others.   If caught, however, he becomes thrower for the next round; otherwise the first
thrower continues in that position.

In a gymnasium a series of circles may be drawn on the floor
in place of the holes or caps, and a beanbag tossed into them.

BALL DRILL

(See *Handball Drill* and *Wall Ball Drill*.)

BALL JUMP RACE

2 to 20 players   *Intermediate*
Indoors or out   *to adult*
                    Basketball; tennis ball

The players stand in files as for relays behind a starting line
at one end of the room, and another line is drawn about a yard
from the opposite end-wall.   On the latter line, in front of each
team, is placed a basketball or tennis ball.   At a signal, each
Number One runs to the far line, places the ball between his feet,
and, holding it there only by the pressure of the feet, jumps back
to the starting line, letting the ball go only when he has crossed
this latter line.   Number Two then picks up the ball in his hands,
runs with it to the far line, and jumps back with it between his
feet.   The couple or team whose last man gets back first wins the
game.

BALLOON BALL

10 to 60 players   *Intermediate grades*
Parties; gymnasium; schoolroom   *to adults*
                        Toy balloon

I. — This game is played with a toy balloon instead of a ball,
the object being to bat it with the hand over a cord as a ball is
played over a net.   All of the balloon games are excellent for
house parties and clubs, as the balloon is too light in weight to
injure any furnishings it may hit; its movements are peculiarly
its own, and afford much sport in the play and some excellent
exercise.

A rope or cord is stretched across each of the two ends of a room,
six feet or more from the floor and a few feet from the end walls.
Players are in two groups, each guarding the rope at its end of the
room and trying to score by batting the balloon over the rope at
the opposite end.   The game is purely recreative and informal,
with only the following rules :

No personal interference is allowed.
The balloon is batted only with the open hand.
No player may bat it twice in succession before another player has
touched it.

Two points are scored for each goal made. The game may be won on gaining ten points, or on the highest score at the end of a fifteen-minute period.

II. FOR THE SCHOOLROOM. — There are two goals as in **I.** The teams are seated in alternate rows, A and B.

OBJECT. — The players of team A try to bat the balloon over goal A; the players of team B try to send it over goal B.

FOULS. — Fouls are called for the following:

> Standing more than half erect.
> Leaving seat entirely.
> Raising desk (if movable).
> Striking ball with clenched hand.

SCORE. — Each goal made counts two points. One point is also awarded to the opposing team for each foul.

III. — This game may be varied by having a goal keeper for each team whose duty shall be to prevent the balloon from crossing his or her goal line. This goal keeper should stand, and should have a free use of the aisle in front of the goal.

This game was originated by Mr. Henry J. Silverman of New York City.

BALLOON CORNER GOAL

10 to 100 players　　　　　　　　　　　*Intermediate grades*
Schoolroom; parlor; gymnasium　　　　　　　*2 balloons*

The game is played with two toy balloons, preferably twelve inches in diameter, one red and one blue, which are struck with the open hand only.

Players are divided into two teams, preferably designated by colors corresponding to the balloons, worn on the arm or otherwise. The teams are assigned by rows across the room from side to side, the first row belonging to the red team, the second to the blue, the third to the red, etc. Four goals are formed by stretching a tape diagonally across each of the four corners of the room about five feet from the floor, the goals in the diagonally opposite corners having the same colors, two of red and two of blue. The game consists in hitting the balloon with the open hand so that it will float down behind a goal tape, the red balloon scoring when it enters the red goals, and the blue balloon when it enters the blue goals. There are no goal guards, but it is the object of all players belonging to the red team to get the red balloon into the red goals, and of the blue team to keep it out. Similarly, the object of the blue team is to get the blue balloon into the blue goals and of the red team to keep it out.

The game starts by the leader's putting the balloons in play by tossing them up in the center of the room, when each side immediately begins to play for them. It has been found that with two balloons and four goals, it is unnecessary to limit the players to any given area. This, however, may be done should play become rough.

A score keeper scores one for each team making a goal with its balloon, but the game continues without interruption, the balloon being at once put in play again by the leader.

A fifteen-minute game should be divided into at least three periods, the leader signaling for a rest at the end of each five minutes.

This game was originated by Mr. Max Liebgold of New York City.

BALLOON VOLLEYBALL

4 to 24 players   *Intermediate grades*
Party; club; gymnasium   *to adults*
Toy balloon

This is somewhat more formal than Balloon Ball, but an excellent game for any free floor space indoors, as for a club or party.

A cord is stretched across the center of the room at a height of six feet or more; a serving line is drawn on the floor on each side of the cord and six feet from it. Players of each team stand in rows across the room as in Volleyball, take turns in serving, and rotate positions as in that game. Follow Volleyball rules for Women as given in this book; allow two attempts at serving; also allow one relay of the balloon on the serve, and five relays on any return. The balloon may not, however, be hit twice in succession by the same player. Score as for Volleyball.

BALL PUSS

3 to 30 or more players   *Primary*
Playground; gymnasium; schoolroom   *grades*
Gas ball; beanbag; basketball; handsizeball

This is a form of ball tag. In it each player chooses a home or corner, as in Puss in the Corner, or Home Tag. When played out of doors, trees may be used for this purpose; in a gymnasium, pillars or different pieces of apparatus; in the schoolroom, the corners of the room, the front and rear corner desks, the teacher's desk, the radiator, or any other objective points. The players who are so stationed beckon to each other to exchange places, and as they run from one place to another the one who is It tries to hit them with the ball. Anyone so hit changes places with the one who is It.

As in all ball-tag games, either a ball or beanbag may be used. If played in the schoolroom, a light gas ball should be used; elsewhere, anything from a light-weight handball to a basketball would be suitable. Hard balls should be avoided.

Where there are many playing, it is advisable to have two or three who take the part of thrower or Puss (It), in which case there will be two or three balls or beanbags in play at the same time, and the game is made more rapid.

BALL STAND

(See *Call-Ball*, *Ring Call-Ball*, and *Spud*.)

BALL TAG

3 to 60 players   *Intermediate*
Playground; gymnasium; schoolroom   *grades*
Gas ball; beanbag; basketball; handsizeball

There are several forms of ball tag, each quite distinctive, and all interesting and making good games. A soft ball or beanbag should be used in all of these games, or with older players a basketball or other large, comparatively light-weight ball.

The players scatter irregularly. One player, who is It, tries to hit one of the other players with a ball or beanbag. Any player thus hit becomes It and must try to tag others in the same way. When a player fails to hit one for whom he aims, the thrower must pick up his own ball or bag, except in the school-room, where the seats and desks interfere with this. There any neighboring player may pick up the ball and throw it back to the one who is It. Players may dodge in any way, as by stooping, jumping, or the usual sideways movements.

Where there are many playing, it is advisable to have two or three who take the part of thrower or It, in which case there will be two or three balls or beanbags in play at the same time, and the game is much more rapid.

BASEBALL

18 players   *Intermediate to adult*
Regulation baseball and bat

(For the less-highly specialized game of Baseball, see *Playground Baseball*, originally known as "Indoor Baseball," though also played out of doors.)

Baseball, called the national game of the United States, is played by two opposing teams of nine men each; hence the term "baseball nine." It is played on a level field in which a square, ninety feet by ninety feet, is outlined obliquely to the boundaries of the larger enclosure, giving it the general appearance of a diamond, from which comes the term "baseball diamond." At the four angles, or corners, of this diamond (or infield) are bases, and in the center is a pitcher's box. The batter's box is beside the home plate (fourth base), one box on each side (for right- or left-handed batters).

The score is made by one team at a time alternately through-out the game. This is the team "at bat." The nine men of the defensive team are disposed over the field in a way that helps to the utmost to protect the bases and get a pitched or batted ball back to the players protecting the bases. Besides the pitcher (in the center) and catcher, beyond but near the batter, the opposing team consists of three basemen, each guarding one of the three bases, first, second, and third; a shortstop, who does the main work in fielding (catching and throwing) batted balls that go between second and third base; and three fielders, who field the balls that are batted far into the outfield (*i.e.*, beyond the diamond). One of the scoring team enters the field as batter and tries to bat a "fair hit," that is, one in which the ball will fall either within the diamond, or beyond it, forward of the foul lines; this ball is thrown to him by the pitcher of the opposing team.

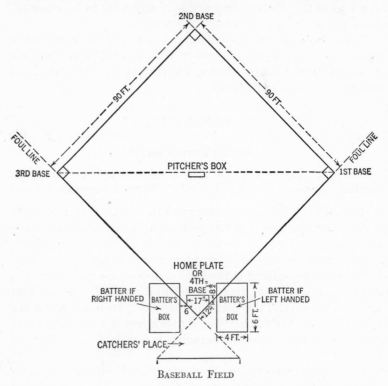

BASEBALL FIELD

The pitcher, catcher, and fielders are opponents of the batter and base runners. If the batted ball is caught on the fly by a fielder, the batter is out. If successful in his strike, the batter instantly becomes a base runner. One point is scored for a team for each player who succeeds in making a "run"; that is, a complete circuit of all four bases, from the home plate over which the batting is done, to first, second, and third bases in their regular order, and so again to the fourth base or home plate. This may be done in one dash, called a "home run," or by stopping in the circuit at any or all of the other bases, as safety points.

When a batter has either been put "out" or has succeeded in making first base, another member of his team comes to the bat, and so on. There can never be more than four men in the field at once from the team having its inning; that is, one man at the bat, and one on each of the other three bases.

Opponents may intercept a base runner by tagging him with the ball (in the hand, not thrown) while he is between bases, or by reaching a base with the ball before he can get there. Either method puts a runner "out" — that is, retires him from the game temporarily, until his turn to bat comes again. After three men on his side have been put out, his team, in its turn, goes into the field and the opposing team goes to bat. An inning lasts until each team has had three men put out in batting and running bases. Nine such innings constitute a game, and that team wins which has the highest score (*i.e.*, has made the largest number of runs) at the end.

BALLS AND STRIKES. — Besides putting out its opponents while they are running bases, the defensive team may be able, through its pitcher, to put out a batter before he becomes a base runner, by pitching the ball so that it takes unexpected curves when it gets near him, making him miss it. A batter is entitled to three "good" balls, or three "strikes." A good ball is one so pitched that it passes over the home plate (the fourth base, beside which the batter stands) and, in passing, is at a height not greater than his shoulder nor lower than his knee. Whether he hits at such a ball or not, it is called a "strike." A poor ball is one that goes outside these limits and is called a "ball," as distinguished from a "strike." If a batter mistakes a ball for a strike and hits at it, it is counted against him as one of the three strikes to which he is entitled. Although the pitcher is his opponent, he is constrained to pitch at least three good balls out of six, as a fourth poor ball from the pitcher entitles the batter to become a base runner, even though he should have missed two good balls pitched to him.

The umpire calls every ball pitched, as either a "ball" or a "strike," as the case may be. "Four balls!" is bad for the pitcher, as it means he has let the batter escape him on poor pitching; and "Three strikes!" is critical for the batter as it means he is "out." When first base is occupied by a base runner and the batter makes a fair strike, the base runner ahead of him must move on to next base to make room for him — a "forced run." This runner is out if the ball gets to the next baseman ahead of him.

The batter's primary object is to hit the ball so far that he will have time to run at least to first base before the ball can be thrown back there to the baseman guarding it. He may be able to make a two-base hit (one on which he can go to both first and second bases), or a three-base hit, or even send the ball so far that he can make all four bases on it — a "home run" and one of the most exciting events in a ball game. The object of the opponents is, of course, to keep the team that is having its inning from scoring runs. This they do by putting out three of its men as soon as possible.

SCORE. — The game is played in nine innings, the highest score at the end winning. In case of a tie, play continues until one team has a higher score for an equal number of innings. If the game is stopped for weather, darkness, or any other cause, before nine innings are played, the highest score wins, provided five innings have been played.

The official who has entire charge of a game is the umpire. He is entirely neutral, favoring neither side more than the other. See *Officials* below.

ASSIST. — A fielder is said to have made an assist whenever he throws a ball to a baseman or other player in time to put out a base runner.

AVERAGES. — *Batting averages* are figured by dividing the number of hits by the number of times at bat.

Fielding averages are found by adding the put-outs and assists and dividing the total by the number of chances for such plays.

BALK. — A feint at throwing by the pitcher. On a balk, each runner except the batter goes ahead one base.

BATTERY. — The pitcher and the catcher.

BATTING ORDER. — The order in which the players of a team go to the bat. The batting order is arranged by the captain of a team and given to the umpire before a game begins. The score keeper calls the players to the bat in the order of this list.

BUNT. — A hit made by simply holding the bat for the ball to hit it without striking at it.

ERRORS. — The misplays made by a baseball player. These are fielding errors and battery errors. Fielding errors may consist of poor handling of the ball, as "muffing" it, or poor judgment or slow work in throwing it when needed to put out a base runner. Battery errors are "balks" by the pitcher, or misplays (mostly passed balls) by the catcher.

FAIR HIT. — A hit by a batter which sends the ball within the diamond or beyond it, between the foul lines.

FLY BALL. — One that goes through the air as distinguished from one that rolls on the ground or bounds.

FOUL HIT. — A ball hit by the batter so that it goes outside the foul lines; that is, back of the diamond, or the extension of its lines from first and third bases.

FOUL STRIKE. — A hit by the batter made with one or both feet outside the batter's box.

GROUNDER. — A ball batted or thrown so that it just skims the surface of the ground.

MUFFED BALL. — An imperfect catch in which the ball slips through the hands.

OFFICIALS. — Two umpires and a scorer are necessary for match games. Informal games are played with one umpire. With two umpires, one stands on the diamond and judges the play of base runners; the other stands behind the catcher and judges the balls and the batter.

PLATE. — A small surface of rubber, metal, or stone which marks the pitcher's plate and fourth or home base (home plate).

SACRIFICE HIT. — The batting of the ball in such a way that there is no chance for the batsman to make his first base, but opportunity is given a base runner to advance. This is usually done by bunting.

STEALING A BASE. — The advance of a base runner to the next base, unaided by a base hit, a put-out, or error in fielding or battery play.

The main technique of playing the ball, and a list of special games for training Baseball skill, are given in the section on *Balls and How to Play Them*.

HISTORY. — While probably a development from the old English game of "Rounders," or the "Old Cat" games of our own country, baseball is essentially an American and modern game.

A commission appointed in 1907, at the suggestion of Mr. A. G. Spalding, to investigate the history of the game, attributed its inception to Mr. Abner Doubleday, of Cooperstown, New York, in 1839. Mr. Doubleday is credited with drawing the first diagram of the "diamond" and bases, evidently in an effort to avoid collisions between players running for a batted ball.

The neighborhood of New York City is credited with contributing most to the evolution of the modern rules, and to the earliest competitive play between clubs. In 1845 the Knickerbocker Base Ball Club was organized in New York. The first baseball convention was held under its auspices in 1857, for the purpose of framing uniform rules.

The professionalizing of the game began in 1863, when the players shared in gate receipts in Brooklyn; the first salaried teams played in 1869, when the Red Stockings of Cincinnati made a tour. The evolution of the game has been in the size and construction of the ball, which at first was slightly larger, heavier, and "livelier"; and more especially in the rules governing the players.

BASEBALL DISTANCE THROW

2 to 20 players   *Intermediate to senior high*

This game gives excellent fielding practice. It is on the principle of the Basketball Distance Throw. Individual or team competition may be used.

I. The throwing line is three feet long; beginning at fifty yards in front of this and parallel to it, a series of parallel distance lines twenty feet long are drawn, ten yards apart, the farthest being one hundred yards from the throwing line.

The player stands behind the throwing line and throws the ball overhand so that it will fall within the distance lines. It scores the number of yards of the line nearest to which it strikes the ground. If it hits a line, it scores the higher number. Each thrower has three (or five) consecutive throws. The highest score wins.

II. This is also played by an actual measurement of distance, the player being given credit for his longest throw.

III. **FOR A PLAYGROUND BALL,** place the first distance line at thirty feet from the throwing line. Use the underhand throw.

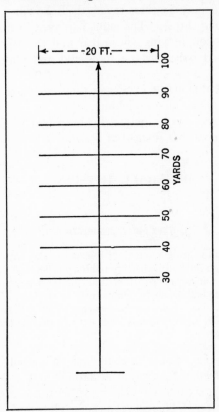

BASEBALL DISTANCE THROW

BASEBALL GROUNDERS

6 to 40 players   *Intermediate grades*

Two parallel lines are drawn fifty to one hundred yards apart.

I. **COUPLE COMPETITION.**—The players face each other in ranks A and B from the outside lines, with a ball for each couple (an A and a B) held by the A's. A rolls the ball with a swift bowling motion towards B ; B runs in to receive the ball, throws it to A, and races back to his base line to receive a long throw from A. The play is then reversed, B bowling the ball and making the long throw. The game is played in from five to ten rounds. The couple wins whose B is first to catch his last long ball. A missed ball must be recovered and played as though caught.

II. TEAM FORMATION in zigzag play with one ball may be used, as in Baseball Quick Fielding.

III. This may also be played by batting the grounder with an indoor baseball bat instead of bowling it.

BASEBALL HIT–PIN — I

18 players   *Junior high*
Gymnasium; playground   *to adult*
Soccer ball; 4 Indian clubs

This is a capital game resembling baseball. The batter kicks instead of batting, though the ball is thereafter thrown. On each base is an Indian club and to put out a runner (kicker) the club must be knocked over by a baseman with the ball before the runner reaches the base. The kicked ball must be fielded and thrown in regular sequence to the first, second, third, and fourth bases. The kicker's run is made entirely outside the diamond with no stop at bases.

The game is played on a baseball diamond measuring thirty-five to forty-five feet on each side according to the playing space. At one corner a six-foot circle is drawn with the angle of the diamond as its center. This serves as home plate and also as batter's (kicker's) box. At each of the other three angles of the diamond a one-foot square is drawn inside, serving as first, second, and third bases. A pitcher's box four feet by twelve feet is drawn in the center of the field with one of its four-foot ends twenty feet in front of the home plate. An Indian club is set up on each of the four bases.

The players are in two teams of nine each. One team is "at bat," its members batting (kicking) in rotation. The other team has a pitcher, catcher, one man for each base, and the balance as fielders.

PITCHER. — The ball is thrown or bowled but only with an underhand swing for which the pitcher must not step out of his box.

KICKER. — For the kick one foot must be in, or (in case of a jump) over, the home-plate circle. A kicker must not hit the ball with any part of his body above the knees. He must not knock down the Indian club on his home plate or he is out.

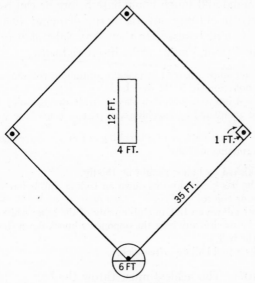

BASEBALL HIT-PIN

STRIKES. — Kicking at a ball and missing it.

Kicking the ball into foul territory except on the third strike, when this may be done.

Not kicking if a bowled (pitched) ball touches within the front half of his home-plate circle.

For three strikes a kicker is retired.

FAIR AND FOUL BALLS. — A kicked ball is fair which strikes (not rolls) anywhere inside or on the foul lines.

A foul ball is one which strikes outside the foul lines.

DEAD BALLS. — If a pitched ball hits the kicker, it is dead and counts neither as a ball nor a strike.

BALLS. — Any pitched or bowled ball which is not a strike or dead ball, and not kicked at by the kicker, is counted as one ball for the latter. For four "balls" he is entitled to a free kick, for which he places the ball in the front half of the home-plate circle.

KICKER IS OUT. — If he or a pitched ball knocks down the club at home plate.

For three "strikes."

If he kicks a foul on a free kick.

BASE RUNNER. — The kicker becomes a base runner when he has kicked a fair ball, his object being to make the entire circuit of the diamond and touch home base before he can be put out.

He must run entirely outside of the diamond, including first, second, and third bases. He there has right of way and while outside the diamond may not be interfered with.

He must not stop at bases but make a continuous run unless put out.

He must not step within the diamond.

He must not interfere with any player within the diamond.

His run is completed by touching any part of home base with one foot.

OUTS. — The runner is out for breaking any of the above-mentioned rules applying to running and also:

If a ball kicked by him is caught on the fly.

If a ball he has kicked knocks down an Indian club before touching any other player or object.

If he knocks down an Indian club on any of the bases while running.

If before he reaches any base the opponents knock down the Indian club there with the ball.

If he kicks a foul ball on a free kick.

FIELDING. — The fielders must throw the ball to first, second, third, and fourth bases in regular rotation.

The baseman covering a base must knock down the Indian club there with the ball before the runner gets there in order to put him out. The club must be standing when hit by the ball. A club knocked over must be replaced before the ball may be thrown to the next baseman.

No fielder may interfere with the runner who is outside the diamond. If this is done the runner scores a run.

SCORE. — The runner scores a run for completing the entire circuit of bases and touching the home plate without being put out. Also, if he is interfered with outside the diamond by an opponent.

Teams change places after three outs for the team at bat. The number of innings is a matter of choice.

BASEBALL HIT–PIN — II

The game of Baseball Hit-Pin is played also with a playground ball and bat (Indoor Baseball equipment), with teams of from ten to fifteen players. Rules are the same as for Baseball Hit-Pin — I, except as required for the different ball : namely, the ball is pitched and batted instead of kicked, this part of the play being as in Playground Baseball.

BASEBALL OVERTAKE

(Beatball: Circular Rounders)

10 players
Baseball; bat; volleyball

Junior to senior
high school

This game is popular in the three different forms here given :

I. On a regular baseball diamond six players are stationed as follows : pitcher in pitcher's box ; catcher and runner both at home plate ; three basemen at first, second, and third bases. All are playing against the runner and his team.

On signal, the pitcher throws the ball to catcher and simultaneously the runner starts on a circuit of first, second, and third bases and back to home plate. As soon as the catcher gets the ball, he throws it to the basemen in the same order — first, second, and third — trying to get it around to home plate before the runner arrives. The runner scores one point for each circuit he finishes ahead of the ball. The players of the running team have each one run and then the teams change places.

II. This is also played with seven players to a team by adding a shortstop and two fielders. The runner is then also a batter as in regular baseball, bats the ball, and runs in an effort to outdistance the ball as it is thrown from base to base. Whoever fields the ball throws it first to the first base, from which it must make the circuit in regular order.

III. As **BEATBALL**, the same game is played with a volleyball or sport ball and without a bat. The runner throws the ball from home base without batting it.

BASEBALL QUICK-FIELDING

4 or more players in couple competition.　　*Junior high to adult*

I. Three parallel lines are drawn from fifty to one hundred feet apart, according to proficiency of players. The two outside lines are base or starting lines. The players stand in two ranks, A and B, facing each other as partners from the baselines. Between each couple, on the center line, is placed a baseball.

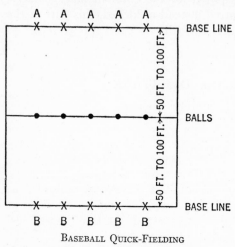

BASELINE

BALLS

BASELINE

BASEBALL QUICK-FIELDING

On signal, all A's race to ball, pick up and throw to B partners, and race back to the base line to receive a long throw from B. Any ball missed must be recovered and played over. Five or ten rounds constitute a game. The couple finishing first wins.

II. This may be played in team competition, each team standing in zigzag formation and using one ball.

BASEBALL TARGET–PITCH

1 to 20 players　　*Intermediate to senior high*

For practice in form and height in pitching, for individual practice, or for competitive scores between individuals or teams.

I. An upright target is painted on a wall or blackboard, and consists of three concentric circles, the inner having a one-foot diameter (six-inch radius), the next a two-foot diameter, and the outer circle a three-foot diameter with its lower edge three feet above the ground.

A pitching line is drawn in front of the target at a distance of from thirty to ninety feet, according to age and proficiency of players.

The pitcher stands behind the pitching line and throws the ball at the target. He scores one point for hitting it anywhere between the outer and middle circles, three points between the middle and inner circles, and five points within the inner circle. If the ball hits a line it scores for the smaller circle. Each player has from five to ten throws, as may be decided in advance. The player or team wins which has the highest score.

For pitching, the player stands with his right foot on or behind the pitching line and must always have one foot on this line until after the ball is delivered. The left foot is in advance. The ball is held in the right hand at the chest, lightly covered by the left. The right arm is either swung or drawn backward, according to whether the throw is to be an underhand or overhand throw. In delivering the ball the force of shoulders, body, and knees is added to the swing and thrust of the arm.

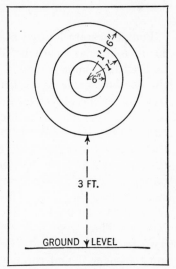

BASEBALL TARGET-PITCH

II. This is also played with a target measuring eighteen by thirty inches, which reproduces the height at which a "good" ball must cross the home plate between the batter's knee and shoulder, the lower edge being twenty-one inches above the ground. For Playground Baseball practice, the distance between pitcher and target is from thirty to forty feet.

"GOOD BALL"
TARGET

BASEBALL THROW AND CATCH

4 players *Baseball* *Intermediate to*
senior high

Four bases are located at the points of a ninety-foot square, as on a regular baseball "diamond." A smaller square may be used for junior players. Four players stand on these bases, the one on "home base" being the one to score. He throws a baseball to the player on first base, who catches it and immediately throws it back to him. The home baseman catches the ball, throws it to second, catches the return and throws it to third, who throws it back to him. Each of the four players thus throws and catches, but the home baseman scores the inning if he makes the complete round of throws and catches successfully; he then continues with other rounds until he misses. A misplay loses the inning, and all four players rotate: Number Three goes to home base for the next inning, Number Two to third base, and so on. Any baseman missing the ball must recover it and throw it from his base. The ball is good if it can be caught by both hands with one foot touching base.

BASKETBALL

10 players *Junior high school*
Basketball; goals *to adults*

Basketball is probably the most popular indoor ball game; nor is any outdoor playground complete without provision for it. The name comes from the goals which were originally (and are still, in effect) suspended baskets. The goals, the marking of the court, the position of teams, the guarding of opponents, and the technique of handling the ball are all distinctive features of the game.

COURT. — The maximum dimensions of the court are ninety-four feet by fifty, minimum forty by thirty-five feet (junior players forty-two by seventy-four feet, to fifty by ninety feet). A line across the center of the court divides it into two equal sections, and at the middle of this is a center circle two feet in diameter, in which, according to early rules, the ball is put in play. A team's front court is that half containing the basket

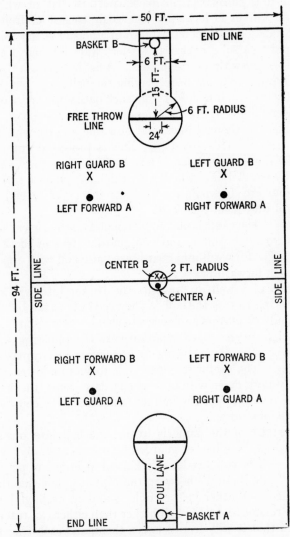

BASKETBALL

(Men's Game; two-division court; teams A and B in position)

for which it is throwing; its back court is that in which the opponents' basket is located. The goals consist of iron rings, eighteen inches in diameter, fastened at a height of ten feet from the ground to a solid backstop, six feet wide by four feet high erected two feet within the end lines. A net hangs from the rings, open at bottom to assist in recovering the ball.

Directly inward, fifteen feet from each backstop (seventeen feet from the end lines), is drawn a free-throw or foul line, twelve feet long, parallel to the end lines, and bisecting a circle which has a six-foot radius. This free-throw line is protected from interference by a free-throw "lane" leading from the goal. This lane is made by parallel lines which start three feet on each side of the basket, and are drawn inward toward the opposite end of the court until they meet the circle.

TEAMS. — The game is played by ten players, five in each team : two forwards, one center, and two guards. One of these is the captain. The forwards and guards are paired off with opponents so that each forward has a guard.

Forwards play well up towards the basket into which their team is trying to toss the ball. They need not be tall but should be agile and fast players and accurate shots. Guards are usually taller and heavier. Each guard covers the opposing forward against whom he plays, trying to prevent or intercept shots at the basket. The center should be able to jump and reach high, constantly alert, down with his own guards, covering the opposing center, or trying to get the ball and pass it up the court to one of his own forwards.

THE OBJECT of the game is to put the ball into one's own basket, namely, the basket guarded by opponents.

START. — The ball (under original rules) is put in play by a "tap-off" or "toss-up" between the centers. For this the two centers face each other in the circle, standing each in his own half; the referee tosses the ball higher than either can reach with a jump so that it will drop between them, and each tries to bat ("tap") it with the open hand to one of his forwards. Neither center may catch the ball until after another player has touched it. If either player should bat it outside the boundary lines of the court on the toss-up it must be centered again.

The ball is thus centered at the beginning of the game and at the opening of the second half. After each goal made, the ball is put in play by the scored-upon team, from a point at the end-court line under its own basket.

When a ball in play goes out of bounds, it is put in play again by a member of the team not responsible, who throws it from outside to a team-mate.

PASSING AND ADVANCING THE BALL. — The ball may be played in a number of ways : it may be thrown with one or both hands, passed, batted (with the open hand), bounced, dribbled, or rolled. (For technique and list of Skill Games see section on *Balls and How to Play Them.*) It may not be kicked, batted with the closed fist, or carried. Players may not strike, charge, tackle, trip, push, or hold an opponent, grasp his clothing, or in any personal contact use the hands or arms to interfere with his progress. The only way to intercept a play is to catch the ball as it is thrown.

A player may not run with the ball; that is, he may not take more than one step with it.

A team may not keep a ball in its own back court more than ten seconds unless it is touched there by an opponent, when a new ten-second period begins.

FOULS AND PENALTIES. — Fouls are technical or personal and are penalized by allowing the opponents a free throw from the foul line. Two such free throws are awarded for interfering with a player when throwing for goal; for minor violations the opponents are given the ball for a throw-in to a team-mate from outside the line near where the foul occurred.

SCORE. — A ball going through a goal scores two points. A goal made from a free throw awarded for a foul scores one point.

The men's game is played in two halves of twenty minutes each, with an intermission of ten minutes. Junior players play the game in quarters of six or eight minutes with one or two minutes' rest after the first and third quarters, and an intermission of ten minutes between halves.

Basketball is a modern invention originated in 1892 by Dr. Naismith, then at the Young Men's Christian Association Training College at Springfield, Massachusetts. The class was studying the elements of successful games under Dr. Luther Halsey Gulick, and was asked to invent new games which should include these elements.

BASKETBALL (FOR WOMEN)

(Line Game; Three-Court Basketball)

12 to 18 players   *Junior high to adult*

Basketball for women has some features that make it less strenuous than the men's game. It is much used by junior players of both sexes.

COURT. — This may be in two divisions, as in the men's game, or the court may have three divisions, from which come the names Line Game, or Three-Court Basketball. The three-division court is ninety by forty-five feet for college players, divided into three equal sections as in the diagram. The division lines may be twelve inches wide, or made of two smaller lines, as in the diagram, measuring twelve inches over all. For high school (junior) players, the court is seventy by thirty-five feet, marked in three equal divisions. If the court is shorter (sixty feet or less), it is marked in halves instead of in three divisions.

TEAMS. — These consist of from six to nine players each. Six is a standard number, but on large courts a larger number can play.

On a two-division court, a team of six has three forwards and three guards. Any one of the forwards (selected by the captain) may serve as center. Only forwards may throw for the basket. Guards may not throw for goal.

On a three-division court, a team of six has two centers, two guards, and two forwards. Only forwards may throw for the basket. Neither centers nor guards may throw for goal.

In both types of court (two or three divisions) players must play in their own division and not leave it during the play.

PLAYING THE BALL. — The ball is put in play either by a toss-up between centers or by a toss from the referee to the center player entitled to it. Play begins on the whistle. Methods of playing the ball are more restricted than in the men's game, being confined to throwing, batting, or bouncing from player to player;

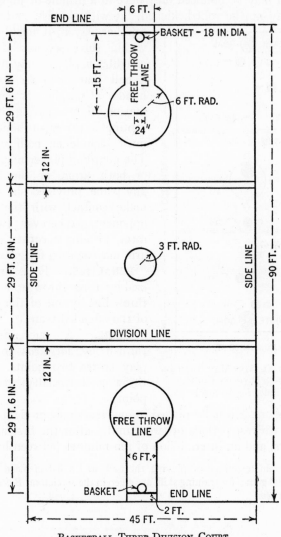

BASKETBALL THREE-DIVISION COURT
(Rules for Women)

the ball may be bounced only once in a dribble or juggle. The ball may not be rolled, kicked, hit with the fist, or handed to

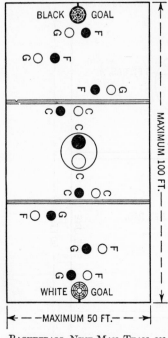

another player; it must be thrown within three seconds after it is caught; a player may not touch a ball that is in an opponent's hands. Guarding is entirely a matter of preventing or intercepting a throw or bounce, and must include no bodily contact. The guarding player may use one or both arms, or the body, in any plane, provided she does not make contact with the ball or opponent. Wherever two walls meet, forming a corner, only one arm may be used for guarding.

PENALTIES. — Fouls are penalized by a free throw from the free-throw line by one of the forwards of the offended team.

SCORE. — A successful goal thrown by forwards in regular play scores two points. A free-throw goal (penalty) scores one point.

BASKETBALL NINE-MAN TEAM ON THREE-DIVISION COURT
(Rules for Women)

The game is usually played in quarters of six or eight minutes each, with rest periods of two minutes after the first and third quarters, and an intermission of ten minutes between halves.

The main technique of playing the ball, and a list of Lead-up games and special games for training skill, are given in the section on *Balls and How to Play Them.*

BASKETBALL DISTANCE THROW

10 to 30 or more players   *Intermediate grades to*
Playground; gymnasium   *senior high school*
Basketball

This is an interesting and simple athletic event, as well as a good game. It is especially useful for players drilling on the handling of the basketball or shotput, and is a good substitute for shotput for girls.

I. A full circle six feet in diameter is drawn on the ground. A heavy line is drawn across its center, which serves as a throwing line. The player stands in the circle and throws the basketball from this throwing line toward other lines drawn in the throwing space as specified below; the ball scores according to its landing in relation to these other lines.

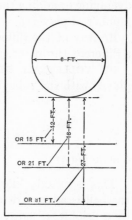

BASKETBALL DISTANCE
THROW

The lines drawn across the throwing space must be parallel with the throwing line in the circle. For players below the seventh year of the elementary school course (below twelve years of age) these three lines should be respectively twelve, eighteen, and twenty-seven feet from the forward edge of the circle. For players from the seventh and eighth year of the school course (that is, thirteen and fourteen years of age) these three lines should be respectively fifteen, twenty-one, and thirty-one feet from the forward edge of the circle. These measurements are for girls. For boys the longer distances given will be found generally advisable, and they may be increased for adults.

The players are divided into competing teams, the players of each team throwing in rapid succession. Each player has but one turn, unless the ball should strike some obstacle before touching the ground, when another trial is allowed. A thrower must at the start stand in the circle and toe the throwing line, drawn across the center of the circle; in completing the throw he must not fall or step forward over the outer line of the circle in front of him.   If at any part of the throw, from its start to finish, the thrower is out of the circle, it is considered a foul and does not score, the number of players in the team being counted as one less when the total or average is figured.

For each throw to the first line (the twelve or fifteen foot line) or any point between it and the next line, a team scores one point. For each throw to the second line (the eighteen or twenty-one foot line), or between it and the next line, a team scores three points.   For each throw to or beyond the third line (the twenty-seven or thirty-one foot line) a team scores five points.   The team averaging or adding the highest score wins (average for an uneven number of players).

II. Any of the different basketball throws may be used or a different throw for each round.

III. **VOLLEYBALL SERVE.** — The game is excellent also when played with the volleyball serve instead of a throw.

BASKETBALL DRIBBLE RACE

8 to 40 players   *Junior high to adult*

This is exactly like the Basketball Juggle Race, except that the ball is advanced to the center line of a wide zigzag formation by a dribble, a series of quick bounces from the floor, being hit down by one hand and bouncing to not more than waist height. At the center line it is caught in both hands and thrown to the next player.   Various means of throwing or passing the ball may be specified.

BASKETBALL DRIBBLE RELAY

2 to 40 players   *Junior high school to adult*

I. Players stand in relay formation behind a starting line; a parallel finish line is drawn at a thirty-foot distance.   The first player of each file has a basketball or volleyball and on signal dribbles it to the finish line, making one bounce on or beyond the line, and then dribbles it back to the starting line, where he hands the ball to his next team-mate, who goes through a similar course. The team finishing first wins.

II. Instead of the finish line, a post, chair, Indian club, or other object may be placed for the player to circle while dribbling the ball.

III. The dribble may also be used for a shuttle relay, the ball being dribbled across from each player to the opposite file of his team.

BASKETBALL FOLLOW–UP GOAL

1 to 20 players   *Junior high school to adult*

This may be played as individual or team competition. Each player shoots for goal from the free-throw line. If he makes the basket, he runs forward and recovers the ball, immediately throwing for goal from that point, and so on until he fails to make the goal, when the next player takes his turn. Each goal scores one point. The game may be played in rounds, the highest score at the fifth or tenth round winning.

BASKETBALL GOAL THROW

Playground; gymnasium   *Intermediate to adult*

I. For each goal there should be from two to ten players. The competition may be between individuals or teams.

Players take turns in shooting for goal from the fifteen-foot free-throw line. Five tries in succession are allowed each player. Each goal made scores one point.

II. For beginners a throwing line may be drawn parallel to the free-throw line but only ten feet from the goal.

BASKET–GOAL CLOCK–THROW

2 to 20 players *Junior high; college*

This may be played in individual or team competition. As indicated by the name (from Clock Golf) it consists of a series of throws from points around the goal.

The free-throw line is extended to form a semicircle, or rim, with the goal as center of the radius. Two, three, or four points (or small circles) are marked on each half of this line, and one

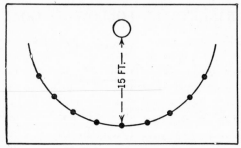

BASKET-GOAL CLOCK-THROW

at the center directly opposite the goal. The player stands on each in turn and throws once for goal, beginning on the right and moving clockwise. He scores one point for the first goal, two for the second, three for the third, and so on.

BASKETBALL JUGGLE RACE

8 to 40 players *Junior high to adult*

1. A throwing line is drawn lengthwise of the playing space. Players of a team stand in zigzag formation, each rank thirty feet back from the throwing line, and each player at two arms' length from his neighbors on the right and left.

Number One of each rank has a volley- or basketball and on signal runs diagonally towards Number Two, juggling the ball until he reaches the center line. The juggle is an upward dribble, tossing the ball lightly upward above head height in a succession of bounces from the open hand. At the center line the player bats

the ball with his open hand (as in a volleyball serve) towards
Number Two and returns to his place.   Number Two catches the
ball, juggles it from his line
to the center in the direction
of Number Three, and there
bats it to Number Three in
the same way. This con-
tinues to the end of the line
and then in reverse direction
back to Number One. The
team wins which first gets its
ball back to Number One.

A dropped ball must be
recovered by the player
dropping it and the play
continued. If a player has
to run out to catch the ball
he must return to his base
line to begin his juggle.

II. The ball may be thrown
from the center line with one
or both hands instead of
batted; or if a basketball is
used, one of the regular

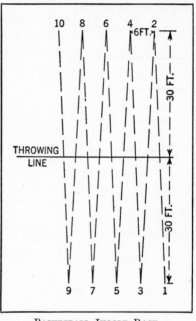

BASKETBALL JUGGLE RACE

basketball passes may be played, but the kind of throw or
pass should be specified before the start.

BASKETBALL LADDER RUN

Any ball   *Junior high school*

This is an excellent game to begin training skill in ball
throwing and catching on the run.

A line is drawn across one end of the court, behind which the
players are lined up in files of competing teams. Ten feet in
front of this starting line another line is drawn across the court,
and at each five-foot interval beyond it still others, until five lines
have been drawn resembling a grill or ladder. Behind the last

line, and facing his team, stands a thrower for each team, holding
a ball.   On a signal the first runner from each team runs forward

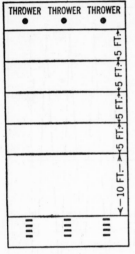

into the first space and receives the
ball tossed by the thrower, runs into
the second space and throws the ball
back to the thrower, runs on into the
third space, and receives the ball again,
then to the fourth space, from which
he passes the ball to the thrower and
returns immediately to the rear of his
file, which has moved up to the starting line.   He touches off the next player
as he passes and the latter repeats the
throwing and catching.   The game may
also be played by having the advancing
player change places with the thrower,
who then passes to the rear of the file.
The team whose last player is first to get
back to the starting line wins the game.

BASKETBALL LADDER RUN

BASKETBALL PASS, CATCH, AND GOAL

4 to 40 players   *Junior high school to adult*

This may be played in either individual or team competition.
Each team lines up outside its free-throw lane with a leader
standing just outside the center circle of the court, facing his
own goal.

One player at a time steps to the free-throw line facing his
leader; he receives a pass from the leader, instantly pivots to
face the goal, and throws for the basket; after which he recovers
the ball, throws it back to the leader, and rejoins his team.   Number Two at once steps to the throwing line and repeats the catch,
turn, and throw.   Each player has but one throw on each
round.   Five rounds are played.   Each goal made scores one
point, and the team (or individual) wins which has the highest
score at the end.

If the pass is not caught, the player recovers the ball and returns it to
the leader for another throw.   If the player must advance beyond the

free-throw line to catch the ball, he must pivot and throw from the point where it was caught. The play should be very deliberate at first and speed up as players become proficient.

BASKETBALL PIVOT RACE

(Pivot and Reverse)

2 to 40 players   *Intermediate grades to adult*

This is not a team game, but one of individual competition to train players for the quick pivot and reversal of direction required in many games.

Players line up side by side behind a starting line at one end of the court. At a whistle from the leader they all run forward until another whistle is heard, when all turn instantly with a pivot motion and run back; before they can reach the starting line the leader again whistles, and they turn and run as before. This running for short or longer distances, and turning on signal, is continued until, at the leader's discretion, the players are allowed to return over the starting line. The first one over wins the game.

For pivoting, the turn is made on either the ball or heel of one foot, while the other foot is advanced in the line of the new direction.

(For pivoting see also *Basketball Pass, Catch, and Goal*.)

BASKETBALL RUN–THROW–AND–CATCH RACE

Basketball; volleyball; rugbyball   *Junior to senior high*

I. Players compete in couples. The play starts with A of each couple on a starting line and B standing five feet to one side and five feet in advance of A. The distances are increased with the skill of players.

On signal the A of each couple throws the ball to B and runs in a straight line forward until five feet ahead of B. B catches the ball (or recovers it if missed) and throws it to A, immediately running forward to receive and throw the ball. This is repeated until B reaches the finish line, where the play is reversed back to the starting line. The couple whose A gets back first wins. This may be played with players catching and throwing the ball in a continuous run, or with only one step after the ball is caught, as

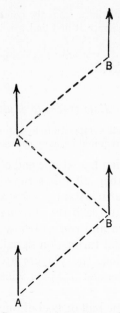

in games in which no running with the ball is allowed.

This game is adapted, by courtesy of the National Council of Girls' Clubs, England.

II. FOR ADVANCED PLAYERS the game should be speeded up so that they throw and catch while moving forward. The spaces may then be wider and the basketball rule enforced which allows not more than one step with the ball.

One point is scored for a team for each proper catch and throw of the ball, and five extra points for a successful tour. A missed or fumbled ball does not score. A catch does not score if the ball is "held" (more than one step taken with it).

BASKETBALL RUN-THROW-AND-CATCH RACE

By courtesy of Miss Dorothy C. Clark of the Polytechnic, London.

BASKETBALL SIDE–PASS RACE

Any large ball   *Intermediate grades*

I. Players stand in two or more competing ranks facing sideways with a distance of from one to two arm's length between each two players.

Number One player of each rank has a basketball which on signal he starts down the line for a series of quick sideways passes. The last player on receiving the ball runs with it up the rear of the rank to the front end position, the entire line progressing one space to the left to make room for him. As soon as he gets to this place, he starts the ball down the line again. This is repeated until Number One gets back to his original place. The team wins whose original Number One is first to return.

A dropped ball must be recovered by the one dropping it and the play continued.

II. Sideways pass is also played in leader and group formation with eight players to a team and a clock-wise rotation. Number One stands at a center point with the others of the team in a semi-circular rank facing him, Number Two at the right and Number Seven at the left. The center player (Number One) passes the ball to Number Two and at once runs forward beside Number Two ready to step into his place when the line moves down; simultaneously the last player from the other end, Number Seven, runs forward to take Number One's place at the center without waiting to receive the ball. This leaves Number Six as the last in the rank to receive the ball on a sideways pass. He passes it at once to the center and follows it to take the center place as the entire rank moves down one place. This continues until each player has thrown the ball, the team winning whose original Number One is first to receive the ball at the center on its last round.

BASKETBALL TWENTY–ONE

Basketball and goal   *Junior high to college*

I. Players throw for goal in turn in individual competition. Each player's turn consists of two tries in succession, one a long shot and the other a short one. He first throws the long shot from behind the circle, which ends the free-throw lane; whether he makes the goal or not, he recovers the ball and throws the short shot from the fifteen-foot line. A goal from the long-shot line scores two points and from the short-shot line one point. The player first making twenty-one points wins.

II. Two balls are used and two goals, each team lined up behind the free-throw line facing its basket. Each first player, on the signal to begin, throws for his basket, and without trying to catch the ball, goes at once to the rear of his team; the next player, meanwhile, runs forward to catch the ball, and from the point where he recovers it throws for goal and in turn goes to the rear of his team, while the third player runs forward to catch the ball, etc. No run, bounce, or dribble with the ball is permitted. A score keeper (for each team) calls the score as made, adding one point for each basket. The team wins which is first to score twenty-one.

BAT AND TAG

10 to 30 players   *Intermediate grades*
Playground; gymnasium   *Baseball and bat; or tennis ball*

I. This is an informal ball game, quickly organized, and good for practice in throwing, batting, or quick dodging.

The ground is marked only at one end, where there is a base or circle for the batsman and for the pitcher, the distance between the two being twenty to thirty feet.

One player is chosen as umpire and scorer. The others are divided into two teams which alternate in batting and pitching. Both teams scatter irregularly over the field.

At the umpire's signal "Play!" the pitcher throws his ball, repeating if necessary until the batsman hits it. On making the hit, the batsman throws down his bat and runs to tag with his hand as many fielders as possible, irrespective of team, keeping count of the number tagged. No one may be tagged twice in immediate succession, but may be touched a second time if another player has been tagged in between. No one may be tagged while fielding the ball.

Meanwhile, any player who catches the batted ball throws it at once to the pitcher, who bounces it once and calls "Halt!" All players stand still. The batsman gives his score of tagged fielders to the umpire, and the next batter and pitcher (from the opposite team) take their places.

II. When a tennis ball is used, it is struck with the open palm instead of a bat. This adapts the game to indoor play or a limited outdoor space.

BATTLE–BALL

6 to 12 players   *Intermediate*
Playground; gymnasium   *to senior high*
Basketball; Indian clubs

This is one of the best and most interesting of the simpler team games. Briefly stated, it consists in trying to dislodge Indian clubs or tenpins placed at the rear of the enemies' territory. Players should be trained to co-operate and to understand the importance of each player's doing well his particular part. Playing into the hands of each other when necessary, as in passing the ball to good throwers, is one of the most important features of team-work.

COURT. — A court measuring about fifty feet long by twenty-five wide should be divided into two equal parts by a line across the center. The rear boundary of each half is the goal or club line on which the Indian clubs are placed. Above these club lines a cord or rope is stretched seven feet from the ground. If desired, back stops may be placed at a distance of five feet beyond the club line to extend beyond the boundaries of the court on either side.

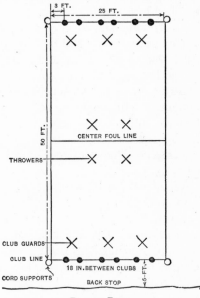

BATTLE-BALL

Indian clubs or tenpins weighing two or three pounds are placed on the club line, there being one pair for each club guard. One pair of these clubs should be placed in the center of the line, and one at each end of it three feet from the posts that hold the cord. The clubs of each pair should be separated by a distance of eighteen inches.

TEAMS AND OFFICIALS. — The teams consist of from three to six players on each side, though five on a side is the most desirable number. The description of this game and the diagram assume five players to a team. Each team chooses a captain, who settles disputes (unless other officers are appointed for this purpose, as hereinafter stated), and who assigns places for the other players as he sees fit. He himself occupies any place he desires.

Each team is divided into club guards and forwards. For five players there should be three club guards, each standing before a pair of clubs, and two forwards or throwers, who stand near the dividing line. In the placing of players it is desirable to place the best catchers as club guards and the best throwers as forwards.

In addition to the team players, it is desirable to have a referee, two judges, and one or two scorers, though all these offices may be filled by the same person.

The referee should keep time, should start the game, should announce scores and settle disputes. The judges, one for each side, should watch for fouls and report points made by their respective sides to their scorers.

OBJECTS. — The objects of the game are (1) to knock over the opponents' clubs with the ball; (2) to make a goal by passing the ball beyond the opponents' club line under the string but not hitting the clubs.

START. — The sides toss up for the ball or choose by drawing cuts.

Whenever a ball goes out of bounds it should be returned to the captain of the opposite (catching) side by a player designated for the purpose.

POINTS OF PLAY. — Successful play will come both from throwing and bowling the ball. (See *Ball Technique — General*, in chapter on *Balls and How to Play Them*.) The ball may be tossed from player to player on the same side, either to get it into the hands of the best thrower or to mislead the opponents as to when it will be aimed at their clubs. Players may move about on their own side, but overstepping the boundary lines is a foul. Club guards should not get far away from their line of duty. The ball should be aimed at the clubs or at open spaces between players, not at the players themselves.

FOULS. — It is a foul for a ball to pass above the cord drawn over the opponents' club line. Such a foul scores one for the defensive side. It is a foul for a thrower to step over the center line. For this the opponents score two points. It is a foul for a club to be overturned by a player on his own side. Each club so overturned scores five points for the opponents.

SCORE. — Overturning an opponent's club with the ball scores five points. Passing the ball beyond the opponents' club line below the cord but without hitting the clubs scores three points.

A ball passing between a pair of clubs scores ten.

A ball passing between the legs of an opposing player scores ten.

No score is made on a ball caught by the opponents.

Fouls score as stated above.

The game is played in ten- or fifteen-minute halves, with five minutes' intermission, the team winning which has the highest score at the end of the second half.

It adds greatly to the interest of the game to post the score in sight of the players, on a blackboard, large paper, or other bulletin.

This game was originated by Dr. Dudley A. Sargent.

BOLOBALL

This game combines various features of Soccer, Basketball, and Handball. It forms the foundation of the game Socco-Smash-Ball described in full in this volume but has the following differences :

The field in Boloball has less detail, and the goal is seven feet wide.

The game is played with a basketball.

There are six players on a team, two forwards, one center, two defence players, and one goalkeeper. Their arrangement on the field is like that of Basketball, except that the centers stand outside the circle as the referee bounces the ball.

The game is played in twenty-minute halves.

Penalty for fouls consists of one minute on the bench.

For all other points see Socco-Smash-Ball.

Boloball was originated by Mr. K. H. Murray.

BOMBARDMENT

10 to 100 players   *Junior high school*
Playground; gymnasium   *Basketball; Indian clubs*

This game resembles Battle Ball in that it consists in trying to overturn Indian clubs or tenpins set up in the opponents' court. The game differs from Battle Ball, however, in being feasible for a much larger number of players, and in being very much simpler in its form, not having the closer team organization or such a

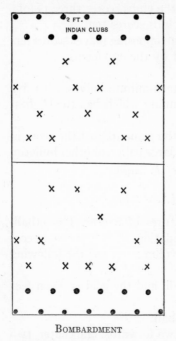

variety in points of scoring as Battle Ball. It may be made one of the liveliest and most interesting games for large numbers of players.

COURT. — The court is divided into two equal parts by a line across the center. At the rear of each half a row of Indian clubs or tenpins is set up, there being the same number of pins as players. Should the number of pins be so great as to require their being closer than two feet apart, a second row should be placed in front of the first, in such a way that each club stands opposite a space in the preceding row of clubs.

PLAYERS. — The players are divided into two teams numbering anywhere from five to fifty each. The players stand between their

BOMBARDMENT

clubs and the dividing line in any scattered formation. With a large number of players several balls should be put in play.

OBJECT AND POINTS OF PLAY. — The object of the game is to knock down the opponents' clubs. Each player will therefore serve both as a guard to protect his clubs, and as a thrower. He may throw whenever he can secure a ball, there being no order in which players should throw. Balls may be made to displace the opponents' clubs by being thrown against the wall behind the clubs, so that they will rebound or carom, knocking the clubs down from the rear. No player may step across the center line. The game is especially interesting when several balls are in play at once.

SCORE. — Each club overturned scores one point for the side which knocked it down. Every club overturned by a player on his own side scores one for the opponents. The game is played in time limits of from ten to twenty minutes, the side winning which has the highest score at the end of that time.

BOUNCEBALL

10 to 30 players   *Intermediate*
Playground; gymnasium   *to junior high*
Tennis ball; regulation handball

I. This game somewhat resembles tennis, but is played over a lower dividing line, and the ball is batted with the hand instead of with a racket; it is always played from a bounce, never "on the fly."

COURT. — Boundary lines for the entire court should be outlined, measuring about fifty feet in length by twenty-five in width, though these dimensions are not invariable. The ground is then divided by a line into two equal parts.

TEAMS. — The players are divided into two equal teams which take their places on either side of the dividing line, scattered over their respective courts without regular formation.

OBJECT. — The game consists in batting a tennis ball or handball with the hand from one side to the other of the dividing line, after it has first bounced in one's own territory.

START. — The leader of the game, or any player on either side, puts the ball in play by throwing it among the players of the opposite side. Whoever catches the ball acts as the first server. The server serves by bouncing the ball once and then hitting or batting it with the open palm on the rebound, so that it will go over into the opponents' court. Should a served ball fail to rebound in the antagonists' court, it is returned to the team from which it came, that they may have a second trial. One player continues to serve until his side scores five, when the ball is thrown to the opponents. The players on a side serve in rotation.

RULES AND POINTS OF PLAY. — In returning a serve or keeping the ball in play at any time, it may be bounced any number of times before being sent into the opponents' court. The one essential point is that it should be kept bouncing, a ball that is dead being thrown back to the server. In bouncing the ball it must always be hit or batted from the upper side with the palm of the hand. Should the ball bounce very low so as to give slight opportunity for batting into the opponents' court, a player may coax it to a higher point before batting. A ball may also be worked forward or to any advantageous point of the ground by bouncing or dribbling in this way before batting it. Whenever a ball enters a court, any member of the team on that side may play upon it. Players will use in this game many points of tennis, such as sending the ball into the opponents' territory with a long glancing stroke, which may make it bounce unexpectedly toward the rear of the opponents' court; or on the contrary, with a small bounce that shall just barely cross the line. A ball going out of bounds is out of play, and must be returned to the server unless it should rebound in the court for which it was intended, when it should still be considered in play.

SCORE. — The score is entirely for a defensive game, being wholly on the opponents' failures. If desired, the score may be the same as in tennis, but is generally as follows:

One point is scored for (*a*) failure to strike the ball as directed (from above with the open palm); (*b*) failure to bounce the ball before sending it into the opponents' ground; (*c*) failure to return a good serve or play. A thirty-minute game, in two halves, if desired.

II. **BOUNCEBALL** is also the name of a game played with a volleyball, with from four to fifteen players on a team, and with a service line drawn on the court eighteen feet from a three-foot net. The playing rules are in several respects, noted below, quite contrary to those of the previous game.

In the serve the ball is batted before it bounces.

A serve may be assisted by one player as a volley, but not after a bounce.

The return may be a volley or after one bounce.

The ball must go over the net from a stroke, not from a bounce.

The ball must not be deliberately bounced or dribbled.

It may be relayed from one player of a team to another, but always as a volley.

Only the playing side scores. They score one point for each failure of opponents. If the serving side fails, the serve goes to opponents. The game is played in two halves of fourteen minutes each. Highest score wins.

BOUNDARY BALL

10 to 100 players   *Intermediate*
Playground; gymnasium   *to junior high*
Basketball

COURT. — The court should measure about twenty feet in width by forty in length, and should be divided in half by a line, marked across it.

PLAYERS. — The players, numbering anywhere from ten to one hundred, are divided into two equal teams. Each team lines up on one side of the dividing line and about ten feet from it.

OBJECT OF THE GAME. — The object of the game is to throw the ball over the opponents' rear boundary line, a team succeeding in doing this scoring one point. As each team lines up at the start ten feet from the center dividing line, it is possible for each to intercept the ball at the point of its line-up. Any players from the line, however, may run back of this line-up to prevent the ball from going over the rear boundary, and the point at which the ball is stopped by any such player indicates the point at which the team must line up for the next play. It therefore becomes a secondary object of the game to force one's adversaries back until they have reached their rear boundary line, where their chances for intercepting the ball are less than in a forward position, as their movements are more restricted.

START. — The teams toss up for which side shall first have the ball. The ball is then given to the center player in the line, who makes the first throw. After this first throw the ball may be put in play by any player in a line.

RULES AND POINTS OF PLAY. — Players may run forward of their first or succeeding line-up to catch the ball, but the line-up never comes forward of its first position. After a line has been forced backward, however, if the ball is caught anywhere between the last line-up and the first, the line moves forward to the new point. Should a ball roll on the ground, the point at which it stops rolling, or is stopped by the players trying to catch it, indicates the line at which they must take their stand. No ball scores a point, however, which rolls beyond the rear boundary line. When a team has been forced back to its rear boundary line, it must stand on that line thereafter, unless it should succeed in stopping the ball forward of that line, when it may move forward to the new position. No player may step over the boundary line.

SCORE. — One point is scored by the throwing team every time a ball is thrown beyond the opponents' rear boundary line. Five points constitute a game.

BOWL–BALL

(See *Bowling, Center Club-Bowls, Circle Club-Bowls,* and *Line Club-Bowls.*)

BOWLING

2 to 10 or more players   *Juniors; adults*
Bowling alley, pins, and balls

Bowling consists in knocking down wooden pins with a ball, which is bowled in wooden alleys specially made to provide smooth runways for the ball, the sides being raised. Each alley is forty-one or forty-two inches in width and long enough to give the ball a clear run of sixty feet to the first pin, counting from the foul line. There are ten pins, made of wood, more or less bottle-shaped, and fifteen inches in height. They are placed at the far end of each alley twelve inches apart in pyramid formation, the apex toward the bowler. The wooden ball (twenty-seven inches in circumference and sixteen pounds in weight) is held in one hand (see *Bowling* in chapter on *Balls and How to Play Them*) and rolled from near ground level, an impetus being given to it by a swing of the arm and a preliminary run or steps. The start may be from as far back from the foul line and include as many steps as the player wishes, but must stop at the foul line at the foot of the alley, though the arm may swing beyond this line in releasing the ball. It is a foul for the foot, hand, or any part of the body to touch the alley beyond the foul line; no score is made on such a foul play, but it counts as one of the "balls" to which the player is entitled. Any pins knocked over by a foul bowl are at once replaced, and the same player, if entitled to another ball, goes on with his play.

Each player has two balls (bowls) at each turn, unless his first bowl knocks over all ten pins, which ends that turn. Players take turns in bowling. Ten turns for each player constitute a game. In a game with four players the play may be independent or in partners. If as partners, the first player of each couple plays, and then the second players. When teams are competing, they play independently in different alleys.

SCORE. — The score and the method of keeping it are peculiar to this game. As shown in the illustration, the score-diagram consists of a series of ten little squares for each player, one for each turn, called a "frame." In each square is marked the score made in that turn and also the total cumulative score up to and including that turn. Expert players sometimes put down only the cumulative totals. A ball scores the number of pins it knocks down; the first ball of a turn has a clear chance at all ten pins and, if these are not all knocked down, the place is cleared of the ball and all fallen pins and the same player's second ball scores all it knocks over of those left standing. When all ten pins are knocked over with one bowl, it is called a **strike** and scores ten points, marked on the frame as a cross, ✕; if the ten pins are knocked over by two balls instead of one, it is called a **spare** and is marked with a slant line (half-cross); this also scores ten points. But the whole scheme of scoring is more complicated than this would appear. After a strike the player adds to his total for that turn the score made by his next two balls, whether played in one or two turns; for a spare he adds the score of one ball only from his next turn. The total for a strike or a spare cannot, therefore, be computed until after the player's next turn or turns. Another point to be noted is that after a strike or spare the score of the player's next turn is added twice to his cumulative total: first, to the total of the strike-turn and, second, to the cumulative total entered in its own turn. If a strike occurs in the last turn (tenth) the player bowls two more balls to complete his score; for a spare, one more ball.

NAME	1	2	3	4	5	6	7	8	9	10	EXTRA
S	5 3	6 3	✗	2 5	7 1	\ 5 5	3 1	✗	\ 8 2	\ 7 3	6
	8	17	34	41	49	62	66	86	103	119	—
R	✗	✗	\ 4 6	3 5	4 1	\ 8 2	1 1	\ 9 1	7 1	2 2	
	24	44	57	65	70	81	83	100	108	112	

BOWLING SCORE

The cumulative scores given above are arrived at as follows:

PLAYER	TURN	SCORE	TOTAL	PLAYER	TURN	SCORE	TOTAL
S	1st	8	$5 + 3 = 8$	R	1st	10	$10 + 10 + 4 = 24$
	2nd	9	$8 + 9 = 17$		2nd	10	$24 + 10 + 10 = 44$
	3rd	10	$17 + 10 + 7 = 34$		3rd	10	$44 + 10 + 3 = 57$
	4th	7	$34 + 7 = 41$		4th	8	$57 + 8 = 65$
	5th	8	$41 + 8 = 49$		5th	5	$65 + 5 = 70$
	6th	10	$49 + 10 + 3 = 62$		6th	10	$70 + 10 + 1 = 81$
	7th	4	$62 + 4 = 66$		7th	2	$81 + 2 = 83$
	8th	10	$66 + 10 + 10 = 86$		8th	10	$83 + 10 + 7 = 100$
	9th	10	$86 + 10 + 7 = 103$		9th	8	$100 + 8 = 108$
	10th	10	$103 + 10 + 6 = 119$		10th	4	$108 + 4 = 112$

The game of Bowling here described is the one most played in American bowling alleys. **Tenpins** is like this game but played with smaller pins on a level surface instead of in alleys. In Germany a much more difficult alley game is played in which the pins stand in oval formation around a king pin which must remain standing after the others are bowled over. Balls of various sizes may be used as needed, and to reach the most difficult pins a ball must be delivered to curve at the end of its course, no carom being allowed.

In many countries outdoor bowling is very popular and a common sight. The French **Boule** and Italian **Boccia** are practically the same game. The British **Bowling on the Green, Lawn Bowls,** or **Skittles** (the latter played both indoors and out) are played with "bowls" that are not completely spherical. All of these outdoor games begin by rolling or throwing a small ball to rest at the far end of the court, after which larger balls are bowled or thrown to rest near it, or to displace it or the opponent's balls; there are also other plays. Each game develops a high degree of skill.

Rules for Lawn Bowls and the Italian game will be found in the volume entitled *Lawn Bowls* in Spalding's Athletic Library.

BOX BALL

2 players   *Intermediate grades*

Regulation handball

This is a game to accustom players to the technique of a small ball. It differs from Hand Tennis only in the ball used and the absence of net and foul lines.

The court is twenty by thirty-two feet, divided across the center by a line on the ground. The server stands behind his end line and bounces a handball, driving it with a stroke of the open hand so that it goes over the line into the opponent's court. The receiver runs out to return the ball, and drives it back with the open hand, either after it has bounced once or as a volley (hitting it on the fly). The returned ball must go into the opponent's court and be returned in the same way.

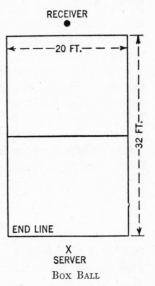

The ball is thus kept in play until one or the other of the players fails to return it properly. If this is the server, he loses his serve and the opponent serves. If the receiver fails, the server scores one point and continues to serve. A ball hitting the lines is in play.

Box Ball

In doubles (four players) the server serves as long as his side scores; the serve then passes to his partner, and when he fails, it goes to the opponents.

Only the serving side scores. They make one point on each failure of the opponents. Eleven points win the game.

BUNT–BALL

16 to 20 players   *Intermediate grades*
Playground; gymnasium

Playground ball (or baseball) and bat

This is an informal game of the baseball type which gives practice in bunting as distinguished from batting.

Four bases are located as on a baseball diamond, and places for pitcher, catcher, and batter as in the regular game.

Players are in two teams, one at bat and the other as pitcher, catcher, three basemen and fielders, the latter placed wherever needed.

The pitcher throws the ball with an underarm swing, as in Playground Baseball, and the batter bunts it. That is, instead of hitting with a swing, he holds the bat loosely, usually in a horizontal position, and allows the ball to meet it so as to fall and roll only a short distance. To hit the ball, or swing at it, puts the batter out. If a flyball is caught, whether fair or foul, the batter is out.

If the ball goes within the fair area, the batter runs to first and succeeding bases and so on around to home base as he has opportunity. He is put out if tagged by a player holding the ball or if the ball is fielded to first base before he gets there. All other rules are as for Playground Baseball.

One point is scored as in baseball for a circuit of bases to home base. The game is played in seven innings.

CALL–BALL

(See also *Ring Call-Ball*, *Ball Stand*, and *Spud*.)

10 to 30 or more players   *Primary grades*
Playground; gymnasium   *Handsizeball*

The players are numbered and scatter irregularly over the playground or gymnasium. One tosses a ball, at the same time calling the number of some other player. This player must run forward and catch the ball before it has bounced more than once. Any player who is successful in this takes the place of the first tosser. Any player who fails rejoins the others, but three failures put him out of the game. For large numbers it is well to have two balls, tossed by two different players.

The one who is tossing the ball will add much to the interest of the game by calling the names of players who are at a considerable distance from the ball, or for any other reason may have a particularly difficult task in reaching the ball in time; or he may take them unaware, as by calling the same name twice in succession, etc. There is no limit to the number of times a player may be called.

CAPTAINBALL

Captainball is one of the best and most popular games for both children and adults, boys and girls. It is one of the most useful forms of games for the period when pupils are beginning to enjoy organization, as it calls for comparatively simple, though pronounced, teamwork.

There are many variations in Captainball, the differences being in (1) the plan of laying out the ground, and consequently the relative position of players; (2) the points of play that score; and (3) the rules restricting the players. While almost any rules of play or points of scoring may be used on almost any plan of ground, certain methods of play seem to have grown out of, and naturally to belong to, certain diagrams. An umpire, referee, and scorer are desirable in any form of the game, but *not absolutely necessary* except for match games.

Seven distinct forms of Captainball are here presented, Captainball I, II, III; (IV) Emperor Ball; (V) Progressive Captainball; also a schoolroom adaptation, (VI), and (VII) Captain Basketball. Some forms which offer minor variations have been omitted in favor of these, which form distinct types.

CAPTAINBALL — I

14 players   *Intermediate grades to*
Basketball; volleyball   *senior high school*

This is in some respects a simpler form of Captainball than those that follow, as there are but three bases or homes on each side of the field, and the captain is on one of these instead of in the center. His position at the farthest point from the dividing line tends to distribute the play equally among all of the players. The number of players is smaller than in other forms of the game. The ball does not score for completing the circle (or triangle) of players, as in other forms of the game. Although very rapid, this form may be less confusing for beginners than in larger formations where there are more players.

COURT. — On each side of the court at corresponding distances from the center three small circles are drawn for bases at the points of a triangle. The circles should be from two to five feet each in diameter, the more skillful the players the smaller the circle. The distance between each two circles forming a triangle should be at least fifteen feet, and the distance across the center of the field between the two inner circles, from fifteen to twenty-five feet.

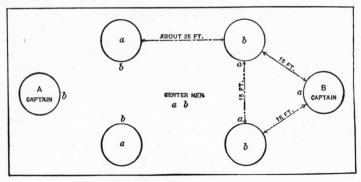

CAPTAINBALL — I

TEAMS. — The players are divided into two teams, each consisting of three basemen, three base guards, and one fielder. One of the basemen is captain and stands in the base at the end of the ground farthest from the center. Each team has a guard stationed near each of its opponents' bases, and a fielder whose general place should be near the center of the ground but who is free to run to any part of the ground, and who should pick up the ball whenever it goes afield. The ball should then be put in play again from the center as at the start.

OBJECT OF THE GAME. — The object of the game is to have a captain catch a ball from one of his basemen. A ball caught by the captain from the guards or fielder of his team does not count. Of course the guards will try to prevent the ball being caught by a captain from one of his basemen, or by one of the basemen from his fielder, and on the other hand will try to secure the ball and send it back to their own basemen or fielder.

START. — The ball is put in play by being tossed up in the center of the ground by a third party between the two fielders, both of whom try to catch it. The one who succeeds has first throw. Touching the ball is not enough for this first catch: it must be caught in both hands. In case of dispute, the ball should be tossed again. The ball is again put in play in this way after each point scored; also after going afield and being picked up by one of the fielders.

RULES. — The basemen may put one foot outside of their bases or circles, but at no time both feet. Each guard must remain near the base he guards but may not step within it even with one foot. Should either side transgress these rules or make any other foul, the ball is thrown to one of the basemen on the opposite side, who is given free play to throw to his captain without interference of his own guard, though the captain's guard may try to prevent its being caught. A ball that goes afield is put in play again at the center, as at the opening of the game.

FOULS. — It is a foul (1) to transgress any of the rules given above; (2) to snatch or bat the ball from an opponent's hands; (3) to bounce the ball more than three times in succession; (4) to run with the ball; (5) to kick it; (6) to hand instead of throwing it; or (7) to hold it longer than time enough to turn once around quickly, or three seconds. Penalty for fouls consists in allowing opponents a free throw from one of their basemen to their captain, as described under Rules.

SCORE. — The ball scores one point whenever a catch is made by a captain from one of his basemen. It does not score when the captain catches it from a guard or fielder.

The game is played by time limits, ranging from ten to thirty minutes. The time is divided in halves, and at the end of the first half the teams have an interval of rest, and the basemen and guards change places. The team wins which has the highest score at the end of the second half. The ball is put newly in play after every point scored.

CAPTAINBALL — II

18 to 60 players   *Intermediate*
Basketball; volleyball   *to senior high*

The distinctive features of this form of Captainball are: (1) The captain occupies a place in the circumference of the circle as in I, instead of in the center as in succeeding forms of the game; (2) the captain's place is near the dividing line, instead of at the farthest point from it as in I; this gives the guards of his team, on the opposite side of the ground, a greater opportunity to reach him than in I, while any increased tendency to concentrate play near the dividing line is offset by the scoring of the ball through completing a round of the circle, and by the greater freedom allowed the guards; (3) the guards may run at large, not being confined to guarding any one baseman; (4) there are no fielders, the free action of the guards making these unnecessary; (5) the ball scores for completing a circle and also for any catch by the captain from one of his team, whether it be baseman or guard; also for a catch by any one baseman from another baseman of his team; or for a catch by the captain after it has passed through the hands of two or three basemen successively; (6) fouls differ from those in some other forms of the game, and are penalized by scoring for the opponents instead of by a toss of the ball.

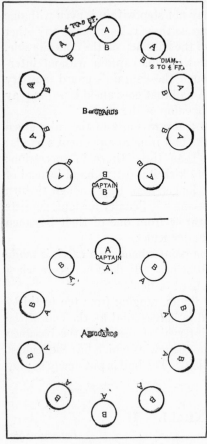

CAPTAINBALL — II

TEAMS. — There should be from eight to thirty players on each side, exclusive of the captain. Half of these players stand in the bases on their own side. The other players of the team (guards) are stationed at the opening of the game each near one of the opponents' bases on the opposite side of the ground from his own basemen. Each guard is chiefly responsible throughout for guarding his particular base; but all guards may move about freely in the opponents' territory without stepping within the rings (bases).

START. — The ball is put in play at the opening of the game, after each catch by a captain, and after each foul, by being tossed by a neutral person in the center of the ground, the guards on both sides trying to get possession of it.

RULES. — It is considered a fair catch for any baseman, including the captain, if the ball be caught from a bounce either from the floor, ceiling, or any other object, or from hitting another player.

A ball that goes afield is secured by the guard standing nearest the point where it left the circle. He puts it in play from the point in the circle where it went out.

Other rules are indicated under "Fouls."

FOULS. — It is a foul (1) to kick the ball; (2) to run with the ball; (3) for a guard to step over the dividing line or inside one of the bases; (4) for a baseman to step outside of his own base, even with one foot; (5) to hand the ball instead of tossing; (6) to snatch or bat the ball from an opponent's hands; (7) to hold the ball longer than time enough to turn around quickly, or three seconds.

One point is scored by the opponents whenever a foul is made, and the ball is then put in play again from the center.

SCORE. — One point is scored for a team every time a baseman catches the ball from another baseman of the same team.

Two points are scored for a team every time its captain makes a fair catch, whether the ball has gone around his circle or not, and whether the ball was thrown by one of his basemen or one of his guards on the opposite side of the field. Three points are scored if the ball reaches two different basemen and the captain successively, whether in regular rotation around the circle or not.

Four points are scored if the ball reaches three different basemen and the captain successively, whether in regular rotation around the circle or not. Five points are scored whenever the ball passes entirely around the circle on one side, in regular rotation of basemen, whether the start and finish of that circle be with the captain or some other baseman. Each foul scores one for the opposing team, as described under "Fouls." After the captain catches the ball, no further points may be scored on it in that play and it then goes back to the center to be put again in play.

CAPTAINBALL — III

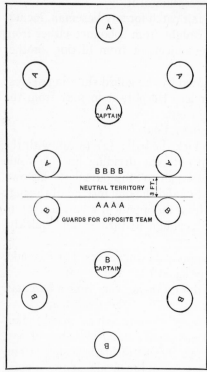

CAPTAINBALL — III

20 to 40 players
Basketball; volleyball

Intermediate to senior high

This form of Captainball is the most strenuous of any, as freer mass play is encouraged among the guards, and there are fewer restrictions in the form of play, batting and hitting the ball being allowed, which are fouls in other forms of the game. The method of punishing fouls is optional and should be determined before the game begins. The court is divided somewhat differently than in other forms of the game, by a neutral space between the two fields, where the ball is tossed for sides. The ball scores both for completing a circle and being caught by a captain, but not for catching from one baseman to another, as in II. The captain is stationed in the center instead of in the circumference of the circle, as in I and II.

CAPTAINBALL — IV

(Emperor Ball)

30 to 40 players   *Junior high school to adult*
Basketball

This game is really a form of Captainball, but differs from any of the previous forms in the following points:

A neutral officer, called the emperor, is stationed in the center of the field between the two teams, and the ball scores its highest when it has been thrown entirely around one of the circles, from there to the captain in the center, and from him to the emperor. There are two fielders, or players at large, who try to intercept the ball before it reaches the emperor, or to block it in any other part of the play.

COURT. — In the center of the court is placed a springboard, box, stool, or other platform for the impartial ruler of the game called the emperor. The court on each side of this point is marked as in the diagram. The two fielders may go anywhere on the field, but their main duty is to prevent the ball reaching the emperor from an opponent. They also pick up the ball when it goes afield and hand it to the emperor for starting again.

Each captain takes his place in a center base; the basemen stand each in a base in the circle surrounding his captain; the guards, of equal number with the basemen, take their places in the opposite field, each being assigned to guard one of the basemen, including the captain, of the opposing team, and may not go from the immediate vicinity of the circle he guards.

OBJECTS OF THE GAME. — The objects of the game for each team consist (1) in throwing the ball from baseman to baseman completely around its circle;

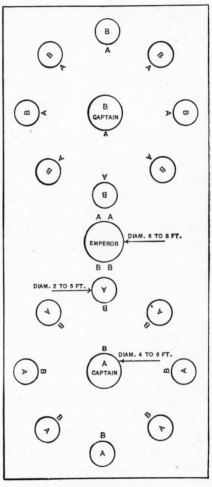

CAPTAINBALL — IV
(Emperor Ball)

(2) around the circle as in (1) and in addition, to throw from the last baseman to the center player or captain; and (3) having completed the previous two points, to throw from the captain to

the emperor, who stands between the two halves of the field. The object of the guards, of course, is (1) to intercept the ball so as to prevent the completion of this play in any of its points; and (2) to gain possession of the ball so as to throw it across the field to their own basemen on the opposite side.

START. — The ball is put in play at the beginning of the game, and always thereafter, when necessary, by the emperor. He must naturally be perfectly impartial, and may toss the ball to either side, in turn, or use his judgment in choosing which side shall have it. He will, of course, do his best to catch the ball for either side that throws it to him. The ball is put newly in play after every point scored, after every foul, and after going afield.

RULES. — No baseman may step outside of his base even with one foot. A ball caught by the captain having one foot out of his base does not score, nor if so caught by a baseman does it count in completing the round of the circle; but this does not count as a foul, and a captain so catching a ball may toss it to one of his team. No mass play is permissible among the guards, each one being obliged to guard only the baseman to whom he is assigned. This does not apply to the two fielders, who may move anywhere on the field, and who pick up balls that go out of the large circles.

FOULS. — It is a foul (1) to hit, bat, or snatch a ball from an opponent; (2) to hand a ball instead of throwing it; (3) to hold a ball longer than time enough to turn around quickly, or three seconds; (4) for a guard to step inside a base. Each foul scores one point for the opponents, and the ball is then put newly in play by the emperor.

SCORE. — A team scores one point when a ball has successfully completed the round of its circle of basemen, but is intercepted in a throw from that to the captain; a team scores two points when its ball has completed the round of the circle of basemen and been caught by its captain in the center, but fails to reach the emperor; a team scores five points when its ball has completed the full play of the circle, its captain, and the emperor. A team scores one point for every foul made by the opponents. The ball is put newly in play by the emperor after every point scored.

The game is played in fifteen-minute halves, with a rest of five or ten minutes between the halves. The highest score wins.

The teams change sides and places for the second half, guards becoming basemen, and *vice versa*.

CAPTAINBALL — V (PROGRESSIVE)

20 to 60 players   *Junior high*
Basketball   *to adult*

This game differs from any other form of Captainball in the fact that the players progress after each score from base to base. Each player thus completes the round of outer bases in his own field, then becomes captain for his team, then a fielder, and then starts on the round as guard for each base, in turn, in the opposite field. The use of progression in this game was originated by Miss Cora B. Clark of New York. It is obviously best adapted to older players — of high school age — but once understood, the progression is simple and well within the ability of younger players.

Use Diagram as for Captainball III.

PROGRESSION. — The distinctive feature of this game is the method of progression. To make this plainer, the players in the diagram are designated by numbers as well as by teams. Thus, "X" indicates all players on one team, and "O" all players on the other team, each player carrying a number, X-1, X-2, X-3, etc. The method of progression is as follows:

After the ball has scored a point, the two fielders, X-13 and O-13, move to base A. O-13, as he is now crossing to his home side of the field, goes inside of base A as baseman, and X-13 becomes his guard; the other two fielders, X-14 and O-14, go to base F, the home man, X-14, going inside the base, and O-14 becoming his guard. It will thus be seen that the two fielders bearing the lower number (13) go to the first base, A, and those bearing the higher number (14) go to the base bearing the highest letter, F. At the same time that the fielders make this change, each baseman and his attendant guard move one base farther up; that is, baseman O-1 and guard X-7 move from base A to base B; baseman O-2 and his guard X-8 move from base B to base C; and so on. The last baseman on this side, O-5, and his guard, X-11, move to the center or captain's base, the previous captain and his guard taking the place of the fielders who stood nearest base E. On the other side of the field the progression is made in the same way, so that the order of pro-

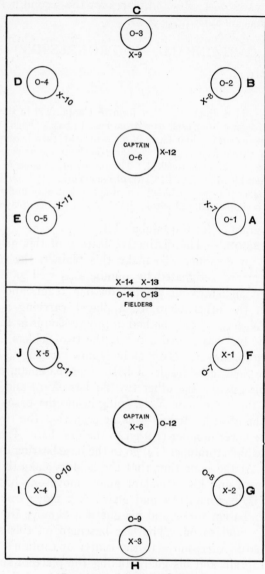

CAPTAINBALL — V (Progressive)

gression is always from bases A, B, C, D, and E to the captain's base, and from the captain's base to fielders. When a player has made the complete circuit of one side, he progresses from fielder's position to the opposite side; that is, after the players who started in base A (basemen O-1 and guard X-7) become fielders, they progress by going to base F, instead of back to base A. This change comes easily if the captain from the base occupied at first by X-6 always takes his place as fielder nearest base A; the fielders nearest A always going to A, and the other fielders to F.

FOULS. — (1) Touching the ball when it is in another player's hands; (2) walking or running with the ball; (3) stepping out of his base by the captain to catch the ball; (4) stepping out of the bases with both feet by the basemen; (5) moving by a guard more than three feet from the base he guards; (6) stepping over the center line into the opponents' territory; (7) two fielders from the same side going after the ball at once when it goes out of bounds.

PENALTY FOR FOULS. — No score is made on fouls, the penalty being the loss of the ball to the opposite side. The ball under these circumstances goes to the player on the other side, who stands in a corresponding position to the one who made the foul.

SCORE. — A ball thrown from a baseman to his captain scores one point. A ball completing a circuit of the outer basemen scores two points. The side wins which has the highest score when time is called. The game may be played in from thirty to sixty minutes' time.

CAPTAINBALL — VI (SCHOOLROOM)

10 to 60 players　　　　　　　　　　　　　　*Intermediate to*
Gas ball　　　　　　　　　　　　　　　　　*junior high*

The class is divided into two teams, with a center captain and five bases on each side. The remaining players of each company serve as guards, and are placed on the opposite side from their captains and bases to prevent opponents from catching the ball.

The teacher or umpire tosses the ball alternately to the guards, the first time to team one, the second time to team two.

The guards, in turn, toss it to their bases, who try to get it to their captains, the opposite guards opposing by guarding with the arms and jumping to catch the ball. The game continues until one captain catches the ball from a *straight throw* (not a bound) from a base (not a guard). The side catching the ball scores a point, and the umpire then tosses the ball to the guards of the opposite team, etc.

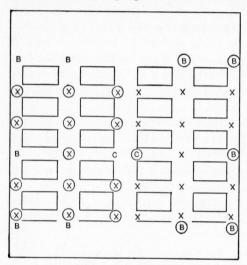

SCHOOLROOM CAPTAINBALL — VI

The game is played in time limits, the side having the highest score at the end of ten or fifteen minutes winning the game.

Fouls are: holding the ball longer than five seconds; snatching the ball; knocking the ball out of an opponent's hand.

In case of a foul the ball is given to the opposite team.

Any number may play the game, provided the sides are even.

This schoolroom adaptation of Captainball was made by Miss Mabel L. Pray of Toledo, Ohio.

CAPTAIN BASKETBALL

12 to 30 players
2 basketballs and 2 goals

Junior high
to adult

1. A basketball court is divided in half with a line across the center. In each half a series of bases is drawn in a circle around the edge as in Captainball II. The number of bases may vary with the number of players but must be the same in each half. The base farthest from each basket is the captain's base for that team. This must be three and a half feet from the

center line between courts, and the base nearest the basket must be three and a half feet in front of that.

Players are divided into two equal teams, consisting of a baseman for each base, one or two captains for each team, and three guards. The number of guards may vary with the number of bases, but it is better to have only one third as many guards as basemen. Guards stand in the opponent's court. If there are two captains to a team they stand on bases opposite each other, one being at the center line and the other near the basket.

The object of the game is for a team to score by: (1) Passing or bouncing the ball in a continuous circuit from captain to captain, if two captains, or back to captain if one; (2) throwing a goal, which may be done by any baseman or captain.

The guards try to intercept the ball and throw it across to their own basemen.

The ball is put in play at the center, between courts, by being tossed between two opposing guards who try each to bat it to his own basemen. This is done after every point scored and at the beginning of halves. The ball is played by throwing, bounding, or batting with the open hand.

FOULS. — The ball may not be held more than three seconds.
It may not be kicked.
Guards may not walk with it.
Basemen may not step out of bases with two feet.
Captains may not step out of bases at all, even with one foot.
Guards must not step over the center line.
Roughness and overguarding are fouls.

PENALTY for a foul is a free throw from the center line by an opposing guard.

OUT OF BOUNDS. — A ball going out of bounds is given to the nearest baseman if it was touched last by a guard, and *vice versa*.

SCORE. — One point is scored for a continuous circuit from captain to captain (if there are two captains) or from captain back to captain if but one.

A goal thrown by a baseman scores two points.

The game is played in two halves, teams changing courts for the second half.

II. In another form of the game, instead of teams changing courts, the basemen rotate, stepping up one base in their own court after each score.   In this form guards do not change courts. Only the four basemen nearest the basket may throw for goal.

III. Where there are but three bases in each court, one point is scored for each pass to the next base instead of for the complete circuit.

CENTER BASE

10 to 30 or more players   *Primary to*
Handsizeball; basketball   *intermediate*

All of the players but one form a circle, with considerable space between each two.   The odd player stands in the center, holding the ball.   He tosses it to any player in the circle, and immediately runs away outside the circle.   The player to whom the ball is thrown must catch it, place it on the ground in the center of the circle, and at once chase the one who threw it.   The one who threw the ball tries to get back to the center of the circle and touch the ball before he can be tagged.   Should he succeed in this, he joins the circle, and the other player throws the ball. If the first center player is tagged before returning to the ball, he throws again, and the one who chased him returns to the circle.

This game is very popular with children.

CENTER CATCH BALL

10 to 30 or more players   *Junior high school to adult*
Handsizeball; basketball; beanbag

I. Simple form for little children.

All of the players but one stand in a circle, with two or three feet distance between players.   The odd player stands in the center of the circle and tries to catch the ball, which is tossed rapidly from one circle player to another.   Should he succeed, the one who last touched the ball changes places with him.

II. Advanced form for skillful players.

This differs from the preceding in the greater distance between players and also in the much greater range and resourcefulness of play.

The players stand in a circle with from six to eight feet between each two, and with one player in the center. The circle players throw a ball from one to another, the object of the game being for the center player to catch the ball or knock it to the floor. The circle players may throw the ball over the heads of one another or across the circle, or make sudden feints of throwing it in one direction, turn suddenly and throw it in another, etc., to deceive the center player.

Any player in the circle who last touched the ball changes places with the center player whenever the latter touches or catches the ball.

CENTER CLUB-BOWLS

(See also *Line Club-Bowls* (*Single*); *Line Club-Bowls* (*Double*); *Circle Club-Bowls*.)

10 to 30 or more players   *Intermediate grades*
Handsizeball; beanbag

The players join in a large circle and number by twos or consecutively. The odd numbers form one team and the even numbers (alternate players) another.
Three Indian clubs are placed at the points of a small triangle (measuring about twelve inches on each side), in the center of the circle. Each player, in turn, bowls at the clubs with a handsizeball or beanbag. Each club bowled over scores one for the bowler's team. The team wins which has the highest score when each player has bowled two or three times, as may be agreed on at the opening of the game. Each player must secure his ball or bag after bowling and replace the overturned clubs. One ball or bag may be used and passed around the circle, but the play is quicker if each player has his own.

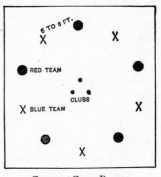

CENTER CLUB-BOWLS

CHINESE BALL

10 or more players   *Intermediate to senior high*
Playground; gymnasium

The players stand in a circle shoulder to shoulder. One player in the circle has a basketball; he throws this to any other player in the circle, who must try to catch it. Immediately that the ball reaches any given player his neighbor on each side must raise vertically the arm next the catcher. Thus the player on the catcher's right will raise his left arm, and the one on the catcher's left will raise his right arm. If a player raises the wrong arm, or none, or both, he leaves the circle. If the circle-man fails to catch the ball, he too must leave the circle. If he does catch it, he throws it instantly to some other circle player, whose neighbors must raise their arms as described. The arms are lowered again as soon as a catcher has thrown the ball. When all but five are eliminated, these are called the winners and the game starts over again. The eliminated players may meanwhile have started another circle. The tempo of the game must be very quick and snappy so as to keep all players alert.

CIRCLE–BALL

10 to 60 or more players   *Primary grades*
Playground; party   *Handsizeball; basketball; beanbag*

The players stand in a circle with from three to five feet between each two. The game consists of merely tossing the ball rapidly from one player to another, but not in regular order. The sport comes from the unexpectedness with which the ball may be thrown across the ring, or reverse the direction in which it is circling the ring, or in any other way taking the players unaware. A leader or teacher should see that this element of sport is put into the game, or else it may be very dull and useless.

Any player failing to catch the ball should sit down, the player winning who remains standing the longest.

When all are seated, the same game may be played in a sitting position.

For a more advanced form of this game, see Round Ball.

For very little children, the spaces between players should be less and the tossing done in regular order from one player to the next, working up gradually to the more varied modes of play suggested above. Several balls or bags may be used, following each other in quick succession. The number of these may be increased until there is but one ball or beanbag (or two) less than the number of players.

CIRCLE CLUB–BOWLS

(See also *Line Club-Bowls (Single); Line Club-Bowls (Double); Center Club-Bowls.*)

6 to 60 or more players　　　　　　　　　*Intermediate to*
Playground; gymnasium　　　　　　　　　*senior high school*
　　　　　　Basketball; football; Indian clubs

The players divide into two teams and take their places in one large circle, the players of one team alternating with those of the

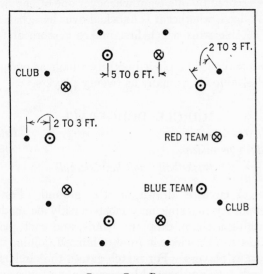

CIRCLE CLUB-BOWLS

other. There should be five or six feet of space between each two players. Each player is provided with an Indian club.

The players of one team distinguish themselves and their clubs in some way, as by tying a handkerchief around the arm and club.

The players, having taken their places in the circle, each places his own club on the floor behind him at a distance of two or three feet. The object of the game is to knock over the opponents' clubs by rolling the ball on the floor, and naturally to protect one's own clubs. Any player may start the game.

While the main form of play for the ball is to roll it, it is permissible to bounce the ball from one player to another, and also permissible to knock over a club with a ball that bounces instead of rolls. It is not permissible to toss a ball from one player to another, or to dislodge a club by a toss unless the ball should hit the floor and bounce before it hits the club.

Whenever a club is dislodged, the owner of the club must set it up again at once; if he also has the ball, he must set up the club before putting the ball again into play.

A point is scored by one team whenever one of the opponents' clubs is dislodged, whether it is knocked over by a ball or by its owner. The side wins which first makes a score of forty-nine points.

The game may also be played with two balls at once, and this is always desirable for as many as twenty players.

CIRCLE DODGEBALL

10 to 60 players　　　　　　　　　　　　　　　*Intermediate*
Playground; gymnasium.　　　　　　　　　　　　*to adults*
　　　　　　　Basketball; soft handsizeball

COURT. — A circle is drawn on the ground. For practice play, a temporary marking may most quickly be made by the players forming a circle, dropping hands, and each player then marking the arc of the circle in front of himself, joining it to those of the adjacent players. For match games the circle should be marked in advance and should be accurate, and measure thirty-five feet in diameter.

TEAMS. — Any number of players may take part. They are divided into two equal teams, one of which stands around and outside of the circle; the other team is grouped promiscuously within the circle. There are no officers of the teams, but for match games a referee is necessary, who should also act as score-keeper.

OBJECT CF GAME. — The object of the game is for the outer or circle team to hit the players of the inner team with a basketball, any player so hit being "out" and having to leave the game. With one slight exception, explained farther on, only the inner players score, and this on the basis of the number of players left in the circle when time limits are called. There is no retaliatory play from the inner team.

START. — The game starts on a signal from the referee with the ball in the hands of the outer circle. The referee blows his whistle for play to cease whenever an inner player is fairly touched with the ball, and again for play to resume. He also signals for time limits explained under "Score."

RULES AND POINTS OF PLAY. — The players in the outer team must not step within the circle when throwing. A center player hit by such a throw is not out.

A ball that does not hit a center player is usually recovered by the outer circle when it rolls or otherwise makes its own way to the opposite side of the circle. If a ball remains in the circle or rebounds into it, one of the outer team may run in to get it. He may throw it while within the circle to one of his teamsmen whh is in place outside the circle; or he may return with it to his own place and throw from there; but he may not throw at one of the inner players while himself within the circle.

The inner team does not play the ball: it only dodges the ball. Any tactics may be used for this except leaving the ring. The dodging may be done by stepping quickly in one direction or another, by twisting, stooping, jumping, or any other methods that suggest themselves.

A player of the inner team hit on any part of his person or clothing by a ball is out. This may be either from the ball on the fly or on a bounce, or rolling. Only one player may be put out for one throw of the ball. Should two players be hit by one throw of the ball, the first one touched by the ball is the one to go out. When a player is hit, the referee blows his whistle, the play ceases, and the player hit quickly leaves the circle. The referee blows his whistle again for the play to resume; but should the hit player not then have left the circle so that he may be hit a second time, such a second hit scores one point for the opponents.

SCORE. — The game is played in two halves of ten minutes each, the teams changing places at the end of the first half. The main scoring is done by the inner team, which scores one point for each player left within the circle at the end of its half. The only other scoring is by the outer team whenever a player is hit a second time before leaving the circle, each such hit scoring one point for the throwing team.

The team wins which at the end of the second half has the highest score from these two sources together.

The game as here given was developed by Mr. William A. Stecher.

CIRCLE PILLAR BALL

12 to 24 players   *Intermediate*
Playground; gymnasium   *to senior high school*
Tennis ball or basketball

This is an excellent preparatory game for regular Basketball.

COURT. — A six-foot circle is drawn in the center of the court and in this is placed a net or goal post, preferably twelve to fifteen feet high. Around this is drawn a circle forty feet in diameter (twenty-foot) radius, and three feet inside of this a similar circle. The space between the two outer circles is called the *track*, and the space between the inner track-circle and the goal is called the *court*. A line is drawn straight across the court and track, dividing the entire space into two halves.

TEAMS. — A variable number of players, from twelve to twenty-four, is divided into two teams. Half of each team are attackers and stand in the track on one side; the other half are defenders or guards and stand in the opposite court semi-circle. They are irregularly placed. Each player must remain in his own track or court, but may move freely within its limits.

GAME. — The object of the game is to hit the center post, one point being scored for each hit. The game is started by a bounce on the crossline between two defending players, who pass the ball to their own attackers. The opposing defenders try to intercept it, but may not enter the goal circle. The ball is played by throwing or passing with one or both hands. It may also be batted with the open hand (not the closed fist), bounced (once), or rolled, but it may not be kicked, nor may a player run with it.

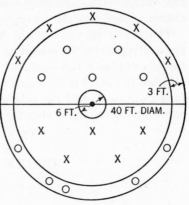

CIRCLE PILLAR BALL

When the ball goes out of bounds, it is returned by the nearest player of the opposite team, who then throws it from the point where it is recovered to a guard of his own team. A player may not tackle another player or touch the ball while it is in the hands of another player.

SCORE. — One point is scored for each hit of the goal post. The game may be played in timed halves, with the higher score winning at the end, or it may be played in one fifteen-minute period.

By courtesy of the National Council of Girls' Clubs, London.

CIRCLE STRIDE–BALL

10 to 30 or more players   *Intermediate grades to*
Playground; gymnasium   *senior high school*
Soccer football; basketball

All but one of the players form a circle, standing in stride position with feet touching those of the next players to make a barricade for the ball.

The odd player stands in the center and tries to throw the ball outside of the circle between the feet of the players. Those in the circle try to prevent the passage of the ball, using only their hands for this. This play is continued until the center player succeeds in sending the ball through the circle, when he changes places with the player between whose feet or on whose right side it passed out. If a circle player moves his feet in any way, he must change places with the center.

The center player will aid his object by using considerable finesse, appearing to intend sending the ball in one direction, turning suddenly and sending it in another, etc.

When the ball has been sent out of the circle, the players turn, facing outward, and the odd man tries to send it back inside according to the same rules.

CIRCLE ZIGZAG

(See *Zigzag Games.*)

CLOCK GOLF

2 or 4 players   *Junior to senior high school*

Clock Golf is a putting game, interesting to both adults and children. In addition it gives excellent practice in the critical art of putting for regular golf.

On a small section of level and closely cut turf is drawn a circle from twenty to twenty-five feet in diameter. Just outside of this, at intervals corresponding to the numbers on a clock face, are placed the Roman numerals one to twelve, the twelve and six being opposite to each other on one diameter, the three and nine at the ends of the other diameter, and the remaining figures in order between them. These numbers are available in ready-made apparatus, but may easily be constructed on disks that can be set in the ground. Inside the circle one putting hole is placed, consisting usually of a cup or can set in the ground to a distance of four to six inches. It should be punctured so as to drain and not hold water. The position of this hole should not be in the exact center of the field, but in one of the quarters, so that in putting there is practice at various angles. The only implements needed are a putter and a golf ball for each player.

The game is played by two or four players who compete either independently or in a foursome (with partners); but each plays his own ball. A foursome may also be played with one ball for each pair, the partners playing it alternately.

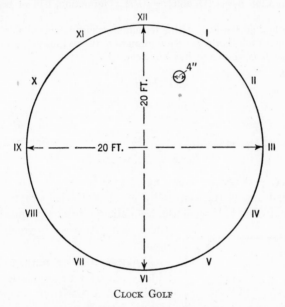

CLOCK GOLF

Each player places his ball on Number One of the clock and putts for the hole, taking as many strokes as necessary to make it. He then recovers his ball and does this from the two o'clock mark, and so on entirely around the clock. His object, as in golf, is to hole out each time with the fewest number of putts.

As in golf, there are two methods of scoring — by strokes or by holes. The most usual method is for each contestant to add the number of strokes necessary to make the hole in his complete round of the clock. The one having the fewest number wins. The second method is for each contestant to putt from each number of the clock, counting as his holes those made in the fewest strokes compared to his opponents. In this case the one who has the greatest number of holes at the end wins.

CLUB–BOWLS

Four forms of this game are given in this volume in alphabetic order. Two are in line formation and two in circle formation, as follows:

   1. **Line Club-Bowls** (Single). — (Relay formation, one club bowled over.)
   2. **Line Club-Bowls** (Double). — (Relay formation, ball or bag bowled between two clubs.)
   3. **Circle Club-Bowls.** — (Ring formation, clubs outside of ring.)
   4. **Center Club-Bowls.** — (Ring formation, three clubs in center.)
   See also *Battle-Ball* and *Bombardment.*

CORNERBALL

(See also *Double Cornerball.*)

10 to 30 or more players   *Intermediate grades to*
Playground; gymnasium   *junior high school*
                    Basketball; volleyball

COURT. — A space measuring at least twenty-five by thirty feet is divided across the center by a straight line. In the further corners of each half so made, a small square goal is marked out, there being two such goals in each court.

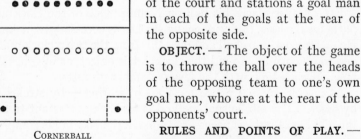

CORNERBALL

PLAYERS. — The players are divided into two even teams, each of which takes position on one side of the court and stations a goal man in each of the goals at the rear of the opposite side.

OBJECT. — The object of the game is to throw the ball over the heads of the opposing team to one's own goal men, who are at the rear of the opponents' court.

RULES AND POINTS OF PLAY. — The players on each side are not bound to any special territory within their own court, but will naturally see that each of the goals at their rear is well protected, and will try to intercept the ball before it can reach these goals. They will also, of course, try to throw the ball **over** the opposing team to their own goal men in the opposite court. No player may cross the line which divides the two halves of the ground. The goal men may not step outside of their goals. Any ball caught in this way fails to score. No opponent may step inside of a goal. When a goal man catches a ball, he must at once throw it back, trying of course to get it to his own team over the heads of the opponents, who try to intercept it.

SCORE. — Every ball caught by a goal man scores one for the throwing team. The side first scoring twenty points wins the game.

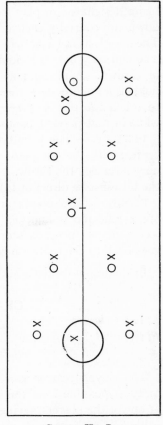

COUPLE HIT-PIN

COUPLE HIT–PIN

18 to 30 players   Intermediate
Playground   to junior high

Basketball or soccer ball;
2 bowling pins or Indian clubs

This is a good game to introduce players to the basketball type of play, in which each player has a guard from the opposite team. It is distinctive in the lengthwise division of the court.

COURT. — A line sixty feet long is drawn down the center of the court. On this, six feet from either end, is drawn a circle six feet in diameter, one as a goal for each team. The center line thus extends about six feet beyond each circle. An Indian club or bowling pin is set up in each circle.

TEAMS. — The players are divided into two teams. A pin-guard is assigned from each team to guard the pin set up in its circle. No one else may enter the circle.

The remaining players are arranged equally on each side of the dividing line in opposing pairs. At no time may a player cross to the other side.

GAME. — The object of the game is to knock down the opponents' club or pin with the ball. The game is started by a bounce midway on the center line by the umpire, two players being designated to play for it. The ball is then passed up or down the court by each team, playing for the opponents' club. The play is as in basketball and must be entirely with the hands. The ball may not be kicked, but may be dribbled (up or down) or thrown. A player may not walk or run with the ball, nor hold it for more than three seconds. Guards are not allowed to touch the players whom they guard, nor to touch the ball while in that player's hands.

PENALTY. — The penalty for a foul is a free throw from the center, with the pin-guard standing outside his circle. No one may intercept the throw. To score from such a penalty-throw, the hit must be direct or from a single bounce inside the circle.

SCORE. — Two points are scored for a team each time the opponents' pin is knocked over. If a guard knocks down his own pin, one point is scored for the opponents, and the ball goes back to the center to be again put in play.

By courtesy of the National Council of Girls' Clubs, London.

CRACKABOUT

10 to 60 players   *Primary to*
Playground; gymnasium   *junior high*
Soft handsizeball

The players scatter over the playground, trying to get as far away as possible from the one who has the ball. He throws it at one of the players, trying to hit him with it, at the same time calling "Crackabout!" All of the players make a rush for the ball, the one who succeeds in getting it being the next thrower. The other players scatter immediately that one has secured it, the ball man at once throwing at some other player, naturally trying to hit the nearest. As soon as the players hear his call of "Crackabout!" they rush together again in the direction of the ball to try and secure it, and so on indefinitely. The game is thus a rapid succession of running away from the ball man and scrimmages to secure the ball. It is one of the strenuous and popular games enjoyed by boys of almost any age, and affords some lively exercise and sport in a few minutes.

CROQUET

2 or 4 players   *Juniors; adults*
Grass lawn, or dirt court   *Croquet set*

Formerly one of the most popular of lawn games, croquet had a period of neglect except by the most expert players; but it is again in favor. It is best played on a closely clipped grass lawn, but may also be played on bare earth, the essential in either case being a level surface.

A CROQUET SET consists of two stakes, nine or ten arches (also called wickets or hoops), and from four to six balls and mallets. A stake is one and one-quarter inches in diameter, pointed at the lower end so that it may be driven into the ground and stand firmly. It should rise from one and one-half to eighteen inches above the surface. Arches are of firm wire with a spread of four to eight inches and are long enough to set firmly in the ground and leave a clearance of eight to ten inches to the top of the arch. Balls are of wood or hard rubber, measure from three and three-eighths to four inches in diameter and are colored for

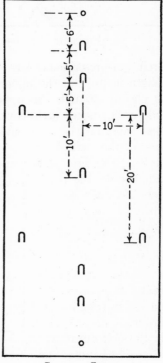

CROQUET COURT

identification; mallets bear a matching color. Markers to attach to the arch next to be played are used in the best games.

THE SIZE OF COURTS varies. Good dimensions are fifty-two feet between stakes, and other dimensions as shown in the diagram. The center arch may be omitted; or it may be single, facing the same way as the end arches; or it may be a double

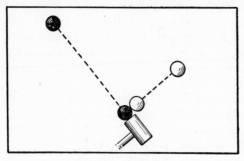

CROQUET; SPLIT-SHOT

arch made of two arches placed one over the other at right angles, requiring a diagonal shot, or eighteen inches apart facing crosswise of the court.

THE GAME consists in each player driving his own ball with his mallet through the arches in prescribed order. Each ball is started at one mallet's length in front of the upper or "home" stake, and from there is played through the upper two arches, to the upper right side arch, center arch, lower right side, two lower arches and then must hit the lower stake, the ball remaining where it then lies for the next shot; the play is then reversed to the home stake. The first player to hit the latter wins the game, or, in a foursome, the part-ners win whose second player is first to get back.

Each player has one shot at the start and thereafter one shot for each arch properly passed and one for the lower stake. A ball is through an arch if a mallet-handle can

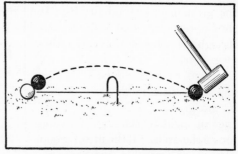

CROQUET; JUMP SHOT

contact the arch on the driving side without touching the ball. A ball hitting an opponent's ball earns two shots. A ball must be played from where it lies, except that balls going beyond the court are returned to the nearest point on the edge and played from there.

Much of the sport of the game is in the play on opponent's ball. Having hit this with his own ball, a player may use the two strokes to which he is entitled to make his own arch; or, he may use one stroke to send the opposing ball to a safe distance and the other for his own arch; or, he may send the opponent's ball to where he can use it again after going through his own arch. Expert players can sometimes accomplish both of these plays with one stroke, called a "split-shot," which sends the two balls in different directions or different distances. Having hit an opponent's ball with his own, a player may lift his own ball by hand and place it anywhere around the other ball in contact with it, for a split-shot; or, having so placed his ball, he may "croquet" the adversary; that is put his foot on his own ball to hold it in place while he delivers a stroke that sends the victim to a distance.

"CROQUET" SHOT

A partner's ball may also be played on and helped in all of these ways. The same ball may not be played on twice without the attacker having made an arch between. There is also a "jump shot" which lofts the ball over an arch or another ball. In a foursome partners do not play in succession: each alternates with an opponent.

The game of croquet here described is one of the best for general use and for beginning players. "Modern Croquet" is the title of a more highly developed game, that has spread widely from the Brooklyn and other New York clubs where it originated, and where the hard rubber ball was evolved. Five-inch arches, long-handled heavy mallets, longer arch distances, and different playing rules (e.g., no "split-shots" allowed) make a highly skillful game. Roque is another admirable and strictly formulated game of croquet, and there is a British Croquet which differs from all of these in layout of court and long, skillful shots.

Rules for all of these games are published in the volume *Lawn Sports*, in Spalding's Athletic Library.

CROSSBALL

24 to 80 players   *Junior to*
Gymnasium; playground   *senior high school*
            Volleyball and nets

This game engages an extremely large number of players. Developed through the doubling up of gymnasium classes, it aroused an interest great enough to displace Basketball in in-

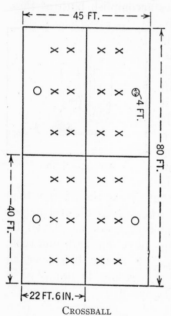

CROSSBALL

tramurals. The game is a variation of Volleyball, and Volleyball rules apply except as noted below.

COURT. — A floor, forty-five by eighty feet, is divided into four courts with Volleyball nets placed at right angles. A circle four feet in diameter, for serving the ball, is drawn in each court according to the diagram.

The players are divided into four equal teams of from six to twenty each, so that as many as eighty players may be taken care of at once.

THE GAME is started by a player, standing within his serving circle and serving the ball into any one of the three opposing courts. The serve is like the Volleyball serve. The server may have three tries but the ball must be played over the net on the third hit without touching the net. The server may be assisted by one of his players on the serve; that is, there may be one relay.

Any player may return the ball on a volley to any of the other courts. The game is very deceptive, as no one knows just where the ball will go; it may start for one court and land in another, either intentionally or otherwise, so that players even in the farthest corners must be alert. It is a failure if the ball is allowed to touch the floor.

SCORE. — The game is purely defensive, the team winning which has the lowest score. The game ends when any team has scored ten points.

A point is scored against a team (*i.e.* added to its score), whenever one of its players (1) volleys the ball into the net, or (2) out of bounds, or (3) allows it to bounce on the floor.

The teams rotate courts after each game until each team has played in each court. Four games thus compose a match. The game may also be played on a time basis; that is, five minutes in each court.

For any other rules of play follow Volleyball.

This game was devised by Mr. Robert E. Bassett and Mr. Wilbur J. Fisher at the Knoxville Junior High School, Pittsburgh, Pennsylvania, and is here reproduced by courtesy of the authors and of *The Journal of Health and Physical Education*, in which it first appeared.

CURTAIN BALL

10 to 100 players   *Intermediate*
Gymnasium; playground   *to junior high*
      Basketball; volleyball

This is one of the best recreative ball games and is adaptable to many conditions. For instance, where a curtain cannot be conveniently hung, the game may be played over a high fence or hedge.

The game consists in throwing a ball backward and forward over a curtain which conceals the opposing players from each other. For a very large number of players, more than one ball may be used.

COURT. — No outside boundaries are necessary for this game. The ground should be divided into two approximately equal parts by an opaque curtain eight feet in height, strung on a rope or wire carried across from side supports. This should touch the ground, so that there is no means of seeing the position of the opposing players on the other side. As stated above, the game may be played across a high fence or hedge instead of over a curtain.

PLAYERS. — The players are divided into two teams of equal number. There is no regular formation or disposition of the players over the ground. Each team should select an umpire, whose duty it is to stand at one end of the curtain on the opponents' side, where he can watch the opponents and keep score.

RULES. — The ball is thrown back and forth from one side to the other over the curtain, and should be caught before it can touch the floor. Players will try to deceive their opponents as to the point where the ball is to cross the curtain, and the more rapid the play is, the more alert the players will have to be. The great sport of the game consists in the unexpectedness with which the ball may appear at any given point.

SCORE. — Opponents score one point whenever the ball touches the ground. The side wins which first scores twenty-one points.

This game was originated by Dr. Dudley A. Sargent.

DEAD–BALL

10 to 60 players   *Intermediates*
Playground; schoolroom   *Gas ball; beanbags*

This game may be played with from one to three balls or beanbags. If with balls, a light gas ball is preferable. The players stand in the aisles or between the seats and desks of the schoolroom, or should be scattered around the playground.

The leader puts the balls in play by tossing them one at a time upward, so they will land in different directions in the room. The players, as opportunity avails, without leaving their places on the floor, try to catch a ball and toss it in the same way to some other player. It is not permissible to throw the ball at another player; it must always be tossed in the air. Any player who does not catch the ball, but instead is touched by it, is "dead" (out of the game), and must retire. Each player tosses the ball upward in some new direction as soon as he receives it. This play continues until only one player remains, who is considered the winner.

DECK HOCKEY

12 to 20 players   *Senior high*
Gymnasium   *to adult*
            Deck-tennis ring; wooden wands

This is a fast and exciting game popular with both boys and girls. One deck-tennis ring is needed and each player has a gymnasium wand of wood.

COURT. — A gymnasium floor of any size may be used, the boundaries being the end and side lines of the basketball court. Where two courts are laid out side by side, two games may be played at the same time. At each end of the court two Indian clubs are set up sixteen feet apart for a goal.

TEAMS. — Teams consist of from six to ten players each, including a goal tender, all placed as in Field Hockey.

OBJECT. — To score a goal by snapping the ring through it.

METHOD OF PLAY. — The game is started by facing-off as in hockey; that is, the referee slides the ring out into mid court between the wands of the two centers and they in turn try to get possession of it or pass it to a teammate.

The ring is advanced by players running about the floor with the wand inserted in the ring, passing the latter to teammates who are free. Each player must keep his wand in contact with the floor at all times whether on offense or defense. When passing the ring to a teammate, or shooting for goal, or advancing the ring to a scoring position, the player must keep the wand inside of the ring. Players who lift the ring from the floor, or lift the wand above the ankles, lose possession of the ring to the opponents, out of bounds.

The ring may be passed only to a teammate who is even with the player or behind him. When within fifteen feet of the opposing goal (the basketball foul line), off-sides do not exist.

Tackling, roughing, tripping, or holding are not allowed, and players using such tactics are suspended from the game for one minute.

The defensive team may play either a man-to-man defense or a zone defense.

Players may intercept passes with their feet to stop the ring in its movement across the floor.

All players on a team are eligible to score goals. In shooting the ring for goal or passing to a teammate, the best method is to give a quick snap of the wrist and let the ring slide across the floor. Many fundamentals of basketball play may be used, such as pivots and reverses.

If two players of opposing sides have their wands inside of the ring at the same time and one of these players does not gain possession of it in ten seconds (a count of ten), the referee blows the whistle to stop play. Play is resumed when the referee slides the ring to these two players for a face-off.

SCORE. — One point is scored for a team each time the ring is put through the opponents' goal. The game is played in quarters of five minutes each.

This game was devised by Mr. Lester G. Bursey, Director of Physical Education, Cooperstown (New York) High School, and is here given by courtesy of the author, and of *The Journal of Health and Physical Education*, in which the game first appeared. Mr. Bursey says of the game that "when mastered it is as fast a floor game as basketball and excellent for 'pepping up' a basketball team which has gone 'stale.'"

DECK TENNIS

2 or 4 players　　　　　　　　　　　　　　*Intermediate grades*
Ship-deck; playground; gymnasium　　　　　　　　　*to adult*
Deck-tennis ring

COURT. — The outside lines of the court measure eighteen by forty feet. An alley is made on each side by drawing a line parallel to each side line, three feet inward. A net is stretched across the center of the court, the posts outside the side lines; the net is four feet high where it is fastened to the posts. Unlike major net games, this court has a foul line drawn entirely across the court, on each side of the net, and three feet from it. The space between the two foul lines is a "dead" space, the ring being considered dead if it falls within it. The space between each foul line and its baseline is divided into two courts by a line drawn down the center.

RING. — In many respects the game is played like Lawn Tennis, but played with a ring instead of a ball. There is an official ring of sponge-rubber, or inflated rubber; or the game may be played with a ring of one-half inch manila rope. The ring must be six inches in diameter.

This is played by an underhand or horizontal toss back and forth across the net, to be caught in the hand and returned without touching the ground.

PLAYERS. — The game is played by one or two players on each side, that is, in singles or doubles, as in Tennis.

START. — The ring is put in play by a serve. In singles the server stands anywhere behind his baseline, and tosses the ring toward any part of his opponent's court except the side alleys. The serve consists of a toss that does not loft the ring more than six inches. The server has but one try and must deliver the

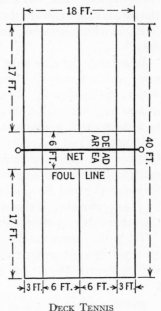

DECK TENNIS

ring without a feint. A ring hitting the net is dead if it falls between the foul lines, and the service then passes to the opponents. A server continues to serve so long as his serve or return is good.

In doubles (two players on a side), the first server stands as in tennis behind his right-hand court and serves the ring into the diagonally opposite court, his partner standing in his own left-hand court. A good serve is followed by another by the same server, but from behind his left-hand court, his partner changing to the right side. This alternation of courts is continued until the server loses his service. He then becomes receiver, standing in his right-hand court. When the service returns to his side, his partner becomes server.

RETURN. — Opponents try to catch and return the ring without allowing it to touch the ground. One hand only may be used, the usual play being to make the catch and return with the same hand. It is permissible to catch the ring against the body, but even then only with one hand. The toss is always an underhand or (horizontal) movement and must always be with the elbow below the shoulder. The only exception to this mode of tossing is when the ring is caught above the shoulder, when the toss may be made from the same elevation, and is then made by dropping the wrist only.

In a catch the ring must be tossed immediately and from the same spot where it was caught. It may not be held nor may a step be taken with it. It may not be batted, juggled, or played in any way but with a toss as here described. The catch must be a clean catch in one motion, no fumbling or juggling.

SCORE. — The server, or serving side, is the only one to score. One point is scored on each failure of the opponents to properly catch or return the ring. A ring falling within the dead area (between the foul lines) scores one point for the server if thrown by the opponents; if thrown by the server, he loses the serve to the other side. A ring falling on the lines is still in play.

The game consists of fifteen points. In case of a tie at *fourteen all*, a player must secure two points in succession to win. Players change courts after each game. The match is the best two games out of three.

While originated as a sport for ship decks, this game is so adaptable that it is used under many other conditions both indoors and out, retaining the name, rules, and equipment of Deck Tennis. Mr. C. F. Schaffer is credited with having evolved the game.

DODGEBALL

This is one of the most popular gymnasium or playground games. It is here described first for an informal game; then in three forms for an athletic contest, the latter as developed by Mr. William A. Stecher; and lastly, for use in the schoolroom. Forms II, III, and IV are for match games. The games will be found in alphabetic order as indicated by their titles.

I. Dodgeball (informal; players not in teams).
II. Circle Dodgeball (one team forming a circle, the other team standing within).
III. Double Dodgeball (two teams in a three-court field).
IV. Progressive Dodgeball (three teams in a three-court field, changing courts at the end of each inning).
V. Schoolroom Dodgeball.

DODGEBALL

(Informal)

(See list of Dodgeball games.)

10 to 60 players
Playground; gymnasium

Primary grades
to adult

Basketball; soft handsizeball

This game is a very popular gymnasium or playground game. An informal mode of play is here described. For match games between competing teams more strict athletic procedure is necessary, and three such forms of the game are given as noted above.

The players are divided into two even groups. One group forms a circle (this need not be marked on the ground). The larger the circle the more sport in the game. The other group stands within the circle, scattered irregularly. The object of the game is for the circle men to hit the center men with a basketball, the center men dodging to evade this. They may jump, stoop, or resort to any means of dodging except leaving the ring. Any player hit on any part of his person at once joins the circle men. The last player to remain in the center is considered the winner. The groups as originally constituted then change places for the next game, the center men becoming circle players and the circle men going to the center.

There is no retaliatory play of the ball by the center players; they merely dodge. The ball is returned to the circle either by a toss from a center man or by a circle man stepping in for it if it should not roll or bounce within reach. When two center men are hit by one throw of the ball, only the first one hit leaves the center.

DOUBLE DODGEBALL

20 to 60 players
Playground; gymnasium

Intermediate
to adults

Basketball; soft handsizeball

The game is played by two opposing teams in a three-court field, instead of by three teams in such a field as in Progressive Dodgeball. One team takes its place in the center court, and the opposing team is equally divided, one half going to each of the end courts. The teams must be of equal numbers, and for match games have sixteen players on each.

The game is played in two halves of ten minutes or less each. At the end of the first half the teams change courts.

The rules for play are exactly the same as for Progressive Dodgeball. The main difference in the games is in the smaller number of opponents in the end courts.

This game was devised by Mr. William A. Stecher.

DOUBLE CORNERBALL

14 to 100 players
Gymnasium; playground

Senior high
school

2 basketballs

This game is one of the comparatively few in which a large number of players may be kept actively engaged at the same time. The game was developed by Miss Caroline M. Wollaston of New York City, through whose kindness it is here given. There are practically two games going on at once, in which each player participates in rotation.

COURT. — The court for this game should be outlined in a square measuring about forty by forty feet. In each corner is marked a small goal, the two goals at one end belonging to one team, say the Blues, and the two goals at the other end belonging to the opposing, or Red, team. Near the center are marked two small circular goals for the throwers of the different teams. The thrower for the Red team stands in the center goal farthest removed from the Red corners; the thrower for the Blue team in the goal farthest removed from the Blue corners.

Two basketballs are needed for the game.

TEAMS. — Any number of players, from fourteen to one hundred, may play. These are divided into two teams. While it is advisable to have the two teams even in numbers, an odd player may be assigned to either team.

Each team chooses its own captain. Each captain selects two goalkeepers, players who can jump and catch well being best for this position. These two goalkeepers are assigned to goals at the same end of the ground, each being guarded by guards from the opposite team. If desired, a halt may be called during the game, and the goalkeepers changed for others designated by the captain. This is sometimes desirable to rest players filling this arduous position, and sometimes for the purpose of distributing among the players opportunities for this kind of play.

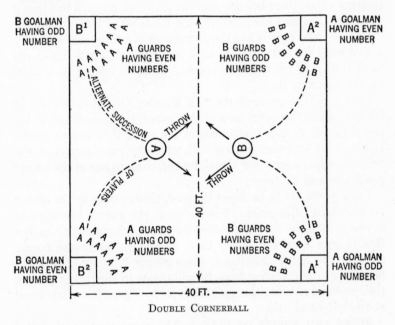

DOUBLE CORNERBALL

The remaining players are guards, and are divided by the captain into two teams, one for each of the opponents' corner goals. The following method has been found to work quickly and well for this purpose : The captain lines up his players and numbers them, taking any number that he chooses for himself. Those having odd numbers are sent to guard one goal, and those having even numbers to guard the other goal. Each guard should remember well his number, as there is a constant rotation of players according to number.

OBJECTS OF GAME. — The first object of the game is for a thrower on the center base to throw a ball to one of the corner goal men of his own team; each ball so caught by the goalkeeper scores. One very distinctive feature of this game is the fact that each guard becomes, in turn, thrower for his team.

Another object of the game is for the guards to prevent the corner goal men from catching the ball. This is not only for defensive play, to prevent the opponents from scoring, but has a positive value, there being a separate guard score, each ball that a guard catches and holds scoring for his team. This scoring for catches by the guards has the advantage of calling for especially active work from the guards, with much jumping in it, and leads to skillful play for catching the ball so as to hold it instead of merely touching it.

START. — The game starts with Number One of each team in his respective throwing base in the center, the guards being disposed in one or two ranks around the goals they are to guard. Each center baseman holds a ball, which he puts in play at the referee's whistle, or other signal, by throwing to one of the corner goalkeepers of his team.

Each guard, as he becomes thrower, throws only to the corner on his side of the court. For instance, the guards bearing odd numbers being on the right side of the court, when player Number One throws from the center base, he will throw to the corner man on the right. Similarly, when player Number Two takes his turn at the throwing base, he will throw to the corner goal on the left-hand side of the court, as his party of guards are stationed at the left-hand side.

RULES AND POINTS OF PLAY. — The game opens with guard Number One in the center base, ready to throw the ball to the corner. Each thrower has but one throw at a turn, whether it is successful or not. Immediately that a thrower has tossed the ball, he steps back to his place among the guards, and the guard bearing the next number steps into the throwing base. The players must keep their own watch for turns to do this, and each should therefore observe at the opening of the game which guard bears the number next before his. This will be a player in the opposite division of guards of his team, as the odd numbers are guarding one corner and the even numbers another.

When each player of a team has thrown from a center base, the numbers begin over again in regular rotation. Thus, if Number Sixteen is the last thrower, Number One follows him.

Whoever catches a ball thrown to a corner, whether it be the corner goalkeeper or one of the guards surrounding him, throws the ball immediately back to the center base, supposedly to the next player, who should have stepped at once to the base when the previous thrower left it. Should this next player not have reached the center base in time to catch the ball, he picks up the ball and throws it to the proper goalkeeper; but it behooves a player to be at the center base in time to catch a ball returned from a corner, because every such catch scores.

A ball caught on the center base is, of course, a return ball from the corner to which a predecessor threw it, and must be a fair throw, whether sent by one of the opponents' guards or his own goalkeeper.

It may make clearer the rotation of the play to illustrate as follows: The game opens with Number One ready on the center base belonging to his team. His group of guards, that is, those bearing the odd numbers, are guarding the corner behind him on the right-hand side of the court. He therefore throws the ball on the referee's signal to the corner goalkeeper for his team at the opposite end of the court on the right-hand side. Immediately that he has thrown the ball, he steps back among his group of guards bearing the odd numbers, and Number Two of his team, who belongs to the group of guards on the left-hand side of the court, steps forward at once to the center base. Meanwhile, the ball may have been caught by the goalkeeper to whom it was thrown, or by one of the guards surrounding him. It is at once tossed back to the center base from which it came, and Number Two guard should be there to catch it.

Number Two then throws the ball to the goalkeeper for his team on the left-hand side of the court. Whoever catches it at once throws it back to the same throwing base, and Number Three should be there to receive it, Number Two having returned to the ranks of his guards. So the game goes on, the guards each taking a turn at the throwing base, and each throwing the ball to the corner goalkeeper on his side of the court.

Meanwhile, the same sort of game is being played by the

opposite team, two balls being in play at once, and each guard taking part in each game for each team, according as he is guard around an opponent's corner goal or a thrower from the center base to his own goal men.

Each goalkeeper and thrower must keep one foot in his goal or base. It is thus permissible for a goalkeeper to step out of his goal with one foot, or lean far out of the goal to catch the ball. Of course the best kind of throw to a goalkeeper is a high curved ball that will go over the heads of the guards and fall within his goal. No guard may step within the goal he guards.

Very alert and rapid play is needed to make this game a success. As one team (Blues) may play faster than the other (Reds), it is not necessary that Number Six of the Red team and Number Six of the Blue team, for example, should be on the center throwing bases at the same time. The two games go on independently of each other.

FOULS. — The overstepping of boundaries in ways not allowed by the rules scores one for the opponents.

SCORE. — A goalkeeper scores one point for his team every time that he catches a ball which has not been touched by one of the guards around his goal. A ball caught by a goalkeeper after being touched by a guard does not score.

In addition to the score made by goalkeepers, a guards' score is kept, each player counting the number of balls he catches and holds, no matter where he is standing, whether in his position as guard or in the center base from which he is to be thrower. Such a catch by a guard scores one point, the guards reporting their points at the end of the game. Touching the ball does not score under any circumstances. It must be caught and held.

The score for the game for either side is the sum of all of the balls caught, according to the above rules, by the goalkeepers and guards on that side. The game is usually played on time limits of from twenty to forty minutes.

For experienced players, scoring by guards may be omitted if desired. The particular object of this feature is to encourage guards to expert work in catching the ball, instead of merely interfering.

DRIVE–BALL

10 to 30 players   *Intermediate*
Playground; gymnasium   *to senior high*
                        Basketball; volleyball

This is one of the most interesting games for players beginning to care for teamwork.

COURT. — A court measuring from thirty to fifty feet in length by twenty to thirty in width is divided into two equal parts, forming two courts, each of which should be a little wider than it is long. A goal about two by four feet is marked in the center rear of each court, within the boundary lines. It facilitates the game if the end of each court may be a wall or fence, and thus make a backstop behind the goal.

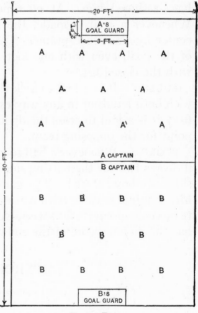

DRIVE-BALL

Each court has bases marked at even distances over its surface, whereon the different players stand. These may be marked simply as a cross for a footmark, or a small circle or square. There is no particular arrangement for these, the only object being to scatter the players, no mass play being allowed in the game.

PLAYERS. — The players, of no stipulated number, are divided into two equal teams. Each team appoints a captain, who stands at the middle of the dividing line and is responsible for the discipline of his team; a goal guard, whose duty it is to keep the ball from the goal and who stands in the goal; and from six to twelve players, each assigned a certain spot marked as his territory and from which he may not move more than two feet.

OBJECT OF GAME. — The object of the game is to throw the ball into the opponents' goal.

START. — The ball is put in play by being placed on the ground at the center of the dividing line between the two captains. At a signal from an umpire, each captain hits the ball with his fist. The ball is thereafter kept moving rapidly back and forth from one court to the other, hit always with the fist. After being caught or otherwise stopped, it should be bounced or thrown from one hand and batted with the fist.

RULES. — No player may move more than two feet from the base assigned him. At no time may players do mass work. Whenever a goal is made, the ball is again started from the center by the two captains. The goal guard may not step out of the goal, even with one foot. The ball must always be hit with the closed fist.

FOULS. — It is a foul to kick the ball; to hold it; to throw it with both hands or in any way except by batting with the closed fist; it is a foul to cross the dividing line. Each foul scores one point for the opposing team.

SCORE. — Whenever a ball touches the ground inside of a goal, it scores two for the batting side. Fouls count for the opposing side, as above stated. The game is played in three rounds of fifteen minutes each, with a rest of five minutes between. The teams change courts for successive rounds. The team wins which has the highest score at the end of the third round.

EMPEROR BALL

(See *Captain Ball — IV.*)

ENDBALL

24 to 40 players　　　　　　　　　　　　　　*Intermediate*
Playground; gymnasium　　　　　　　　　　*to junior high*
　　　　　　　　　　Basketball

COURT. — This is played on a court measuring at least thirty by thirty feet, though a larger area is desirable. This space is divided across the center and at either end a narrow goal strip, three feet wide, is drawn by a second line within and parallel to the end line.

TEAMS number from twelve to twenty each; one third of each team are basemen and stand within the goal area; the remainder are fielders (guards) and stand on the side of the field opposite their basemen, in rows parallel to the center line.   Players should

ENDBALL

be numbered in consecutive order from the right-hand forward fielder to the left-hand baseman, and after each goal made the scoring team should rotate one place, so that in the course of the game each player will probably play in each position.

THE OBJECT OF THE GAME is for the fieldmen on one side to throw the ball over the heads of the fieldmen on the opposite side to reach their own basemen.   Each ball so caught by a baseman who has both feet within the base, or goal area, scores one point for the side catching it.   The baseman may either throw it at once over the heads of his opponents to his own fieldmen on the opposite side of the court, or it may be thrown first from baseman to baseman, seeking a better opportunity for the long throw.

The object of the intervening fieldmen or guards is, of course, to intercept the ball before it can reach the opposing basemen at their rear, and to throw it to their own basemen at the rear of the opposite court over the heads of the intervening opponents.

START. — The game is started by the referee who tosses the ball between two opposing guards at the center of the field; each of the latter tries to catch it, the one whose hands touch it first being the possessor of the ball. After the start the ball remains continuously in play from any point where it may be.

OUT-OF-BOUNDS. — If the ball goes out of bounds over the end or side lines, the nearest baseman or fieldman, as the case may be, retrieves it and throws it to his nearest teammate.

FOULS. — Fieldmen may not step over the division line nor over any other lines except to recover the ball.

No player may walk or run with or hold the ball; that is, he may not take more than one step with it and must throw it within five seconds after catching it.

No player may touch a ball in the hands of another player.

It is a foul to hold or push another player.

PENALTY. — One point is scored by the opponents for any foul, and the ball is immediately put in play by the nearest opponent.

SCORE. — The game is played in halves of ten minutes each. Teams change sides at the end of the first half, keeping their respective positions in the new court.

One point is scored by a team for each catch of the ball by one of its basemen who has both feet within the goal area. One point is scored for each foul by the opponents.

FIELD HOCKEY

22 players *Senior high school to adult*

GENERAL DESCRIPTION. — Field Hockey is played on a large turf field, having a goal at each end. Each half of the field is defended by a team of eleven players. The ball, about the size of a baseball, is rolled over the ground with a curved stick, not kicked nor played by the hand. A goal is scored each time a team puts the ball through the opponents' goal with a shot made from within the striking circle — an area which is marked in front of each goal. The game is played in two halves.

EQUIPMENT. — The ball is a regulation hockey ball (about nine inches in circumference), covered with white leather, the inner construction being of cork and twine.

Sticks for Field Hockey are made mainly of wood and may not weigh more than twenty-three ounces. The handle is rounded, but the head or blade has the left-hand side flat and the reverse convex. A four-inch rubber ring may be used on the stick to protect the hands, but is included in the weight.

Shoes, boots, or shin-guards are advisable for protection, and each team should wear a distinctive color.

FIELD. — The game is usually played on a level turf field; the fewer inequalities in the surface, the better the game. The turf should have frequent cutting and rolling. The length of a hockey field is one hundred yards and its width from fifty to sixty yards.

For juniors, minimum measurements may be eighty-five by forty-five yards, but then the twenty-five-yard line, five-yard line, striking circle, and goal, all retain the same measurements as on the larger field.

The boundaries are marked in white — the longer lines called *side lines*, and those connecting them at the end, *goal lines*. Flags are placed at the four corners and outside the cross lines, one yard beyond the side lines.

The field is divided into halves by a transverse line, and each half has another transverse line twenty-five yards from its goal line, called the twenty-five-yard line. A spot is marked in the exact center of the field on the halfway line for the "bully-off."

A dotted line is marked parallel with the side lines and five yards within them. This is called the five-yard line and, though not required by official rules, assists very much in carrying out the regulations of the game.

Goals. — In the center of each goal line is erected a goal made of posts seven feet high, placed four yards apart, inside measurement. These are connected by a crossbar. Neither crossbar nor uprights may extend beyond the point where they intersect.

Goal Net. — Each goal should be fitted with a net to catch the ball and assist in determining whether or not the goal has been made. The net is cubical in shape, the rear being from four to six feet back of the goal.

Striking Circle. — In front of each goal is an area enclosed by a line called the "striking circle." To score, a ball going through the goal must have been hit from within this circle.

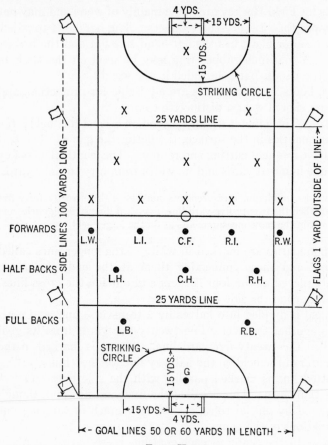

FIELD HOCKEY

The striking circle is made by drawing, fifteen yards in front of each goal, a line four yards long and parallel with the goal lines. Each end of this line is then joined to the goal line with a quarter circle for which the goal post on that side is the center (fifteen-yard radius).

TEAMS. — There are two teams of eleven players each, — five forwards, three halfbacks, two fullbacks, and one goalkeeper.

The line-up of the players of each team at the opening of the game is usually, though not invariably, as follows:

Left Wing, Left Inside, Center Forward, Right Inside, Right Wing,
Left Halfback, Center Halfback, Right Halfback,
Left Fullback Right Fullback
Goalkeeper

The players take these positions whenever the ball is bullied-off from the center of the field.

THE GAME. — The captains toss a coin for choice of goals. Goals are changed for the second half of the game.

BULLY-OFF. — The ball is put in play by a "bully-off." This is done by two players, one from each team (usually center forwards), who stand squarely facing the side lines with the ball between them; each touches the ground with his stick on his own side of the ball, then hits his opponent's stick above the ball, repeating these two movements alternately three times in succession; after which, each of the two players tries to hit the ball toward his opponent's territory. Every other player of a team must be between the ball and his own goal, and not nearer to the ball than three yards.

The ball is thus bullied-off at the center of the field at the beginning of each half and after each goal scored. The bully-off is also given as a penalty for certain fouls at the spot where the foul occurred.

For failure to observe any of the rules connected with it, a bully-off must be repeated.

OUT OF BOUNDS. — After being "in touch" (going out of bounds over the side lines) the ball is put in play by what is called a "roll-in." It must be entirely over the line to be considered out of bounds.

For the roll-in, a player of the opposing side to the one that sent it out rolls the ball in by hand along the ground (not thrown or bounced) from the point at which it crossed the line; it may be sent in any direction. This player must stand with both feet and stick beyond the side line, and may not touch the ball again until it has been touched or hit by another player.

A ball sent out of bounds behind the goal line, not between the goal posts, by the attacking or defending team, is bullied-off, or awarded a penalty bully, as the umpire may decide.

METHODS OF PLAYING THE BALL. — A distinguishing feature of hockey is that it is played on the run and most strokes are calculated for that type of play. The ball is played wholly with the stick by passing, dribbling, or any of several other strokes. The ball is supposed to be rolled, and never kicked by any player except the goalkeeper, who may so defend his goal.

The ball may be stopped (but not otherwise played) by the foot, or by any other part of the person or apparel, if it is not bounced forward or is not to the advantage of the player; it may even be caught in the hand but must then be dropped at once perpendicularly (not thrown to a distance). The ball may not be kicked, picked up, thrown, or carried (except by the goalkeeper within the striking circle); nor may it be kept, or knocked back and forth in any way except with the stick.

PASSING. — The play consists largely of passes from one member of a team to another. Short passes are far more frequent and safer than long ones. A player may receive and return a pass on the run without stopping the ball; or he may stop the ball (as with stick or foot), and then hit it. The ball may not be undercut except in the scoop stroke, when that is permissible to surmount an obstacle. A ball being played between opponents may be intercepted in a pass.

The main technique of playing the ball and a list of games for training Field Hockey skills are given in the section on *Balls and How to Play Them.*

RULES FOR PLAYERS. — No personal interference is allowed, either kicking, tripping, charging, body-checking, or obstructing a player in any way. A player may not run between an opponent and the ball.

OFFSIDE PLAY. — This is one of the most important points for players to understand. A player is offside and may not play the ball if he is nearer the opponents' goal line than the ball when it is hit or rolled in, unless at least three of the opponents are nearer their own goal line than himself. If he is offside when the ball is hit, he may not touch the ball or in any way interfere with any other player until the ball has been hit by a player of the opposite team. He is not offside in his own half of the field, nor may he be penalized for merely standing in an offside position. It is *playing* in that position that constitutes breach of rules.

RULES FOR THE STICK. — No part of a stick may be raised above the shoulder during any part of a hit, either at the beginning or at the end of the stroke. For this error the umpire or captain should at once call "Sticks!" and enforce the penalty.

It is not permissible to hit, strike, lift, hold, hook, or interfere in any way with an opponent's stick.

All hits or stops of the ball with the stick must be with its flat side, never with the rounded side.

The stick may be used to take the ball, but it must not trip or block the opponent. In tackling from the left, the stick must touch the ball before touching the opponent's person or stick.

No player without a stick in the hand may interfere in the game in any way.

PENALTIES FOR FOULS. — These are a free-hit, a corner, a penalty corner, or a penalty bully-off, and they vary for the same foul, according to whether it is committed within or without the striking circle or is made by the attacking or defending side.

Outside the Striking Circle. — For any foul by either team outside the striking circle, a free hit is awarded the opponents from the point where the foul occurred.

Inside the Striking Circle. — For a foul committed by the *attacking* team inside the striking circle, a free hit is awarded the defending team from any point inside the circle.

For a foul committed by the *defending* team within the striking circle, the attacking team is awarded a penalty corner. If the foul was intentional or made when a goal would probably have been scored, a penalty bully-off is given, on a spot three yards in front of the goal line.

Free-Hit. — For a free-hit, no other player than the striker may be within five yards of the spot where the hit is made. Any stroke but a "scoop" may be used. The striker may not touch the ball again until another player of either team has touched it. Should a striker miss the ball on a free-hit, he may repeat the stroke.

Corner (*"Long Corner"*). — A free-hit with the ball on either the side line or goal line, but three feet from the corner, all other players being at least five yards away.

Penalty Corner (*"Short Corner"*). — A penalty corner is a free-hit made from any point on the goal line within ten yards of the nearest goal post, at whichever side of the field the attacking team may choose.

No goal may be scored from a corner hit until the ball has been stopped by one of the attacking team, or has touched the person or stick of a player of the defending team. All players of the defending team must be behind their own goal line, and the attacking team must be outside the striking circle in the field of play.

A player making a corner hit may not play again until another player has played on the ball. Should the first stroke miss the ball, the player may hit again.

SCORE. — One point is scored for a team for each ball put through the opponents' goal below the bar from the front, by a hit made by the attacking team within the striking circle. A glance-off from the stick scores the same as a shot if the ball goes through the goal. To score a goal, a ball must go entirely over the line.

Should a goal post be displaced, the umpire may award a goal if in his judgment the ball passed within what would have been the goal boundaries.

The ball is bullied-off at the center of the field after each goal is scored and at the beginning of the second half.

The game is *played in two halves* of thirty minutes each, with a rest between. For juniors, halves may be fifteen, twenty, or twenty-five minutes in length. Quarters are not officially authorized.

OFFICIALS. — Two umpires, two scorers, and two timekeepers constitute the officials. Each umpire has charge of half the field.

HISTORY. — In its primitive form Field Hockey is one of the oldest ball games in the world. It was known in ancient Greece. In the Copenhagen National Museum is an altar dish from 1330 showing, in the decoration, two players bullying a ball. The present name is thought to have been derived from the hooked stick used in the game and to be of old French origin, from the word *hoquet*, meaning a shepherd's crook.

The modern development of the game is distinctively English. No attempt to formulate rules was made prior to 1875, at which date an association of hockey clubs was formed near London, and a few rules formulated, which formed the basis of the later development.

The game was introduced into the United States in 1901, by Miss Constance M. K. Applebee, who in that year started it in several of the leading women's colleges (Vassar, Bryn Mawr, and Smith) and in the Harvard Summer School of Physical Training.

FIELD–HOCKEY DRIBBLE AND DRIVE

12 to 22 players   *Senior high to adult*

Players in two teams stand in two lines in zigzag formation, feet apart, with a center line between ranks as for Basketball Juggle Race (diagram, page 461). The first A player dribbles the ball to the center line, then drives it to his first B player, who stops it, dribbles to center, and drives to his second A, and so on down the ranks, when a return play is made. If the drive does not send the ball as far as his baseline, the next player must go out for it, dribble it back to his baseline, and from there begin his dribble to the center. The team wins whose original A is first to receive back the ball.

FIELD–HOCKEY DRIBBLE AND TURN

12 to 22 players   *Senior high to adult*

Players in teams of six to eleven stand in relay files behind a starting line. A second (parallel) line is drawn at a thirty-foot distance, and on this an Indian club is placed in front of each file. On signal, Number One of each team dribbles a hockey ball to the Indian club, around it to the right, and back to Number Two, passing at once to the rear of the file. Number Two repeats the play, and so on for each member of the team. It helps to good relay work to have but one stick, a player starting only when the returning player hands him the stick. The team wins which finishes first.

FIELD–HOCKEY DRIBBLE RACE

This is played like the Hockey Drive Relay in zigzag formation. A player finishing his turn passes to the rear of the opposite rank.

FIELD–HOCKEY DRIVE RELAY

12 to 22 players   *Senior high to adult*

I. For gymnasium or other limited space, teams are divided into A's and B's who face each other in files, in shuttle relay formation. On signal, each first A drives to his own first B, hands the stick to second A at his starting line, and moves down to the rear of the file. First B's repeat this on their side of the shuttle, and so on until the first A gets back to the starting line and receives the ball, which finishes the round. The first team to finish wins.

II. Teams are divided into A's and B's who face each other in ranks in zigzag formation, as in Zigzag Ball — I, at a distance of six to ten yards according to proficiency. On signal the first A of each team drives a hockey ball to first B, who sends it back to second A and so on down the line; the last B to receive the ball immediately starts its return in reverse order. The first team to get the ball back to the player who started it wins the game.

FIELD–HOCKEY GOAL DRIVE

5 to 22 players   *Senior high to*
Individual or team competition   *adult*

Three points are marked on the striking circle — one directly in front of the goal and one on each side fifteen feet from the center mark. Each player of each team has one drive for goal from each mark: (1) standing on the mark; (2) from a walk; and (3) from a run. There must be no halt for driving in the run and walk.

Each successful goal scores one point.

FIELD–HOCKEY PASSES

(See *Keep-Ball*.)

FIELD–HOCKEY SCOOP–OVER RACE

12 to 22 players   *Senior high to adult*

Two starting lines are drawn fifteen yards apart and halfway between them is placed an obstacle such as a baseball bat. Teams are divided into halves, A and B, which face each other in files behind the starting lines in shuttle-relay formation. On signal the first of each team dribbles a hockey ball to the obstacle, negotiates this with a scoop, dribbles on to teammate B opposite, and passes to the rear of that file while B repeats the play. Each player has but one try at the scoop. The team scores five points whose last player is the first to the opposite starting line; and in addition, each team scores one point for each successful scoop. The highest score wins.

FIST BALL

6 to 30 or more players   *Intermediate*
Playground; gymnasium; parlor   *to senior high*
Volleyball; basketball; gas ball

This game is very similar to Volleyball, but differs from that game in the fact that the ball is hit with the fist instead of the open hand; that the ball may bounce on the ground; and that the general rules are simpler. For large numbers two balls may be used, as described at the end.

COURT. — The court should be, if possible, one hundred feet long and sixty feet wide, with clearly defined boundaries. Across the center a rope or cord is stretched, head high, which divides it into two equal courts. If desired, each court may be divided into small squares, one for each player, to prevent mass play.

PLAYERS. — The players are divided into two equal teams, each of which scatters irregularly over the court unless assigned to squares as described above. The players in each team should be numbered consecutively to facilitate rotation in serving. One officer will be needed to act as umpire and scorer.

OBJECT OF GAME. — The object of the game is to send the ball back and forth across the stretched cord, striking it only with the fist. The game is defensive; that is, the scoring is done by a team when the opponents fail to return the ball or to keep it properly in play.

START. — The ball is put in play by a regular serve at the opening of the game, after each point scored, and after going out of play. The players take turns in serving for their team, being numbered before the game opens. The sides alternate in serving after a score.

The player who serves the ball should stand at a central point ten feet from the dividing line, and may serve the ball in two ways. He may bounce it and bat it with the fist over into the opponents' court, or he may hold it in his hand, toss, and serve it with his fist. The ball must go over the line to be in play. Should a server fail in this, the ball must be handed to the opposite side, which then has a trial. After a ball has otherwise gone out of play, it is served anew by the side responsible for the failure.

RULES AND POINTS OF PLAY. — The ball must cross into the opponents' court above the cord to score or be properly in play.

A ball to score its highest (two points) must be returned after a serve without bouncing, although any number of players may hit it or keep it in the air before sending it back over the line. A ball may bounce once before being returned and score less (one point). It is out of play if it bounces twice without being hit between the bounces.

Several methods of play are permissible, but the rule is invariable that the ball must always be hit with the closed fist, and always from underneath, except for sending it across the line. It must reach the opponents' court from a blow and not from a bounce. Either fist may be used in striking a ball, but never both at once. A player may "juggle" the ball before batting it over the line to the opponents by hitting it from underneath with his closed fist. A ball hit with the forearm is considered properly in play except for a service. Several players on one team may play on the ball before sending it into the opponents' court. In doing this the ball may bounce once after every time it is hit with the fist.

A ball is out of play (1) when it passes under the line or touches the line; (2) when it touches the ground twice in succession without being hit between the bounces; (3) when it touches the ground outside the boundaries from a blow; (4) when it bounces out of boundaries. Whenever a ball is put out of play in these ways, it is sent back to the team responsible for the failure, and they must put it in play again.

Whenever a team scores a point, the ball must again be put into play with a regular serve, the teams taking turns in this and each player on a team serving in turn.

SCORE. — The score is made by both teams and is for returning the ball. If returned to the opponents without touching the ground, it counts two points for those returning it. A ball which touches the ground once before being hit back over the lines scores one point. The game consists of twenty-five points.

After each game the two teams exchange courts.

FOR LARGE NUMBERS it is very desirable to have two or more balls in play at once. They are served simultaneously from opposite sides of the court, at the opening of the game. There should be one scorekeeper for each ball.

FOR THE PARLOR. — This game may be played in the parlor with a light gas ball measuring four or five inches in diameter, or with a child's gas balloon. The same rules apply as in other forms of the game.

FOOTBALL

(Soccer Football; Rugby Football: American Collegiate)

Two major games of Football are in general use — Rugby and Soccer, both of English origin. The two games have radical differences in the balls used and in the manner of playing them.

Soccer Football is a kicking game played with a round ball. The ball may not be carried nor played with hands nor arms, nor is any bodily interference of players allowed. The goalkeeper is largely exempt from these restrictions. A goal is made by kicking the ball between the goal posts and under the bar. The description will be found in its alphabetic order in this section under **S**.

Rugby is played with a so-called oval ball which is carried, passed, thrown, and kicked; players may be tackled. A goal is scored (1) when a ball is kicked over the bar or over a goal post, or (2) on a touchdown, which consists of carrying the ball over the opponents' goal line. The Rugby game described in this book is the American, or Collegiate, game. The description will be found in this section under **R**.

FOOTBALL TAG

3 to 30 or more players　　　　　　　　　　　　*Intermediate*
Playground; gymnasium　　　　　　　　　　　　*to senior high*
　　　　　　　　　Soccer football

Each of the players has three points at the beginning of the game. The players are scattered irregularly over the ground or gymnasium. One player, who is It, has a football which he kicks lightly toward any other player, the idea being to tag some other by mere touch of the ball. Anyone so touched or tagged by the ball loses one of the three points with which he started, and also becomes It, trying in turn to kick the ball so it will tag one of his fellows. There are no restrictions as to the moving about of players to evade the ball. The latter must not be touched with the hands, nor may it be kicked higher than the chests of the players. Anyone infringing these rules loses one point for each offense, and remains It until he successfully tags someone according to rules. Any player who loses his three points is out of the game, and the player wins who remains longest in the field.

GOLF

1 to 4 players　　　　　　　　　　　　　　　　*Juniors; adults*

Golf is almost the only walking game played with a ball. Its popularity is doubtless due largely to this fact as well as to the combination of skill with delightful outdoor surroundings.

The game is played over "links" (called preferably a golf course), which may be laid out on any grass-covered or sand-covered stretch of sufficient length. Throughout the course, at distances of several hundred yards, are holes in the ground about four inches in diameter. The game consists in driving a small ball, by means of clubs, from hole to hole, using as few strokes as possible. The first stroke toward each hole is called a "drive," and is made from a smooth area called the "teeing ground." Each hole is surrounded by very level, smooth turf called a "putting green." Between the teeing ground and the putting green are sections of ground having varied characteristics which present difficulties to be negotiated in the play. These sections are called "fair green," "the rough," and "hazards." The selection and laying out of golf grounds is a very critical matter and should have the advice of experienced experts.

THE COURSE OR LINKS. — A standard course may have nine or eighteen holes, though most courses are for eighteen-hole games, and nine-hole links have to be played twice around. The total length of a course would vary from two to three and three-fourths miles. The distance between holes is rarely less than one hundred yards or longer than six hundred yards.

TEES. — At the start for each hole is a teeing ground, which is a smooth area from ten to twenty feet square, covered with level, close-cut turf. The ball is usually set on a small mound of sand or earth about one inch high called a "tee." This is termed *teeing the ball*. The teeing ground for each hole is placed comparatively near to the putting green of the previous hole.

FAIRWAY is the general name given to the strip of ground, about four hundred yards long, that lies between a teeing ground and its putting green.

HAZARDS. — Occasionally in the fairway there are hazards of various kinds; that is, obstacles to the play or flight of the ball. A hazard may, for instance, be a bunker — that is, a mound of earth or an embankment — or a pond, marsh, road, fence, tree, stream, or sand-trap. These hazards may be natural or artificial; they add to the zest of a game by catching the ball from poorly played shots.

HOLES: PUTTING GREEN. — Each hole is located in an area of closely cut, smooth turf, called a putting green, generally at least twenty yards square. Each hole is a four-inch cup sunk in the ground. A flag marks the position of each hole. This is taken away when players are on the putting green, but must immediately be replaced after holing out. After making a hole, the ball is taken out by hand.

BALLS. — Golf balls are made of hard gutta-percha and are slightly over one and one-half inches in diameter and one and one-half ounces in weight.

CLUBS vary in length, weight, and shape:

The *driver* has a long shaft and wooden head; it is used for long shots from the tee.

The *brassie* is quite similar to the driver, except that the head is more laid back or pitched and has a brass sole. It is used to play long shots from the top of a fairly good lie and when a maximum distance is desired.

A *cleek* or *iron* has an iron head with very little pitch and a long shaft; it is used for long shots when the lie is not quite good enough for a brassie, or the distance desired not quite so great.

The *midiron* has a shorter shaft than the cleek and a deeper head, is heavier, has more pitch, and is used to throw the ball into the air when approaching the hole.

The *mashie* has a shorter iron blade than the midiron, has more pitch to its head, and is used for short approaches or to play the ball out of difficult lies.

The *niblick* has a small round head and is used to play the ball out of sand holes or other hazards.

The *putter* has a short handle and stands upright. It is used for the short shots played on the putting green.

There are other clubs, but those mentioned above are the most important.

The matter of gripping and playing the clubs is very technical and should have personal instruction.

TECHNICAL TERMS. — The *stance* is the manner of standing when about to strike the ball.

Addressing the ball includes the movements of a player and club preparatory to a stroke.

Long shots are called *drives*.

The *approach* involves the strokes that place a ball on the putting green.

Lofting the ball is lifting the ball with a stroke more than enough to clear the ground. This is necessary over bunkers and often for a bad lie. The face of the different clubs is laid back at different angles to facilitate or avoid lofting.

To draw the ball with the club toward the left side instead of driving it straight ahead is called *pulling the ball.*

To send the ball toward the right instead of straight ahead is called *slicing* it.

To hit the ball near the top instead of full on the face is called *topping the ball.*

No means of propelling the ball by the club other than with a stroke with the head of the club is permissible. That is, the ball may not be drawn along (spooned), or pushed, or scraped.

DIFFERENT KINDS OF GAMES. — There are two established modes of play called (1) Match Play; and (2) Stroke Competition or Medal Play. A third is called "Bogey Competition."

In *Match Play* the object is to win the hole; that is, to make each hole in fewer strokes than the opponent. The score is of holes won and not the total number of strokes over the entire course.

In *Medal Play* or *Stroke Competition* the object is to go over the entire course with as few strokes as possible. The score is therefore primarily of total strokes rather than of holes won.

Bogey Competition is a form of play in which each player compares his score for each hole with an arbitrary, imaginary score, fixed by a committee. The player wins, loses, or halves each hole with this "Bogey" exactly as he would with an opponent. The Bogey score represents the number of strokes in which a good player might reasonably be expected to make each hole.

Par means an ideal score for an expert player on any given links, and usually averages from seventy-two to seventy-five strokes for an eighteen-hole course. Par is used as a standard of comparison; also a player alone may make an imaginary opponent of Par as he plays around the links.

Twosome means a game between two players.

Foursome means four players in a game, two on each side. Each plays his own ball.

Two-ball Foursome is played by four players but with only two balls, one for each side. The partners play their ball with alternate strokes.

RULES AND ETIQUETTE. — The playing of golf is governed both by official rules and by etiquette. equally binding and usually published together. They include such points as prece-dence on the links, the removal of obstacles or loose impediments, moving a ball, playing or interfering with a ball in motion, playing wrong balls, lost balls, what advice or information may be asked, how near one may stand to another player during a stroke, talking under such circumstances, etc.

The United States rules for golf are based on those of the Royal and Ancient Golf Club of St. Andrews, near Edinburgh, the most famous golf club in the world.

HISTORY. — Golf is well termed "The Royal and Ancient Game." For several centuries it has been the national game of Scotland. As early as the fifteenth century it was so popular there that an act of Parliament forbade its play because it hindered the practice of archery, then used for national defense. Toward the end of that century indictments were frequent in Scotland for breaking the Sabbath by playing "Gowff."

Many old tombstones in Scotland recite the achievements in golf of the departed, as a famous general's victories in battle might be noted.

Whether or not the game originated in Scotland is not known. Old Dutch tiles picture what might have been the crude beginnings of the game, but no certainty attaches to this. It is known, however, that balls for the game were early imported into Scotland from Holland — to such an extent that in 1618 this was forbidden as taking too much money out of the country.

Golf balls at that time were made of leather stuffed with feathers. The modern development of the game is due largely to the discovery of gutta-percha and its use in balls, which marked an epoch in the history of the game. Such balls were in general use about the middle of the nineteenth century.

The popularity of the game outside of Scotland is even more recent. In England, although some golf organizations are almost as old as those in Scotland, the game was not general until the end of the century. It was first played in the English universities about 1880, and became general only in the early '90's. Apparently it was about that time that women began to play.

The seriousness of the British golfer's regard for his game is shown by the following quotation from a modern English work : "It is difficult for a whole-souled golfer to reconcile the addiction of the royal family of Stuart for golf with their unsatisfactory character in some other particulars."

In the United States the game became general in the last few years of the nineteenth century. No other outdoor game engages actively so many men of all ages, or does so much to keep overworked business and professional men in health.

HANDBALL

2 or 4 players   *Junior high to adult*

GENERAL DESCRIPTION. — Handball consists in volleying a small rubber ball with the open hand toward a wall, from which it should rebound within the playing court, to be returned by another (opposing) player. Failure to return the ball to the

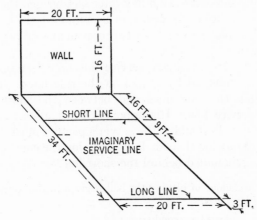

HANDBALL COURT

wall is a miss. The score, as in tennis, is made only by the side which serves: they score on the opponents' failures. The game calls for strenuous, all-over muscular exercise and great skill and quickness. It may be played on any outdoor or indoor court having a smooth wall surface. The official game of the most expert players is played on all six surfaces of an enclosed room, front, rear, and side walls, floor and ceiling. For junior players, or as a recreational game, a one-wall game is popular, and this is the form here described.

COURT. — The game may be played on any smooth wall surface. Special outdoor walls are constructed of concrete or wood, and consist of a front wall and floor; short sidewalls are sometimes included, to hold the ball. Such a handball wall should be twenty feet wide and at least sixteen feet high; the depth of the court from the wall is thirty-four feet. A wire backstop should

top an outdoor wall, and be placed also at the sides if there are
no other sidewalls.

Two lines are drawn on the ground parallel to the wall. The
first, called the *short line*, should be sixteen feet from the wall:
a served ball, to be good, must bound on the player's side of
this line; the second line, called the *long line*, marks the rear
boundary of the court, thirty-four feet from the wall, to which it is
connected by side lines extending three feet beyond the long line.

PLAYERS. — Two or four players are required, the latter called
doubles. The players are thus two opponents, or two teams of
two men each.

SERVING. — An imaginary service line nine feet back of the
short line is indicated by marks on the side lines. The server
stands within the side lines and between the short line and
imaginary service line. His opponent must also stand behind
the short line.   In doubles, the server's partner must stand during the serve outside the side lines, entering the court only when
the ball has rebounded behind the short line.

The main technique of playing the ball is given in the section on *Balls
and How to Play Them.*

The server is allowed a second try:

(*a*) If the serve is a *short ball*, that is, does not rebound behind the short
line.

(*b*) If the serve is a *long ball*, one that rebounds behind the long line.

(*c*) If the served ball hits an opponent.

The server is out:

(*a*) If the served ball goes outside the side lines.

(*b*) If the served ball hits the server or his partner.

(*c*) If the served ball hits any obstruction, including the ceiling.

(*d*) If two long or two short balls, or a long and a short, are served in
succession.

(*e*) If a partner in doubles serves out of turn.

The server continues to serve until he or his partner fails to
return the ball.

In doubles the two players on one team serve in succession and
then the two opponents.

RETURNING THE BALL. — As soon as a served ball recrosses the
short line, the opponent returns it to the wall with an open-hand

strike, hitting it either on the fly or after one bounce. Such a returned ball must hit the wall and rebound to the court. The opposing sides strike the ball alternately until one or the other fails to return it properly.

When the receiving side fails properly to return the ball, it goes again to the same server.

When the serving side fails to return the ball, the server is out, and the serve passes to the opponent.

HINDERS. — Certain interferences with player or ball are called *hinders*, as follows:

(*a*) *When a ball hits an opponent* before touching the wall or floor. Such a ball must be served again.

(*b*) *When a player is unintentionally blocked or interfered with* by an opponent, the ball is served over.

Interference from a partner is not a hinder.

Intentional blocking or interference of an opponent is penalized by one point to the offended team.

SCORE. — Twenty-one points constitute a game for men; women often play fifteen points as a game.

The serving side is the only one to score: they score one point for each failure of the opponents to properly return the ball. When the serving side fails to return the ball, they are out as servers and become receivers. A match is two out of three games.

HISTORY. — To bounce a ball against a wall is an instinctive form of play; but just when or where this became formulated into a game with rules is not definitely known. The fully developed game of Handball, as known in America, was introduced from Ireland about 1840. It is generally considered to have originated in Ireland, where it has the importance of a national game.

HANDBALL DRILL

1 to 100 players   *Elementary grades*

Handsizeball; beanbags

When little children first begin to handle a ball of ordinary hand size, the acquirement of skill in tossing and catching is not altogether easy. Experience with such children has shown that some preliminary drill is very desirable as a preparation for the ball games. This drill may itself be done in the play spirit and made very interesting.

The various movements described may be general (by the class in unison) in time to music or counting; or they may be done individually or with partners as indicated, irrespective of the time in which other individuals or partners are working.

In the latter method the play may be competitive, the pupils counting the number of times in which they bounce or toss or catch without missing, the one reaching the highest number winning.

It will be noted that the drill seeks to cultivate equal skill of both hands. This is very desirable in many games and should be done aside from any theories as to the value of ambidexterity.

See also the game *Rosemary*.

HANDBALL DRILL — I. (ELEMENTARY)

A. BOUNCING

INDIVIDUAL PLAY

1. Bounce, and catch with both hands, palms *upward*.

2. Bounce, and catch with one hand (right, then left), palm *upward*.

3. Bounce, hit to rebound once, and catch with one hand (right, then left), palm *upward*.

4. Bounce, and catch with one hand (right, then left), the palm *downward* in catching ("dog snack").

5. Bounce, hit to rebound twice, or more times, and catch with one hand (right, then left).

WITH PARTNERS

If there are many players they may stand in long ranks facing each other for these drills, or in separate couples scattered promiscuously over the ground. In either case they should begin with a comparatively short distance, say of three feet, between partners, and gradually increase the distance.

1. Bounce to partner, who will catch with both hands.

2. Bounce to partner, who will catch with one hand (right, then left), palm *upward*.

3. Bounce to partner, who will catch with one hand (right, then left), palm *downward*.

4. Bounce to partner, who will return ball by hitting it for a rebound without catching it. This may be kept up between the two indefinitely.

B. TOSSING

INDIVIDUAL PLAY

1. Toss, and catch ball with both hands.

2. Toss, and catch with one hand (right, then left), palm *upward*.

3. Toss, and hit it to retoss in the air without catching (right hand, then left), palm *upward*.

WITH PARTNERS

1. Toss ball to partner, who will catch with both hands.

2. Toss ball to partner, who will catch with one hand (right, then left), palm *upward*.

3. Toss ball to partner, who will catch with one hand (right, then left), palm *outward* ("dog snack").

C. BOUNCING AGAINST WALL

INDIVIDUAL PLAY

1. Throw ball against a wall, allow it to bounce once on the floor, and catch with both hands.

2. Throw ball against wall, bounce once, and catch with one hand (right, then left), palm *upward*.

3. Throw against wall, bounce once, and catch with one hand (right, then left), palm *downward*.

4. Throw against wall and catch without bouncing on the ground, with one hand (right, then left), palm *upward*.

5. Throw, and catch without bouncing on ground, with one hand (right, then left), palm *outward*.

WITH PARTNERS

1. Repeat the above throws against the wall, the partner catching in each case as designated in the list.

HANDBALL DRILL — II. (ADVANCED)

1 to 100 players   *Intermediate to junior high*

A. TOSSING

INDIVIDUAL PLAY

1. Toss or throw the ball straight upward as high as possible; catch it in one hand (right, then left), with palm *upward*.

2. Toss or throw the ball straight upward as high as possible; catch it in one hand (right, then left), palm *outward* ("dog snack").

3. Hold out one arm, say the left, straight in front at shoulder level; holding the ball in the right hand, swing the right arm outward in a full circle; toss the ball upward from under the outstretched arm, and catch with the hand that threw, palm *outward*.

4. Repeat this throwing with the left hand, holding out the right.

5. Toss the ball sideways over one's own head, and catch on the opposite side. This is done as follows: Holding the ball in the right hand, swing the right arm out sideways, and from about shoulder level toss the ball over the head toward the left side. Catch it on the left side near shoulder level with the left hand, palm upward or outward.

6. Reverse, tossing from the left hand and catching with the right.

7. Toss the ball under the upraised knee as follows: Holding the ball in the right hand, raise the right knee upward, bent at an angle, swing the right arm in circle outward, and toss the ball upward from under the knee; that is, from the inner side of the leg; catch with the hand that threw, palm *outward*. Repeat with the left hand and knee.

8. Throw the ball upward behind the back, so that it comes forward over the opposite shoulder, as follows: Holding the ball in the right hand, circle the right arm outward, bend the arm behind the back, toss the ball upward over the left shoulder, and catch it over the head or in front with the hand that threw, palm outward. Reverse, using the left arm and throwing over the right shoulder. When this is first tried the ball may not be thrown very high or very well as to direction; but it is a fascinating throw to practice and may soon be done with a high toss and very accurately.

HAND BATBALL

(See also *Long Ball I and II*.)

8 to 20 players   *Intermediate grades*
Playground   *to adult*
Volleyball, basketball, soccer ball, or handsizeball

A home base two feet square is drawn on the ground. At a distance of forty feet from it is placed a net-post, jump standard, chair, or other objective.

Players are divided into two teams which are alternately batters and fielders. The fielders scatter irregularly over the field. Each batter serves in turn until his team has three outs, when the teams change places.

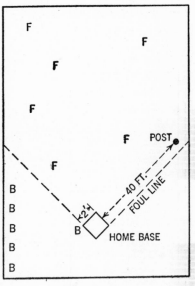

The batter, standing on home base, tosses the ball and bats it with his open hand (a handsizeball is bounced and batted), immediately running to and around the post and back to home base. He has three tries at batting, and is out (1) if failing on the third try; (2) if the batted ball is caught on the fly; (3) if he is

HAND BATBALL

hit by the ball before getting back to home base; (4) if he interferes with a fielder; (5) if he touches the goal-post in rounding it.

The fielders try to get the ball and to hit the runner with it (below the waist) before he can get back to his base. A fielder may not hold the ball more than five seconds, nor may he run with it, more than one step being considered a run. Fielders may pass the ball back and forth to each other, but no two players may do this more than twice in succession. A fielder may not interfere with the batter.

Only the batting team scores. It gains one point for each successful run and one point for each infringement of rules by the fielding team. Teams change places on a failure of the batter. Any number of innings may be played, the highest score winning.

HAND TENNIS

(See also *Bounceball* and *Box Ball*.)

2 or 4 players   *Junior high school*
Tennis court   *Tennis ball*

The court is sixteen by forty feet with a net across the center, two feet four inches high at the posts. Three feet on each side of

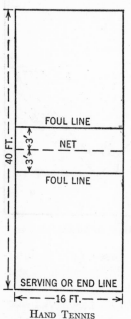

HAND TENNIS

the net a foul line is drawn parallel to the net. Players must never step across these lines and a ball falling within them is dead.

A tennis ball or any small handsizeball is served from behind the end line and may go into any part of the opponent's court beyond the foul line, as may also a return ball.

The serve is made by bouncing the ball and hitting it with the open hand before it is waist high (underhand swing). The return is also an open-hand strike; the first return must be after a bounce, but thereafter the return may be a volley after a bounce.

The game is played like Lawn Tennis except for the layout of the court and the absence of a racket.

The serving side scores one point for each failure of the opponents to properly return the ball. Either side scores one point if opponents step over the foul line. Fifteen points make a game.

HOCKEY

Three major forms of Hockey are described in alphabetic order in this section on Ball Games — namely, Deck Hockey (under D), Field Hockey (under F), and Ice Hockey (under I). Skill Games for Field Hockey follow that game (under F), and the technique of fundamental plays for that game is described in the chapter on *Balls and How to Play Them*.

HOME RUN

10 to 60 players   *Intermediate grades*
Schoolroom   *Gas balls or beanbags*

Arrange the players so that all seats are filled with the same number in each row. No. 1 in each row has a beanbag or ball, and at the word "Start!" stands and throws the bag or ball to No. 2, who also stands at the word "Start." No. 2 throws it back to No. 1 and sits down while No. 1 throws the ball to No. 3, who stands up as soon as No. 2 is seated. No. 3 throws it back to No. 1 and the game continues until No. 1 has thrown the ball to the last player in the row. When No. 1 receives the ball from the last player, he lays it down on the desk and runs to the seat of the last player, while all players move up toward the front one seat. No. 2 in the row then becomes No. 1, and tosses the ball as his predecessor did. The game continues until the original No. 1 reaches his original place and calls "Home run!" thus scoring a point for his row and starts again. The row scoring the most points during fifteen minutes becomes the winner.

This game was originated by Miss Amy A. Young of Cleveland, Ohio.

ICE HOCKEY

12 players   *Senior high school to adult*

GENERAL DESCRIPTION. — Ice Hockey is probably the most popular and widely used of skating games. The object for each of the competing teams is to put through the opponents' goal a small cylindrical piece of rubber called a *puck*. The puck is played entirely by long slender sticks flattened out into a curving blade at the end. The game in its general formation and rules is very similar to Field Hockey and also bears a strong resemblance to Lacrosse.

RINK. — Hockey is played on the ice — the field, whether outdoors or in, being called a "rink." The size officially recommended is two hundred by eighty-five feet (maximum measurements are two hundred fifty by one hundred ten feet and minimum one hundred sixty-five by sixty feet). A board fence or banking three or four feet high surrounds the field from which the puck rebounds. Corners of the rink are rounded to a fifteen-foot radius. The rink is divided into three zones, a center zone and two end zones, by a transverse line drawn sixty feet inward from each goal. Two goals are placed at either end of the rink ten to fifteen feet from the end boards or edge of the ice. Goal posts are four feet in height and six feet apart. Attached to them is a net cage to capture the puck when a goal is shot. The entire goal box is usually movable. A six-foot goal line is drawn on the ice between posts and around each goal a goalkeeper's crease six by ten feet, extending forward and back of the goal line as in the diagram. A two-foot square is marked in the exact center of the field, and similar squares diagonally outward fifteen feet from each goal center, for face-offs.

Thirty-eight feet in front of each goal is a penalty-shot mark in a ten-foot circle.

EQUIPMENT. —

Sticks. — Official Ice Hockey sticks are made of wood and of varying lengths up to fifty-four inches (to the heel) ; fifteen inches for the blade ; three and one-half inches at the widest part.

Pucks. — Pucks are made of vulcanized rubber, cylindrical in shape, one-inch thick throughout, and three inches in diameter.

Skates must not be sharply pointed nor sharpened so as to injure other players, nor extend far beyond the shoe.

Dress. — Gloves are usually made of leather with a special gauntlet to protect the hand from injury from opponents' sticks. The goalkeeper wears leg guards to the hips and also a padded stomach protector.

TEAMS. — Six players constitute a team — the goalkeeper, two defense men (right and left), and three forwards (center, right wing, and left wing).

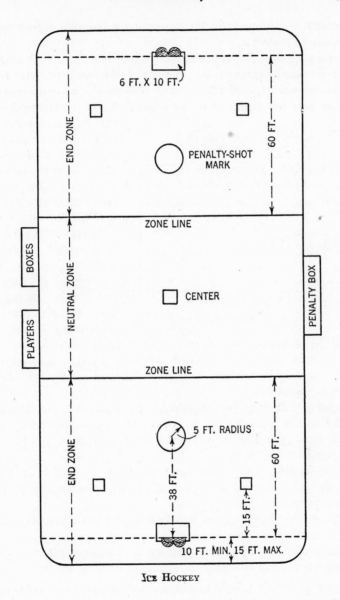

6 FT. X 10 FT.

END ZONE

60 FT.

PENALTY-SHOT
MARK

ZONE LINE

BOXES

NEUTRAL ZONE

CENTER

PLAYERS

PENALTY BOX

ZONE LINE

END ZONE

60 FT.

5 FT. RADIUS

38 FT.

15 FT.

10 FT. MIN. 15 FT. MAX.

Ice Hockey

START. — The puck is put in play by a face-off. The referee drops it (or throws it gently to avoid bouncing) between the sticks of two opposing players. These players must stand each with his right side towards his own end of the rink (*i.e.* toward the goal he is defending), and sticks must rest on the ice with twelve inches between them. On the referee's signal the two players try to get possession of the puck or play it to a teammate. All other players must be at least ten feet from the puck and between it and their own goal.

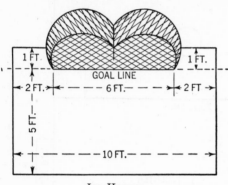

ICE HOCKEY
(Detail of Goalkeeper's Crease)

PLAYING THE PUCK. — The puck is played with the stick by "carrying" it; that is, shoving or sliding it over the ice, though it is often lofted. It may be stopped with the stick when below shoulder height, and batted with it when below knee height (two feet off the ice). It may be stopped, carried, or kick-passed by the skate. It may be stopped, but not carried nor held, by any part of the body. It may be stopped by the hand but not thrown, and must be immediately dropped. It may be batted by the open hand, but the player who batted it must be the first to recover it for his team.

A defending team must keep the puck in motion in their defense zone and advance it toward the opponents' goal line unless prevented by an opponent.

When a puck leaves a defensive zone, all but three players of the defense must leave at once.

Body checking is permissible by a defending player in his defense zone, but charging, elbowing, or kneeing are fouls.

A fair body check is made by a player in his defensive zone and in front of an opponent who is playing the puck, the latter standing still or skating slowly. To check when the opponent is skating fast or is not in front of the checking player is *charging*. It is *kneeing* or *elbowing* if the checking player uses his knee or elbow. Legitimate body checking must be done only with the trunk of the body (hips to shoulders), must be above the opponent's knees, not from the side or back, or unnecessarily rough.

USE OF THE STICK. — It is permissible for a player to hook with his stick the stick of an opponent who is playing or attempting to play the puck. The hooking may not be near the handle of the opponent's stick nor may there be any cross-checking, which consists of thrusting the stick, held in two hands, across an opponent's face or body. Permissible hooking is simply a means of obtaining the puck. There may be no tripping or slashing with the stick, nor may it be thrown. Tripping is an attempt to trip with the leg, foot, or stick. Holding a stick stiffly as it touches the skate of an opponent is a trip. Slashing is swinging the stick with unnecessary force in playing the puck or otherwise. Charging, roughing, or interfering with the goalkeeper inside his crease are major offenses.

ZONE PLAY. — The central zone is called the neutral zone, and the zone containing a goal which the team is defending is its defending zone and the opposite end its attacking zone.

Any player, regardless of his position on the rink, has the right to attempt to get possession of the puck from an opponent, within certain provisions for off-side and on-side play, which are governed by the zones.

If the puck does not go out of a zone in which it is played, any player in that zone at the time is eligible to play it, or, any player in a zone nearer his own end of the rink.

A puck carried, passed, or shot into an attacking zone may be followed up by the player or his teammates provided no member of their team was in the attacking zone when the puck crossed the line.

A puck sent out of the defensive zone by a defender may not be played by a teammate who was in the neutral zone at the time; but if sent out by the attacking team a defender in the neutral zone may play it directly.

PENALTIES. — A minor penalty is suspension of the offending player from the game for two minutes, and a major penalty for five minutes of actual playing time. The player must immediately leave the rink and remain in the penalty box until the time-keeper indicates his return.

After a foul the puck is put in play again by a face-off either at the point where the foul occurred or at the center, or at the side face-off squares, according to the foul. For a foul in preventing the puck going through the goal a penalty shot is awarded from the penalty-shot mark in front of the goal cage.

SCORE. — One point is scored for a team for each time that it sends the puck through the opponents' goal. The team having the higher score at the end wins. The game is played in three twenty-minute periods with intermissions of ten minutes between. If a score is tied at the end of the third period, an over-time period of ten minutes is allowed after a ten-minute intermission. This may occur twice.

OFFICIALS. — The supreme official for a game of Ice Hockey is a referee. He has an assistant referee, two goal umpires, a time-keeper, assistant timekeeper, and a penalty timekeeper.

HISTORY. — The early history of Ice Hockey is rather obscure, but it is thought to be a development from games known in Great Britain in very early times under the names of Shinny, Shinty, and Hurling. The name of hockey is said to be first mentioned in some English statutes as early as 1527.

In its present highly developed form, hockey is due to the Canadians, among whom the game is widely used. Teams for shinny were organized in Canada in 1881. Montreal is credited with the first organized Hockey Club, in which the game was definitely defined with the beginning of modern rules. The first League games in Canada were played in 1884. The game was introduced in the United States at Johns Hopkins University by Mr. C. Shearer, a student from Montreal.

International games between Canada and the United States were first played in 1895.

The game was introduced in Europe by Mr. George A. Meagher of Montreal. The first European team was in Paris, with London and Scotland soon following.

INDOOR BASEBALL

(See *Playground Baseball*.)

KEEP–BALL

(Keep Away)

(See also *Volleyball Keep-over*.)

20 to 40 players   *Intermediate*

Gymnasium or field   *to adult*

Hockey ball and sticks; basketball

I. The players, in two teams of from ten to twenty each, have distinctive colors or marks and are scattered over the field irregularly in pairs of opponents. The ball is put in play from the center, and the team which gets it tries to pass it as many times as possible from teammate to teammate before the opponents can get it and start similar play. Each player in a series of passes calls the number of the pass, the first calling "One!" the second "Two!" etc. Each such pass between members of the same team scores one point. Or the game may be scored for the greatest number of passes in a single series, the team winning which has made the longest series in a given playing time.

The game is equally good for Basketball or Hockey.

II. FOR VOLLEYBALL (also called KEEP–IT–UP). — Any number of teams may play, as there is no interplay between them except the competition of score. Each stands in its own court and has its own volleyball. On signal each group starts play by one player serving the ball to a teammate. Thereafter the ball is volleyed from one player to another, always of the same team, each player calling the number of his volley, the first calling "One!" the second "Two!" etc. When the ball hits the floor, or another player, or any obstacle, or when it goes out of bounds, it is dead, and is at once put in play again by another serve for a new score-series. The team scoring the longest series wins. Another method of scoring is for the longest continuous series, the first team to score one hundred being the winner.

KICK LONG BALL

10 to 30 players   *Junior to*

Soccer ball   *senior high school*

I. This is the same as Long Ball except that the batter kicks the ball instead of batting it. He may place-kick or drop-kick the ball, and to be a fair ball it must hit the ground beyond a sixteen-foot line drawn in front of the home plate. He then tries to run to the long base and back to home before being put out. Fielders may catch the ball on the fly, which puts the kicker out, or they can put him out (1) by tagging him with the thrown ball (always below the waist) before he gets back to home base, or (2) by a fielder on base with the ball before the runner gets there, or (3) by a fielder dribbling or kicking the ball across the sixteen-foot line before he gets back to it.

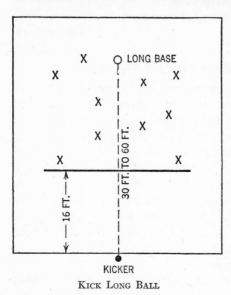

KICKER

KICK LONG BALL

A kicker has two tries and is out if he fails the second time. He must stand behind the home plate when kicking. When three kickers are out, the teams change places.

One point is scored for a team for each successful run. The number of innings is not limited.

II. The same game may be played by obliging fielders to kick the ball to tag the runner instead of throwing it after a fly catch.

LACROSSE

RULES FOR WOMEN'S GAME

24 players   *Senior high*
Open field   *to adult*

Lacrosse goals, crosse, and balls

Lacrosse is one of the most beautiful of the outdoor team games. Formerly played only by men, and considered extremely strenuous, it has undergone an evolution that brings it within the powers of junior players and women. The play of the ball is by tossing and catching with long, loosely strung crosses, somewhat resembling tennis rackets, and in finally throwing it by means of these through the opponent's goal.

FIELD. — In the center of the field is drawn a circle having a ten-yard radius; in the center of this is a twelve-foot line parallel to the goal lines.

Goals are erected from forty-five to fifty-five yards from this center line, making them from ninety to one hundred ten yards apart. They consist of upright posts six feet apart and six feet above ground, joined across the top by a rigid crossbar and all painted white; a goal line is drawn on the ground from post to post; a net is fastened to the rear of the posts and crossbar, carried back six feet and pegged firmly to the ground all around, giving it a pyramidal shape. Surrounding the goal is a goal crease which consists of a square twelve feet by twelve feet marked on the ground. It extends six feet forward from and six feet back of the goal line and its sides are three feet from the goal posts.

EQUIPMENT. — The ball is of rubber sponge not more than eight inches in circumference nor

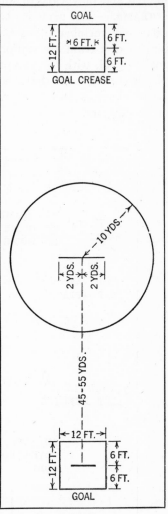

LACROSSE

five ounces in weight. The crosse is made from a long stick drawn around in a curve, the opening being loosely strung and not more than one foot at its widest part. The length, considerably greater than that of a tennis racket, is not officially limited and may vary to suit the individual player.

TEAMS. — The game is played by two teams of twelve players each, one member of each team being elected captain. The players of a team are stationed on one side of the ground from goal to goal, with the exception of one attack and one defence player stationed on the opposite half as shown in the diagram. Each player is paired off with one of similar position of the opposing team.

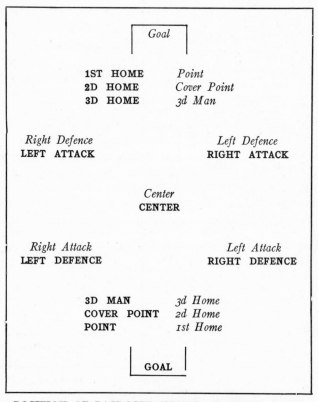

POSITION OF LACROSSE TEAMS, WOMEN'S GAME
(AS PLAYED IN GREAT BRITAIN)

OFFICIALS. — One umpire, two goal umpires, two scorekeepers, and two timekeepers.

THE GAME. — The ball is put in play at the center of the field by what is called a "draw." For this the centers toe the center line and hold their crosses touching each other in the air, reverse up, about hip level and parallel to the ground. Each center faces so that the crosse is between the ball and the goal he is defending. The ball is placed on the crosses by the umpire, and on signal the two crosses are drawn *up* and away from one another, when immediately each center plays for possession.

The ball is played by being passed from crosse to crosse, with a special technique for catching, cradling, and tossing. There is no batting of the ball with the crosse, as in tennis. Much of the play is on the run. No player may touch the ball with the hands, but may propel it with foot or leg if opportunity occurs. It is permissible to check any opponent's crosse, but not roughly or recklessly. Body checking is allowable, but consists merely in getting in the way of an opponent to block progress: no charging or shouldering is permissible. Any player may put the ball through the goal; it must be propelled entirely by the crosse, not by the person, and to score a goal the entire ball must go completely over the goal line and under the crossbar from the front. Should the defending team put it through in any manner it scores for the opposite team.

The goalkeeper may not catch or throw the ball with the hands, but he may block it with them or with the crosse or body in any manner.

PENALTY. — A "free position" is awarded opponents as penalty for a foul. For this the umpire indicates where a player shall stand (not within ten yards of the goal lines), and the latter then takes the ball in the crosse and on the umpire's signal may either shoot for goal, pass the ball, or run with it.

SCORE. — The game is played in two periods of fifteen to twenty-five minutes each with a ten-minute rest period between if either side claims it. The team wins which scores the greater number of goals. Each goal made scores one point. Ends are changed for the second period.

LACROSSE

RULES FOR MEN AND BOYS

20 players *Senior high school to adult*

The game differs in a few points from that described for women. The playing field is outlined by ground marking, being one hundred twenty yards long and from seventy to eighty-five yards wide, entirely enclosed by a five-foot fence ten feet back from the boundary line. The field is divided across the center by a line drawn from the side lines to the center circle. Goals are eighty yards apart and of the same dimensions as in the fuller description, having twenty yards of free space behind each goal.

Teams number ten players each and their positions are the traditional ones shown in the diagram, forming an unbroken line-up from goal to goal. The game tends toward less running and more throwing of the ball from player to player. Rules for body checking are somewhat different. There is an off-side, at least two players of each team being required between the center line and the goal being attacked. The game is played in four quarters of fifteen minutes each with one minute after first and third quarters and ten minutes between halves.

HISTORY. — Lacrosse originated with the North American Indians, by whom it was called "The ball game." It appears to have been played in all parts of the country, and was substantially the same game in different localities, though there may have been some differences in the construction of the crosses and balls. Like most Indian events, the game was preceded by religious rites which invoked the aid of the Great Spirit. These rites consisted partly of an all-night dance around the goals, followed by water rites in the morning. From several hundred to one thousand players are said to have taken part on each side. It is unnecessary to say that each player did not have an assigned part in the game as under modern team rules. Squaws entered the game, not to play, but to urge on their husbands by switching them.

The modern game of Lacrosse, with its improved implements, highly developed skill, different functions assigned to different players, and team co-operation, is the result of an interest taken in the game by the white men of Canada. Dr. George Beers, of Montreal, is credited with having recognized the possibilities of the game, commencing its development in 1850.

The present name was given to the Indian game by the French Canadians, who saw in the curved stick making the crosse resemblance to a Bishop's crozier (*la croix*).

The game was introduced into England in 1865 by Canadian boys at school near Reading. The United States took it up somewhat later than the Canadians.

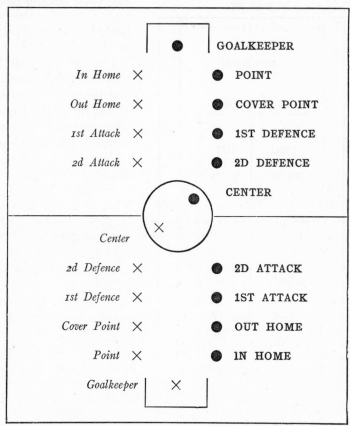

POSITION OF LACROSSE TEAMS, MEN'S GAME

LAWN TENNIS

2 to 4 players   *Junior high to adults*
Tennis court   *Tennis ball and racket*

GENERAL DESCRIPTION. — Lawn Tennis is played on a diagramed court outlined on a level of turf or dirt. It is played by two, three, or four persons who alternately send a ball across a net to each other, batted with a tennis racket. The player, or partners, who fail to send the ball back properly over the net to the opponent forfeit a point; that is, the opponent scores one point on this failure.

Putting the ball in play is called serving, and the player who does this is called the server. The opponent is the receiver. For technique, see chapter on *Balls and How to Play Them.*

COURT. — The outer lines of a tennis court measure thirty-six by seventy-eight feet. The long lines are side lines, and the ends, baselines. Within this rectangle are drawn two side service lines, parallel to the side lines and four feet six inches within them. These are connected by two service lines eighteen feet inward from the baselines, and parallel to them. This leaves an inner

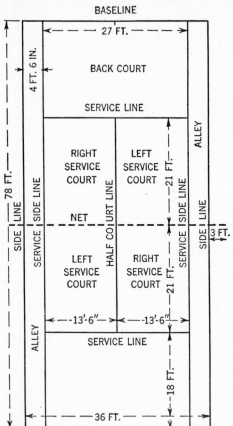

REGULATION LAWN TENNIS COURT

rectangular space which is divided in the center lengthwise by a line drawn from service line to service line. When the net is placed across the center of the court, this leaves four service courts in the center, each thirteen feet six inches in width.

The net must be stretched across the center of the court on posts set three feet outside of the side lines. The top of the net must be three feet six inches high at the posts and three feet at the center.

It is advisable to enclose a tennis court with side stops and backstops of twine or wire netting from seven to twelve feet high, to catch the ball. These should not be nearer than four feet to the side lines, or twelve feet to the baselines.

EQUIPMENT. — The ball is about two and a half inches in diameter, made of rubber and filled with air under pressure. The rubber is covered with white cloth.

The racket should have an oval-shaped frame of wood with handle about eighteen inches long. It is interlaced with catgut strings. Rackets of different weights are used.

Shoes without heels should be worn on the tennis court.

THE GAME is played either by two players, called *singles*, by four, called *doubles*, or by three, called a *three-handed game*.

Choice of Court or Service. — Players determine by the toss of a coin or the racket in which end of the court they will play and which side shall have the first serve. The winner of the toss may choose either the end or the serve but not both.

Service. — A player serves throughout one entire game. The ball is put in play by a serve, which consists in tossing it and striking it toward the opponent's court with the racket, with either an underhand or overhand stroke. The ball must bounce within the diagonally opposite service court before it is returned. In serving, the server must stand with both feet back of the baseline. His first serve for every game must be from behind the right half of this line as he faces the net, and his second serve will be from the opposite (left) half, and thereafter his service must be alternately from the right and left halves.

A server may, if necessary, have two tries or efforts for any one serve.

If a served ball should not be delivered correctly in any way, it is called a *fault*. For two consecutive faults an opponent scores one point.

A ball touching a line is considered to be within the court.

If a served ball hits the net, it does not count as a serve, even though it afterwards strikes the ground within the proper court. Such a ball is a *let*, that is, it does not count in any way, even as a fault. But a returned ball that touches the net and goes over is considered a good return.

The server must not serve until the receiver is in position and ready. Should he do so, the serve does not count in any way, either as a try or a fault. It is a let. A receiver may not claim that he was not ready after he has made any attempt to return the ball.

The second game is begun with a service by the player who was receiver in the previous game.

The receiver must return a served ball after it has bounced once in his own service court and send it so that, if it drops, it will fall within the opponent's court. He may not return it before it bounces, as that would be to volley it. After this first return from the serve, the receiver and his opponent are both at liberty to volley the ball or to play it after a first bounce as they may choose. In singles the ball must not fall in an alley; in doubles it may fall anywhere on the opponents' side of the net.

Should either player fail to return the ball properly, the opponent scores one point.

FAULTS, LETS, FORFEITED STROKES. — The term "foul" is not used ordinarily in tennis, as in most games, to denote misplay or an infringement of playing rules. The terms "fault" and "let" are used instead, and some misplays have no specific name but are penalized by the opponent's scoring one point.

The term "fault" applies to play of the server only and covers a failure to observe the conditions of correct serving, either as to his own form of delivery or as to the place where the ball drops.

The penalty for a first fault is loss of one of the two trials at the time of service. After a fault on his first try, the server tries again to serve from the same half of his court. A second fault from behind the same half (two consecutive faults) entitles the opponent to score a point and the server then serves from the other half of his baseline.

Opponent's score. — For some misplays, opponents score one point as follows:

The receiver scores one point if the server:

serves two faults in succession;
fails to return the ball;
returns the ball so that it drops outside the proper court.

The server scores one point if the receiver:

volleys the service instead of waiting for the ball to bounce;
fails to return the ball;
returns the ball so that it drops outside the proper court.

Either player scores a point if the opponent :

touches the net or its fixtures with his person or racket while the ball is in play;

volleys the ball before it has completely crossed the net ;

touches the ball more than once with his racket on the same play ;

allows the ball in play to touch him personally or anything worn or carried by him except his racket.

DOUBLES OR FOUR-HANDED GAME. — All rules and methods of play for singles apply also to doubles.

When four are playing, the side alleys are used as part of the court.

The two partners stand on the same side of the net ; they decide between them which shall be the first to serve and keep that order thereafter. The opponents decide which of the two shall receive the first service.

The served ball must drop within the diagonally opposite court as in the singles game ; but in returning the ball the player has a larger court into which to return it as it may drop anywhere on either half of the opponents' court.

The service remains on the same side of the net throughout the games of a set, but is taken alternately by the two partners.

For the second game the service is taken by the partner of the first receiver, and the partner of the server becomes first receiver.

THREE-HANDED GAME. — In the three-handed game the two partners stand on the same side of the net, and the single player serves every alternate game.

All served balls must fall within the service court on the diagonally opposite side.

Balls returned by the single player may drop anywhere in the doubles' court, but the two partners, in returning the ball to the single player, must keep the ball within the singles court.

SCORE. — A player (or partners) scores on the opponent's failure to return the ball, one point for each such failure. Either side may score, irrespective of which is serving. In stating the score, the server's score is named first. The first point scored in each game counts *fifteen;* the second also fifteen, making *thirty;* the third counts ten, making *forty*, and the first side to score four times wins the game.

The scoring is not so simple as this may appear. If both opponents have scored one point, the score stands *fifteen all;* or, if both have tallied two points, *thirty all;* but if both have made three points (*forty*), it is called *deuce*.

When the game has gone to *deuce*, neither one can win the game by making one additional point. Two consecutive points must be made to win the game. If after *deuce* one player makes an additional point, his score is called *advantage;* if he makes the next one, he wins the game; if he loses it, the score goes back to *deuce,* and so on until one or the other makes two consecutive points.

When the server wins the first point after *deuce,* it is called *advantage in;* when the receiver wins the first point after *deuce,* it is called *advantage out.*

The player who first wins six games wins a *set,* unless both players have won five games, when the score in games is *five all,* or *games all.* After such a score one side must win two games in succession to win; for example *six-eight* or *seven-nine,* etc.

Love is a term in tennis that signifies *naught.*

Love all means that neither side has made a point.

Love-fifteen is the score when the server has made no point and the opponent one.

Fifteen-love is the score when the server has made his first point and the receiver has not yet scored.

Love set is the score when either one of the two players has not won a game while the other has won six games.

In the three- and four-handed games partners score as one person.

SUMMARY OF POINTS. — A point is won if an opponent fails to return a ball; volleys a served ball; serves a double fault; allows the ball in play to hit him; touches the net during play; strikes a ball before it has passed the net.

In match play it is usual for the team winning two sets out of three to be considered winners of the match. In finals of a tournament, however, three out of five are usually required.

OFFICIALS. — It is not usual to have officials for Lawn Tennis except for tournament games. For tournaments a referee, umpire, and linesmen are appointed.

HISTORY. — Lawn Tennis is said to be an adaptation of indoor court tennis. Some authorities maintain that it is a descendant of an old outdoor French game, played with a cork ball and batted by hand over a mound of dirt two feet high. In 1874 Major Walter C. Wingfield of the British Army patented the game. At that time the court was shaped like an hourglass and the net at its center was more than a foot higher than our nets at the present time.

LINE–BALL

10 to 60 players   *Primary grades*
Schoolroom   *Gas balls; beanbags*

For this game a line should be drawn on the floor across the front of the schoolroom, a short distance in front of the blackboard. One player from each row of seats takes his place toeing this line. Another line is drawn at the front of each aisle even with the edge of the front desks. The game consists in a tossing of the ball from the leader on the forward line to different players, who take their places in turn on the line at the head of the aisle. Each row of seats should contain an even number of players, as the different lines compete with each other.

The first players in the rows rise from their seats on a given signal, toe the line at the head of their aisle, and catch the ball, which should be tossed to them immediately by the leader who stands opposite. This player quickly returns the ball to the leader by means of another toss, and sits down at once. His sitting is a signal for the player next behind him to run forward to the line, catch the ball from the leader, toss it back to the leader, and reseat himself. This continues until every player in the line has caught and returned the ball, when the leader should return to his seat and hold the ball up at arm's length, as a signal that his line has finished. The line wins whose leader is the first to do this.

For a more advanced form of this game, see *Home Run*.

LINE CLUB–BOWLS (DOUBLE)

(See also *Line Club-Bowls* [*Single*]; *Center Club-Bowls; Circle Club-Bowls*.)

2 to 60 or more players   *Junior*
Playground; gymnasium   *high school*
        Handsizeball; beanbag; Indian clubs

This game is like Single Club-Bowls, except that the object of the play is to pass the ball or beanbag between a pair of upright Indian clubs, instead of trying to knock one over.

I. If there are but *few players*, one pair of clubs is set up for each player, with an interval between them two inches wider than the diameter of the ball that is used. At from ten to twenty feet from the clubs a line is drawn on which the players stand to throw. The players slide the bag over the floor or roll the ball; all play at once, each player scoring one if his ball or bag goes between the clubs without knocking them over. The clubs are then put in order if displaced, the balls or bags gathered up, and the players return to the starting line and bowl again.

The player wins who first scores twenty-five or fifty, as may be determined before the game opens.

II. Where there is a *large number of players*, the same form of play is used with the players in relay formation, each member of the group bowling in turn.

The group or team with the highest score when all have bowled wins.

LINE CLUB–BOWLS (SINGLE)

(See also *Line Club-Bowls [Double]; Center Club-Bowls; Circle Club-Bowls.*)

2 to 60 or more players   *Junior*
Playground; gymnasium   *high school*
           Basketball; handsizeball; beanbag; Indian club

This game differs from Double Club-Bowls only in the object of the play. In Single Club-Bowls the object is to knock over one Indian club which stands alone. In Double Club-Bowls the object is to bowl the ball or bean-bag between two upright Indian clubs without knocking them over.

I. Any kind of ball or beanbag may be used for this game. For *few players*, one Indian club is set up for each player, all clubs being widely separated and on a given line. At from ten to thirty feet from this club line a second line is drawn, on which the players must stand to play. The players all slide the bag over the floor at once, or roll the ball, each player scoring one when he knocks over his Indian club. The clubs are then replaced, the balls or bags gathered up, and the players return to the starting line and bowl again.

The player wins who first scores twenty-five or fifty, as may be determined before the game opens.

II. Where there is a *large number of players*, the same form of play is used with the players in relay formation. Each member of a group bowls in turn. · After each player has bowled, he should replace the club and bring back the ball or beanbag to the next player. In this form of the play it is not necessary for the different rows to throw simultaneously, unless that be desired as a question of order or to facilitate the scoring. The row or team which makes the highest score wins.

LINE ZIGZAG

(See *Zigzag Games*.)

LONG–BALL

6 to 20 players	*Intermediate grades*
Playground; gymnasium	*to senior high school*

Baseball and bat

I. This game differs from Batball in being more distinctively a baseball game in its equipment, distances, and mode of play. It is a very popular game.

A home plate is outlined, and thirty to forty feet from it a pitcher's box. At a distance of sixty-five feet from the home plate, and at an angle less than that of a baseball "diamond," a field base is outlined, to measure about four by eight feet.

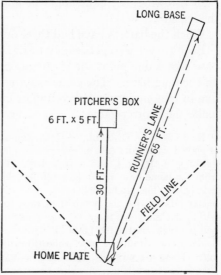

The game is played with a regular baseball and bat. Players are in two teams of from three to twenty each. With pitcher and catcher in their usual places, and a baseman near the field base, the rest of the fielding team scatters anywhere forward of the foul lines. The batter continues to bat until he touches the ball. Any touch of the ball with the bat entitles the batter to run to the field base, but only on a fair strike may he at once return to home plate and score a run; for any foul tip or foul strike he must stay on field base until some other batter on his side makes a fair hit. Any number of runners may be waiting in the long base (field base) for a chance to run home; this comes with any fair strike, when all may run at once. Having left the long base, a runner may not return to it. Should all the players of a team be on the field base at one time, the side is out.

A batter is out (1) if his batted ball is caught on the fly, (2) if an opponent is in either the long base or home base with the ball before he gets there, (3) when he is tagged off base with the ball in the hands of a fielder, (4) when he is hit while off base with the ball thrown by the fielding team.

The fielding team catches the ball and tries (1) to tag the runner with it either by a throw or in the hand, (2) to get to either base with the ball ahead of the runner, or (3) to throw the ball to a teammate in better position for one of these plays.

In throwing, the ball should be aimed to hit the runner below the waist.

When the batters have had three outs, the teams change places.

Each player who gets safely to the field base and back to home base scores one point for his team, whether or not he is held up on the long base. The game may be won on points or played in five to nine innings. For young or inexperienced players, points make the shorter game.

II. LONG–LANE BALL. — Under the name of Long Ball another game is played with from ten to twenty-five players on each team, a different marking of the field, and a volleyball. The pitcher's box is twenty feet from the home base, and a lane ten feet wide connects the home base and field base. The pitcher delivers the ball with an underhand throw, and the batter hits it with the hand, then runs to field base and returns, entirely within the lane. He is out (1) if stepping outside the lane, (2) if the batted ball is caught on the fly, (3) if hit with the ball while between bases. If a fielder steps within the base while throwing at a runner, the latter is not out. There are no fouls. The runner may wait on field base for a good chance to return home, in which case the next player comes to bat. Any number may be waiting on field base. A point is scored for each runner who makes the field base and returns, whether held up on the base or not. The game is played in innings. Teams change places when three runners are out.

MOUNT BALL

10 to 100 players

Playground; gymnasium

Junior to senior high school

Basketball; handsizeball

This is a game of ball played by half of the players while mounted on the backs of the other players. It is therefore desirable that the players be paired off so that the two in each pair should be of nearly equal weight and size.

The players form a circle in pairs, each with his selected partner. There should be considerable space between couples; in other words, the circle should be rather large in comparison with the number of players. It is then decided by a toss-up or otherwise which of each couple shall first be "pony" and which shall be rider. The ponies bend forward from the hips, pressing their hands against the knees, or thighs just above the knees. The knees should be stiff, not bent. The backs are thus bent forward and the riders mount, straddling the shoulders of the players who are ponies.

The ball is put in play by being tossed from any player to another, and the game consists on the part of the riders in trying to keep the ball in as active play as possible in a simple game of toss and catch, and on the part of the ponies in trying to prevent the catching of the ball. To do this the ponies may grow restive and turn around in any way they see fit, but must not lose their general places in the circle.

When a rider fails to catch a ball, all of the riders must at once dismount and run in any direction; the pony belonging to the rider who missed the ball picks up the ball immediately, and as soon as he has it calls "Halt!" All of the riders must then stand still, and the player who holds the ball tries to hit his recent rider. The rider aimed at may try to evade the ball by stooping or jumping, but must not otherwise leave his place on the floor. During this part of the play the other ponies remain in their position in the circle, so that the one who is throwing the ball will not confuse them with the riders. If the player (pony) who throws the ball at his dismounted rider succeeds in hitting him, all of the ponies and riders exchange places, the riders becoming ponies and the former ponies mounting them. If the player aiming the ball at his dismounted rider does not succeed in hitting him, the riders remount and the game goes on as before.

It is not permissible for a rider to hold a ball at any time, no matter how difficult his position at the moment may be ; he must toss it at once. It is well to have a leader, whether one of the players or not, who watches for mistakes, gives the commands to mount and dismount, and announces misses and hits.

This game was played by the ancient Greeks, and is found in various forms in many countries. It is needless to say that it is one of the more strenuous games. When properly played it contains great sport.

NEWCOMB

16 to 40 players   *Junior to senior high school*
Volley-, basket-, or soccerball; net or rope

COURT. — The dimensions of the court may be adapted to almost any playing space, but twenty-five by fifty feet are good. Across the center of this court a rope or volleyball net is stretched at a height of seven feet from the ground, dividing the space into two courts. On each side of the net, parallel to it and six feet from it, a line is drawn on the ground making a neutral zone twelve feet wide.

TEAMS. — Players are in two teams of from eight to twenty each, including a captain. They are scattered over the field at equal distances, each team in its own court. A player covers his assigned position and does not wander over the court.

OBJECT AND METHOD OF PLAY. — The object of the game is to throw the ball over the net into the opponent's court; opponents must catch it before it can touch the floor.

Play is started by one of the captains, who throws the ball into the opponent's court. Any player of the opposing side may catch it but must immediately throw it back into the other court. The ball is played only by throwing and catching; it may not be kicked, batted (volleyed), or bounced. No relaying is allowed, no holding of the ball, nor may a player step into the neutral zone. Long throws to the rear of the opponent's court are obviously desirable, but a throw outside the court is a foul. Play should be rapid, and it continues until a point is scored.

OUT OF BOUNDS. — A ball hitting the wall is out of bounds and does not score.

A ball thrown beyond the opponent's court scores as a foul if not touched by the defending team. It is recovered and played by the nearest player.

FOULS. — A foul is scored (one point) for the opponents for any of the following misplays:

If the ball is relayed or touched by two players on one side before going over the net; touches the net or goes under it; or is thrown out of bounds.

If a player holds or walks with the ball or steps into the neutral zone while playing it.

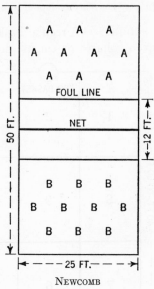

NEWCOMB

SCORE. — One point is scored for the opposing team every time (1) the ball touches the floor or (2) a foul is made.

The team first scoring twenty-one points wins the game.

The game is sometimes played in halves or quarters of from five to ten minutes each and then the team wins which has the highest score at the end.

After a score the ball is put in play again by the nearest player of the team at fault. He at once picks it up and throws it for the opponent's court.

NINE–COURT BASKETBALL

18 to 60 players   *Junior to senior high school*
Playground; gymnasium   *Basketball*

This is one of the comparatively few games that give a large amount of activity to a large number of players playing at the same time. The game as here given was the invention of Miss Cora B. Clark and Miss Caroline M. Wollaston of New York City. Not only has it proven to be a most popular and interesting game, but its basic ideas of multiple courts and progression of players have been adapted to a large variety of games.

COURT. — A regular basketball court is used, divided into nine even squares or courts, numbered in consecutive order around

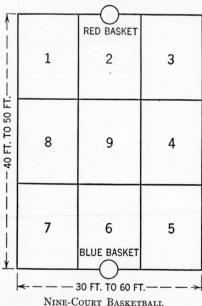

NINE-COURT BASKETBALL

the outside, starting in one corner; the ninth one is in the center.

TEAMS. — While from eighteen to sixty players may play this game at once, eighteen make the best playing number. A larger number is better divided into two sets, to play for ten minutes alternately.

The players are in two teams, each with a captain. The teams are paired off; the two opponents forming a couple should be of practically equal height.

The couples are numbered as they pair off, the number indicating to which court they shall go for the opening of the game. Thus, couple Number One will go to court one, couple Number Two to court two, etc. Should there be more than nine couples, the tenth couple will go to court one, the next couple to court two, etc. Each court thus contains an equal number of players of each team.

OBJECTS OF THE GAME. — The objects of the game for each team are (1) to throw the ball into its own basket; this may be done from any court in the diagram; and (2) to prevent the opponents from putting the ball into their basket.

PROGRESSION OF PLAYERS. — One of the marked characteristics of this game is the constant progression in the position of players, as every time that a goal is made all move to the next court. Those in court nine go to court one, those in one to court two, etc. Each player has an opportunity to play from all positions on the field.

START. — The game is started by the referee tossing the ball between two opposing players in court nine, each facing his own basket. Each tries to send the ball toward his own basket, others playing upon the ball immediately.

RULES AND POINTS OF PLAY. — The ball may be thrown for a basket from any of the courts. In other words, it is not necessary for the ball to be passed to a player in court two to be thrown for the Red basket, or to court six in order to be thrown to the Blue basket, though that may be a desirable play.

Players must remain in their own small courts except when progressing. Whether any penalty shall be attached to momentary stepping over the lines between small courts in the excitement of rapid catching and passing should be decided before the game opens. No player may step over the outer boundary lines, except to get the ball when it goes afield. A throw for a basket made with even one foot outside of the outer boundary lines is a foul.

Guarding is done by placing the hands or arms to intercept a throw, but neither ball nor thrower may be touched. Only one player may guard a thrower, no matter how many players may be in the small court where the thrower stands. The two opponents who first pair off at the opening of the game when places are assigned act thereafter as guards one to the other, no other players being allowed to fill that office.

When two players have possession of a ball, the one who touched it first has the right to it. If this cannot be decided instantly, the ball is thrown up between them as at the start of the game, the nearest player tossing it.

When the ball goes outside of the outer boundaries of the court, only one player may go after it. All of the players in the small court through which it left this boundary may start for it, but the first one over the line continues and secures the ball. Players from other courts may not try to get a ball that thus goes afield. When a ball has gone afield, the player picking it up must throw it from the point where it is picked up to any court player. No running or walking with the ball is allowed in thus returning the ball to the courts.

In playing on the ball, no player is allowed to hold the ball or to run or walk with it or bounce it. A player may turn around quickly with the ball, but must throw it at once. A player transgressing these rules must give the ball to his opponent — that is, to the opponent who has been paired off with him.

FOULS. — No scoring is made on the fouls. Transgression of any of the rules given above is punished by giving the ball to the opponents, the transgressor in each case giving it to the opponent paired off with him.

SCORE. — A team scores one point for each goal. The game is played on time limits. Where a large number of players is divided into two groups to take turns at playing, the time limits for each are generally ten minutes; with such rest intervals they may play indefinitely. Where all of the players are engaged in one game, the period may be from thirty to sixty minutes.

OVER–AND–UNDER RELAY

10 to 100 players   *Intermediate*
Playground; schoolroom   *to senior high*
Various balls

This game is a combination of Arch Ball and Stride Ball.

The players stand in stride position in single relay formation. The leaders of each file have several balls of contrasting sizes, as a basketball, handsizeball, Rugby ball, ping-pong ball, etc. On signal each leader starts passing the balls backward down his file, in quick succession, the first one passed overhead, the next between the feet, and so on alternately until all have been passed. The player at the end accumulates them and when the last ball is received must gather them all up and carry them to the front, immediately starting the play over again. This continues, the file moving backward one space each time the series is completed when the original leader, having received all the balls at the rear, gets back to the front with his load. The team wins whose leader is first to return.

OVERTAKE

20 to 60 players   *Intermediate*
Playground   *to senior high*
                 2 balls or beanbags

OBJECTS OF GAME. — This is a scoring game of toss and catch between a captain and the players of his team who are lined up around a circle alternated with the players of an opposing team. The objects of the game are (1) to complete the round of tossing and catching quicker than the opponents; (2) to "overtake" or outdistance the bag or ball which the opponents are tossing.

The players are evenly divided in two teams designated by colors or otherwise. The two Number-One players of each team stand opposite each other. A captain for each team stands in the center of the circle; the captains may not step outside of a four-foot circle drawn as their base, but they may there move around each other as the play may require. A referee is desirable to start the game, keep score, and return balls that go afield.

The game starts on signal with the captains standing back to back in the center, each facing his Number-One player, to whom he throws the ball for an immediate return; he then throws it to Number Two and so on clockwise around the circle. If a captain drops a ball three times, he changes places with Number One; this captain, failing three times, changes with Number Two, etc.

A ball which overtakes (passes) the opponent's ball scores five points. The ball that first completes the circuit to its Number-One player scores two points. The game is won on a score of ten points.

OVER–THE–CORD CATCH

10 to 40 players   *Intermediate to adult*
        Volleyball; basketball; Rugby ball

1. Players are lined up in relay formation behind a starting line, which is drawn at a distance of from twenty to thirty feet from a cord or rope stretched across the court at a height of from seven to ten feet above the ground. The first player of each team

holds a large ball. On signal, each first player runs forward, tosses the ball over the cord, and runs on to catch it on the far side of the cord; instantly on catching he reverses direction (pivots) and runs back to hand the ball to Number Two of his team, keeping on to take his place at the rear of the team. Number Two runs and tosses the ball in the same way as soon as he receives it. A missed ball must be recovered by the player missing it and thrown again. The team wins whose last player is first to recross the starting line.

II. For beginners the ball should bounce before being caught.

III. For advanced players the throw of the ball over the cord and its catch on the other side are made on the return run as well as on the outward run.

PADDLE TENNIS

2 to 16 players　　　　　　　　　　　　　　　　*Intermediate*
Playground; gymnasium　　　　　　　　　　　　　*to senior high*
　　　　　Special paddle and ball

This is an adaptation of Lawn Tennis to a very small court and a comparatively large number of players. In addition to its interest and adaptability, it is an excellent game for introducing players to the general procedure of regulation Tennis. Mr. F. P. Beal is credited with having originated this form of Tennis.

The court is one quarter the size of a regulation Lawn Tennis court, the area of the latter (thirty-six by seventy-eight feet) being divided into four small courts as shown in the diagram. Each court is marked as for Lawn Tennis but in smaller dimensions, its outside measurements being eighteen by thirty-nine feet with a two-foot alley between courts. The length of these smaller courts is extended one foot and a half at each end beyond the side lines of the large court. The top of the net should be two feet four inches from the ground at the posts and two feet two inches at the center. Instead of a tennis racket a paddle is used made of hard wood, measuring slightly over fourteen inches in length and seven and one-half inches in width. Balls are of sponge rubber and somewhat smaller than tennis balls, though a regular tennis ball may be used. Official Paddle Tennis equipment is available.

The play in general is like Lawn Tennis; the ball is served in singles by a server standing with both feet back of the baseline (end line of court). The service is delivered from the right and left sides of the court alternately, beginning from the

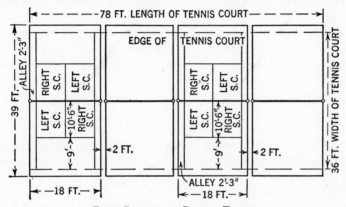

FOUR COURTS FOR PADDLE TENNIS
(Placed crosswise of a Lawn Tennis court)

right in every game, and the ball served must strike the ground in the service court diagonally opposite. The server has two tries from the same spot. If the second ball is incorrectly served, the server must change to the other side of the court and the opponent scores one point. In singles the same server serves through an entire game, when the serve passes to the opponent. In doubles the serve remains on the same side throughout a game but alternates between the two partners.

The ball is returned, as in Lawn Tennis, after it has bounced (not more than once), and must go within the bounds of the opposite court. A failure in such a return scores one for the opponent and the ball is again served by the same server. After the first return of a served ball players continue to keep the ball in motion, either with a volley or after one bounce. The score is stated in Lawn Tennis terms, " Fifteen-Love," etc.

PASS–BALL RELAY

10 to 100 players   *Intermediate*
Playground; gymnasium   *to adult*
Basketball

I. The teams line up in relay formation, and the game consists in passing a basketball backward overhead.

The players in a team must not stand close enough together to touch. An objective point or post is placed in front of each team at a distance of at least fifty or seventy-five feet if space admits. When the starter says "Go!" the first player hands the ball backward overhead to the next player, and each one in turn passes it in a similar way down the line. When the last player receives the ball, he runs forward with it around the goal, returns, and passes it to the player at the head of the line, when it again travels backward to the rear as before. A returning player may hand the ball to the front player, either facing him or turning with his back to him and passing the ball overhead; but he may not toss it to him. A returning player takes his place at the head of the line. The original leader of the line will thus move gradually backward until he is at the rear of the file; he will be the last runner forward, and should be plainly marked. When he receives the ball, he runs forward with it around the goal like his predecessors, but on his return, instead of lining up and passing the ball backward, dashes with it over the finish line. The finish line should be a tape (strand of worsted) stretched parallel with the starting line, but three feet to the rear of the files. Should the playing space not admit of this, the starting line may be used as a finish line.

Should the ball be dropped as it is passed down the line, the player next behind the one who last touched it must leave his place in the line, pick up the ball, return, and put it in play from where it left the line. If so rectified, this dropping of the ball does not score as a foul.

Rules used by the Girls' Branch of the Public Schools Athletic League of New York call for a judge of fouls for each team and two judges at the finish. One foul is scored against a team for —

    1. Every player who does not touch the ball as it is passed backward.

2. Every player (except a returning player) who turns to face the next one and hand the ball instead of passing it backward overhead.

3. A returning player tossing the ball to the head of the file.

4. The head player standing forward of the starting line.

5. A runner touching the goal as he encircles it.

The teams win in the order of finishing if there are no fouls. One foul disqualifies a team unless the competing teams have made an equal or greater number of fouls. In such a case the teams win in the order of finishing, plus consideration of the smallest record on fouls. A team finishing second, for example, with no fouls, would win over a team finishing first with one or more fouls.

Teams	Order of Finishing	Number of Fouls	Order of Winning
A	1	3	
B	4	2	Third place
C	2	2	Second place
D	3	0	First place

II. AS A RECREATIONAL GAME. — This is made more rapid by dispensing with the distance run; the player at the rear of the file then merely runs to the front and at once passes the ball back.

III. In still another form, instead of the rear player running to the front of his file, as soon as he gets the ball he commands "About Face!" The whole file then faces to the rear and passes the ball backward again to the front. Several such "about facings" may be stipulated to constitute a game.

PASS THE BAT

5 to 12 players   *Intermediate grades*
Playground   *Tennis or other soft ball*

Two bases are marked fifteen or twenty feet apart, one for a pitcher and one for a batter. On a line at right angles to these, and beginning sixty feet away from them, small bases in a row are marked about ten feet apart, one for each of the remaining players. The game is an effort of the pitcher to become batter, all other players being his opponents.

Play begins with all players in their places. The pitcher throws the ball to the batter, who bats it off into the field. Immediately the ball is hit, the pitcher runs to recover it and get back to batter's base before the last base player can reach it with the bat. Meanwhile the batter, as soon as he has hit the ball, runs to the first baseman in the row of bases, hands him the bat,

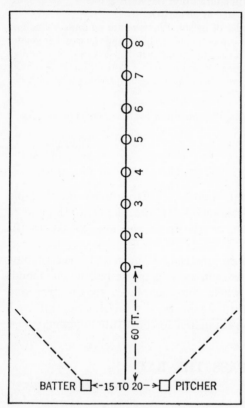

PASS THE BAT

stays on that base and the first baseman runs to second and hands the bat to him, and so on until the bat is relayed to the end of the line and each player has moved up one base. The last man in the row, on receiving the bat, runs to the batter's base, trying to reach it before the pitcher arrives. Whoever gets there first becomes batter and the man who is out becomes pitcher.

The pitcher, however, has another resource to put out his antagonists: that is, he may hit with the ball any player in the row who is off base (running between bases) or the last player before he can get to batter's base with the bat. Any player so hit becomes pitcher and the pitcher wins by becoming batter.

If any baseman in the row is hit off base by the ball, he becomes pitcher, the last man in the row takes his base, and the remaining basemen move up one base.

For this game, played in Czechoslovakia, the author is indebted to Prof. M. Vejchoda-Ambros, of Prague.

PIG IN A HOLE

10 to 60 players   *Junior high*
Playground; seashore; gymnasium   *Basketball*

Each player should be provided with a stick about three feet
long.   This may be made by whittling branches, or a gymnasium
wand or piece of broom-
stick may be used.   A
hole is dug in the
ground measuring
twelve or fifteen inches
in diameter.   All of the
players but one stand
in a circle around this,
with several feet be-
tween each two players
so that they may move
freely.   Each player
digs a small hole in the
ground in front of his
place in the circle, the
hole to measure about
four inches in diameter.

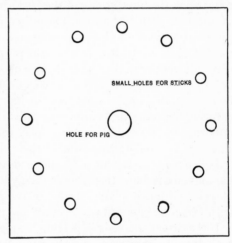

PIG IN A HOLE

The game is played with a basketball, although a smaller ball
may be used, in which case the center hole need not be quite
so large, though it should be somewhat larger than the ball used.

The game consists in the odd player's trying (1) to get the ball
(the "pig") into the center hole with his stick, which all of the
other players will try to prevent; and (2) the odd player's trying
to be released from his position by placing the end of his stick
in one of the small holes belonging to one of the circle players,
which he can only do when the player in question has his own
stick out of it.

The game starts by all of the players putting their sticks in the
center hole under the ball.   They count, "One, two, three!"
and on the last word all lift the ball with the sticks and then rush
for the small holes, each player placing the end of his stick in a
hole.   As there is one less hole than the number of players, one

odd player will be left out.　It thereupon becomes his duty to drive the pig into the hole from whatever point it may have landed through the combined effort and toss with which the game opened.　The circle players try to prevent the pig getting into the hole by blocking its passage with their sticks.　They may not kick it or play upon it in any other way.　The odd player will try to ward off the interference of the sticks by clearing a way in front of the ball with his own.　The other players may leave their places at any time to block the passage of the ball; but this is a dangerous thing to do, for the odd player may at any moment leave his work with the ball and place his stick in one of the vacant holes.　It therefore behooves the circle players to leave their holes unguarded only when there is imminent danger of the ball entering the center hole from that side of the ring, or when a good opportunity comes for aggressive play to drive the ball out of the ring, which should also be one of their objects.

It is not necessary for a player to return to his own hole after having removed his stick from it.　Any hole may be taken by any player, and much of the interest of the game lies in the freedom with which players will move about and take chances in this way.

If the driver succeeds in getting his pig in the center hole, he is considered to have won, and the game begins again.　Should the driver succeed in placing his stick in an unoccupied hole in the circle, the odd player thus left out must become driver.

FOR THE GYMNASIUM. — This game may be adapted to the gymnasium by drawing chalk circles in place of those that would be dug in the ground out of doors.　The same rules apply for the game, which may be played either with a basketball or a beanbag.

This game is found in many countries.　Several of the forms of play here given are from the Chinese.　It is an old traditional game in England and popular there today.

PING–PONG

(See *Table Tennis*.)

PLAYGROUND BASEBALL

(Indoor Baseball)

20 players *Intermediate grades to adult*
Playground ball and bat

GENERAL DESCRIPTION. — Playground Baseball, or Indoor Baseball, is an adaptation of the regular game of baseball to limited space indoors or out, and is suitable for men or women, senior or junior players.

The ball is larger and softer than for regular baseball, being made to cover a shorter distance when batted. The bat is shorter and smaller in circumference. These differences in equipment call for some differences in the technique of play, especially in the throwing and batting of the ball. (See chapter on *Balls and How to Play Them.*) The game is more adaptable to varied surroundings than regular Baseball, and more recreational in character, being less highly specialized and strenuous, though a very lively game. These qualities account for its great popularity.

FIELD. — A regular baseball diamond is laid out, measuring from twenty-seven feet to sixty feet on each side according to space available. Adults and senior boys usually play on a sixty-foot diamond out of doors; girls and juniors on one measuring thirty-five feet.

The game is played like regular baseball, except for the following modifications:

TEAMS. — Ten players constitute a team instead of the usual baseball nine, the additional player being a short fielder.

The positions of players are not strictly defined, except as to pitcher and catcher.

PLAY. — Pitching the ball is done in most games with the underhand throw, though in some localities, on large fields, an overhand throw is allowed. The method should be understood before the game begins.

The batter may not run after third strike but is out at once.

No bunting is allowed in some localities, any attempt to bunt putting the batter out. This also varies in different sections of the country and is probably related somewhat to the size of the field; it also should be clearly understood in advance.

A batted ball must strike in fair ground and is then a "fair" ball whether it rolls into foul ground or not.

The batter must lay down the bat — never throw it.

STEALING BASES. — A base runner may not take his foot from his base until a pitched ball has reached or passed the batter; if he does, he is out.

INNINGS. — The game is played in seven innings instead of the nine of regular baseball. Five innings must have been played to score a called game.

PROGRESSIVE CAPTAINBALL

(See *Captainball* — *V.*)

PROGRESSIVE DODGEBALL

15 to 100 players   *Intermediate*
Playground; gymnasium   *to senior high school*
Basketball

COURT. — The ground is divided into three equal courts, each thirty by thirty feet. The end courts may be shorter if full space is not available.

TEAMS. — The players are in three equal teams, here designated by colors, Red, White, and Blue. There are no officers for the teams, but one referee for the game, who should also act as scorekeeper, is desirable, and for match games necessary.

OBJECT OF THE GAME. — The game consists in hitting players with a flying ball (not a bounce), any player so hit being out and leaving the field. For this purpose the two end teams play against the center team (but not against each other); and the center team also plays the ball in a retaliatory or aggressive game, trying to hit players on either of the end teams.

START. — At the opening of the game the two outer teams line up, each on its inner boundary line, each player standing with one foot on the line. The center team is grouped irregularly near the middle of the center court. The teams change courts at the end of each inning, and the formation or line-up just described is resumed at the opening of each inning.

The referee puts the ball in play by tossing it to the center team and signals for the game to open. He also blows his whistle when a player is out (*i.e.* hit by a ball "on the fly," not on a bounce) and again tosses the ball. After the ball is in play, teams may secure the ball when it is "dead," *i.e.* when it has not just been played by an opponent, but has stopped, rolled, or bounced into its own court.

RULES AND POINTS OF PLAY. — The center player catching the ball, throws it at one of the opposing players (Red or Blue).

A ball thrown by either end team across the center court may be caught, however, by a player on the opposite end.

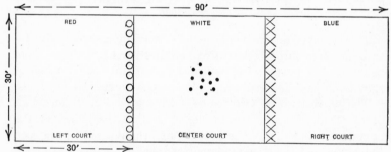

PROGRESSIVE DODGEBALL

A player is not out if hit by a ball that rebounds, whether from the floor, another player, a wall, or any other object.

A player is not out if the thrower of the ball overstepped the boundary lines while throwing.

The only kind of hit that puts a player out is from a fly ball thrown from behind a boundary line.

Players may dodge in any way they choose, but a hit from a flying ball on any part of the person or clothing puts a player out.

At the close of each inning (of five or more minutes) the teams progress or change courts in regular order, from right to left. That is, the Blue team moves to the center, the White team to the left court, and the Red team to the right court. For the third inning another change is made in the same direction, the Reds going to the center, the Blues to the left court, and the Whites to the right court. Thus, in the three innings each team will have played in each court.

When a new inning is started and the teams change courts, all players who have been hit and are out return to their teams. Each inning begins, therefore, with full teams.

SCORE. — The team wins which at the close of the three innings has the smallest score; that is, has had the smallest number of players hit.

This game was devised by Mr. William A. Stecher.

PUNCH BALL

12 to 40 players   *Intermediate*
Large field   *to adult*

Playgroundball

This is played on a rather large field, maximum seventy-five by three hundred yards. The entire rear lines are the goal lines, there being no goal posts. The ball is the comparatively soft ball of the Playground Baseball type. It is a fast game with few fouls.

The players are in two teams, each starting in its own half of the field. The game consists in getting the ball over the opponents' goal line. The ball is put in play halfway between the center and the serving team's own goal by a toss and punch with the fist. Thereafter it is played entirely with the hands or body, but never thrown or kicked. It may be punched with the closed fist, slapped with the open hand, or butted with the body. No dribbling is allowed, and no running with the ball. More than one step is a run. The ball may be tossed, but only to be punched or slapped. It may be caught, but not held.

For a foul the ball is given to the opponents, being thrown in to them from the side line nearest where the foul occurred. A ball out of bounds over the side lines is thrown in by the opposite team from that which sent it out.

One point is scored by a team for each time it puts the ball beyond the opponents' goal line. The ball then goes to the opposite team, to be put in play as at the start. The game is played in four periods of ten minutes each, with one-minute rests between first and second, third and fourth, and an intermission of ten minutes between halves. The team having the highest score at the end wins.

RING CALL–BALL

(See also *Call-Ball*.)

10 to 30 or more players   *Primary grades*
Playground; gymnasium   *Handsizeball; beanbag*

This game is similar in some respects to Call-Ball, but being played in a circle formation, is much simpler and less difficult and exciting, being suited particularly to younger players.

The players form a circle, with one in the center, who throws a ball in the air, at the same time calling the name of one of the circle players. The one called must run forward and catch the ball before it bounces more than once. If he catches it, he returns to the circle. If he does not catch it, he changes places with the thrower.

ROLEY POLEY

(Hat Ball)

5 to 20 players   *Primary to intermediate grades*
Playground; gymnasium   *Handsizeball; beanbag*

A row of holes three or four inches in diameter is made in the ground, with about one foot space between.   There should be one hole less than the number of players.   Boys' caps may be placed in a similar row instead of digging holes.   Parallel with the row of holes, and about twenty feet away from it, a baseline is drawn. A pile of pebbles (called "babies") should be collected before the game begins.

The game consists primarily of rolling a ball into one of the holes or caps, followed by ball tag, and a scoring with the pebbles. The players stand each a little distance behind a hole except one, who is chosen to be the first roller.   He rolls the ball from the baseline into one of the holes or caps.   Immediately he and all of the players except the one into whose hole the ball has fallen, run, scattering in any direction.   The one to whose lot the ball has fallen lifts the ball as quickly as possible, calling "Stand!" as soon as he has it in his hand.   The running players must halt when they hear this order, and the one who holds the ball tries to hit one of them with it from where he stands.   If he succeeds in doing so, one of the pebbles is put in the cap of the player who is hit. Should he miss hitting anyone, a pebble is put in his own cap. Should the player who tries to roll the ball into one of the holes or caps miss getting it in, a pebble is put in his own cap, and he makes other trials until he succeeds. When a player is hit by the ball, he becomes roller, and all of the others return to their places. The game continues until one player gets six (or ten) stones ("babies") in his hole or cap. When this happens, he must be "court-martialed," that is, stand with his face against a wall or fence and let each player take three shots at him with the rubber ball, the first time with the thrower's eyes closed and then with them open. The distance of the throwers from the fence is determined by the victim's throwing the ball at the fence three times so it will rebound; the farthest point to which the ball rebounds becomes the throwing line for the court-martialing. If no fence or wall is available, the throwing is done from an agreed distance at the back of the victim.

This game may be played by drawing a series of circles on the ground or floor in place of the holes or caps, and sliding a beanbag into them. This form is serviceable for a gymnasium.

ROSEMARY

Individual play   *Handsizeball*   *Elementary*

This is a delightful little folk game from Holland, which may be used by one player alone, or by a class of any number in unison. It is admirable for acquiring the early skill of ball tossing and catching.

The game is played with any handsizeball about like a tennis ball or larger. This is tossed as the player asks a question of herself about Rosemary; the question is answered and acted out while the ball is in the air, and then the ball is caught. The questions refer to Rosemary getting dressed in the morning and ready for school.

> *1st toss:* Where was Rosemary?
> *Ans.* Sitting behind the curtain. (*Cover the face with both hands; then catch.*)

2d toss: What was she doing there?

    Ans. She combed her hair. (*Motions of combing hair; catch.*)

3d toss: What else did she do?

    Ans. She washed her hands. (*Motions of washing hands; catch.*)

4th toss: What else did she do?

    Ans. She cleaned her teeth. (*Act out; catch.*)

5th toss: Then what else did she do?

    Ans. She put on her dress. (*Act; catch.*)

6th toss: Then what did she do?

    Ans. She jumped and danced. (*Act; catch.*)

An indefinite number of items may be added, such as putting on her shoes, eating her breakfast, getting her books, skipping to school, etc.

ROUND BALL

20 to 60 players   *Intermediate grades*
Playground; gymnasium   *Handsizeball; basketball*

This is an advanced form of Circle Ball, there being two competing teams standing alternately in a circle, with wide spaces between, all facing inward.

Each team has a captain and a ball. The game consists in each team's throwing the ball around the circle, started by its captain. The team wins whose ball first completes the circle five times. Each time that the captain receives the ball he calls out the number of

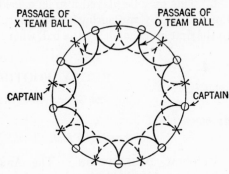

ROUND BALL

times the ball has circulated, "One" for the first time, "Two" for the second, etc. The play should be rapid. Any player dropping the ball must pick it up and throw in regular form.

The game may be varied by requiring different methods of throwing and catching, such as catching with the right hand, left hand, both hands, etc., if a handsizeball is used; or throwing from below, above, or from the chest if a basketball pass is used.

RUGBY DISTANCE THROW

Rugby football field; playground　　　　*Junior high school*
Rugby football　　　　　　　　　　　　　　*to college*

This may be played as individual or team competition.

I. The ground, if not a regular Rugby field, is marked with a throwing line and a series of parallel lines at ten- (or five-) yard intervals, as in *Baseball Distance Throw*. The player stands behind the throwing line and on each throw scores a number of points corresponding to the yard-line nearest to which the ball strikes the ground. Each player has three (or five) consecutive throws.

Another method of scoring is to credit each player with only his longest throw. In team competition the total score of the members gives the team score.

II. This may be played also on a field that does not have distance lines, by measuring the distance from the throwing line to the first mark made by the ball where it strikes the ground.

RUGBY FOOTBALL

(American Game; Collegiate Football)

22 players　　　　　　　　　　　　　　*Senior high to adults*
Rugby football and goals

GENERAL DESCRIPTION. — The American game of Rugby (Collegiate Football) is played by two opposing teams of eleven players each; they start the game facing each other in scrimmage formation, in a large rectangular field, each standing in its own half. At the far end of each half is a goal of upright posts supporting a crossbar. The ball is commonly called the oval or Rugby ball and is prolate spheroid in shape.

The object of the game is for a team to advance the ball beyond the opponents' goal. There are two ways of doing this. The ball may be kicked over the goal above the crossbar between the two upright posts, which is called "kicking a goal," or it may be carried over the goal line by a player of the opposing team and there touched to the ground, or otherwise declared dead, called a "touchdown." After a touchdown a team has a free (unimpeded) try at goal with a kick. The ball is usually advanced but short distances in each attempt, called a "down."

Rugby Football differs from Soccer Football in the layout of the field, the shape of the ball,

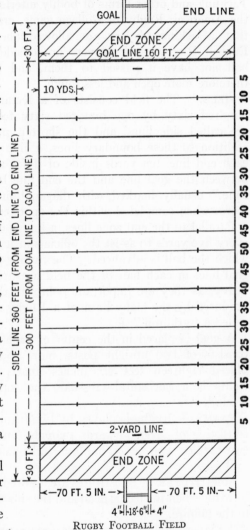

RUGBY FOOTBALL FIELD

the manner in which the ball is played, and the way in which goals are made and points scored. The hands and arms are used so that the ball is passed, thrown, and carried as well as kicked, whereas in Soccer kicking alone is permissible. Tackling and other forms of bodily interference are features of the American Rugby or College game, growing out of the fact that attacking players are allowed ahead of the ball. In English Rugby, such players are offside, may not play the ball nor have it passed to them, and the English game is therefore more open and less rough.

FIELD. — The field consists of a rectangle measuring three hundred sixty by one hundred sixty feet. The longer lines are called side lines, and the shorter are the end lines. In addition to these boundary lines, a line is drawn parallel to each end line, ten yards inside of it for a goal line, the space between the goal line and the end line being called the "end zone," usually marked with diagonal lines. A forward pass scores when completed within the opponent's end zone.

Parallel to the end zone lines, a line is drawn across the field every five yards to assist the officials in judging the distances to which the ball is advanced. The twenty-yard, forty-yard, and goal lines in each half of the field are usually made especially heavy, as they are important points in the game. The effect produced by the many lines of a Rugby field led to its being called a "gridiron."

A goal is placed in the center of each of the end lines and consists of two upright posts, more than twenty feet high, placed eighteen feet six inches apart. Between these uprights is a horizontal crossbar, the top ten feet from the ground.

TEAMS. — Rugby is played by two teams of eleven men each, consisting of seven forwards (namely, one center, two guards, two tackles, two ends), one quarterback, two halfbacks, and a fullback.

SUBSTITUTES. — Substitutes are allowed, but the change must be made when the ball is dead and the substitute must first report to the umpire.

A player leaving the game may not return in the same period or intermission in which he left, but may return in the following period unless disqualified or suspended from the game.

CHOICE OF GOALS. — At the start of the game the captains toss a coin, the winner having his choice of goal, and of kick-off or receiving the kick-off. The loser of the toss may then choose between the two remaining options.

The game is played in four quarters; at the beginning of the second and fourth quarters the teams change goals. The team that then has possession of the ball retains the relative position of the ball and distance to be gained. For the beginning of the second half the captain of the team that lost the toss has the same choice that the winner of the toss had at the beginning of the game. The ball is put in play by a kick-off, scrimmage, or free-kick.

KICK-OFF. — The opening play of a game is a kick-off — either a drop-kick or place-kick from anywhere on or back of the team's own forty-yard line. The kicker's team must be behind the ball, and opponents at least ten yards in advance of the ball — with at least five players within five yards of this line — until after the kick-off. The ball must pass the opponents' forty-yard line to be in play, unless touched by an opponent. The kick-off also opens the third period, and starts play after each try-for-point or goal from field.

SCRIMMAGE. — The ball is put in play by a scrimmage except as otherwise specified. For a scrimmage, opposing teams line up opposite each other, the seven rushers or forwards on a line, and the backs in formation behind them as shown in the diagram. The quarterback or captain of the team having the ball usually signals, by calling numbers, letters, or other words unintelligible to any but his team, what is to be the next play.

ADVANCING THE BALL. — A team must advance the ball at least ten yards in every four attempts (downs), or the ball goes to the opponents. The three such plays that follow the first down are numbered consecutively second, third, and fourth downs. Should a team make the required distance in the fourth or an earlier down, the next play becomes the first down in a new series. A down occurs when the ball becomes dead.

A *down* is declared when a player having the ball falls so that at least one knee touches the ground. It is not a down if only his hands or feet touch the ground. A forward pass hitting the ground before being caught is also a down, called an incompleted pass.

A goal may be kicked from the field by either a drop-kick or a place-kick, not a punt.

TOUCHDOWN. — The highest score is made by carrying the ball over the goal line, where, if declared dead, it is called

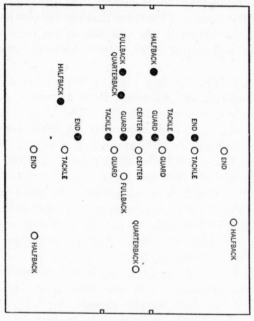

RUGBY SCRIMMAGE FORMATION
(The far team has the ball at the center)

a "touchdown." The successful team, in addition to scoring for this, has a try at goal.

SAFETY AND TOUCHBACK. — A safety consists in the downing of a ball by a defending player behind the goal line, provided the play is from his own team. This scores two points for the attacking team. If the ball is dead behind the goal line, held by the defense but sent there by the attackers, no score is made and the play is called a "touchback." The ball is returned to play after a safety by a free kick made by the team scored upon anywhere on or back of its own twenty-yard line. After a touchback the defending team puts the ball in play by a scrimmage anywhere on its own twenty-yard line.

TACKLING. — Only the man with the ball may be tackled. For this, hands and arms may be used to grasp and throw him to the ground. Teammates protecting the man with the ball may not use hands and arms until after the kick, but may run against opponents with hips or shoulders, their arms held in against the body. Opponents may use hands and arms freely.

PLAYING THE BALL. — This is done by running with the ball and with forward and sideways passes and the various kicks.

Kicks. — These are punt, drop-kick, and place-kick. For technique of these see *Rugby* in section on *Balls and How to Play Them*, page 418.

In the case of a punt, players of the kicker's team who are ahead of the ball are off-side and may not play the ball.

Forward Pass. — The ball is thrown end first to a teammate in the direction of the opponents' goal. To be on-side this teammate must have been at the end of the line of scrimmage or behind it. The pass may be intercepted by any opponent.

Lateral Pass. — This consists in passing the ball by a runner to a teammate not in front of him; that is, to one on a line with him or behind him.

Fouls and Penalties. — Fouls involve the manner of playing the ball, the position of players in reference to the ball, interference, etc., as explained above. Penalties consist mostly of loss of distance or loss of the ball and are subject to change in the official rules.

SCORE. — A touchdown scores six points for the team making it.

The side making a touchdown may score one further point on a try-for-point.

A goal kicked from the field scores three points.

A safety is penalized by two points added to the score of the attacking team.

The game is played in four fifteen-minute periods.

OFFICIALS. — For a match game the officials are a referee, an umpire, a field judge, a linesman, and two assistant linesmen.

REFEREE. — The referee is the head official in charge of the game. He is the judge of all rules relating to the ball and sole authority for the score.

UMPIRE. — This official judges of the position and conduct of players as distinguished from the supervision and progress of the ball. The umpire judges of such fouls as holding, offside play, and unfair tackling. When he sees a foul, the umpire signals and reports it to the referee, who alone has power to suspend the play and enforce penalties. The umpire usually stands back of the defensive team.

FIELD JUDGE. — The field judge usually takes a position back of the defending team at the side and opposite from the linesmen. The field judge keeps the time (when the ball is actually in play), and acts as an assistant to the other officials in observing fouls.

LINESMAN. — This official is charged with noting the distance which the ball has advanced, the position of players in relation to the ball when it is put in play, and fouls which involve personal conduct. After each down, the assistants mark a point on the side line even with the ball.

HISTORY. — The beginnings of modern football are very far in the past. The Ancient Greeks played a seizing game of ball, in which two opposing sides tried to seize and carry away a ball (called harpastum). Another form of play, exactly opposite, was their epikoinos, in which, starting the ball on a certain line, each party tried to send it over the opponent's goal line.

For centuries in England whole village communities divided annually in two opposing parties that drove a ball from one end of the village to another.

Like many other games, football earned the distinction of several royal edicts forbidding its play in England in the fourteenth and fifteenth centuries. Doubtless the game had undergone considerable modifications from the wild play of these early days, when it was adopted, about 1800, by English schools and universities.

The beginning of the modern Rugby is indicated by a tablet at Rugby School which reads:

This stone
commemorates the exploit of

WILLIAM WEBB ELLIS

who with a fine disregard for the rules of football as
played in his time
first took the ball in his arms and ran with it thus
originating the distinctive feature of
The Rugby Game

A.D. 1823.

Harvard University is credited with introducing this game to the United States in 1875, after its teams had played the game in Canada. Doubtless cruder forms of football had already existed here. The Collegiate game of today is a distinct variety of football differing from the English Rugby as explained in opening paragraphs of this text.

RUGBY KICKS FOR ACCURACY

(For technique see page 418)

DROP-KICK FOR GOAL. — This is a drop-kick for accuracy to put the ball over the crossbar between the goal posts. It is made from a twenty-five-yard line (shorter distance for juniors). Each player is allowed ten kicks and is given one point for each successful kick.

PLACE-KICK FOR GOAL. — The object is to kick the ball over the bar between the goal posts of a regular Rugby goal. The ball is set on end on a line thirty yards from the goal (twenty yards for juniors), and kicked on the run. Each player is allowed ten kicks and scores one point for each that is successful.

RUGBY KICKS FOR DISTANCE

DROP-KICK FOR DISTANCE. — Standing behind the goal line, the player drops the ball to the ground and kicks it on the bound. Measurement and scoring are as for the *Rugby Distance Throw* described above.

PLACE-KICK FOR DISTANCE. — The player stands the ball on end on the goal line, and kicks it in on the run. Measurement and scoring as for *Baseball Distance Throw* with five-yard intervals between the lines if specially drawn.

PUNT FOR DISTANCE. — Standing behind the goal line until his kick is made, the player drops the ball and kicks it before it strikes the ground. Measurement and scoring are as for *Rugby Distance Throw* described above.

RUGBY PASSES

FORWARD PASS FOR ACCURACY. — Contestants try to throw the ball through a hoop suspended firmly at twenty yards from the throwing line. One foot must remain in contact with the line. Each player has five tries, and scores one point for each that is successful.

RUGBY RUN, THROW, AND CATCH RACE. — This is like the *Basketball Run, Throw, and Catch Race, page 463.* The competition is between couples, who stand facing in the direction of the run, the right-hand player (B) being from three to ten feet in advance of his partner (A) who has the ball. This is thrown from the first player to his partner, the first then running forward on his own line of direction to receive the return pass. The ball may be thrown and caught while players are standing or running, but the method used should be specified and used throughout the distance covered. A ball dropped is recovered and returned to play by the one missing it. On a long field the couple wins whose player is first to catch the pass on the opposite goal line. On a short field, players should turn at the far end of the course and play back to the starting line.

RUGBY SIDE-PASS RACES. — See the two forms described under *Basketball Side-Pass Race, page 464;* namely, (I) players in ranks; (II) leader-and-group formation with clockwise rotation and passing.

RUSSIAN HOLE BALL

3 to 10 players   *Out of doors; seashore; snow*
                    Ball; beanbag; stone

This game is played with one small ball, in size anywhere from that of a golf to a tennis ball. If played in the snow, a hard frozen snowball may be used, or a stone will do.

A series of holes is made in the ground, sand, or snow, large enough to contain the ball. These holes are placed in a straight line, one beyond the other, about three feet apart, there being as many holes as there are players. All holes are numbered, corresponding to the numbers of the players, from one to ten, or whatever the maximum may be. About ten feet from the first hole, and at right angles to the row, a straight line is drawn on the ground, behind which the players stand to throw. The first player stands directly in line with the row of holes and throws

for one of them. This is a toss of the ball. The ball scores
for the player according to the number of the hole in which it falls,
and this number also designates the next player.
For instance, if the ball falls in the third hole,
it scores three for the first player, who at once
gives place to Number Three, who in turn has
one throw. Should this ball fall in hole number five, it scores five for this player, and the
fifth player will have the next turn. The game
may be played according to score, the one first
scoring twenty-five or fifty winning; or it may
be played according to time, the one having
the highest score at the end of fifteen or
twenty minutes being the winner.

This is one of the few games that may be
adapted to the snow or to the damp sand
of the seashore, though it may be played
anywhere out of doors where holes can be
dug.

RUSSIAN HOLE
BALL

This game comes from the Russian province of Bessa-
rabia, which formerly belonged to Turkey.

SCHOOLROOM DODGEBALL

10 to 60 players   *Gas ball*   *Intermediate*

The players are evenly divided into two teams. One team
takes its place around the outer edge of the room; the players of
the other team scatter through the aisles or seats, which latter
should be turned up if possible. The outer team tries to hit the
inner team with the ball, any player so hit taking his place in
the outer team and joining in its play. The player who remains
longest in the center is considered to have won.

Only a hit from a ball on the fly counts. A hit from a bounce
does not put a player out. If a ball touches any part of the clothing or person, it is considered a hit. If two players are hit by the
same throw, only the first one hit is considered out. Players
may dodge the ball in any way. The ball is returned to the circle

players by a toss from one of the inner team, should it be out of reach of any player of the circle team.

If desired, the hit players may leave the game instead of joining the outer circle. This leaves the teams intact, and each then keeps a separate score.

If successive games are played, the teams change places, the inner players going to the circle, and *vice versa*. The game may then be played in innings if desired, each team to be given three minutes in the circle. One point is then scored against a team while in the center for every player hit, and the team wins which has the smallest score at the end.

SCHOOLROOM VOLLEYBALL

10 to 60 players   *Intermediate*
Gas ball   *to junior high*

The players are divided into two teams, and the players in each team number consecutively. A net or string is placed across the

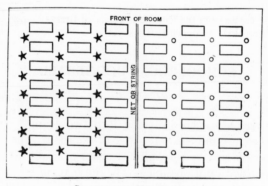

SCHOOLROOM VOLLEYBALL

schoolroom, dividing it into two equal parts. The top should be six feet from the floor. The game consists in batting the ball with the hand back and forth over the string, a point being scored by either team whenever its opponents allow the ball to touch the floor. The ball may be batted (not thrown) in any way, but by only one hand at a time.

The players stand in the aisles, each having a required place.

The game starts by serving the ball.

Two failures to bat the ball over the net changes the serve to the other side; otherwise, the server continues until the ball is not returned by his own side; the serve then changes to No. 1 of team 2, then to No. 2 of team 1, then to No. 2 of 2, etc.

The team wins which has the highest score at the end of a ten- or fifteen-minute period.

Every time that the ball touches the floor (not a desk) it scores against that side on which it falls, counting one point for the opposing team, irrespective of which team served the ball.

SHOOTER

10 to 20 players   *Primary to*
Playground   *intermediate grades*
                Tennis or other light ball

Two bases are marked on the ground from thirty to sixty feet apart. Midway between them, and at right angles to an imaginary line connecting them, are places for a shooter and his helper. The shooter should be from thirty to forty-five feet from the base line. Players are chosen for shooter and helper (catcher) and the remaining players line up in single file behind one of the bases, as for a relay. The object of the game for the file is for each player in turn to run across to the opposite base without being tagged with the ball; the object for the shooter is to hit the players with the ball as they run

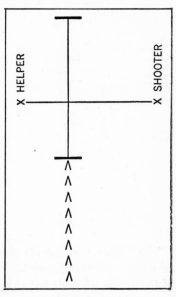

SHOOTER

from base to base. He scores one point for each hit and continues to be shooter so long as he is successful. If he shoots without hitting he loses his position and goes to the rear of the file, while the player at whom he aimed unsuccessfully becomes shooter. A runner who is hit takes the place of helper (catcher) and the helper goes to the rear of the file of runners.

This game is from Czechoslovakia.

SKYLARK

20 to 30 players   *Intermediate*
Playground   *to junior high*
Handsizeball, support, and bat

A short, thick peg is driven into the ground in the center of a six-foot circle; across it is laid a strip of wood with a slight hollow at one end on which the ball rests. This strip is called the

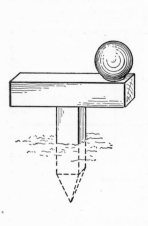

SKYLARK

"spoon"; or the spoon may rest on a stone instead of on a peg. The ball is light of weight, like a tennis ball, and the bat usually short, about two feet in length. A touch-base is marked at a distance of about sixty feet. Players are in two teams, one at bat, lined up behind the batting base, each member to bat in turn; the other team is on the opposite side of the circle, facing the batter, and scattered irregularly in the field.

The batter does not hit the ball, but the "spoon," his object being to send the ball so high in the air by hitting the free end of the spoon with his bat that he can run to the touch-base and back again before the opponents can catch the ball. If he is successful in this or if the ball is caught by his own team, it scores one point for his team. Both teams try to catch the ball and may run freely, but no personal interference is allowable. It is, however, a risk for any member of the batting team to run out for the ball, as he is then vulnerable to be tagged by the ball, the same as the batter, and if hit (tagged), it puts his batter out. If the ball falls to the ground, anyone may recover it and go on with the play.

Each batter has two tries at lofting the ball. When each member of the batting team has had his turn, teams change sides.

This traditional game, from Czechoslovakia, is kindly contributed by Prof. M. Vejchoda-Ambros, of Prague. In its oldest form there is no division of players into "sides" or teams; the batter plays against all others as opponents.

SOCCER DRIBBLE AND KICK

2 to 40 players   *Junior high to college*

For each team three long parallel lines are drawn twenty to forty feet apart as in Basketball Juggle Race, page 460. Each team is in two ranks which stand facing each other in zigzag formation behind the outside line. Number One of each team has a soccer ball and on signal dribbles this to the center line and from there kicks it to Number Two on the opposite line. Number Two blocks the ball with any permissible soccer play (*i.e.* with foot or body, not with the hands), dribbles it to his starting line if it has not stopped there, and goes through a similar play to Number Three on the first line. When the ball reaches the end of the line, a return play is made in the opposite direction back to Number One.

SOCCER DRIBBLE RELAY

1 to 40 players   *Junior high to college*

I. SINGLE-FILE RELAY FORMATION behind a starting line, with a jump stand, chair, or other object as a goal post, placed at from twenty to forty feet distant. Each first player has a soccer ball and on signal dribbles this with his foot to and around the post and back to the starting line where the next player takes it for similar play while the first one moves to the rear of his line. At first the play is slow for accuracy; it scores one point for each player who makes the tour without, in the umpire's opinion, losing control of the ball. Later, for speed play, the team whose last player gets back first wins.

II. SERPENTINE DRIBBLE. — Several posts or obstacles are placed in a line twenty feet apart and the ball dribbled around them alternately to the right and left (serpentine).

SOCCER FOOTBALL

22 or more players   *Junior high school to adult*

BALL. — Soccer is played with a round, laced, leather-covered ball somewhat smaller than a basketball.

FIELD. — The Soccer field is a quadrangle measuring from fifty by one hundred yards to one hundred by one hundred thirty yards. A halfway line is drawn across the field, separating it into even halves. In the exact center, bisected by this line, is drawn a circle having a ten-yard radius (twenty-yard diameter). The side lines are called the *touch lines*. The end lines are called the *goal lines*.

Flags should be placed at each corner of the field, preferably of light color and on staffs (not pointed), which are not less than five feet high.

Goals. — In the center of each goal line are placed two goal posts, eight yards apart, connected by a bar eight feet from the ground.

Net. — While not required by the rules, a goal net to catch the ball adds much in determining when a goal is made.

Goal Area. — A goal area is marked in front of each goal by drawing lines from the goal line six yards inward into the field, there connecting them by a line twenty yards long, parallel with the goal line.

Penalty Area. — Enclosing the goal area is a larger quadrangle called a penalty area. The side lines for these are drawn forward into the field of play eighteen yards. There they are connected with a transverse line parallel to the goal line.

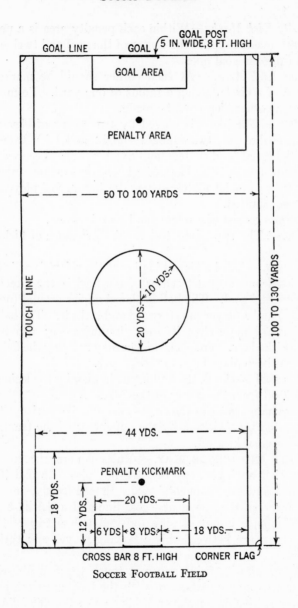

Soccer Football Field

Penalty-Kick Mark. — Within each penalty area is a penalty-kick mark made opposite the center of the goal and twelve yards inward from the goal line.

Corner Kick Area. — At each corner should be marked the quadrant of a circle having a radius of one yard. From within this area a corner kick must be made.

TEAMS. — The game is played by two teams of eleven men each: a goalkeeper, two fullbacks (right and left), three half-backs (right, left, and center), and five forwards (a center, inside and outside, and right and left wings (the outside forwards)).

In any but official match games the number of players on a team is not limited.

OFFICIALS consist of a referee and two linesmen.

START. — The two teams toss a coin for choice of kick-off or goal.

KICK–OFF. — The ball is put in play at the referee's whistle by a place kick from the exact center of the field in the direction of the opponents' goal. The ball is placed on the ground (not on a raised tee) and a player runs forward and kicks it. The ball must move forward more than its own circumference; otherwise it must be kicked off again. The kicker may not play the ball again until it has been played by another player.

After a goal is scored, the ball is put in play by the losing team by a kick-off from the center of the field.

Teams change goals at the end of each playing period, the play being started by a kick-off by the opponents of the team which had the original kick-off.

OFFSIDE AND ONSIDE PLAY. — Rules govern the conditions under which a player may or may not play the ball if he is between it and the opponents' goal. Stated briefly, any player who is between the opponents' goal line and a ball last played by a teammate is out of play (offside) unless two of the defending team are between this attacking player and their own goal line.

A player who is offside may not touch the ball himself, nor interfere with any opponent or with the ball, until the ball has been played by another player of his own or the defending side. A player behind the ball is onside. Also, any player is onside while a goal kick or corner kick is made. To quote from official rules:

> "A player who is in his own half of the field of play at the moment the ball is last played cannot be offside. The point to notice is not where a player is when he plays the ball, but where he is at the moment it is played by a player of the same side."

Official rules in regard to offside and onside play are quite complicated and are often dispensed with for junior players. For others, see Official Rules, *Spalding's Athletic Library*.

Opponents may not pass the center nor into the circle until the ball has been kicked off.

As soon as the ball is kicked off, it is in play, to be kicked anywhere within the lines of the field. To the forwards falls the most aggressive play in advancing the ball and trying to score goals. The halfbacks play behind the forwards, feeding the ball to them or blocking opponents' balls. Fullbacks are practically assistant goalkeepers and must play near the goal, to prevent entry of the ball.

The ball is played entirely by kicking. No catching, handling, nor carrying of the ball is allowed except by the goalkeeper within the penalty area. An exception is the throw-in after the ball has been in touch (over the side lines). Aside from this, the hands may not be used on the ball nor on any opponent by any player. No tripping, kicking, pushing with the knee, charging or jumping at a player is permissible. Nor may an opponent be held or pushed with the hands. The referee's judgment is final in deciding between intentional rough play and unintentional contact of players.

The goalkeeper, while within the penalty area, may catch or throw the ball with his hands or obstruct it with any part of his body. He may not carry the ball for more than two steps. The goalkeeper may be charged while he is holding the ball or obstructing a player either when he is within or without the goal area, but such charging must not be rough.

A FREE KICK is awarded for fouls committed outside the penalty area, opponents being ten yards from the ball. A goal may be scored from a free kick awarded for intentional misplay of the ball or an opponent.

PENALTY KICK. — For a foul committed by the defensive team within the penalty area, a penalty kick is awarded the attacking team. For this the ball is kicked from the penalty-kick mark with no other players in the penalty area except a kicker and goalkeeper; and the goalkeeper may not advance beyond his goal line until the ball is kicked. A goal may be scored from a penalty kick. The ball is in play as soon as kicked, but the player may not kick it again until it has been played by another player.

CORNER KICK. — If a defending player sends the ball intentionally or accidentally behind the goal line, the attacking side is awarded a corner kick. This is taken from within the corner kick area nearest where the ball went out. A goal may be scored directly from a corner kick. The kicker may not play the ball again until it has been played by another player. No opponent may be within ten yards until the ball is kicked.

THROW-IN. — A ball passing beyond the side lines either in the air or on the ground is in "touch" and out of play. It is returned by a player on the opposite team to the one that put it out. The returning player (wing or halfback) must stand at the point on the touch line where the ball left the field of play. He must have some part of both feet on the line, and throw the ball in over his own head with both hands, aiming in any direction that he chooses; but a goal may not be scored from a throw-in. The thrower may not again play the ball until another player of either side has played it.

GOAL KICK. — After a ball has passed the goal line (not a "goal"), propelled by the attacking team, it is put in play by a goal kick made by the defending goalkeeper or fullback from that half of the goal area nearest the point where it left the field.

AFTER SUSPENSION OF PLAY for any reason such as putting in a substitute, injury to a player, etc., the ball is again put in play by the referee. He throws it down at the place where it was when time was called. It is in play when it touches the ground.

FOULS. — To play the ball contrary to rules.

To tackle or interfere bodily with a player except as noted for the goalkeeper.

If occurring outside the penalty area, such fouls as noted above are penalized by a free kick from which a goal may be scored.

If occurring within the penalty area by the defending team, such a foul is penalized by a penalty kick awarded the offended team. A goal may be scored on such a kick.

SCORE. — A goal scores one point. To score a goal the ball must be kicked between the goal posts and under the bar. No other form of getting it through may score.

The official game for men is played in halves of forty-five minutes each with a five-minute intermission between.

For junior players the game is in quarters, usually of eight or ten minutes each, with a rest of one or two minutes after first and third quarters and a ten-minute rest between halves.

Teams change goals after each playing period. For the new period the ball is kicked off by the opponents of the team which had the original kick-off.

After a goal is scored, the losing team kicks off from the center.

The team scoring the largest number of goals wins the game.

SOCCER FOOT–TRAP AND PASS

10 to 40 players   *Junior high to college*

Players stand in a straight rank or circle from four to twenty feet apart sideways. The ball is passed to the left with the right foot, trapped by the next player with his left foot, passed with his right, and so on to the end of the line when a return play is made in the opposite direction. A player scores one point for each pass and one for each trap which does not require more than one step from place to recover (or touch) the ball. Each player calls his score aloud as his play is completed. This score is for accuracy, not speed. When skill is acquired, competitive teams may play in relay form.

Practice without scoring is advisable for new players.

SOCCER KICK FOR ACCURACY

1 to 30 players   *Junior high to college*

I. If a soccer goal is not available, an enclosure of the same dimensions (eight by eight yards) is marked on a wall. A point is marked on the ground directly in front of this at a distance of from thirty to thirty-six feet. The ball is placed on this mark and players take turns in kicking for goal, each having ten tries and scoring one point for each successful kick.

II. Instead of a place kick, the ball may be rolled toward the player, who will trap it and then kick for goal.

SOCCER KICK FOR DISTANCE

1 to 30 players   *Junior high to college*

I. The ball is placed on a baseline and the player may make a standing or running kick. The distance is marked from the baseline to the point where the ball first touches the ground.

If competitive, the play may be between individuals or teams.

II. This may also be played and scored with distance lines as for Baseball Distance Throw.

SOCCER LINE–BALL

7 to 20 players   *Junior high school*

Soccerball

I. This is a beginning game in soccer technique, played on a small field thirty to fifty feet on the ends and forty to sixty feet on the sides. Players are in two teams of equal number, ranging from seven to twenty on each. Players of each team are numbered, Number One being the first forward. The others line up as guards in front of the end line which they are to defend. The game consists in the forwards trying to kick the ball over the opponents' end line, through the line of guards, not over their heads.

The ball is put in play by the two forwards facing each other a short distance apart in the center of the field. The referee rolls the ball between them, and on signal each forward tries to kick or dribble it toward and over the opponents' goal, through the opposing rank of guards. The guards defend only with soccer plays and only these plays may be used anywhere in the game; that is, with blocking, trapping with the foot or body, or kicking; when more expert, heading

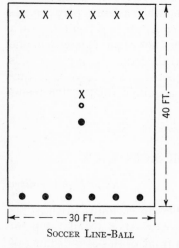

SOCCER LINE-BALL

may be used.   Neither guards nor forwards may use the hands.
A ball going over the end line above the heads of the guards does
not score.   A goal scores one point when the ball goes over the
line through the line of guards.   It is then put again in play at
the center by the referee, but the players rotate after every goal
scored, the Numbers Two, for instance, becoming forwards after
the first goal, and the previous forwards becoming guards at the
far end of their respective lines.   After a second goal the
Numbers Three become forwards, etc.

A ball going over a goal line is recovered by one of the defending guards and put in play with a kick from the line.   A
ball going out-of-bounds over a side line is thrown in from the
point where it went out by an opponent of the player who last
touched it.

SCORE. — Goal made between guards, two points.

Goal made from a free kick, one point.

It is a foul for any player to use his hands on the ball or to
push or hold an opponent.   For this a free kick from the spot
where the foul occurred is awarded to the opposing forward.

II. SQUARE SOCCER. — This is played like Line Soccer, but a
team is lined up along one side and end of their half of the field
instead of only at the end.   The opponents line up along the end
and opposite side of their half.   Or there may be four teams lined
up on the four sides.

SOCCER PIN–BALL

10 to 14 players   *Junior high*
Soccerball; 6 Indian clubs   *to adult*

On a field thirty by forty feet a goal area is marked in the center
of each end, measuring twelve feet long and extending into the
field six feet.   In each goal area three Indian clubs or "pins" are
set up at the points of a fifteen-inch triangle.   Each team stands
in the half of the field which it guards.   Two members are fullbacks and stand in front of the goal; a center for each team stands
in the middle of the field and the balance of the players support
him as forwards in a line across the field.

Each team tries to knock down the pins in the opponents' goal by a kicked ball.

Centers toss for the first play on the ball. It is then placed in the center of the field, and only the player winning the toss may play it when the referee whistles to begin. The ball is played entirely without the hands, mainly by kicking, passing, or dribbling; but all soccer plays may be used, such as trapping the ball with the foot or body, or by heading. No one may enter the goal area except to recover a ball. Fouls and penalties, and ball out-of-bounds are the same as for Soccer Line-Ball. It is well to begin team play by assigning a funnel-shaped territory to each player to be responsible for, as shown in the diagram for Socco-Smash Ball; also to encourage passing the ball to teammates who are in a better position to play for the pins.

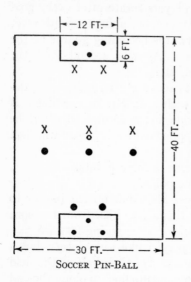

SOCCER PIN-BALL

One point is scored by a team for each pin it knocks over.

SOCCER STRIDE–BALL

20 or more players   *Junior high school to adult*

Players stand in a circle facing inward, feet wide astride and touching the feet of neighbors. One player is kicker and stands in the center with a soccer ball. He kicks the ball in an effort to send it between the legs of any circle man. For blocking the ball the circle players may use any of the soccer methods, such as foot trapping, body trapping, or heading, but may not block with the hands. Any player who allows the ball to pass either between his legs or between himself and his neighbor on the right changes places with the kicker. If the kicker does not succeed on his sixth try, he changes places with the last one to block the ball.

SOCCO–SMASH BALL

(Modification of Boloball)

20 players   *Intermediate*
Gymnasium; playground   *to senior high*
                        Soccerball

The following game is a modification of Boloball and was developed for the use of boys of eleven and twelve years of age in the public schools of Oakland, California, under the supervision of Miss Lois A. Lear. The game is based on Boloball and many of the rules are the same, but there are also numerous differences which are noted at the end.

COURT. — The game is played in an entire gymnasium, with the walls as boundaries, or on an open field approximately sixty by one hundred feet. This may be varied to meet local conditions. A three-foot circle is drawn in the center of the field, in which the ball is put in play. At each end is a goal consisting of two standards seven feet in height and nine feet apart, connected by a crossbar or rope on top. A penalty area, twelve feet in radius, is drawn around each goal, and outside of this, a parallel line at a three-foot distance. The inner line (toward the goal) is a penalty-area line, from which most penalty shots are played, and the outer line, fifteen feet in front of the goal, is used for other penalties, when the foul is committed by the defensive team.

TEAMS. — There are *ten players* in each team: two left forwards, two right forwards, one center, two half-backs, two full-backs, and one goalkeeper. They stand in formation similar to Soccer, as shown in the diagram; the two centers must stand outside the center circle. The forwards are charged with playing in funnel-shaped lanes converging at the goal. These are not marked on the court, but each forward is supposed to be responsible for such territory.

One *referee* is needed.

Substitutes may be put in at any time in the game when the referee has the ball.

OBJECT OF GAME. — The object of the game is to drive the ball between the goal posts and under the crossbar with distinct modes of play, hereinafter described, and without the aid of the body below the waist, the ball being kept in the air as much as possible.

START. — The game is started by the referee who bounces the ball on the ground in the center of the circle. He is the only one who may enter the circle. The two centers play for the ball as soon as it reaches shoulder height. The ball is thus put in play at the center of the court at the beginning of the game, at the beginning of the second half, and after a goal. After a foul the ball is put in play again in the same manner at the point where the foul was committed.

ADVANCING THE BALL. —

The ball is never kicked.

The ball is played by *only one hand at a time*.

The ball is hit by *the open hand*, never by the fist.

It is advanced by an *overhead dribble* (tapping the ball up off the palm of the hand, not more than three taps), while the player advances;

Or by the *basketball dribble* (bouncing on the floor while advancing, only three bounces being permitted).

One dribble may be followed by the other, but the ball must then be passed without returning to the initial dribble.

By the *smash* with the hand as in Handball.

By the *scoop throw* off the ground. In this method the ball is scooped off the ground and leaves the hand in a *single* movement. However, the player may retain possession of the ball if he wishes to dribble it.

By *bouncing off the head, chest, or shoulders*, or by any other method, provided the player does not deliberately touch the ball with the body below the waist. He *may not kick* it.

The ball is *never thrown* except in the scoop throw, or by the goalkeeper.

A player *may not run* with the ball held stationary in the hand. It must be advanced by a dribble or a smash.

A bounce-smash may be used at any time during the play to recover or advance the ball.

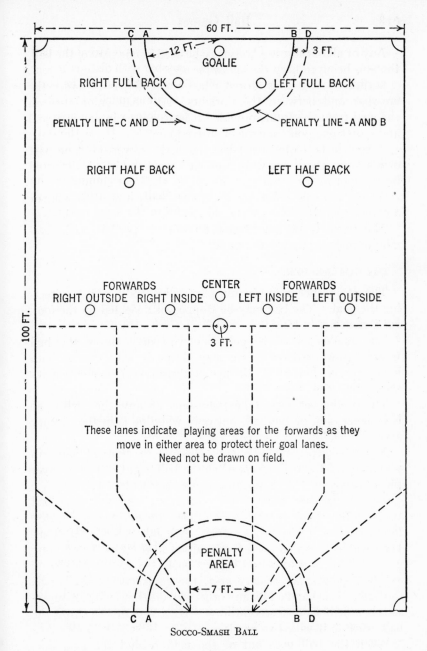

SOCCO-SMASH BALL

617

Any or all of these methods may be used in one play of the ball, the aim being to keep *the ball in the air*.

SCORE. — A goal is scored when the ball passes under the crossbar and between the uprights. Any ball going through the goal from the front, provided it is scored as in (2), is a goal and scores one point for the offensive team.

A goal to be scored must last touch the scorer on some part of his body above his waist. A goal made by a ball deflected by the foot or leg of an *offensive* player shall not count.

A goal may be made by a dribble, scoop-throw, smash, or a corner (penalty) bounce-smash.

The game is played in two ten-minute periods with five-minute rests between halves.

THE GOALKEEPER. —

The goalkeeper may use any part of his body while protecting the goal. The ball may be stopped or deflected by the foot, *but it must not be kicked*.

The goalkeeper is the only one who may throw the ball (scoop-throw excepted). He may throw it with one or both hands at any time within the penalty area *except* when a penalty shot is being played.

The goalkeeper may take two steps at any time when he is in possession of the ball, but only when he is in the penalty area.

The goalkeeper may be body-checked or charged while in possession of the ball, *except* when the ball is out of bounds over the end line, or when a penalty shot is being played.

The goalkeeper may score a goal by throwing the ball through the opposite goal. *He is the only one who may throw the ball while in the penalty area.* A good play for the goalkeeper is to throw the ball to a position in front of the opposite goal for a forward to deflect in for a goal.

When *outside the penalty area*, the goalkeeper must handle the ball as it is handled by any other player, that is, by a bounce-smash, a dribble, or a scoop-throw. He may not then throw the ball or catch it with two hands.

When the ball goes out of the field behind the goal line.

the goalkeeper is not obliged to return it, but he may do so; this speeds up the game.

BALL OUT OF BOUNDS. — A ball going out of bounds at the side lines is given to the player of the opposing team opposite the man who last touched the ball. The player returning the ball must stand outside the field of play near where the ball went out, and put it in play again by a bounce-smash.

Balls going over the end lines (except the goal) and touching the *offensive team last* are given to the goalkeeper for a free throw or a free smash.

Balls touching the *defensive team last* are given to the offensive team for a corner-bounce-smash.

PENALTIES. — For fouls committed *outside the penalty area*, a bounce-smash is given to the opponents on the spot where the foul was committed and is made by the man playing the opposite position from the man who committed the foul. When such a penalty shot is made, guards *must stand back* at least nine feet.

Fouls committed *in the penalty area* by the *defensive team* are penalized by a free bounce-smash from the penalty-area line. No one is allowed in the area while this is played except the goalkeeper, who must be on the goal line but is not then allowed his privilege of two steps.

THE FREE BOUNCE–SMASH IS GIVEN FOR THE FOLLOWING INFRACTIONS OF THE RULES:

Throwing the ball (except by the goalkeeper).

Touching the ball with two hands at the same time (except by the goalkeeper).

Hitting the ball with the closed fist (the open hand only must be used).

Charging or body-checking an opponent; tripping or unnecessary rough play.

Running with the ball held *stationary* in the hand. The ball must be advanced by either a dribble or a smash.

Taking more than three bounces in either a bouncing or upward dribble.

Kicking or deliberately touching the ball with the hips or legs.

The goalkeeper's taking more than two steps with the ball.

PLAYING HINTS. —

1. Hit the ball up instead of down.
2. Use relays to develop skills and team play.

3. The *offensive team* may go into the *defensive* penalty area at any time except when a penalty bounce-smash is being played.

4. The players should be in their own territory for the bounce-smash at the start of the game. As teams become proficient, however, it is suggested that the two outside forwards play in the opposing territory at the start of the game or after a goal has been made.

5. When the referee cannot decide which player smashed the ball out of bounds, it is bounced between the two players nearest the point, and these two try for it.

The differences between this and Bolo Ball include the kind of ball used, adaptation to an open field, several points in the formation of the teams, and in the play of the ball, the length of periods, and penalties. These developments tend toward the cultivation of team play. Miss Althea Sims Bunker, Supervisor of Recreation in the Oakland, California, schools, to whom the author is indebted for the game writes: "We like it because it affords fifth- and sixth-grade boys an opportunity to enjoy a team game which does not require the development of the highly technical skills of Basketball and Soccer, but which includes several elements of these games. Boys enjoy it because of the fine team play which it develops."

SPEEDBALL

14 to 22 players   *Junior high to adult*
Football field   *Speedball or soccer ball*

Speedball is one of the best games for players of average ability. It is distinctive for the variety of plays allowed on the ball, which, under prescribed conditions, may be played as in Soccer Football, Rugby Football, or Basketball.

Speedball was invented in 1921 by Prof. Elmer D. Mitchell of the University of Michigan. It is here given by courtesy of the author.

FIELD. — The official field is the same as that used in Rugby Football. The fifty-yard line is called the *middle line* and the two forty-yard lines are the *restraining lines*. The ten-yard area between the goal line and the end line on which the goal posts stand is called the *end zone* and *penalty area*. Ten yards in front of each goal and midway between the side lines, a penalty mark is placed. The official football goals are used, with posts eighteen feet six inches apart and crossbar ten feet from the ground.

The size of the field should be reduced for younger players. Two small speedball fields may be made crosswise on a football field. The goal posts are then placed ten yards back from the side lines, making the field two hundred and twenty feet long.

EQUIPMENT. — An official speedball or soccer ball is used. The speedball is a round ball slightly larger than a soccer ball and smaller than a basketball.

TEAMS.—The official size of a team is eleven players. On a smaller field, the teams may consist of nine or seven players.

KICK-OFF. — The team winning the toss has the privilege of selecting to kick-off or to receive at the goal of its choosing.

The game starts by a place kick from the center of the field in the direction of the opponents' goal. Each team must be at its own end of the field at the time of the kick-off.

THE PLAY. — After the kick-off each team attempts to work the

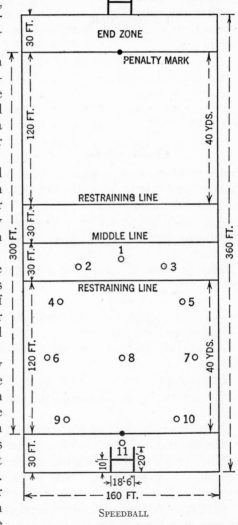

SPEEDBALL

ball down the field and score. A "fly ball" (one lofted by a kick) may be caught and thrown to teammates and in this respect the game resembles Basketball. A "ground ball" must be kicked or dribbled without the use of arms, and in this respect the game resembles Soccer.

The ball may be played by throwing, punting, drop kicking, and dribbling with feet or hands, under specified conditions.

A fly ball may be caught or played with the hands until it again hits the ground.

A ground ball (one that is stationary, rolling, or bouncing) may not be played by the hands or arms. Even though in the air, such a ball is considered a ground ball unless it rises direct from a kick or comes from a pass.

A player may dribble with his feet, or use one overhead dribble, but may not score a touchdown by this last method. He may bat or tip fly balls at will. He may kick a ground ball into the air and catch it himself.

A player standing still when he catches the ball is allowed one step; two steps if running; if at full speed he must stop *as soon as possible* (referee's decision). Violation of these rules is called "carrying the ball." A player cannot step over the goal line to score.

A player may guard an opponent who has the ball but in no way hold the opponent. An opponent who does not have the ball may not be obstructed.

A ball held by two opponents is tossed up as in Basketball.

OUT OF BOUNDS. — A ball over the side lines is thrown in by a member of the opposing team at the point where it went out.

A ball over the end line is a touchback or safety.

TOUCHBACK. — When the offensive team puts the ball over the end line (not a score), it is a touchback and is put in play by an opponent by a punt, place kick, or pass at the point where it crossed the line.

SAFETY. — When a defensive player last touches a ball before it goes over the end line (no score), a member of the offensive team puts it in play at that point by a punt, place kick, or pass.

SCORING. — Points are scored as follows:

Field goal	3 points
Touchdown	2 points
End kick	1 point
Penalty kick	1 point
Drop kick	1 point

A field goal is made when the ball is kicked or legally given impetus with the body over the goal line between the goal posts and under the crossbar.

A touchdown is scored when a player standing in the end zone catches a forward pass.

An end kick is scored when a ground ball is kicked or legally given impetus over the goal line from within the end zone.

For a foul, a penalty kick is awarded from the penalty mark, the kicker trying to kick it between the goal posts under the crossbar. One defensive player may guard the goal on the end line between the goal posts.

A drop kick is scored when a ball legally caught is drop kicked over the crossbar from the field outside the defensive zone area.

FOULS. — The following are *personal fouls:* (1) kicking, tripping, charging, pushing, holding, or blocking an opponent; (2) unnecessary roughness.

The following are *technical fouls:* (1) making an illegal substitution; (2) taking more than three time-outs in a game; (3) having more than eleven men on the field; (4) delaying the game.

The following are *violations:* (1) carrying the ball; (2) touching a ground ball with the hands; (3) making two successive overhead dribbles; (4) violating the kick-off rule; (5) violating the penalty-kick restrictions; (6) violating the rules in returning an out-of-bounds ball to play; (7) violating free-kick restrictions; (8) violating the tie-ball rule; (9) kicking or kneeing a fly ball by a player unless he has caught it.

PENALTIES. — The penalty for a *personal foul*, committed outside the player's end zone, is a penalty kick by the offended player. If missed, a touchback is declared. For a personal foul in a player's own end zone, the penalty is two penalty kicks by the offended player.

The penalty for a *technical foul* committed outside the player's own penalty area is a penalty kick by any member of the offended team.   If missed, a touchback is declared.   If the technical foul is committed inside the player's own penalty area, the penalty is a penalty kick by any member of the offended team.   The ball is in play as soon as kicked.

The penalty for a *violation* outside the player's own penalty area is the award of the ball out of bounds to a member of the offended team.

The penalty for a *violation* inside the player's own penalty area is a penalty kick by the opponents with the opportunity of a follow-up if missed.

PENALTY KICK. — For a personal or technical foul, the ball is placed on the penalty mark and the kicker tries to kick it through the goal posts under the crossbar.   On penalty kicks where no follow-up is allowed, only the kicker and the goal guard may play the ball.   When a follow-up play is allowable, teammates of neither kicker nor goaltender may enter the end zone until the ball is kicked.

LENGTH OF GAME. — The game is played in four periods of ten minutes each with an intermission of two minutes after the first and third quarters, and ten minutes between halves.   For high schools periods should be five to eight minutes.

In case of a tie, one or more overtime periods of three minutes are played.

SUBSTITUTES. — A player may be taken out of the game and resubstituted once during the game.

OFFICIALS. — A referee and two linesmen.

SPEEDBALL FOR WOMEN

The maximum dimensions of the field are one hundred yards by sixty yards; for high-school players eighty by forty yards is best.   The end zone is only six yards wide, and the penalty mark twelve yards from the goal.   In other respects, the field corresponds to that used by men.

The rules differ from those used by men in the following respects :

A drop kick scores two points instead of one.

The ball is thrown in from out of bounds, with a two-handed overhand throw and is in play as it hits the ground.

Guarding rules are like Women's Basketball.

The penalty for a violation is a free kick, with the opponents at least six yards away.

SPONGEBALL

12 players   *Junior to senior high*
Playground; gymnasium   *Sponge ball; paddle racket*

This is an inexpensive recreational game. The ball used is made from an ordinary vegetable sponge (not sponge rubber) which is cut round to measure approximately three and one-half inches in diameter, or about the size of a playground or sport ball. The action of the sponge is very different from that of any other ball. It is batted by paddle-tennis rackets, though regular tennis rackets may be used. The game is played on a field measuring sixty by thirty feet, divided across the center by a regular tennis or volleyball net. The height of the net at the top is from seven and one-half to eight feet.

The twelve players are divided into two teams of six each. They stand in two lines parallel to the net, each team in its own court. Players are numbered consecutively so as to rotate as in Volleyball.

The ball is put in play by a server who stands behind the baseline and serves by tossing and batting the ball with the paddle, using either an overhand or an underhand swing. The server may have two tries.

When Number One server is out, his team rotates as in Volleyball so that Number Two steps to his place as the next server, and the retiring server goes to place Number Six.

The return is made as in Tennis, the object being to bat the ball back and forth over the net into the opponents' court. For failure to keep the ball going, the opponents score one point. No player may hit the ball twice in succession; not more than three players may hit the ball before it goes across the net; the net may not be touched with the paddle or body; the ball may not be played in any way except with the paddle; no player may strike another's paddle. Infringement of any of these rules constitutes a foul.

Only the serving side scores. It scores one point each time the opponents commit a foul or fail to return the ball fairly into the servers' court. When fifteen or more points have been scored, the team wins which has a two-point lead.

This game was originated by Mr. A. B. Wegener and is here reproduced by courtesy of the author and of the *Journal of Health and Physical Education*, in which the game first appeared.

SPUD

10 to 100 players　　　　　　　*Junior to senior high school*
Playground; gymnasium　　　　　　*Any soft ball or beanbag*

This is a combination of Call-Ball and Ball Tag, with scoring and penalties added. It is very popular with boys of almost any age.

The players stand in a group, with one in the center holding the ball. The center player drops the ball, at the same time calling the name of one of the other players. All but the one called immediately scatter, as they are liable to be tagged with the ball. The player called secures the ball as quickly as possible, calls "Halt!" all stand still and the ball man tries to hit one of the other players with it. He may not run to do this, but must stand where he secured the ball. If he misses, he recovers the ball, stands where he gets it, and tries again, the other players running from him as before. If he hits a player, that one immediately secures the ball, tries to hit someone else with it, the second one hit tries to hit a third, and so on.

Whenever a player misses hitting another with the ball, it is called a "spud," and counts one against him. Any player hit also has one "spud" counted against himself. When any player has three spuds against him, he must stand twenty feet from the other players, with his back to them, and his hands on his knees, and they each have one shot at him with the ball. An additional optional feature is for the victim to be allowed to return each ball thrown at him with a similar shot at the thrower; in this the latter about-faces and puts his hands on his knees. The victim then starts the play again from the center of the ground.

SQUARE BALL

8 to 32 players   *Intermediate grades*
Playground; gymnasium   *Basketball*

COURT. — This consists of one large square with a base at each corner, and, should there be enough players, bases are placed at intervening points along the sides of the square.

PLAYERS. — The players are divided into two teams, one of which stands on the bases; the other team assembles in the center of the square and is on the defensive.

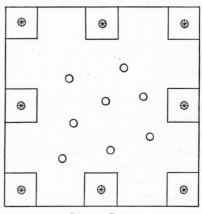

SQUARE BALL

OBJECT. — The ball is thrown from one to another of the players on bases, always following the lines of the square and not its diagonals. The chief object of the game, however, is suddenly to interrupt this circuit of the ball by throwing it so as to hit one of the center players. The object of any center player who is hit is, in his turn, to hit with the ball any member of the outer team, who all turn and run as soon as a center man is hit. A center player who is hit picks up the ball quickly and calls "Halt!" When this is heard the runners must stand still, and the center player tries to hit one of them with the ball.

SCORE. — The scoring of the game is done entirely according to whether the center player hits or misses his opponent in this throw of the ball after he has called a halt. Every player thus hit scores one for the centers. Every throw made and missed under these circumstances scores one for the opponents or outside team. The team wins which first scores twenty-five.

This game is also played without score, any member of the outer team hit by a center man being obliged to join the centers. In this form the game ends when all of the outer players have been so recruited.

SQUARE SOCCER
(See *Soccer Line-Ball II.*)

STOOL BALL

5 to 20 players   *Intermediate*
Playground; gymnasium   *to junior high*
Handsizeball

A stool, box, or inverted pail is set in an open place, and from ten to twenty feet away from this a throwing line is drawn. One player is appointed stool defender, and stands beside the stool. It is well also to appoint a scorer and linesman who disqualify any players who cross the throwing line; also have one player behind the stool defender to return the balls that may go afield. The players, in turn, throw the ball from the throwing line in an effort to hit the stool. The stool defender tries to prevent this by batting the ball away with his hand. If the ball hits the stool, the one who threw it changes places with the stool defender; if the ball batted by the defender is caught on the fly by another of the players, that one changes places with the stool defender. The object of the stool defender should therefore be not only to hold his place by preventing the ball from hitting the stool, but to bat it in such a way that the other players may not catch it.

This game has been very successfully adapted by adding scoring as a feature of it; in this case any player hitting the stool with the ball, or catching it when it is returned by the stool defender, scores one point, while the stool defender scores one for each time he successfully prevents the ball's hitting the stool without being "caught out." The player wins who has the highest score at the end of the playing time.

This is one of the old games that has come down through centuries. Chronicles of Queen Elizabeth's reign tell of the Earl of Leicester and his train setting forth to play the game, though it is supposed to have originated with the milkmaids and their milking stools. In Sussex the game is played with upright boards instead of a stool, forming a wicket as in Cricket. It was formerly for women and girls as popular as the game of Cricket for boys and men, and the rules of play are quite similar.

STRIDE–BALL RELAY

(Straddle Club)

10 to 100 players   *Intermediate to senior high*
Playground or gymnasium   *Any ball; Indian club; beanbag*

The players are divided into two or more teams which stand in single file relay formation, and in leapfrog position, feet wide apart to form a tunnel through which the ball is passed. Each team has a ball. The first players (captains) of each file toe a line, and at a signal put the ball in play by passing it backward between the feet. When players become expert, one long shot will send the ball to the end of the line. The other players may strike it to help it along as it passes them if it goes slowly. Should the ball stop, or go out of bounds at any place, the player before whom this occurs must put it in play again, starting it between his feet. When the ball reaches the rear of the file, the last player runs with it to the front, the line moving backward quickly one place to make room for him, and immediately rolls the ball back again between the feet. This is repeated until the "captain" is the last player. He runs forward with the ball, places it on a marked spot twenty feet in front of his line, and returns to his place at the head of the file. The file wins whose captain is first to return to his original position.

Should there not be space for a point at which to leave the ball, the game may be finished by the last player holding up the ball when it reaches the end of the line, or by his running forward with it to the head of the line.

An Indian club instead of a ball makes a much more skillful game, the club being shoved over the ground, neck first. It is much more difficult to guide than a ball, requires greater deliberation for a long shot, and more easily stops or goes out of bounds.

This is one of the best games for training self-control under excitement, as the precision needed for a long shot, especially with the Indian club, is very difficult under the circumstances.

TABLE TENNIS
(Ping Pong)

2 or 4 players   *Elementary to adult*
Special table, ball, and racket

Ping Pong is a form of Tennis played on a table with a light, hollow ball, the play being quite the same as in Lawn Tennis, though the technique of the game is greatly changed by the type of the equipment as well as its use.

The surface of a Ping Pong court is the surface of the table, which should be nine by five feet. This is painted dark green, with a white line around the outside edge and down the center. It should stand thirty inches above the floor. Smaller tables may be used, measuring eight by four feet. A special net of dark material bound with white at the top divides the table across the center, the top being six and three-fourths inches above the table.

Ping Pong balls are made of celluloid about four and one-half inches in circumference, and rackets of wood, though the latter may have a surface of sand paper, rubber, cork, or leather. The choice of courts is determined by a toss as in Tennis, and the play and score throughout follow the rules of Lawn Tennis.

For the service the server must stand behind his end of the table. The ball is served as in Tennis, tossed and batted, but so that it first bounces on the server's side of the net, crosses the net and then bounces on any portion of the receiver's side. Neither the server nor his racket nor ball may be over the table when the serve is made.

A returned ball must pass over the net and touch anywhere in the opponent's court. The ball is always played from a bounce and never volleyed. Improper play includes touching or moving the table with the free hand while the ball is in play, and the ball's touching a player before it has touched the playing ground.

LETS are the same as in Lawn Tennis, namely:

Allowing a served ball to touch the net or its supports;

Serving before the receiver is ready;

An incident beyond the control of a player causing him to lose a point. In this case another ball is served.

FAULTS. — These consist in improper service as to rules either for ball or server. In Ping Pong two faults are not allowed as in Lawn Tennis, one fault scores a point for the receiver.

SCORE. — Scoring is the same as in Lawn Tennis. The player first winning twenty-one points wins the game. If a score stands at *twenty all*, the game is won by the player who first makes two more points than his opponent. The opponent scores one point on any failure to play the ball properly.

A match consists in winning two games out of three, or three out of five.

TENNIS

Five forms of Tennis are described in this section on Ball Games and will be found in their alphabetic order as follows: Deck Tennis (under D); Hand Tennis (under H); Lawn Tennis (under L); Paddle Tennis (under P); Table Tennis (Ping Pong) (under T).

(See also *Badminton.*)

TENNIS WALL–BALL

1 to 10 players   *Junior high to adult*

On a smooth wall surface draw two horizontal lines, one to be three and a half feet from the floor and the other parallel to this and two feet above it.

The player stands five feet from the wall with his left (or right) side toward the wall and the foot on that side advanced. He grasps the racket in the hand farthest from the wall, with a grip close to its head. The ball is tossed from the left (forward) hand, batted with the racket to hit the wall between the lines, allowed to bounce from the floor, hit again, and so on indefinitely until a failure. The weight changes to the forward foot with each stroke. Successful strokes are counted as played and constitute the player's score. On failure the play passes to the next player.

When sufficiently skillful, the play is made more difficult by grasping the racket half way down the handle, and standing ten or fifteen feet from the wall, admitting of a freer swing in the stroke.

For a still further progression, the player stands thirty feet from the wall and grasps the racket at the end of the handle.

TEN–TRIPS

6 to 21 players   *Junior to senior high school*
Playground   *Baseball; tennis ball*

This game is a competition between two or more teams, and consists in rapid pitching and catching of a baseball or tennis ball by each team.

A team consists of three players, two of whom stand thirty yards or more apart for a baseball, with the third player (Number One) halfway between and on a line with them. Number One (the pitcher) starts the game by throwing the ball to one of the end players (Number Two); he, in turn, throws it over the head of the pitcher to the opposite end player (Number Three), who throws it back again to Number Two, and he makes the last throw, sending it to the center player, or pitcher, Number One, from whom it started. This is called one trip, and the pitcher, as he catches it, calls out "One!" or "One trip!" and immediately begins the next round. The players standing in the following order, 2, 1, 3, the order of throwing is thus, 1, 2, 3, 2, 1. Ten trips complete a game.

Competing teams stand in parallel files, and the pitchers of all teams start at once on a signal. The team wins which first completes ten trips. Any number of teams may play at once.

This game is from Williams College, where it probably originated.

TETHERBALL

2 to 8 players   *Junior high school to adult*
Out of doors   *Special tether-ball outfit*

This is one of the most delightful and vigorous games that is adapted to small playing space, a plot twenty feet square being enough for it. The paraphernalia for the game includes a wooden pole placed upright, so it shall stand ten feet above the ground, and be embedded deeply enough, probably three feet below the surface, to be firm during the strain of play. A pole should measure seven and a half inches in circumference at the ground,

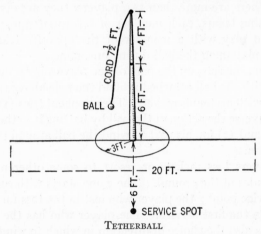

TETHERBALL

and should taper toward its upper end. A black stripe should be painted around it six feet above the ground.

To the top of this pole a ball is attached by a stout linen cord or fishing line. The ball is either a tennis ball, having a netted cover, by means of which it is attached to the cord, or a stuffed or sponge-rubber ball made with a tape for attaching the rope. No metal should be used around it in any way. When hanging at rest, the ball should be seven and a half feet from the top of the pole, and two and a half feet from the ground. The ball is played upon by any sort of tennis racket.

A tether-ball outfit, consisting of pole, ball, cord, and marking ropes, with staples for the ground, may be bought of sport dealers, but any of the paraphernalia may be improvised, the pole being cut from a sapling, and even the bats whittled from strips of thin board about the size of a shingle.

On the ground around the pole a circle should be drawn three feet in radius; that is, six feet in diameter. A straight line twenty feet in length should bisect the circle to separate the territory for the players. In addition to the circle and line, two spots should be marked on the ground, from which the ball is served. These should be at the ends of an imaginary line crossing the first line at right angles, and should be six feet from the pole, one on each side of the ground.

Where there are more than two players, they are divided into two opposing teams, each member of a team stepping forward, in turn, to play with a member of the opposite team. Only these two play upon the ball during one game.

The game consists, on the part of one player, in trying to wind the cord with the ball attached around the pole above the line by batting it with his tennis racket. The opponent tries (1) to inter-- fere and reverse the action of the ball by batting it in the opposite direction, and (2) for his part to wind the ball around the pole in his direction.

The players toss rackets or resort to some other method of choosing sides of the ground. The game starts with each player on his service point; the player who lost in the toss for choice of ground has the first service. The player who has the choice of ground has also the choice of direction in which to wind the ball.

The ball is then put in play by the server with a regular serve (toss and hit); he may hit the ball but once. Should he fail to send it across the line with his first serve, he loses his serve and the opposite player has the ball. After the serve both players are free to hit the ball whenever they can. It is sometimes possible to send the ball so high and with so much force that the entire cord will wind around the pole in one stroke, before the opponent can hit it with his racket. Of course such strokes should be the endeavor of both sides.

Should a player fail to hit the ball, the opponent has the next turn, either on service or after the ball is once in play.

Each player must keep entirely on his own side of the dividing line, his feet, arms, and racket. Neither player may step on or over the circle about the pole. If the string winds around the handle of a racket of one of the players, it is a foul. It is also a foul for the string to wind about the pole below the black mark, and counts against the player in whose direction it is wound; that is, if it winds in the direction in which he is trying to send the ball. Penalty for transgression of any of the above rules (fouls) is allowing the opponent a free hit from his service mark. When a ball is taken for service in this way, if it has to be either wound or unwound on the pole a half turn, so as to reach the other side, it shall be unwound.

The game is won when the string has been entirely wound around the pole above the limit line. When there are but two players, the one wins who has the majority out of eleven games. Where there are more than two players, the team wins which has the greatest number of games to its credit at the end of from two to five rounds, as may be decided at the opening of the series.

THREE HOLES

2 to 10 or more players   *Elementary*
Out of doors; seashore   *to junior high*
                         Small ball

This game is played by rolling a ball about the size of a golf ball into holes made in the ground. Three holes are made by spinning on the heel. They should be in a straight line, at a distance of from six to fifteen feet apart. At the same distance from them and at right angles to them, a line is drawn from which the players roll their balls. The first player stands with his heel on the bowling line and rolls his ball into hole number one. If successful, he takes his ball out of the hole, places his heel in the hole, and rolls the ball to hole two. If successful, he repeats this play for hole three, and then turns around and rolls the ball back again into hole two and then into hole one. Having done this, he starts again at the line and rolls the ball successively into each of the three holes until he reaches number three a second time. When this is accomplished, he has won the game.

The probabilities, however, are that the player will not succeed in making the holes so quickly as here described. Whenever a player's ball fails to get into a hole, he leaves it where it lies and gives place to the next player. The next player has the choice of aiming for the hole or for his antagonist's ball. Having hit this ball, he then rolls from that position to the hole. Should he fail to make either his opponent's ball or the hole, his ball must lie where it stopped, and the next player takes a turn. Whether the play be interrupted by failures of different players or not, the player wins who first rolls his ball up the line, down again, and back to the third hole, as first described.

TOSS–BALL

10 to 60 players   *Intermediate grades*
Party; schoolroom   *Gas ball; beanbag*

This game should be played with a light gas ball or a beanbag, which the leader holds, standing in front of the other players who are seated.   The leader throws the ball suddenly in any direction at any player, who must stand at once to catch the ball and immediately toss it back.   A player failing to catch the ball, or catching it without standing, has one point counted against him. Any player having failed in this way three times is out of the game and must take his place at one side of the room.

TREE BALL

5 to 15 or more players   *Elementary*
Camp   *to adult*
                    Football; handsizeball; beanbag

This game is a form of Ball Tag, and may be played with any light-weight football, or with a bag or sack filled with leaves or grass.

Each of the players but one chooses a tree, as for the games Puss in the Corner or Ball Puss.   The object of the game for the odd player is (1) to kick the ball so as to tag one of the tree men with it, and (2) to secure a tree for himself, which he may do when no one else has it.   The object of the tree players should be not only to avoid the ball by dodging, which may include running around the trees, but they should also try to exchange places as frequently as possible, their prowess in this way serving as an aggravation to the odd man.   The game should be played where there is not much undergrowth, and under such conditions may be very lively and full of sport.

This game may also be played with a handball or beanbag.
This should be tossed instead of kicked. The game differs from
Ball Puss in that the players are tagged by the ball while at their
stations instead of while changing.

TWO–TEAM CIRCLE PASSING

(Variations of Round Ball)

20 to 30 players   *Intermediate grades*
Playground; gymnasium; party   *Various balls or articles*

I. The players are divided into two teams, plainly marked,
as with colored armband, necktie, or other insignia. They

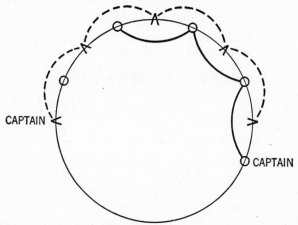

TWO-TEAM CIRCLE PASSING

stand alternately in one circle, one team facing outward and
the other inward, as in the diagram. Each team has a captain,
and the two captains stand opposite each other in the circle,
taking part in the game. On signal, the two captains start
passing a football to the right to their own teammates. When
a captain receives the ball, he lays it on the floor and picks up
at once another object which lies there and starts that also
to the right. When this is received from the circuit of his
team, he places it on the floor and picks up another. When
this third object is received, the captain holds it up at arm's

length and cries "Sit!" and the team sits on the floor. The first team to sit wins the game.

The articles passed should be as different in weight, size, and shape as possible, such as balls large and small, light and heavy, Indian club, ball-bat, etc.

II. CIRCLE PASS AND FACE. — Members of two teams stand alternately in one circle, one team facing outward and the other inward. On signal, each captain starts passing an oval football to the right. When the captain receives the ball at the end of its circuit, he calls "Face!" and his team faces in the opposite direction and begins immediately passing the ball again to the right. This changes the direction of the ball. The play is repeated until each team has faced four times. The fourth time the captain calls "Sit!" and the first team to sit wins the game.

This game is reprinted by courtesy of Miss Dorothy C. Clark of the Polytechnic, London, from her Collection of "Twenty-five Relay Races."

VOLLEYBALL (MEN'S RULES)

12 to 24 players   *Junior high to adult*
Gymnasium; playground   *Volleyball*

GENERAL DESCRIPTION. — Volleyball is played as one of the major team games and also in simpler forms; the rules here given are for major games. It is played by two teams who stand one on each side of a high net dividing the court into halves. The object of the game for each team is to keep a volleyball in lively play over the net toward its opponents' court, as each team scores only on its opponents' failures to properly return the ball or to keep it in the air. The ball must not touch the floor. It is played mainly by batting with the hand (one or both) and may not be caught or held; but it may also be played by any part of the body above the hips. The necessity of keeping the ball off the floor leads to a very rapid game with much agility and skill. A distinctive feature of the original game is the rotation of players so that each one plays in each position.

COURT. — The court is sixty feet long by thirty wide. For younger players it may be twenty-five by fifty. A tennis or

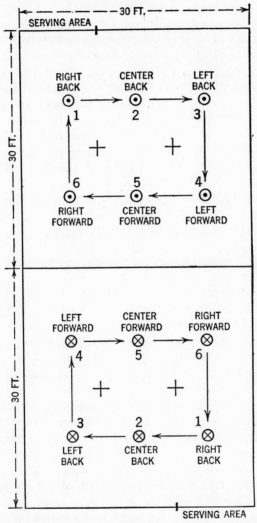

MEN'S VOLLEYBALL COURT AND POSITION OF PLAYERS AT START OF
A GAME

volleyball net is stretched across the center and extends a foot on each side. The upper edge of the net is eight feet from the ground for men, seven feet six inches for women. For elementary players service lines are indicated five feet inward from the end lines and parallel to the latter. Two crosses on each side serve as half-way marks.

TEAMS. — Match games for men are played with six players on a team; but in other games there may be as many as eleven or twelve to a team. The players stand in line formation across the field, parallel to the net. The order is according to the diagram. Players are numbered and shift clockwise, or in large teams, in serpentine order to the next position each time the server is out; that is, for each inning.

Each player plays mostly in the vicinity of his assigned place and in the course of the rotation may play all positions from forward to server, but in exigencies of the game he may leave his point.

Officials for match games are: referee, scorer, and two linesmen, one for each serving line.

START. — The ball is put in play by Right Back, who becomes server and stands back of the right-hand third of the baseline of his court, with both feet back of it. The serve consists in batting the ball with one hand, open or closed, to any part of opponent's court. It is thus put in play at the opening of the game, after every point scored, for any violation of rules, or whenever the referee declares the ball dead. The same server continues until "side out," — *i.e.* a failure by his team.

To be a successful serve, the ball must go over the net, not touching it, must not be touched by any other player of the server's team, and must fall in the opponents' court. In match games for men one serve only is allowed.

RETURNING THE BALL. — The object of the receiving team is to return the ball over the net without allowing it to touch the floor in their court. The opponents score on such failure.

The ball must be kept in the air.

Catching the ball *or holding* it are not allowed.

Dribbling is not allowed. For one player to touch the ball twice in succession in any manner is dribbling.

Relaying is not allowed on a serve, but in returns it may be permitted. No one may play it twice in succession: it must be touched by another player in between. In match games the ball may be hit only three times before being returned over the net.

Any but a served ball *may be recovered from the net*, but the net must not be touched. Such a recovered ball is considered still in play.

The ball is dead when it hits any object outside the court, touches the floor inside or outside the court, or touches any part of a player below the hips, or when for any reason the play is suspended by the referee's whistle.

A player may not touch the net or reach over it to strike the ball.

A player may not be supported by any other player or object while striking the ball.

PENALTIES. — *The serving side* loses its serve ("side out") for any illegal play of the ball.

The receiving side is penalized for any infringement of rules by the addition of a point to the opponents' score.

SCORES. — One point is scored for opponents every time the receiving team fails legally to return the ball; that is, allows it to touch the floor in their own court, or go out of bounds, or plays it contrary to rules.

Only the serving side scores.

The men's official game is won after one team scores fifteen points, if it is then two points ahead of the opponents. If not two points ahead, play continues until one or the other team is two points ahead.

The serving side is out whenever the server fails, or whenever the team in its turn fails to return the ball.

Teams change courts for each game. The losers of the previous game serve for the new game.

HISTORY. — Volleyball, like Basketball, is one of America's contributions to modern sport. Its invention is attributed to Mr. William G. Morgan, of Holyoke, Massachusetts, in 1895.

VOLLEYBALL FOR WOMEN AND JUNIORS

Playground; gymnasium   *Junior high to adults*

This game is played exactly like the match game for men with the following modifications:

COURT. — The court is slightly smaller, for juniors, measuring fifty by twenty-five feet.

NET. — The net height is seven and one-half feet, and for younger players may be six feet six inches.

TEAMS. — Eight players are on a team instead of six.

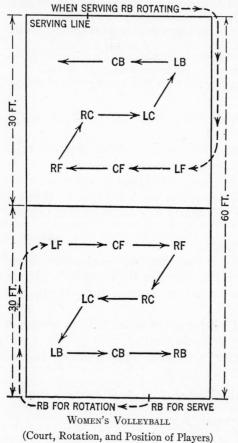

WOMEN'S VOLLEYBALL
(Court, Rotation, and Position of Players)

START. — The server has two tries and the ball may be relayed once.

PLAYING THE BALL. — In the women's game the ball is played only with the arms and hands. It is batted with one or both hands, open or closed.

One player may touch the ball twice in succession.

Teams may relay the ball any number of times, not being limited to three players as in the men's game.

SCORE. — The game is played in two halves of fifteen minutes each, and is won by the team having the higher score at the end of the second half.

Rotation of position was a feature of the original game, but in the evolution of rules some localities have adopted a nonrotation regime, the serve only going from one player to the next.

VOLLEYBALL CLOCK-SERVE

Playground; gymnasium   *Junior high school to adult*

I. This game trains skill in aiming, as well as in serving, a volleyball.

A semicircle is drawn on the ground having a radius of from ten to thirty feet from a central base.   This circle is divided into

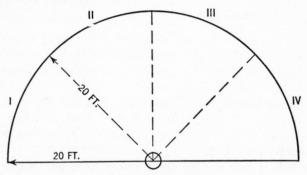

VOLLEYBALL CLOCK-SERVE

quarters by lines on the rim, each quarter being numbered, beginning at the left.

One to four players stand outside the circle to field the ball.

Players are divided into two teams and take alternate turns in serving.   The first player stands at the center point and serves a volleyball over the first quarter of the circle; one foot must remain on the center; the fielder tosses the ball back and the player serves over space two.   This is repeated for spaces three and four, after which the next team has an inning.   A server may have but one try for each space.   The ball must land within an imaginary extension of the radial lines.

One point is scored for each successful serve, and if a ball is served across each of the four spaces in succession, one extra point is given for the series.   In case of a failure to send the ball over any space, the player serves over the next space.

The team wins which has the largest combined score.

II. The skill of this game may be increased by marking an eight-foot area for each quarter of the circle, twenty feet beyond

it and on a radius from its center.   The serve then scores only
if the ball falls within the proper square.

VOLLEYBALL KEEP–OVER

(Keep-Away)

(See also the game *Keep-Ball II*.)

20 to 80 players   *Intermediate to senior high*
Playground; gymnasium   *Volleyball and net*

I.   This is a simple form of Volleyball, intended to occupy large
numbers and introduce players to the handling of a volleyball.

The game consists in keeping the ball in the air across a net
by striking it with the open hand.

The players are in two teams and stand in their own court
in successive rows parallel to the net.   A player must guard
his particular territory throughout the game; there is no rotation
as in official Volleyball.

The ball is put in play by a volley from any player.   He
tosses it wherever he stands and hits it with the other hand, open
or closed, so that, if possible, it goes over the net.   The opposing
team returns it without allowing it to touch the ground.   Any
number of players may relay or touch the ball in returning it
from either side.

The score is made mostly on the opponents' allowing the
ball to touch the floor on their side of the net.   This scores one
point.   A ball volleyed out of bounds scores one point for the
opponents.   The nearest player then puts the ball again in play
with the usual volley.

The team wins which has the higher score at the end of the
playing time.

II.   As *Volleyball Mass-Play* this same game is played with
serpentine rotation of players after every score.

VOLLEYBALL PASSING RACE

Playground; gymnasium   *Junior high to adults*

Teams stand in relay formation in ranks, with from six to ten
feet between shoulders.   The ball is passed up the line and back

again to the first player, being kept in the air throughout. A high arc is the best play. No player may catch the ball, hold it, or touch it more than once (twice optional) in his play, or it scores a minus point for his team, as does a ball touching the floor, or one played out of order. A dropped ball is recovered by the player missing it and continued at once in play. The team wins which finishes first with the lowest minus score.

VOLLEYBALL SERVE–AND–RETURN RELAY

Playground; gymnasium   *Junior high to adults*

I. A volleyball net is stretched across the court and a service line drawn on the ground on each side, parallel to it, and at a distance of from ten to thirty feet according to proficiency of players. The players are equally divided into two teams, which serve and return in succession. Each team stands behind its own service line. The first player of the first team serves a volleyball from anywhere behind his line. As he takes his position, the first player of the opposite team steps into his own court to receive the ball. The receiver returns the ball on the fly, hitting it only with the open hand (one or both) and not allowing it to bounce. Both served and returned balls must fall within the opponents' court. The ball is received by Number Two of the serving team, who at once serves from behind his line, while the first receiver steps back to his original position and Number Two of his team steps forward to return the next serve. This rotation continues until each player of each team has had his turn, when the serving team become receivers and the receiving team serve. One point is scored for a team for each good serve or return.

A service is not good if the ball touches the net, but a returned ball is good if it touches and goes over.

II. In a simpler form of this game for beginners, only the serve is scored and the return is merely a tossback. Each player has two tries.

III. In still another form, one player acts as server throughout and all of the other players are on the opposite side and act as receivers, having but one try each. The score is then only on a successful return.

VOLLEYBALL–SERVE RELAY

10 to 40 players   *Junior high school*
Playground; gymnasium   *to adults*

Players are divided into teams of equal number and stand in relay formation behind a starting line. Ten feet in front of this starting line a volleyball net or tennis net is stretched across the court, the top being from six to eight feet from the ground. Each team has a ball, or all may play with one ball.

One player of each team stands on the opposite side of the net to catch and return the ball. The players of each team serve the ball over the net in turn. Each player has one try on each round. The returned ball is caught by the next player of the team, the preceding server passing at once to the rear of the line when his serve is completed.

One point is scored for a team each time the ball is served over the net. According to the number of players, each team has from one to five rounds. The team wins which at the end has had the greatest number of successful serves.

WALL–BALL DRILL

(See also *Handball Drill* and *Tennis Wall Ball.*)

2 to 10 players.   *Intermediate grades*
Out of doors; gymnasium   *Handsizeball or regulation handball*

This drill consists in throwing a ball against a wall, and catching it, with the following variations. It may be used for individual play, or for competition between two players, or as a game for large numbers. When used for large numbers, the players should be divided into several teams of equal numbers, each player throwing in turn for as many feats as he can perform without failure, each successful feat or play scoring one point for his team. He gives place to the next player upon failing.

Each play should be first performed by allowing the ball to bounce once on the ground before catching it; later it should be caught without the bounce.

1. Throw the ball against the wall, let it bounce once, and catch it; repeat this three times.

2. Throw, and clap hands three times before catching.

3. Throw, and twirl the hands around each other before catching.

4. Throw, and clap hands and touch the right shoulder.

5. Throw, clap hands, and touch the left shoulder.

6. Throw three times with the right hand and catch with the same hand.

7. Throw three times with the left hand and catch with the same hand.

8. Throw with the right hand and catch with the right with the palm downward (knuckles up, "dog snack" fashion).

9. Throw with the left hand and catch with the left in the same manner as in 8.

10. Throw, clap the hands, touch the right knee, and catch.

11. Throw, clap the hands, touch the left knee, and catch.

12. Throw the ball; clap the hands in front, behind, in front again, and catch the ball.

13. Throw, lift the right knee, clap the hands under it, and catch.

14. Throw, lift the left knee, clap the hands under, and catch.

15. Throw, turn around, and catch.

WANDERING BALL

10 or more players   *Intermediate to adult*
Playground; gymnasium

All but one of the players stand in a circle, one arm's length apart. They pass a ball rapidly from one to another, but always to the neighbor on the right or left, never to one at a greater distance. The odd player, who must remain outside the circle, tries to catch or touch the ball as it is being passed. He may not guard it to prevent a pass. When successful he changes places with the passer whose ball he has touched.

This game is from the Russian by courtesy of Mademoiselle Marie Barsky.

WAR

10 to 60 players   *Intermediate*
Playground; gymnasium   *to junior high*

Basketball

Two concentric circles are drawn at each end of the playground,
the size of the circles depending on the number of players. When
there are thirty on each side, the diameter of the inner circle
should be fifteen feet and that of the outer circle thirty feet. The
inner circle is the fortress, and the space between the two circles
is the trench. Behind each trench is drawn a prison ten feet
square. The rest of the floor is the battlefield. The players are
divided into two teams, which take possession of the two fortresses.
Then one side advances to attack the fortress of the other side.
The attacking party has a basketball, which represents ammunition. The object is to throw the ball in such a way as to strike
within the opponents' fortress. The assailants surround the
trench and pass the ball among themselves until a favorable
opportunity offers for a well-directed shot. By making this
preliminary passing of the ball very rapid, the enemy is confused
as to the quarter from which the ball may be expected. If one
of the assailing party enters the enemy's trench, he may be
tagged, and so become a prisoner, being placed in the prison and
therefore out of the play. If the shot (throw of the ball), when
finally made for the enemy's fortress, is successful, the assailing
party scores one, and all of its men who are held prisoners are set
free.

The defending team during the attack stand within their trench
or their fortress, as they see fit, and try to block the ball. If at
any time the ball falls into their hands, they immediately rush
out in an attack on the enemy's fortress at the opposite end of
the ground, and in transit may tag with the ball, and so make
prisoners of, as many of the enemy as they can touch. The enemy
must therefore, when a ball lands within its opponents' fortress,
flee immediately for the safety of its own fortress. The attacking
en route may be done either by throwing the ball or by touching
the opponent with the ball held in hand; but it may only be done
with the ball and not with the hand alone.

When the opposite fortress has been reached, the attacking team tries to throw the ball within it, and the game goes on as before. Members of the defending team may at any time go outside of their trench to get the ball, but run great risk of being made prisoners in doing so by having the ball thrown from the enemy so as to hit them. When a ball is aimed for this purpose, if the player at whom it is aimed touches or intercepts it in any way, he is a prisoner. Of course he may dodge it.

Each single point that is made is called a battle, and the side that wins the greater number of battles within the time limit wins the game.

This game was originated by Mr. J. E. Doldt, and is here printed by kind permission of members of the Alumni Association of the Boston Normal School of Gymnastics, from their book, *One Hundred and Fifty Gymnastic Games.*

ZIGZAG GAMES

These games may be played with any kind of ball or with beanbags.

There are several forms of Zigzag Ball. The simpler forms are useful in getting young players or those unused to play accustomed to the skill of handling balls. The more complicated forms make very lively games, interesting to players of any age. The different games are played in line and circle formation. The main characteristics of the different line forms are as follows:

(1) The players are divided into groups of two ranks each, each group forming a separate team. The ball is zigzagged from one rank to another of a team without skipping any players. The teams are competitive, as in relay races.

(2) The players stand in groups of two lines each, but these groups are composed of two different teams, the alternate players of one rank and the alternate players of the opposite rank forming one team, and the intervening players of the two ranks another.

Other forms of the game are also here given; namely, the Zigzag Circle and the Zigzag Overhead Toss, in which latter game the ball is tossed over the heads of intervening ranks, the players of alternate ranks belonging to the same team.

In all of these forms the game may be made more lively and complicated by advancing from the use of one ball to that of two or more. The kind of ball used will also make a great difference in the play, anything from a beanbag to a basketball or medicine ball being suitable. Where beanbags are used, it is desirable to have different colored bags for the different teams.

As in all zigzag games, the play is made easier by a distinctive dress or color for each team, or a handkerchief tied on the arm for one team; but

much keener play is required without this.   Then each player should
observe closely before the game begins from which player he is to catch the
ball, and to which player he is to throw.   This will facilitate the rapidity
of the play, a feature on which much of the sport depends.   For very young
or unskilled players the action should be rather slow, especially when the
game is being learned.

ZIGZAG BALL — I

20 to 100 players   *Primary grades*
Playground; gymnasium   *Any ball; beanbag*

The players are divided into two or more teams which compete
against each other.   Each team is divided into two ranks, the

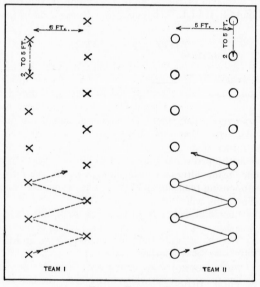

ZIGZAG BALL — I

players standing side by side, with a distance of from two to five
feet between each two players.   The ranks of a team face each
other, with a distance of five feet between them and so that each
player is opposite a space instead of a player.

The first player in one rank of each team has a ball.   At a
given signal this is thrown to the first player in the opposite rank.

This player throws it quickly to the second player of the first rank, and so on in zigzag form to the end of the line, where the ball is immediately sent back again in the same way to the front. The group which first gets its ball back to the head wins.

When players have had a little practice with one ball, two or more should be used, the starters starting the second ball down the line as soon as the first ball has reached the third player. Where several balls are used in this way, the last player of the line must hold the balls until all are received before starting them on their return journey.

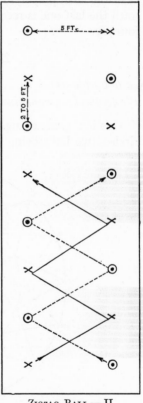

ZIGZAG BALL — II

20 to 100 players
Playground; gymnasium

Intermediate grades
Any ball; beanbag

In this form of zigzag ball the players are all in two ranks, which comprise two competing teams, rather than in teams of two ranks each, as in the preceding game. The players of one team alternate with the players of the opposing team in each of the two ranks. The balls will cross in starting and repeatedly thereafter unless one should outdistance the other.

The players of two teams stand alternately, and form two ranks which face each other, with five feet space between ranks and two to five feet apart sideways. Each

ZIGZAG BALL — II

faces directly a player of the opposing team, instead of facing a space between players as in the previous game. If desired, one team may be designated by color or a handkerchief on one arm, though this help to memory detracts much from the alertness demanded and cultivated by the game and from its sport.

The first player in each rank holds a ball. At a signal this is thrown to the first player of his own team in the opposite rank, who throws it to the second player of his team in the rank from which he received it, etc.

The team wins whose ball first gets back to the front.

After some practice, more than one ball may be used, in which case the last· player in each team will have to hold the balls until the last one is received before starting them on their return journey.

ZIGZAG CIRCLE

12 to 60 players   *Junior high school*
Playground; gymnasium   *Basketball; handsizeball; beanbag*

This is a game of zigzag ball (or beanbag) between concentric circles, two balls being used, played in opposite directions. The

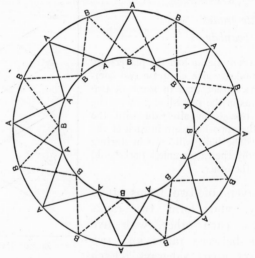

ZIGZAG CIRCLE

players form two teams who line-up alternately and form two concentric circles, facing each other. The leader of one team is in the outer circle and the leader of the opposing team is in the inner circle and each has a ball. These are put in play at a signal, the play consisting in throwing the balls backward and forward in a zigzag line between teammates from one circle to the other. The inner circle should start its ball to the right; the outer circle to the left. The team wins which first completes the circle three times.

This game may be made more interesting and require much more alertness on the part of the players by putting more balls into play. This may be done by the starters starting a second ball around the circle as soon as the first has reached the third player. In this way several balls may be used at once.

ZIGZAG OVERHEAD TOSS

20 to 100 players   *Junior high school*
Playground; gymnasium   *Handsizeball; basketball; beanbag*

This game is a variation of Zigzag Ball, and is more difficult and interesting for older players. The players are divided into two

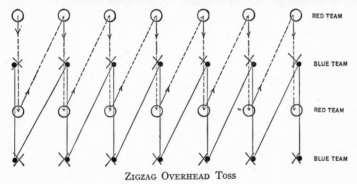

ZIGZAG OVERHEAD TOSS

teams, best distinguished by colors — say Red and Blue. The two teams stand in even ranks alternately about five feet apart; for instance, the Red team will form ranks one and three, and will play together, facing each other; while the Blue team will form ranks two and four, which will face each other and play together.

The first player in each team has a ball which is put in play upon a signal by being tossed over the heads of the intervening rank to Number One in the other rank of his team. This player tosses the ball back to Number Two in the first rank, and so the ball is tossed in zigzag form from one player to another in ranks of the same color until it reaches the end of the line, when it is zigzagged back to the starting point in the same way. This is all done over the heads of an intervening rank of the opposite color. Simultaneously the competing team is playing in the same way.

The team wins which first gets the ball back to the starting point.

With a large number of players the number of ranks may be increased beyond four if desired.

This game may be made more interesting and require much more alertness on the part of the players by putting more balls into play. This may be done by the starters starting a second ball or more balls, tossing down the line as soon as a predecessor has reached the third player. When this is done, the game is won (*a*) by the team whose last player at the foot of the line is first to receive the last ball; or (*b*) the last player may accumulate the balls and return them to the front in reverse order, the team winning which first gets its last ball back to the original starter.

TRACK AND FIELD EVENTS

TRACK AND FIELD EVENTS

These include various running, jumping, and weight-throwing contests. Although often called Track and Field Games they are essentially individual or team contests of strength, skill, speed, and endurance.

RUNNING RACES

These include sprints or dashes from forty to one hundred yards in length, middle distance races from three hundred yards to one mile, and distance races from one to ten miles or more. The latter include cross-country races and the longest race known — the Marathon — twenty-five miles or over.

The Marathon has usually been run only at Olympic Games revived in 1896 and commemorates one of the most famous incidents in classic history (490 B.C.), in which, after the Greeks were victorious in a great battle against the invading Persians on the plain of Marathon, an unknown soldier ran the entire distance from the battlefield to the city of Athens ($26\frac{1}{4}$ miles) to tell of the victory. He dropped dead immediately after delivering the message.

It has become customary in America to call any running race of from ten to twenty miles a "Marathon."

The physiological difference between distance races and sprint races, or dashes, lies largely in the strain upon nervous energy made by short distances and the endurance, especially of heart and lungs, required by the long races which are not run at so intense a speed.

START

Two different forms of starting are used in running races: Where speed is the main object, as with sprinting, the crouching start is used; in middle-distance races either the crouch or standing start is used; and for races above a quarter mile in length a standing start is usual.

CROUCHING START. — A starting line or "scratch" is drawn on the ground. The contestant crouches to this and places his fingers and thumbs on, or just behind, the line, the thumbs stretched apart from the fingers. No part of the hands or any other part of the body must touch the ground over the line, or it counts as a false start. The hands should be only shoulder-width apart. The left foot should be placed from four to eight inches behind the starting line and the right knee bent and resting on the ground in line with the left toes or instep. If running on a soft track, the contestant digs a small hole for the toes of each foot, the rear of the hole being perpendicular to form a solid resistance against which he may push in getting his start. A block of wood is often used to further this resistance.

STANDING START. — The runner toes the line with his left foot; usually the forward (left) knee is bent and the weight thrown over it. The toe may be on the line but not over it. Usually the left arm is forward, elbow slightly bent, and the right arm diagonally backward and downward.

SIGNALS. — For either the crouching or standing start three signals are given by the starter:

(1) "On your mark!" The player assumes position on the starting line, relaxed.

(2) "Get set!" At this the runner tenses the muscles, inclines the body forward with eyes looking ahead on the track, and listens intently for the final signal, ready to spring forward.

In the crouching start he lifts the rear knee and straightens the arms.

It is a foul for any part of the body to be in motion, or to touch ground or be beyond the line before the starting signal. To do this is called a "false start" and the starter inflicts a penalty by moving the offender back.

(3) The signal to start is the word: "Go!" or, in official races, a pistol shot.

SPRINTING (DASHES)

These are made in lanes at least three feet wide for each runner. There is a starting line, and at the end a finish line on the ground and above it (four feet high for adults) a length of soft worsted is stretched from side to side. This is called the "tape," and the runner first to get over the finish line carries this with him on his breast, called "breasting the tape." It is a foul to touch this with the hands, and in all races it is customary for the runner to finish with his arms thrown upward (in some sections downward and backward).

In the start of a sprint the runner recovers his upright position in the first few strides, but not on the first step. This position is never entirely upright, but should always have a forward inclination. The run is made by lifting the knees high (nearly to the hip) and putting the feet down vigorously without entirely straightening the knees. The arms are bent at the elbows, the hands moving forward and backward freely.

The runner should never slow up at the finish but cross the line at full speed, being careful, as previously stated, not to grasp the tape.

Officials necessary are a starter and a judge at the finish line. It is customary for the starter to drop a handkerchief as he says "Go!" as a signal for the judge at finish to note the time by the second hand of his watch. It is advisable to have a stopwatch, otherwise the second hand is noted for the finish also.

FOULS. — It is a foul for a runner to run out of his lane, to cross in the path of another runner, to throw out his arms sidewise, or in any way impede other competitors.

TRACK RELAY RACE

A relay race is one in which the competitors are teams instead of individuals. In the track race here described, each competitor runs but part of the distance to be covered, and is then relieved by another member of his team, these various runners being stationed at regular places on the track.

Four is the usual number on a relay team, but the number is not invariable. These races are usually run on a regular running track, indoors or out. The scratch, or starting line, is drawn on the ground across the track as for all other races. A similar line is drawn for each runner on the team, these being at equal distances; thus, for a race a mile long, to be run by a four-man team, four starting lines would be drawn at distances of 440 yards.

All of the members of a team should be marked in some uniform way to distinguish them from other teams and make sure of a correct touch-off and also to assist the judges.

No member of a relay team may run more than once in a given heat. Should his team come in first or second in the race he would run with them in further trial heats or in the finals.

The change of runners is made by a touch-off of the hands, or, more customary, an exchange of a baton, — a small length or rod of wood. Official batons measure approximately one foot in length, but junior players often use longer ones. Twenty feet beyond each starting line another and parallel line is drawn which makes a twenty-foot zone within which the touch-off or exchange of baton must take place. It is a foul for a player to start over the twenty-foot line without the baton or touch-off, or to touch off outside these limits.

In the touch-off the hands must actually touch. To overlap the hands without touching or to make an attempt to touch and fail count as failures, disqualifying the team. If the baton is dropped, the team is disqualified, unless the runner stops and recovers it.

The waiting relay may toe his line toward the rear if he wishes, reaching back to the incoming relay, but he may not step back of this line to meet him. The two runners may run together throughout the twenty-foot distance, but the touching of hands must take place before the outgoing runner crosses the twenty-foot line.

At the start the teams draw for their positions, as to whether they shall be next to the inner edge of the track, or second or third from it, etc. The start itself is like that for any other race, and either the crouching start or the standing start is used according to whether the runner is to cover a short or long distance. The method of running also conforms to this usage. At the finish, hands should be thrown up as for any race as the runner breasts the tape.

MIDDLE DISTANCE AND DISTANCE RACES

Distances and starts are explained at the beginning of this section.

These races are not run in lanes like sprints or dashes, although each contestant is assigned a place on the starting line. It is permissible to cross in front of another runner at not less than two paces (about six feet) in advance of him, but, on an oval track, this may not be done after the last turn. The finish is a straightaway. There is no rule about starting, but up to one quarter mile it is customary to use the crouching start and for greater distances the standing start. The gait is easier than in sprinting, having less tension and usually being not so far up on the toes, except at the start and finish, when sprinting is often used. The movement of the arms is not so tense. The finish is made under the same rules as sprinting.

CROSS-COUNTRY RUN

This is a running race, presumably without rest, over the open country. It may be along roadways or across fields and streams and through woods. It is usually taken over a well-marked trail.

The length of the run varies from two and one-half miles for boys of high school age, to ten miles for adults. The cross-country run should not be undertaken without previous training, as it is a test of endurance, especially for the heart and lungs.

The competition may be individual or between teams. All of the runners of all teams start at once. The first runner to return to the starting point scores one point; the second runner to return scores two points, the third three points, and so on. In a race between individuals, the one finishing first wins. If the runners are in competing teams, each team scores the total number of points made by the first five of its members to finish. The team wins which scores the fewest number of points.

HURDLE RACES

A hurdle race is a combination of running and jumping. It is a running race in which the contestants jump over hurdles which are obstacles generally of the nature of a gate.   In America these hurdles are made to swing or turn over easily, so that they give if kicked and a jumper is not tripped by hitting one.   The distances for hurdles vary from forty yards with three hurdles to two hundred twenty yards with ten hurdles.   The hurdles are from two to two and one-half feet in height.   It is customary to start the hurdle race with a crouching start as for sprints.

All rules for races apply, such as those for false starts, not leaving one's lane, and impeding another runner.   Each hurdle must be jumped over with both feet.   It is a foul to trail one foot beside the hurdle and disqualifies the runner.   Two hurdles may be knocked over but a third disqualifies the contestant.   (Sometimes this is limited to one hurdle.)   The finish is the same as for dashes.

JUMPING

STANDING BROAD JUMP

For the Standing Broad Jump there is a take-off board six or eight inches wide and at least two inches deep, sunk firmly in the ground.   This serves as a scratch line; usually a jumping pit is dug in front of this from five to six feet wide and twenty-five to thirty feet long, filled with sand or soft earth.

The contestant stands on the take-off board, or toeing a scratch line, and for the Standing Broad Jump may take no preliminary step or jump.   To do so disqualifies him.   He may bend the knees and sway the body and arms backward and forward to get impetus, but may not lift the feet.   He takes off and lands with both feet.

The measure of the jump is taken from the front edge of the take-off board or line to the first break in the ground, whether that is made with his feet or any other part of his body.   In landing, he should therefore fall forward or sideways, as even a touch of the hand behind him constitutes a point for measurement.

Each contestant is allowed three or four trials (number to be decided in advance), the longest one being considered his record.

THREE STANDING BROAD JUMPS

This event is exactly like the Standing Broad Jump, except that instead of stopping when he lands, the contestant jumps again immediately, making a second and then a third jump. He may not stop between jumps even for any of the preparatory movements made before a first jump. The jump is made with both feet and the measurement is made from the outer edge of the take-off or scratch line to the heel mark of the last jump unless some other part of the body touches the ground nearer the take-off, when that constitutes the mark for measurement. All rules and fouls are the same as for Standing Broad Jump.

RUNNING BROAD JUMP

This event requires a long runway, a take-off board and a jumping pit. There is no rule limiting the distance of the preliminary run; about six paces is customary. The jump is made at the finish of the run and is a spring from one foot, made from the forward edge of the take-off. For the foot to touch the ground in front of the take-off as the jump is made counts as a trial. The jump is measured to the first mark. The jumper should have good balance in landing and fall forward to avoid lessening the measurement of his jump. Each contestant is given three or four trials — the number to be decided in advance.

RUNNING HOP, STEP, AND JUMP

This event is exactly like the Running Broad Jump except that the first leap is a hop, followed without stopping by a step, and then by a jump. All rules, fouls, and procedure are the same as for the Running Broad Jump.

The landing from the first spring is made on the foot that made the take-off — the hop. The second landing is made with the opposite foot — the step. This may be made as long as possible, propelled by the foot that remains on the ground. The spring to the third and final effort (the jump) is made from the one foot then on the ground, but the landing is on both feet. There must be no stop between any of the three efforts.

The measurement is made from the scratch line or forward edge of the take-off to the final mark of the heels, subject to the same measurement of any fall or mark of the body backward.

RUNNING HIGH JUMP

Jump standards should be placed twelve feet apart. On them should be placed a light bar, either rectangular of light wood, or of bamboo, resting on pins that do not extend more than three inches from the posts. This bar should be easily displaced if hit while jumping. The height of the jump is measured from the ground to the bar at the center between the standards. Three feet in front of the bar is drawn a balk line parallel to the bar. Running over this line constitutes a balk, two of which count as one trial. In other words, the contestant must jump from three feet in front of the bar.

It is customary to have a fan-shaped approach, as the jump is usually made from the side. Neither the take-off nor the landing should be where the ground is slippery. Out-of-doors it is customary to have a jumping pit dug and filled in. This needs particular care indoors. It is customary to hang a handkerchief or a white cloth in the center of the bar to aid the jumper in judging the height.

The jump is made from one foot at the end of a short run. There is no limit to the length of the approach, but it is usually made in an oblique direction from the side, the spring being made from the foot on the side toward the bar. The "scissors" jump is usual, the landing being made on the same leg from which the jump was made. The first height (the lowest) is usually with the bar at two feet six inches from the ground (lower for juniors). If a contestant clears this on the first jump it is set higher, but he has three trials, if necessary, at each height. Displacing the bar at any height on the third trial disqualifies him, the previous height cleared being considered his record.

WEIGHT THROWING

SHOT–PUT

The shot is put (thrown) from within a circle seven feet in diameter (inside measurements); a toe-board is placed on one quarter of the circumference of this circle and fastened firmly in the ground toward the front of the circle. The put is made over this, but neither the feet nor any part of the contestant's body may touch the top of this toe-board nor the ground outside of it. Women usually throw from behind a straight ten-foot line two inches wide.

The shot is of metal. For adult- and college-championship contests the weight is sixteen pounds. High schools use a twelve-pound shot, junior high schools eight-pound, and women from six- to eight-pound.

Each competitor has four trials (women three trials) and his best (farthest) put is his record in the event, whether it be made on his first, second, or third trial.

The measurement is made from the outer edge of the circle or line where the competitor stood to the nearest mark made in the earth by the shot.

The put is made with a thrust of the arm from the top of the shoulder, and the force of the entire body is added to that of the arm by a quick spring of the feet.

Should the contestant step on or over the circle it is a foul, and the put so made counts as a trial but does not score. It is also a foul to drop the shot during any part of the trial.

Field judges take charge of the event.

THROWING THE DISCUS

The discus throw was introduced to general athletic practice after the first of the modern Olympic Games, in 1896.

The classic discus is, roughly stated, the shape of two saucers placed edge to edge, and weighs four and a half pounds. Sometimes a hurl ball is used, especially for women and elementary schools, weighing four pounds in the latter and six pounds for college use. Where women use a discus it weighs a little over two pounds.

The throw is made from a circle slightly over eight feet (women from a straight ten-foot line the same as for Shot-Put).

Two methods of throwing are in use: the so-called "free" style and a classic or "Greek" style. The discus should fall within a ninety-degree sector in front of the throwing line. Fouls count as trials but the throw is not measured. Fouls consist of dropping the discus at any time during the trial, stepping on or over the line, or touching the ground in front of it in any way before the throw is measured.

JAVELIN THROW

This is a Swedish event that has grown in popularity since the first of the modern Olympic Games, in 1896.

The field is a level, across which is marked a straight line called a scratch line or restraining line. This is ten or twelve feet long and two inches or more in width.

The javelin is a simple wooden shaft of hard wood, usually fitted with a metal point at the end. The length varies from six feet eight inches for high schools to seven feet two inches for colleges, and the weight from one pound for high schools to nearly one and a half pounds for adults.

The throw is made either from a stand or a run. Any grip may be used, but only one hand for the approach and the throw. The throw is made without stepping on or over the line. Such a step disqualifies the throw, and counts as one of the three trials allowed each contestant.

The measurement is made from the restraining line to the point on the ground first touched by the point of the javelin. A throw does not count in which any part of the shaft touches the ground before the point. There are judges as for the shot-put.

INDEX

This Index is first a guide (in black-faced type) to the pages of this book on which games are described. In the five columns at the right of the page numbers it further indicates by X's the grades or ages at which games may appropriately be used.

	Page	Primary Grades 1, 2, 3	Inter-mediate Grades 4, 5, 6	Junior High School	Senior High School	College and Adult
All Run	**426**	X	X			
All Up Relay	**57**	X	X	X	X	
Animal Blind Man's Buff .	**58**	X	X			
Animal Chase	**58**		X			
Arch Ball	**426**		X	X	X	
Arch Goal Ball . . .	**428**		X	X		
Arrow Chase	**59**	X	X	X	X	X
Author's Initials	**269**					
Automobile Treasure Hunt	**269**					X
"B" Game	**271**			X	X	X
Badminton (Battledore and Shuttlecock)	**428**			X	X	X
Bag — Pile	**389**		X			
Ball Chase	**432**	X	X			
Ball Drill (*See* Handball Drill and Wall-Ball Drill)						
Ball Games	**425**					
Ball Games suitable for Beanbags	**403**					
Ball Jump Race	**433**		X	X	X	X
Ball Puss	**436**	X				
Balls	**407**					
Ball Stand (*See* Call-Ball, Ring Call-Ball, and Spud)						
Ball Tag	**436**		X			
Ball Technique	**408**					
General Technique . .	**409**					

667